MOULTON'S
LIBRARY OF LITERARY CRITICISM
of English and American Authors

MOULTON'S LIBRARY

of English

THROUGH THE BEGINNING

IN FOUR VOLUMES

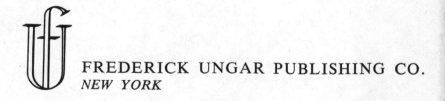

FREDERICK UNGAR PUBLISHING CO.
NEW YORK

OF LITERARY CRITICISM

and American Authors

OF THE TWENTIETH CENTURY

Abridged, revised, and with additions by

MARTIN TUCKER

Associate Professor of English
Long Island University

VOLUME II

Neo-Classicism
to the Romantic Period

Material that has been added to this revised edition is reprinted by permission of the following:

Constable and Company Limited. For excerpt on George Meredith, from *Poetry and Philosophy of George Meredith* by G. M. Trevelyan, published 1890.

Hutchinson & Co. Ltd. For excerpt on Ernest Dowson, in *Twenty Years in Paris* by R. H. Sherard, published 1906.

Jonathan Cape Limited. For excerpt on Oscar Wilde and Ernest Dowson, in *The Eighteen-nineties: A Review of Art and Ideas at the Close of the Nineteenth Century* by Holbrook Jackson, published 1927.

Macmillan & Co. Ltd. For excerpt on W. S. Gilbert, from *Coasting Bohemia* by J. C. Carr, published 1914.

The Society of Authors, literary representative of the author's estate. For excerpt on George Meredith, in *George Meredith* by Richard Le Gallienne, published 1890.

Every effort has been made to trace and to acknowledge properly all copyright owners. If any acknowledgment has been inadvertently omitted, the necessary correction will be made in the next printing.

CONTENTS

AUTHORS INCLUDED

BIBLIOGRAPHICAL NOTE

Below the introductory paragraph for each writer included in these volumes, the reader will find bibliographic entries of standard editions and biographical and/or critical studies published through 1964. The scheme of these entries is as follows:

The standard edition (or editions) of the writer's work is placed first; where one-volume texts and selected editions of excellence merit attention, these are listed next; on occasion convenient school texts are also noted; following the list of editions are standard biographical and critical studies. In cases where scholarly study has been particularly active, or literary issues remain in the realm of disputation and/or doubt, several biographical and critical works may be noted. Short titles are sometimes used, especially in editions of an author's work. In certain selected cases a study of a single work, as distinct from the collected edition of an author's work, will be found in the bibliographical listings.

Abbreviations used in the entries are: *repr.* for reprint; *rev.* for revision; *OSA* for Oxford Standard Authors one-volume editions; *ed.* for "edited by"; and *tr.* for "translated by."

Early standard editions listed in the original Moulton headnotes are usually not repeated in the bibliographical entries. Standard editions in the new listings, and their revisions and reprints, indicate availability, although they do not guarantee it.

THE EARLY
EIGHTEENTH CENTURY

GEORGE FARQUHAR
1678-1707

George Farquhar, 1678-1707. Born, in Londonderry, 1678. Educated at Londonderry. To Trinity Coll., Dublin, as sizar, 17 July 1694. Left college, 1695 (?); appeared soon after on Dublin stage. To London, 1697 (?). First play, *Love and a Bottle*, produced at Drury Lane, 1699; *The Constant Couple*, in 1700; *Sir Harry Wildair*, in 1701. Presented by Earl of Orrery with lieutenant's commission, 1700(?). In Holland, 1700. Married, 1703 (?). Visit to Dublin, 1740; continued to produce plays. Sold commission to pay debts. Died, April 1707. WORKS: *Love and a Bottle*, 1699; *Sir Harry Wildair*, 1701; *The Inconstant*, 1702; *The Twin Rivals*, 1702; *The Stage-coach* (with Motteux; anon.), 1705; *The Recruiting Officer* 1706; *The Beaux Stratagem*, 1707; *Love's Catechism* (anon.; compiled by Farquhar from preceding), 1707. POSTHUMOUS: *The Constant Couple*, 1710. *Collected Works*: *Comedies*, 1710; *Works* (in 2 vols.), 1718-36; in 2 vols., 1892. *Life*: by Wilkes, in 1775 edn. of *Works;* by A. C. Ewald, in 1892 edn.

R. Farquharson Sharp, 1897, *A Dictionary of English Authors,* p. 96

SEE: *Works,* ed. Charles Stonehill, 1930, 2v.; Willard Connely, *Young George Farquhar: the Restoration Drama at Twilight,* 1949.

PERSONAL

Mr. Farquhar had now been about a twelve-month married, and it was at first reported, to a great fortune; which indeed he expected, but was miserably disappointed. The lady had fallen in love with him, and so violent was her passion, that she resolved to have him at any rate; and as she knew Farquhar was too much dissipated in life to fall in love, or to think of matrimony unless advantage was annexed to it, she fell upon the stratagem of giving herself out for a great fortune, and then took an opportunity of letting our poet know that she was in love with him. Vanity and interest both uniting to persuade Farquhar to marry, he did not long delay it, and, to his immortal honour let it be spoken, though he found himself deceived, his circumstances embarrassed, and his family growing upon him, he never once upbraided her for the cheat, but behaved to her with all the delicacy, and tenderness of an indulgent husband. . . . If he was not a man of the highest genius, he seems to have had excellent moral qualities.

Theophilus Cibber, 1753, *Lives of the Poets,* vol. III, p. 133

3

We can follow him pretty closely through his day. He is a queer mixture of profanity and piety, of coarseness and loyalty, of cleverness and density; we do not breed this kind of beau nowadays, and yet we might do worse, for this specimen is, with all his faults, a man. He dresses carefully in the morning, in his uniform or else in his black suit. When he wants to be specially smart, as, for instance, when he designs a conquest at a birthday-party, he has to ferret among the pawnbrokers for scraps of finery, or secure on loan a fair, full-bottom wig. But he is not so impoverished that he cannot on these occasions give his valet and his barber plenty of work to do preparing his face with razors, perfumes and washes. He would like to be Sir Fopling Flutter, if he could afford it, and gazes a little enviously at that noble creature in his French clothes, as he lounges luxuriantly past him in his coach with six before and six behind.

Edmund Gosse, 1891, *Gossip in a Library,* p. 150

The Beaux' Stratagem (1707)

The reader may find some faults in this play, which my illness prevented the amending of; but there is great amends made in the representation, which cannot be matched, no more than the friendly and indefatigable care of Mr. Wilks, to whom I chiefly owe the success of the play.

George Farquhar, 1707, *The Beaux-Stratagem,* Advertisement

It is an honour to the morality of the present age, that this most entertaining comedy is but seldom performed; and never, except some new pantomime, or other gaudy spectacle, be added, as an afterpiece, for the attraction of an audience. The well-drawn characters, happy incidents, and excellent dialogue, in *The Beaux' Stratagem,* are but poor atonement for that unrestrained contempt of principle which pervades every scene.

Mrs. Elizabeth Inchbald, 1808, "Remarks" on *The Beaux Stratagem,* in *The British Theatre,* ed. Elizabeth Inchbald, vol. VIII

Its plot is new, simple, and interesting; the characters various, without confusing it; the dialogue sprightly and characteristic; the moral bold, healthy, admirable, and doubly needed in those times, when sottishness was a fashion. *Archer* and *Aimwell* who set out as mere intriguers, prove in the end true gentlemen, candid, conscientious, and generous. *Scrub* and *Boniface,* though but a servant and an innkeeper, are quotable fellows both, and have made themselves prominent in theatrical recollection,—the former especially, for his quaint ignorance and sordid cunning. And *Mrs. Sullen* is the more touching in her distress, from the cheerfulness with which she wipes away her tears. *Sullen* is an awful brute, yet not thoroughly inhuman; for he feels, after all, that he has no right to such a wife.

Leigh Hunt, 1840, ed. *The Works of Wycherley, Congreve,
Vanbrugh, and Farquhar*, p. lviii

In *The Beaux' Stratagem* (1707) Farquhar achieved his masterpiece. This comedy, justly the most celebrated of his plays and destined to an enduring life on the stage, deserved its success in the first instance by the cleverness of the plot, which is ingenious without being improbable. Some of the incidents, indeed, are of dubious import, including one at the close,—a separation by mutual consent,—which throws a glaring light on the view taken by the author and his age of the sanctity of the marriage-tie. But the comedy is also an excellent picture of manners. The inn with its rascally landlord and highwaymen-guests and the country-house into which the Beau is carried in a fainting-fit, stand before us as scenes from real life; and some of the characters are drawn with much humour and spirit. The most successful conception is that of Archer, who pretends to be the valet of his friend the Beau, but carries on adventures on his own account. This became one of Garrick's most famous parts; and indeed the easy volubility of the pretended servant furnishes an admirable opportunity for a fine actor of light comedy. Altogether this play is written in the happiest of veins; and may be regarded as the prototype of Goldsmith's *She Stoops to Conquer,* like which it hovers rather doubtfully on the borders—not always easy to determine—of comedy and farce.

Adolphus William Ward, 1875-99, *A History of
English Dramatic Literature*, vol. III, p. 484

GENERAL

Farquhar is a light and gay writer, less correct and less sparkling than Congreve; but he has more ease; and perhaps fully as great a share of the vis comica. The two best and least exceptionable of his plays, are *The Recruiting Officer,* and *The Beaux' Stratagem.* I say, the least exceptionable; for, in general, the tendency of both Congreve and Farquhar's plays is immoral. Throughout them all, the rake, the loose intrigue, and the life of licentiousness, are the objects continually held up to view; as if the assemblies of a great and polished nation could be amused with none but vicious objects.

Hugh Blair, 1783, *Lectures on Rhetoric and Belles-Letters,*
ed. Mills, p. 542

He makes us laugh from pleasure oftener than from malice. He somewhere prides himself in having introduced on the stage the class of comic heroes here spoken of, which has since become a standard character, and which represents the warm-hearted, rattle-brained, thoughtless, high-spirited young fellow, who floats on the back of his misfortunes without repining, who forfeits appearances, but saves his honour—and he gives us to understand that it was his own. He did not need to be ashamed of it. Indeed there is internal evidence that this sort of character is his own, for it pervades his works generally, and is the moving spirit that informs them. His comedies have on this account probably a greater appearance of truth and nature than almost any others. His incidents succeed one another with rapidity, but without premeditation; his wit is easy and spontaneous; his style animated, unembarrassed, and flowing; his characters full of life and spirit, and never overstrained so as to "o'erstep the modesty of nature," though they sometimes, from haste and carelessness, seem left in a crude, unfinished state. There is a constant ebullition of gay, laughing invention, cordial good humour, and fine animal spirits, in his writings. Of the four writers here classed together, we should perhaps have courted Congreve's acquaintance most, for his wit and the elegance of his manners; Wycherley's, for his sense and observation on human nature; Vanbrugh's, for his power of farcical description and telling a story; Farquhar's, for the pleasure of his society, and the love of good fellowship.

William Hazlitt, 1818, *Lectures on the English Comic Writers*

He extended the list of the comic dramatic personages of the day, and his Captain Plume, the fine gentleman officer, Boniface, the innkeeper, Cherry, his lively daughter, Scrub, the country servant who guesses they are talking of *him,* "for they laughed consumedly," and above all the inimitable recruiting officer, Sergeant Pike—are all invaluable additions to our stock of comedy characters. His plots are simpler and better than those of his brother playwrights, they have more life and movement, and the episodes succeed each other in an unforced way which must have made his pieces very pleasant to audiences.

Oswald Crawfurd, 1883, ed. *English Comic Dramatists,* p. 172

It is fortunate for Farquhar that he could not emulate the exquisitely civilized depravities of Congreve's urban Muse. But his dialogue is not "low" to modern tastes; it has, in general, a simple, natural zest, infinitely preferable to the Persian appartus of the early eighteenth century. Even he, however, can rant and deviate into rhetoric, as soon as his lovers drop upon one knee. More plainly in Farquhar's work than in that of any contemporary, we mark the glamour of the Caroline literature fading, and the breath of life blowing in. . . . His mind was a Medea's kettle, out of which everything issued cleaner and more wholesome. . . . Though

Farquhar did not live, like Vanbrugh and the magnanimous Dryden, to admit the abuse of a gift, and to deplore it, he alone, of the minor dramatists, seems all along to have had a negative sort of conscience better than none. His instincts continually get the better not only of his environment, but of his practice. Some uneasiness, some misgiving, are at the bottom of his homely materialism. He thinks it best, on the whole, to forswear the temptation to be sublime, and to keep to his cakes and ale; and for cakes and ale he had an eminent and inborn talent.

Louise Imogen Guiney, 1894, *A Little English Gallery*,
pp. 132, 136, 137

ANTHONY ASHLEY COOPER
Third Earl of Shaftesbury

1671-1713

Born, in London, 26 Feb. 1671. Early education under tutorship of John Locke. At a private school, 1682-83; at Winchester, Nov. 1683 to 1686. Travelled on Continent, 1686-89. M. P. for Poole, May 1695; re-elected, Nov. 1695. Retired from Parliament, owing to ill-health, July 1698. Visit to Holland, 1698-99. Succeeded to Earldom, on death of his father, 10 Nov. 1699. Took his seat in House of Lords, 19 Jan. 1700. In Holland, Aug. 1703 to Aug. 1704. Married Jane Ewer, Aug. 1709. To Italy, for health, autumn of 1711. Died, in Naples, 15 Feb. 1713. Buried at St. Giles's. WORKS: *An Inquiry concerning Virtue* (anon.), 1699; *A Letter Concerning Enthusiasm* (anon.), 1708; *Sensus Communis* (anon.), 1709; *The Moralists* (anon.), 1709; *Soliloquy or Advice to an Author* (anon.), 1710; *Characteristics of Men, Manners, Opinions, Times* (3 vols.), 1711; *A Notion of the Historical Draught . . . of the Judgment of Hercules* (anon.), 1713; *Several Letters written by a Noble Lord to a Young Man at the University* (anon.), 1716. POSTHUMOUS: *Letters . . . to R. Molesworth*, 1721; *Letters, collected*, 1746; *Original Letters by Locke, Sidney, and Shaftesbury*, ed. by T. Foster, enlarged edn. 1847. He *edited*: B. Whichcot's *Selected Sermons*, 1689.

R. Farquharson Sharp, 1897, *A Dictionary of English Authors*, p .253

SEE: *The Life, Unpublished Letters and Philosophical Regimen*, ed. Benjamin Rand, 1900; J. M. Robertson, *Shaftesbury*, 1907; R. L. Brett, *The Third Earl of Shaftesbury: A Study in Eighteenth-Century Literary Theory*, 1951.

PERSONAL

As regards personal habits, Shaftesbury is reported to have been remarkably abstemious at a time when riotous living was the rule amongst the upper classes of society, and not the exception. . . . As an earnest student, an ardent lover of liberty, an enthusiast in the cause of virtue, and a man of unblemished life and untiring beneficence, Shaftesbury probably had no superior in his generation. His character and pursuits are the more remarkable, considering the rank of life in which he was born and the circumstances under which he was brought up. In many respects, he reminds us of the imperial philosopher, Marcus Aurelius, whose works we know him to have studied with avidity, and whose influence is unmistakably stamped upon his own productions. . . . Though Shaftesbury was one of the earliest of English moralists, and died so long ago as 1712-13, the present Earl is only his great-grandson.

Thomas Fowler, 1882, *Shaftesbury and Hutcheson*
(*English Philosophers*), pp. 39, 40, 41

Shaftesbury was a man of lofty and ardent character, forced by ill-health to abandon politics for literature. He was liberal, though much fretted by the difficulty of keeping out of debt. He was resolved, as he tells his steward, not to be a slave to his estates, and never again to be "poorly rich." He supported several young men of promise at the university or elsewhere. He allowed a pension of £20 a year to the deist Toland, after Toland's surreptitious publication of his papers, though he appears to have dropped it in his fit of economy in 1704. He gives exceedingly careful directions for regulating his domestic affairs during his absence. His letters to his young friends are full or moral and religious advice, and the "Shaftesbury Papers" show many traces of his practical benevolence to them. He went to church and took the sacrament regularly, respecting religion though he hated the priests. He is a typical example of the whig aristocracy of the time, and with better health might have rivalled his grandfather's fame.

Leslie Stephen, 1887, *Dictionary of National Biography*,
vol. XII, p. 132

There is nothing that demands concealment in his career, whatever his mistakes or shortcomings; the more closely one presses home upon the inner motives and exalted purpose of his life the richer and more ennobling does his character appear.

Benjamin Rand, 1900, ed., *The Life, Unpublished Letters, and*
Philosophical Regimen of Anthony, Earl of Shaftesbury,
Introduction, p. vi

GENERAL

The generality of moralists and philosophers have hitherto agreed that there could be no virtue without self-denial; but a late author, who is now much read by men of sense, is of a contrary opinion, and imagines that men, without any trouble or violence upon themselves, may be naturally virtuous. He seems to require and expects goodness in his species, as we do a sweet taste in grapes and China oranges, of which, if any of them are sour, we boldly pronounce that they are not come to that perfection their nature is capable of. This noble writer fancies that, as man is made for society, so he ought to be born with a kind affection to the whole, of which he is a part, and a propensity to seek the welfare of it. In pursuance of this supposition, he calls every action performed with regard to the public good, virtuous; and all selfishness, wholly excluding such a regard, vice. In respect to our species, he looks upon virtue and vice as permanent realities that must ever be the same in all countries and all ages, and imagines that a man of sound understanding, by following the rules of good sense, may not only find out that *"Pulchrum et Honestum"* both in morality and the works of art and nature, but likewise govern himself, by his reason, with as much ease and readiness as a good rider manages a well-taught horse by the bridle. . . . Two systems cannot be more opposite than his Lordship's and mine.

Bernard de Mandeville, 1723, *A Search into the Nature of Society*

The rest of his time he employed in ordering his writings for publication, which he placed in the order they now stand. The several prints then first interspersed in the work were all designed by himself, and each device bears an exact affinity to the passage to which it refers. That no mistake might be committed, he did not leave to any other hand, even so much as the drudgery or correcting the press. In the three volumes of the *Characteristics* he completed the whole of his writings which he intended should be made public, though some people have, however, in a very ungenerous manner, without any application to his family, or even their knowledge, published several of his letters, and those too of a private nature, many of which were written in so hasty and careless a manner, that he did not so much as take copies of them.

Fourth Earl of Shaftesbury, c 1734-41, *A Sketch of the Life of the Third Earl of Shaftesbury*

It hath been the fate of Lord Shaftesbury's *Characteristics,* beyond that of most other books, to be idolized by one party, and detested by another. While the first regard it as a work of perfect excellence, as containing everything that can render mankind wise and happy; the latter are disposed to rank it among the most pernicious of writings, and brand it as one continued heap of fustian, scurrility, and falsehood. . . . The noble writer hath mingled beauties and blots, faults and excellencies, with a liberal and unsparing hand.

John Brown, 1751, *Essays on the Characteristics*

You say you cannot conceive how Lord Shaftesbury came to be a philosopher in vogue; I will tell you: First, he was a Lord; secondly, he was as vain as any of his readers; thirdly, men are very prone to believe what they do not understand; fourthly, they will believe anything at all, provided they are under no obligation to believe it; fifthly, they love to take a new road, even when that road leads nowhere; sixthly, he was reckoned a fine writer, and seemed always to mean more than he said. Would you have any more reasons? An interval above forty years has pretty well destroyed the charm. A dead Lord ranks with Commoners; Vanity is no longer interested in the matter, for the new road has become an old one.

Thomas Gray, 1758, *Letters,* Aug. 18

The writings of the latter breathe the virtues of his mind, for which they are much more estimable than for their style and manner. He delivers his doctrines in ecstatic diction, like one of the Magi inculcating philosophic visions to an eastern auditory.

Horace Walpole, 1758, *A Catalogue of the Royal and Noble Authors, of England, Scotland and Ireland,* ed. Park, vol. IV, p. 55

The philosophical manner of Lord Shaftesbury's writing is nearer to that of Cicero than any English author has yet arrived at; but perhaps had Cicero written in English, his composition would have greatly exceeded that of our countryman. The diction of the latter is beautiful, but such beauty as, upon nearer inspection, carries with it evident symptoms of affectation. This has been attended with very disagreeable consequences. Nothing is so easy to copy as affectation, and his lordship's rank and fame have procured him more imitators in Britain than any other writer I know; all faithfully preserving his blemishes, but unhappily not one of his beauties.

Oliver Goldsmith, 1759, *The Bee,* No. 8, Nov. 24

Considerable merit, doubtless, he has. His works might be read with profit for the moral philosophy which they contain, had he not filled them with so many oblique and invidious insinuations against the christian religion; thrown out, too, with so much spleen and satire, as do no honour to his memory, either as an author or a man. His language has many beauties. It is firm, and supported in an uncommon degree; it is rich and musical. No English author, as I formerly showed, has attended so much to the regular construction of his sentences, both with respect to propriety, and with respect to cadence. All this gives so much elegance and pomp to his language, that there is no wonder it should have been highly admired by some. It is greatly hurt, however, by perpetual stiffness and affectation. This is its capital fault. His lordship can express nothing with simplicity. He seems to have considered it as vulgar, and beneath the dignity of a man of quality, to speak like other men. Hence he is ever in buskins; and dressed out with magnificent elegance. In every sentence, we see the marks of labour and art; nothing of that ease which expresses a sentimnt coming natural and warm from the heart. Of figures and ornament of every kind, he is exceedingly fond, sometimes happy in them; but his fondness for them is too visible; and having once laid hold of some metaphor or allusion that pleased him, he knows not how to part with it. . . . Lord Shaftesbury possessed delicacy and refinement of taste, to a degree that we may call excessive and sickly; but he had little warmth of passion; few strong or vigorous feelings, and the coldness of his character, led him to that artificial and stately manner which appears in his writings. He was fonder of nothing than of wit and raillery; but he is far from being happy in it. He attempts it often, but always awkwardly; he is stiff, even in his pleasantry; and laughs in form, like an author, and not like a man.

> Hugh Blair, 1783, *Lectures on Rhetoric and Belles-Letters,*
> ed. Mills, pp. 209, 210

For a considerable time he stood in high repute as a polite writer, and was regarded by many as a standard of elegant composition: his imitators as well as admirers were numerous, and he was esteemed the head of the school of sentimental philosophy. Of late years he has been as much depreciated as he was before extolled, and in both cases the matter has been carried to an extreme.

> Thomas Park, 1806, ed. *Walpole's Royal and Noble Authors,*
> vol. IV, p. 59

Shaftesbury retains a certain place as one of the few disciples of idealism who resisted the influence of Locke; but his importance is purely historical. His cold and monotonous though exquisitely polished dissertations have fallen into general neglect, and find few readers and exercise no influence. The shadow of the tomb rests upon them all; a deep unbroken silence, the chill of death surrounds them. They have long ceased to wake any interest, or to suggest any enquiries, or to impart any impulse to the intellect of England.

> William Edward Hartpole Lecky, 1865, *Spirit of Rationalism*
> *in Europe,* vol. I

Shaftesbury's relation to Christianity involves some difficult questions. If all we had to settle were simply whether or not he went with the Christianity prevalent in his time, the answer would be easy. He stood apart from the clergy, ridiculed "the heroic passion of *saving souls,*" and the Christian who had "his conversation in heaven." He said, with a sneer, that he dutifully and faithfully embraced the holy mysteries, conforming to the Church by law established, and making no researches into the origin of the rites and symbols. If he were to exercise himself in such speculations, he was quite sure that the further he inquired the less satisfaction he would find; for inquiry was the sure road to heterodoxy. This was a mode of writing common with the Deists. It must have been provoking and offensive, not only to the clergy, against whom it was aimed, but to all right-minded people. It is evident, however, that he was only bantering the clergy, whose ignorance and prejudice may have been equally provoking to all sensible men. He immediately after asserts the right of every man to examine the Scriptures for himself; and not only to examine them, but to know their history, what they profess to be, and what authority they claim. If Scripture be the only religion of Protestants, we ought, surely, as Protestants, to know what Scripture is.

John Hunt, 1868, "Anthony Earl of Shaftesbury,"
The Contemporary Review, vol. 8, p. 521

Shaftesbury, it is plain, took great pains in the elaboration of his style, and he succeeded so far as to make his meaning transparent. The thought is always clear. We are spared the trouble of deciding between different interpretations of his doctrines, a process so wearisome in the case of most philosophical authors. But, on the other hand, he did not equally succeed in attaining elegance, an obect at which he seems equally to have aimed. There is a curious affectation about his style, a falsetto note, which, notwithstanding all his efforts to please, is often irritating to the reader. The main characteristic of Shaftesbury's style is, perhaps, best hit off by Charles Lamb, when he calls it "genteel." He poses too much as a fine gentleman, and is so anxious not to be taken for a pedant of the vulgar, scholastic kind, that he falls into the hardly more attractive pedantry of the æsthete and *virtuoso*. The *limæ labor* is almost everywhere apparent. The efforts at raillery and humour are sometimes so forced as to lose their effect, and he is too apt to inform his reader beforehand, when he is about to put on his light and airy manner.

Thomas Fowler, 1882, *Shaftesbury and Hutcheson*
(English Philosophers), p. 61

He writes in a style which is consummately easy and lucid. There are none of those obscurities and experimental reaches of thought which in other thinkers one sometimes finds so puzzling and so suggestive; his meaning may not be very profound, but it is at least expressed for the better understanding of the plain man. He brings into English prose an order and a clearness of which it was beginning to stand in some need. The worst that can be said of him is that he is terribly affected—"genteel" was Charles Lamb's epithet. He is not always in buckram; he will unbend to you; but all the same his treatises invariably smack of the superior person, the man of birth, debarred by circumstances from his natural pursuit of politics, and condescending to while away a part of his too abundant leisure in unravelling some niceties of the intellect. Unwilling to appear a pedant, he falls into the opposite vices of desultoriness and superficiality.

E. K. Chambers, 1894, English Prose, ed. Craik, vol. III, p. 448

Judged by his influence on the age Shaftesbury's place in the history of literature and of philosophy is an important one. Seed springs up quickly when the soil is prepared for it, and Shaftesbury by his belief in the perfectability of human nature through the aid of culture, appealed as Mandeville also did from a lower and opposite platform, to the views current in polite society. According to Shaftesbury men have a natural instinct for virtue, and the sense of what is beautiful enables the virtuoso to reject what is evil and to cleave to what is good. Let a man once see that to be wicked is to be miserable, and virtue will be dear for its own sake apart from the fear of punishment or the hope of reward. He found salvation for the world in cultivated taste, but had no gospel for the men whose tastes were not cultivated.

John Dennis, 1894, The Age of Pope, p. 214

The influence of Shaftesbury's Characteristics, 1711, was far more literary than metaphysical. He condemned metaphysics, but his philosophy, such as it was, inspired Pope and his cultivated thinking on several subjects made many writers in the next generation care for beauty and grace.

Stopford A. Brooke, 1896, English Literature, p. 190

Although the philosophy of Shaftesbury is thus founded on stoicism, this Philosophical Regimen is a new and brilliant presentation of that moral system. The discourses of Epictetus were uttered, it is believed, extempore. They have a popular form, but often lack in continuity of expression. The thoughts of Marcus Aurelius, on the other hand, were written down merely for personal use. They bear the evidence of private honesty, but are stated in short paragraphs which are often obscure. The merits rather than the defects of these two works are combined in the Philosophical Regimen of Shaftesbury. It is written in a style that can at all times be readily understood, and it likewise possesses all the sincerity of personal writing where the purpose is "only to improve by these, not publish, profess, or teach them." The eloquence of the utterance is frequently such as could only have proceeded from Shaftesbury, whose method of philosophical rhapsody so captivated his contemporary Leibnitz. The permanent strength of this Regimen, however, consists in the fact that it is one of the most consistent and thorough-going attempts ever made to transform a philosophy into a life. Just as Spinoza was "God-intoxicated," so Shaftesbury was "intoxicated with the idea of virtue." He is the greatest Stoic of modern times. Into his own life he wrought the stoical virtue for virtue's sake. This exalted purpose he sought to attain by means of this Regimen. It thus embodies a philosophy which must compel a renewed and critical study from the stoical standpoint of his *Characteristics*. Indeed, it may be said, we believe, with perfect truth that there has been no such strong expression of stoicism since the days of Epictetus and Marcus Aurelius as that contained in the Philosophical Regimen of Shaftesbury. The Greek slave, the Roman Emperor, and the English nobleman, must abide the three great exponents of stoical philosophy.

> Benjamin Rand, 1900, ed. *The Life, Unpublished Letters, and Philosophical Regimen of Anthony, Earl of Shaftesbury*, Introduction, p. xii

WILLIAM WYCHERLEY
1640?–1715

> William Wycherley, 1640-1715. Born, in London, 1640. Educated in France, 1655. Became a Roman Catholic. Abjured Church of Rome, and matriculated at Queen's Coll., Oxford. Took no degree. Student of Inner Temple, 1659. Served in Army during war with Holland. Play, *Love in a Wood*, produced at Drury Lane, 1671; *The Gentleman Dancing Master*, Dorset Gardens Theatre, Jan. 1672; *The Country Wife,* Lincoln's Inn Fields Theatre, 1673(?); *The Plain Dealer,* Lincolns Inn Fields Theatre, 1674. Married (i.) Countess of Drogheda, 1678(?). After her death was imprisoned for seven years in the Fleet for debt. Debts paid by James II., who gave him a pension of £200. Friendship with Pope begun, 1704. Married (ii.) Miss Jackson, Nov. 1715. Died, in London, Dec. 1715. Buried in St. Paul's, Covent Garden. WORKS: *Love in a Wood*, 1672; *The Gentleman Dancing Master*, 1673; *The Country Wife*, 1675; *The Plain Dealer*, 1677; *Epistles to the King and Duke* (anon.), 1682; *Miscellany Poems*, 1704; *Works*, 1713. POSTHUMOUS: *Posthumous Works*, ed. by L. Theobald, 1728. COLLECTED WORKS: *Plays, etc.* (2 vols.), 1720.
>
> R. Farquharson Sharp, 1897, *A Dictionary of English Authors*, p. 306
>
> SEE: *Complete Works*, ed. Montague Summers, 1924, 4v.; Willard Connely, *Brawny Wycherley*, 1930.

PERSONAL

Wycherley died a Romanist, and has owned that religion in my hearing.— It was generally thought by this gentleman's friends, that he lost his memory by old age; it was not by age, but by accident, as he himself told me often. He remembered as well at sixty years old, as he had done ever since forty, when a fever occasioned that loss to him. . . . Wycherley was a very handsome man. His acquaintance with the famous Duchess of Cleveland commenced oddly enough. One day, as he passed that duchess's coach in the ring, she leaned out of the window, and cried out loud enough to be heard distinctly by him; "Sir, you're a rascal: you're a villain!" Wycherley from that instant entertained hopes. He did not fail waiting on her the next morning: and with a very melancholy tone begged to know, how it was possible for him to have so much disobliged her Grace? They were very good friends from that time; yet, after all, what did he get by her? He was to have travelled with the young Duke of Richmond; King Charles gave him, now and then, a hundred pounds, not often. . . . We were pretty well together to the last: only his memory was so totally bad, that he did not remember a kindness done to him, even from minute to minute. He was peevish too latterly; so that sometimes we were out a little, and sometimes in. He never did any unjust thing to me in his whole life; and I went to see him on his death-bed.

Alexander Pope, 1728-30, Spence's Anecdotes,
ed. Singer, pp. 2, 13

Wycherley was in a bookseller's shop at Bath, or Tunbridge, when Lady Drogheda came in and happened to inquire for The Plain Dealer. A friend of Wycherley's, who stood by him, pushed him toward her, and said, "There's the Plain Dealer, Madam, if you want him?" Wycherley made his excuses; and Lady Drogheda said, "that she loved plain-dealing best." He afterwords visited that day, and in some time after married her. This proved a great blow to his fortunes; just before the time of his courtship, he was designed for governor to the late Duke of Richmond; and was to have been allowed fifteen hundred pounds a year from the government. His absence from court in the progress of this amour, and his being yet more absent after his marriage, (for Lady Drogheda was very jealous of him), disgusted his friends there so much, that he lost all his interest with them. His lady died; he got but little by her: and his misfortunes were such, that he was thrown into the Fleet, and lay there seven years.

John Dennis, 1728-30, Spence's Anecdotes, ed. Singer, p. 33

A man who seems to have had among his contemporaries his full share of reputation, to have been esteemed without virtue, and caressed without good nature. Pope was proud of his notice. Wycherley wrote verses in his praise, which he was charged by Dennis with writing to himself, and they agreed for awhile to flatter one another. It is pleasant to remark how soon Pope learnt the cant of an author, and began to treat critics with contempt, though he had yet suffered nothing from them. But the fondness of Wycherley was too violent to last. His esteem of Pope was such that he submitted some poems to his revision; and when Pope, perhaps proud of such confidence, was sufficiently bold in his critcisms and liberal in his alterations, the old scribbler was angry to see his pages defaced, and felt more pain from the detection than content from the amendment of his faults. They parted; but Pope always considered him with kindness; and visited him a little before he died.

Samuel Johnson, 1779-81, *Pope, Lives of the English Poets*

In reading this author's best works, those which one reads most frequently over, and knows almost by heart, one cannot help thinking of the treatment he received from Pope about his verses. It was hardly excusable in a boy of sixteen to an old man of seventy.

William Hazlitt, 1818, *Lectures on the English Comic Writers*

So high did Wycherley stand in the royal favour, that once, when he was confined by a fever to his lodgings in Bow-street, Charles, who, with all his faults, was certainly a man of a social and affable disposition, called on him, sat by his bed, advised him to try change of air, and gave him a handsome sum of money to defray the expense of the journey. Buckingham, then master of the horse, and one of that infamous ministry shown by the name of the Cabal, had been one of the duchess's innumerable paramours. He at first showed some symptoms of jealousy, but soon, after his fashion, veered round from anger to fondness, and gave Wycherley a commission in his own regiment, and a place in the royal household.

Thomas Babington Macaulay, 1841, "Comic Dramatists of the Restoration," *Edinburgh Review; Critical and Miscellaneous Essays*

He ended as he had begun, by unskilfulness and misconduct, having succeeded neither in becoming happy nor honest, having used his vigorous intelligence and real talent only to his own injury and the injury of others.

H. A. Taine, 1871, *History of English Literature,* tr. Van Laun, vol. I, bk. iii, ch. i., p. 480

The Country Wife (1673)

This evening the comedy called the Country Wife was acted in Drury-lane, for the benefit of Mrs. Bignell. . . . The poet, on many occasions, where the propriety of the character will admit of it, insinuates, that there is no defence against vice but the contempt of it; and has, in the natural ideas of an untainted innocent, shown the gradual steps to ruin and destruction which persons of condition run into, without the help of a good education to form their conduct. The torment of a jealous coxcomb, which arises from his own false maxims, and the aggravation of his pain by the very words in which he sees her innocence, makes a very pleasant and instructive satire. The character of Horner, and the design of it, is a good representation of the age in which that comedy was written; at which time love and wenching were the business of life, and the gallant manner of pursuing women was the best recommendation at Court. To this only it is to be imputed, that a gentleman of Mr. Wycherley's character and sense condescends to represent the insults done to the honour of the bed, without just reproof; but to have drawn a man of probity with regard to such considerations had been a monster, and a poet had at that time discovered his want of knowing the manners of the Court he lived in, by a virtuous character in his fine gentleman, as he would shew his ignorance by drawing a vicious one to please the present audience.

Richard Steele, 1709, *The Tatler*, No. 3, Apr. 16, pp. 96, 97

Wycherley was before Congreve; and his *Country Wife* will last longer than anything of Congreve's as a popular acting play. It is only a pity that it is not entirely his own; but it is enough so to do him never-ceasing honour, for the best things are his own. His humour is, in general, broader, his characters more natural, and his incidents more striking than Congreve's. It may be said of Congreve, that the workmanship overlays the materials: in Wycherley, the casting of the parts and the fable are alone sufficient to ensure success. We forget Congreve's characters, and only remember what they say: we remember Wycherley's characters, and the incidents they meet with, just as if they were real, and forget what they say, comparatively speaking.

William Hazlitt, 1818, *Lectures on the English Comic Writers*

In *The Country Wife* there are no such scenes and dialogue of continued excellence as those of Olivia and her visitors in the second act of *The Plain Dealer,* but the principal female character hits a point of more lasting nature, and is an exquisite meeting of the extremes of simplicity and cunning; so that with some alterations, especially of the impudent project of Horner, which would have been an affront in any other age to a decent audience, this comedy outlasted the performances of the graver one.

Leigh Hunt, 1840, ed., *The Dramatic Works of Wycherley, Congreve, Vanbrugh, and Farquhar*

The play itself, with all its extravagant coarseness, is not without its home-speaking moral: for the unrestricted woman of society, Alithea, vindicates her own self-respect by a steadiness and constancy towards the man to whom she had pledged her truth, till he himself, by wanton absurdity and self-seeking, forces her to marry the man she preferred, but had resolutely refused, because of her previous engagement; while the "cribbed and cab-ined" country wife, mewed up before marriage, and jealously watched, and mistrusted, and locked up afterwards, is ready to rush into any eccen-tricity of conduct from pure ignorance, with resentment at the injustice exercised towards her. Bad education, and want of confidence, from first to last, was the cause of all the evil; for her nature is frank and generous, and even lovable. She is a wild weed brought suddenly into the hothouse of artificial and licentious society. Another unfavourable feature in the play is the hollowness and utter absence of all confidence in the men towards each other: there is no restingplace for the heart—all are "dear friends," and all would be traitors at the first glance of an inducement. They cer-tainly are not hypocrites to each other, for no one is deceived in his estimate of his companion's friendship.

Charles Cowden Clarke, 1871, "On the Comic Writers of England,"
The Gentleman's Magazine, n. s., vol. 7, p. 827

The Plain Dealer (1674)

> Since the Plain Dealer's scenes of manly rage
> Not one has dared to lash this crying age.

William Congreve, 1695, Love for Love, Prologue

There is a heaviness about it, indeed, an extravagance, an overdoing both in the style, the plot, and characters, but the truth of feeling and the force of interest prevail over every objection. The character of Manly, the Plain Dealer, is violent, repulsive, and uncouth, which is a fault, though one that seems to have been intended for the sake of contrast; for the portrait of consummate, artful hypocrisy in Olivia, is, perhaps, rendered more striking by it. The indignation excited against this odious and pernicious quality by the masterly exposure to which it is here subjected, is "a discipline of humanity." No one can read this play attentively without being the better for it as long as he lives. It penetrates to the core; it shows the immorality and hateful effects of duplicity, by showing it fixing its harpy fangs in the heart of an honest and worthy man. It is worth ten volumes of sermons.

William Hazlitt, 1818, Lectures on the English Comic Writers

The feelings of the public saw better than the court-wits, and instinctively revolted against this play in spite of the exquisite scenes of the scandal-mongering fine ladies and gentlemen.

Leigh Hunt, 1840, ed., *The Dramatic Works of Wycherley, Congreve, Vanbrugh, and Farquhar*

One of the most brutally cynical, but none the less one of the best-constructed pieces which have ever held the stage. With his magnificent gaiety and buoyancy, Wycherley exaggerated and disfigured the qualities which should rule the comic stage, but they were there; he was a ruffian, but a ruffian of genius.

Edmund Gosse, 1897, *Short History of Modern English Literature*, p. 191

The coarseness of Wycherley's touch is nowhere more obvious than when we compare the picture of Fidelia, the girl who loves Manly and follows him to sea in man's clothes, with Shakespeare's Viola in *Twelfth Night*. Fidelia, with whom we are expected to be in sympathy, aids Manly in his revolting plot against Olivia. But much may be forgiven on account of the underplot of the litigious widow Blackacre, and her son Jerry, a raw squire. They are the forerunners of Goldsmith's Mrs. Hardcastle and Tony Lumpkin, and of Steele's Humphry Gubbin, and the scenes in which they appear enabled Wycherley to make use of such knowledge of the law as he had picked up at the Temple, and supply a much-needed lighter element to the play.

G. A. Aitken, 1900, *Dictionary of National Biography*, vol. LXIII, p. 197

GENERAL

   . . . Wycherley earns hard whate'er he gains;
He wants no Judgment, and he spares no Pains:
He frequently excels; and at the least,
Makes fewer Faults than any of the rest.

John Wilmot Earl Rochester, 1678, *An Allusion to the Tenth Satire of the First Book of Horace*

If he had composed nothing but his poems, he would have been one of the most neglected writers in the English language.

James Granger, 1769-1824, *Biographical History of England*, vol. V, p. 248

Translated into real life, the characters of . . . Wycherley's dramas, are profligates and strumpets,—the business of their brief existence, the undivided pursuit of lawless gallantry. No other spring of action, or possible motive of conduct, is recognized; principles which, universally acted upon, must reduce this frame of things to a chaos. But we do them wrong in so translating them. No such effects are produced in *their* world. When we are among them, we are amongst a chaotic people. We are not to judge them by our usages. No reverend institutions are insulted by their proceedings,—for they have none among them. No peace of families is violated,—for no family ties exist among them. No purity of the marriage bed is stained,—for none is supposed to have a being. No deep affections are disquieted,—no holy wedlock bands are snapped asunder,—for affection's depth and wedded faith are not of the growth of that soil. There is neither right or wrong,—gratitude or its opposite,—claim or duty,— paternity or sonship. Of what consequence is it to virtue, or how is she at all concerned about it, whether Sir Simon, or Dapperwit, steal away Miss Martha; or who is the father of Lord Froth's, or Sir Paul Pliant's children?

Charles Lamb, 1824? On the Artificial Comedy of the
Last Century

Wycherley's plays are said to have been the produce of long and patient labour. The epithet of "slow" was early given to him by Rochester, and was frequently repeated. In truth, his mind, unless we are greatly mistaken, was naturally a very meager soil, and was forced only by great labour and outlay to bear fruit, which, after all, was not of the highest flavour. He has scarcely more claim to originality then Terence. It is not too much to say, that there is hardly anything of the least value in his plays, of which the hint is not to be found elsewhere. The best scenes in *The Gentleman Dancing-Master* were suggested by Calderon's *Maestro de Danzar,* not by any means one of the happiest comedies of the great Castilian poet. *The Country Wife* is borrowed from the *Ecole des Maris* and the *Ecole des Femmes.* The groundwork of *The Plain Dealer* is taken from the *Misanthrope* of Molière. One whole scene is almost translated from the *Critique de l'Ecole des Femmes;* Fidelia is Shakespeare's Viola stolen, and marred in the stealing; and the Widow Blackacre, beyond comparison Wycherley's best comic character, is the Countess in Racine's *Plaideurs,* talking the jargon of English instead of that of French chicane.

Thomas Babington Macaulay, 1841, "Comic Dramatists of the
Restoration," Edinburgh Review; Critical and Miscellaneous Essays

Wycherley, the coarsest writer who has polluted the stage. . . . His style is laboured, and troublesome to read. His tone is virulent and bitter.

He frequently forces his comedy in order to get at spiteful satire. Effort and animosity mark all that he says or puts into the mouths of others. . . . We find in him no poetry of expression, no glimpse of the ideal, no system of morality which could console, raise, or purify men. . . . If Wycherley borrows a character anywhere, it is only to do it violence, or degrade it to the level of his own characters. If he imitates the Agnes of Molière, as he does in *The Country Wife,* he marries her in order to profane marriage, deprives her of honour, still more of shame, still more of grace, and changes her artless tenderness into shameless instincts and scandalous confessions. If he takes Shakespeare's Viola, as in *The Plain Dealer,* it is to drag her through the vileness of infamy, amidst brutalities and surprises. If he translates the part of Célimène, he wipes out at one stroke the manners of a great lady, the woman's delicacy, the tact of the lady of the house, the politeness, the refined air, the superiority of wit and knowledge of the world, in order to substitute the impudence and cheats of a foulmouthed courtesan. If he invents an almost innocent girl, Hippolita, he begins by putting into her mouth words that will not bear transcribing. Whatever he does or says, whether he copies or originates, blames or praises, his stage is a defamation of mankind, which repels even when it attracts and which sickens one while it corrupts. A certain gift hovers over all—namely, vigour—which is never absent in England, and gives a peculiar character to their virtues as to their vices.

H. A. Taine, 1871, *History of English Literature,*
tr. Van Laun, vol. I, bk. iii, ch. i, pp. 480, 481, 483

His merits lie in the vigour with which his characters are drawn, the clearness with which they stand out from one another, and the naturalness with which he both constructs his plots and chooses his language. As for his plots, they are rarely original, and in the main based upon Molière; but Wycherley neither borrows without reflexion, nor combines without care. The wit of his dialogue is less sparkling and spontaneous than that of Congreve's or of Vanbrugh's; he is, as Leigh Hunt says, somewhat heavy as well as brawny in his step, and he lacks in general the gaiety of spirit which is the most charming phase of comic humour. On the other hand, he excels in satire of an intenser kind; his sarcasms are as keen as they are cruel; and the cynicism of his wit cannot prevent us from acknowledging its power. But while he ruthlessly uncloaks the vices of his age, his own moral tone is affected by their influence to as deplorable a degree as is that of the most light-hearted and unthinking of the dramatists contemporary with him.

Adolphus William Ward, 1875-99, *A History of
English Dramatic Literature,* vol. III, p. 462

Whatever the cause, he was lost to the stage at thirty, and his occasional poetical productions . . . were far from qualifying him to sit in the seat of Dryden. He enjoyed, nevertheless, supremacy of another kind. Regarded as an extinct volcano, he gave umbrage to no rivals; his urbane and undemonstrative temper kept him out of literary feuds; all agreed to adore so benign and inoffensive a deity, and the general respect of the lettered world fitly culminated in Pope's dedication of his *Homer* to him, the most splendid literary tribute the age could bestow.

Richard Garnett, 1895, *The Age of Dryden*, p. 126

JOSEPH ADDISON
1672–1719

Joseph Addison, 1672-1719. Born, at Milston, Wilts, 1 May 1672. Educated at private schools at Amesbury and Salisbury; at Lichfield School, 1683; at Charterhouse (1685-87?); to Queen's Coll., Oxford, 1687. Demyship at Magdalen Coll., 1689; B.A., 6 May 1691; M.A., 14 Feb. 1693; Fellowship, 1697-1711. Crown Pension of £300 a year, 1697. To France, autumn of 1699; lived in Blois and Paris (1700). Tour in Italy, winter of 1700-01. At Geneva, 1701; Vienna, 1702. In Germany, Holland, and return to England, 1703. Member of Kitcat Club. Commissioned to write poem to celebrate Battle of Blenheim, 1704; appointed to Under-Secretaryship of State, 1706. With Halifax on Mission to Hanover, 1707. M.P. for Lostwithiel, Nov. 1708; election quashed, Dec. 1709. Sec. to Lord Lieut. of Ireland, and Keeper of Records, 1709. Contributed to Steele's *Tatler*, 1709-10. M.P. for Malmesbury, 1710. Published *Whig Examiner*, (5 nos.) Sept.-Oct., 1710. Bought estate of Bilton in Warwickshire, 1711. *Spectator* published daily, 1 March 1711 to Dec 1712. *Cato* produced at Drury Lane, 14 April 1713. Contrib. to *The Guardian*, May-Sept. 1713; to Steele's *Lover*, and to a revived *Spectator*, June-Sept. 1714. Comedy *The Drummer* anonymously produced, 1715. Resumed political appointments, 1715-16. *The Freeholder* (55 nos.), published anonymously, Dec. 1715-June 1716. Married Countess of Warwick, 3 Aug. 1716. Retired from appointments, March 1718, owing to ill-health. Daughter born in Jan. 1718. Controversy with Steele in *Old Whig* (2 nos., 19 March and 2 April 1719). Died, in London, 17 June 1719. WORKS: *Dissertatio de insignioribus Romanis poetis*, 1692; *A Poem to His Majesty*, 1695; Latin Poem on the Peace of Ryswick, 1697; Lat. poems in *Examen Poeticum Duplex*, 1698, and *Musarum Anglicanarum Analecta*, vol. II., 1699; *Letters from Italy to the Rt. Hon. Charles, Lord Halifax*, 1703; *Remarks on several Parts of Italy*, 1705; *The Campaign*, 1705; *Fair Rosamond* (anon.), 1707; *The Present State of the War* (anon.), 1708; *Papers in "Tatler,"* 1709-10; *Whig Examiner*, 1710; 274 nos. in *Spectator*, 1711-12; *The Late Tryal and Conviction of Count Tariff*, (anon.), 1713; *Cato*, 1713; Papers in *Guardian*, 1713; in *Love* and new *Spectator*, 1714; *Essay concerning the Error in distributing modern Medals*, 1715; *The Drummer* (anon.), 1716; (Poetical addresses to Princess of Wales and Sir G. Kneller, 1716); *The Freeholder* (anon.), 1715-16; Translations of Ovid's *Metamorphoses* with Dryden and others, 1717; *Two Poems; viz., I. On the Deluge. . . . An ode to Dr. Burnet; II. In praise of Physic and Poetry. An ode to Dr. Hannes* (Lat. and Eng.), 1718; *The Resurrection: a poem,* 1718; *The Old Whig* (anon), 1719; *The Patrician* (anon.), 1719. POSTHUMOUS: *Notes upon the twelve books of Paradise Lost* (from *Spectator*), 1719; *Skating: a poem* (Lat. and Eng.), 1720; *Evidences of the Christian Religion,* 1730; *Discourse on Ancient and Modern Learning,* 1739. Collected *Works:* first published by T. Tickell in 1721. *Life:* by Miss Aikin, 1843; by W. J. Courthope, 1844.

R. Farquharson Sharp, 1897, *A Dictionary of English Authors,* p. 2

SEE: *Miscellaneous Works in Verse and Prose,* ed. A. C. Guthkelch, 1914, 2 v.; *Letters,* ed. W. Graham, 1941; Peter Smithers, *Life,* 1954; J. Lannering, *Studies in the Prose Style of Addison,* 1951; also see *The Tatler,* ed. G. A. Aitken, 1894, 4 v.; *The Spectator,* ed. Donald F. Bond, 1965, 5 v.; W. J. Graham, in *English Literary Periodicals,* 1930.

PERSONAL

I dined to-day with Dr. Garth and Mr. Addison at the Devil Tavern, by Temple Bar; and Garth treated. And it is well I dine every day, else I should be longer making out my letters. . . . Mr. Addison's election has passed easy and undisputed, and I believe if he had a mind to be chosen King he would not be refused.

Jonathan Swift, 1710, *Journal to Stella,* Oct. 12

Were there One whose fires
True Genius kindles, and fair Fame inspires;
Blest with each talent and each art to please,
And born to write, converse, and live with ease:
Should such a man, too fond to rule alone,
Bear, like the Turk, no brother near the throne.
View him with scornful, yet with jealous eyes,
And hate for arts that caus'd himself to rise;
Damn with faint praise, assent with civil leer,
And without sneering, teach the rest to sneer;
Willing to wound, and yet afraid to strike,
Just hint a fault, and hesitate dislike;
Alike reserv'd to blame, or to commend,
A tim'rous foe, and a suspicious friend;
Dreading ev'n fools, by Flatterers besieg'd,
And so obliging that he ne'er oblig'd;
Like *Cato,* give his little Senate laws,
And sit attentive to his own applause;

While Wits and Templars ev'ry sentence raise,
And wonder with a foolish face of praise:—
Who but must laugh, if such a man there be?
Who would not weep, if ATTICUS were he?

Alexander Pope, 1715-23-27-35, Epistle to Dr. Arbuthnot

Mr. Jo. Addison, who was made, about Easter last, secretary of state, is *turned out of office,* and made one of the tellers of the exchequer. His under-secretary was Mr. Tho. Tickell, that pretender to poetry, of Queen's college. Mr. Addison was by no means qualifyed for the office of secretary, being not skilled in business, and not knowing how to speak. This is what is commonly said.

Thomas Hearne, 1717, Reliquiæ Hearnianæ, ed. Bliss,
Nov. 9, vol. II, p. 54

It could not be imagined that to diminish a worthy man, as soon as he was no more to be seen, could add to him who had always raised, and almost worshipped, him when living. There never was a more strict friendship than between those gentlemen; nor had they ever any difference but what proceeded from their different way of pursuing the same thing. The one with patience, foresight, and temperate address always waited and stemmed the torrent; while the other often plunged himself into it, and was as often taken out by the temper of him who stood weeping on the brink for his safety, whom he could not dissuade from leaping into it.

Richard Steele, 1720, The Theatre, No. 12

Mr. Addison wrote very fluently; but he was sometimes very slow and scrupulous in correcting. He would show his verses to several friends; and would alter almost everything that any of them hinted at as wrong. He seemed to be too diffident of himself; and too much concerned about his character as a poet: or (as he worded it) too solicitous for that kind of praise, which, God knows, is but a very little matter after all! . . . Many of his Spectators he wrote very fast; and sent them to the press as soon as they were written. It seems to have been best for him not to have had too much time to correct. . . . Addison was perfect good company with intimates; and had something more charming in his conversation than I ever knew in any other man: but with any mixture of strangers, and sometimes only with one, he seemed to preserve his dignity much; with a stiff sort of silence.

Alexander Pope, 1728-30, Spence's Anecdotes,
ed. Singer, pp. 37, 38

Atticus could be a friend to men, without awaking their resentment, and be satisfied with his own virtue without seeking popular fame: he had the reward of his wisdom in his transquality, and will ever stand among the few examples of true philosophy, either ancient or modern. . . . You will think I have been too long on the character of Atticus. I own I took pleasure in explaining it. Pope thought himself covertly very severe on Addison, by giving him that name; and I feel indignation whenever he is abused, both from his own merit, and because he was ever your father's friend; besides that it is naturally disgusting to see him lampooned after his death by the same man who paid him the most servile court while he lived, and was besides highly obliged by him.

Lady Mary Wortley Montagu, 1755, Letter to the Countess
of Bute, July 20

Dr. Young has published a new book, on purpose, he says himself, to have an opportunity of telling a story that he has known these forty years. Mr. Addison sent for the young Lord Warwick, as he was dying, to show him in what peace a Christian could die—unluckily he died of brandy—nothing makes a Christian die in peace like being maudlin! but don't say this in Gath, where you are.

Horace Walpole, 1759, Letters, May 16, ed. Cunningham,
vol. III, p. 227

Addison, a crawling sycophant, full of envy and spleen; frantic when a friend prospered; happy only when misfortune lighted on his associates; a hypocrite who would take you by the hand, and if he heard you utter a sentiment which in his heart he knew to be erroneous, would labour to confirm you in it with all his zeal, rejoicing in your inexperience, as Satan might exult over the fall of a young novice.

Edward Wortley Montagu, 1776? An Autobiography, vol. I, p. 57

Of this memorable friendship the greater praise must be given to Steele. It is not hard to love those from whom nothing can be feared; and Addison never considered Steele as a rival; but Steele lived, as he confesses, under an habitual subjection to the predominating genius of Addison, whom he always mentioned with reverence, and treated with obsequiousness. Addison, who knew his own dignity, could not always forbear to shew it, by playing a little upon his admirer; but he was in no danger of retort: his jests were endured without resistance or resentment. But the sneer of jocularity was not the worst. Steele, whose imprudence of generosity, or vanity of profusion, kept him always incurably necessitous, upon some pressing exigence, in an evil hour, borrowed an hundred pounds of his friend, probably without much purpose of repayment; but Addison, who seems to have had other notions of a hundred pounds, grew impatient of delay, and reclaimed his loan by an execution. Steele felt with great sensibility the obduracy of his creditor; but with emotions of sorrow rather than of anger.

Samuel Johnson, 1779-81, *Addison, Lives of the English Poets*

Many persons having doubts concerning this fact, I applied to Dr. Johnson to learn on what authority he asserted it. He told me he had it from Savage, who lived in intimacy with Steele, and who mentioned that Steele told him the story with tears in his eyes. Ben Victor, Johnson said, likewise informed him of this remarkable transaction, from the relation of Mr. Wilks the comedian, who was also an intimate of Steele's. Some, in defence of Addison, here said, that "the act was done with the good-natured view of rousing Steele and correcting that profusion which always made him necessitous." "If that were the case," said Johnson, "and that he only wanted to alarm Steele, he would afterwards have *returned* the money to his friend, which it is not pretended he did.

Edmond Malone, 1781, March 15, *Boswell by Croker*, p. 671

Addison. Dick! I am come to remonstrate with you on those unlucky habits which have been so detrimental to your health and fortune.

Steele. Many thanks, Mr. Addison; but really my fortune is not much improved by your arresting me for the hundred pounds; nor is my health, if spirits are an indication of it, on seeing my furniture sold by auction to raise the money.

Addison. Pooh, pooh, Dick! what furniture had you about the house.

Steele. At least I had the arm-chair, of which you never before had dispossessed me longer than the evening; and happy should I have been to enjoy your company in it again and again, if you had left it me.

Addison. We will contrive to hire another. I do assure you, my dear Dick, I have really felt for you.

Steele. I only wish, my kind friend, you had not put out your feelers quite so far, nor exactly in this direction; and that my poor wife had received an hour's notice; she might have carried a few trinkets to some neighbour. She wanted her salts; and the bailiff thanked her for the bottle that contained them, telling her the gold head of it was worth pretty nearly half-a-guinea.

Walter Savage Landor, 1828, *Imaginary Conversations,*
Third Series, Works, vol. V, p. 50

Some blemishes may undoubtedly be detected in his character; but the more carefully it is examined, the more will it appear, to use the phrase of the old anatomists, sound in the noble parts—free from all taint of perfidy, of cowardice, of cruelty, of ingratitude, of envy. Men may easily be named in whom some particular good disposition has been more conspicuous than in Addison. But the just harmony of qualities, the exact temper between the stern and the humane virtues, the habitual observance of every law, not only of moral rectitude, but of moral grace and dignity, distinguished him from all men who have been tried by equally full information.

Thomas Babington Macaulay, 1843, "Life and Writings of
Addison," Critical and Miscellaneous Essays

When this man looks from the world whose weaknesses he describes so benevolently, up to the Heaven which shines over us all, I can hardly fancy a human face lighted up with a more serene rapture; a human intellect thrilling with a purer love and adoration than Joseph Addison's. Listen to him: from your childhood you have known the verses; but who can hear their sacred music without love and awe?

"Soon as the evening shades prevail,
  The moon takes up the wonderous tale," etc.

It seems to me those verses shine like the stars. They shine out of a great deep calm. When he turns to heaven, a Sabbath comes over that man's mind: and his face lights up from it with a glory of thanks and prayer. . . . If Swift's life was the most wretched, I think Addison's was one of the most enviable. A life prosperous and beautiful—a calm death—an immense fame and affection afterwards for his happy and spotless name.

William Makepeace Thackeray, 1853, English Humourists of
the Eighteenth Century

It seems to have been in Holland House (for he died shortly afterwards) that Addison was visited by Milton's daughter, when he requested her to bring him some evidences of her birth. The moment he beheld her he exclaimed: "Madam, you need no other voucher; your face is a sufficient testimonial whose daughter you are." It must have been very pleasing to Addison to befriend Milton's daughter, for he had been the first to popularize the great poet by his critiques on Paradise Lost, in the Spectator.

Leigh Hunt, 1855, The Old Court Suburb, ch. xv

There is not a name in the annals of English literature more widely associated with pleasant recollections than that of Addison. His beautiful hymns trembled on our lips in childhood; his cheerful essays first lured us, in youth, to a sense of the minor philosophy of life; we tread his walk at Oxford with loving steps; gaze on his portrait, at Holland House or the Bodleian Gallery, as on the lineaments of a revered friend; recall his journey into Italy, his ineffectual maiden speech, his successful tragedy, his morning studies, his evenings at Button's, his unfortunate marriage, and his holy death-bed, as if they were the experiences of one personally known, as well as fondly admired; and we muse beside the marble that designates his sepulchre in Westminster Abbey, between those of his first patron and his most cherished friend, with an interest such as is rarely awakened by the memory of one familiar to us only through books. The harmony of his character sanctions his writings; the tone of the *Spectator* breathes friendliness as well as instruction; and the tributes of contemporaries to his private worth, and of generations to his literary excellence, combine with our knowledge of the vicissitudes of his life, to render his mind and person as near to our sympathies as they are high in our esteem. Over his faults we throw the veil of charity, and cherish the remembrance of his benevolence and piety, his refinement and wisdom, as the sacred legacy of an intellectual benefactor.

Henry T. Tuckerman, 1857, *Essays, Biographical and Critical,*
p. 394

He was an amiable and highly gifted, rather than a strong or great man. His shrinking timidity of temperament, his singular modesty of manners, his quiet, sly power of humorous yet kindly observation, his minute style of criticism, even the peculiar cast of his piety, all served to stamp the lady-man. In taciturnity alone he bore the sex no resemblance. And hence it is that Campbell in poetry, and Addison in prose, are, or were, the great favourites of female readers. He had many weaknesses, but, as in the character of woman, they appeared beautiful, and cognate to his gentle nature. His fear of giving offence was one of the most prominent of these. In his writings and in his life, he seems always treading on thin ice.

George Gilfillan, 1859, ed., *Poetical Works of Joseph Addison,*
etc., Life, p. xxx

Next came the age of the *Tatler* and *Spectator.* Steele, editor of the first, is buried at his seat near Carmarthen. His second wife, "his dearest Prue," is laid amongst the poets. But the great funeral of this circle is that of Addison. The last serene moments of his life were at Warwick House. "See how a Christian can die." . . . The spot selected was the vault in the north aisle of that Chapel, in the eastern recess of which already lay the coffins of Monk and his wife, Montague Earl of Sandwich, and the two Halifaxes. Craggs was to follow within a year. Into that recess, doubtless in order to rest by the side of his patron, Montague Earl of Halifax, the coffin of Addison was lowered. At the head of the vault, Atterbury officiated as Dean, in his prelate's robes. Round him stood the Westminster scholars, with their white tapers, dimly lighting up the fretted aisle. One of them has left on record the deep impression left on them by the unusual energy and solemnity of Atterbury's sonorous voice. Close by was the faithful friend of the departed—Tickell, who has described the scene in poetry yet more touching than Macaulay's prose.

> Arthur Penrhyn Stanley, 1867-96, *Historical Memorials*
> *of Westminster Abbey*

The harmony and symmetry of this winning personality has, in a sense, told against it; for men are prone to call the well-balanced nature cold and the well-regulated life Pharisaic. Addison did not escape charges of this kind from the wild livers of his own time, who could not dissociate genius from profligacy nor generosity of nature from prodigality. It was one of the greatest services of Addison to his generation and to all generations, that in an age of violent passions, he showed how a strong man could govern himself. In a time of reckless living, he illustrated the power which flows from subordination of pleasure to duty. In a day when wit was identified with malice, he brought out its power to entertain, surprise, and delight, without taking on the irreverent levity of Voltaire, the bitterness of Swift, or the malice of Pope.

> Hamilton Wright Mabie, 1896, *Library of the World's*
> *Best Literature,* ed. Warner, vol. I, p. 153

Addison's individuality stands in striking contrast with that of his friend, Steele. He was a man of pure and noble character, of lofty ideals, and genuine piety; but we miss in him the fervour and spontaneity that make Steele, with all his errors and infirmities, so delightful and engaging a figure. He was proud, shy, reserved, intensely self-conscious, and thus often left with those about him an impression of coldness and austerity. But he was, in reality, one of the kindest and most sympathetic of men. In the annals of literature he may well bear "without abuse the grand old name of gentleman," for along with exquisite breeding and urbanity he possessed masculine courage and feminine sensibility and grace.

> William Henry Hudson, 1899, ed., *The Sir Roger De Coverley*
> *Papers,* Introduction, p. xiii

An Account of the Greatest English Poets (1694)

His *Account of the Principal English Poets* is just but tame; he probably wrote it in metre merely because Roscommon had done something of the same kind before him; at any rate, by the side of the animated judgments of Pope in his *Epistle to Augustus,* his historical survey of English poetry seems flat and languid.

W. J. Courthope, 1880, *English Poets,* ed. Ward, vol. III, p. 1

It would be a great mistake to confound these verses, which are scarcely more than an exercise in penmanship, with Addison's real work.

Thomas Sergeant Perry, 1883, *English Literature in the Eighteenth Century*, p. 133, note

The Campaign (1705)

The next composition is the far-famed *Campaign,* which Dr. Warton has termed a "Gazette in Rhyme," with harshness not often used by the good-nature of his criticism. Before a censure so severe is admitted, let us consider that War is a frequent subject of Poetry, and then enquire who has described it with more justness and force. Many of our own writers tried their powers upon this year of victory: yet Addison's is confessedly the best performance; his poem is the work of a man not blinded by the dust of learning; his images are not borrowed merely from books. The superiority which he confers upon his hero is not personal prowess, and "mighty bone," but deliberate intrepidity, a calm command of his passions, and the power of consulting his own mind in the midst of danger. The rejection and contempt of fiction is rational and manly.

Samuel Johnson, 1779-81, *Addison, Lives of the English Poets*

Addison's "Blenheim" is poor enough; one might think it a translation from some German original of those times. Gottsched's aunt, or Bodmer's wet-nurse, might have written it.

Thomas De Quincey, 1847-58, *Schlosser's Literary History, Works,* ed. Masson, vol. XI, p. 27

His principal piece, *The Campaign,* is an excellent model of becoming and classical style. Each verse is full, perfect in itself, with a clever antithesis, or a good epithet, or a figure of abbreviation.

H. A. Taine, 1871, *History of English Literature,* tr. Van Laun, vol. II, bk. iii, ch. iv, p. 92

As a poem, *The Campaign* shows neither loftiness of invention nor enthusiasm of personal feeling, and it cannot therefore be ranked with such an ode as Horace's *Qualem ministrum,* or with Pope's very fine *Epistle* to the Earl of Oxford after his disgrace. Its methodical narrative style is scarcely misrepresented by Warton's sarcastic description of it; but it should be remembered that this style was adopted by Addison with deliberate intention. . . . The design here avowed is certainly not poetical, but it is eminently business-like and extremely well adapted to the end in view. What Godolphin wanted was a set of complimentary verses on Marlborough. Addison, with infinite tact, declares that the highest compliment that can be paid to the hero is to recite his actions in their unadorned grandeur. This happy turn of flattery shows how far he had advanced in literary skill since he wrote his address "To the King."

W. J. Courthope, 1884, *Addison* (*English Men of Letters*), pp. 61, 62

The poem, like all Addison's performances of the kind, shows facility and poetic sensibility, stopping short of poetic genius. It is better than a similar poem of Halifax's on the battle of the Boyne, but does not stand out at any great elevation above the work of the time; and Macaulay's remark that it is not absurdly mythological is praise which might equally be applied to Halifax and others. Macaulay notes that the simile of the angel owed its great effect to its allusion to the famous storm of 1703; and Johnson quotes the remark of Dr. Madden that if he had proposed the same topic to ten schoolboys, he should not have been surprised if eight had brought him the angel. Warton unkindly calls the poem a "Gazette in rhyme." We may be content to say that it was on the higher level of official poetry, and helped Addison's rise in literature and politics.

Leslie Stephen, 1885, *Dictionary of National Biography,* vol. I, p. 124

Fair Rosamond (1707)

A criticism on this most wretched performance is more than it deserves, but, to account for the bad reception it met with, it is necessary to mention that the music preponderating against the elegance and humour of the poetry, and the reputation of its author, bore it down the third night of representation. To begin with the overture; it is in three parts, and in the key of D with the greater third; the first movement pretends to a great deal of spirit, but is mere noise. The two violin parts are simple counterpoint, and move in thirds almost throughout; and the last movement intended for an air is the most insipid ever heard. As to the songs, they have neither air nor expression. There is one that sings thus:—

O the pleasing, pleasing, pleasing, pleasing, pleasing anguish.

An ingenious and sensible writer, mentioned in a preceding note, who was present at the performance, says of *Rosamond* that it is a confused chaos of music, and that its only merit is its shortness.

Sir John Hawkins, 1776, A General History of the Science and
Practice of Music, ch. clxxi

The whole drama is airy and elegant; engaging in its process, and pleasing in its conclusion. If Addison had cultivated the lighter parts of poetry, he would probably have excelled.

Samuel Johnson, 1779-81, Addison, Lives of the English Poets

It is the highest and easiest style of Dryden,—that in which he wrote *Alexander's Feast,* and some other of his lyrics,—but is sustained for some fifteen hundred lines with an energy and a grace which we doubt if even Dryden could have equalled. Its verses not only move but dance. The spirit is genial and sunny, and above the mazy motions shines the light of genuine poetry.

George Gilfillan, 1859, ed., Poetical Works of Joseph Addison,
etc., Life, p. xxiv

Addison lacked the qualities of a successful libretto writer. He was too serious, and despite the lightness of his touch, there was a certain rigidity in him which made him unapt at versification which required quickness, agility, and variety. When he attempted to give his verse gayety of manner, he did not get beyond awkward simulation of an ease which nature had denied him.

Hamilton Wright Mabie, 1896, Library of the World's
Best Literature, ed. Warner, vol. I, p. 152

The Tatler (1709-10)

A finer piece of humour was never written, than Addison's Journal of the Court of honour in *The Tatler;* in which every reader perceives the opposition of dignity and meanness: the latter arising from the insignificance of the causes; the former from the serious air of the narrative, from the accuracy of detail and minuteness of enquiry in the several examinations, and from the grave deportment of the judge and jury. Indeed, through the whole work, the personage of Isaac Bickerstaff is supported with inimitable pleasantry. The conjurer, the politician, the man of humour, the critic; the seriousness of the moralist, and the mock dignity of the astrologer; the vivacities and the infirmities peculiar to old age, are all so blended and contrasted in the censor of Great Britain, as to form a character equally complex and natural, equally laughable and respectable.

James Beattie, 1776-9, Essays, p. 356

It has been too much the fashion to depreciate the *Tatler,* and to contrast it with its more elaborate and finished successor the *Spectator.* The attempt, however, is not just; they are built upon very different plans; and if it be allowed, as it probably must upon comparison, that there is more unity, regularity, and polish in the conduct and plan of the *Spectator,* it may, I think, with equal truth be asserted of the *Tatler,* that it possesses more vivacity, wit, and variety, than any periodical paper extant.

Nathan Drake, 1804, Essays Illustrative of the Tatler,
Spectator and Guardian, vol. I, p. 342

We now enter on those parts of Mr. Addison's prose works, which have done him the greatest honour, and have placed him at the head of those whom we call our polite writers. I know that many readers prefer Dr. Swift's prose to his:—but, whatever other merit the Dean's writings may have, (and they have, certainly, a great deal,) I affirm it with confidence, (because I have examined them both with care,) that they are not comparable to Mr. Addison's, in the correctness, propriety, and elegance of expression. Mr. Addison possessed two talents, both of them very uncommon, which singularly qualified him to excel. . . . I mean an exquisite knowledge of the English tongue in all its purity and delicacy; and a vein of humour, which flowed naturally and abundantly from him on every subject; and which experience hath shown to be inimitable. But it is in the *former* respect only that I shall criticise these papers; and I shall do it with severity, lest time, and the authority of his name, (which, of course, must become sacred,) should give a sanction even to his defects. If any man of genius should be so happy, as to equal all the excellencies of his prose, and to avoid the few blemishes which may, haply, be found in it, he would be a perfect model of style, in this way of writing: but of such an one, it is enough to say at present, (and I shall, surely, offend no good writer in saying it,)

"—hunc nequeo monstrare, et sentio tantúm."

Richard Hurd, 1808-10, ed., Works of Joseph Addison, The Tatler

Apart from the fortunate popularity attaching to the central figure, and the advantage arising from a narrower field of operation, it can scarcely be affirmed that the *Spectator* greatly excelled the *Tatler,* especially when attention is confined to its more enduring characteristics. If we withdraw the critical work of Addison, part of which, according to Tickell, was not prepared expressly for its pages, and to-day has lost much of its value,— if we withdraw the moral essays of Steele, now grown tedious by frequent imitation, what remains is neither better nor worse than the staple material of the *Tatler.* In the social paper neither writer surpassed what he had done before. As already stated, Addison's best work in the *Spectator,* though perhaps more sustained, is not superior to his best work in its predecessor; while Steele in that predecessor is distinctly stronger.

Austin Dobson, 1886, *Richard Steele (English Worthies),* p. 141

The Spectator (1711-12)

It would have been impossible for Mr. Addison, who made little or no use of letters sent in by the numerous correspondents of the *Spectator,* to have executed his large share of this task, in so exquisite a manner, if he had not ingrafted into it many pieces, that had lain by him in little hints and minutes, which he from time to time collected, and ranged in order, and moulded into the form in which they now appear.

Thomas Tickell, 1721, ed., *The Works of Joseph Addison,*
Preface, vol. I, p. xiii

I have lately studied *The Spectator,* and with increasing pleasure and admiration. Yet it must be evident to you that there is a class of thoughts and feelings, and these, too, the most important, even practically, which it would be impossible to convey in the manner of Addison, and which, if Addison had possessed, he would not have been Addison. . . . *The Spectator* itself has innocently contributed to the general taste for unconnected writing, just as if "Reading made easy" should act to give men an aversion to words of more than two syllables, instead of drawing them *through* those words into the power of reading books in general.

Samuel Taylor Coleridge, 1810, *Letters,* ed., E. H. Coleridge,
vol. II, p. 557

Not many years ago, it was very generally the custom, I remember, for every young person, male and female, to go through a course of reading of the papers of the *Spectator.* This has fallen quite into disuse now-a-days, and I do not know that it is much to be regretted. The *Spectator* contains, undoubtedly, much sensible and sound morality; but it is not a very high order of Christian ethics. It contains much judicious criticism, but certainly not comparable to the deeper philosophy of criticism which has entered into English literature in the present century. Those papers will always have a semi-historical interest, as picturing the habits and manners of the times—a moral value, as a kindly, good-natured censorship of those manners. In one respect, the *Spectator* stands unrivalled to this day: I allude to the exquisite humour in those numbers in which Sir Roger de Coverley figures. If any one desire to form a just notion of what is meant by that very indefinable quality called "humour," he cannot more agreeably inform himself than by selecting the Sir Roger de Coverly papers, and reading them in series.

Henry Reed, 1855, Lectures on English Literature
From Chaucer to Tennyson, p. 231

He has, in his imaginary Club, created a number of characters which will be recognized and loved wherever English is read. The prose of these exquisite Essays is perfect, as a specimen of the very best work of the era. To the young student it will, of course, have something of an old-world flavour, but its quaintness and pleasantness will amply repay him for any unfamiliarity with the terms of the expression of the day. It is always clear and easy, free from pomposity, pedantry, and verbosity, deeply religious in feeling, and tenderly humorous in expression.

Kathleen Knox, 1882, English Lessons, p. 61

The treatment of the character-sketch by Steele and Addison in the *Spectator* (1711-12) was highly original. They drew portraits of representative Englishmen, and brought them together in conversation in a London club. They conducted Sir Roger de Coverley through Westminster Abbey, to the playhouse, to Vauxhall, into the country to Coverley church and assizes; they incidentally took a retrospective view of his life, and finally told the story of his death. When they had done this they had not only created one of the best defined characters in our prose literature, but they had almost transformed the character-sketch into a novel of London and provincial life. From the *Spectator* the character-sketch, with its types and minute observation and urbane ridicule passed into the novel, and became a part of it.

Wilbur L. Cross, 1899, Development of the English Novel, p. 24

SIR ROGER DE COVERLEY

It is recorded by Budgell, that of the characters feigned or exhibited in the *Spectator,* the favourite of Addison was Sir Roger de Coverley, of whom he had formed a very delicate and discriminate idea, which he would not suffer to be violated; and therefore, when Steele had shewn him innocently picking up a girl in the Temple, and taking her to a tavern, he drew upon himself so much of his friend's indignation, that he was forced to appease him by a promise of forbearing Sir Roger for the time to come. The reason which induced Cervantes to bring his hero to the grave, *para mi sola nacio Don Quixote, y yo para el,* made Addison declare, with undue vehemence of expression, that he would kill Sir Roger; being of opinion that they were born for one another and that any other hand would do him wrong.

Samuel Johnson, 1779-81, *Addison, Lives of the English Poets*

Sir Roger de Coverley is one of those truthful types of character, which, though created by the mind of man, yet, by the ordination of Nature herself (for Nature includes art among her works), outlasts the successive generations of flesh and blood which it represents. The individuals perish, and leave no memorial; nay, we hardly care to know them while living. We might find them tiresome. We feel that Nature has done well in making them; we are grateful for the race; especially on behalf of others, and of the poor; but we do not particularly see the value of their society; when, lo! in steps one of Nature's imitators—called men of genius—and, by the mere fact of producing a likeness of the species to the mind's eye, enchants us forever both with it and himself. A little philosophy may easily explain this; but perhaps a little more may still leave it among the most interesting of mysteries.

Leigh Hunt, 1849, *A Book for a Corner*

No truer or more winning picture of worthy old English knighthood can you find anywhere in literature; nowhere such a tender twilight color falling through brooks upon old English country homes. Those papers made the scaffolding by which our own Irving built up his best stories about English country homesteads, and English revels of Christmas; and the De Coverley echoes sound sweetly and surely all up and down the pages of *Bracebridge Hall.*

Donald G. Mitchell, 1890, *English Lands, Letters and Kings,*
Vol. II: From Elizabeth to Anne, p. 291

Of all things else that Addison has done there remains one preëminent figure which is his chief claim to immortality. *The Campaign* has disappeared out of literature; *Cato* is known only by a few well-known lines; the *Spectator* itself, though a work which no gentleman's library can be without, dwells generally in dignified retirement there, and is seldom seen on any table but the student's, though we are all supposed to be familiar with it: but Sir Roger de Coverley is the familiar friend of most people who have read anything at all, and the acquaintance by sight, if we may so speak, of everybody. There is no form better known in all literature. His simple rustic state, his modest sense of his own importance, his kind and genial patronage of the younger world, which would laugh at him if it were not overawed by his modesty and goodness, and which still sniggers in its sleeve at all those kind, ridiculous ways of his as he walks about in London, taken in on all sides, with his hand always in his purse, and his heart in its right place, are always familiar and delightful. We learn with a kind of shock that it was Steele who first introduced this perfect gentleman to the world, and can only hope that it was Addison's idea from the first, and that he did not merely snatch out of his friend's hands and appropriate a conception so entirely according to his own heart.

Mrs. M. O. W. Oliphant, 1894, *Historical Characters of the Reign of Queen Anne,* p. 193

It is a rather singular circumstance that we have in our literature one well-drawn character—fulfilling all the requirements of a "study" from the life, one of our important and most classic characters indeed—existing entirely outside the pages of a novel, a drama, or of any formal fiction. This is genial, worthy old Sir Roger de Coverley, who in the year 1711 strolled into England quietly and unannounced, introduced and hospitably entertained by Joseph Addison and Richard Steele. Addison, it is true, produced no novel; he did as great a thing, for he drew a character so strongly individualized, so amiable in its attributes, that he has lived from that day to ours one of the best beloved in English fiction. Thus Joseph Addison may be regarded as at the very beginning of the century suggesting if not inventing the novel form, and as setting a pattern in the portrayal of real character which has rarely been surpassed.

William Edward Simonds, 1894, *Introduction to the Study of English Fiction,* p. 39

While *The Spectator* contains ample material for a fully developed novel, it only just falls short of making a fully developed novel out of it. Had the various detached episodes in which the essayist and his companions figure been more closely related to one another—had they been gathered up and carefully woven into the definite pattern of the plot—then the *Sir Roger de Coverley Papers* here reprinted would have been to all intents and purposes a serial novel running through a periodical. As it is, we can never properly neglect them in any historical survey of English prose fiction.

William Henry Hudson, 1899, ed., *The Sir Roger de Coverley Papers,* Introduction, p. xxiii

Cato (1713)

Cato, a most noble play of Mr. Addison, and the only one he writ, is to be acted in Easter week. The town is full of expectation of it, the Boxes being already bespoke, and he designing to give all the Benefit away among the Actors in proportion to their performing.

George Berkeley, 1712-13, Letter to Sir John Perceval

Cato was not so much the wonder of Rome in his days as he is of Britain in ours; and though all the foolish industry possible has been used to make it thought a party play, yet what the author once said of another may the most properly in the world be applied to him on this occasion:

> Envy itself is dumb, in wonder lost,
> And factions strive who shall applaud him most.

The numerous and violent claps of the Whig-party on the one side of the theatre were echoed back by the Tories on the other, while the author sweated behind the scenes with concern to find their applause proceeding more from the hand than the head. This was the case, too, of the prologue-writer, who was clapped into a stanch Whig at almost every two lines. I believe you have heard, that after all the applauses of the opposite faction, my Lord Bolingbroke sent for Booth, who played Cato, into the box between one of the acts, and presented him with fifty guineas in acknowledgement (as he expressed it) for defending the cause of liberty so well against a perpetual dictator. The Whigs are unwilling to be distanced this way, as it is said, and therefore design a present to the same Cato very speedily; in the meantime they are getting ready as good a sentence as the former on their side, so betwixt them it is probable that Cato (as Dr. Garth expressed it) may have something to live upon after he dies.

Alexander Pope, 1713, Letter to Sir William Trumbull, April 30

But now let us sum up all these absurdities together. Sempronius goes at noonday, in Juba's guards, to Cato's palace, in order to pass for Juba, in a place where they were both so very well known: he meets Juba there, and resolves to murder him with his own guards. Upon the guards appearing a little bashful, he threatens them:

> Hah! Dastards, do you tremble!
> Or act like men; or, by yon azure heav'n!

But the guards still remaining restive, Sempronius himself attacks Juba, while each of the guards is representing Mr. Spectator's sign of the Gaper, awed, it seems, and terrified by Sempronius's threats. Juba kills Sempronius, and takes his own army prisoners, and carries them in triumph away to

Cato. Now, I would fain know, if any parts of Mr. Bayes's tragedy is so full of absurdity as this?

John Dennis, 1713, *Criticism on Cato*

It is in every body's memory, with what applause it was received by the public; that the first run of it lasted for a month; and then stopped, only because one of the performers became incapable of acting a principle part. The Author received a message, that the Queen would be pleased to have it dedicated to her: but as he had designed that compliment elsewhere, he found himself obliged by his duty on the one side, and his honour on the other, to send it into the world without any dedication. The fame of this Tragedy soon spread through *Europe,* and it has not only been translated, but acted in most of the languages of Christendom. The translation of it into *Italian,* by Signor *Salvini,* is very well known; but I have not been able to learn, whether that of Signor *Valetta,* a young *Neapolitan* nobleman, has ever been made public.

Thomas Tickell, 1721, ed., *The Works of Joseph Addison,*
Preface, vol. I, p. xiv

In 1703, nine years before it was acted, I had the pleasure of reading the first four acts (which was all of it then written) privately with Sir Richard Steele: it may be needless to say it was impossible to lay them out of my hand until I had gone through them; or to dwell upon the delight his friendship to the author received, upon my being so warmly pleased with them; but my satisfaction was as highly disappointed when he told me, whatever spirit Mr. Addison had shown in his writing it, he doubted he would never have courage enough to let his *Cato* stand the censure of an English audience; that it had only been the amusement of his leisure hours in Italy, and was never intended for the stage. The poetical diffidence Sir Richard himself spoke of with some concern, and in the transport of his imagination could not help saying, "Good God! what a part would Betterton make of Cato!" But this was seven years before Betterton died, and when Booth (who afterwards made his fortune by acting it) was in his theatrical minority. In the latter end of Queen Anne's reign, when our national politics had changed hands, the friends of Mr. Addison then thought it a proper time to animate the public with the sentiments of Cato. In a word, their importunities were too warm to be resisted; and it was no sooner finished than hurried to the stage, in April 1712.

Colley Cibber, 1739, *An Apology for His Life*

Is a glaring instance of the force of party; so sententious and declamatory a drama would never have met with such rapid and amazing success, if every line and sentiment had not been particularly tortured and applied to recent events, and the reigning disputes of the times. The purity and energy of the diction, and the loftiness of the sentiments, copied in a great measure from Lucan, Tacitus, and Seneca the philosopher, merit approbation. But I have always thought, that those pompous Roman sentiments are not so difficult to be produced, as is vulgarly imagined; and which, indeed, dazzle only the vulgar. A stroke of nature is, in my opinion, worth a hundred such thoughts as

> When vice prevails, and impious men bear sway,
> The post of honour is a private station.

Cato is a fine dialogue on liberty, and the love of one's country; but considered as a dramatic performance, nay, as a model of a just tragedy, as some have affectedly represented it, it must be owned to want action and pathos; the two hinges, I presume, on which a just tragedy ought necessarily to turn, and without which it cannot subsist. It wants also character.

Joseph Warton, 1756, *Essay on the Genius and Writings of Pope,*
vol. I, p. 270

Addison possesses an elegant mind, but he was by no means a poet. He undertook to purify the English tragedy, by a compliance with the supposed rules of good taste. We might have expected from a judge of the ancients, that he would have endeavoured to approach the Greek models. Whether he had any such intention I know not, but certain it is, that he produced nothing but a tragedy after the French cut. *Cato* is a feeble and frigid piece, almost destitute of action, without one truly overpowering moment. Addison has so narrowed a great and heroic picture by his timid manner of treating it, that he could not even fill up the frame without foreign intermixtures. . . . Addison took his measures well; he brought all the great and small critics, with Pope at their head, the whole militia of good taste under arms, that he might excite a high expectation of the piece which he had produced with so much labour. *Cato* was universally praised, as a work without an equal. And on what foundation do these boundless claims rest? On regularity of form? This had been already observed by the French poets for nearly a century, and notwithstanding the constraint, they had often attained a much stronger pathetic effect. Or on the political sentiments? But in a single dialogue between Brutus and Cassius, in Shakespeare, there is more of a Roman way of thinking, and republican energy, than in all *Cato.*

Augustus William Schlegel, 1809, *Dramatic Art and Literature,*
Lecture xiii, tr. Black

Addison's *Cato,* in spite of Dennis's criticism, still retains possession of the stage with all its unities. My love and admiration for Addison is as great as any person's, let that other person be who he will; but it is not founded on his *Cato,* in extolling which Whigs and Tories contended in loud applause. The interest of this play (bating that shadowy regret that always clings to and flickers round the form of free antiquity) is confined to the declamation, which is feeble in itself, and not heard on the stage. I have seen Mr. Kemble in this part repeat the Soliloquy on Death without a line being distinctly heard; nothing was observable but the thoughtful motion of his lips, and the occasional extension of his hand in sign of doubts suggested or resolved; yet this beautiful and expressive dumb-show, with the propriety of his costume, and the elegance of his attitude and figure, excited the most lively interest, and kept attention even more on the stretch, to catch every imperfect syllable or speaking gesture. There is nothing, however, in the play to excite ridicule, or shock by absurdity, except the love scenes, which are passed over as what the spectator has no proper concern with; and however feeble or languid the interest produced by a dramatic exhibition, unless there is some positive stumbling-block thrown in the way, or gross offence given to an audience, it is generally suffered to linger on to a *euthanasia,* instead of dying a violent and premature death.

William Hazlitt, 1820, Lectures on the Dramatic Literature
of the Age of Elizabeth, Lecture viii

Its dramatic weakness has never been denied. The love scenes are incongrous. It consists in the great part of declamation which Addison's taste restrained within limits, and polished into many still familiar quotations, but which remains commonplace.

Leslie Stephen, 1885, Dictionary of National Biography,
vol. I, p. 128

Criticisms

It gives one pain to refuse to such a writer as Mr. *Addison,* any *kind* of merit, to which he appears to have laid claim, and which the generality [of his readers] have seemed willing to allow him. Yet it must not be dissembled, that *criticism* was, by no means, his talent. His taste was truly elegant; but he had neither that vigour of understanding, nor chastised, philosophical spirit, which are so essential to this character, and which we find in hardly any of the antients, besides Aristotle, and but in a very few of the moderns. For what concerns his *criticism on Milton* in particular, there was this accidental benefit arising from it, that it occasioned an admirable poet to be read, and his excellencies to be observed. But for the merit of the work itself, if there be anything just in the *plan,* it was, because

Aristotle and Bossu had taken the same route before him. And as to his *own* proper observations, they are for the most part, so general and indeterminate, as to afford but little instruction to the reader, and are, not unfrequently, altogether frivolous.

Richard Hurd, 1751, *Comments on Horace's
Epistola ad Augustum*

It is already well known, that Addison had no very intimate acquaintance with the literature of his own country. It is known, also, that he did not think such an acquaintance any ways essential to the character of an elegant scholar and *littérateur*. Quite enough he found it, and more than enough for the time he had to spare, if he could maintain a tolerable familiarity with the foremost Latin poets, and a very slender one indeed with the Grecian. *How* slender, we can see in his *Travels*. Of modern authors, none as yet had been published with notes, commentaries, or critical collations of the text; and accordingly, Addison looked upon all of them, except those few who professed themselves followers in the retinue and equipage of the ancients, as creatures of a lower race. Boileau, as a mere imitator and propagator of Horace, he read, and probably little else amongst the French classics. Hence it arose that he took upon himself to speak sneeringly of Tasso. To this, which was a bold act for his timid mind, he was emboldened by the countenance of Boileau. Of the elder Italian authors, such as Ariosto, and, *a fortiori,* Dante, he knew absolutely nothing. Passing to our own literature, it is certain that Addison was profoundly ignorant of Chaucer and of Spenser. Milton only,—and why? simply because he was a brilliant scholar, and stands like a brigade between the Christian literature and the Pagan,—Addison had read and esteemed.

Thomas De Quincey, 1847? *Shakspeare, Works,* ed. Masson,
vol. IV, p. 22

Addison brought to the study of literature a mind which was open to receive impressions from every side. He commenced, as he was bound to do, with an application of the rules of Aristotle, but he acquired confidence in his own judgment as he proceeded in his researches, and finally availed himself freely of new elements of human knowledge which were unknown to Aristotle. His application of the Aristotelian canons to *Paradise Lost* was undertaken in deference to the spirit of the age, but in his essay on "The Pleasures of the Imagination," he discovers a new principle to which the charm and power of poetic literature is to be referred: a principle which, unlike the appeal to "fear and pity," is applicable not to one but to every form of poetry and fiction. And in so doing he introduces fresh considerations, which affect all manifestations of art, but of which the rules of Aristotle take no account, and notices new effects for which these rules provide no tests; and in supplying these omissions he has permanently widened the scope of criticism, whether the object of its inquiry be a picture or a poem, form or thought. . . . By the work of Addison criticism was brought into line with modern thought; and the critic was provided with a test which he could apply with equal success to every fresh form which literature had developed.

W. Basil Worsfold, 1897, *The Principles of Criticism*, pp. 59, 107

GENERAL

Mr. Addison, for a happy and natural style, will be always an honour to British literature. His diction indeed wants strength, but it is equal to all the subjects he undertakes to handle, as he never (at least in his finished works) attempts anything in the argumentative or demonstrative way.

Oliver Goldsmith, 1759, *The Bee,* No. 8, Nov. 24

His poetry is first to be considered; of which it must be confessed that it has not often those felicities of diction which gave lustre to sentiments, or that vigour of sentiment that animates diction: there is little of ardour, vehemence, or transport; there is very rarely the awfulness of grandeur, and not very often the splendour of elegance. He thinks justly; but he thinks faintly. This is his general character; to which, doubtless, many single passages will furnish exception. Yet, if he seldom reaches supreme excellence, he rarely sinks into dulness, and is still more rarely entangled in absurdity. He did not trust his powers enough to be negligent. There is in most of his compositions a calmness and equability, deliberate and cautious, sometimes with little that delights, but seldom with anything that offends.

Samuel Johnson, 1779-81, *Addison, Lives of the English Poets*

Addison was a mere lay preacher, completely bound up in formalism, but he did get to say many a true thing in his generation; an instance of one formal man doing great things. Steele had infinitely more *naïveté,* but he was only a fellow-soldier of Addison, to whom he subordinated himself more than was necessary. It is a cold vote in Addison's favor that one gives.

Thomas Carlyle, 1838, *Lectures on the History of Literature,* p. 176

Well, but Addison's prose is Attic prose. Where, then, it may be asked, is the note of proviniciality in Addison? I answer, in the commonplace of his ideas. This is a matter worth remarking. Addison claims to take leading rank as a moralist. To do that, you must have ideas of the first order on your subject,—the best ideas, at any rate, attainable in your time,—as well as be able to express them in a perfectly sound and sure style. . . . Now Addison has not, on his subject of morals, the force of ideas of the moralists of the first class,—the classical moralists; he has not the best ideas attainable in or about his time, and which were, so to speak, in the air then, to be seized by the finest spirits; he is not to be compared for power, searchingness, or delicacy of thought to Pascal, or La Bruyère, or Vauvenargues; he is rather on a level, in this respect, with a man like Marmontel; therefore, I say, he has the note of provinciality as a moralist; his is provincial by his matter, though not by his style.

Matthew Arnold, 1865, "The Literary Influence of Academies,"
Essays in Criticism, pp. 58, 59

Greater energy of character, or a more determined hatred of vice and tyranny, would have curtailed his usefulness as a public censor. He led the nation gently and insensibly to a love of virtue and constitutional freedom, to a purer taste in morals and literature, and to the importance of those everlasting truths which so warmly engaged his heart and imagination. The national taste and circumstances have so much changed during the last century and a half, that these essays, inimitable as they are, have become antiquated, and are little read.

Robert Chambers, 1876, Cyclopædia of English Literature,
ed. Carruthers, p. 281

His style, with its free, unaffected movement, its clear distinctness, its graceful transitions, its delicate harmonies, its appropriateness of tone; the temperance and moderation of his treatment, the effortless self-mastery, the sense of quiet power, the absence of exaggeration or extravagance, the perfect keeping with which he deals with his subjects; or again the exquisite reserve, the subtle tenderness, the geniality, the pathos of his humour—what are these but the literary reflection of Addison himself, of that temper so pure and lofty yet so sympathetic, so strong yet so lovable.

John Richard Green, 1880, ed., Essays of Joseph Addison,
Introduction, p. xxiv

It is difficult in a short summary of facts to give any impression of the influence exercised on the mind and feelings of his country by Addison. It was out of proposition with the mere outcome of his literary genius.

It was the result of character almost more than of intellect, of goodness and reasonableness almost more than of wit. His qualities of mind, however, if not of the very loftiest order, were relatively harmonised to an astonishing degree, so that the general impression of Addison is of a larger man than the close contemplation of any one side of his genius reveals him as being. He has all the moral ornaments of the literary character; as a writer he is urbane, cheerful, charming, and well-mannered to a degree which has scarcely been surpassed in the history of the world. His wit is as penetrating as a perfume; his irony presupposes a little circle of the best and most cultivated listeners; his fancy is so well tempered by judgment and observation that it passes with us for imagination. We delight in his company so greatly that we do not pause to reflect that the inventor of Sir Roger de Coverley and Will Honeycomb had not half of the real comic force of Farquhar or Vanbrugh, nor so much as that of the flashing wit of Congreve. Human nature, however, is superior to the rules, and Addison stands higher than those more original writers by merit of the reasonableness, the good sense, the wholesome humanity that animates his work. He is classic, while they are always a little way over on the barbaric side of perfection. The style of Addison is superior to his matter, and holds a good many flies in its exquisite amber. It did not reach its highest quality until Addison had become acquainted with *A Tale of a Tub,* but it grew to be a finer thing, though not a greater, than the style of Swift.

Edmund Gosse, 1888, A History of Eighteenth Century
Literature, p. 193

SIR JOHN VANBRUGH
1664-1726

Born, in London, Jan. 1664; baptized, 24 Jan. Probably spent some time in Paris in youth; afterwards served in Army. Play, *The Relapse,* performed at Drury Lane, Dec. 1696; *Æsop,* Drury Lane, Jan. 1697; *The Provok'd Wife,* Lincoln's Inn Fields, May 1697; *The False Friend,* Drury Lane, Jan. 1702. Practised as an architect. Built Castle Howard, Blenheim, and other important houses. Appointed Controller of Royal Works, 1702. Play, *Squire Trelooby* (written with Congreve and Walsh), produced at Lincoln's Inn Fields, 30 March 1704; *The Country House,* 1705. Built a theatre in the Haymarket. His play, *The Confederacy,* produced there, 30 Oct. 1705; *The Mistake,* 27 Dec. 1705. Clarencieux King-at-Arms, 1705-26. To Hanover, on embassy to convey Order of Garter to the Elector, May 1706. Knighted, 19 Sept. 1714. Surveyor of Gardens and Waters, 1715. Surveyor of Works, Greenwich Hospital, 1716. Member of Kit-Kat Club. Married Henrietta Maria Yarburgh, 14 Jan. 1719. Died, in London, 26 March 1726. Buried in St. Stephen's, Walbrook. WORKS: *The Relapse* (anon.), 1697 (afterwards known, in Sheridan's adaptation, as *A Trip to Scarborough*); *The Provok'd Wife* (anon.), 1697; *Æsop*, 1697; *A Short Vindication of "The Relapse" and "The Provok'd Wife"* (anon), 1698; *The Pilgrim* (adapted from Dryden; anon.), 1700; *The False Friend* (anon.), 1702; *The Confederacy* (anon.), 1705; *The Mistake* (anon.), 1706; *The Country House* (trans. from the French of Carton D'Ancourt), 1715. POSTHUMOUS: *The Provok'd Husband* (completed by Cibber from Vanbrugh's *A Journey to London*), 1728; *The Cornish Squire* (trans. from Molière), 1734. COLLECTED WORKS: in 2 vols., ed. by W. C. Ward, 1893.

> R. Farquharson Sharp, 1897, *A Dictionary of English Authors*, p. 288

SEE: *Complete Works*, ed. Bonamy Dobrée and Geoffrey Webb, 1927-28, 4v.; Bonamy Dobrée, in *Restoration Comedy*, 1924; L. Whistler, *Sir John Vanbrugh, Architect and Dramatist*, 1938.

PERSONAL

Under this stone, reader, survey
Dead Sir John Vanbrugh's house of clay:
Lie heavy on him, Earth, for he
Laid many a heavy load on thee.

> Abel Evans, c 1699, *On Sir John Vanbrugh*

A silly fellow, who is the architect at Woodstock.

> Thomas Hearne, 1714, *Reliquiæ Hearnianæ*, ed Bliss, Sept. 25, vol. I, p. 310

The only architect in the world who could have built such a house, and the only friend in the world capable of contriving to lay the debt upon one to whom he was so highly obliged.

> Sarah Dutchess Marlborough, 1718, *Case of the Duke of Marlborough and Sir John Vanbrugh*

The Relapse (1697)

The character of Amanda is interesting, especially in the momentary wavering and quick recovery of her virtue. This is the first homage that the theatre had paid, since the Restoration, to female chastity; and notwithstanding the vicious tone of the other characters, in which Vanbrugh has gone as great lengths as any of his contemporaries, we perceive the beginnings of a re-action in public spirit, which gradually reformed and elevated the moral standard of the stage.

> Henry Hallam, 1837-39, *Introduction to the Literature of Europe*, pt. iv, ch. vi, par. 53

We know of no better comic writing in the world than the earlier scenes of Lord Foppington in *The Relapse.*

Leigh Hunt, 1840, ed., *The Dramatic Works of Wycherley, Congreve, Vanbrugh and Farquhar*

Of Vanbrugh's ten or eleven plays, that which has longest kept the stage is *The Relapse,* still acted, in its altered form, by Sheridan, as the *Trip to Scarborough.* The piece was produced at the Theatre de l'Odeon, in Paris, in the spring of 1862, as a posthumous comedy of Voltaire's! It was called the *Comte de Boursoufle,* and had a "run." The story ran with it that Voltaire had composed it in his younger days for private representation, that it had been more than once played in the houses of his noble friends, under various titles, that he had then locked it up, and that the manuscript had only recently been discovered by the lucky individual who persuaded the manager of the Odeon to produce it on his stage? The bait took. All the French theatrical world in the capital flocked to the Faubourg St. Germain to witness a new play by Voltaire. Critics examined the plot, philosophized on its humour, applauded its absurdities, enjoyed its wit, and congratulated themselves on the circumstances that the Voltairean wit especially was as enjoyable then as in the preceding century! Of the authorship they had no doubt whatever; for, said they, if Voltaire did not write this piece, who *could* have written it? The reply was given at once from this country; but when the mystification was exposed, the French critics gave no sign of awarding honor where honor was due, and probably this translation of the *Relapse* may figure in future French editions as an undoubted work of Voltaire.

John Doran, 1863, *Annals of the English Stage,* vol. I, p. 158

The Relapse is a delightful play to read; its spirit is sustained without effort to the end; and although the characters are somewhat farcical, yet are they more so than many an anomaly we all and each of us meet in every day life? Lord Foppington, for instance, is a delicious coxcomb; but that man must be deaf, blind and insensible, who cannot in his own experience verify a Lord Foppington in absurdity, conceit, and stolid selfishness. This character is perhaps a reflex of the Sir Fopling Flutter of Etheredge; more so however in the externals than in the inner structure of the specimen.

Charles Cowden Clarke, 1872, "On the Comic Writers of England," *Gentleman's Magazine,* n. s., vol. 8, p. 39

The play remained a prime favourite with the public throughout the eighteenth century, and has passed through several transformation. A three-act farce, called *The Man of Quality,* was carved out of it by Lee and given at Covent Garden in 1776; and in the following year Sheridan, reflecting that it was "a pity to exclude the productions of our best writers for want of a little wholesome pruning," recast it as *A Trip to Scarborough.* The original play was seen at the Olympic in 1846, and at the Strand as late as 1850. A version by Mr. John Hollingshead, also called *The Man of Quality,* was produced at the Gaiety on 7 May 1870 with Miss Nellie Farren as Miss Hoyden, a part in which Mrs. Jordan had excelled; and another, called *Miss Tomboy,* by Mr. Robert Buchanan, at the Vaudeville on 20 March 1890.

Thomas Seccombe, 1899, *Dictionary of National Biography,*
vol. LVIII, p. 87

The Provoked Wife (1697)

In 1725 we were called upon, in a manner that could not be resisted, to revive *The Provoked Wife,* a comedy which, while we found our account in keeping the stage clear of those loose libertines it had formerly too justly been charged with, we had laid aside for some years. The author, sir John Vanbrugh, who was conscious of what it had too much of, was prevailed upon to substitute a new written scene in the place of one in the fourth act, where the wantonness of his wit and humour had (originally) made a rake talk like a rake, in the borrowed habit of a clergyman; to avoid which offence, he clapt the same debauchee into the undress of a woman of quality. Now the character and profession of a fine lady not being so indelibly sacred as that of a churchman, whatever follies he exposed in the petticoat, kept him at least clear of his former profaneness, and were now innocently ridiculous to the spectator.

Colley Cibber, 1739, *An Apology for His Life*

The characters in this play, especially that of Sir John Brute, are drawn with consummate skill, and the dialogue is easy, brilliant, and natural: but the plot is more licentious in its conduct and situations than any contemporary production with which we are acquainted, and absolutely demoralising in the principle of domestic retaliation it attempts to justify. A surly and unfeeling husband is here retorted upon by his wife, who sacrifices her own honour by way of taking revenge upon him for his ill-treatment of her: and this mode of avenging herself is admitted by the catastrophe to be perfectly reasonable and correct.

S. Astley Dunham, 1838, ed., *Literary and Scientific Men of
Great Britain and Ireland,* vol. III, p. 216

The Provoked Wife, to my own feelings and taste, is a nauseous production. Sir John Brute, the chief person, is a monster-curiosity, and fit only for a museum. There are anomalies in the world, it is true, and Sir John Brute is one: he is an awful hog. His wife is an natural character, and tells her own tale clearly and well. The other characters, Belinda (her niece), Constant, Heartfree, and Lady Fanciful, are little better than common stock from the dramatic warehouse. The play is considerably licentious, and yet the spirit of its moral is less revolting, from the tone of unselfishness and an unconsciously developed tone of justice towards the party against whom the question is always begged, a frankness and liberality of sentiment that one may look for in vain in the heartless and passionless intrigueries of Congreve.

> Charles Cowden Clarke, 1872, "On the Comic Writers of England," *Gentleman's Magazine,* n. s., vol. 8, p. 42

ARCHITECTURE

> For building famed, and justly reckon'd
> At court, Vitruvius the Second:
> No wonder, since wise authors shew,
> That best foundations must be low:
> And now the duke has wisely ta'en him
> To be his architect at Blenheim.
> But, raillery for once apart,
> If this rule holds in every art;
> Or if his grace were no more skill'd in
> The art of battering walls than building,
> We might expect to see next year
> A mouse-trap man chief engineer.

> Jonathan Swift, 1708, *Works*

Belongs only to this work in a light that is by no means advantageous to him. He wants all the merit of his writings to protect him from the censure due to his designs. What Pope said of his comedies is much more applicable to his buildings—

"How Van wants grace!"—

Grace! He wanted eyes, he wanted all ideas of proportion, convenience, propriety. He undertook vast designs, and composed heaps of littleness. The style of no age, of no country, appears in his works; he broke through all rule, and compensated for it by no imagination. He seems to have hollowed quarries rather than to have built houses; and should his edifices, as they seem forced to do, outlast all record, what architecture will posterity think was that of their ancestors? The laughers, his contemporaries, said, that having been confined in the Bastile, he had drawn his notions on building from that fortified dungeon.

Horace Walpole, 1762-86, *Anecdotes of Painting in England,*
p. 310

There is, however, no doubt but that Vanbrugh was justly accused by the Duchess of extravagance in many instances, and of exceeding his commission in others. She even taxed him with building one entire court at Blenheim without the Duke's knowledge. She detected his bad taste and grasping spirit, and despised his mismanagement,—of which latter the best proof was, that when, upon the death of the Duke, the whole charge of the building fell into her hands, she completed it in the manner, and at the reduced expense, which has been described. That "wicked woman of Marlborough," as Sir John Vanbrugh termed the Duchess, had perhaps no greater error in his eyes than the penetration with which she discovered his narrow pretensions, his inadequacy, and wanton taste, not to say peculation.

Katherine Thomson, 1838, *Memoirs of Sarah Jennings,*
Duchess of Marlborough, vol. II, p. 458

Sir John Vanbrugh's merits as an architect—his fire, his daring, his picturesqueness, his solidity and grandeur—have been recognised and very handsomely acknowledged by the best judges of art. Sir Joshua Reynold's judgment of him, though often quoted, may be quoted once again:—"In the buildings of Vanbrugh, who was a poet as well as an architect, there is a greater display of imagination than we shall find perhaps in any other; and this is the ground of the effect we feel in many of his works, notwithstanding the faults with which many of them are charged." It was the peculiarity of Vanbrugh's genius that he was a poet even more than a builder, and designed a palace as he designed a play—in masses, with so much unity of thought in the stone construction as he would have studied in his action and dialogue, the whole relieved and enlivened by artistic contrasts and surprises. No man, probably, not a slave of rules, will deny to Blenheim and to Castle Howard a certain splendour and originality not to be seen in the works of commen men. Seen from the bridge, or from the grassy upland above the bridge, what secular edifice in England will compare in force, solidity, and cheeriness, with the front of Blenheim? Is it not wonderfully bright, and bold, and various, striking in the detail and in the mass? Does it not gloriously cap and adorn the voluptuous site on which it stands? Does not the work, too, thoroughly embody the idea out of which it grew—the memorial of a nation's gratitude and of a hero's deeds?

Duke of Manchester, 1864, *Court and Society from Elizabeth to Anne*, p. 226

The verdict of Vanbrugh's literary rivals as to the architectural merit of Blenheim was wholly unfavourable. In the minds of less prejudiced critics there has been great divergence of opinion; but it must be conceded that Vanbrugh hardly rose to his opportunities. The general plan of a grand central edifice, connected by colonnades with two projecting quadrangular wings, and of the approaches(including the "Titanic bridge"), is admirable in its way. The sky-line is broken in a picturesque fashion, and the light and shade are balanced and contrasted in a manner which evoked the enthusiastic eulogy of Sir Joshua Reynolds, Uvedale Price, Allan Cunningham, and other connoisseurs of scenic effect. On the other hand, the ornament, when not positively uncouth, is unmeaning and there is a sensible coarseness in matters of detail throughout the work. Voltaire remarked upon Blenheim that if the rooms were as wide as the walls were thick, the chateau would be convenient enough. The last thing that Vanbrugh had in his mind was personal comfort for his clients.

Thomas Seccombe, 1899, *Dictionary of National Biography*, vol. LVIII, p. 91

GENERAL

Sir *John Vanbrugh* has writ several comedies which are more humorous than those of Mr. *Wycherley,* but not so ingenious. Sir *John* was a man of pleasure, and likewise a poet and an architect. The general opinion is, that he is as sprightly in his writings as he is heavy in his buildings.

François Marie Arouet Voltaire, 1732? *Letters Concerning the English Nation*, p. 147

How Van wants grace, who never wanted wit!

Alexander Pope, 1733, *First Epistle of the Second Book of Horace*

Though to write much in a little time is no excuse for writing ill, yet sir John Vanbrugh's pen is not to be a little admired for its spirit, ease, and readiness, in producing plays so fast upon the neck of one another; for notwithstanding this quick despatch, there is a clear and lively simplicity in his wit, that neither wants the ornament of learning, nor has the least smell of the lamp in it. As the face of a fine woman, with only her locks loose about her, may be then in its greatest beauty, such were his productions only adorned by nature. There is something so catching to the ear, so easy to the memory in all he wrote, that it has been observed by all the actors of my time, that the style of no author whatsover gave their memory less trouble than that of sir John Vanbrugh; which I myself, who have been charged with several of his strongest characters, can confirm by a pleasing experience. And indeed his wit and humour were so little laboured, that his most entertaining scenes seemed to be no more than his common conversation committed to paper. Here I confess my judgment at a loss, whether in this I give him more or less than his due praise.

Colley Cibber, 1739, An Apology for His Life

Sir John Vanbrugh, it is said, had great facility in writing, and is not a little to be admired for the spirit, ease, and readiness, with which he produced his plays. Notwithstanding his extraordinary expedition, there is a clear and lively simplicity in his wit, that is equally distant from the pedantry of learning, and the lowness of scurrility. As the face of a fine lady, with her hair undressed, may appear in the morning in its brightest glow of beauty; such were the productions of Vanbrugh, adorned with only the negligent graces of nature.

Theophilus Cibber, 1753, Lives of the Poets, vol. IV, p. 103

Sir John Vanburgh has spirit, wit, and ease; but he is, to the last degree, gross and indelicate. He is one of the most immoral of all our comedians. His *Provoked Wife* is full of such indecent sentiments and allusions, as ought to explode it out of all reputable society. His *Relapse* is equally censurable; and these are his only two considerable pieces.

Hugh Blair, 1783, Lectures on Rhetoric and Belles-Lettres,
ed. Mills, Lecture xlvii, p. 542

He is no writer at all, as to mere authorship; but he makes up for it by a prodigious fund of comic invention and ludicrous description, bordering some what on caricature. Though he did not borrow from him, he was much more like Moliere in genius than Wycherley was, who professedly imitated him. He has none of Congreve's graceful refinement, and as little of Wycherley's serious manner and studied insight into the springs of character; but his exhibition of it in dramatic contrast and unlooked-for situations, where the different parties play upon one another's failings, and into one another's hands, keeping up the jest like a game of battledore and shuttlecock, and urging it to the utmost verge of breathless extravagance, in the mere eagerness of the fray, is beyond that of any other of our writers. . . . He has more nature than art; what he does best, he does because he cannot help it. He has a masterly eye to the advantages which certain accidental situations of character present to him on the spot, and executes the most difficult and rapid theatrical movements at a moment's warning.

William Hazlitt, 1818, Lectures on the English
Comic Writers, Lecture iv

Of the four great Restoration playwrights, Vanbrugh had most of the "trick of the stage." Like Wycherley, he has the rare and great merit that he wrote to be acted, not to be read. He is less cynical than Wycherley, more civilized and human in his satire, and far less gross. He lacks the wit and style of Congreve, but has greater natural flow and natural ease: the players are said to have found his pieces particularly easy to get by heart, and this would seem to be a proof that he spoke the language natural to his day. Vanbrugh goes further afield for his plots than his contemporaries, and brings more than mere fine ladies and gentlemen on to the stage.

Oswald Crawfurd, 1883, ed., English Comic Dramatists, p. 84

This very clear and original writer had, indeed, erred by an extraordinary licence, and owes to his coarseness the obscurity into which his plays have fallen. . . . Where Congreve is volatile and sparkling, Vanbrugh does not attempt to compete with him, but reserves himself for carefully studied effects, for passages where every touch is marked by the precision and weight of the author's style. He is perhaps more like Molière than other English dramatist; he is like him in the abundance of his stage-knowledge, and in the skill he shows in rapid and entertaining changes of situation. At the same time he is English to a fault, saturated with the brutality of the fox-hunting squire of the period. This very coarseness of fibre, added to Vanbrugh's great sincerity as a writer, gives his best scenes a wonderful air of reality.

Edmund Gosse, 1888, A History of Eighteenth
Century Literature, p. 67

COTTON MATHER
1663-1728

Son of Increase Mather. A famous Congregational clergyman of Boston, pastor of the North Church, 1683-1728, and his father's colleague for the greater part of that period. He was a prolific author, publishing nearly four hundred works, large and small, but it is upon the *Magnalia Christi Americana* that his reputation rests. Among other works are *Wonders of the Invisible World; Christian Philosopher; Psalterium Americanum;*

Manductio ad Ministerium; Memorable Providences Relating to Witch-craft; Essays to Do Good; The Armour of Christianity; Batteries upon the Kingdom of the Devil; Death made Easie and Happy. His style is disfigured by pedantry and strained analogies, and is at all times far removed from simplicity, but the author is nevertheless easily seen to be intensely earnest in his endeavors to be of service to his generation.

> Oscar Fay Adams, 1897, *A Dictionary of American Authors,* p. 249

SEE: *Diary, from the Year 1712,* ed. William R. Manierre, 1964; *Selections from Cotton Mather,* ed. K. B. Murdock, 1926; Barrett Wendell, *Cotton Mather, The Puritan Priest,* 1891, repr. 1963.

PERSONAL

By his learned works and correspondence, those who lived at the greatest distance might discern much of his superior light and influence; but they could discern these only by a more mediate and faint reflection. These could neither see nor well imagine that extraordinary luster of pious and useful literature, wherewith we were, every day, entertained, surprised, and satisfied, who dwelt in the directer rays, in the more immediate vision.

> Thomas Prince, 1729, *Life and Times of Cotton Mather,* by Marvin, p. 575

When I was a boy, I met with a book, entitled *Essays to do Good,* which I think was written by your father. It had been so little regarded by a former possessor, that several leaves of it were torn out; but the remainder gave me such a turn of thinking, as to have an influence on my conduct through life. . . . It is now more than sixty years since I left Boston: but I remember well both your father and grandfather, having heard them both in the pulpit, and seen them in their houses. The last time I saw your father was in the beginning of 1724, when I visited him after my first trip to Pennsylvania. He received me in his library, and on my taking leave, showed me a shorter way out of the house through a narrow passage, which was crossed by a beam overhead. We were still talking as I withdrew, he accompanying me behind, and I turning partly towards him, when he said hastily, "Stoop, stoop!" I did not understand him, till I felt my head hit against the beam. He was a man that never missed any occasion of giving instruction, and upon this he said to me, "You are young, and have the world before you; stoop as you go through it, and you will miss many hard thumps." This advice, thus beat into my head, has frequently been of use to me; and I often think of it, when I see pride mortified, and misfortunes brought upon people by their carrying their heads too high.

> Benjamin Franklin, 1784, *Letter to Samuel Mather,* May 12

His early reputation, and the prominent part he took in the ecclesiastical affairs of New England; the great and long-continued consideration which he enjoyed with the people at large; his literary attainments and unquestionable ability of a certain kind; the contributions he made to the materials of our early history, ample at least, if not so exact as might be desired; and last, though not least, his grievous errors of conduct, on several important occasions, give him an undoubted eminence above most of his contemporaries, and make him one of the most remarkable characters that belong to the early period of New England.

John Gorham Palfrey, 1836, "Spark's *American Biography*," *North American Review*, vol. 43, p. 518

To cover his confusion, Cotton Mather got up a case of witchcraft in his own parish. . . . Was Cotton Mather honestly credulous? . . . He is an example how far selfishness, under the form of vanity and ambition, can blind the higher faculties, stupefy the judgment, and dupe consciousness itself.

George Bancroft, 1840, *History of the United States,* vol. III

He incurred the responsibility of being its chief cause and promoter. In the progress of the superstitious fear, which amounted to frenzy, and could only be satisfied with blood, he neither blenched nor halted; but attended the courts, watched the progress of invisible agency in the prisons, and joined the multitude in witnessing the executions.

Josiah Quincy, 1840, *History of Harvard University,* vol. I, p. 63

The suggestion, that Cotton Mather, for purposes of his own, deliberately got up this witchcraft delusion, and forced it upon a doubtful and hesitating people, is utterly absurd. . . . Mather's position, convictions, and temperament alike called him to serve on this occasion as the organ, exponent, and stimulator of the popular faith.

Richard Hildreth, 1849, *History of the United States of America,* vol. II, p. 151

As Cotton Mather was a very distinguished man, Grandfather took some pains to give the children a lively conception of his character. Over the door of his library were painted these words, BE SHORT,—as a warning to visitors that they must not do the world so much harm as needlessly to interrupt this great man's wonderful labors. On entering the room you would probably behold it crowded, and piled, and heaped with books. They were huge, ponderous folios, and quartos, and little duodecimos, in English, Latin, Greek, Hebrew, Chaldaic, and all other languages that either originated at the confusion of Babel or have since come into use. All these books,

no doubt, were tossed about in confusion, thus forming a visible emblem of
the manner in which their contents were crowded into Cotton Mather's
brain. And in the middle of the room stood a table, on which, besides
printed volumes, were strewn manuscript sermons, historical tracts, and
political pamphlets, all written in such a queer, blind, crabbed, fantastical
hand, that a writing-master would have gone raving mad at the sight of
them. By this table stood Grandfather's chair, which seemed to have contracted an air of deep erudition, as if its cushion were stuffed with Latin,
Greek, and Hebrew, and other hard matters. In this chair, from one year's
end to another, sat that prodigious bookworm, Cotton Mather, sometimes
devouring a great book, and sometimes scribbling one as big. In Grandfather's younger days there used to be a wax figure of him in one of the
Boston museums, representing a solemn, dark-visaged person, in a minister's
black gown, and with a black-letter volume before him.

> Nathaniel Hawthorne, 1850, *Grandfather's Chair,* ch. iv

Mather was always exercising his ingenuity to contribute something useful
to the world. He was one of the first to employ the press extensively in the
dissemination of tracts; he early lifted his voice in favor of temperance; he
preached and wrote for sailors; he instructed negroes; he substituted moral
and sagacious intellectual restraints with his children for flogging; conversation he studied and practised as an art; and he was a devoted histori-
ographer of his country for posterity—besides his paramount employment,
according to the full measure of his day and generation, of discharging the
sacred duties of his profession. Pity that any personal defects of temperament or "follies of the wise" should counterbalance these noble achievements—that so well freighted a bark should at times experience the want
of a rudder. Good sense was the one stick occasionally missing from the
enormous faggot of Mather's studies and opinions. . . . One thing he never
could attain, though he nearly inherited it, though his learning almost irre-
sistibly challenged it, though he spiritually anticipated it—the prize of the
Presidency of Harvard College. One and another was chosen in preference
to him. The ghostly authority of the old priestly influence was passing
away. Cotton Mather was, in age a disheartened and disappointed man.
The possession, in turn, of three wives had proved but a partial consolation.
One of his sons he felt compelled to disown; his wife was subject to fits of
temper bordering on insanity; the glooms of his own disposition grew darker
in age as death approached, a friend whom he was glad to meet, when he
expired, at the completion of his sixty-fifth year, the 13th February, 1728.
His last emphatic charge to his son Samuel was, "Remember only that one
word, 'Fructuosus.' "

> Evert A. and George L. Duyckinck, 1855-65-75, *Cyclopædia of*
> *American Literature,* ed. Simmons, vol. I, p. 67

He is the greatest of American scholars. It is doubtful if any one in the New World has ever equalled his acquaintance with theological and classic literature, his readiness in using his knowledge, his wonderful industry, his intense literary ardor. No moment of his life was wasted, and all his life was given to study.

> Eugene Lawrence, 1880, *A Primer of American Literature*, p. 20

He became the greatest pulpit power in his day, and unsurpassed since, unless, perhaps, by a very few in later generations. During the week he made the most faithful preparation by reading, meditation, prayer, and writing. Study of the Bible in the original languages kept his mind fresh and unhackneyed. Praying as he wrote, he went into the house of God surcharged with God's truth and spirit. Nothing was left till Saturday night or Sunday morning to tax his strength by way of mental toil and worry over a sermon. Saturday evening and Sunday morning were sacred to devotions. He went to the sanctuary as to the "gate of heaven." Full of matter and fervent in prayer, he was like a charged battery, and he represented Christ as he stood before his auditory. They were instructed, they were aroused, their consciences were quickened, their affections were kindled, their reason was satisfied by the words spoken, and all was sent home by the intense spiritual energy with which he spoke and prayed.

> Abijah P. Marvin, 1892, *The Life and Times of Cotton Mather*,
> p. 58

It was, perhaps, fear that the belief in the supernatural, and notably in the supernatural agency of the Evil One, was dying out which led Cotton Mather, a minister of prodigious though ill-digested learning and at the same time full of spiritual self-conceit, to countenance the horrible delusion of Salem Witchcraft which has left a dark stain on New England history, as readers of Hawthorne's *House of the Seven Gables* know. . . . Cotton Mather afterwards partly redeemed himself by countenancing, at a great sacrifice of his popularity and at some risk of his life, the introduction of inoculation, which excited the ignorant fury of the mob. Even in him learning begot something of liberality.

> Goldwin Smith, 1893, *The United States, An Outline of*
> *Political History, 1492-1871*, pp. 37, 38

On February 15, 1728, the Reverend Benjamin Colman, first minister of the Brattle Street church, preached the Boston lecture in memory of Cotton Mather, who had died two days before. Cotton Mather had lived all his life in Boston; there is no record, they say, of his ever having travelled farther from home than Ipswich or Andover or Plymouth. Of sensitive temperament, and both by constitution and by conviction devoted to the traditions in which he was trained, he certainly presented, to a degree nowhere common, a conveniently exaggerated type of the characteristics that marked the society of which he formed a part.

Barrett Wendell, 1893, *Stelligeri and other Essays Concerning America,* p. 47

GENERAL

The true place of Cotton Mather in our literary history is indicated when we say, that he was in prose writing, exactly what Nicholas Noyes was in poetry,—the last, the most vigorous, and, therefore, the most disagreeable representative of the Fantastic school in literature; and that, like Nicholas Noyes, he prolonged in New England the methods of that school even after his most cultivated contemporaries there had outgrown them, and had come to dislike them. The expulsion of the beautiful from thought, from sentiment, from language; a lawless and a merciless fury for the odd, the disorderly, the grotesque, the violent; strained analogies, unexpected images, pedantries, indelicacies, freaks of allusion, monstrosities of phrase;—these are the traits of Cotton Mather's writing, even as they are the traits common to that perverse and detestable literary mood that held sway in different countries of Christendom during the sixteenth and seventeenth centuries. Its birthplace was Italy; New England was its grave; Cotton Mather was its last great apostle. His writings, in fact, are an immense reservoir of examples in Fantastic prose. Their most salient characteristic is pedantry,— a pedantry that is gigantic, stark, untempered, rejoicing in itself, unconscious of shame, filling all space in his books like an atmosphere. The mind of Cotton Mather was so possessed by the books he had read, that his most common thought had to force its way into utterance through dense hedges and jungles of quotation.

Moses Coit Tyler, 1878, *A History of American Literature, 1676-1765,* vol. II, p. 87

Aptly styled by the historian of American literature "the literary behemoth" of New England. . . . Cotton Mather was a man of undoubted ability and vast erudition, and much of his work may still be read with curiosity and interest; but as a historian he was untrustworthy, and his style, overcharged and involved, was the worst, as it was the last, in the fantastic fashion of the seventeenth century.

Henry Cabot Lodge, 1881, *A Short History of the English Colonies in America,* pp. 469, 470

His work can be reckoned up, but the worker eludes comprehension. It is easier to misjudge than to judge him. His mind was pendulous, as one of his most discriminating biographers has observed, and though attached at its highest point to eternal justice, it was ever swaying over a wide range of notions and impulses. Oftentimes a riddle to himself, it is no wonder that the measuring of him must still be so largely conjectural with us.

> Eliot Lord, 1893, "Harvard's Youngest Three,"
> *New England Magazine,* vol. 13, p. 645

His *Memorable Providences Relating to Witchcraft,* written apparently with perfect honesty and published in 1789, served as a fan for the fire smouldering in Salem. Four years later, when men like Justice Sewall were bitterly repenting of their part in the terrible tragedy, Mather published his *Wonders of the Invisible World,* a cold-blooded account of the trials and executions at Salem, every word pregnant with the belief that devils and not human beings had been dealt with. That he was intensely honest in all this need not be said. His terrible convictions triumphing over his naturally kind heart would not have allowed him to hesitate even had the evidence involved his son Samuel.

> Fred Lewis Pattee, 1896, *A History of American Literature,* p. 47

WILLIAM CONGREVE
1670-1729

Born, at Bardsey, near Leeds, Jan. (?) 1670. Soon after his birth, family removed to Lismore. Educated at Kilkenny School. To Trinity Coll., Dublin, 5 April 1685; M.A., 1696. Entered Middle Temple, but soon abandoned law. Play, *The Old Batchelor,* produced, Jan. 1693; *The Double Dealer,* Nov. 1693; *Love for Love,* 30 April 1695; *The Mourning Bride,* 1697; *The Way of the World,* 1700. Commissioner for Licensing Hackney Coaches, July 1695 to Oct. 1707. Abandoned playwriting. Joined Vanburgh in theatrical management for short time in 1705. Commissioner of Wine Licenses, Dec. 1705 to Dec. 1714. Appointed Secretary for Jamaica, Dec. 1714. Member of Kit-Kat Club. Intimacy with Duchess of Marlborough in later years of life. Died, in London, 19 Jan. 1729. Buried in Westminster Abbey. WORKS: *The Mourning Muse of Alexis,* 1659; *The Old Batchelor,* [1693], *The Double Dealer,* [1694]; *A Pindarique Ode, humbly offer'd to the King,* 1695; *Love for Love,* 1695; *Amendments upon Mr. Collier's false and imperfect Citations* (anon.), 1698; *The Birth of the Muse,* 1698; *The Mourning Bride,* 1697 (2nd edn. same year); *Incognita* (anon.), 1700; *The Way of the World,* 1700; *The Judgment of Paris,* 1701; *A Pindarique Ode, humbly offer'd to the Queen,* 1706; *Works* (3 vol.), 1710; *A Letter to . . . Viscount Cobham,* 1729. He *translated:* Book

III. of Ovid's *Art of Love,* 1709; Ovid's *Metamorphoses* (with Dryden, Addison, etc.), 1717; La Fontaine's *Tales and Novels* (with other translators), 1762: and assisted Dryden in revision of translation of Virgil, 1697. He *edited:* Dryden's *Dramatick Works,* 1717. COLLECTED WORKS: 1731, etc.

> R. Farquharson Sharp, 1897, *A Dictionary of English Authors,* p. 65

SEE: *Works,* ed. Bonamy Dobrée, 1925-28, 2v.; John C. Hodges, *Congreve the Man: A Biography from New Sources,* 1941; Kathleen M. Lynch, *A Congreve Gallery,* 1951; Emmett L. Avery, *Congreve's Plays on the Eighteenth-Century Stage,* 1951.

PERSONAL

I have a multitude of affairs, having just come to town after nine weeks' absence. I am growing fat, but you know I was born with somewhat of a round belly. . . . Think of me as I am, nothing extenuate. My service to Robin, who would laugh to see me puzzled to buckle my shoe, but I'll fetch it down again.

> William Congreve, 1704, *Letter to Keally*

Be pleased to direct your eyes toward the pair of beaux in the next chariot. . . . He on the right is a near favourite of the Muses; he has touched the drama with truer art than any of his contemporaries, comes nearer nature and the ancients, unless in his last performance, which indeed met with most applause, however least deserving. But he seemed to know what he did, descending from himself to write to the Many, whereas before he wrote to the Few. I find a wonderful deal of good sense in that gentleman; he has wit without the pride and affectation that generally accompanies, and always corrupts it. His Myra is as celebrated as Ovid's Corinna, and as well known. How happy is he in the favour of that lovely lady! She, too, deserves applause, besides her beauty, for her gratitude and sensibility to so deserving an admirer. There are few women, who, when they once give in to the sweets of an irregular passion, care to confine themselves to him that first endeared it to them, but not so the charming Myra.

> Mrs. Mary de la Riviere Manley, 1709, *The New Atalantis*

I was to-day to see Mr. Congreve, who is almost blind with cataracts growing on his eyes; and his case is, that he must wait two or three years, until the cataracts are riper, and till he is quite blind, and then he must have them couched; and besides he is never rid of the gout, yet he looks young and fresh, and is as cheerful as ever. He is younger by three years or more than I, and I am twenty years younger than he. He gave me a pain in the great toe, by mentioning the gout. I find such suspicions frequently, but they go off again.

Jonathan Swift, 1710, Journal to Stella, Oct. 26

The uncommon praise of a man of wit, always to please, and never to offend. No one, after a joyful evening, can reflect upon an expression of Mr. Congreve's that dwells upon him with pain.

Richard Steele, 1713, Poetical Miscellanies, Dedication

Instead of endeavouring to raise a vain monument to myself, . . . let me leave behind me a memorial of my friendship with one of the most valuable of men, as well as finest writers of my age and country. One who has tried, and knows by his own experience, how hard an undertaking it is to do justice to Homer, and one who I'm sure sincerely rejoices with me at the period of my labours. To him, therefore, having brought this long work to a conclusion, I desire to dedicate it, and have the honour and satisfaction of placing together in this manner, the names of Mr. Congreve and of . . .

Alexander Pope, 1720, Homer's Iliad, Postscript, March 25

Mr. *Congreve* had one defect, which was, his entertaining too mean an idea of his first profession, (that of a writer) tho' 'twas to this he owed his fame and fortune. He spoke of his works as of trifles that were beneath him; and hinted to me, in our first conversation, that I should visit him upon no other foot than that of a gentleman, who led a life of plainness and simplicity. I answered, that had he been so unfortunate as to be a mere gentleman I should never have come to see him; and I was very much disgusted at so unseasonable a piece of vanity.

François Marie Arouet Voltaire, 1732? Letters Concerning
the English Nation, p. 148

His place in the custom-house, and his office of secretary in Jamaica, are said to have brought him in upwards of 1200 *l.* a year; and he was so far an œconomist, as to raise from thence a competent estate. No man of his learning ever pass'd thro' life with more ease, or less envy; and as in the dawn of his reputation he was very dear to the greatest wits of his time, so during his whole life he preserved the utmost respect of, and received continual marks of esteem from, men of genius and letters, without ever being involved in any of their quarrels, or drawing upon himself the least mark of distaste, or even dissatisfaction. The greatest part of the last twenty years of his life were spent in ease and retirement, and he gave himself no trouble about reputation.

Theophilus Cibber, 1753, Lives of the Poets, vol. IV, p. 93

Congreve was very intimate for years with Mrs. Bracegirdle, and lived in the same street, his house very near hers; until his acquaintance with the young Duchess of Marlborough. He then quitted that house. The duchess showed me a diamond necklace (which Lady Di. used afterwards to wear) that cost seven thousand pounds, and was purchased with the money Congreve left her. How much better would it have been to have given it to poor Mrs. Bracegirdle.

Edward Young, 1757, Spence's Anecdotes, ed. Singer, p. 286

The body lay in state in the Jerusalem Chamber and was buried with great pomp in Westminster Abbey. A monument was erected in the abbey by the Duchess of Marlborough, with an inscription of her own writing, and a hideous cenotaph was erected at Stowe by Lord Cobham. It was reported that the duchess afterwards had a figure of ivory or wax made in his likeness, which was placed at her table, addressed as if alive, served with food, and treated for "an imaginary sore on its leg." The story, if it has any foundation, would imply partial insanity.

Leslie Stephen, 1887, Dictionary of National Biography,
vol. XII, p. 8

No defence can serve for our poet's abandonment of Mrs. Bracegirdle with the paltry legacy, and nothing can extenuate the mortal comedy of his end as bon viveur when the Duchess of Marlborough, whom he had made his heir, placed his waxen effigy at her table, so contrived as to nod when she spoke to it, wrapped its feet in cloths, and had a physician to attend upon it and render a daily diagnosis. With the seven thousand pounds remaining from the legacy, after this pleasant whim was satisfied, the young Duchess bought a diamond necklace. Mrs. Bracegirdle, the favorite of his early years, the woman for whom he had written the best of his characters and who shares his theatrical fame, was poor, but she shielded Congreve's memory by her silence, while the Duchess blazoned his infatuation by her diamonds. This was a death scene for a comic dramatist to observe.

George Edward Woodberry, 1888, The Nation, vol. 47, p. 256

The Old Bachelor (1693)

Mr. Congreve was of the Middle Temple, his first performance was an Novel, call'd incognita, then he began his Play the old Batchelor, haveing little Acquaintance withe the traders in that way, his Cozens recommended him to a friend of theirs, who was very usefull to him in the whole course of his play, he engag'd Mr. Dryden in its favour, who upon reading it sayd he never saw such a first play in his life, but the Author not being acquainted with the stage or the town, it would be pity to have it miscarry for want of a little Assistance: the stuff was rich indeed, it wanted only the fashionable cutt of the town. To help that Mr. Dryden, Mr. Manwayring, and Mr. Southern red it with great care, and Mr. Dryden putt it in the order it was playd, Mr. Southerne obtaind of Mr. Thos: Davenant who then governd the Playhouse, that Mr. Congreve should have the privilege of the Playhouse half a year before his play was playd, wh. I never knew allowd any one before: it was playd with great success that play made him many friends.

Thomas Southerne, 1735-36? *Add. MSS.,* 4221, British Museum

The writing here is already excellent, and distinguished, especially by its lightness, from anything that had preceded it in the post-Restoration drama. The majority of the leading characters, however, contain nothing quite original; it would be easy to find in Molière or elsewhere prototypes or analogues of Heartwell, who sets up for a misogynist but is in reality a victim to female wiles, of the blustering coward, Captain Bluffe, and of the demure but deep Mrs. Fondlewife. Yet these in company with a number of other personages furnish an abundant variety, and the action is both brisk and diverting. Morally, both the plots of which the play is composed are objectionable; but the dramatic life in this comedy is unmistakable, and more than any other quality justified a success so rarely achieved by the work of a novice hand.

Adolphus William Ward, 1875-99, *A History of English Dramatic Literature,* vol. III, p. 471

The Double Dealer (1694)

But there is one thing at which I am more concerned than all the false criticism that are made upon me; and that is, some of the ladies are offended. I am heartily sorry for it; for I declare, I would rather disoblige all the critics in the world than one of the fair sex. They are concerned that I have represented some women vicious and affected. How can I help it? It is the business of a comic poet to paint the vices and follies of human kind. . . . I should be very glad of an opportunity to make my compliments to those ladies who are offended. But they can no more expect it in a comedy, than *to be tickled by a surgeon when he is letting their blood.*

William Congreve, 1693, *Double-Dealer,* Epistle Dedicatory

Congreve's *Double Dealer* is much censured by the greater part of the town, and is defended only by the best judges, who, you know, are commonly the fewest. Yet it gains ground daily, and has already been acted eight times.

The women think he has exposed their witchery too much, and the gentlemen are offended with him for the discovery of their follies and the way of their intrigue under the notions of friendship to their ladies' husbands. My verses, which you will find before it, were written before the play was acted; but I neither altered them, nor do I alter my opinion of the play.

John Dryden, 1793, Letter to Walsh

The Double Dealer, with the solemn reciprocities of *Lord* and *Lady Froth,* and the capital character of *Lady Plyant,* "insolent to her husband, and easy to every pretender," is far superior to *The Old Bachelor.* Congreve excels in mixtures of impudence, hypocrisy, and self-delusion. The whole of the fifth scene of the second act, between *Lady Plyant* and *Mellefont,* is exquisite for the grossness of the overtures made under pretence of a delicacy in alarm. But it is no wonder a comedy did not succeed that has so black a villain in it as *Maskwell,* and an aunt who has a regularly installed gallant in her nephew. *Sir Paul Plyant* also says things to his daughter, which no decent person could hear with patience between father and child. The writer's object might have been a good one; but it is of doubtful and perilous use to attempt to do good by effrontery.

Leigh Hunt, 1840, ed., The Works of Wycherley,
Congreve, Vanbrugh and Farquhar

Notwithstanding certain repulsive features in the action, this is undoubtedly one of the best comedies in our dramatic literature.

Adolphus William Ward, 1875-99, A History of
English Dramatic Literature, vol. III, p. 472

Love for Love (1695)

This play is as full of character, incident, and stage-effect, as almost any of those of his contemporaries, and fuller of wit than any of his own, except perhaps *The Way of the World.* It still acts, and is still acted well. The effect of it is prodigious on the well-informed spectator. In particular, Munden's Foresight, if it is not just the thing, is a wonderfully rich and powerful piece of comic acting. His look is planet-struck; his dress and appearance like one of the signs of the Zodiac taken down. Nothing can be more bewildered; and it only wants a little more helplessness, a little more of the doating, querulous garrulity of age, to be all that one conceives of the superannuated, star-gazing original.

William Hazlitt, 1818, Lectures on the English
Comic Writers, Lecture iv

The comedy of *Love for Love* has been commonly accounted Congreve's masterpiece, and perhaps with justice. It is not quite so uniformly brilliant in style as *The Way of the World,* but it has the advantage of possessing a much wholesomer relation to humanity than that play, which is almost undiluted satire, and a more theatrical arrangement of scenes. In *Love for Love* the qualities which had shown themselves in *The Old Bachelor* and *The Double Dealer* recur, but in a much stronger degree. The sentiments are more unexpected, the language is more picturesque, the characters have more activity of mind and vitality of nature. All that was merely pink has deepened into scarlet; even what is disagreeable,—the crudity of allusion and the indecency of phrase,—have increased. The style in all its parts and qualities has become more vivid. We are looking through the same telescope as before, but the sight is better adjusted, the outlines are more definite, and the colours more intense. So wonderfully felicitous is the phraseology that we cannot doubt that if Congreve could only have kept himself unspotted from the sins of the age, dozens of tags would have passed, like bits of Shakespeare, Pope, and Gray, into habitual parlance. In spite of its errors against decency, *Love for Love* survived on the stage for more than a century, long after the remainder of Restoration and Orange drama was well-nigh extinct.

Edmund Gosse, 1888, *Life of William Congreve*
(*Great Writers*), p. 69

The Mourning Bride (1697)

The incidents succeed one another too rapidly. The play is too full of business. It is difficult for the mind to follow and comprehend the whole series of events; and, what is the greatest fault of all, the catastrophe, which ought always to be plain and simple, is brought about in a manner too artificial and intricate.

Hugh Blair, 1783, *Lectures on Rhetoric and Belles-Lettres,*
ed. Mills, Lecture xlv

The Mourning Bride is not uninteresting in its story, nor so bad in its poetry as one might expect from the want of faith and passion natural to a town-wit of that age. . . . If the tragedy were revived now, the audience would laugh at the inflated sentences and unconscious prose. The revival of old English literature, and the tone of our best modern poets, have accustomed them to a higher and truer spirit. Yet some of the language of Almeria, as where, for instance, she again meets with Osmyn, is natural and affecting; and it is pleasing to catch a man of the world at these evidences of sympathy with what is serious. Nor are sensible and striking passages wanting.

Leigh Hunt, 1840, ed., *The Works of Wycherley,*
Congreve, Vanbrugh and Farquhar

It has been the habit to quote *The Mourning Bride* as the very type of bad declamatory tragedy. No doubt Dr. Johnson did it harm by that extravagant eulogy in which he selected one fragment as unsurpassed in the poetry of all time. But if we compare it, not with those tragedies of the age of Elizabeth, studded with occasional naïve felicities, which it is just now the fashion to admire with some extravagance, but with what England and even France produced from 1650 to the revival of romantic taste, *The Mourning Bride* will probably take a place close after what is best in Otway and Racine. It will bear comparison, as I would venture to assert, with Southerne's *Fatal Marriage* or with Crébillon's *Rhadamiste et Zénobie,* and will not be pronounced inferior to these excellent and famous tragedies in dramatic interest, or genuine grandeur of sentiment, or beauty of language. It has done what no other of these special rivals has done, outside the theatre of Racine, it has contributed to the everyday fashion of its country several well-worn lines. But it is not every one who says that "Music has charms to soothe a savage breast" or that "Hell knows no fury like a woman scorn'd," who would be able to tell where the familiar sentiment first occurs.

Edmund Gosse, 1888, Life of William Congreve
(Great Writers), p. 87

The Way of the World (1700)

The Way of the World was the author's last and most carefully finished performance. It is an essence almost too fine; and the sense of pleasure evaporates in an aspiration after something that seems too exquisite ever to have been realised. After inhaling the spirit of Congreve's wit, and tasting "love's thrice reputed nectar" in his works, the head grows giddy in turning from the highest point of rapture to the ordinary business of life; and we can with difficulty recall the truant Fancy to those objects which we are fain to take up with here, *for better, for worse.*

William Hazlitt, 1818, Lectures on the English
Comic Writers, Lecture iv

The great art of Congreve is especially shown in this, that he has entirely excluded from his scenes,—some little generosities in the part of Angelica perhaps excepted,—not only anything like a faultless character, but any pretensions to goodness or good feelings whatsoever. Whether he did this designedly, or instinctively, the effect is as happy, as the design (if design) was bold. I used to wonder at the strange power which his *Way of the World* in particular possesses of interesting you all along in the pursuits of characters, for whom you absolutely care nothing—for you neither hate nor love his personages—and I think it is owing to this very indifference for any, that you endure the whole. He has spread a privation of moral light, I will call it, rather than by the ugly name of palpable darkness over his creations; and his shadows flit before you without distinction or preference. Had he introduced a good character, a single gush of moral feeling, a revulsion of the judgment to actual life and actual duties, the impertinent Goshen would have only lighted to the discovery of deformities, which now are none, because we think them none.

> Charles Lamb, 1824, *On the Artificial Comedy of the Last Century*

The coquetry of Millamant, not without some touches of delicacy and affection, the impertinent coxcombry of Petulant and Witwood, the mixture of wit and ridiculous vanity in Lady Wishfort, are amusing to the reader. Congreve has here made more use than, as far as I remember, had been common in England, of the all-important soubrette, on whom so much depends in French comedy.

> Henry Hallam, 1837-39, *Introduction to the Literature of Europe,* pt. iv, ch. vi, par. 52

I do not think it too much to say in its praise, that it comprises the most quintessentialised combination of qualities requisite to compound an artificially legitimate comedy to be found in the whole range of our dramatic literature. I do not say, the comedy of *primitive* and *natural* life; but the comedy of the furbelows and flounces; of powder and essences; of paint and enamelling; of high-heels, hoops, and all hideous artificialities, concealments, intrigues, plots, and subterfuges. In reading the play, one's faculties are retained in a perpetual suspension of pleasure at the unabating and highly sustained succession of flights of wit, gaily tinctured imageries, flashing repartees, and skilfully contrasted characters on the scene.

> Charles Cowden Clarke, 1871, "On the Comic Writers of England," *The Gentleman's Magazine,* n. s., vol. 7, p. 842

The comic work of Congreve, though different rather in kind than in degree from the bestial and blatant license of his immediate precursors, was inevitably for a time involved in the sentence passed upon the comic work of men in all ways alike his inferiors. The true and triumphant answer to all possible attacks of honest men or liars, brave men or cowards, was then as ever to be given by the production of work unarraignable alike by fair means or foul, by frank impeachment or furtive imputation. In 1700 Congreve thus replied to Collier with the crowning work of his genius,—the unequalled and unapproached master-piece of English comedy. The one play in our language which may fairly claim a place beside or but just beneath the mightiest work of Molière is *The Way of the World*.

Algernon Charles Swinburne, 1877, Encyclopædia Britannica,
vol. VI

Successive critics, seeing, what we must all acknowledge, the incomparable splendour of the dialogue in *The Way of the World,* have not ceased to marvel at the caprice which should render dubious the success of such a masterpiece on its first appearance. But perhaps a closer examination of the play may help us to unravel the apparent mystery. On certain sides, all the praise which has been lavished on the play from Steele and Voltaire down to Mr. Swinburne and Mr. George Meredith is thoroughly deserved. *The Way of the World* is the best-written, the most dazzling, the most intellectually accomplished of all English comedies, perhaps of all the comedies of the world. But it has the defects of the very qualities which make it so brilliant. A perfect comedy does not sparkle so much, is not so exquisitely written, because it needs to advance, to develop. To *The Way of the World* may be applied that very dubious compliment paid by Mrs. Browning to Landor's *Pentameron* that, "were it not for the necessity of getting through a book, some of the pages are too delicious to turn over."

Edmund Gosse, 1888, Life of William Congreve
(Great Writers), p. 135

GENERAL

Among all the efforts of early genius which literary history records, I doubt whether anyone can be produced that more surpasses the common limits of nature than the plays of Congreve. . . . Congreve has merit of the highest kind, he is an original writer, who borrowed neither the models of his plot, nor the manner of his dialogue. Of his plays I cannot speak distinctly; for since I inspected them years have passed; but what remains upon my memory is, that his characters are commonly fictitious and artificial, with very little of nature and not much of life. . . . Of his miscellaneous poetry, I cannot say anything very favourable. The powers of Congreve seem to desert him when he leaves the stage.

Samuel Johnson, 1779-81, Congreve, Lives of the English Poets

They are too cold to be mischievous: they keep the brain in too incessant inaction to allow the passions to kindle. For those who search into the powers of intellect, the combinations of thought which may be produced by volition, the plays of Congreve may form a profitable study. But their time is fled—on the stage they will be received no more; and of the devotees of light reading such as could read them without disgust would probably peruse them with little pleasure.

Hartley Coleridge, 1833, Biographia Borealis, p. 693

The poetical remains of Congreve, especially when considered in connection with those remarkable dramatic works which achieved for him so swift and splendid a reputation, have but a slender claim to vitality. His brilliant and audacious Muse seems to have required the glitter of the foot-lights and the artificial atmosphere of the stage as conditions of success; in the study he is, as a rule, either trivial or frigidly conventional.

Austin Dobson, 1880, English Poets, ed. Ward, vol. III, p. 10

Congreve was essentially a man of letters; his style is that of a pupil not of Molière but of the full, the rich, the excessive, the pedantic Jonson; his Legends, his Wishforts, his Foresights, are the lawful heirs—refined and sublimated but still of direct descent—of the Tuccas and the Bobadils and the Epicure Mammons of the great Elizabethan; they are (that is) more literary than theatrical—they are excellent reading, but they have long since fled the stage and vanished into the night of mere scholarship.

William Ernest Henley, 1890, Views and Reviews, p. 206

Where Congreve excels all his English rivals is in his literary force, and a succinctness of style peculiar to him. He had correct judgment, a correct ear, readiness of illustration within a narrow range, in snap shots of the obvious at the obvious, and copious language. He hits the mean of a fine style and a natural in dialogue. He is at once precise and voluble. If you have ever thought upon style you will acknowledge it to be a signal accomplishment. In this he is a classic, and is worthy of treading a measure with Molière. . . .

George Meredith, 1897, An Essay on Comedy and the
Uses of the Comic Spirit, p. 32, 33

SIR RICHARD STEELE
1672-1729

Born, in Dublin, March 1672. Early education at Charterhouse, Nov. 1684 to Nov. 1689. Matric., Ch. Ch., Oxford, 13 March 1690; Postmaster Merton Coll., 1691. Left Oxford, 1694. Took no degree. Entered the army, 1695. Priv. Sec. to Lord Cutts, 1696-97. Commission in the Guards, 1697. Play, *The Funeral,* produced at Drury Lane, Dec. 1701; *The Lying Lover,* Dec. 1703; *The Tender Husband,* April 1705. Married (i) Mrs.

Margaret Stretch, 1705. Gentleman-Waiter to Prince George of Denmark, Aug. 1706 to Oct. 1708. Wife died, Dec. 1706. Gazetteer, May 1707 to Oct. 1710. Married (ii) Mary Scurlock, Sept. 1707. Contrib. to *The Muses Mercury,* 1707; to *Spectator,* March 1711 to Dec. 1714; to *Guardian,* March to Oct. 1713; to *The Englishman,* Oct. 1713 to Nov. 1715. Commissioner of Stamp Office, Jan. 1710 to June 1713. M. P. for Stockbridge, 1713; expelled from House of Commons on account of passages in writings, 1714. Surveyor of Royal Stables at Hampton Court, 1714. Lieutenant for County of Middlesex, and J. P., 1714. Governor of Royal Company of Comedians, 1715-20. Knighted, 1715. M. P. for Boroughbridge, 1715. Commissioner of Forfeited Estates in Scotland, 1715. Edited *The Theatre* (under pseud. "Sir John Edgar"), Jan. to April 1720. M. P. for Wendover, March 1722. Comedy, *The Conscious Lovers,* produced at Drury Lane, Nov. 1722. Later years spent in retirement, mainly in Wales. Died at Carmarthen, 1 Sept. 1729. WORKS: *The Procession* (anon.), 1695; *The Christian Hero,* 1701; *The Funeral,* 1702; *The Lying Lover,* 1704; *The Tender Husband,* 1705; *Letter to Dr. Sacheverell* (under pseud. "Isaac Bickerstaff"), 1709; *The Tatler* (under pseud. "Isaac Bickerstaff,"* 4 vols.), 1709-11; Contributions to *The Spectator,* 1711-14; to *The Guardian,* 1713; to *The Englishman,* 1713-15; *The Importance of Dunkirk Considered,* 1713; *The Englishman's Thanks to the Duke of Marlborough* (anon.), 1712; *The Crisis,* 1713; *Letter to the Tongue-loosed Doctor* (under pseud. "Isaac Bickerstaff"), 1713; *Speech on the proposal of Sir T. Hanmer for Speaker,* 1714; *Letter to a Member of Parliament,* 1714; *Apology for Himself and his Writings,* 1714; *A Defence for drinking to the pious memory of K. Charles I.,* 1714; *Romish Ecclesiastical History of Late Years,* 1714; *Letter from the Earl of Mar to the King,* 1715; *The Lover; to which is added, the Reader,* 1715; *Political Writings,* 1715; *Town-Talk* (9 nos.), 1715-16; *Chit-Chat* (under pseud. "Humphrey Philroye"), 1716; *The British Subjects' Answer to the Pretender's Declaration,* 1716; *Speech for Repealing of the Triennial Act,* 1716; *The Tea Table,* 1716; *An Account of the Fish-Pool* (with J. Gilmore), 1718; *Letter to the Earl of O————d,* 1719; *The Spinster,* 1719; *The Antidote* (2 nos.; anon.), 1719; *Inquiry into the Manner of Creating Peers* (anon.), 1719; *The Plebeian* (anon.), 1719; *The Theatre* (under pseud. "Sir John Edgar"), 1720; *The Crisis of Poverty,* 1720; *A Nation a Family,* 1720; *The D————n of W————r still the same* (anon.), 1720; *State of the Case between the Lord Chamberlain,* etc., 1720; *The Conscious Lovers,* 1723; *Dramatick Works,* 1723; *Woods' Melancholly Complaint* (anon.), 1725. POSTHUMOUS: *Epistolary Correspondence,* ed. by J. Nichols, 1787. He translated: Cerri's *Account of the State of the Roman Catholic Religion,* 1715; and edited: *Poetical Miscellanies,* 1714; *The Ladies' Library,* 1714. Life: by G. A. Aitken, 1889.

R. Farquharson Sharp, 1897, A Dictionary of
English Authors, p. 267

SEE: *Plays,* ed. George A. Aitken, 1894 (Mermaid edition); *The Christian Hero,* ed. Rae Blanchard, 1932; *Steele's Tracts and Pamphlets,* ed. Rae Blanchard, 1944; *Poetical Miscellanies,* ed. Rae Blanchard, 1952; *The Englishman,* ed. Rae Blanchard, 1955; *Richard Steele's Periodical Journalism, 1714-16,* ed. Rae Blanchard, 1959; *The Correspondence,* ed.

Rae Blanchard, 1941; George A. Aitken, *Life,* 1889, 2v.; Willard Connely, *Life,* 1934; J. Loftis, *Steele and Drury Lane,* 1952; Calhoun Winton, *Captain Steele: The Early Career of Richard Steele,* 1964.

PERSONAL

On Sunday night last, Captain Keely and one Mr. Steele, an officer of the Guards, fought a duel in Hide-Park, in which the latter was mortally wounded, and some say he is since Dead.

Flying Post, 1700, June 18-20

After the first Bottle he is no disagreeable Companion. I never knew him taxed with Ill-nature, which hath made me wonder how Ingratitude came to be his prevailing Vice; and I am apt to think it proceeds more from some unaccountable sort of Instinct, than Premeditation. Being the most imprudent Man alive, he never follows the Advice of his Friends, but is wholly at the mercy of Fools or Knaves, or hurried away by his own Caprice; by which he hath committed more Absurdities in Oeconomy, Friendship, Love, Duty, good Manners, Politics, Religion and Writing, than ever fell to one Man's share.

Jonathan Swift, 1713, *The Importance of the*
Guardian Considered

D'ye see that black beau (stuck up in a pert chariot), thickset, his eyes in his head with hanging eyebrows, broad face, and tallow complexion. . . . I long to inform myself if that coach be his own. . . . He is called M. L'Ingrate. . . . Though he's a most incorrect writer, he pleases in spite of his faults. . . . I remember him almost t'other day but a wretched common trooper. He had the luck to write a small poem, and dedicated it to a person he never saw. . . . His morals were loose.

Mrs. Mary de la Riviere Manley, 1709, *New Atalantis,*
vol. I, p. 131

Richard Steel, esq., member of parliament, was on Thursday last, about 12 o'clock at night, expelled the house of commons for a roguish pamphlett called "The Crisis," and for several other pamphletts, in which he hath abused the queen, &c. This Steel was formerly of Christ Church in Oxford, and afterwards of Merton college. He was a rakish, wild, drunken spark; but he got a good reputation by publishing a paper that came out daily, called *The Tatler,* and by another called *The Spectator;* but the most ingenious of these papers were written by Mr. Addison, and Dr. Swift, as 'tis reported. And when these two had left him, he appeared to be a mean, heavy, weak writer, as is sufficiently demonstrated in his papers called *The Guardian, The Englishman,* and *The Lover.* He now writes for bread, being involved in debt.

Thomas Hearne, 1713-14, *Reliquiæ Hearnianæ,* ed. Bliss,
March 23, vol. I, p. 296

Sir John Edgar is of a middle stature, broad shoulders, thick legs, a shape like the picture of somebody over a farmer's chimney—a short chin, a short nose, a short forehead, a broad flat face, and a dusky countenance. Yet with such a face and such a shape, he discovered at sixty that he took himself for a beauty, and appeared to be more mortified at being told that he was ugly, than he was by any reflection made upon his honour or understanding. . . . He is a gentleman born, witness himself, of very honourable family; certainly of a very ancient one, for his ancestors flourished in Tipperary long before the English ever set foot in Ireland. He has testimony of this more authentic than the Herald's Office or any human testimony. For God has marked him more abundantly than he did Cain, and stamped his native country on his face, his understandings, his writings, his actions, his passions, and, above all, his vanity. The Hibernian brogue is still upon all these, though long habit and length of days have worn it off his tongue.

John Dennis, 1720, *The Character and Conduct of
Sir John Edgar*

Sir Richard Steele having one day invited to his house a great number of persons of the first quality, they were surprised at the number of liveries which surrounded the table; and after dinner, when wine and mirth had set them free from the observations of a rigid ceremony, one of them inquired of Sir Richard how such an expensive train of domesticks could be consistent with his fortune. Sir Richard very frankly confessed that they were fellows of whom he would willingly be rid. And then, being asked why he did not discharge them, declared that they were bailiffs, who had introduced themselves with an execution, and whom, since he could not send them away, he had thought it convenient to embellish with liveries, that they might do him credit while they staid.

Samuel Johnson, 1744, *Life of Richard Savage*

He had survived much, but neither his cheerful temper nor his kind philosophy. He would be carried out in a summer's evening, where the country lads and lasses were at their rural sports, and with his pencil give an order on his agent for a new gown to the best dancer. That was the last thing seen of Richard Steele. And the youths and maidens who saw him in his invalid-chair, enfeebled and dying, saw him still as the wits and fine ladies and gentlemen had seen him in his gaiety and youth, when he sat in the chair of Mr. Bickerstaff, creating pleasure for himself by the communication of pleasure to others, and in proportion to the happiness he distributed increasing his own.

John Forster, 1855, "Sir Richard Steele,"
Quarterly Review, vol. 96, p. 568

Who has not heard of Sir Richard Steele? Wordsworth says of one of his characters—

> "She was known to every star,
> And every wind that blows."

Poor Dick was known to every sponging-house, and to every bailiff that, blowing in pursuit, walked the London streets. A fine-hearted, warm-blooded character, without any atom of prudence, self-control, reticence, or forethought; quite as destitute of malice or envy; perpetually sinning and perpetually repenting; never positively irreligious, even when drunk; and often excessively pious when recovering sobriety,—Steele reeled his way through life, and died with the reputation of being an orthodox Christian and a (nearly) habitual drunkard; the most affectionate and most faithless of husbands; a brave soldier, and in many points an arrant fool; a violent politician, and the best natured of men; a writer extremely lively, for this, among other reasons, that he wrote generally on his legs, flying or meditating flight from his creditors; and who embodied in himself the titles of his three principal works—The Christian Hero, The Tender Husband, and The Tatler;—being a "Christian Hero," in intention, one of those intentions with which a certain place is paved; a "Tender Husband," if not a true one, to his two ladies; and a "Tatler" to all persons, in all circumstances and at all times.

George Gilfillan, 1859, ed., Poetical Works of Joseph Addison,
etc., Life, p. xiv

He had two wives, whom he loved dearly and treated badly. He hired grand houses, and bought fine horses for which he could never pay. He was often religious, but more often drunk. As a man of letters, other men of letters who followed him, such as Thackeray, could not be very proud of him. But everybody loved him; and he seems to have been the inventor of that flying literature which, with many changes in form and manner, has done so much for the amusement and edification of readers ever since his time.

Anthony Trollope, 1879, Thackeray (English Men of Letters),
p. 162

I am confident that the result of the fuller study of his life, which is now rendered practicable, will be the conviction that, in spite of weaknesses, which are among the most apparent of all those to which mortals are liable,

Steele's character is more attractive and essentially nobler than, perhaps that of any of the greatest of his contemporaries in the world of letters.

> George A. Aitken, 1889, *The Life of Richard Steele,*
> vol. I, Preface

The Christian Hero (1701)

Steele began his career as a writer, with a poem, his *Christian Heroes,* which justified no great expectations. This poem could have little of soul or of nature in it, because the contents stood in a most surprising contradiction with Steele's scandalous and dissolute course of life.

> Friedrich Christoph Schlosser, 1823-43, *History of the*
> *Eighteenth Century,* vol. I, p. 102

One would hardly have looked to him for any early talk about the life of a true *Christian Hero.* But he did write a book so entitled, in those wild young days, as a sort of kedge anchor, he says, whereby he might haul out from the shoals of the wicked town, and indulge in a sort of contemplative piety. It was and is a very good little book, but it did not hold a bit, as an anchor.

> Donald G. Mitchell, 1890, *English Lands, Letters and Kings,*
> *From Elizabeth to Anne,* p. 281

It differs considerably both in style and teaching from the ordinary devotional manual, and without much straining may be said to exhibit definite indications of that faculty for essay-writing which was to be so signally developed in the *Spectator,* in which indeed certain portions of it were afterwards embodied.

> Austin Dobson, 1898, *Dictionary of National Biography,*
> vol. LIV, p. 131

The Funeral (1702)

Nothing can establish a better proof of the admirable merit of this play . . . than the diligence with which the critics have attempted, to no purpose, to discover that it is not genuine; for the plot and the style are unquestionably the author's own, and the last is so peculiar, which is indeed the characteristic of Steele's writings, that nothing can be more difficult to get by heart; but when attached to the memory, nothing can be more easy to retain. . . . Every thing is perfectly in nature, and the moral is complete.

> Charles Dibdin, 1795, *A Complete History of the Stage,*
> vol. IV, pp. 307, 308

Very sprightly and pleasant throughout, it was full of telling hits at lawyers and undertakers, and, with a great many laughable incidents, and no laugh raised at the expense of virtue or decency, it had one character (the widow on whom the artifice of her husband's supposed death is played off) which is a masterpiece of comedy.

> John Forster, 1855, "Sir Richard Steele,"
> *Quarterly Review*, vol. 96, p. 540

His sense of humour enlivens some of the scenes, and is, perhaps, chiefly visible in *The Funeral;* but for the most part dulness is in the ascendant, and the sentiment is frequently mawkish.

> John Dennis, 1894, *The Age of Pope*, p. 137

The Tender Husband (1705)

In *The Tender Husband* he seems to have contented himself with the more modest aim of being harmless, instead of didactic,—in other words, he tried to be simply amusing.

> Austin Dobson, 1886, *Richard Steele (English Worthies)*, p. 45

In this play he gave unmistakable evidence of his happy genius for conceiving and embodying humorous types of character, putting on the stage the parents or the grandparents of Squire Western, Tony Lumpkin, and Lydia Languish.

> William Minto, 1887, *Encyclopædia Britannica*,
> Ninth ed., vol. 22, p. 555

The Tender Husband, though not so good as *The Funeral*, contains a great deal of genuine comedy. The weakness of the play lies in the "moral" scenes in which Clerimont, senior, makes trial of his wife by means of Fainlove. This part of the story, together with Fainlove's marriage with Humphery Gubbin, is farfetched and out of place.

> George A. Aitken, 1889, *The Life of Richard Steele*, vol. I, p. 109

The Tatler (1709-11)

It must, indeed, be confessed that never man threw up his pen under stronger temptations to have employed it longer; his reputation was at a greater height than, I believe, ever any living author's was before him. . . . There is this noble difference between him and all the rest of our polite and gallant authors: the latter have endeavoured to please the age by falling in with them, and encouraging them in their fashionable vices and false notions of things. It would have been a jest some time since, for a man to have asserted that anything witty could be said in praise of a married state; or that devotion and virtue were anyway necessary to the character of a fine gentleman. . . . It is incredible to conceive the effect his writings have had on the town; how many thousand follies they have either quite banished, or given a very great check to; how much countenance they have added to virtue and religion; how many people they have rendered happy, by showing them it was their own fault if they were not so; and, lastly, how entirely they have convinced our fops and young fellows of the value and advantages of learning.

John Gay, 1711, *Present State of Wit*

Steele appears to have begun the paper without any concert, or hope of other assistance than what came spontaneously. His chief dependence was on his intelligence, which gave him a superiority over his contemporaries, who were merely news-writers, and had never discovered that a periodical paper might furnish instruction of a better and more lasting kind. In the other parts of the *Tatler,* he was at first less careful; his style had a familiar vulgarity not unlike that of the journalists of the age, which he adopted either in compliance with the prevailing manner, or by way of disguise. In one paper he acknowledges "incorrectness of style," and writing "in an air of common speech." All this however became a *Tatler,* and for some time he aimed at no higher character. But when associated with Addison, he assumed a tone more natural to a polished and elegant mind, and dispersed his coarser familiarity among his characteristic correspondents. If he did not introduce, he was the first who successfully employed the harmless fiction of writing letters to himself, and by that gave a variety of amusement and information to his paper, which would have been impracticable had he always appeared in his own character. All succeeding Essayists have endeavoured to avail themselves of a privilege so essential to this species of composition, but it requires a mimicry of style and sentiment which few have been able to combine.

Alexander Chalmers, 1803, ed., *The Tatler,*
Biographical Preface, p. 44

I have . . . always preferred the *Tatler* to the *Spectator*. Whether it is owing to my having been earlier or better acquainted with the one than the other, my pleasure in reading these two admirable works is not at all in proportion to their comparative reputation. The *Tatler* contains only half the number of volumes, and, I will venture to say, at least an equal quantity of sterling wit and sense. "The first sprightly runnings" are there—it has more of the original spirit, more of the freshness and stamp of nature. The indications of character and strokes of humour are more true and frequent; the reflec-tions that suggest themselves arise more from the occasion, and are less spun out into regular dissertations. They are more like the remarks which occur in sensible conversation, and less like a lecture. Something is left to the understanding of the reader. Steele seems to have gone into his closet chiefly to set down what he observed out of doors. Addison seems to have spent most of his time in his study, and to have spun out and wire-drawn the hints, which he borrowed from Steele, or took from nature, to the utmost. I am far from wishing to depreciate Addison's talents, but I am anxious to do justice to Steele, who was, I think, upon the whole, a less artificial and more original writer. The humorous descriptions ôf Steele resemble loose sketches, or fragments of a comedy; those of Addison are rather comments, or ingenious paraphrases, on the genuine text.

William Hazlitt, 1818, Lectures on the English Comic Writers,
Lecture V

At a time in no way remarkable for refinement, Steele's gallantry to women, thus incessantly expressed in *The Tatler* to the last, was that of a Sir Tristan or Sir Calidore; and in not a small degree, to every houshold into which it carried such unaccustomed language, this was a ground of its extraordinary success. Inseparable always from his passion is the exalted admiration he feels; and his love is the very flower of his respect.

John Forster, 1855-58, "Sir Richard Steele," Quarterly Review;
Biographical Essays, vol. II, pp. 119, 122

It is fortunately not necessary nowadays to argue as to the comparative merits of the papers by Steele and Addison, and such a discussion would be the last thing that Steele would wish; but this may be said, that Steele was the originator of nearly every new departure in the periodicals which the two friends produced; and if Steele had not furnished Addison with the opportunity for displaying his special power, Addison would in all proba-bility have been known to us only as an accomplished scholar and poet of no great power. The world owes Addison to Steele. . . . It is just because the *Tatler* is more thoroughly imbued with Steele's spirit than the *Spectator*, that many competent judges have confessed that they found greater pleasure in the earlier periodical than in its more finished and more famous successor.

George A. Aitken, 1889, The Life of Richard Steele,
vol. I, pp. 248, 249

Steele has the merit of having been the first to feel the new intellectual cravings of his day and to furnish what proved to be the means of meeting

them. His *Tatler* was a periodical of pamphlet form, in which news was to
be varied by short essays of criticism and gossip. But his grasp of the new
literature was a feeble grasp. His sense of the fitting form for it, of its fitting
tone, of the range and choice of its subjects, were alike inadequate. He
seized indeed by a happy instinct on letter-writing and conversation as the
two molds to which the essay must adapt itself; he seized with the same
happy instinct on humour as the pervading temper of his work and on
"manners" as its destined sphere. But his notion of "manners" was limited
not only to the external aspects of life and society, but to those aspects as
they present themselves in towns; while his humor remained pert and superficial. The *Tatler,* however, had hardly been started when it was taken in
hand by a greater than Steele.

Susan Hale, 1898, *Men and Manners of the Eighteenth Century,*
p. 76

The *Tatler*—Swift's own suggestion to Steele—is full of happy illustration
and communication of ideas. Dated from coffee-houses, it was the first
paper to unite the record of news with the portrayal of manners, to dissemi-
nate at once fact and fiction, to publish Whig principles and puff friendly
authors. How good is his description of the "Club!" Sir Geofrey Notch,
who appropriates the "right-hand" chair, and "calls every thriving man
a pitiful upstart;" Major Matchlock, who "has all the battles by heart . . .
and brags every night of his having been knockt off his horse at the rising
of the London apprentices." Dick Reptile, the "good-natured indolent man,
who speaks little himself, but laughs at our jokes;" the Bencher, who is "the
greatest wit next to myself," and "shakes his head at the dullness of the
present age." They meet at six and disperse at ten. The maid comes with
a lantern "to light me home." Literature for the first time descends to the
people. Not without reason does Swift, under the *nom de plume* of Humphry
Wagstaffe, boast that the Staffian style is *"to describe things exactly as they
happen."* Realism made its bow to the world; and, then, too, for the first
time women claimed the lion's share of attention, and button-holed mankind. Steele's letters from flirts and prudes, scolds and shrews, languishers
and rebels, are the lineal precursors of the *Spectator.* Children, too, win an
audience. That really wonderful essay (which Thackeray has mentioned),
where Steele records the impressions of his early fatherlessness, abounds in
pathetic touches—the same that soften us in his *Spectator* paper about the
poor Anonyma in the Piazza of Covent Garden. Does not the sentence of
his "delight in stealing from the crowd" reveal the whole nature of the
sensitive lad? There is a sob in the style. To Steele and Prior belong the
domain of childhood.

Walter Sichel, 1901, *Bolingbroke and His Times,* p. 116

The Spectator (1711-14)

Memorandum, That there is a daily paper comes out, called *The Spectator,* written, as is supposed, by the same hand that writ the *Tatler,* viz. Captain Steel. In one of the last of these papers is a letter from Oxon at four o'clock in the morning, and subscribed *Abraham Froth.* It ridicules our hebdomadal meetings. The *Abraham Froth* is designed for *Dr. Arthur Charlett,* an empty, frothy man, and indeed the letter personates him incomparably well, being written, as he uses to do, upon great variety of things, and yet about nothing of moment. It brings in his cronys, Gorge Clarke, of All Souls, Dr. William Lancaster, provost of Queen's, and Dr. Gardiner, warden of All Souls. Dr. Lancaster is called in it *Sly-Boots,* and Dr. Gardiner is called in it *Dominick.* Queen's people are angry at it, and the common-room say there, 'tis silly, dull stuff, and they are seconded by some that have been of the same college. But men that are indifferent commend it highly, as it deserves.

Thomas Hearne, 1711, *Reliquiæ Hearnianæ,* ed. Bliss,
April 22, vol. I, p. 218

There is scarcely a department of essay-writing developed in the *Spectator* which does not trace its origin to Steele. It is Steele who first ventures to raise his voice against the prevailing dramatic taste of the age on behalf of the superior morality and art of Shakespeare's plays. . . . Steele, too, it was who attacked, with all the vigor of which he was capable, the fashionable vice of gambling. . . . The practice of duelling, also, which had hitherto passed unreproved, was censured by Steele. . . . The sketches of character studied from life, and the letters from fictitious correspondents, . . . appear roughly, but yet distinctly, drafted in the *Tatler.* Even the papers of literary criticism, afterward so fully elaborated by Addison, are anticipated by his friend, who may fairly claim the honor to have been the first to speak with adequate respect of the genius of Milton. In a word, whatever was perfected by Addison was begun by Steele.

W. J. Courthope, 1884, *Addison (English Men of Letters),*
pp. 98, 99, 100

The Guardian (1713)

The character of Guardian was too narrow and too serious: it might properly enough admit both the duties and the decencies of life, but seemed not to include literary speculations, and was in some degree violated by merriment and burlesque. What had the Guardian of the Lizards to do with clubs of tall or of little men, with nests of ants, or with Strada's prolusions? Of this paper nothing is necessary to be said, but that it found many contributors, and that it was a continuation of the Spectator, with the same elegance, and the same variety, till some unlucky sparkle from a Tory paper set Steele's politicks on fire, and wit at once blazed into faction. He was soon too hot for neutral topicks, and quitted the *Guardian* to write the *Englishman*.

> Samuel Johnson, 1779-81, *Addison, Lives of the English Poets*

Conscious Lovers (1723)

Parson Adams—"I never heard of any plays fit for a Christian to read but *Cato* and the *Conscious Lovers,* and I must own in the latter there are some things almost solemn enough for a sermon."

> Henry Fielding, 1742, *Joseph Andrews*

In the year 1722, he brought his *Conscious Lovers* on the stage, with prodigious success. This is the last and most finished of all Sir Richard's Comedies, and 'tis doubtful if there is upon the stage, any more instructing; that tends to convey a finer moral, or is better conducted in its design. We have already observed, that it is impossible to witness the tender scenes of this Comedy without emotion; that is, no man of feeling and humanity, who has experienced the delicate solicitudes of love and affection, can do it.

> Theophilus Cibber, 1753, *Lives of the Poets,* vol. IV, p. 119

Nor can it be doubted that it was with Steele the unlucky notion began, of setting comedy to reform the morals, instead of imitating the manners, of the age. Fielding slily glances at this when he makes Parson Adams declare the *Conscious Lovers* to be the only play fit for a Christian to see, and as good as a sermon; and in so witty and fine a writer as Steele, so great a mistake is only to be explained by the intolerable grossness into which the theatre had fallen in his day.

> John Forster, 1848-54, *The Life and Times of Oliver Goldsmith,*
> vol. II, p. 93

LETTERS

These Letters manifest throughout, with irresistible conviction, the very many excellent and amiable qualities, which greatly endeared this public Benefactor to society; and, in proof of their authenticity, we see in them with regret, indubitable marks of "that imprudence of generosity, or vanity of profusion, which kept Steele always incurably necessitous," and shaded

his fine character. Considering the constant vexation and serious incon-
veniences of which it was the cause or the occasion, to himself and his
family, nothing can be said to excuse Steele's inattention to œconomy; it
was however more pardonable, and the less reproachable, as in the end
he did ample justice to his creditors. Our regret on every instance which
these Letters afford of this indiscretion, is very greatly augmented, by our
admiration and love of that extensive and indefatigable philanthropy, to
which we are principally indebted for a long series of well-written papers,
fraught with valuable lessons of morality and good-breeding, which have
doubtless contributed very much to the intellectual improvement, and moral
refinement, of both sexes, in this country. Excepting however what refers
in these Letters to the lamentable failure of conduct above mentioned, too
well ascertained before; no publication of Steele redounds more to his
honour as a man, than the present. It shews him to have been a firm and
conscientious patriot; a faithful, affectionate husband; a fond, indulgent
parent; and, even at this period, if it does not illustrate, it very much enhances the value of his writings, both moral and political, to know with
certainty, that the salutary instructions and sublime preceps, so much admired, and so well received, from the fictitious Isaac Bickerstaff, esq., were
no other than the genuine sentiments, and habitual practice, of the real
Sir Richard Steele.

> John Nichols, 1787-1809, ed., *The Epistolary Correspondence of*
> *Sir Richard Steele*, Preface, p. vi

The earliest letters we have from Steele to Miss Scurlock are supposed to
have been written in August 1707, and the marriage seems to have taken
place on the 9th September following. Steele's wife treasured up the letters
and notes she received from her husband, and for the next eleven years we
have a record of events, passing troubles, successes, hopes and fears, such
as cannot be paralleled in all literature. Swift's *Journal* is to some extent
a similar unfolding of private thoughts and feelings, but Steele was entirely
exempt from the limitations imposed upon Swift by his relations towards
his correspondents. In judging of these letters it must be remembered that
they were meant only for a wife's eye. In one of the earliest in the series
Steele said expressly: "I beg of you to show my letters to no one living, but
let us be contented with one another's thoughts upon our words and actions
without the intervention of other people, who cannot judge of so delicate
a circumstance as the commerce between man and wife." But, notwithstanding this, the whole series of 400 notes was published in 1787, without any
suppression, by John Nichols, who purchased the originals from Mr. Scurlock, next of kin to Steele's daughter, Lady Trevor, who had received them
from her mother. Steele himself, it should be remembered, published some
of these letters in the *Tatler* (No. 35) and *Spectator* (No. 142). Few men's

character and innermost life have been exposed to anything approaching such a searching scrutiny, and very few could have passed through the ordeal with the honour that attaches to Steele. The marriage was one of affection, and it remains so on both sides until the end. There were, of course, defects of character in each; it would be absurd to contend that Steele was not faulty in many ways, and the faults were such as are seen most easily, especially by those who read to prove to their own satisfaction that the noblest of men fall short even as they; but the great fact remains that during all the years of married life Steele retained the affection of his wife unimpaired. At the end she was still his "dear Prue" and "dear Wife."

George A. Aitken, 1889, *The Life of Richard Steele*, vol. I, p. 172

The "fond fool of a husband," writing while his ragged boy tumbles on the floor, or the "brats his girls" stand on either side of the table, presents a picture which one would not exchange for all the immaculate primness of Joseph Addison. The letters to "Prue" should be read side by side with the *Journal to Stella*. Both have the supreme merit of perfect sincerity, simplicity and devotion. The difference between them is the difference between the strongly contrasted natures of the two writers. No one can doubt which was the more lovable, any more than which was the greater, man.

Stanley Lane Poole, 1898, *Eighteenth Century Letters*,
ed. Johnson, Introduction, p. xxvii

DANIEL DEFOE
1660-1731

Born (Daniel Foe, name changed to Defoe in 1703,) in Cripplegate, 1660 or 1661. To school at Newington Green, 1674 or 1675. Went into business about 1685 (?). Sided with Monmouth in Rebellion, 1685. Liveryman of City of London, 26 Jan. 1688. With William's army, 1688. Bankrupt, about 1692(?). Accountant to the Commissioners of the Glass Duty, 1695-99. Vigorous partisan of King William. Prosecuted for libelling the Church, 1703. Sentenced to fine, pillory, and imprisonment during Queen's pleasure, July 1703. Stood in pillory, which populace guarded and wreathed with flowers, July 1703. Imprisoned in Newgate. Released from prison, Aug. 1704. Wrote *The Review*, Feb. 1704 to June 1713. Sent to Edinburgh as secret agent in favour of Union, autumn 1706. Returned to England, spring 1708. On another mission to Scotland, 1708; again in 1712. Active political controversialist and pamphleteer. Prosecuted for libel and imprisoned, 22 April 1713, but pardoned immediately. Found guilty of libelling Lord Annesley, 12 July 1715, but escaped sentence. Wrote periodical *Mercurius Politicus*, 1716-20; edited *Mist's Journal*, Aug. 1717 to Oct. 1724. Started *Whitehall Evening Post*, 1718, and *Daily Post*, 1719; wrote in *Whitehall Evening Post*, 1718-20; in *Daily Post*, 1719-25;

in *Applebee's Journal*, 1720-26. Died, in Moorfields, 26 April 1731. Buried in Bunhill Fields. WORKS: A complete list of Defoe's works, numbering upwards of 250, is given in William Lee's *Life of Defoe*, 1869. His political, religious, and social Controversial Tracts date from 1694 to 1731. In fiction, some of his best-known works are: *The Life and Strange Surprising Adventures of Robinson Crusoe*, 1719; *The Further Adventures of Robinson Crusoe*, 1719; *Life of Captain Singleton*, 1720; *Moll Flanders*, 1722; *Journal of the Plague Year*, 1722; *Life of John Sheppard*, 1724. COLLECTED WORKS: *A True Collection of the Writings of the Author of The True Born Englishman, Corrected by Himself* (anon.), 1703; *Novels*, 1810; *Novels and Miscellaneous Works*, 20 vols., 1840-41; *Works*, with memoir by Hazlitt, 1840-43. *Life*, by W. Lee, 1869.

> R. Farquharson Sharp, 1897, *A Dictionary of*
> *English Authors*, p. 76

SEE: *Works*, ed. G. H. Maynadier, 1903-4, 16 v.; *Novels and Selected Writings*, 1927-28, 14 v.; *The Review*, ed. A. W. Secord, 1938, 22 v. (Facsimiles); *An Index to Defoe's "Review,"* ed. W. L. Payne, 1948; *The Best of Defoe's "Review,"* ed. W. L. Payne, 1951; *Letters*, ed. George Harris Healey, 1955; A. W. Secord, *Studies in the Narrative Method of Defoe*, 1924; James Sutherland, *Defoe*, 1937, rev. 1950; John Robert Moore, *Defoe in the Pillory and Other Studies*, 1939; W. L. Payne, *Mr. Review*, 1947; John Robert Moore, *Daniel Defoe, Citizen of the Modern World*, 1958.

PERSONAL

DANIEL DE-FOE
BORN 1661
DIED 1731
AUTHOR OF

ROBINSON CRUSOE.

This monument is the result of an appeal,
in the *Christian World* newspaper,
to the boys and girls of England, for funds
to place a suitable memorial upon the grave
of
Daniel De-Foe.
It represents the united contributions
of seventeen hundred persons.
Septr. 1870.

> Inscription on Monument, Erected 1870

Whereas Daniel De Foe, alias De Fooe, is charged with writing a scandalous and seditious pamphlet, entitled *The Shortest Way with the Dissenters;* he is a middle-sized, spare man, about forty years old, of a brown complexion, and dark brown-coloured hair, but wears a wig; a hooked nose, a sharp chin, gray eyes, and a large mole near his mouth; was born in London, and for many years was a hose-factor, in Freeman's yard, in Cornhill, and now is owner of the brick and pantile works near Tilbury Fort, in Essex. Whoever shall discover the said Daniel De Foe to one of her majesty's principal secretaries of state, or any of her majesty's justices of the peace, so as he may be apprehended, shall have a reward of fifty pounds, which her majesty has ordered immediately to be paid on such discovery.

London Gazette, 1702-3, *Proclamation*, Jan. 10

The person who discovered Daniel Foe—for whom a reward of £50 was promised in the *Gazette*—sends to me for his money, but does not care to appear himself. If, therefore, your lordship will order the sum to be paid to Mr. Armstrong, I will take care that the person shall have it who discovered the said Foe, and upon whose information he was apprehended.

Nottingham, 1703, *Letter to Godolphin*, May; *Calendar Treasury Papers*, vol. II, p. 153

One of those authors (the fellow that was pilloried, I have forgot his name) is indeed so grave, sententious, dogmatical a rogue, that there is no enduring him.

Jonathan Swift, 1708, *A Letter from a Member of the House of Commons in Ireland to a Member of the House of Commons in England, concerning the Sacramental Test*

I remember an Author in the World some years ago, who was generally upbraided with Ignorance, and called an "Illiterate Fellow," by some of the *Beau-Monde* of the last Age. . . . I happened to come into this Person's Study once, and I found him busy translating a Description of the Course of the River Boristhenes, out of *Bleau's* Geography, written in *Spanish*. Another Time I found him translating some Latin Paragraphs out of *Leubinitz Theatri Cometici,* being a learned Discourse upon Comets; and that I might see whether it was genuine, I looked on some part of it that he had finished, and found by it that he understood the Latin very well, and had perfectly taken the sense of that difficult Author. In short, I found he understood the *Latin,* the *Spanish,* the *Italian,* and could read the *Greek,* and I knew before that he spoke *French* fluently—*yet this Man was no Scholar*. As to Science, on another Occasion, I heard him dispute (in such a manner as surprised me) upon the motions of the Heavenly Bodies, the Distance, Magnitude, Revolutions, and especially the Influences of the Planets, the Nature and probable Revolutions of Comets, the excellency of the New Philosophy, and the like; *but this Man was no Scholar*. . . . This put me upon wondering, ever so long ago, what this *strange Thing* called a Man of Learning *was,* and what is it that constitutes a *Scholar?* For, *said I,* here's a man speaks five Languages and reads the Sixth, is a master of Astronomy, Geography, History, and abundance of other useful Knowledge (which I do not mention, that you may not guess at the Man, who is too Modest to desire it), and yet, they say *this Man is no Scholar.*

Daniel Defoe, 1720-26, Applebee's Journal

That De Foe was a man of powerful intellect and lively imagination, is obvious from his works; that he was possessed of an ardent temper, a resolute courage, and an unwearied spirit of enterprise, is ascertained by the events of his changeful career: and whatever may be thought of that rashness and improvidence by which his progress in life was so frequently impeded, there seems no reason to withold from him the praise of . . . integrity, sincerity, and consistency.

John Ballantyne, 1810, ed. De Foe's Novels,
Edinburgh ed., Memoir

When, or upon what occasion it was, that De Foe made the alteration in his name, by connecting with it the foreign prefix, no where appears. His enemies said, he adopted it because he would not be thought an Englishman; but this notion seems to have no other foundation than the circumstance of his having, in consequence of his zeal for King William, attacked the prejudices of his countrymen, in his well-known satire of *The True-born Englishman.* Oldmixon intimates, that it was not until after he had stood in the pillory, that he changed his name; and Dr. Browne tells us, that he did it at the suggestion of Harley:

"Have I not chang'd by your advice my name."

But no reliance is to be placed upon the testimony of either of these writers when speaking of De Foe. His motive was, probably, a dislike to his original name, either for its import, or its harshness; or he might have been desirous of restoring it to its Norman origin.

Walter Wilson, 1830, Memoirs of the Life and Times of
Daniel De Foe, vol. I, p. 231

He was a great, a truly great liar, perhaps the greatest liar that ever lived. His dishonesty went too deep to be called superficial, yet, if we go deeper still in his rich and strangely mixed nature, we come upon stubborn foundations of conscience. . . . Shifty as Defoe was, and admirably as he used his genius for circumstantial invention to cover his designs, there was no other statesman of his generation who remained more true to the principles of the Revolution, and to the cause of civil and religious freedom. No other public man saw more clearly what was for the good of the country, or pursued it more steadily. . . . Defoe cannot be held up as an exemplar of moral conduct, yet if he is judged by the measures that he laboured for and not by the means that he employed, few Englishmen have lived more deserving than he of their country's gratitude. He may have been self-seeking and vainglorious, but in his political life self-seeking and vain-glory were elevated by their alliance with higher and wider aims. Defoe was a wonderful mixture of knave and patriot. Sometimes pure knave seems to be uppermost, sometimes pure patriot; but the mixture is so complex, and the energy of the man so restless, that it almost passes human skill to unravel the two elements. The author of *Robinson Crusoe* is entitled to the benefit of every doubt.

William Minto, 1879, *Daniel Defoe* (*English Men of Letters*),
pp. 165, 166, 167

Defoe was temperate in his habits: unlike so many of his contemporaries, he never drank to excess. He did not smoke or take snuff. He considered smoking as "conducive to intemperate drinking"; and in his younger days, thanks to a fine constitution, he rarely troubled the doctor. The theatre, the ball-room, and the card-table were to him the very devil. In manly sports and athletic exercises he had always found an attraction; nor was there wanting in him the Puritan love of horse-play; and his reputation for swordsmanship was always a protection to him. In that "frenzy of the tongue," as he puts it, called swearing he could see "neither pleasure nor profit." He loved a good tale and a merry jest; but "low-prised wit," indulged in at the expense of decency and morals, his soul abhorred. His talk, when he was excited, was pungent with witticisms; but he was in the habit of repeating favourite quotations with too great frequency.

Thomas Wright, 1894, *The Life of Daniel Defoe*, p. 316

The Review (1704-1713)

The poor *Review* is quite exhausted, and grown so very contemptible that, though he has provoked all his brothers of the quill, none will enter into a controversy with him. The fellow, who had excellent natural parts, but wanted a small foundation of learning, is a lively instance of those wits who, as an ingenious author says, will endure but one skimming.

John Gay, 1711, *Present State of Wit*

One of the leading objects of the *Review,* after the discussion of politics, was to correct the vices of the times. Throughout the work, the writer carries on an unsparing warfare against folly and vice, in all their forms and disguises. In forcible terms he inveighs against the fashionable practice of immoderate drinking, the idle propensity to swearing, the little regard that was paid to the marriage vow, and the loose conversation and habits of men in general. In well-pointed satire, he chastises the licentiousness of the stage; and condemns, in strong language, the barbarous practice of duelling. He has also some just remarks upon the rage for gambling speculations, which, in this reign, had risen to a great height. Upon all these subjects, he brings forth his capacious stores of wit and humour to the assistance of grave reasoning, adducing examples occasionally of the flagitious courses he condemns; but with sufficient delicacy to shew that his aim was the reformation, rather than the exposure, of the offender. No man paid a greater regard to those decencies of expression which have so much influence in regulating the intercourses of life; and although few individuals had greater provocation, from the coarse and illiberal writers of the day, yet he rarely suffers his temper to be disturbed, or departs from courtesy of language towards even his bitterest opponents.

Walter Wilson, 1830, *Memoirs of the Life and Times of Daniel De Foe,* vol. II, p. 201

Defoe's greatest work, greatest undoubtedly, as to its magnitude, and perhaps, in value and importance; yet the least known of his multifarious writings. . . . When it is remembered, that no other pen was ever employed than that of Defoe, upon a work appearing at such frequent intervals, extending over more than nine years, and embracing, in more than five thousand printed pages, essays on almost every branch of human knowledge, the achievement must be pronounced a great one, even had he written nothing else. If we add that, between the dates of the first and last numbers of the *Review,* he wrote and published no less than eighty other distinct works, containing 4,727 pages, and perhaps more, not now known, the fertility of his genius must appear as astonishing as the greatness of his capacity for labour. . . . Only those who have read *The Review* can be thoroughly acquainted with Daniel Defoe.

William Lee, 1869, *Daniel Defoe: His Life and Recently Discovered Writings,* vol. I, pp. 84, 85

Apparition of Mrs Veal (1706)

An adventurous bookseller had ventured to print a considerable edition of a work by the Reverend Charles Drelincourt, minister of the Calvinist Church in Paris, and translated by M. D'Assigny, under the title of the *Christian's Defence against the Fear of Death, with several directions how to prepare ourselves to die well.* But however certain the prospect of death, it is not so agreeable (unfortunately) as to invite the eager contemplation of the public; and Drelincourt's book, being neglected, lay a dead stock on the hands of the publisher. In this emergency he applied to De Foe to assist him (by dint of such means as were then, as well as now, pretty well understood in the literary world) in rescuing the unfortunate book from the literary death to which general neglect seemed about to consign it. De Foe's genius and audacity devised a plan which, for assurance and ingenuity, defied even the powers of Mr. Puff in the *Critic;* for who but himself would have thought of summoning up a ghost from the grave to bear witness in favour of a halting body of divinity? There is a matter-of-fact, businesslike style in the whole account of the transaction, which bespeaks ineffable powers of self-possession. . . . The effect was most wonderful. *Drelincourt upon Death,* attested by one who could speak from experience, took an unequalled run. The copies had hung on the book-seller's hands as heavy as a pile of lead bullets. They now traversed the town in every direction, like the same balls discharged from a field-piece. In short, the object of Mrs. Veal's apparition was perfectly attained.

Sir Walter Scott, c 1821, Memoir of Daniel De Foe,
Miscellaneous Works, vol. IV, pp. 267, 273

Never, perhaps, has a story been so misunderstood as this apparition of Mrs. Veal. The idle tradition that it was written to promote the sale of Drelincourt's work on *The Fear of Death,* has been conclusively disposed of by Mr. Lee, who proves that when *Mrs. Veal* appeared *Drelincourt* was already a popular work in its third edition, and, furthermore, that Mrs. Veal's recommendation, contrary likewise to tradition, did not have any appreciable effect on the sale of *Drelincourt.* These traditions, which arose from the fact that the printer of *Drelincourt* was permitted to reprint Defoe's pamphlet in the fourth edition of *Drelincourt,* deceived even so acute a critic as Sir Walter Scott. *Drelincourt,* which long continued popular, was subsequently printed sometimes with and sometimes without *Mrs. Veal.* But there is another erroneous notion concerning *Mrs. Veal* that requires to be dealt with, and that is the assumption that the narrative is a fiction. Whoever will read the story, says Sir Walter Scott, "as told by Defoe himself will agree that, could the thing have happened in reality, so it would have been told." But the extraordinary thing is that nobody should have inquired whether it was not true, that is to say, whether a lady of Defoe's acquaintance, to whom he gives the name of Mrs. Bargrave, did not tell him, and in good faith, this story; and that such was certainly the case, no one who reads carefully Defoe's works on "Magic and Apparitions," can possibly doubt. Defoe, as we shall show, when dealing with those books, believed firmly in apparitions; he had had stories told him which there was no getting over, and this of Mrs. Bargrave's was one of them.

Thomas Wright, 1894, The Life of Daniel Defoe, p. 131

The fact that there is no record of Defoe's story being contradicted by contemporary writers might have suggested that it was at least based on fact; for enemies were not slow to blame Defoe for saying that *Robinson Crusoe* and other tales were true. It has become the fashion of late to assume that Defoe was romancing when he said that his narratives were true histories, and the more he has asserted it the more critics have laughed at his skill or abused him for the immorality of his devices, according to the way the matter struck them. This scepticism has been extended to matters relating to Defoe's own life and character, and the late Professor Minto went so far as to say that he was "perhaps the greatest liar that ever lived." The result of this attitude has been a marked change in the common estimate of Defoe, as shown by the chance notices of him in the newspapers. . . . But does not the story told in this paper show that we should be at least as likely to arrive at the truth by believing what Defoe says, in the absence of proof to the contrary?

George A. Aitken, 1895, "Defoe's *Apparition of Mrs. Veal*,"
The Nineteenth Century, vol. 37, pp. 99, 100

Robinson Crusoe (1719)

If ever the story of any private man's adventures in the world were worth making public, and were acceptable when published, the Editor on this account thinks this will be so. The wonders of this man's life exceed all that (he thinks) is to be found extant; the life of one man being scarce capable of a greater variety. The story is told with modesty, with seriousness, and with a religious application of events to the uses to which wise men always apply them, viz., to the instruction of others by this example, and to justify and honour the wisdom of Providence in all the variety of our circumstances, let them happen how they will. The Editor believes the thing to be a just history of fact; neither is there any appearance of fiction in it; and, however, thinks, because all such things are despatched, that the improvement of it, as well to the diversion as to the instruction of the reader, will be the same. And as such, he thinks, without farther compliment to the world, he does them a great service in the publication.

Daniel Defoe, 1719, *Robinson Crusoe*, Preface

We may remember that we have been most of us, when Children, wonderfully pleased with the achievements of *Tom Thumb, Jack the Giant-Killer, Don Bellianis of Greece, The Seven Champions of Christendom,* and such like extraordinary Heroes; and many of us, in our more advanced Age, are little less delighted with such Books as, *The Life and Adventures of Robinson Crusoe;* which seems to have had that uncommon Run upon the Town for some Years past, for no other Reason but that it is a *most palpable Lye,* from Beginning to End; and I doubt not that the famous Passage of his *Swimming to Shore* Naked, *with his* Pockets *full of Biscuits,* tho' a most notorious *Blunder* in the Author, has pass'd for a very good Jest, and been received with abundance of Pleasure by many of his Readers.

Benjamin Hoadley, 1725, *London Journal,* Sept. 4

Since we must have books, there is one which, to my mind, furnishes the finest of treatises on education according to nature. My Emile shall read this book before any other; it shall for a long time be his entire library, and shall always hold an honorable place. It shall be the text on which all our discussions of natural science shall be only commentaries. It shall be a test for all we meet during our progress toward a ripened judgment, and so long as our taste is unspoiled, we shall enjoy reading it. What wonderful book is this? Aristotle? Pliny? Buffon? No; it is *Robinson Crusoe.*

Jean Jacques Rousseau, 1762-67, *Emile,* tr. Worthington, p. 147

Robinson Crusoe must be allowed, by the most rigid moralists, to be one of those novels which one may read, not only with pleasure, but also with profit. It breathes throughout a spirit of piety and benevolence; it sets in a very striking light . . . the importance of the mechanic arts, which they, who know not what it is to be without them, are apt to undervalue: it fixes in the mind a lively idea of the horrors of solitude, and, consequently, of the sweets of social life, and of the blessings we derive from conversation and mutual aid; and it shows, how, by labouring with one's own hands, one may secure independence, and open for one's self many sources of health and amusement. I agree, therefore, with Rousseau, that this is one of the best books that can be put in the hands of children.

James Beattie, 1783, *Dissertations, Moral and Critical*

Robinson Crusoe, the favourite of the learned and the unlearned, of the youth and the adult; the book that was to constitute the library of Rousseau's Emilius, owes its secret charm to its being a new representation of human nature, yet drawn from an existing state; this picture of self-education, self-inquiry, self-happiness, is scarcely a fiction, although it includes all the magic of romance; and is not a mere narrative of truth, since it displays all the forcible genius of one of the most original minds our literature can boast. The history of the work is therefore interesting. It was treated in the author's time as a mere idle romance, for the philosophy was not discovered in the story; after his death it was considered to have been pillaged from the papers of Alexander Selkirk, confided to the author, and the honour, as well as the genius, of De Foe were alike questioned. . . .

Robinson Crusoe was not given to the world till 1719, seven years after the publication of Selkirk's adventures. Selkirk could have no claims on De Foe; for he had only supplied the man of genius with that which lies open to all; and which no one had, or perhaps could have, converted into the wonderful story we possess but De Foe himself. Had De Foe not written *Robinson Crusoe,* the name and story of Selkirk had been passed over like others of the same sort; yet Selkirk has the merit of having detailed his own history, in a manner so interesting, as to have attracted the notice of Steele, and to have inspired the genius of De Foe.

Isaac Disraeli, 1791-1824, "Robinson Crusoe,"
Curiosities of Literature

Perhaps there exists no work, either of instruction or entertainment, in the English language, which has been more generally read, and more universally admired, than *The Life and Adventures of Robinson Crusoe.* It is difficult to say in what the charm consists, by which persons of all classes and denominations are thus fascinated: yet the majority of readers will recollect it as among the first works which awakened and interested their youthful attention; and feel, even in advanced life, and in the maturity of their understanding, that there are still associated with Robinson Crusoe, the sentiments peculiar to that period, when all is new, all glittering in prospect, and when those visions are most bright, which the experience of afterlife tends only to darken and destroy.

John Ballantyne, 1810, ed, *De Foe's Novels,*
Edinburgh ed., Memoir

Never did human being excite more sympathy in his fate than this shipwrecked mariner: we enter into all his doubts and difficulties, and every rusty nail which he acquires fills us with satisfaction. We thus learn to appreciate our own comforts, and we acquire, at the same time, a habit of activity; but, above all, we attain a trust and devout confidence in divine mercy and goodness. The author also, by placing his hero in an uninhabited island in the Western Ocean, had an opportunity of introducing scenes which, with the merit of truth, have all the wildness and horror of the most incredible fiction. *That* foot in the sand—*those* Indians who land on the solitary shore to devour their captives, fill us with alarm and terror, and, after being relieved from the fear of Crusoe perishing by famine, we are agitated by new apprehensions for his safety. The deliverance of Friday, and the whole character of that young Indian, are painted in the most beautiful manner; and, in short, of all the works of fiction that have ever been composed, Robinson Crusoe is perhaps the most interesting and instructive.

John Dunlop, 1814-42, *The History of Fiction,* vol. II, p. 420

Compare the contemptuous Swift with the contemned De Foe, and how superior will the latter be found! But by what test?—Even by this; that the writer who makes me sympathize with his presentations with the whole of my being, is more estimable than he who calls forth, and appeals but to, a part of my being—my sense of the ludicrous, for instance. De Foe's excellence it is, to make me forget my specific class, character, and circumstances, and to raise me while I read him, into the universal man.

> Samuel Taylor Coleridge, 1818, *Mythology, Imagination, and
> Superstition; Miscellanies, Æsthetic and Literary*, ed. Ashe, p. 154

What man does not remember with regret the first time that he read *Robinson Crusoe*? Then, indeed, he was unable to appreciate the powers of the writer; or rather, he neither knew nor cared whether the book had a writer at all. He probably thought it not half so fine as some rant of Macpherson about dark-browed Foldath and white-bosomed Strinadona. He now values Fingal and Temora only as showing with how little evidence a story may be believed, and with how little merit a book may be popular. Of the romance of Defoe, he entertains the highest opinion. He perceives the hand of a master in ten thousand touches, which formerly he passed by without notice. But though he understands the merits of the narrative better than formerly, he is far less interested by it. Xury, and Friday, and pretty Poll, the boat with the shoulder-of-mutton sail, and the canoe which could not be brought down to the water's edge, the tent with its hedge and ladders, the preserve of kids, and the den where the old goat died, can never again be to him the realities which they were.

> Thomas Babington Macaulay, 1828, "Dryden," *Edinburgh Review;
> Critical and Miscellaneous Essays*

It has become a household thing in nearly every family in Christendom. Yet never was admiration of any work—universal admiration—more indiscriminately or more inappropriately bestowed. Not one person in ten—nay, not one person in five hundred—has, during the perusal of *Robinson Crusoe,* the most remote conception that any particle of genius, or even of common talent, has been employed in its creation! Men do not look upon it in the light of a literary performance. Defoe has none of their thoughts—Robinson all. The powers which have wrought the wonder have been thrown into obscurity by the very stupendousness of the wonder they have wrought! We read, and become perfect abstractions in the intensity of our interest; we close the book, and are quite satisfied that we could have written as well ourselves. All this is effected by the potent magic of verisimilitude. Indeed the author of *Crusoe* must have possessed, above all other faculties, what has been termed the faculty of *identification*—that dominion exercised by volition over imagination, which enables the mind to lose its own in a fictitious individuality.

Edgar Allan Poe, 1836, Marginalia, Works, vol. VII, p. 300

It sinks into the bosom while the bosom is most capable of pleasurable impressions from the adventurous and the marvellous; and no human work, we honestly believe, has afforded such great delight. Neither the *Iliad* nor the *Odyssey,* in the much longer course of ages, has incited so many to enterprise, or to reliance on their own powers and capacities. It is the romance of solitude and self-sustainment; and could only so perfectly have been written by a man whose own life had for the most part been passed in the independence of unaided thought, accustomed to great reverses, of inexhaustible resource in confronting calamities, leaning ever on his Bible in sober and satisfied belief, and not afraid at any time to find himself Alone, in communion with nature and with God.

John Forster, 1845-58, "Daniel De Foe," Edinburgh Review,
Historical and Biographical Essays, vol. II, p. 95

While he was not a great artist, he was a wonderful craftsman. That is to say, he studied his fellow-creatures from the point of view of their relations to society; he writes as a reformer with a direct practical end, with the end that was foremost in the minds of his generation, that of promoting civilization. Take his *Robinson Crusoe,* for example; full as it is of fine things, as when Robinson sees with terror the print of a human foot upon the sand, it is singularly devoid of any expression of the feeling of vast loneliness that would weigh down on the spirit of any such hero in a novel of the present day. The problem that lay before him, and which he accomplished, was how to make himself over from a worthless person into a peaceable, God-fearing citizen. The shadow of the municipal law and of the English Sunday seems to lie over the lonely island. The moral of the book, in short, is this: If a man in solitude, with a few scraps from a wreck and an occasional savage, dog, and cat to help him, can lead so civilized a life, what may we not expect of good people in England with abundance about them? This moral is what now makes the value of the book as a means of education for boys, that they may see, as Rousseau put it, that the stock of an ironmonger is better than that of a jeweller, and glass better than diamonds.

Thomas Sergeant Perry, 1883, English Literature in the
Eighteenth Century, p. 310

When a boy I loved those books that other boys love, and I love them still. I well remember a little scene which took place when I was a child of eight or nine. *Robinson Crusoe* held me in his golden thrall, and I was expected to go to church. I hid beneath a bed with *Robinson Crusoe,* and was in due course discovered by an elder sister and a governess, who, on my refusing to come out, resorted to force. Then followed a struggle that was quite Homeric. The two ladies tugged as best they might, but I clung to *Crusoe* and the legs of the bed, and kicked till, perfectly exhausted, they took their departure in no very Christian frame of mind, leaving me panting, indeed, but triumphant.

H. Rider Haggard, 1887, *Books which Have Influenced Me,* p. 66

Defoe would hardly recognize *Robinson Crusoe* as "a picture of civilization," having innocently supposed it to be quite the reverse; and he would be as amazed as we are to learn from Mr. Frederic Harrison that his book contains "more psychology, more political economy, and more anthropology than are to be found in many elaborate treatises on these especial subjects," —blighting words which I would not even venture to quote if I thought that any boy would chance to read them, and so have one of the pleasures of his young life destroyed.

Agnes Repplier, 1891, "A Plea of Humor," *Points of View,* p. 4

Defoe's narratives all aim at exhibiting the processes of memory, untouched by the shaping imagination. And unambitious though such an aim may be, it was perhaps a necessary exercise for the modern novel in its infancy. . . . Robinson Crusoe typifies the spirit of the Anglo-Saxon race, and illustrates in epitome the part it has played in India and America. He keeps his house in order, stores the runlets of rum, and converts Friday, telling him that God is omnipotent, that he "could do everything for us, give everything to us, take everything from us." Poor Friday believed in a Great Spirit, and held that "All things say O to him"—an unpractical view that receives no manner of notice from Crusoe, who nevertheless reports their conversations, and honestly admits that he was "run down to the last degree" by some of Friday's theological arguments. But the very deficiencies in the story of Crusoe, and the imagination of Defoe, only gave the writer fuller scope for the exhibition of his particular talent. On a blank canvas small splashes are striking, and Defoe forces the reader to take the deepest interest in the minutest affairs of the castaway. It is a testimony to the practical nature of childhood that the book is so widely regarded as the best boy's book in the world. When the story leaves the magic limits of the island, it must be said the interest flags; and at last, in the "Serious Reflections," subjoined by an afterthought, it positively stagnates. But the main piece of original narrative is a masterpiece, and marks a new era in the writing of prose fiction.

Walter Raleigh, 1894, *The English Novel,* pp. 132, 133

The first of my favorite authors of fiction is Daniel Defoe, and he comes to the front as naturally as if he saw a sail upon the horizon and was anxious to discover to what sort of craft it belonged. . . . Defoe's prominence in my mind is based upon his ability to transmute a fictional narrative into a record of facts; things which might have been became, in his hands, things which actually were. But it is to the story itself that his supremacy as a fictional writer is confined; it does not extend to his personages. It is in the relation of a story, not in the delineation of character, that this great author excels. . . . To reduce romance to realism without depriving the former of any of its charms was the example set by Defoe to the writers of English fiction. His characters, his situations, his incidents, his material, and his machinery, have all been surpassed, but his story telling never. . . . I may sum up what I have to say about Defoe in the statement that it is the telling of his story and not the story itself which charms me and holds me to my allegiance. *Robinson Crusoe* is not the best work of English fiction, but it is, in my opinion, the best told story.

Frank R. Stockton, 1897, "My Favorite Novelist and His Best Book,"
Munsey's Magazine, vol. 17, pp. 351, 352, 353

Moll Flanders (1722)

The various incidents in the eventful life of Moll Flanders, from the time of her seduction to that of her becoming a convict and a quiet settler in Maryland, are those of real life, as exemplified by multitudes of individuals, who have run the career of their vicious propensities. The artless disposition of the narrative, the lively interest excited by unlooked-for coincidences, the rich natural painting, the moral reflections, are all so many proofs of the knowledge and invention of the writer; but the facts were furnished him by the annals of Newgate. . . . From the character of the incidents that compose the present narrative, De Foe was fully aware of the objections that would be urged against it by the scrupulous. To conceal a single fact, would have taken so much from the fidelity of the portrait; all that he could do, therefore, was to neutralize the poison, by furnishing the strongest antidotes. Accordingly, whilst he paints the courses of an every-day profligate in their natural colours, he shows us with the same faithfulness their natural tendency; and that, first or last, vice is sure to bring down its own punishment. His villains never prosper; but either come to an untimely end, or are brought to be penitents. In dressing up the present story, he tells us, he had taken care to exclude every thing that might be offensive; but conscious that he had a bad subject to work upon, he endeavours to interest the reader in the reflections arising out of it, that the moral might be more enticing than the fable.

Walter Wilson, 1830, *Memoirs of the Life and Times
of Daniel De Foe,* vol. III, pp. 489, 490

Of these novels we may, nevertheless, add, for the satisfaction of the inquisitive reader, that *Moll Flanders* is utterly vile and detestable: Mrs. Flanders was evidently born in sin. The best parts are the account of her childhood, which is pretty and affecting; the fluctuation of her feelings between remorse and hardened impenitence in Newgate; and the incident of her leading off the horse from the inn-door, though she had no place to put it in after she had stolen it.

William Hazlitt, 1830, "Wilson's *Life and Times of Daniel Defoe*,"
Edinburgh Review, vol. 50, p. 422

Deals with the sore of society in very much the spirit of M. Zola and his followers. Defoe lays bare the career of an abandoned woman, concealing nothing, extenuating nothing, but also hoping nothing. It could only be when inspired by the hope of amelioration, that such a narrative could be endurable. But Defoe's novel is inspired merely by hope of the good sale which of course it achieved: the morbid way in which he, like M. Zola, lingers over disgusting detail, and the perfunctory manner in which any necessary pieces of morality are introduced, preclude us from attributing any moral purpose to a vivid and clever, but most revolting novel.

P. F. Rowland, 1894, *A Comparison, Criticism and Estimate of
the English Novelists from 1700 to 1850*, p. 6

Journal of the Plague Year (1722)

The History of the Great Plague in London is one of that particular class of compositions which hovers between romance and history. Undoubtedly De Foe embodied a number of traditions upon this subject with what he might actually have read, or of which he might otherwise have received direct evidence. The subject is hideous almost to disgust, yet, even had he not been the author of *Robinson Crusoe,* De Foe would have deserved immortality for the genius which he has displayed in this work, as well as in *Memoirs of a Cavalier*.

Sir Walter Scott, c 1821, *Memoir of Daniel De Foe,
Miscellaneous Works*, vol. IV, p. 255

Such is the veri-similitude of all the writings of Defoe, that unless we have had some other means of refuting their authenticity than internal evidence, it would be a very difficult task to dispute their claims to credit. Such is the minuteness of detail; such a dwelling is there upon particular circumstances, which one is inclined to think would have struck no one but an actual spectator; such, too, is the plainness and simplicity of style; such the ordinary and probable nature of his materials, as well as the air of conscientiousness thrown over the whole, that it is a much easier thing to say the narrative is tedious, prolix, or dull, than to entertain a doubt of its veracity. All these marks of genuineness distinguish the work before us perhaps more than any other compositions of the same author.

H. Southern, 1822, "Defoe's *History of the Plague,*"
Retrospective Review, vol. 6, p. 2

Of all the prolific Daniel's two hundred and fifty-odd works, none better exhibits his most striking features of style. The minute detail, the irresistible verisimilitude, the awful realism, are all there, and almost persuade us that he saw all that he describes, in spite of our knowledge that he was a boy— though a precocious one—of five, when the pestilence was raging.

Josiah Renick Smith, 1895, "New Presentments of Defoe,"
The Dial, vol. 19, p. 16

GENERAL

Poetry was far from being the talent of De Foe. He wrote with more perspicuity and strength in prose, and he seems to have understood, as well as any man, the civil constitution of the kingdom, which indeed was his chief study. . . . Considered as a poet, Daniel De Foe is not so eminent, as in a political light: he has taken no pains in versification; his ideas are masculine, his expressions coarse, and his numbers generally rough. He seems rather to have studied to speak truth by probing wounds to the bottom, than, by embellishing his versification, to give it a more elegant keenness. This, however, seems to have proceeded more from carelessness in that particular, than want of ability.

Theophilus Cibber, 1753, *Lives of the Poets,* vol. IV, pp. 315, 324

De Foe is our only famous politician and man of letters, who represented, in its inflexible constancy, sturdy dogged resolution, unwearied perseverance, and obstinate contempt of danger and of tyranny, the great Middle-class English character. We believe it to be no mere national pride to say, that, whether in its defects or its surpassing merits, the world has had none other to compare with it. . . . He was too much in the constant heat of the battle, to see all that we see now. He was not a philosopher himself, but he helped philosophy to some wise conclusions. He did not stand at the highest point of toleration, or of moral wisdom; but, with his masculine active arm, he helped to lift his successors over obstructions which had stayed his own advance. He stood, in his opinions and in his actions, alone and apart from his fellow men; but it was to show his fellow men of later times the value of a juster and larger fellowship, and of more generous modes of action.

John Forster, 1845-58, "Daniel De Foe," *Edinburgh Review;*
Historical and Biographical Essays, vol. II, p. 90

In his greatest works Defoe remains, in his own way, unsurpassed; it is when we turn to the tales which are less known that we see how later writers have developed the art of fiction. . . . If Defoe's narratives are generally less thrilling, if there is less humour or sentiment, if there is a want of imagination and a neglect of the aid furnished by picturesque descriptions of scenery or past times, the honour remains to him of having a great share in the education and inspiration of those who carried the art to a higher level than that to which he usually attained. If his range of vision was limited, it was very vivid; and he was so great a master of the simple style of narration, that all his readers, whether illiterate or refined, can understand and find pleasure in his works.

George A. Aitken, 1893, "John Gay," *Westminster Review,*
General Introduction, vol. I, pp. xlvi, xlvii

JOHN GAY
1685-1732

Born, at Barnstaple, 1685; baptized 16 Sept. 1685. Educated at Barnstaple Grammar School. For short time apprentice in a London shop; returned to Barnstaple; thence again to London, probably as secretary to Aaron Hill. Sec. to Duchess of Monmouth, 1712-14. Contrib. to *Guardian,* 1713. *The Wife of Bath* produced at Drury Lane, 12 May 1713. In Hanover as sec. to Lord Clarendon, 8 June to Sept., 1714. *What-d'ye-Call-it* produced at Drury Lane, 23 Feb. 1715. *Three Hours after Marriage* (written with Pope and Arbuthnot), Drury Lane, 16 Jan. 1717. To Aix with William Pulteney (afterwards Earl of Bath), 1717. At Cockthorpe with Lord Harcourt, 1718. Severe losses in South Sea Bubble. Under patronage of Duchess of Queensberry from 1720. *The Captives* produced at Drury Lane, 15 Jan. 1724; *The Beggar's Opera,* Lincoln's Inn Fields, 29 Jan. 1728; sequel, *Polly,* forbidden by Lord Chamberlain, 1729; *Acis and Galatea,* Haymarket, May 1732; *Achilles* (posthumous), Covent Garden, 10 Feb. 1733. Died, in London, 4 Dec. 1732. Buried in Westminster Abbey. WORKS: *Wine,* 1708; *The Present State of Wit* (anon.), 1711; *The Mohocks* (anon.), 1713; *Rural Sports,* 1713; *The Wife of Bath,* 1713; *The Fan,* 1714; *The Shepherd's Week,* 1714; *A Letter to a Lady* (anon.), 1714; *What-d'ye-Call-it,* 1715; *A Journey to Exter,* 1715; *Court Poems,* 1716; *God's Revenge against Punning* (under pseud. of "Sir James Baker"), 1716; *Trivia,* 1716; *An Admonition . . . to the famous Mr. Frapp* (under pseud. of "Sir James Baker"), 1717; *Letter to W—L—, Esq.,* 1717; *Epistle to Pulteney,* 1717; *Three Hours after Marriage* (with Pope and Arbuthnot), 1717; *Two Epistles,* (1720?); *Poems* (2 vols.), 1720; *A Panegyrical Epistle* (anon.; attrib. to Gay), 1721; *An Epistle to . . . Henrietta, Duchess of Marlborough,* 1722; *The Captives,* 1724 (2nd edn. same year); *Fables,* first series, 1727, second ser., 1738; *The Beggar's Opera,* 1728 (2nd and 3rd edns. same year); *Polly,* 1729 (another edn.

same year); *Acis and Galatea* (anon.), 1732. POSTHUMOUS: *Achilles,*
1733; *The Distress'd Wife,* 1743; *The Rehearsal at Goatham,* 1754; *Gay's
Chair: poems never before printed,* 1820. COLLECTED WORKS: *Plays,* 1760;
Works (4 vols.), 1770; ed. by Dr. Johnson (2 vols.), 1779; ed. J. Underhill (2 vols.), 1893. *Life:* by Coxe, 1797; by W. H. K. Wright, in 1889
edn. of *Fables,* by J. Underhill in 1893 edn. of *The Poetical Works.*

R Farquharson Sharp, *A Dictionary of
English Authors,* p. 110

SEE: *Poetical Works,* ed. G. C. Faber, 1926; *Selected Poems,* ed. A. Ross,
1950; *"The Beggar's Opera," by John Gay: A Faithful Reproduction of
the 1729 Edition . . . with Commentaries,* 1961; F. Kidson, *The Beggar's
Opera: Its Predecessors and Successors,* 1922; W. H. Irving, *John Gay,
Favorite of the Wits,* 1940; Sven M. Armens, *John Gay, Social Critic,*
1954.

PERSONAL

Gay was quite a natural man, wholly without art or design, and spoke just
what he thought, and as he thought it.—He dangled for twenty years about
a court, and at last—was offered to be made Usher to the young Princesses.
—Secretary Craggs made Gay a present of stock in the South Sea year: and
he was once worth twenty thousand pounds, but lost it all again. He got
about four hundred pounds by the first *Beggar's Opera,* and eleven or twelve
hundred by the second.—He was negligent and a bad manager:—latterly
the Duke of Queensbury took his money into his keeping, and let him have
only what was necessary out of it: and as he lived with them he could not
have occasion for much: he died worth upwards of three thousand pounds.

Alexander Pope, 1737-39, *Spence's Anecdotes,* ed. Singer, p. 161

In the great society of the wits, John Gay deserved to be a favourite, and
to have a good place. In his set all were fond of him. His success offended
nobody. He missed a fortune once or twice. He was talked of for court
favour, and hoped to win it; but the court favour jilted him. Craggs gave
him some South Sea Stock; and at one time Gay had very nearly made his
fortune. But Fortune shook her swift wings and jilted him too: and so his
friends, instead of being angry with him, and jealous of him, were kind and
fond of honest Gay.

William Makepeace Thackeray, 1853, *The English Humourists
of the Eighteenth Century,* p. 146

In character Gay was affectionate and amiable, but indolent, luxurious,
and very easily depressed. His health was never good, and his inactive habits
and tastes as a gourmand did not improve it. But his personal charm as
a companion must have been exceptionable, for he seems to have been

a universal favourite, and Pope, Swift, and Arbuthnot (with none of whom he ever quarrelled) were genuinely attached to him.

Austin Dobson, 1890, *Dictionary of National Biography,* vol. XXI

Fables (1727-38)

For a Fable he gives now and then a Tale, or an abstracted Allegory; and from some, by whatever name they may be called, it will be difficult to extract any moral principle. They are, however, told with liveliness; the versification is smooth; and the diction, though now-and-then a little constrained by the measure or the rhyme, is generally happy.

Samuel Johnson, 1779-81, *Gay, Lives of the English Poets*

Gay was sometimes grosser than Prior, not systematically, but inadvertently —from not being so well aware of what he was about; nor was there the same necessity for caution, for his grossness is by no means so seductive or inviting. Gay's *Fables* are certainly a work of great merit, both as to the quantity of invention implied, and as to the elegance and facility of the execution. They are, however, spun out too long; the descriptions and narrative are too diffuse and desultory; and the moral is sometimes without point. They are more like Tales than fables. The best are, perhaps, the Hare with Many Friends, the Monkeys, and the Fox at the Point of Death.

William Hazlitt, 1818, *Lectures on the English Poets,* Lecture VI

As a fabulist he has been sometimes hypercritically blamed for presenting us with allegorical impersonations. The mere naked apologue of Æsop is too simple to interest the human mind, when its fancy and understanding are past the state of childhood or barbarism. La Fontaine dresses the stories which he took from Æsop and others with such profusion of wit and *naïveté,* that his manner conceals the insipidity of the matter. *"La sauce vaut mieux que le poisson."* Gay, though not equal to La Fontaine, is at least free from his occasional prolixity; and in one instance, (the Court of Death,) ventures into allegory with considerable power. Without being an absolute simpleton, like La Fontaine, he possessed a *bonhomie* of character which forms an agreeable trait of resemblance between the fabulists.

Thomas Campbell, 1819, *Specimens of the British Poets*

Thackeray confessed that he had not been able to peruse them since his very early youth; but probably he would have found no difficulty in digesting them if he had made some slight effort. It is true that there is a certain want of variety both in the subject and tone of the fables; but they abound in touches of humour, and are written in an easy style. Many of them are tales and sometimes allegories, rather than fables, properly so called, and in the posthumous collection the fable forms a very small part of each poem. But what can be neater than the description of the election of the Fox as regent to the Lion?

> George A. Aitken, 1893, "John Gay," *Westminster Review*,
> vol. 140, p. 402

The Beggar's Opera (1728)

Dr. Swift had been observing once to Mr. Gay, what an odd pretty sort of thing a Newgate Pastoral might make. Gay was inclined to try at such a thing, for some time, but afterwards thought it would be better to write a comedy on the same plan. This was what gave rise to *The Beggar's Opera*. He began on it, and when first he mentioned it to Swift, the Doctor did not much like the project. As he carried it on, he showed what he wrote to both of us; and we now and then gave a correction, or a word or two of advice: but it was wholly of his own writing. When it was done, neither of us thought it would succeed. We showed it to Congreve, who, after reading it over, said, "It would either take greatly, or be damned confoundedly."— We were all at the first night of it, in great uncertainty of the event; till we were very much encouraged by overhearing the Duke of Argyle, who sat in the next box to us, say, "It will do,—it must do!—I see it in the eyes of them."—This was a good while before the first act was over, and so gave us ease soon; for the duke (besides his own good taste) has a more particular knack than any one now living, in discovering the taste of the public. He was quite right in this, as usual; the good nature of the audience appeared stronger and stronger every act, and ended in a clamour of applause.

> Alexander Pope, 1734-36, *Spence's Anecdotes,* ed. Singer, p. 120

Cato, it is true, succeeded, but reached not by full forty days the progress and applause of *The Beggar's Opera.* Will it however admit of a question which of the two compositions a good writer would rather wish to have been the author of? Yet, on the other side, must we not allow, that to have taken a whole nation, high and low, into a general applause, has shown a power in poetry which, though often attempted in the same kind, none but this one author could ever yet arrive at.

> Colley Cibber, 1739, *An Apology for His Life*

The effects of *The Beggar's Opera* on the minds of the people have fulfilled the prognostications of many that it would prove injurious to society. Rapine and violence have been gradually increasing ever since its first representation: the rights of property, and the obligation of the laws that guard it, are disputed upon principle. Every man's house is now become what the law calls it, his castle, or at least it may be said that, like a castle, it requires to be a place of defence; young men, apprentices, clerks in public offices, and others, disdaining the arts of honest industry, and captivated with the charms of idleness and criminal pleasure, now betake themselves to the road, affect politeness in the very act of robbery, and in the end become victims to the justice of their country: and men of discernment, who have been at the pains of tracing this evil to its source, have found that not a few of those, who, during these last fifty years have paid to the law the forfeit of their lives, have in the course of their pursuits been emulous to imitate the manners and general character of Macheath.

Sir John Hawkins, 1776, A General History of the
Science and Practice of Music, ch. cxc, p. 875

Often and often had I read Gay's *Beggar's Opera,* and always delighted with its poignant wit and original satire, and if not without noticing its immorality, yet without any offence from it. Some years ago, I for the first time saw it represented in one of the London theatres; and such were the horror and disgust with which it impressed me, so grossly did it outrage all the best feelings of my nature, that even the angelic voice and perfect science of Mrs. Billington lost half their charms, or rather increased my aversion to the piece by an additional sense of incongruity. Then I learned the immense difference between reading and seeing a play.

Samuel Taylor Coleridge, 1812, Omniana, ed. Ashe, p. 386

This piece has kept possession of the stage for upwards of a century. "Macheath" and "Polly" have been favourite parts with most of our principal vocal performers; and, when well represented, it has rarely failed to draw crowded audiences in every part of the kingdom. Its effects on public morals have been the subject of much discussion and controversy. Soon after its appearance it was praised by Swift, as a piece which placed all kinds of vice in the strongest and most odious light. Others, however, censured it, as giving encouragement not only to vice but to crime, by making a highwayman the hero, and dismissing him at last unpunished. It was even said that its performance had a visible effect in increasing the number of this description of freebooters. The celebrated police magistrate, Sir John Fielding, once told Hugh Kelly, the dramatist, on a successful run of *The Beggar's Opera,* that he expected, in consequence of it, a fresh cargo of highwaymen at his office. Upon Kelly's expressing his surprise at this, Sir John assured him, that, ever since the first representation of that piece, there had been, on every successful run, a proportionate number of highwaymen brought to the office, as would appear by the books any morning he chose to look over them. Kelly did so, and found the observation to be strictly correct. . . . Recently, however, *The Beggar's Opera* has been rarely performed. Whether this has arisen from a growing sense of its impropriety, or from the want of fitting representatives of the hero and heroine, we shall not pretend to say. We believe that its licentiousness has contributed, no less than its wit and the beauty of its music, to the favour it has so long enjoyed: but it may be presumed that the time is come, or at least approaching, when its licentiousness will banish it from the stage, notwithstanding its wit and the beauty of its music.

George Hogarth, 1838, Memoirs of The Musical Drama,
vol. II, pp. 50, 55

It was Polly, however, as impersonated by the fascinating Lavinia Fenton (in 1728) that made the success of *The Beggar's Opera*. She dressed the part in the most simple manner, and the pathetic naiveté with which she delivered the lines—

> For on the rope that hangs my dear
> Depends poor Polly's life,

had such an effect that applause burst forth from every part of the house. The work had up to this moment gone but poorly. Its triumph was now assured, and the enthusiasm of the public went on increasing until the fall of the curtain. The opera soon made its way to Wales, Scotland, and Ireland. The principal songs were inscribed on fans and screens, and the enemies of foreign art boasted that *The Beggar's Opera* (which is really a semi-burlesque comedy, interspersed with songs set to popular tunes) had driven out the opera of the Italians.

Henry Sutherland Edwards, 1888, The Prima Donna:
Her History and Surroundings

Polly (1729)

The inoffensive John Gay is now become one of the obstructions to the peace of Europe, the terror of the ministers, the chief author of the *Craftsman,* and all the seditious pamphlets which have been published against the government. He has got several turned out of their places; the greatest ornament of the court (*i.e.* Duchess of Queensberry) banished from it for his sake; another great lady (Mrs. Howard, afterwards Countess of Suffolk) in danger of being chasée likewise; about seven or eight duchesses pushing forward, like the ancient circumcelliones in the church, who shall suffer martyrdom on his account first. He is the darling of the city. . . . I can assure you, this is the very identical Jno. Gay whom you formerly knew and lodged with in Whitehall two years ago.

John Arbuthnot, 1728-29, Letter to Jonathan Swift, March 19

Among the remarkable occurrences of this winter, I cannot help relating that of the Duchess of Queensberry being forbid the Court, and the occasion of it. One Gay, a poet, had written a ballad opera, which was thought to reflect a little upon the Court, and a good deal upon the Minister. It was called *The Beggar's Opera,* had a prodigious run, and was so extremely pretty in its kind, that even those who were most glanced at in the satire had prudence enough to disguise their resentment by chiming in with the universal applause with which it was performed. Gay, who had attached himself to Mrs. Howard and been disappointed of preferment at Court, finding this couched satire upon those to whom he imputed his disappointment succeeded so well, wrote a second part to this opera, less pretty but more abusive, and so little disguised that Sir Robert Walpole resolved, rather than suffer himself to be produced for thirty nights together upon the stage in the person of a highwayman, to make use of his friend the Duke of Gafton's authority, as Lord Chamberlain, to put a stop to the representation of it. Accordingly, this *theatrical Craftsman* was prohibited at every play-house. Gay, irritated at this bar thrown in the way both of his interest and his revenge, zested the work with some supplemental invectives, and resolved to print it by subscription. The Duchess of Queensberry set herself at the head of this undertaking, and solicited every mortal that came in her way, or in whose way she could put herself, to subscribe. To a woman of her quality, proverbially beautiful, and at the top of the polite and fashionable world, people were ashamed to refuse a guinea, though they were afraid to give it. Her solicitations were so universal and so pressing, that she came even into the Queen's apartment, went round the Drawing-room, and made even the King's servants contribute to the printing of a thing which the King had forbid being acted. The King, when he came into the Drawing-room, seeing her Grace very busy in a corner with three or four men, asked her what she had been doing. She answered, *"What* must be agreeable, she was sure, to anybody so humane as his Majesty, for it was an act of charity, and a charity to which she did not despair of bringing his Majesty to contribute." Enough was said for each to understand the other. . . . Most people blamed the Court upon this occasion. What the Duchess of Queensberry did was certainly impertinent; but the manner of resenting it was thought impolitic.

Lord Hervey, 1729, Letter to Swift, Hervey's Memoirs,
vol. I, chap. vi

Which brought in more money to Gay from its not having been allowed to get on the stage than its brilliant predecessor had done after all its unexampled run. The measure of Walpole's wrath was filled by the knowledge that a piece was in preparation in which he was to be held up to public ridicule in the rudest and most uncompromising way. Walpole acted with a certain boldness and cunning. The play was brought to him, was offered for sale to him. This was an audacious attempt at blackmailing; and at first it appeared to be successful. Walpole agreed to the terms, bought the play, paid the money, and then proceeded at once to make the fact that such a piece had been written, and but for his payment might have been played, an excuse for the introduction of a measure to put the whole English stage under restriction, and to brand it with terms of shame. He picked out carefully all the worst passages, and had them copied, and sent round in private to the leading members of all parties in the House of Commons, and appealed to them to support him in passing a measure which he justified in advance by the illustrations of dramatic licentiousness thus brought under their own eyes. By this mode of action he secured beforehand an amount of support which made the passing of his Bill a matter of almost absolute certainty. Under these favorable conditions he introduced his Playhouse Bill.

Justin McCarthy, 1884, *A History of the Four Georges,*
Vol. II, Chap. 27

GEORGE LILLO
1693-1739

Born, in London, 4 Feb. 1693. Assisted his father in jewellery business. Play *Silvia* produced at Drury Lane, 10 Nov. 1730; *The Merchant* (afterwards called: *The London Merchant, or the History of George Barnwell*), Drury Lane, 22 June 1731; *Britannia, or the Royal Lovers,* Covent Garden, 11 Feb. 1734; *The Christian Hero,* Drury Lane, 13 Jan. 1735; *Fatal Curiosity,* Haymarket, 1736; *Marina* (adapted from *Pericles*), Covent Garden, 1 Aug. 1738; *Elmerick,* posthumously produced, Drury Lane, 23 Feb. 1740; adaptation of *Arden of Faversham,* posthumously produced, Drury Lane, 19 July 1759. Died, in London, 3 Sept. 1739. Buried in St. Leonard's, Shoreditch. WORKS: *Silvia* (anon.), 1731; *The London Merchant,* 1731 (2nd edn. same year); *The Christian Hero,* 1735; *Fatal Curiosity,* 1737; *Marina,* 1738. POSTHUMOUS: *Britannia and Batavia,* 1740; *Elmerick,* 1740; *Arden of Faversham* (adapted), 1762. COLLECTED WORKS: ed. by T. Davies, with *memoir* (2 vols.), 1755.

R. Farquharson Sharp, 1897, *A Dictionary of
English Authors,* p. 169

George Barnwell (1731)

A tragedy which has been acted thirty-nine times consecutively at Drury Lane, amidst unflagging applause from a constantly crowded house; which has met with similar success wherever it has been performed; which has been printed and published to the number of many thousand copies, and is read with no less interest and pleasure than it is witnessed upon the stage— a tragedy which has called forth so many marks of approbation and esteem must occasion in those who hear it spoken of one or other of two thoughts: either that it is one of those master-pieces the perfect beauty of which is perceived by all; or that it is so well adapted to the particular taste of the nation which thus delights in it that it may be considered as a certain indication of the present state of that nation's taste.

Abbé Prévost, 1740, *Le Pour et Contre,* vol. III, p. 337

As this was almost a new species of tragedy, wrote on a very uncommon subject, he rather chose it should take its fate in the summer, than run among the more hazardous fate of encountering the winter criticks. The old ballad of "George Barnwell" (on which the story was founded) was on this occasion reprinted, and many thousands sold in one day. Many gaily-disposed spirits brought the ballad with them to the play, intending to make their pleasant remarks (as some afterwards owned) and ludicrous comparisons between the antient ditty and the modern drama. But the play was very carefully got up, and universally allowed to be well performed. The piece was thought to be well conducted, and the subject well managed, and the diction proper and natural; never low, and very rarely swelling above the characters that spoke. Mr. Pope, among other persons distinguished by their rank, or particular publick merit, had the curiosity to attend the peformance, and commended the actors, and the author; and remarked, if the latter had erred through the whole play, it was only in a few places, where he had unawares led himself into a poetical luxuriancy, affecting to be too elevated for the simplicity of the subject. But the play, in general, spoke so much to the heart, that the gay persons before mentioned confessed, they were drawn in to drop their ballads, and pull out their handkerchiefs. It met with uncommon success; for it was acted above twenty times in the summer season to great audiences; was frequently bespoke by some eminent merchants and citizens, who much approved its moral tendency: and, in the winter following, was acted often to crowded houses: And all the royal family, at several different times, honoured it with their appearance. It gained reputation, and brought money to the poet, the managers, and the performers.

Theophilus Cibber, 1753, *Lives of the Poets,* vol. V, p. 339

Read again to-day, the "master-piece" of this remarkable character seems less sublime. It is a melodrama of a decidedly sombre type, highly moral, and in parts, but in parts only, full of pathos. . . . *Manon* was as yet unwritten, and who shall say that Lillo's play, which Prévost saw performed in

London, and spoke of with such enthusiasm, did not count for something in the creation of his romance? However this may be, there is a touch of the rogue about Des Grieux, and Manon is too lovable; the lesson conveyed is less direct and less tragic. The manner in which the humble dissenter George Lillo determined to produce was very different. He aimed at producing a more forcible impression, and wrote, not a dramatic work, but a sermon in the form of a play. Nevertheless, crude as it is from an artistic point of view, this drama contains a presage of something great. . . . *George Barnwell*, which in England was regarded as a common and rather vulgar drama of some merit, produced on the continent the impression of a work of genius, and gave the theater a new lease of life. The Germans became as enthusiastic over Lillo as over Shakespeare; Gottsched and Lessing extolled him to the skies, and the latter imitated him in *Sara Sampson*. He became one of the classics of the modern drama. Yet, strange as it may seem, even to the Germans he appeared too brutal, and Sébastian Mercier's *Jenneval,* a modified but inferior adaption, was played in preference.

Joseph Texte, 1895-99. *Jean-Jaques Rousseau and the Cosmopolitan Spirit in Literature,* tr. Matthews, pp. 134, 135, 138

GENERAL

Notwithstanding the power of Lillo's works, we entirely miss in them that romantic attraction which invites to repeated perusal of them. They give us life in a close and dreadful semblance of reality, but not arrayed in the magic illusion of poetry. His strength lies in conception of situations, not in beauty of dialogue, or in the eloquence of the passions. Yet the effect of his plain and homely subjects was so strikingly superior to that of the vapid and heroic productions of the day, as to induce some of his contemporary admirers to pronounce that he had reached the acmè of dramatic excellence, and struck into the best and most genuine path of tragedy. . . . It is one question whether Lillo has given to his subjects from private life the degree of beauty of which they are susceptible. He is a master of terrific, but not of tender impressions. We feel a harshness and gloom in his genius even while we are compelled to admire its force and originality.

Thomas Campbell, 1819, *Specimens of the British Poets*

One of the prominent offenders who followed in Steele's wake was George Lillo whose highly moral tragedies, written for the edification of playgoers, have the kind of tragic interest which is called forth by any commonplace tale of crime and misery. In Lillo's two most important dramas, *George Barnwell,* a play founded on the old ballad, and *The Fatal Curiosity,* there is a total absence of the elevation in character and language which gives dignity to tragedy. His plays are like tales of guilt arranged and amplified from the Newgate Calendar. The author wrote with a good purpose, and the public appreciated his work, but it is not dramatic art, and has no pretension to the name of literature.

John Dennis, 1894, *The Age of Pope*, p. 138

ALEXANDER POPE
1688-1744

1688 (May 21), Birth of Pope. 1700, (Circ), Pope takes up his residence with his father at Binfield. 1704, Commencement of intimacy with Sir Wm. Trumbull, 1705, and Walsh. 1707, First acquaintance with the Blount family. 1709, *Pastorals* published. 1711, *Essay on Criticism*, Pope introduced to Gay, 1712, and Addison, *Rape of the Lock* (original edition), *The Messiah*. 1713, (April), Addison's *Cato* first acted, *Prologue to Cato*. Pope's attack on Dennis reproved by Addison, *Windsor Forest*, Pope introduced to Swift, *Ode on St. Cecilia's Day*, Pope studies painting under Jervas. (November), Subscription for *Translation of Iliad* opened. 1713-4, Meetings of the Scriblerus Club. 1714, Death of Queen Anne, *Rape of the Lock* (enlarged), *Temple of Fame*. 1715, *Iliad* (vol. i). 1715-6, Quarrel with Addison. 1716, (April), Pope settles with his parents at Chiswick, Departure for the East of Lady Mary Wortley Montagu. 1717, *Elegy to the Memory of an Unfortunate Lady, Epistle of Eloisa to Abelard, Three Hours after Marriage* produced, First quarrel with Cibber. (October), Death of Pope's father. 1718. Pope settled with his mother at Twickenham, Return from the East of Lady Mary Wortley Montagu. 1720, South-Sea Year, *Iliad* (last volume). 1722, Correspondence with Judith Cowper. 1723, First return of Bolingbroke, Banishment of Atterbury. 1725, Edition of *Shakspere*, Pope attacked by Theobald, *Odyssey* (vols. i-iii), Second return of Bolingbroke, who settles at Dawley. 1726, *Letters to Cromwell* (Curll), Swift pays a long visit to Twickenham. 1727, (June), Death of George I., *Miscellanies* (vols. i. and ii.); containing, among other pieces by Pope, the "Treatise on the Bathos." 1728, *The Dunciad* (Books i.-iii.). 1730, *Grub Street Journal* (continued by Pope and others till 1737). Quarrels with Aaron Hill and others. 1731, *Epistle on Taste*, The remaining *Moral Essay* up to 1735. 1732, *Essay on Man* (Ep. 1.), The remaining Epistles up to 1734. (December), Death of Gay. 1733, Quarrel with Lord Hervey. (June), Death of Pope's mother. 1735, *Epistle to Arbuthnot*, Death of Arbuthnot, Pope's *Correspondence*, (Curll). 1736, Pope's *Correspondence* (Authorised edition). 1737, *Imitations of Horace*. 1738, *Epilogue to Satires*. 1740. (March), Close of Correspondence with Swift, First meeting with Warburton. 1742. *The New Dunciad* (in four books). 1743, *The Dunciad* (with Cibber as hero). 1744, (May 30), Death of Pope.

Adolphus William Ward, 1869, ed., *The Poetical Works of Alexander Pope*, Chronological Table, p. lii

SEE: *Poems*, Twickenham Edition, General Editor John Butt, 1939-   ,
6 v. (Vol. I: *Pastoral Poetry* and *An Essay on Criticism* (not published),
Vol. II: *The Rape of The Lock and Other Poems*, ed. Geoffrey Tillotson,
1940, Vol. III: *An Essay on Man*, part I, ed. Maynard Mack, 1950,
part II, *Epistles to Several Persons* (Moral Essays), ed. F. W. Bateson,
1951; Vol. IV: *Imitations of Horace*, ed. John Butt, 1939; Vol. V: *The
Dunciad*, ed. James Sutherland, 1943; Vol VI: *Minor Poems*, ed. Norman
Ault and John Butt, 1954); *Prose Works*, ed. Norman Ault, 1936; *Correspondence*, ed. George Sherburn, 1956, 5 v. (abridged by John Butt,
1960, one volume); *The Rape of the Lock*, ed. J. S. Cunningham (*Studies
in English Literature*, No. 2), 1961; *Pope's Essay on Criticism 1709:
A Study of the Bodleian Manuscript Text, with Facsimiles, Transcripts
and Variants*, by Robert M. Schmitz, 1962; *Life*, in *Works*, ed. W. Elwin
and W. J. Courthope, 1871-79, 10 v.; George Sherburn, *The Early Career
of Alexander Pope*, 1934; R. K. Root, *The Poetical Career of Pope*, 1938;
Geoffrey Tillotson, *On the Poetry of Pope*, 1938, rev. 1958; Geoffrey
Tillotson, *Pope and Human Nature*, 1958; D. M. Knight, *Pope and the
Heroic Tradition: A Critical Study of His Iliad*, 1951; A. L. Williams,
Pope's Dunciad, 1955; R. W. Rogers, *The Major Satires of Pope*, 1955.

PERSONAL

If you have a mind to enquire between Sunninghill and Oakingham, for
a young, squab, short gentleman, an eternal writer of amorous pastoral
madrigals, and the very bow of the god of Love, you will be soon directed
to him. And pray, as soon as you have taken a survey of him, tell me
whether he is a proper author to make personal reflections on others. This
little author may extol the ancients as much, and as long as he pleases, but
he has reason to thank the good gods that he was born a modern, for had
he been born of Grecian parents, and his father by consequence had by law
the absolute disposal of him, his life had been no longer than that of one
of his poems,—the life of half a day.

> John Dennis, 1711, *Reflections, Critical and Satirical on a
> Rhapsody, Call'd An Essay on Criticism*, p. 29

Dick Distick we have elected president, not only as he is the shortest of us
all, but because he has entertained so just a sense of his stature as to go
generally in black, that he may appear yet less; nay, to that perfection is he
arrived that he stoops as he walks. The figure of the man is odd enough:
He is a lively little creature, with long arms and legs—a spider is no ill
emblem of him; he has been taken at a distance for a small windmill.

> Alexander Pope, 1713, "The Little Club," *The Guardian*, June 26

... Pope, the monarch of the tuneful train!
To whom be Nature's, and Britannia's praise!

All their bright honours rush into his lays!
And all that glorious warmth his lays reveal,
Which only poets, kings, and patriots feel!
Tho' gay as mirth, as curious though sedate,
As elegance polite, as pow'r elate;
Profound as reason, and as justice clear;
Soft as compassion, yet as truth severe;
As bounty copious, as persuasion sweet,
Like Nature various, and like Art complete;
So fine her morals, so sublime her views,
His life is almost equall'd by his Muse.

Richard Savage, 1729, The Wanderer, Canto I

Mr. Alexander Pope, the poet's father, was a poor ignorant man, a tanner
at Binfield in Berks. This Mr. Alex. Pope had a little house there, that he
had from his father, but hath now sold it to one Mr. Tanner, an honest man.
This Alexander Pope, though he be an English poët, yet he is but an indifferent scholar, mean at Latin, and can hardly read Greek. He is a very
ill-natured man and covetous, and excessively proud.

Thomas Hearne, 1729, Reliquiæ Hearnianæ, ed. Bliss,
July 18, vol. III, p. 23

To believe nothing is yours but what you own, would be merely ridiculous.
Did you not deny The Dunciad for seven years? Did you not offer a reward
of three guineas, by an advertisement in the Post-man, to know the publisher of your version of the First Psalm? and when you were informed,
did you ever pay the premium? Did you not publish the Worms yourself?
And do you own any of these in the preface of the second volume of your
works? In short, sir, your conduct as to your poetical productions is
exactly of a piece with what I once met with at the Old Bailey. A most
flagrant offender was put upon his trial for a notorious theft, and by his
egregious shuffling he put Mr. Recorder Lovel into a violent passion.
Sirrah, says he, you have got a trick of denying what you ought to own, and
by owning what you might as well deny. "An' please your honour," quoth
culprit, "that's the way not to be hanged."

Edmund Curll, 1735, Epistle, Pope's Literary Correspondence,
vol. II

Mr. Pope's not being richer may be easily accounted for.—He never had
any love for money: and though he was not extravagant in anything, he
always delighted, when he had any sum to spare, to make use of it in giving,
lending, building, and gardening; for those were the ways in which he dis-

posed of all the overplus of his income.—If he was extravagant in anything it was in his grotto, for that, from first to last, cost him above a thousand pounds.

Mrs. Blount, 1737-39, *Spence's Anecdotes,* ed. Singer, p. 160

I can say no more for Mr. Pope (for what you keep in reserve may be worse than all the rest). It is natural to wish the finest writer, one of them, we ever had, should be an honest man. It is for the interest even of that virtue, whose friend he professed himself, and whose beauties he sung, that he should not be found a dirty animal. But, however, this is Mr. Warburton's business, not mine, who may scribble his pen to the stumps and all in vain, if these facts are so. It is not from what he told me about himself that I thought well of him, but from a humanity and goodness of heart, ay, and greatness of mind, that runs through his private correspondence, not less apparent than are a thousand little vanities and weaknesses mixed with those good qualitics, for nobody ever took him for a philosopher.

Thomas Gray, 1746, *Letter to Horace Walpole,* Feb. 3

Pope had but one great end in view to render this world supportable to him. That was *Friendship, the peculiar gift of heaven.* This did he nobly deserve and obtain; but for how short a time! Jealousy deprived him of the affection he assiduously sought from Mr. Wycherly, and many others; but Death cruel Death was far more cruel. The dearest ties of his heart all yielded to his stroke. The modest Digby, the gentle virtuous Gay, the worthy Arbuthnot, the exiled Atterbury—but why should I enumerate these excellent men, when their very names dejected me? But in nothing does Pope equally charm me as in his conduct to his mother: it is truly noble.

Frances Burney, 1771, *Early Diary,* Dec. 8, vol. I, p. 140

Pope, who was all malice, hatred, and uncharitableness; false as a Jesuit; fickle as a fool; mercenary as a waiting woman; and with a prurient fancy, which, had his body permitted it, would have led him into excesses as gross as any that Chartres was accused of.

Edward Wortley Montagu, 1776? *An Autobiography,* vol. I, p. 57

Pope was, through his whole life, ambitious of splendid acquaintance; and he seems to have wanted neither diligence nor success in attracting the notice of the great; for from his first entrance into the world (and his entrance was very early) he was admitted to familiarity with those whose rank or station made them most conspicuous. . . . He is said to have been beautiful in his infancy; but he was of a constitution originally feeble and weak; and as bodies of a tender frame are easily distorted, his deformity was probably in part the effect of his application. His stature was so low, that, to bring him to the level with common tables, it was necessary to raise his seat. But his face was not displeasing, and his eyes were animated and vivid. . . . When he rose, he was invested in a bodice made of stiff canvas, being scarcely able to hold himself erect till they were laced, and he then put on a flannel waistcoat. One side was contracted. His legs were so slender that he enlarged their bulk with three pair of stockings, which were drawn on and off by the maid; for he was not able to dress or undress himself, and neither went to bed nor rose without help. His weakness made it very difficult for him to be clean. . . . He sometimes condescended to be jocular with servants or inferiors; but by no merriment, either of others or his own, was he ever seen excited to laughter. . . . In the duties of friendship he was zealous and constant; his early maturity of mind commonly united him with men older than himself, and therefore, without attaining any considerable length of life, he saw many companions of his youth sink into the grave; but it does not appear that he lost a single friend by coldness or by injury; those who loved him once, continued their kindness.

Samuel Johnson, 1779-81, Pope, Lives of the English Poets

Pope's character and habits were exclusively literary, with all the hopes, fears, and failings, which are attached to that feverish occupation,—a restless pursuit of poetical fame. Without domestic society, or near relations; separated by weak health and personal disadvantages from the gay; by fineness of mind and lettered indolence, from the busy part of mankind, surrounded only by a few friends, who valued these gifts in which he excelled, Pope's whole hopes, wishes, and fears, were centered in his literary reputation. To extend his fame, he laboured indirectly, as well as directly; and to defend it from the slightest attack, was his daily and nightly anxiety. Hence the restless impatience which that distinguished author displayed under the libels of dunces, whom he ought to have despised, and hence too the venomed severity with which he retorted their puny attacks.

Sir Walter Scott, 1814, Memoirs of Jonathan Swift

As a Christian, Pope appears in a truly estimable light. He found himself a Roman Catholic by accident of birth; so was his mother; but his father was so upon personal conviction and conversion,—yet not without extensive study of the questions at issue. It would have laid open the road to preferment, and preferment was otherwise abundantly before him, if Pope would have gone over to the Protestant faith. And in his conscience he found no obstacle to that change; he was a philosophical Christian, intolerant of nothing but intolerance, a bigot only against bigots. But he remained true to his baptismal profession, partly on a general principle of honour in adhering to a distressed and dishonoured party, but chiefly out of reverence and affection to his mother. In his relation to women Pope was amiable and gentlemanly, and accordingly was the object of affectionate regard and admiration to many of the most accomplished in that sex. This we mention especially, because we would wish to express our full assent to the manly scorn with which Mr. Roscoe repels the libellous insinuations against Pope and Miss Martha Blount. A more innocent connexion we do not believe ever existed.

Thomas DeQuincey, c1838-90, *Pope, Works,* ed. Masson,
vol. IV, p. 277

His own life was one long series of tricks, as mean and as malicious as that of which he suspected Addison and Tickell. He was all stiletto and mask. To injure, to insult, to save himself from the consequence of injury and insult by lying and equivocating, was the habit of his life. He published a lampoon on the Duke of Chandos; he was taxed with it; and he lied and equivocated. He published a lampoon on Aaron Hill; he was taxed with it; and he lied and equivocated. He published a still fouler lampoon on Lady Mary Wortley Montagu; he was taxed with it; and he lied with more than usual effrontery and vehemence. He puffed himself and abused his enemies under feigned names: He robbed himself of his own letters, and then raised the hue and cry after them. Besides his frauds of malignity, of fear, of interest, and of vanity, there were frauds which he seems to have committed from love of fraud alone. He had a habit of stratagem—a pleasure in outwitting all who came near him. Whatever his object might be, the indirect road to it was that which he preferred.

Thomas Babington Macaulay, 1843, "Life and Writings of
Addison," *Edinburgh Review; Critical and Miscellaneous Essays*

Thanks to his father, Pope's fortune was enough to place him above dependence. No matter what was the amount of his patrimony, his spirit was independent, and he resolved, from the first, to limit his desires to his means. . . . Pope greedy of money! Why Johnson admits that he gave away an eighth part of his income; and where is the man, making no ostentatious profession of benevolence—subscribing to no charities, as they are called, or few—standing in no responsible position before the world, which indeed he rather scorned than courted, of whom the same can be said? Pope, we suspect, with all his magnificent subscriptions, did not leave behind him so much as he had received from his father. His pleasure was in scattering, not in hoarding, and that on others rather than on himself. He was generous to the Blounts and because one proof has accidentally become known, it has been winged with scandal;—he was generous to his half-sister,—gen-

erous to her sons,—generous to Dodsley, then struggling into business,—
nobly generous to Savage; for though the weakness and the vice of Savage
compelled Pope to break off personal intercourse, he never deserted him.
These facts were known to his biographers; and we could add a bead-roll
of like noble actions, but that it would be beside our purpose and our limits.
Pope, indeed, was generous to all who approached; and though his bodily
weakness and sufferings made him a troublesome visitor, especially to servants,—though one of Lord Oxford's said that, "in the dreadful winter of
forty, she was called from her bed by him four times in one night," yet this
same servant declared, "that in a house where her business was to answer
his call, she would not ask for wages." What more could be told of the
habitual liberality of a man who never possessed more than a few hundred
a year? It startled persons accustomed to the munificence of the noble
and the wealthy.

Charles Wentworth Dilke, 1854-75, "Pope's Writings,"
The Papers of a Critic, vol. I, pp. 110, 111

Bolingbroke had given to Pope the manuscript of The Patriot King, and the
letter on Patriotism, in order to get five or six copies printed for private
circulation. Pope, however, had given orders for fifteen hundred additional
copies to be worked off, under the strictest injunctions of secrecy. The
secret was kept until Pope's death. Soon afterwards Bolingbroke received
a letter from the printer, asking him what was to be done with these fifteen
hundred copies? Bolingbroke was astonished to find so much artifice and
meanness in his former friend. He requested Lord Marchmont to get all
the edition into his hands. . . . The edition was, however, not burnt at the
house Lord Marchmont was furnishing in London. He thought it more satisfactory to have the sheets, destroyed under Bolingbroke's own eyes. They
were all taken down to Battersea, and burned on the terrace. Bolingbroke
himself set fire to the pile. It is impossible to defend Pope. That he greatly
admired The Patriot King, and was afraid so valuable a work would be lost
to posterity, unless he took this method of preserving it, as Warburton afterwards alleged, is at best scarcely an excuse. No adequate motive for Pope's
conduct has ever been discovered nor imagined. The simplest explanation
is the most satisfactory. Stratagem and double-dealing were habitual to him:
he could not act straightforwardly, nor understand a straightforward course
in others; he frequently lied when lying was quite useless to him, and answered no purpose of deception; and when he could not deceive his enemies,
he with a weak kind of cunning appears to have taken a pleasure in outwitting his best friends.

Thomas Macknight, 1863, The Life of Henry St. John,
Viscount Bolingbroke, pp. 666, 667

In Pope, then, we have to do with a remarkably complex character. It will not do simply to brand him as a hypocrite, for the essence of hypocrisy consists in unreality; but behind the falsities of Pope there is an eagerness and intensity which gives them a human interest, and makes us feel, that, in his poetry, we are in contact with the nature of the man himself. To separate that moral nature into various elements, so as to decide how much is deliberately false, how much may be accepted as true, and how much is self-deception, we ought, following his own rule, to examine his

> Proper character,
> His fable, subject, scope in every page,
> Religion, country, genius of his age.

On this principle much of the inconsistency in his conduct will be found to correspond with the union of opposite conditions in his nature: the piercing intelligence and artistic power, lodged in the sickly and deformed frame; the vivid perception of the ridiculous in others, joined to the most sensitive consciousness of his own defects; the passionate desire for fame, aggravated by a fear of being suspected by his countrymen on account of his religion; the conflicting qualities of benevolence and self-love; the predominance of intellectual instinct; the deficiency of moral principle. It might be predicted of a character so highly strung, so variously endowed, so "tremblingly alive" to opinion, and so capable of transformation, that it would exhibit itself in the most diverse aspects, according to the circumstances by which it was tested. And this is just what we find. Perhaps no man of genius was ever more largely influenced by his companions and his surroundings than Pope.

> William John Courthope, 1881, ed., *The Works of Alexander Pope, Introduction to The Moral Essays and Satires,* vol. III, p. 26

Pope's disease was that of Malvolio and one or two others—he was sick of self-love. He knew himself to be warm-hearted and generous, he forgot he was also vain and disingenuous, and so remembering and thus forgetting, he loved himself unsparingly. A cripple and a Catholic, he was prevented by nature and by law from either active pursuits or the public service. Crazy for praise and fame, and conscious of enormous ability, he determined to make himself felt, as an independent force in verse. Resentful to the last degree, writhing under a dunce's sneer, maddened by a woman's laugh, he grasped his only weapon with a fierce hand and made his hatreds "live along the line." I do not believe any just man can read Dr. Johnson's and Mr. Courthope's Lives of Pope without liking him. Some of the bad poets (e.g. Kirke White) have been better men, but very few of the good ones.

> Augustine Birrell, 1889, "Noticeable Books,"
> *The Nineteenth Century,* vol. 26, p. 988

LADY MARY

To say that he had any right to make love to her is one thing; yet to believe that her manners, and cast of character, as well as the nature of the times, and of the circles in which she moved, had given no license, no encouragement, no pardoning hope to the presumption, is impossible; and to trample in this way upon the whole miserable body of his vanity and humility, upon all which the consciousness of acceptability and glory among his fellow-creatures, had given to sustain himself, and all which in so poor, and fragile, and dwarfed, and degrading a shape, required so much to be so sustained; —assuredly it was inexcusable,—it was inhuman. . . . She had every advantage on her side:—could not even this induce her to put a little more heart and consideration into her repulse? Oh, Lady Mary! A duke's daughter wert thou, and a beauty, and a wit, and a very triumphant and flattered personage, and covered with glory as with lute-string and diamonds; and yet false measure didst thou take of thy superiority, and didst not see how small thou becamest in the comparison when thou didst thus, with laughing cheeks, trample under foot the poor little *immortal!*

Leigh Hunt, 1847, *Men, Women and Books,* vol. II, p. 196

The friendship with Pope, conspicuous in the letters written during the embassy, is an unfortunate episode in the life of Lady Mary. All the stories which have gained credence, to the injury of her reputation, are probably due to his subsequent quarrel with her, the hatred and unscrupulousness with which he pursued her, and his fatal power of circulating scandalous insinuations. It is certain that the tenor of her life up to the period of her quarrel with Pope, was wholly unlike that career of profligacy which has been popularly attributed to her since the publication of Pope's Satires and the Letters of Horace Walpole—who, it must be remembered, wrote after Pope's celebrated attacks; and it is no less certain that, on a careful investigation, not one of the charges brought against her will be found to rest on any evidence.

W. Moy Thomas, 1861, ed., *Letters and Works of
Lady Mary Wortley Montagu,* Memoir, vol. I, p. 21

Why Pope and Lady Mary quarreled is a question on which much discussion has been expended, and on which a judicious German professor might even now compose an interesting and exhaustive monograph. A curt English critic will be more apt to ask why they should *not* have quarreled. We know that Pope quarreled with almost every one: we know that Lady Mary quarreled or half quarreled with most of her acquaintances: why then should they not have quarreled with one another? It is certain that they were very intimate at one time; for Pope wrote to her some of the most pompous letters of compliment in the language. And the more intimate they were to begin with, the more sure they were to be enemies in the end. . . . We only know that there was a sudden coolness or quarrel between them, and that it was the beginning of a long and bitter hatred. In their own times Pope's sensitive disposition probably gave Lady Mary a great advantage,—her tongue perhaps gave him more pain than his pen gave her; but in later times she has fared the worse.

> Walter Bagehot, 1862-89, "Lady Mary Wortley Montagu," *Works*,
> ed. Morgan, vol. I, pp. 377, 379

The stroke, when it came, was delivered on the most sensitive part of the poet's nature. It is quite unnecessary to suppose that he was passionately in love with Lady Mary. The "declarations" which he is constantly making to her in his letters, he made, with as much sincerity, and almost in identical words, to Judith Cowper and Martha Blount; and, in using language of this kind, he was only conforming with the gallantry fashionable in his age. He calls himself in one of his poems the "most thinking rake alive." His love-making was like his description of Stanton-Harcourt, purely ideal, but his vanity and his artistic sensibility were so strong that he was vexed when he was not believed to be in earnest. To have the declaration of his elaborate passion received with laughter, must have been a rude shock to his vanity, and his acute self-consciousness would have no doubt associated Lady Mary's behaviour with his own physical defects. After all his well-considered expressions of devotion, after the exquisite lines in which he had connected her name with his grotto, ridicule was the refinement of torture. It humiliated him in his own esteem, and the recollection of the light mockery, with which she had always met his heroics, added to his sense of insult and injury. These considerations, though they help us to understand the condition of Pope's feelings, afford no excuse whatever for the character of his satire on Lady Mary.

> Whitwell Elwin and William John Courthope, 1881, ed.,
> *The Works of Alexander Pope*, vol. III, p. 282

MARTHA BLOUNT

Patty Blount was red-faced, fat, and by no means pretty. Mr. Walpole remembered her walking to Mr. Bethell's, in Arlington Street, after Pope's death, with her petticoats tucked up like a sempstress. She was the decided mistress of Pope, yet visited by respectable people.

> Edmond Malone, 1792, *Maloniana, From Horace Walpole*,
> ed. Prior, p. 437

He was never indifferent to female society; and though his good sense prevented him, conscious of so many personal infirmities, from marrying, yet he felt the want of that sort of reciprocal tenderness and confidence in a female, to whom he might freely communicate his thoughts, and on whom, in sickness and infirmity, he could rely. All this Martha Blount became to him; by degrees, she became identified with his existence. She partook of his disappointments, his vexations, and his comforts. Wherever he went, his correspondence with her was never remitted; and when the warmth of gallantry was over, the cherished idea of kindness and regard remained.

William Lisle Bowles, 1806, ed. *Pope's Works,* vol. I

Ode to Solitude

The first of our author's compositions now extant in print, is an *Ode on Solitude,* written before he was twelve years old: Which, consider'd as the production of so early an age, is a perfect masterpiece; nor need he have been ashamed of it, had it been written in the meridian of his genius. While it breathes the most delicate spirit of poetry, it at the same time demonstrates his love of solitude, and the rational pleasures which attend the retreats of a contented country life.

Theophilus Cibber, 1753, *Lives of the Poets,* vol. V, p. 221

Pope never wrote more agreeable or well-tuned verses than this interesting effusion of his boyhood. Indeed there is an intimation of sweetness and variety in the versification, which was not borne out afterwards by his boasted smoothness: nor can we help thinking, that had the author of the *Ode on Solitude* arisen in less artificial times, he would have turned out to be a still finer poet than he was. But the reputation which he easily acquired for wit and criticism, the recent fame of Dryden, and perhaps even his little warped and fragile person, tempted him to accept such power over his contemporaries as he could soonest realize. It is observable that Pope never repeated the form of verse in which this poem is written. It might have reminded him of a musical feeling he had lost.

Leigh Hunt, 1849, *A Book for a Corner*

Pastorals (1709)

The author seems to have a particular genius for this kind of poetry, and a judgment that much exceeds his years. He has taken very freely from the ancients. But what he has mixed of his own with theirs is no way inferior to what he has taken from them. It is not flattery at all to say that Virgil had written nothing so good at his age. His preface is very judicious and learned.

William Walsh, 1705, *Letter to William Wycherley,* April 20

It is somewhat strange that in the pastorals of a young poet there should not be found a single rural image that is new; but this, I am afraid, is the case in the Pastorals before us. The ideas of Theocritus, Virgil, and Spenser are, indeed, here exhibited in language equally mellifluous and pure; but the descriptions and sentiments are trite and common. To this assertion, formerly made, Dr. Johnson answered, "that no invention was intended." He, therefore, allows the fact and the charge. It is a confession of the very fault imputed to them. There *ought* to have been invention. It has been my fortune from my way of life, to have seen many compositions of youths of sixteen years old, far beyond these Pastorals in point of genius and imagination, though not perhaps of correctness. Their excellence, indeed, might be owing to having had such a predecessor as Pope.

Joseph Warton, 1797, ed. Pope's Works

Warton's observations are very just, but he does not seem sufficiently to discriminate between the softness of individual lines, which is the chief merit of these Pastorals, and the general harmony of poetic numbers. Let it, however, be always remembered, that Pope gave the first idea of mellifluence, and produced a softer and sweeter cadence than before belonged to the English couplet. Dr. Johnson thinks it will be in vain, after Pope, to endeavour to improve the English versification, and that it is now carried to the *ne plus ultra* of excellence. This is an opinion the validity of which I must be permitted to doubt. Pope certainly gave a more correct and finished tone to the English versification, but he sometimes wanted a variety of pause, and his nice precision of every line prevented, in a few instances, a more musical flow of modulated passages. But we are to consider what he did, not what might be done, and surely there cannot be two opinions respecting his improvement of the couplet though it does not follow that his general rhythm has no imperfection. Johnson seems to have depreciated, or to have been ignorant of, the metrical powers of some writers prior to Pope. His ear seems to have been caught chiefly by Dryden, and as Pope's versification was more equably (couplet with couplet being considered, not passage with passage) connected than Dryden's, he thought therefore that nothing could be added to Pope's versification. I should think it the extreme of arrogance and folly to make my own ear the criterion of music; but I cannot help thinking that Dryden, and of later days, Cowper, are much more harmonious in their general versification than Pope. I ought also to mention a neglected poem, not neglected on account of its versification, but on account of its title and subject—Prior's *Solomon*. Whoever candidly compares these writers together, unless his ear be habituated to a certain recurrence of pauses precisely at the end of a line, will not (though he will give the highest praise for compactness, skill, precision, and force, to the undivided couplets of Pope, separately considered)—will not, I think, assent to the position, that in versification "what he found brickwork he left marble." I am not afraid to own, that with the exception of the *Epistle to Abelard,* as musical as it is pathetic, the verses of Pope want variety, and on this account in some instances they want both force and harmony. In variety, and variety only, let it be remembered, I think Pope deficient.

William Lisle Bowles, 1806, ed. Pope's Works

There is no evidence, except the poet's own assertion, to prove that the Pastorals were composed at the age of sixteen. They had been seen by Walsh before April 20, 1705, if any dependence could be placed upon the letter of that date which he wrote to Wycherley, when returning the manuscript, but the letter rests on the authority of Pope alone, and there is reason to question the correctness of the date. . . . Whatever may be the true date of the Pastorals, a portion of them certainly existed before April 20, 1706.

Whitwell Elwin, 1871, ed., The Works of Alexander Pope,
Pastorals, vol. I, pp. 240-41

Pope's manner is intolerably artificial; he bears the graceless yoke of the Miltonic epithet; his matter is a mere pastiche from Virgil and Theocritus, Dryden and Spenser; but for melodious rhythm and dignity of phrase his pastorals reach a point which he never afterwards surpassed. The musical possibilities of the heroic couplet are exhausted in the eclogue entitled "Autumn," and though we may perhaps think the meter inappropriate to the subject, we cannot fail to be sensible of the ease and dignity of the verse.

Edmund K. Chambers, 1895, English Pastorals, p. xlv

An Essay on Criticism (1711)

The Art of Criticism, which was published some months since, and is a masterpiece in its kind. The observations follow one another like those in Horace's *Art of Poetry,* without that methodical regularity which would have been requisite in a prose author. They are some of them uncommon, but such as the reader must assent to, when he sees them explained with that elegance and perspicuity in which they are delivered. As for those which are the most known, and the most received, they are placed in so beautiful a light, and illustrated with such apt allusions, that they have in them all the graces of novelty, and make the reader, who was before acquainted with them, still more convinced of their truth and solidity.

Joseph Addison, 1711, The Spectator, No. 253, Dec. 20

I dare not say anything of the *Essay on Criticism* in verse; but if any more curious reader has discovered in it something *new* which is not in Dryden's prefaces, dedications, and his *Essay on Dramatic Poetry,* not to mention the French critics, I should be very glad to have the benefit of the discovery.

John Oldmixon, 1728, Essays on Criticism in Prose

A work which displays such extent of comprehension, such nicety of distinction, such acquaintance with mankind, and such knowledge both of ancient and modern learning, as are not often attained by the maturest age and longest experience. . . . One of his greatest, though of his earliest, works is *Essay on Criticism,* which, if he had written nothing else, would have placed him among the first critics and the first poets, as it exhibits every mode of excellence that can embellish or dignify didactic composition,— selection of matter, novelty of arrangement, justness of precept, splendour of illustration, and propriety of digression. I know not whether it be pleasing to consider that he has produced this piece at twenty, and never afterwards excelled it: he that delights himself with observing that such powers may be soon attained, cannot but grieve to think that life was ever after at a stand. To mention the particular beauties of the Essay would be unprofitably tedious; but I cannot forbear to observe, that the comparison of a student's progress in the sciences with the journey of a traveller in the Alps, is perhaps the best that English poetry can shew.

Samuel Johnson, 1779-81, Pope, Lives of the English Poets

The quantity of thought and observation in this work, for so young a man as Pope was when he wrote it, is wonderful: unless we adopt the supposition that most men of genius spend the rest of their lives in teaching others what they themselves have learned under twenty. The conciseness and felicity of the expression are equally remarkable. . . . Nothing can be more original and happy than the general remarks and illustrations in the Essay: the critical rules laid down are too much those of a school, and of a confined one.

William Hazlitt, 1818, Lectures on the English Poets,
Lecture IV

The *Essay* has many incorrect observations, and, in spite of its own axioms, many bad rhymes, many faulty grammatical constructions. But these cannot weigh against the substantial merit of the performance. They cannot obscure the truth that the poem is, what its title pretends, an *Essay on Criticism,* an attempt made, for the first time in English literature, and in the midst of doubts, perplexities, and distractions, of which we, in our position of the idle heirs of that age, can only have a shadowy conception, to erect a standard of judgment founded in justice of thought and accuracy of expression. Nor will it be denied that, as a poem, the critical and philosophical nature of the subject is enlivened by bold, brilliant, and beautiful imagery.

> William John Courthope, 1889, *The Life of Alexander Pope,*
> *Works,* ed. Elwin and Courthope, vol. V, p. 70

Pope impaired the vitality of English poetry for fifty years by his futile "to advantage dressed," and succeeded in teaching "a school of dolts to smooth, inlay, and clip, and fit," as the excited Keats has it. Horace is very modern, we say; we can read him nowadays with great comfort, with greater comfort than we can get from Pope. Not only is Horace nearer to us in his ideas on language and on style; he understood criticism better than did Pope.

> Edward E. Hale, Jr., 1897, "The Classics of Criticism,"
> *The Dial,* vol. 22, p. 246

The Messiah (1712)

This is certainly the most animated and sublime of all authors' compositions, and it is manifestly owing to the great original which he copied. Perhaps the dignity, the energy, and the simplicity of the original, are in a few passages weakened and diminished by florid epithets, and useless circumlocutions.

> Joseph Warton, 1797, ed. *Pope's Works*

All things considered, *The Messiah* is as fine and masterly a piece of composition as the English language, in the same style of verse, can boast. I have ventured to point out a passage or two, for they are rare, where the sublimity has been awakened by epithets; and I have done this, because it is a fault, particularly with young writers, so common. In the most truly sublime images of Scripture, the addition of a single word would often destroy their effect. It is therefore right to keep as nearly as possible to the very words. No one understood better than Milton where to be general, and where particular; where to adopt the very expression of Scripture, and where it was allowed to paraphrase.

> William Lisle Bowles, 1806, ed. *Pope's Works*

It is an admirable *tour de force,* and should be regarded like his *Pastorals* as an exercise in diction and versification. Though, by the conditions under which he has bound himself, he was forced to lower the grandeur of the Scripture language, the artfulness with which he adapts his imagery to the

Virgilian manner, and combines scattered passages of prophecy in a volume of stately and sonorous verse, is deserving of high admiration; and the concluding lines ascend to a height not unworthy of the original they paraphrase.

> William John Courthope, 1889, *The Life of Alexander Pope,*
> *Works,* ed. Elwin and Courthope, vol. V, p. 36

The Rape of the Lock (1712-14)

The stealing of Miss Belle Fermor's hair, was taken too seriously, and caused an estrangement between the two families, though they had lived so long in great friendship before. A common acquaintance and well-wisher to both, desired me to write a poem to make a jest of it, and laugh them together again. It was with this view that I wrote the *Rape of the Lock;* which was well received, and had its effect in the two families.—Nobody but Sir George Brown was angry, and he was a good deal so, and for a long time. He could not bear, that Sir Plume should talk nothing but nonsense.— Copies of the poem got about, and it was like to be printed; on which I published the first draught of it (without the machinery), in a Miscellany of Tonson's. The machinery was added afterwards, to make it look a little more considerable, and the scheme of adding it was much liked and approved of by several of my friends, and particularly by Dr. Garth: who, as he was one of the best natured men in the world, was very fond of it.

> Alexander Pope, 1737-39, *Spence's Anecdotes,* ed. Singer, p. 147

I have been assured by a most intimate friend of Mr. Pope's, that the Peer in *Rape of the Lock* was Lord Petre; the person who desired Mr. Pope to write it, old Mr. Caryl, of Sussex; and that what was said of Sir George Brown in it, was the very picture of the man.

> Joseph Spence, 1737-39, *Anecdotes,* ed. Singer, p. 148

This seems to be Mr. Pope's most finished production, and is, perhaps, the most perfect in our language. It exhibits stronger powers of imagination, more harmony of numbers, and a greater knowledge of the world, than any other of this poet's works: and it is probable, if our country were called upon to shew a specimen of their genius to foreigners, this would be the work here fixed upon.

> Oliver Goldsmith, 1767, *The Beauties of English Poetry*

The most airy, the most ingenious, and the most delightful of all his compositions. . . . To the praises which have been accumulated on *The Rape of the Lock* by readers of every class, from the critic to the waiting-maid, it is difficult to make any addition. Of that which is universally allowed to use the most attractive of all ludicrous compositions, let it rather be now inquired from what sources the power of pleasing is derived.

Samuel Johnson, 1779-81, Pope, Lives of the English Poets

It is the most exquisite specimen of *filigree* work ever invented. It is admirable in proportion as it is made of nothing. . . . It is made of gauze and silver spangles. The most glittering appearance is given to every thing, to paste, pomatum, billets-doux and patches. Airs, languid airs, breathe around; the atmosphere is perfumed with affectation. A toilette is described with the solemnity of an altar raised to the goddess of vanity, and the history of a silver bodkin is given with all the pomp of heraldry. No pains are spared, no profusion of ornament, no splendour of poetic diction, to set off the meanest things. The balance between the concealed irony and the assumed gravity is as nicely trimmed as the balance of power in Europe. The little is made great, and the great little. You hardly know whether to laugh or weep. It is the triumph of insignificance, the apotheosis of foppery and folly. It is the perfection of the mock-heroic.

William Hazlitt, 1818, Lectures on the English Poets,
Lecture IV

No more brilliant, sparkling, vivacious trifle is to be found in our literature than *Rape of the Lock,* even in this early form. . . . Pope declared, and critics have agreed, that he never showed more skill than in the remodelling of this poem; and it has ever since held a kind of recognized supremacy amongst the productions of the drawing-room muse. . . . The successive scenes are given with so firm and clear a touch—there is such a sense of form, the language is such a dexterous elevation of the ordinary social twaddle into the mock-heroic, that it is impossible not to recognize a consummate artistic power. The dazzling display of true wit and fancy blinds us for the time to the want of that real tenderness and humour which would have softened some hard passages, and given a more enduring charm to the poetry. It has, in short, the merit that belongs to any work of art which expresses in the most finished form the sentiment characteristic of a given social phrase; one deficient in many of the most ennobling influences, but yet one in which the arts of converse represent a very high development of shrewd sense refined into vivid wit.

Leslie Stephen, 1880, Alexander Pope (English Men of Letters),
pp. 39, 40, 42

The Rape of the Lock is very witty, but through it all don't you mark the sneer of the contemptuous, unmanly little wit, the crooked dandy? He jibes among his compliments; and I do not wonder that Mistress Arabella Fermor was not conciliated by his long-drawn cleverness and polished lines.

Andrew Lang, 1889, *Letters on Literature,* p. 152

The Temple of Fame (1714)

It was probably the similarity of taste that induced Pope when young to imitate several of the pieces of Chaucer, and in particular to write his *Temple of Fame,* one of the noblest, although one of the earliest of his productions. That the hint of the piece is taken from Chaucer's *House of Fame,* is sufficiently obvious, yet the design is greatly altered, and the descriptions, and many of the particular thoughts, are his own; notwithstanding which, such is the coincidence and happy union of the work with its prototype, that it is almost impossible to distinguish those portions which are originally Pope's, from those for which he has been indebted to Chaucer.

William Roscoe, 1824-47, ed., *The Works of Alexander Pope,*
vol. II, p. xiv

Pope, who reproduced parts of the *House of Fame,* in a loose paraphrase, in attempting to improve the construction of Chaucer's work, only mutilated it.

Adolphus William Ward, 1880, *Chaucer (English Men
of Letters),* p. 96

Homer's Iliad (1715-20)

I am pleased beyond measure with your design of translating Homer. The trials you have already made and published on some parts of that author have shown that you are equal to so great a task; and you may therefore depend upon the utmost services I can do in promoting this work, or anything that may be for your service.

George Granville (Lord Lansdown), 1713,
Letter to Alexander Pope, Oct. 21

I borrowed your Homer from the bishop, (mine is not yet landed), and read it out in two evenings. If it pleases others as well as me, you have got your end in profit and reputation: yet I am angry at some bad rhymes and triplets; and pray in your next do not let me have so many unjustifiable rhymes to war, and gods. I tell you all the faults I know, only in one or two places you are a little too obscure, but I expected you to be so in one or two-and-twenty. . . . Your notes are perfectly good, and so are your preface and essay.

Jonathan Swift, 1715, *Letter to Pope,* June 28

The *Iliad* took me up six years; and during that time, and particularly the first part of it, I was often under great pain and apprehension. Though I conquered the thoughts of it in the day, they would frighten me in the night.—I sometimes, still, even dream of being engaged in that translation; and got about half way through it: and being embarrassed and under dread of never completing it.

Alexander Pope, 1742-43, Spence's Anecdotes, ed. Singer, p. 214

They can have no conception of his [Homer's] manner, who are acquainted with him in Mr. Pope's translation only. An excellent poetical performance that translation is, and faithful in the main to the original. In some places, it may be thought to have even improved Homer. It has certainly softened some of his rudenesses, and added delicacy and grace to some of his sentiments. But withal, it is no other than Homer modernized. In the midst of the elegance and luxuriancy of Mr. Pope's language, we lose sight of the old bard's simplicity.

Hugh Blair, 1783, Lectures on Rhetoric and Belles-Lettres,
ed. Mills, Lecture XLIII

Pope's translation is a portrait endowed with every merit, excepting that of likeness to the original. The verses of Pope accustomed my ear to the sound of poetic harmony.

Edward Gibbon, 1794, Memoirs of My Life and Writings

To what a low state knowledge of the most obvious and important phenomena had sunk, is evident from the style in which Dryden has executed a description of Night in one of his Tragedies, and Pope his translation of the celebrated moonlight scene in the *Iliad*. A blind man, in the habit of attending accurately to descriptions casually dropped from the lips of those around him, might easily depict these appearances with more truth. Dryden's lines are vague, bombastic, and senseless; those of Pope, though he had Homer to guide him, are throughout false and contradictory. The verses of Dryden, once highly celebrated, are forgotten; those of Pope still retain their hold upon public estimation.—nay, there is not a passage of descriptive poetry, which at this day finds so many and such ardent admirers. Strange to think of an enthusiast, as may have been the case with thousands, reciting those verses under the cope of a moonlight sky, without having his raptures in the least disturbed by a suspicion of their absurdity!

William Wordsworth, 1815, Poetry as a Study

In the course of one of my lectures, I had occasion to point out the almost faultless position and choice of words in Pope's original compositions, particularly in his Satires, and Moral Essays, for the purpose of comparing them with his translation of Homer, which I do not stand alone in regarding as the main source of our pseudo-poetic diction.

Samuel Taylor Coleridge, 1817, *Biographia Literaria*

One hundred and seventy years have since gone by, and many attempts have been made by writers of distinction to supply the admitted deficiencies in Pope's work. Yet his translation of the *Iliad* occupies a position in literature which no other has ever approached. It is the one poem of the kind that has obtained a reputation beyond the limits of the country in the language of which it is written, and the only one that has fascinated the imagination of the unlearned. Many an English reader, to whom the Greek was literally a dead language, has followed through it the action of the Iliad with a livelier interest than that of *The Faery Queen* or of *Paradise Lost*. The descriptions of the single combats and the funeral games have delighted many a schoolboy, who has perhaps revolted with an equally intense abhorrence from the syntax of the original.

William John Courthope, 1889, *The Life of Alexander Pope,*
Works, ed. Elwin and Courthope, vol. V, p. 162

We may add that neither its false glitter nor Pope's inability—shared in great measure with every translator—to catch the spirit of the original, can conceal the sustained power of this brilliant work. Its merit is the more wonderful since the poet's knowledge of Greek was extremely meagre, and he is said to have been constantly indebted to earlier translations. Gibbon said that his "Homer" had every merit except that of faithfulness to the original; and Pope, could he have heard it, might well have been satisfied with the verdict of Gray, a great scholar as well as a great poet, that no other version would ever equal his. All that has been hitherto said with regard to Pope and Homer relates to his version of the *Iliad*. On that he expended his best powers, and on that it is evident he bestowed infinite pains.

John Dennis, 1894, *The Age of Pope,* p. 37

He could not have turned out a true translation, indeed, when his lack of Greek learning threw him back upon French and Latin versions, upon earlier English translations, or upon assistance of more scholarly but less poetic friends. He worked from a Homer minus Homer's force and freedom, a Homer ornamented with epigrams to suit the taste of the age. His tools were a settled diction and a ready-made style, regular, neat, and terse. The result could never have been Homer, but it is an English poem of sustained

vivacity and emphasis, a fine epic as epics went in the days of Anne—
"A very pretty poem, Mr. Pope, but not Homer."

> James Warwick Price, 1896, ed., *The Iliad of Homer,*
> Books i, vi, xxii and xxiv, Introduction, p. 11

The Odyssey (1725)

He made over 3500£. after paying Broome 500£. (including 100£. for
notes) and Fenton 200£.—that is, 50£. a book. The rate of pay was as
high as the work was worth, and as much as it would fetch in the open
market. The large sum was entirely due to Pope's reputation, though obtained, so far as the true authorship was concealed upon something like
false pretences. Still, we could have wished that he had been a little more
liberal with his share of the plunder. . . . The shares of the three colleagues
in The *Odyssey* are not to be easily distinguished by internal evidence. On
trying the experiment by a cursory reading, I confess (though a critic does
not willingly admit his fallibility) that I took some of Broome's work for
Pope's, and, though closer study or an acuter perception might discriminate
more accurately, I do not think that the distinction would be easy. This
may be taken to confirm the common theory that Pope's versification was
a mere mechanical trick. Without admitting this, it must be admitted that
the external characteristics of his manner were easily caught; and that it
was not hard for a clever versifier to produce something closely resembling
his inferior work, especially when following the same original. But it may
be added that Pope's *Odyssey* was really inferior to the *Iliad,* both because
his declamatory style is more out of place in its romantic narrative, and
because he was weary and languid, and glad to turn his fame to account
without more labour than necessary.

> Leslie Stephen, 1880, *Alexander Pope (English Men of Letters),*
> pp. 79, 80

Eloisa to Abelard (1717)

The harmony of numbers in this poem is very fine. It is rather drawn out to
too tedious a length, although the passions vary with great judgment. It
may be considered as superior to anything in the epistolary way; and the
many translations which have been made of it into the modern languages
are in some measure a proof of this.

> Oliver Goldsmith, 1767, *The Beauties of English Poetry*

I read it again, and am bored: this is not as it ought to be; but, in spite of
myself, I yawn, and I open the original letters of Eloisa to find the cause of

my weariness. . . Declamation and commonplace; she sends Abelard discourses on love and the liberty which it demands, on the cloister and peaceful life which it affords, on writing and the advantages of the post. Antitheses and contrasts, she forwards them to Abelard by the dozen; a contrast between the convent illuminated by his presence and desolate by his absence, between the tranquillity of the pure nun and the anxiety of the culpable nun, between the dream of human happiness and the dream of divine happiness. In fine, it is a *bravura* with contrasts of *forte* and *piano,* variations and change to key. Eloisa makes the most of her theme, and sets herself to crowd into it all the powers and effects of her voice. Admire the *crescendo,* the shakes by which she ends her brilliant *morceaux.* . . Observe the noise of the big drum, I mean the grand contrivances, for so may be called all that a person says who wishes to rave and cannot. . . . This kind of poetry resembles cookery; neither heart nor genius is necessary to produce it, but a light hand, an attentive eye, and a cultivated taste.

> H. A. Taine, 1871, *History of English Literature,*
> tr. Van Laun, vol. II, bk. iii, ch. vii, pp. 200, 201, 202

A mystery surrounds the *Elegy*—we do not know the circumstances by which it was conceived; but the warmth of *Eloisa* may be largely explained on purely personal grounds, which fact, of course, robs it of much of its significance as an index to Pope's general taste in poetry. No one who reads Pope's correspondence with Lady Mary can avoid the conclusion that the poet embodied in this *Epistle* much of his own sentimental longings; for Pope's attitude toward the brilliant society woman was certainly more than that of conventional gallantry.

> William Lyon Phelps, 1893, *The Beginnings of the*
> *English Romantic Movement,* p. 24

Edition of Shakespeare (1725)

He [Pope] never valued himself upon it enough to mention it in any letter, poem, or other work whatsoever.

> William Ayre, 1745, *Memoirs of Pope,* vol. II, p. 15

Mr. Pope discharged his duty so well, as to make his editions the best foundation for all future improvements.

> William Warburton, 1747, ed. *Shakspeare,* Preface

Pope, in his edition, undoubtedly did many things wrong, and left many things undone; but let him not be defrauded of his due praise. He was the first that knew, at least the first that told, by what helps the text might be improved. If he inspected the early editions negligently, he taught others to be more accurate. In his preface he expanded with great skill and elegance the character which had been given to Shakespeare by Dryden; and he drew the public attention upon his works, which, though often mentioned, had been little read.

Samuel Johnson, 1779-81, *Pope, Lives of the English Poets*

Pope asserts, that he [Shakespeare] wrote both better and worse than any other man. All the scenes and passages which did not suit the littleness of his taste, he wished to place to the account of interpolating players; and he was in the right road, had his opinion been taken, of mangling Shakspeare in a most disgraceful manner.

Augustus William Schlegel, 1809, *Dramatic Art and Literature,*
tr. Black

This was, perhaps, the first decided failure in any of the publications by Pope. He was deficient in some important requisites for the task he had undertaken. The irksome but necessary duty of collation was indifferently performed; he wanted patience, and he could not command all the early copies. He was not sufficiently read in the literature of Shakspeare's contemporaries, and thus missed many points of illustration confirming or elucidating the text. He also somewhat arbitrarily and unwarrantably altered or suppressed lines and passages, which he conceived to have been interpolated or vitiated by the players and transcribers.

Robert Carruthers, 1853-57, *The Life of Alexander Pope,* p. 231

Rowe was succeeded, as an editor of Shakespeare, by Pope, who published a superb edition, in six volumes, quarto, in 1725. Pope, like most of those authors of eminence in other departments of literature, who have undertaken to regulate the text of Shakespeare, made a very poor editor. He used the quartos somewhat to the advantage, but more to the detriment of his author; foisting into the text that which Shakespeare himself had rejected. He gave us a few good, and several very pretty and plausible conjectural emendations of typographical errors; but he added to these so many which were only exponents of his own conceit and want of kindred appreciation of Shakespeare's genius, that his text, as a whole, is one of the poorest which remain to us.

Richard Grant White, 1854, *Shakespeare's Scholar,* p. 9

Pope had few qualifications for the task, and the venture was a commercial failure. . . . His innovations are numerous, and are derived from "his private sense and conjecture," but they are often plausible and ingenious. He was the first to indicate the place of each new scene, and he improved on Rowe's subdivision of the scenes.

Sidney Lee, 1900, Shakespeare's Life and Works, p. 175

The Dunciad (1728-42)

There is a general outcry against that part of the poem which is thought an abuse on the Duke of Chandos. Other parts are quarrelled with as obscure and inharmonious; and I am told that there is an advertisement that promises a publication of Mr. Pope's Epistle verified. . . . I am surprised Mr. Pope is not weary of making enemies.

Patrick Delany, 1731, Letter to Sir Thomas Hanmer, Dec. 23,
Hanmer's Correspondence, p. 217

On the 12th of March, 1729, at St. James's, that poem was presented to the King and Queen (who had before been pleased to read it) by the Right Honourable Sir Robert Walpole: and some days after the whole impression was taken and dispersed by several noblemen and persons of the first distinction. It is certainly a true observation, that no people are so impatient of censure as those who are the greatest slanderers: which was wonderfully exemplified on this occasion. On the day the book was first vended, a crowd of authors besieged the shop; entreaties, advices, threats of law, and battery, nay, cries of treason were all employed, to hinder the coming out of the *Dunciad;* on the other side, the booksellers and hawkers made as great efforts to procure it: what could a few poor authors do against so great a majority as the public? There was no stopping a torrent with a finger, so out it came. Some false editions of the book having an owl in their frontispiece, the true one, to distinguish it, fixed in its stead an ass laden with authors. Then another surreptitious one being printed with the same ass, the new edition in octavo returned for distinction to the owl again. Hence arose a great contest of booksellers against booksellers, and advertisements against advertisements; some recommended the "Edition of the Owl," and others the "Edition of the Ass"; by which names they came to be distinguished, to the great honour also of the gentlemen of the *Dunciad.*

Richard Savage, 1732, Account of the Dunciad

The Dunciad cost me as much pains as anything I ever wrote.

Alexander Pope, 1734-36, Spence's Anecdotes, ed. Singer, p. 107

It was a victory over a parcel of poor wretches, whom it was almost co-wardice to conquer. A man might as well triumph for having killed so many flies that offended him. Could he have let them alone by this time, poor souls! they had all been buried in oblivion.

Colley Cibber, 1742, *Letter to Mr. Pope*, July 7, p. 12

The fifth volume contains a correcter and completer edition of the *Dunciad* than hath been hitherto published, of which, at present, I have only this further to add, that it was at my request he laid the plan of a fourth book. I often told him, it was a pity so fine a poem should remain disgraced by the meanness of its subject, the most insignificant of all dunces, — bad rhymers and malevolent cavillers; that he ought to raise and ennoble it by pointing his satire against the most pernicious of all,—minute philosophers and free-thinkers. I imagined, too, it was for the interest of religion to have it known, that so great a genius had a due abhorrence of these pests of virtue and society. He came readily into my opinion; but, at the same time, told me it would create him many enemies. He was not mistaken, for though the terror of his pen kept them for some time in respect, yet on his death they rose with unrestrained fury in numerous coffee-house tales, and Grub Street libels. The plan of this admirable satire was artfully contrived to show, that the follies and defects of a fashionable education naturally led to, and necessarily ended in, freethinking, with design to point out the only remedy adequate to so destructive an evil.

William Warburton, 1751, ed. *Pope's Works*

He (Dryden) died, nevertheless, in a good old age, possessed of the king-dom of wit, and was succeeded by king Alexander, surnamed Pope. This prince enjoyed the crown many years, and is thought to have stretched the prerogative much farther than his predecessor: he is said to have been extremely jealous of the affections of his subjects, and to have employed various spies, by whom if he was informed of the least suggestion against his title, he never failed of branding the accused person with the word *dunce* on his forehead in broad letters; after which the unhappy culprit was oblig-ed to lay by his pen forever, for no bookseller would venture to print a word that he wrote. He did indeed put a total restraint upon the liberty of the press; for no person durst read anything which was writ without his license and approbation; and this license he granted only to four during his reign, namely, to the celebrated Dr. Swift, to the ingenious Dr. Young, to Dr. Arbuthnot, and to one Mr. Gay, four of his principal courtiers and favourites. But, without diving any deeper into his character, we must allow that king Alexander had great merit as a writer, and his title to the kingdom of wit was better founded, at least, than his enemies have pretended.

Henry Fielding, 1752, *Covent Garden Journal,* No. 23, March 21

The Dunciad is blemished by the offensive images of the games; but the poetry appears to me admirable; and, though the fourth book has obscurities, I prefer it to the three others: it has descriptions not surpassed by any poet that ever existed, and which surely a writer merely ingenious will never equal. The lines on Italy, on Venice, on Convents, have all the grace for which I contend as distinct from poetry, though united with the most beautiful.

Horace Walpole, 1785, Letter to J. Pinkerton, June 26

The condition of authorship began to fall from the days of *The Dunciad:* and I believe in my heart that much of that obloquy which has since pursued our calling was occasioned by Pope's libels and wicked wit. Everybody read those. Everybody was familiarised with the idea of the poor devil author. The manner is so captivating, that young authors practise it, and begin their career with satire. It is so easy to write, and so pleasant to read! to fire a shot that makes a giant wince, perhaps; and fancy one's self his conqueror. It is easy to shoot—but not as Pope did—the shafts of his satire rise sublimely.

William Makepeace Thackeray, 1853, The English Humourists
of the Eighteenth Century

However great his merit in expression, I think it impossible that a true poet could have written such a satire as *The Dunciad,* which is even nastier than it is witty. It is filthy even in a filthy age, and Swift himself could not have gone beyond some parts of it. One's mind needs to be sprinkled with some disinfecting fluid after reading it. I do not remember that any other poet ever made poverty a crime. And it is wholly without discrimination. De Foe is set in the pillory forever; and George Wither, the author of that charming poem, *Fair Virtue,* classed among the dunces. And was it not in this age that loose Dick Steele paid his wife the finest compliment ever paid to woman, when he said "that to love her was a liberal education?"

James Russell Lowell, 1871-90, Pope, Prose Works,
Riverside ed., vol. IV, p. 49

Moral Essays (1731-35)

In the "Moral Poem," I had written an address to our Saviour; imitated from Lucretius's compliment to Epicurus: but omitted it by the advice of Dean Berkley.—One of our priests, who are more narrow-minded than yours, made a less sensible objection to the *Epistle on Happiness:* he was very angry that there was nothing said in it of our eternal happiness hereafter, though my subject was expressly to treat only of the state of man here.

Alexander Pope, 1734-36, *Spence's Anecdotes,* ed. Singer, p. 107

These Epistles, in which Poetry has condescended to become the handmaid of Philosophy, to decorate, and set her off to advantage, are written with a spirit and vivacity not exceeded by any production of the kind in any country or language. Their nearest prototypes are the Epistles of Horace and Boileau, and the Satires of Ariosto and Bentivoglio, to none of which they are inferior. In our own language they may be considered as the first attempt to unite sound sense and deep research with the lighter graces of elegant composition, and to promote the cause of virtue and morality by conveying the purest precepts in the most impressive language, and illustrating them by examples which strike the imagination with all the force of reality. As they had in this country no example, so they have as yet had no rival; nor until a genius shall arise that shall unite in himself, in an equal degree, the various endowments by which their author was distinguished, is it likely they ever will.

William Roscoe, 1824-47, ed., *The Works of Alexander Pope,*
vol. IV, p. 170

Warton preferred *Windsor Forest* and *Eloisa* to the *Moral Essays* because they belonged to a higher kind of poetry. Posterity likes the *Moral Essays* better because they are better of their kind. They were the natural fruit of Pope's genius and of his time, while the others were artificial. We can go to Wordsworth for nature, to Byron for passion, and to a score of poets for both, but Pope remains unrivaled in his peculiar field. In other words, we value what is characteristic in the artist; the one thing which he does best, the precise thing which he can do and no one else can.

Henry A. Beers, 1898, *A History of English Romanticism
in the Eighteenth Century,* p. 220

An Essay on Man (1733-34)

If I had undertaken to exemplify Pope's felicity of composition before a rigid critic, I should not select the *Essay on Man,* for it contains more lines unsuccessfully laboured, more harshness of diction, more thoughts imperfectly expressed, more levity without elegance, and more heaviness without strength, than will easily be found in all his other works.

Samuel Johnson, 1779-81, *Pope, Lives of the English Poets*

Dr. Joseph Warton, talking last night at Sir Joshua Reynold's of Pope's *Essay on Man,* said that much of his system was borrowed from King's book on the *Origin of Evil.* This was first published in Dublin, in Latin, in 1704, and translated into English by Bishop Law, in 1731, not very long before the *Essay on Man* was written. Dr. Warton mentioned that Lord Lyttleton told him that he lived much with Pope at that time, and that Pope was then undoubtedly a Free-thinker; though he afterwards either changed his opinion or thought it prudent to adopt Warburton's explanation and comment, who saw his meaning as he chose to express it, "better than he did himself." Dr. Warton forbore to state this in his "Essay on Pope."

Edmond Malone, 1789, Jan. 18, Life by Prior, p. 149

Various and discordant have been the opinions of critics and commentators respecting this celebrated performance. That it possesses a distinguished share of poetic excellence none, however, have yet ventured to deny. M. Voltaire goes so far as to affirm, that to this Essay Pope stands indebted for that pre-eminence which he ascribes to him, when compared with his illustrious predecessor Dryden. But that Pope is actually entitled to this claim of superiority is, at least, very problematical; and if it was allowed, the *Rape of the Lock,* the *Epistle of Eloise,* the *Eclogue of the Messiah,* and some other pieces that might be mentioned, would generally be considered as affording a better foundation for this claim to rest upon than the *Essay on Man,* in which poetry holds a subordinate place; and in which it is merely employed, though with the happiest success, to embellish and illustrate the most abstruse lessons of philosophy. . . . It is well known that the general plan of this Essay was originally framed by Lord Bolingbroke, and it is universally believed that Pope was ignorant of the ultimate, and indeed the obvious tendency of his own arguments.

W. Belsham, 1799, Essays Philosophical and Moral,
Historical and Literary, vol. I, pp. 346, 347

Bolingbroke had himself sufficient vigor of imagination and brilliancy of style to have written a prose essay which might engage the attention of persons fond of moral and philosophical speculation; but by judiciously borrowing the Muse of Pope, he has diffused his sentiments on these topics through all classes and ages of English literature; has made them familiar to our early and our mature conceptions; and stamped them in indelible characters on the language of the country. This conversion of a dry and argumentative subject into a splendid and popular one, is a miracle of the poetic art; and an inquiry into the means by which it has been effected will probably go far into the elucidation of that *essential character* of poetical composition which distinguishes it from prose.

John Aikin, 1820, Observations on Pope's Essay on Man

The success of this enterprise was astonishing. Be the philosophy what and whose it may, the poem revived to the latest age of poetry the phenomenon of the first, when precept and maxim were modulated into verse, that they might write themselves in every brain, and live upon every tongue. The spirit and sweetness of the verse, the lucid and vivid expressions, the pregnant brevity of the meanings, the marrying of ardent and lofty poetical imaginings to moral sentiments and reflections, of which every bosom is the birth-home, the pious will of the argument, which humbles the proud and rebellious human intellect under the absolute rectitude and benevolence of the Deity—nor, least of all, the pleasure of receiving easily, as in a familiar speech, thoughts that *were* high, and *might be* abstruse, that, at all events, wore a profound and philosophical air—with strokes intervening of a now playful, now piercing, but always adroit wit—and with touches, here and there strewn between, of natural painting, and of apt unsought pathos— these numerous and excellent qualifications met upon the subject of all subjects nearest to all—MAN—speedily made the first great, original, serious writing of Pope a text-book and a manual for its branch of ethico-theosophy, in every house where there were books in England. These powerful excellences of this great poem did more. They inwove its terse, vigorous, clear, significant, wise, loving, noble, beautiful, and musical sentences—east, west, north, south,—with all memories, the mature and the immature—even as in that old brave day of the world or ever books were.

John Wilson, 1845, "Dryden and Pope," Blackwood's Magazine

If the question were asked, What ought to have been the best among Pope's poems? most people would answer, the *Essay on Man*. If the question were asked, what is the worst? all people of judgment would say, the *Essay on Man*. Whilst yet in its rudiments, this poem claimed the first place by the promise of its subject; when finished, by the utter failure of its execution, it fell into the last.

Thomas DeQuincey, 1848-58, The Poetry of Pope, Works,
ed. Masson, vol. XI, p. 86

Every word is effective: every passage must be read slowly; every epithet is an epitome; a more condensed style was never written.

H. A. Taine, 1871, History of English Literature,
tr. Van Laun, Vol. II, bk. iii, ch. vii, p. 210

His attempt to "vindicate the ways of God to man" is confused and contradictory, and no modern reader, perplexed with the mystery of existence, is likely to gain aid from Pope. Nominally a Roman Catholic, and in reality a deist, apart from poetry he does not seem to have had strong convictions on any subject, and was content to be swayed by the opinions current in society. In undertaking to write an ethical work like the *Essay* his ambition was greater than his strength, yet if Pope's philosophy does not "find" us, to use Coleridge's phrase, it did appeal to a large number of minds in his own day, and had not lost its popularity at a later period. The poem has been frequently translated into French, into Italian, and into German; it was pronounced by Voltaire to be the most useful and sublime didactic poem ever written in any language; it was admired by Kant and quoted in his lectures; and it received high praise from the Scotch philosopher, Dugald Stewart. The charm of poetical expression is lost or nearly lost in translations, and while the sense may be retained the aroma of the verse is gone. The popularity of the *Essay* abroad is therefore not easily to be accounted for, unless we accept the theory that the shallow creed on which it is based suited an age less earnest than our own.

John Dennis, 1894, *The Age of Pope,* p. 52

Imitations of Horace (1737)

I have perused the last lampoon of your ingenious friend, and am not surprised you did not find me out under the name of Sappho, because there is nothing I ever heard in our characters and circumstances to make a parallel; but as the town (except you, who know better) generally suppose Pope means me, whenever he mentions that name, I cannot help taking notice of the horrible malice he bears against the lady signified by that name, which appears to be irritated by supposing her writer of the Verses to the Imitator of Horace.

Lary Mary Wortley Montagu, 1735, *Letter to Arbuthnot,* Jan. 3

Few portions of the poetry of Pope have been more popular than these *Imitations of Horace,* with their accompanying Prologue and Epilogue. Though the satire be often too severe, and too much tinged with party rancour, or private spleen, the allusions are so apt, and the parallel passages so happy, that every reader must feel gratified in comparing the two poets, and in remarking the exquisite art and address of the *English* satirist, who has never in any instance servilely copied his original, but has merely pursued the train of thought which Horace had suggested; and in so doing has ably filled up the outline which is sometimes but faintly traced on the page of the Roman classic. The Prologue and Epilogue, especially the latter, are still more poignant and keen than the Imitations, to which, perhaps, they were at first, with no great propriety, annexed.

Nathan Drake, 1804, *Essays Illustrative of the Tatler,*
Spectator and Guardian, vol. III, p. 103

In these Pope's verse is as perfect as it is anywhere, and his subject is borrowed, not from his commonplace book, but from his own experiences. He wants the careless ease, the variety, the unemphatic grace of Horace, it is true. But he has many of the qualities of his master, and it is probable that only when men weary of hearing how Horace strolled down the Sacred Way and met an intolerable Bore—only then, or perhaps a little earlier, will they cease to hearken how Alexander Pope bade John Searle bar the door at Twickenham against the inroads of Bedlam and Parnassus.

Austin Dobson, 1888, "Alexander Pope," *Scribner's Magazine,*
vol. 3, p. 547

LETTERS

I have read the collection of letters you mention and was delighted with nothing more than that air of sincerity, those professions of esteem and respect, and that deference paid to his friend's judgement in poetry which I have sometimes seen expressed to others, and I doubt not with the same cordial affection. If they are read in that light, they will be very entertaining and useful in the present age; but in the next, Cicero, Pliny, and Voiture may regain their reputation.

Elijah Fenton, 1726, *Letter to Broome,* Sept.

There cannot be a stronger proof of his being capable of any action for the sake of gain than publishing his literary correspondence, which lays open such a mixture of dulness and iniquity, that one would imagine it visible even to his most passionate admirers.

Lady Mary Wortley Montagu, 1752, *Letter to the Countess*
of Bute, June 23

No one can read them without feeling that they were written for more eyes than those of his correspondents. There is a laboured smartness, a constant exhibition of fine sentiment, which is strained and unnatural. His repeated deprecation of motives of aggrandizement argues "a thinking too precisely" on the very subject; and no man whose chief ambition was to gain a few friends would so habitually proclaim it. These tender and delicate aspirations live in the secret places of the heart. . . . True sentiment is modest.

Henry Theodore Tuckerman, 1846, *Thoughts on the Poets,*
Third ed., p. 76

Every examination into the history of the letters was slight before Mr. Dilke engaged into the laborious task. His familiarity with the books, pamphlets and periodicals of the time could not be exceeded, and his doubts once awakened he accepted nothing upon trust. With an immense amount of research and skill he proceeded to track Pope through his tortuous courses. He laid bare the ramifications of the plot against Curll, which was only known in a few of its prominent particulars. He detected, what none of the editors and biographers had perceived, base manœuvres and deceit which accompanied the publication of the *Letters to and from Dr. Swift*. He was originally put upon his investigations by the manuscript collection of Pope's letters to Caryll and these revealed a new set of frauds in the evidence they supplied of letters converted into a fictitious correspondence. His inclination was to favour Pope whenever there was an opening for a liberal interpretation, and it was not from hostitlity that he exposed the network of fraud, and brought out the dark traits of a dishonourable disposition with new and terrible force. He printed his discoveries in the *Athenæum,* and after studying the facts afresh by the light of his essays, I am compelled to adopt his conclusions. The evidence, upon which they rest is often circumstantial and intricate, and cannot be followed to the end without steady attention, and some trial of patience.

> Whitwell Elwin, 1871, ed., *The Works of Alexander Pope,*
> vol. I, Introduction, p. xxvii

GENERAL

I am always highly delighted with the discovery of any rising genius among my countrymen. For this reason I have read over, with great pleasure, the late miscellany published by Mr. Pope, in which there are many excellent compositions of that ingenious gentleman.

> Joseph Addison, 1712, *The Spectator,* No. 523, Oct. 30

He is, in my opinion, the most elegant, the most correct poet; and at the same time the most harmonious (a circumstance which redounds very much to the honour of this muse) that *England* ever gave birth to. He has mellowed the harsh sounds of the *English* trumpet to the soft accents of the flute. His compositions may be easily translated, because they are vastly clear and perspicuous; besides, most of his subjects are general, and relative to all nations.

> François Marie Arouet Voltaire, 1732, *Letters Concerning the*
> *English Nation,* p. 170

Pope's talent lay remarkably in what one may naturally enough term the condensation of thoughts. I think no English poet ever brought so much sense into the same number of lines with equal smoothness, ease, and poetical beauty. Let him who doubts of this peruse the *Essay on Man* with attention.

William Shenstone, 1763, Essays on Men and Manners

Pope is a satirist, and a moralist, and a wit, and a critic, and a fine writer, much more than he is a poet. He has all the delicacies and proprieties and felicities of diction—but he has not a great deal of fancy, and scarcely ever touches any of the greater passions. He is much the best, we think, of the classical Continental school; but he is not to be compared with the masters —nor with the pupils—of that Old English one from which there had been so lamentable an apostasy. There are no pictures of nature or of simple emotion in all his writings. He is the poet of town life, and of high life, and of literary life; and seems so much afraid of incurring ridicule by the display of natural feeling or unregulated fancy, that it is difficult not to imagine that he would have thought such ridicule very well directed.

Francis, Lord Jeffrey, 1819-44, Contributions to the Edinburgh Review,
vol. 2, p. 292

Neither time, nor distance, nor grief, nor age can ever diminish my veneration for him, who is the great moral poet of all times, of all climes, of all feelings, and of all stages of existence. The delight of my boyhood, the study of my manhood, perhaps (if allowed to me to attain it) he may be the consolation of my age. His poetry is the Book of Life. Without canting, and yet without neglecting religion, he has assembled all that a good and great man can gather together of moral wisdom clothed in consummate beauty.

Lord Byron, 1821, A Second Letter on Bowles's Strictures
on the Life and Writings of Pope

Pope formed his style on that of Dryden. He has less enthusiasm, less majesty, less force of thought, than his great model, but he has more delicacy of feeling, more refinement and more correctness. If he never soars to the height which Dryden reached when "the full burst of inspiration came," he never sinks so low as his master ofttimes fell. While soothed by the exquisitely sweet, but somewhat monotonous couplets of Pope, we occasionally long for the bolder and more varied music of Dryden's lines.

Alexander Dyce, 1831-51, Memoir of Pope

He was, some one we think has said, the sort of a person we cannot even conceive existing in a barbarous age. His subject was not life at large, but fashionable life. He described the society in which he was thrown, the people among whom he lived; his mind was a hoard of small maxims, a quintessence of petty observations. When he described character, he described it, not dramatically nor as it is in itself, but observantly and from without; calling up in the mind not so much a vivid conception of the man—of the real, corporeal, substantial being—as an idea of the idea which a metaphysical bystander might refine and excruciate concerning him. Society in Pope is scarcely a society of people, but of pretty little atoms, colored and painted with hoops or in coats,—a miniature of metaphysics, a puppet-show of sylphs. He elucidates the doctrine that the tendency of civilized poetry is towards an analytic sketch of the existing civilization.

Walter Bagehot, 1855, "William Cowper," Works,
ed. Morgan, vol. I, p. 424

I hold Pope to be the most perfect representative we have, since Chaucer, of the true English mind; and I think *The Dunciad* is the most absolutely chiselled and monumental work "exacted" in our country. You will find, as you study Pope, that he has expressed for you, in the strictest language and within the briefest limits, every law of art, of criticism, of economy, of policy, and, finally, of a benevolence, humble, rational, and resigned, contented with its allotted share of life, and trusting the problem of its salvation to Him in whose hands lies that of the universe.

John Ruskin, 1870, Lectures on Art, Lecture III

The mention of Pope reminds me that he is the traditional exemplar of the didactic heresy, so much so that the question is still mooted whether he was a poet at all. As to this, one can give only his own impression, and my adverse view has somewhat changed,—possibly because we grow more sententious with advancing years. Considering the man with his time, I think Pope was a poet; one whose wit and reason exceeded his lyrical feeling, but still a poet of no mean degree. Assuredly he was a force in his century, and one not even then wholly spent. His didacticism was inherent in the stiff, vicious, Gallic drum-beat of his artificial style—so falsely called "classical," so opposed to the true and live method of the antique—rather than in his genius and quality. It is impossible that one with so marked a poetic temperament, and using verse withal as almost his sole mode of expression, should not have been a poet. In the manner of his time, how far above his rivals!

Edmund Clarence Stedman, 1892, The Nature and Elements
of Poetry, p. 213

JONATHAN SWIFT
1667-1745

Born, in Dublin, 30 Nov. 1667. At school at Kilkenny, 1673-82. Matric.,
Trin. Coll., Dublin, as Pensioner, 24 April 1682; B. A. 1686. Emigrated to
England, and joined his mother at Leicester, 1688. Lived in house of Sir
W. Temple, at Moor Park, as his Secretary, and Tutor to Esther Johnson,
1689-92. Entered at Hart Hall, Oxford, 14 June 1692; M. A., 5 July
1692. Ordained Deacon, 18 Oct. 1694; Priest, 13 Jan. 1695. Prebend of
Kilroot, Ireland, 1695. Returned to Moor Park, 1696-98. To Dublin, as
Chaplain to Earl of Berkeley, 1699; Rector of Agher, and Vicar of Laracor
and Rathbeggan, March 1699. Prebend of Dunlavin, 1700. Returned to
England with Earl of Berkeley, 1701. B. D. and D. D., Dublin, 1702.
Subsequent life spent partly in Ireland, partly in England. Edited *The
Examiner*, Nov. 1710 to June 1711. Founded the Brothers' Club, 1711;
the Scriblerus Club, 1712. Dean of St. Patrick's, 23 Feb. 1713. Friend-
ship with Esther Johnson ("Stella") begun, 1700. Friendship with Esther
Vanhomrigh ("Vanessa") begun, 1710; she died, 1723. Contributed to
London, 1734. Mind began to give away, 1737. Died, in Dublin, 19 Oct.
1745. Buried in St. Patrick's Cathedral. WORKS: *A Discourse of the
Contests . . . between the Nobles and the Commons, etc.* (anon.), 1701;
A Tale of a Tub (anon.), 1704; *Predictions* (under pseud.: "Isaac Bickerstaff"), 1707; *Vindication* of preceding, 1709; *Meditation upon a Broom-
stick* (anon.), 1710; *A New Journey to Paris* (under pseud. "Sieur Du
Baudrier"), 1711; *Miscellanies*, 1711; *The Conduct of the Allies* (anon.),
1711; *Some Advice . . . to the Members of the October Club* (anon.),
1712; *Letter to the Lord High Treasurer*, 1712; *A Proposal for Correcting . . . the English Tongue*, 1721; *Some Reasons to prove that no person
is obliged, by his principles as a Whig, to oppose Her Majesty* (anon.),
1712; *The Publick Spirit of the Whigs* (anon.), (1714); *A Preface to the
B—p of S—r—m's. Introduction* (under pseud. "Gregory Misosarum"),
1713; *The Conduct of the Purse of Ireland*, 1714; *Essays*, 1714; *The Art
of Punning*, 1719; *Proposal for the Universal Use of Irish Manufacturers*
(anon.), 1720; *Defence of English Commodities*, 1720; *Right of Prece-
dence* (anon.), 1720; *The Wonderful Wonder of Wonders* (anon.),
(1720?); *Letter of Advice to a Young Poet*, 1721; *Letter to a Gentleman
lately entered into Holy Orders*, 1721; *The Journal* (anon.), 1722; *Letter
from a Lady of Quality* (anon.), 1724; *Two Letters under pseud. "M. B.
Drapier,"* 1724; *Gulliver's Travels* (anon.), 1726; *Cadenus and Vanessa*
(anon.), 1726; *The Intelligencer* (with Sheridan), 1729; *The Journal of a
Modern Lady* (anon.), 1729; *Proposal for Preventing the Children of the
Poor from Being a Burthen, etc."* (anon.), 1730; *The Presbyterians' plea
. . . examined* (anon.), 1731; *The Advantages proposed by repealing the
Sacramental Test, etc.*, 1732; *On Poetry* (anon.), 1733; *Scheme for a
Hospital for Incurables* (anon.), 1733; *Poems on Several Occasions*, 1734;
Proposals for erecting a Protestant Nunnery in the City of Dublin (anon.),
1736; *The Beast's Confession to the Priest*, 1738; *Complete Collection of
Genteel and Ingenious Conversation* (under pseud. "Simon Wagstaff"),
1738; *An Imitation of the Sixth Satire of the Second Book of Horace,*

1738; *Verses on the Death of Dr. Swift, written by himself,* 1739; *Some Free Thoughts upon the Present State of Affairs* (anon.), 1741; *Literary Correspondence,* 1741; *Three Sermons,* 1744; *The Difficulty of Knowing One's Self,* 1745. (Also a number of small controversial tracts, anonymous ballads printed on single sheets, etc.) POSTHUMOUS: *Brotherly Love,* 1754; *History of the Four Last Years of the Queen,* 1758; *Letters* (3 vols.), 1767; *Letters* (6 vols.), 1761-69; *Sermons* (1790?). He *edited* Sir W. Temple's *Letters,* 1700; Sir W. Temple's *Works,* 1720; Arbuthnot and Pope's *Miscellaneous Works,* 1742. COLLECTED WORKS: ed. by Sir Walter Scott (19 vols.), 1814. *Life:* by H. Craik, 1882; by J. Churton Collins, 1895.

R. Farquharson Sharp, 1897, *A Dictionary of English Authors,* p. 272

SEE: *Prose Works,* ed. Herbert Davis, 1937-59, 14 v. (Shakespeare Head Edition); *Poems,* ed. Harold Williams, 1937, rev. 1958, 3 v.; *Journal to Stella,* ed. Harold Williams, 1948, 2 v.; *Correspondence,* ed. Harold Williams, 1964-65, 5 v.; Ricardo Quintana, *The Mind and Art of Jonathan Swift,* 1936, repr. 1953; Herbert Davis, *The Satires of Jonathan Swift,* 1947; Irvin Ehrenpreis, *Swift: The Man, His Works and The Age, 1963* (Vol. I); Edward W. Rosenheim, Jr., *Swift and the Satirist's Art,* 1963; Milton Voigt, *Swift and The Twentieth Century,* 1964; also see *Gulliver's Travels,* ed. Harold Williams, 1926; A. E. Case, *Four Essays on Gulliver's Travels,* 1945.

PERSONAL

Now, I know a learned man at this time, an orator in the Latin, a walking Index of books, who has all the libraries in Europe in his head, from the Vatican at Rome to the learned collection of Doctor Salmon at Fleet Ditch; but he is a cynic in behaviour, a fury in temper, unpolite in conversation, abusive in language, and ungovernable in passion. Is this to be learned? Then may I still be illiterate.

Daniel DeFoe, 1704-13, *The Review*

Swift came into the coffee-house, and had a bow from everybody but me. When I came to the antechamber to wait before prayers Dr. Swift was the principal man of talk and business, and acted as Minister of Requests. He was soliciting the Earl of Arran to speak to his brother, the Duke of Ormond, to get a chaplain's place established in the garrison of Hull for Mr. Fiddes, a clergyman in that neighbourhood, who had lately been in jail, and published sermons to pay fees. He was promising Mr. Thorold to undertake with my Lord Treasurer that according to his petition he should obtain a salary of 200*l* per annum, as minister of the English Church at Rotterdam. He stopped F. Gwynne, Esq., going in with the red bag to the Queen, and told him aloud he had something to say to him from my Lord Treasurer. He talked with the son of Dr. Davenant to be sent abroad, and took out his pocket-book and wrote down several things as *memoranda* to do for him. He turned to the fire, and took out his gold watch, and telling him the time of day, complained it was very late. A gentleman said, "it was too fast." "How can I help it," says the Doctor, "if the courtiers give me a watch that won't go right?" Then he instructed a young nobleman that the best poet in England was Mr. Pope (a Papist), who had begun a translation of Homer into English verse for which, he said, he must have them all subscribe. "For," says he, "the author *shall not* begin to print till I *have* a thousand guineas for him." Lord Treasurer, after leaving the Queen, came through the room, beckoning Dr. Swift to follow him; both went off just before prayers.

White Kennett, Bishop of Peterborough, 1713, *Diary*

Dr. Swift has an odd blunt way, that is mistaken, by strangers, for ill-nature. —'Tis so odd that there's no describing it but by facts.—I'll tell you one that just comes into my head. One evening Gay and I went to see him: you know how intimately we were all acquainted. On our coming in; "Hey-day, gentlemen," says the Doctor, "what's the meaning of this visit? How come you to leave all the great lords, that you are so fond of, to come hither to see a poor Dean?"—Because we would rather see you than any of them.— "Ay, any one that did not know you so well as I do, might believe you. But, since you are come, I must get some supper for you, I suppose?"—No, Doctor, we have supped already.—"Supped already! that's impossible: why, 'tis not eight o'clock yet."—Indeed we have.—"That's very strange: but if you had not supped, I must have got something for you.—Let me see, what should I have had? a couple of lobsters? ay, that would have done very well;—two shillings: tarts; a shilling. But you will drink a glass of wine with me, though you supped so much before your usual time, only to spare my pocket?"—No, we had rather talk with you, than drink with you.— "But if you had supped with me, as in all reason you ought to have done, you must have drank with me.—A bottle of wine; two shillings.—Two and two, is four; and one is five: just two and sixpence a piece. There, Pope, there's half-acrown for you; and there's another for you sir: for I won't save anything by you I am determined." This was all said and done with his usual seriousness on such occasions; and in spite of everything we could say to the contrary, he actually obliged us to take the money.

Alexander Pope, 1728-30, *Spence's Anecdotes,* ed. Singer, p. 15

Violent party-men, who differed in all things besides, agreed in their turn to show particular respect and friendship to this insolent derider of the worship of his country, till at last the reputed writer is not only gone off with impunity, but triumphs in his dignity and preferment.

Sir Richard Blackmore, 1716, *Essays,* vol. I, p. 217

Dean Swift has had a statute of lunacy taken out against him. His madness appears chiefly in most incessant strains of obscenity and swearing.—habits, to which the more sober parts of his life were not absolutely strangers, and to which his writings themselves have some tincture.

Charles Yorke, 1742, Letter to his Brother, June

He assumed more the air of a patron than of a friend. He affected rather to dictate than advise. . . . His hours of walking and reading never varied. His motions were guided by his watch, which was so constantly held in his hand, or placed before him on his table that he seldom deviated many minutes in the daily revolution of his exercises and employments.

John Boyle (Lord Orrery), 1751-53, Remarks on the Life and Writings of Dr. Jonathan Swift, pp. 29, 44

My lord when you consider Swift's singular, peculiar, and most variegated vein of wit, always rightly intended (although not always so rightly directed), delightful in many instances, and salutary even where it is most offensive; when you consider his strict truth; his fortitude in resisting oppression and arbitrary power; his fidelity in friendship; his sincere love and zeal for religion; his uprightness in making right resolutions, and steadiness in adhering to them; . . . his invincible patriotism, even to a country which he did not love; his very various, well-devised, well-judged, and extensive charities throughout his life, and his whole fortune (to say nothing of his wife's) conveyed to the same Christian purposes. . . . To conclude. No man ever deserved better of his country than Swift did of his. A steady, persevering, inflexible friend; a wise, a watchful, and a faithful counsellor, under many severe trials and bitter persecutions, to the manifest hazards both of his liberty and fortune. He lived a blessing, he died a benefactor, and his name will ever live an honour, to Ireland.

Patrick Delany, 1754, Observations on Lord Orrery's Remarks on the Life and Writings of Dr. Jonathan Swift, p. 291

He could not endure to be treated with any sort of familiarity, or that any man living, his three or four acquaintances with whom he corresponded to the last only excepted, should rank himself in the number of his friends.

Deane Swift, 1755, An Essay upon the Life, Writings and Character of Dr. Jonathan Swift, p. 361

I remember as I and others were taking with him an evening walk, about a mile from Dublin, he stopped short; we passed on; but perceiving he did not follow us, I went back, and found him fixed as a statue, and earnestly gazing upward at a noble elm, which in its uppermost branches was much withered and decayed. Pointing at it, he said, "I shall be like that tree, and shall die at the top."

Edward Young, 1759, Letter to Richardson

The person of Swift had not many recommendations. He had a kind of muddy complexion, which, though he washed himself with Oriental scrupulosity, did not look clear. He had a countenance sour and severe, which he seldom softened by any appearance of gaiety. He stubbornly resisted any tendency to laughter. . . . His beneficence was not graced with tenderness of civility; he relieved without pity, and assisted without kindness; so that those who were fed by him could hardly love him. . . . Of Swift's general habits of thinking, if his letters can be supposed to afford any evidence, he was not a man to be either loved or envied. He seems to have wasted life in discontent, by the rage of neglected pride, and the languishment of unsatisfied desire. He is querulous and fastidious, arrogant and malignant; he scarcely speaks of himself but with indignant lamentations, or of others but with insolent superiority when he is gay, and with angry contempt when he is gloomy.

Samuel Johnson, 1779-81, Jonathan Swift,
Lives of the English Poets

Though the greatness of Swift's talents was known to many in private life, and his company and conversation much sought after and admired, yet was his name hitherto little known in the republic letters. The only pieces which he had then published, were *The Battle of the Books,* and *The Contests and Dissentions in Athens and Rome,* and both without a name. Nor was he personally known to any of the wits of the age, excepting Mr. Congreve, and one or two more, with whom he had contracted an acquaintance at Sir William Temple's. The knot of wits used at this time to assemble at Button's coffee-house: and I had a singular account of Swift's first appearance there from Ambrose Philips, who was one of Mr. Addison's little senate. He said that they had for several successive days observed a strange clergyman come into the coffeehouse, who seemed utterly unacquainted with any of those who frequented it; and whose custom it was to lay his hat down on a table, and walk backward and forward at a good pace for half an hour or an hour, without speaking to any mortal, or seeming in the least to attend to anything that was going forward there. He then used to take up his hat, pay his money at the bar, and walk away without opening his lips. After having observed this singular behaviour for some time, they concluded him to be out of his senses; and the name that he went by among them, was that of "the mad parson." This made them more than usually attentive to his motions; and one evening, as Mr. Addison and the rest were observing him, they saw him cast his eyes several times on a gentleman in boots, who seemed to be just come out of the country, and at last advanced towards him as intending to address him. They were all eager to hear what this dumb mad parson had to say, and immediately quitted their seats to get near him. Swift went up to the country gentleman, and in a very abrupt manner, without any previous salute, asked him, "Pray, sir, do you remember any good weather in the world?" The country gentleman, after staring a little at the singularity of his manner, and the oddity of the question, answered, "Yes, sir, I thank God I remember a great deal of good weather in my time."—"That is more," said Swift, "than I can say; I never remember any weather that not not too hot, or too cold; too wet or too dry; but however God Almighty contrives it, at the end of the year 'tis all very well." Upon saying this, he took up his hat, and without uttering a syllable more, or taking the least notice of any one, walked out of the coffeehouse; leaving all those who had been spectators of this odd scene staring after him, and still more confirmed in the opinion of his being mad.

Thomas Sheridan, 1784, *Life of Dean Swift*

The disease under which he laboured so long, and which we have ventured to term "cerebral congestion," might, from the symptoms, be styled by some pathologists "epileptic vertigo," such as that described by Esquirol—an affection to which, it is well known, many men of strong intellect have been subject. For the last few years of his embittered existence, from his seventy-fifth to his seventy-eight year, his disease partook so much of the nature of senile decay, or the *dementia* of old age, that it is difficult, with the materials now at command, to define by any precise medical term his actual state.

Sir William R. Wilde, 1845, *On the Closing Years of Swift's Life*

A man strangely compounded of contrary extremes, uniting many natures within his own. . . . A strenuous and even merciless defender of the Church as by the law established, he sometimes brought discredit upon his profession, and upon the institution he so much revered, by the freedom of his behaviour and the recklessness of his wit. A vehement lover of liberty, he was guilty of no compassion for hostile scribblers, whose arrest and punishment he often urged on the Tory leaders; while he constantly inveighed against any relaxation of the disabilities that shut out Dissenters from offices under the Crown. A friend to the principles of the Revolution in the State, he cleaved to the principles of the reaction in the Church; Somers was his friend, while Sacheverell seemed his exemplar. A man of piquant and at times charming manner, of social sensibilities, enjoying company, tolerant of foibles, he was nevertheless a stern censor and an unsparing censurer of the race, which he hated and contemned. A despiser of mankind, incessantly aflame with rage against the cruelties of the dominant and the cowardice of the subject, he was full of good works, such as only the truest and largest benevolence could dictate. A student of economy, parsimonious to a fault in private affairs, in philanthropic and literary relations he was a very Mæcenas for his generous munificence; and many men owed their fortune to one who neither sued nor intrigued for himself. An ardent admirer and tender friend of not a few women, he disappointed the love of two who were deeply and fatally devoted to him, and heartily despised the sex. A marvel of cold purity in his personal life, in his poems and satires he rushed repeatedly into grossness and downright filthiness worthy only of a man who had passed the stage in vice at which sexual pleasures cease to give the desired satisfaction to the appetites. A coward in many trivial matters of daily incident—dreading smallpox and other such mischances of our civilisation—in his public life he was fearless, when freedom of speech brought him face to face with an enraged and tyrannical law. . . . A lover of anonymity, a courtier of obscurity, a despiser of pretence, a hater of show, his genius made him the familiar of Princes, the friend and counsellor of Ministers, the pride of a whole country, the peculiar trust and boast of the poor within its borders. In two things alone was he throughout consistent: in the thorough and even offensive personal independence, into which the unhappy experience of his youth but too harshly trained him; and in the unextinguishable love of liberty, the incorruptible patriotism, that guided his political career from the first to the last.

D. Laing Purves, 1868, The Works of Jonathan Swift, Life,
pp. 38, 39

Jonathan Swift remains what he was a century ago, the sphinx of English literature. Prominent: in his own line, as probably no other author ever was before; the observed of all, as the bosom friend of the leading wits and statesmen of the most classic modern age; the most illustrious polemic that the modern world has ever seen, he yet stands to this day, the greatest mystery among distinguished men of letters. Even the secret of Junius yields, in importance and interest, to that which attaches to the name of the Dean of St. Patrick's. Gifted with the capacity to entrance the intellect of men, and inthrall the passions of women, he seems to have been at home in ridiculing the former, and bringing down the love of the latter to despair. Who, on regarding the portrait of him left by Jervas, which exhibits a noble and placid expanse of brow, serene eyes, and a mouth not noticeable for its bitterness or agitation, could imagine that one of the most restless spirits which ever inhabited a human breast found lodgment there?

George Barnett Smith, 1876, "Dean Swift," *The International Review,* vol. 3, p. 306

The last indignity was reserved for our own century and for philosophers in the Flying Island of the British Association. In 1835, in making alterations under the aisle of St. Patrick's Cathedral, the coffins of Swift and Stella were found side by side. The British Association was holding its meeting in Dublin, and, as the genius of irony would have it, phrenology was then the fashion. Doubtless with the permission of Swift's successor at that day in the deanery of the Cathedral, two dainty toys were provided for the perambulating professors and their fair entertainers. The skulls of Swift and of Esther Johnson went the rounds of the drawingrooms; they were patted and poised and peeped at; pretty, sentimental speeches and ponderous scientific phrases flew to right and left; here hung "only a woman's hair," and there the condyloid processes projected into the foramen magnum of the occipital bone. The bumps of veneration and amativeness were measured, and it was ascertained that wit was small. Drawings and casts were made. Finally when all the pretty speeches had run dry; and the spectacles were all taken off, and wisdom had departed from the land, the desecrated bones were restored to darkness, to be once more discovered within a few days past, but not again to have their nakedness exposed to the gaping inhabitants of Laputa.

Edward Dowden, 1882, "Literature," *The Academy,* vol. 22, p. 233

Into a particular account of Swift's last years it would be almost agony to enter. Nothing in the recorded history of humanity, nothing that the imagination of man has conceived, can transcend in horror and pathos the accounts which have come down to us of the closing scenes of his life. His memory was gone, his reason was gone; he recognised no friend; he was below his own Struldbrugs. Day after day he paced his chamber, as a wild beast paces its cage, taking his food as he walked, but refusing to touch it as long as any one remained in the room. During the autumn of 1742 his state was horrible and pitiable beyond expression. At last, after suffering unspeakable tortures from one of the most agonising maladies known to surgery, he sank into the torpor of imbecility. By the mercy of Providence it generally happens that man so degraded is unconscious of his degradation. But this mercy was withheld from Swift. On one occasion he was found gazing at his image in a pierglass and muttering piteously over and over again, "Poor old man!" On another he exclaimed, frequently repeating it, "I am what I am." "He never talked nonsense," says Deane Swift, "nor said a foolish thing." In this deplorable condition he continued for two years, and then maintained unbroken silence till death released him from calamity.

John Churton Collins, 1893, Jonathan Swift, p. 235

He was a profoundly sensitive man, yet he was also matter-of-fact. His honest recognition of things as they were was mitigated by no intervening haze of romance, and no spiritual revelation of distant hopes. . . . His was not a temperament to manufacture ideals; and the times had no ideals to offer. What wonder if fierce wrath filled his great, sad soul; if the worlds of politics, of society, of the great mass of men, seemed to him equally contemptible and pitiful. . . . The social sarcasm of Swift is unequaled in fervor of ironic power, but is also alone among the chief satires of England in the bitterness of its tone. The terrible epitaph which, by his own command, was placed over his tomb speaks of the only peace possible to him.

Vida D. Scudder, 1898, Social Ideals in English Letters, p. 97

STELLA

This day, being Sunday, January 28, 1727-8, about eight o'clock at night, a servant brought me a note, with an account of the death of the truest, most virtuous, and valuable friend, that I, or perhaps any other person, was ever blessed with. She expired about six in the evening of this day; and as soon as I am left alone, which is about eleven at night, I resolve, for my own satisfaction, to say something of her life and character. . . . She was sickly from her childhood, until about the age of fifteen; but then grew into perfect health, and was looked upon as one of the most beautiful, graceful, and agreeable young women in London, only a little too fat. Her hair was blacker than a raven, and every feature of her face in perfection. . . . Never was any of her sex born with better gifts of the mind, or who more improved them by reading and conversation. Yet her memory was not of the best, and was impaired in the latter years of her life. But I cannot call to mind that I ever once heard her make a wrong judgment of persons, books, or affairs. Her advice was always the best, and with the greatest freedom, mixed with the greatest decency. She had a gracefulness, somewhat more than human, in every motion, word, and action. Never was so happy a conjunction of civility, freedom, easiness, and sincerity. There seemed to be a combination among all that knew her, to treat her with a dignity much beyond her rank; yet people of all sorts were never more easy than in her company. . . . All of us who had the happiness of her friendship agree unanimously, that, in an afternoon or evening's conversation, she never failed, before we parted, of delivering the best thing that was said in the company. Some of us have written down several of her sayings, or what the French call *bons mots,* wherein she excelled beyond belief. She never mistook the understanding of others; nor ever said a severe word, but where a much severer was deserved.

Jonathan Swift, 1727-8, The Character of Mrs. Johnson

Stella was the concealed but undoubted wife of Dr. Swift, and if my informations are right, she was married to him in the year 1716 by Dr. Ash, then Bishop of Clogher. . . . Stella was a most amiable woman both in mind and person: She had an elevated understanding, with all the delicacy, and softness of her own sex. Her voice, however sweet in itself, was still rendered more harmonious by what she said. Her wit was poignant without severity: Her manners were humane, polite, easy and unreserved.—Wherever she came, she attracted attention and esteem. As virtue was her guide in morality, sincerity was her guide in religion. She was constant, but not ostentatious in her devotions: She was remarkably prudent in her conversation; she had great skill in music; and was perfectly well versed in all the lesser arts that employ a lady's leisure. Her wit allowed her a fund of perpetual cheerfulness within proper limits. She exactly answered the description of Penelope in Homer.

"A woman, lovliest of the lovely kind,
 In body perfect, and compleat in mind."

John Boyle (Lord Orrery), 1751, Remarks on the Life and
Writings of Dr. Jonathan Swift

The general rule, I think, between him and Mrs. Johnson was this: when the Doctor was absent from home she lived at his house; but when he was at home she lodged either somewhere at Trim, or was resident at the house of Dr. Raymond, the vicar of Trim, a gentleman of great hospitality, a friend of Dr. Swift, a man of learning and fine address, with the advantage of a tall, handsome, and graceful person.

Deane Swift, 1755, An Essay upon the Life, Writings and
Character of Dr. Jonathan Swift, p. 90

Notwithstanding Dr. Delany's sentiments of Swift's marriage, and notwithstanding all that Lord Orrery and others have said about it, there is no authority for it but a hearsay story, and that very ill-founded. It is certain that the Dean told one of his friends, whom he advised to marry, that he himself never wished to marry at the time he ought to have entered into that state; for he counted upon it as the happiest condition, especially towards the decline of life, when a faithful, tender friend, is most wanted. While he was talking to this effect, his friend expressed his wishes to have seen him married: the Dean asked why? "Because," replied the other, "I should have the pleasure of seeing your offspring; all the world would have been pleased to have seen the issue of such a genius." The Dean smiled, and denied his being married, in the same manner as before, and said he never saw the woman he wished to be married to. The same gentleman, who was intimate with Mrs. Dingley for ten years before she died, in 1743, took occasion to tell her that such a story was whispered of her friend Mrs. Johnson's marriage with the Dean, but she only laughed at it as an idle tale, founded only on suspicion. . . . Had he been married, he could not have lived in a state of separation from her, he loved her so passionately; for he admired her upon every account that can make a woman amiable or valuable as a companion for life. Is it possible to think that an affectionate husband could first have written, and then have used, those several prayers, by a dying wife with whom he never cohabited, and whose mouth must have been filled with reproaches for denying her all conjugal rights for a number of years, nay, from the very period (1716) that is pretended to be the time of the marriage?

William Monck Mason, 1820, *History and Antiquities of St. Patrick's Cathedral, near Dublin*

One final consideration is that the oppressive and disabling nature of Swift's life-long disease has been greatly underrated in the more severe of the criticisms which have been made with regard to his conduct to Esther Johnson. I do not know that labyrinthine vertigo would necessarily incapacitate a man for the performance of marital duties, but it certainly might be a barrier to them more formidable than unprofessional critics are likely to suppose possible. Dr. Beddoes suggested that Swift was impotent from youthful dissipation, of which there is not a tithe of evidence. May not the great and grave disease of which I have adduced such copious evidence have been the real reason why Swift did not live with the woman whom it was certain that he loved with the most tender and persistent devotion?

Dr. (F. R. S.) Bucknill, 1881, *Dean Swift's Disease, Brain*

The relation between the two was from the first, so far as the world was concerned, free from all doubt or ambiguity. Stella shared in all Swift's interests, remained his constant companion, and by degrees became the centre of his circle. But they never met alone: they never lived in the same house: and though all his thoughts and cares were shared by her, the bond was never in reality a closer one. And these strict limits of their friendship were so carefully maintained, that slander never ventured to assert otherwise, except in some vulgar outbursts which forgot even appropriateness of attack. Strange and abnormal as were its conditions, fettered and cramped as it was by Swift's pride and waywardness, or by the mysteries of disease, the romance of that mutual devotion still forms one of the threads of the deepest interest running through Swift's dark and somber life.

Henry Craik, 1882, *The Life of Jonathan Swift*, p. 89

If there was any person entitled to speak with authority on the subject, that person was assuredly Mrs. Dingley. For twenty-nine years, from the commencement, that is to say, of Swift's intimate connection with Stella till the day of Stella's death, she had been her inseparable companion, her friend and confidante. She had shared the same lodgings with her; it was understood that Swift and Esther were to have no secrets apart from her. When they met, they met in her presence; what they wrote, passed, by Swift's special request, through her hands. Now it is well known that Mrs. Dingley was convinced that no marriage had ever taken place. The whole story was, she said, an idle tale. Two of Stella's executors, Dr. Corbet and Mr. Rochford, distinctly stated that no suspicion of a marriage had ever even crossed their minds, though they had seen the Dean and Esther together a thousand times. Swift's housekeeper, Mrs. Brent, a shrewd and observant woman, who resided at the deanery during the whole period of her master's intimacy with Miss Johnson, was satisfied that there had been no marriage. So said Mrs. Ridgeway, who succeeded her as housekeeper, and who watched over the Dean in his declining years. But no testimony could carry greater weight than that of Dr. John Lyon. He was one of Swift's most intimate friends, and, when the state of the Dean's health was such that it had become necessary to place him under surveillance, Lyon was the person selected to undertake the duty. He lived with him at the deanery; he had full control over his papers; he was consequently brought into contact with all who corresponded with him, and with all who visited him. He had thus at his command every contemporary source of information. Not long after the story was first circulated, he set to work to ascertain, if possible, the truth. The result of his investigations was to convince him that there was absolutely no foundation for it but popular gossip, unsupported by a particle of evidence.

John Churton Collins, 1893, *Jonathan Swift*, p. 150

Vanessa

Near twenty years ago I heard from a gentleman now living, with whom Vanessa lived, or lodged, in England, an account of the Dean's behaviour to the unhappy woman, much less to his reputation than the account my Lord [Orrery] gives of that affair. According to this gentleman's account she was not the creature that she became when she was in Ireland, whither she followed him, and, in hopes to make herself an interest with his vanity, threw herself into glare and expense; and, at last, by disappointment, into a habit of drinking, till grief and the effects of that vice destroyed her. You may gather from the really pretty piece of his, *Cadenus and Vanessa,* how much he flattered her, and that he took great pains to gloss over that affair. I remember once to have seen a little collection of letters and poetical scraps of Swift's, which passed between him and Mrs. Van Homrigh, this same Vanessa, which the bookseller then told me were sent him to be published, from the originals by this lady, in resentment of his perfidy.

Samuel Richardson, 1752, *To Lady Bradshaigh,* April 22, *Correspondence,* ed. Barbauld, vol. VI, p. 175

His affection was never free from the egoistic element which prevented him from acting unequivocally, as an impartial spectator would have advised him to act, or as he would have advised another to act in a similar case. And therefore, when the crisis came, the very strength of his affection produced an explosion of selfish wrath, and he escaped from the intolerable position by striking down the woman whom he loved, and whose love for him had become a burden. The wrath was not the less fatal because it was half composed of remorse, and the energy of the explosion proportioned to the strength of the feeling which had held it in check.

Leslie Stephen, 1882, *Swift* (*English Men of Letters*), p. 144

He lodged close to her mother, and was a frequent guest at her table. Vanessa insensibly became his pupil, and he insensibly became the object of her impassioned affection. Her letters reveal a spirit full of ardour and enthusiasm, and warped by that perverse bent which leads so many women to prefer a tyrant to a companion. Swift, on the other hand, was devoid of passion. Of friendship, even of tender regard, he was fully capable, but not of love. The spiritual realm, whether in divine or earthly things, was a region closed to him, where he never set foot. As a friend he must have greatly preferred Stella to Vanessa; and from this point of view his loyalty to the original object of his choice, we may be sure, never faltered. But Vanessa assailed him on a very weak side. The strongest of all his instincts was the thirst for imperious domination. Vanessa hugged the fetters to which Stella merely submitted. Flattered to excess by her surrender, yet conscious of his binding obligations and his real preference, he could neither discard the one beauty nor desert the other. It is humiliating to human strength and consoling to human weakness to find the Titan behaving like the least resolute of mortals, seeking refuge in temporizing, in evasions, in fortuitous circumstance.

Richard Garnett, 1887, *Encyclopædia Britannica,* Ninth ed., vol. XXII

The Battle of the Books (1697?-1704)

Swift for the Ancients has argued so well,
'Tis apparent from thence that the Moderns excel.

Mrs. Barker, 1735, On the Celebrated Dispute between the
Ancients and the Moderns, p. 285

Of all that constituted once the so famous controversy, its prodigious learning and its furious abuse, this triumphant piece of humour alone survives. It was circulated widely before Temple died, and not until four years later appeared in print, as portion of a volume which weakened the side of which the writer had engaged as much as it strengthened that of the enemy. Swift could not help himself. The ancients could show no such humour and satire as *The Tale of a Tub* and *The Battle of the Books*.

John Forster, 1875, The Life of Jonathan Swift, vol. I, p. 104

Its object is satire, not criticsm. Where it touches on the points in dispute, it is in such broad and far-reaching metaphor as that by which he illustrates the "sweetness and light" of the ancients through the fable of the Spider and the Bee, which has supplied a telling phraseology to a phase of latter-day criticism. Like all the satire that Swift ever wrote, it goes directly to the point by its personal reference. For Swift the main issue is one between Temple and Bentley, between the Christchurch wits and Wotton, not between the arguments of the critics. His preference for the ancients was thorough and sincere: but it went deeper than literary criticism.

Henry Craik, 1882, The Life of Jonathan Swift, p. 72

A Tale of the Tub (1704)

I am of your mind as to the Tale of a Tub. I am not alone in the opinion, as you are there; but I am pretty near it, having but very few on my side, but those few are worth a million. However, I have never spoke my sentiments, not caring to contradict a multitude. Bottom admires it, and cannot bear my saying I confess I was diverted with several passages when I read it, but I should not care to read it again. That he thinks not commendation enough.

William Congreve, 1704, Letter to Keally, Oct. 28

I beg your Lordship (if the book is come down to Exon), to read *The Tale of a Tub*, for, bating the profaneness of it, it is a book to be valued, being an original of its kind, full of wit, humour, good sense, and learning. It comes from Christ Church, and a great part of it is written in defence of

Mr. Boyle against Wotton and Bentley. The town is wonderfully pleased with it. . . . The author of *A Tale of a Tub* will not as yet be known; and if it be the man I guess, he hath reason to conceal himself because of the profound strokes in that piece, which would do his reputation and interests in the world more harm than the wit can do him good. I think your lordship hath found out a very proper employment for your pen, which he would execute very happily. Nothing·can please more than that book doth here at London.

Francis Atterbury, 1704, *Letters to Bishop Trelawney,*
June 15, July 1

The *Tale of a Tub* is a work, of perhaps greater felicity of wit, and more ludicrous combinations of ideas, than any other book in the world. It is however, written in so strange a style of "banter," to make use of one of the author's words, or rather in so low and anomalous a slang, which perhaps Swift considered as the necessary concomitant of wit; that it is by no means proper to be cited as an example of just composition.

William Godwin, 1797, "Of English Style," *The Enquirer,* p. 444

The literary merit of the *Tale of a Tub* is great, and, in this respect, exceeding everything which he afterwards produced. The style has more nerve, more imagery, and spirit, than any other portion of his works: the wit and humour are perfectly original, and supported throughout with undiminished vigour; but, it must be confessed, occasionally coarse and licentious; and the digressions exhibit erudition of no common kind, though not always applied in illustration of that side of the question on which justice and impartiality have since arranged themselves.

Nathan Drake, 1804, *Essays Illustrative of the Tatler,*
Spectator and Guardian, vol. III, p. 143

With this for my whole fortune, I was trudging through Richmond in my blue smock-frock, and my red garters tied under my knees, when, staring about me, my eyes fell upon a little book in a book-seller's window, on the outside of which was written *The Tale of a Tub,* price threepence. The title was so odd that my curiosity was excited. I had the threepence; but, then, I could not have any supper. In I went and got the little book, which I was so impatient to read, that I got over into a field at the upper corner of Kew Gardens, where there stood a haystack. On the shady side of this I sat down to read. The book was so different from any thing I had ever read before, it was something so new to my mind, that, though I could not understand some parts of it, it delighted me beyond description, and produced what I have always considered a sort of birth of intellect. I read on until it was dark without any thought of supper or bed. . . . My *Tale of a Tub,* which I carried about with me wherever I went, and when I—at about twenty years old—lost it in a box that fell overboard in the Bay of Fundy, in North America, the loss gave me greater pain than I have since felt in losing thousands of pounds.

William Cobbett, c1810, *Evening Post*

Although the object of the *Tale of a Tub* was undoubtedly to defend the Church of England, and to ridicule its opponents, it would be difficult to find in the whole compass of literature any production more utterly un-restrained by considerations of reverence or decorum. Nothing in Voltaire is more grossly profane than the passages in Swift about the Roman Catholic doctrine concerning the Sacrament, and the Calvinistic doctrine concerning inspiration. And although the *Tale of a Tub* is an extreme example, the same spirit pervades many of his other performances. His wit was perfectly unbridled. His unrivalled power of ludicrous combination seldom failed to get the better of his prudence; and he found it impossible to resist a jest. It must be added that no writer of the time indulged more habitually in coarse, revolting, and indecent imagery; that he delighted in a strain of ribald abuse peculiarly unbecoming in a clergyman; that he lived in an atmosphere deeply impregnated with scepticism; and that he frequently expressed a strong dislike for his profession.

William Edward Hartpole Lecky, 1861-71, *The Leaders of Public Opinion in Ireland,* p. 19

Swift had, indeed, little enough in common with the philosophy of Lucretius. But in both we have the same gloom of cynicism. In both there is the same profound scorn of superstition, and yet the same belief that in superstition we must find the main source of most human action. In Swift as in Lucretius, the literary instinct has made the general and wide-reaching satire far more strong in its impression than the ostensible object of the book. If we read the *Tale of a Tub* with understanding of its real meaning, we have as little impression, at the end, of the quarrels of Peter and Martin and Jack, as we have, after reading the poem of Lucretius, of the niceties of the Epicurean system. Divided by eighteen centuries, there is yet much in the mental at-titude of the two men that brings them close together. Swift's supposed debt to Rabelais is almost proverbial. But, after all, it is more in the following of a recognised vehicle of satire, than in anything else. Swift read Rabelais, as the acknowledged master of a peculiar style of sarcasm. The style has al-ready become antiquated: and yet his adoption of it leaves the essential qualities of the *Tale of a Tub* absolutely unimpaired.

Henry Craik, 1882, *The Life of Jonathan Swift,* p. 112

The reader of such vigorous and effective English, employed with so much directness and point, cannot but sympathize with the feeling which prompted him to say in his old age, when his mind was gradually failing, "Good God, what a genius I had when I wrote that book!" Not only is the book his masterpiece, but it is also his best allegory; indeed one would hazard little in making the assertion that it is the best sustained allegory that ever was written.

Herbert Eveleth Greene, 1889, "The Allegory in Spenser, Bunyan and Swift," *Publications of the Modern Language Association of America*, vol. IV, p. 168

The Examiner

No modern leader-writer, however common-place, would write such heavy stuff now.

Stanley Lane-Poole, 1883, ed. *Selections from the Prose Writings of Jonathan Swift*, Preface, p. xxv

At the beginning of November Swift undertook the editorship of *The Examiner,* and for upwards of three years he fought the battles of the Ministry as no one had ever yet fought the battles of any Ministry in the world. With a versatility unparalleled in the history of party warfare, he assailed his opponents in almost every form which satire can assume; in Essays which are still read as models of terse and luminous disquisition; in philippics compared with which the masterpieces of Cicero will, in point of vituperative skill, bear no comparison; in pamphlets which were half a century afterwards the delight of Burke and Fox: in ribald songs, in street ballads, in Grubstreet epigrams, in ludicrous parodies. He had applied his rare powers of observation to studying the peculiarities of every class in the great family of mankind, their humours, their prejudices, their passions; and to all these he knew how to appeal with exquisite propriety. He was a master of the rhetoric which casts a spell over senates and tribunals, and of the rhetoric which sends mobs yelling to the tar-barrel or the clubstick. With every weapon in the whole armoury of scorn he was equally familiar. In boisterous scurrility he was more than a match for Oldmixon. In delicate and subtle humour he was more than a match for Addison. In an age when the bad arts of anonymous polemics had been brought to perfection, his lampoons achieved a scandalous pre-eminence. His sarcasm and invective were terrific. His irony made even the Duchess of Marlborough quail; his pasquinades drove Eugene in ignominy from our shores; his broadsides made it perilous for the Opposition to show their faces in the streets. But however remarkable were his abilities as an unscrupulous assailant, his abilities as an unscrupulous advocate were not less consummate. Where his object was persuasion, he was indifferent to everything but effect. He hesitated at nothing. When the testimony of facts was against him, he distorted them beyond recognition. When testimony was wanting, he invented it. When the statements of his opponents admitted of no confutation, he assumed the air of an honest and stout-hearted Englishman who refused to be duped. His diction—plain, masculine, incisive— came home to every one; and the monstrous effrontery of his assumptions was seldom suspected by readers whose reason was enthralled by the circumstantial conclusiveness with which he drew his deductions. In truth, of all writers who have ever entered the arena of party politics, Swift had, in a larger measure than any, the most invaluable of all qualifications—the art of making truth assume the appearance of elaborate sophistry, and the art of making elaborate sophistry assume the appearance of self evident truth.

John Churton Collins, 1886, Bolingbroke, A Historical Study,
and Voltaire in England, p. 59

The style of Swift's *Examiners* is perfect of its kind and for its purpose. His own rather bald definition of a good style—"proper words in proper places" —expresses the form of these papers precisely, while their matter like the lead of a bullet, is calculated nicely, and only to serve a single object—to go straight and strong and true to its mark. The admiration Swift's political tracts excites is of the kind excited by a steam-engine—admiration of power, precision, and such exquisite adaptation of means to a single end that there is neither waste nor want, friction nor dispersion.

Richard Ashe King, 1895, Swift in Ireland, p. 61

The Drapier Letters (1724)

A proclamation for discovering ye Author of ye Pamphlet intitled A letter to ye whole people of Ireland, by M. B. Drapier, author of the letter to the shopkeepers, &c.

£300 REWARD.

By the Lord Lieutenant and Council of

Ireland.

A PROCLAMATION

Content:

Whereas a wicked and malicious pamphlet, intitled A letter to the whole people of Ireland, by M. B. Drapier, author of the letter to the shopkeepers, &c., printed by John Harding, in Molesworth's Court, in Fishamble Street,

Dublin, in which are contained several seditious and scandalous paragraphs highly reflecting upon his Majesty and his ministers, tending to alienate the affections of his good subjects of England and Ireland from each other, and to promote sedition among the people, hath been lately printed and published in this kingdom: We, the Lord Lieutenant and Council do hereby publish and declare that, in order to discover the author of the said seditious pamphlet, we will give the necessary order for the payment of three hundred pounds sterling, to such person or persons as shall within the specified six months from this date hereof, discover the author of the said pamphlet, so as he be apprehended and convicted thereby. . . .

GOD save the KING.

Proclamation Against the Drapier, 1724, Oct. 27

Let Ireland tell, how wit upheld her cause,
Her trade supported, and supplied her laws;
And leave on Swift this grateful verse engraved,
"The rights a Court Attacked, a poet saved."
Behold the hand that wrought a nation's cure,
Stretched to relieve the idiot and the poor,
Proud vice to brand, or injured worth adorn,
And stretch the ray to ages yet unborn.

Alexander Pope, 1737, *Imitations of Horace*,
bk. ii, ep. i, v. 221-228

His object was, not to do good to Ireland, but to vex and annoy the English ministry. To do this however with effect, it was necessary that he should speak to the interests and feelings of some party who possessed a certain degree of power and influence. This unfortunately was not the case in that day with the Catholics; and though this gave them only a stronger title to the services of a truly brave or generous advocate, it was sufficient to silence Swift. They are not so much as named above two or three times in his writings—and then only with scorn and reprobation. In the topics which he does take up, it is no doubt true, that he frequently inveighs against real oppression and acts of indisputable impolicy; yet it is no want of charity to say, that it is quite manifest that these were not his reasons for bringing them forward, and that he had just as little scruple to make an outcry, where no public interest was concerned, as where it was apparent. It was sufficient for him, that the subject was likely to excite popular prejudice and clamour, —or that he had some personal pique or animosity to gratify. The Drapier's letters are sufficient proof of the influence of the former principle.

Francis, Lord Jeffrey, 1816, "The Works of Jonathan Swift,"
Edinburgh Review, vol. 27, p. 22

Believing, however erroneously, that Swift had delivered them from a great public danger, their gratitude to him knew no bounds, nor ended even with his powers of mind. "The sun of his popularity," says a great poet, "remained unclouded, even after he was incapable of distinguishing its radiance." The Drapier's Head became a favourite sign; his portrait, we are told, was engraved, woven upon handkerchiefs, and stuck upon medals (not of copper I presume). His health was quaffed at every banquet, his presence everywhere welcomed with blessings by the people. They bore with all the infirmities of genius, all the peevishness of age. In vain did he show contempt and aversion to those who thus revered him: in vain did he deny them even the honour of his birth-place, frequently saying, "I was not dropped in this vile country, but in England." In vain did he sneer at the "savage Old Irish." No insult on his part could weaken their generous attachment. Even at this day, as I am assured, this grateful feeling still survives; and all parties in Ireland, however estranged on other questions, agree in one common veneration for the memory of Swift.

> Philip Henry Earl Stanhope (Lord Mahon), 1836-58, *History of England from the Peace of Utrecht to the Peace of Versailles, 1713-1783*, vol. II., p. 67

Is it fair to call the famous *Drapier's Letters* patriotism? They are masterpieces of dreadful humour and invective: they are reasoned logically enough too, but the proposition is as monstrous and fabulous as the Lilliputian island. It is not that the grievance is so great, but there is his enemy—the assault is wonderful for its activity and terrible rage. It is Samson with a bone in his hand, rushing on his enemies and felling them: one admires not the cause so much as the strength, the anger, the fury of the champion.

> William Makepeace Thackeray, 1853, *The English Humourists of the Eighteenth Century*

Because Swift takes the Irish, not the English, view of the question,—because he goes to battle armed with the strength of his genius, the fire of his indignation,—he is therefore no patriot! What is it to be a patriot? To sit in the chimneycorner and make fine phrases about loving your country, or to go out and do battle for her? There was nothing in Ireland, in Swift's day, to which the affections could cling. The first thing to be done was to constitute a state worthy of love, the first steps to that end were in resistance to oppressive measures; the first feeling to be encouraged was hatred of the oppressor. It is true that Swift often spoke with contempt of the Irish, and that he regarded his appointment to the Deanery of St. Patrick's as a decree of banishment from civilization and friendship. He showed little sentimental patriotism; but he understood the duties of a patriot, and did his best to discharge them. He may sometimes have displayed the temper of Coriolanus; but, unlike the Roman, he endured unto the end.

Adams Sherman Hill, 1868, "The Character of Jonathan Swift,"
North American Review, vol. 106, p. 86

The public joy knew no bounds. In a few hours Dublin presented the appearance of a vast jubilee. In a few days there was scarcely a town or a village in Ireland which was not beside itself with exultation. The whole island rang with the praises of the Drapier. It was the Drapier, they cried, who saved them, it was the Drapier who had taught them to be patriots. Had Swift rescued the country from some overwhelming calamity, had he done all and more than all that the Œdipus of story is fabled to have done for the city of Amphion, popular gratitude could not have gone further. Medals were struck in his honour. A club, the professed object of which was to perpetuate his fame, was formed. His portrait stamped on medallions, or woven on handkerchiefs, was the ornament most cherished by both sexes. When he appeared in the streets all heads were uncovered. If for the first time he visited a town, it was usual for the Corporation to receive him with public honours. Each year, as his birthday came around, it was celebrated with tumultuous festivity. "He became," says Orrery, "the idol of the people of Ireland to a degree of devotion that in the most superstitious country scarcely any idol ever attained." "Spirit of Swift!" exclaimed Grattan on that memorable day when he brought foward his Declaration of Legislative Independence, "Spirit of Swift! your genius has prevailed; Ireland is now a nation." Even now no true Irishman ever pronounces his name without reverence.

John Churton Collins, 1893, Jonathan Swift, p. 188

The Drapier's Letters are epochmaking in that they first taught Ireland the policy and the power of union, of dogged inert resistance, and of strategically organized and directed agitation. Their effect was, in fact, commensurate with their power, and their power of its kind was supreme. It is the power of a deft, vigorous, intent and unerring-eyed wielder of a hammer, who hits each nail on the head and home without one single feint, or flourish, or one single short, or weak, or wasted stroke. Swift's consummate mastery of the art which conceals art was never shown to such perfection as in these letters, whose naked simplicity is so like naked truth as to be confounded with it. . . . It is, in fact, incontestable that Swift's service to Ireland deserves the distinction he gives it in his epitaph. Look at it how you will, either from the point of view of the need of the service, or of its righteousness, or of its greatness, or of its difficulty, and Swift's work in Ireland is his supreme achievement. When "in the reign of Queen Anne he dictated for a time the policy of the English nation," he had at his back a powerful and compact party, all the influence (then enormous) of the Court, Harley's serviceable cunning and the brilliant intellect of Bolingbroke. But of his work in Ireland he might say with literal truth, "Alone I did it!"

Richard Ashe King, 1895, Swift in Ireland, pp. 108, 202

Gulliver's Travels (1726)

Here is a book come out, that all our people of taste run mad about; 'tis no less than the united work of a dignified clergyman, an eminent physician, and the first poet of the age; and very wonderful it is, God knows!—great eloquence have they employed to prove themselves beasts, and shew such veneration for horses, that since the Essex quaker, nobody has appeared so passionately devoted to that species; and to say truth, they talk of a stable with so much warmth and affection, I cannot help suspecting some very powerful motive at the bottom of it.

Lady Mary Wortley Montagu, 1726,
Letter to the Countess of Mar

Gulliver's Travels, I believe, will have as great a run as John Bunyan. It is in everybody's hands. Lord Scarborough, who is no inventor of stories, told me that he fell in company with a master of a ship, who told him that he was very well acquainted with Gulliver; but that the printer had mistaken; that he lived in Wapping, and not in Rotherhithe. I lent the book to an old gentleman who went immediately to his map to search for Lilliput.

John Arbuthnot, 1726, Letter to Swift, Nov. 8

About ten days ago a book was published here on the Travels of one Gulliver, which has been the conversation of the whole town ever since: the whole impression sold in a week; and nothing is more diverting than to hear the different opinions people give of it, though all agree in liking it extremely. 'Tis generally said that you are the author, but I am told the bookseller declares he knows not from what hand it came. From the highest to the lowest it is universally read, from the cabinet council to the nursery. You may see by this you are not much injured by being supposed the author of this piece. If you are, you have disobliged us, and two or three of your best friends, in not giving us the least hint of it. Perhaps I may all this time be talking to you of a book you have never seen, and which has not yet reached Ireland; if it have not I believe what we have said will be suf-

ficient to recommend it to your reading, and that you will order me to send
it to you.

John Gay, 1726, Letter to Swift, Nov. 17

Gulliver's Travels is a book in which the author seems to have called up
all his vigilance and skill in the article of style: and, as the plan of his fiction
led to that simplicity in which he delighted, no book can be taken as a fairer
specimen of the degree of cultivation at which the English language had at
that time arrived. Swift was perhaps the man of the most powerful mind of
the time in which he lived.

William Godwin, 1797, "Of English Style," The Enquirer, p. 446

It would, perhaps, be too much to say that the author had an express design
to blacken and culminate human nature, but at least his work displays evident marks of a diseased imagination and a lacerated heart—in short, of
that frame of mind which led him in the epitaph he composed for himself,
to describe the tomb as the abode, *Ubi saeva indignatio ulterius cor lacerare
nequit.* We rise, accordingly, from *Gulliver's Travels,* not as from the work
of De Foe, exulting in our nature, but giddy, and selfish, and discontented,
and, from some parts, I may almost say brutified. The general effect, indeed, of works of satire and humour is perhaps little favourable to the mind,
and they are only allowable, and may be read with profit, when employed
as the scourges of vice or folly.

John Dunlop, 1814-42, The History of Fiction, vol. II, p. 421

He has taken a new view of human nature, such as a being of a higher
sphere might take of it; he has torn the scales from off his moral vision; he
has tried an experiment upon human life, and sifted its pretensions from
the alloy of circumstances; he has measured it with a rule, has weighed it
in a balance, and found it, for the most part, wanting and worthless, in
substance and in show. Nothing solid, nothing valuable is left in his system
but virtue and wisdom. What a libel is this upon mankind! What a convincing proof of misanthropy! What presumption and what *malice pre-
pense,* to show men what they are, and to teach them what they ought to be!
What a mortifying stroke, aimed at national glory, is that unlucky incident
of Gulliver's wading across the channel and carrying off the whole fleet of
Blefuscu! After that, we have only to consider which of the contending
parties was in the right. What a shock to personal vanity is given in the
account of Gulliver's nurse Glumdalclitch! Still, notwithstanding the dis-
paragement to her personal charms, her good nature remains the same
amiable quality as before. I cannot see the harm, the misanthropy, the

immoral and degrading tendency of this. The moral lesson is as fine as the intellectual exhibition is amusing.

William Hazlitt, 1818, *Lectures on the English Poets,*
Lecture VI

The part of Dean Swift's satire which relates to the "Stulbrugs" may possibly occur to some readers as bearing upon this topic. That the staunch admirers of that singularly-gifted person should have been flung into ecstasies on the perusal of this extraordinary part of his writings, need not surprise us. Their raptures were full easily excited; but I am quite clear they have given a wrong gloss to it, and heaped upon its merits a very undeserved praise. They think that the picture of the Stulbrugs was intended to wean us from a love of life, and that it has well accomplished its purpose. I am very certain that the dean never had any such thing in view, because his sagacity was far too great not to perceive that he only could make out this position by a most undisguised begging of the question. How could any man of the most ordinary reflection expect to wean his fellow-creatures from love of life by describing a sort of persons who at a given age lost their faculties and became doting, drivelling idiots? Did any man breathing ever pretend that he wished to live, not only for centuries, but even for threescore years and ten, bereaved of his understanding, and treated by the law and by his fellowmen as in hopeless incurable dotage? The passage in question is much more likely to have proceded from Swift's exaggerated misanthropy, and to have been designed as an antidote to human pride, by showing that our duration is necessarily limited,—if, indeed, it is not rather to be regarded as the work of mere whim and caprice.

Henry, Lord Brougham, 1835, *A Discourse of Natural Theology,*
Sect. v, note

The most admirable satire ever conveyed in a narrative, and the most plausible disguise that fiction ever bore. So well is the style of the old English navigators copied—so much does there seem of their honest simplicity and plain common sense—so consistent is every part of the story— so natural all the events after the first improbability,—that the fable, even in its wildest flights, never loses an air of real truth.

Philip Henry Earl Stanhope (Lord Mahon), 1836-58,
History of England from the Peace of Utrecht to the
Peace of Versailles, 1713-1783, vol. II, p. 228

With what power, what genius in ludicrous invention, these stories are written, no one needs to be reminded. Schoolboys, who read for the story only, and know nothing of the satire, read *Gulliver* with delight; and our literary critics, even while watching the allegory and commenting on the philosophy, break down in laughter from the sheer grotesqueness of some of the fancies, or are awed into pain and discomfort by the ghastly significance of others. Of Swift we may surely say, that, let our literature last for ages, he will be remembered in it, and chiefly for his fictions, as one of the greatest and most original of our writers—the likest author we have to Rabelais, and yet with British differences. In what cases one would recommend Swift is a question of large connexions. To all strong men he is and will be congenial, for they can bear to look round and round reality on all sides, even on that which connects us with the Yahoos. Universality is best.

David Masson, 1859, *British Novelists and Their Styles,* p. 94

The reason few persons were angry at Gulliver was that the satire was seldom felicitous enough to wound. Sometimes it is obscure, sometimes revolting and extravagant, and is invariably feeblest when most elaborate. The genius of the book is in the original and diverting incidents, and especially in the skill with which the fabulous is converted into the real. This must always have been the charm of the work, which flags, as Jeffrey remarked, whenever the satire predominates over the story.

Whitwell Elwin, 1871, ed. *The Works of Alexander Pope,*
vol. VII, p. 86, note

What Swift has really done is to provide for the man who despises his species a number of exceedingly effective symbols for the utterance of his contempt. A child is simply amused with Bigendians and Littleendians; a philosopher thinks that the questions really at the bottom of Church quarrels are in reality of more serious import; but the cynic who has learnt to disbelieve in the nobility or wisdom of the great mass of his species finds a most convenient metaphor for expressing his disbelief. In this way *Gulliver's Travels* contains a whole gallery of caricatures thoroughly congenial to the despisers of humanity.

Leslie Stephen, 1882, *Swift (English Men of Letters),* p. 176

Swift's great work, after storming the outposts of human policy and human learning, breaks at last in a torrent of contempt and hatred on the last stronghold of humanity itself. The strength of Swift's work as a contribution to the art of fiction lies in the portentous gravity and the absolute mathematical consistency wherewith he develops the consequences of his modest assumptions. In the quality of their realism the voyages to Lilliput and Brobdingnag are much superior to the two later and more violent satires; he was better fitted to ridicule the politics of his time than to attack the "men of Gresham," of whose true aims and methods he knew little or nothing; and the imagination stumbles at many of the details of the last book. But the wealth of illustration whereby he maintains the interest of his original conception of pigmies and giants is eternally surprising and delightful.

Walter Raleigh, 1894, *The English Novel*, p. 137

So ends *Gulliver's Travels*. In the verses which he wrote on the subject of his own death, Swift said that perhaps he "had too much satire in his vein," but added that:

"His satire points at no defect
But what all mortals may correct."

The imperfections and contradictions in the "Voyage to the Houyhn- hnms" are obvious. There is a total want of probability in the general conception, and the Houyhnhnms are made to do many things which it was physically impossible for them to perform. It is difficult to believe that, as some have said, the Houyhnhnm represents Swift's ideal of morality. Houyhnhnm and Yahoo are alike imperfect, and Swift falsely assumes that the natural affections are opposed to reason, instead of showing how the one should be influenced by the other. It is a counsel of despair.

George A. Aitken, 1896, *Gulliver's Travels*, p. 396, note

His modern fame mainly rests on *Gulliver's Travels*, the object of which, as he said, apart from the three hundred pounds realized, was to vex the world. The sixth chapter of "A Voyage to Brobdingnag" in this immortal book stands unrivalled, unless by More's *Utopia*, as an ironical descrip- tion of English political institutions of the time.

W. H. S. Aubrey, 1896, *The Rise and Growth of the English Nation*, vol. III, p. 112

Journal to Stella

It is a wonderful medley, in which grave reflections and important facts are at random intermingled with trivial occurrences and the puerile jargon of the most intimate tenderness.

Sir Walter Scott, 1814, *Memoirs of Jonathan Swift*

Never, surely, was there a stranger picture of human character than Swift's daily record of his hopes and fears, his love and his ambition, his small miseries, strange affectations, and tender communings. But it is not an elevating picture as we look upon it; neither the reverend doctor nor the young lady to whom this journal is really addressed rises in our estimation.

We are almost inclined to apologize even for the licentiousness of St. John, when we find it plainly recorded for the instruction and amusement of this young lady by her middle-aged companion. The explanation that the manners of Queen Anne's reign were grosser than ours, and that people were much more accustomed to plain speaking, is not at all satisfactory. There are indelicate allusions enough in the *Spectator,* and in Lady Montague's letters; but nothing like what we find in this journal, written in confidence to a young lady for whom Swift professed the most platonic affection. Coarse jokes and coarse oaths, the plainest allusions and double meanings of the broadest kind, are all mingled together in this strange medley of wit, vanity, affection, and secret history.

Thomas Macknight, 1863, *The Life of Henry St. John,*
Viscount Bolingbroke, p. 128

Its gossip, its nonsense, its freshness and ease of style, the tenderness concealed, or half-revealed, in its "little language," and the illustrations it supplies incidentally of the manners of the court and town, these are some of the charms that make us turn again and again to its pages with ever-increasing pleasure. We enjoy Swift's egotism and trivialities, as we enjoy the egotism of Pepys or Montaigne, and can imagine the eagerness with which the *Letters* were read by the lovely woman whose destiny it was to receive everything from Swift save the love which has its consummation in marriage. The style of the *Journal* is not that of an author composing, but of a companion talking; and it is all the more interesting since it reveals Swift's character under a pleasanter aspect than any of his formal writings. We see in it what a warm heart he had for the friends whom he had once learnt to love, and with what zeal he exerted himself in assisting brother-authors, while receiving little beyond empty praise from ministers himself.

John Dennis, 1894, *The Age of Pope,* p. 166

Some seven years only divide the close of his almanac and the threshold of *The Journal to Stella,* but the gulf between them in attraction is immeasurable. Swift's diary of two worlds—his own and hers whose letters have unfortunately perished—stands out unique, the most entrancing and the most tragic of all extant journals. It haunts one like a refrain. The mere step in style from the quaint affectations of Pepys and the colourless gravity of Evelyn to Swift's nervous diction, his terse impetuosity, his repressed fondness, his emphasised hardness, his little pathetic language, his large indignant irony, is the step from still life to breathing, from lecture to literature, from what must always remain ancient to what will never cease to be modern.

W. Sichel, 1899, "Men Who Have Kept a Diary,"
Blackwood's Magazine, vol. 165, p. 74

Poems

I heard my father say, that Mr. Elijah Fenton, who was his intimate friend, and had been his master, informed him that Dryden, upon seeing some of Swift's earliest verses, said to him "Young man, you will never be a poet!"

Joseph Warton, 1756-97, *Essay on the Genius and Writings of Pope*

Swift, whose muse seems to have been mere misanthropy: he was a cynick rather than a poet; and his natural dryness and sarcastick severity would have been unpleasing had he not qualified them by adopting the extravagant humour of Lucian and Rabelais.

Tobias George Smollett, 1757-58, *History of England, George I,* notes

His verse is only, apparently, distinguished by the accident of measure; it has no quality of poetry, and, like his prose, is remarkable for sense and wit.

Sir James Macintosh, *Diary, Memoirs* ed. Mackintosh, vol. II, p. 182

His imitations of Horace, and still more his "Verses on his own Death," place him in the first rank of agreeable moralist in verse. There is not only a dry humour, an exquisite tone of irony, in these productions of his pen, but there is a touching, unpretending pathos, mixed up with the most whimsical and eccentric strokes of pleasantry and satire. His "Description of the Morning in London," and of a "City Shower," which were first published in the *Tatler,* are among the most delightful of the contents of that very delightful work. Swift shone as one of the most sensible of the poets; he is also distinguished as one of the most nonsensical of them. No man has written so many lack-a-daisical, slip-shod, tedious, trifling, foolish, fantastical verses as he, which are so little an imputation on the wisdom of the writer; and which, in fact, only show his readiness to oblige others, and to forget himself. He has gone so far as to invent a new stanza of fourteen and sixteen syllable lines for Mary the cookmaid to vent her budget of nothings, and for Mrs. Harris to gossip with the deaf old housekeeper. Oh, when shall we have such another Rector of Laracor!

William Hazlitt, 1818, *Lectures on the English Poets,* Lecture VI

Rhyme and rhythm are only businesslike tools, which have served him to press and launch his thought; he has put nothing but prose into them: poetry was too fine to be grasped by those coarse hands. But in prosaic subjects, what truth and force! How this masculine nakedness crushes the artificial poetry of Addison and Pope! There are no epithets; he leaves his thought as he conceived it, valuing it for and by itself, needing neither ornaments, nor preparation nor extension; above the tricks of the profession, scholastic conventionalisms, the vanity of the rhymester, the difficulties of the art; master of his subject and of himself. This simplicity and naturalness astonish us in verse. Hcre, as elsewhere, his originality is entire, and his genius creative; he surpasses his classical and timid age; he tyrannises over form, breaks it, dare utter anything, spares himself no strong word. Acknowledges the greatness of this invention and audacity; he alone is a superior, who finds everything and copies nothing. . . . He drags poetry not only through the mud, but into the filth; he rolls in it like a raging madman, he enthrones himself in it, and bespatters all passers-by. Compared with his, all foul words are decent and agreeable.

H. A. Taine, 1871, History of English Literature, tr. Van Laun,
vol. II, bk. iii, ch. v, pp. 137, 139

Swift's poetry is perfect, exactly as the old Dutch artists were perfect painters. He never attempted to rise above this "visable diurnal sphere." He is content to lash the frivolities of the age, and to depict its absurdities. In his too faithful representatons, there is much to condemn and much to admire. Who has not felt the truth and humour of his "City Shower," and his description of "Morning?" Or the liveliness of his "Grand Question Debated," in which the knight, his lady, and the chambermaid, are so admirably drawn?

Robert Chambers, 1876, Cyclopædia of English Literature,
ed. Carruthers

Few give themselves the trouble to study his beginnings, and few, therefore, give weight enough to the fact that he made a false start. He, the ground of whose nature was an acrid commonsense, whose eye magnified the canker till it effaced the rose, began as what would now he called a romantic poet. With no mastery of verse, for even the English heroic (a balancing-pole which has enabled so many feebler men to walk the ticklish rope of momentary success) was uneasy to him; he essayed the Cowleian Pindarique, as the adjective was the rightly spelled with a hint of Parisian rather than Theban origin. . . . He who could not be a poet if he would, angrily resolved that he would not if he could. Full-sail verse was beyond his skill, but he could manage the simpler fore-and-aft rig of Butler's octosyllabics. As Cowleyism was a trick of seeing everything as it was not, and calling everything something else than it was, he would see things as they were—or as, in his sullen disgust, they seemed to be,—and call them all by their right names with a resentful emphasis. He achieved the naked sincerity of a Hottentot— nay, he even went beyond it in rejecting the feeble compromise of the breech-clout. Not only would he be naked and not ashamed, but everybody else should be so with a blush of conscious exposure, and human nature should be stripped of the hypocritical fig-leaves that betrayed by attempting to hide its identity with the brutes that perish. His sincerity was not unconscious, but self-willed and aggressive. But it would be unjust to overlook that he began with himself.

James Russell Lowell, 1876, "Forster's Life of Swift,"
The Nation, vol. 22, p. 265

How admirable also is his poetry—easy, yet never slip-shod! It lacks one quality only—imagination. There is not a fine phrase, a magical line to be found in it such as may occasionally be found in—let us say—Butler. Yet as a whole, Swift is a far more enjoyable poet than Butler. Swift has unhappily written some abominable verses, which ought never to have been set up in type; but the "Legion Club," the verses on his own death, *Cadenus and Vanessa,* the "Rhapsody on Poetry," the tremendous lines on the "Day of Judgement," and many others, all belong to enjoyable poetry, and can never lose their freshness, their charm, their vitality. Amongst the poets of the eighteenth century Swift sits secure, for he can never go out of fashion.

Augustine Birrell, 1894, Essays about Men, Women and
Books, p. 7

Cadenus and Vanessa (1726)

Cadenus and Vanessa is, of itself, complete proof that he had in him none of the elements of poetry. It was written when his faculties were in their perfection, and his heart animated with all the tenderness of which it was ever capable—and yet it is as cold and as flat as the ice of Thulé. Though describing a real passion, and a real perplexity, there is not a spark of fire, nor a throb of emotion in it from one end to the other. All the return he makes to the warmhearted creature who had put her destiny into his hands, consists in a frigid mythological fiction, in which he sets forth, that Venus and the Graces lavished their gifts on her in her infancy, and moreover got Minerva, by a trick, to inspire her with wit and wisdom. The style is mere prose—or rather a string of familiar and vulgar phrases tacked together in rhyme, like the general tissue of his poetry.

Francis, Lord Jeffrey, 1816, "Works of Jonathan Swift,"
Edinburgh Review, vol. 27, p. 49

In the walk of satire and familiar poetry, wit and knowledge of mankind, joined to facility of expression, are the principal requisites of excellence, and in these Swift shines unrivalled. *Cadenus and Vanessa* may be considered as his chief d'œuvres in that class of poems which is not professedly satirical.

It is a poem on manners, and, like one of Marmontel's Contes moraux, traces the progress and circulation of passion, existing between two persons in modern society, contrasted strongly in age, manners, and situation. Yet even here the satirical vein of Swift has predominated. We look in vain for depth of feeling or tenderness of sentiment, although, had such existed in the poet's mind the circumstances must have called it forth. The mythological fable, which conveys the compliments paid to Vanessa, is as cold as that addressed to Ardelia, or to Miss Floyd. It is in short a kind of poetry which neither affects sublimity nor pathos; but which, in the graceful facility of the poet, unites the acute observation of the observer of human nature, to commemorate the singular contest between Cadenus and Vanessa, as an extraordinary chapter in the history of the mind.

John Mitford, 1833, *Life of Swift*

LETTERS

Dean Swift's also are unaffected; and as a proof of their being so, they exhibited his character fully, with all its defects; though it were to be wished, for the honour of his memory, that his epistolary correspondence had not been drained to the dregs, by so many successive publications as have been given to the world.

Hugh Blair, 1783, *Lectures on Rhetoric and Belles-Letters,*
ed. Mills, Lecture XXXVII

Swift's masculine power is manifest in his letters, for affection, unless the affection of rudeness, came not nigh him. There is, too, in his letters, a sad reality, from the connection with that strange control which his stern nature gained over the affections of two women at the same time; his mystterious marriage with one, and the final heart-breaking of them both.

Henry Reed, 1855, *Lectures on English Literature
from Chaucer to Tennyson,* p. 405

Swift's own letters, however, have the true genius ring. In so far as he came under the spirit of the age, and found himself in correspondence with men who would have shuddered at incorrect syntax or bad logic, they are careful compositions. But he was an exceedingly quick writer; and, as most of his letters are addressed to friends of tried fidelity, they afford us a real insight into the man and his being. They describe his manner of life: they show how the solitary chafed against exile without being able to summon up strength to quit it; and they enable us to trace his gradual decline, from attempted resignation, into a bitterness which no philosophy could soothe.

Gerald P. Moriarty, 1892, *Dean Swift and his Writings,* p. 278

GENERAL

To Jonathan Swift, the most agreeable companion, the truest friend, and the greatest genius of his age, this work is presented by his most humble servant the author.

> Joseph Addison, 1705, Inscription to Presentation
> Copy of *Travels in Italy*

There is just published Swift's History. . . . Pope and Lord Bolingbroke always told him it would disgrace him, and persuaded him to burn it. Disgrace him indeed it does,—being a weak libel, ill written for style, uninformed, and adopting the most errant mob stories. He makes the Duke of Marlborough a coward, Prince Eugene an assassin, my father remarkable for nothing but impudence, and would make my Lord Somers anything but the most amiable character in the world, if unfortunately he did not praise him while he tries to abuse.

> Horace Walpole, 1758, *To Sir Horace Mann,* March 21;
> *Letters* ed. Cunningham, vol. III, p. 130

In Swift's writings there is a false misanthropy, grounded upon an exclusive contemplation of the vices and follies of mankind, and this misanthropic tone is also disfigured or brutalized by his obtrusion of physical dirt and coarseness. . . . Swift's style is, in its line, perfect; the manner is a complete expression of the matter, the terms appropriate, and the artifice concealed. It is simplicity in the true sense of the word.

> Samuel Taylor Coleridge, 1818, *Miscellanies, Æsthetic and*
> *Literary,* ed. Ashe, pp. 128, 181

By far the greatest man of that time, I think, was Jonathan Swift; Dean Swift, a man entirely deprived of his natural nourishment, but of great robustness; of genuine Saxon mind, not without a feeling of reverence, though, from circumstances, it did not awaken in him, for he got unhappily, at the outset, into the Church, not having any vocation for it. It is curious to see him arranging, as it were, a little religion to himself. . . . He saw himself in a world of confusion and falsehood. No eyes were clearer to see into it than his. He was great from being of acrid temperament: painfully sharp nerves in body as well as soul, for he was constantly ailing, and his mind, at the same time, was soured with indignation at what he saw around him. He took up therefore, what was fittest for him, namely, sarcasm, and he carried it quite to an epic pitch. There is something great and fearful in his irony, for it is not always used for effect, or designedly to depreciate. There seems often to be a sympathy in it with the thing he satirizes; occasionally it was even impossible for him so to laugh at any object without a sympathy with it, a sort of love for it; the same love as Cervantes universally shows for his own objects of merit.

> Thomas Carlyle, 1838, *Lectures on the History of Literature,*
> Lecture X, p. 177

Jonathan Swift, though writing upon the gross side of human life, was a writer, nevertheless, who was conscious that he was treading the paths of greatness. Had he always received due encouragement, and had the burden of his life been lightened, there is no knowing of what height he could not have attained in the roll of letters. On the severe and thoroughly caustic side of satire, he has no equal; he is a giant wielding the weapons of ridicule; and had not his existence been so overshadowed by disappointments, it would be hazardous, we repeat, to affirm what triumphs he might not have achieved in English literature. As it is, he enjoys the position of one of its finest and most honored classics.

> George Barnett Smith, 1876, "Dean Swift," *The International*
> *Review,* vol. 3, p. 316

It may well be doubted whether in absolute command over language, any English prose author has ever equalled Swift. His style defies description or classification. It lends itself less than any, to imitation or to parody. It varies according to every mood. Its lucid simplicity is so perfect that its phrases once read, seemed to be only the natural utterances of careless thought, produced effort and without art. Its very neglect of rule, and its frequent defiance of grammatical regularity, help to give to it force and directness. But such a style refuses to transmit the secret of its power, and must needs remain unique and solitary in its kind.

> Henry Craik, 1894, *English Prose,* Introduction, vol. III, p. 6

JAMES THOMSON
1700-1748

> Born at Ednam manse Kelso, 11th Sept. 1700, but brought up at South-dean, Jedburgh. He had studied for the ministry at Edinburgh, when in 1725 he removed to London, and in 1726 published "Winter," the first of his poems on the *Seasons;* it was immediately successful. "Summer" and "Spring" followed in 1727-28, and in 1730 "Autumn" completed the work. In 1729 his *Sophonisba* was produced. One luckless line, "O Sophonisba, Sophonisba O," is still remembered for the parody, "O Jemmy Thomson, Jemmy Thomson O," which killed what little life the piece possessed. His other tragedies were *Agemmnon* (1738), *Edward and*

Eleonora (1739), *Tancred and Sigismunda* (1745), and *Coriolanus* (1748). In 1731 Thomson was chosen to accompany the son of Lord Chancellor Talbot on the Grand Tour. The poem of *Liberty* (1732), inspired by his travels, was dedicated to the Prince of Wales, who in 1737 gave the poet a pension of £100 a year. He also obtained the sinecure post, worth £300 more, of surveyor-general of the Leeward Islands. In 1740 the *Masque of Alfred* was produced before the Prince and Princess of Wales. It contains "Rule Britannia" (claimed also for Mallet.) Thomson's finest work, *The Castle of Indolence,* was published in May 1748. He died at Richmond, 27th August following.

> Patrick and Groome, eds., 1897, *Chambers's Biographical Dictionary,* p. 914

SEE: *Complete Poetical Works,* ed. J. Logie Robertson, 1908; Douglas Grant, *James Thomson,* 1951.

PERSONAL

Mr. Thomson was at the Leasowes in the summer of 1745, and in the autumn of 1746, and promised when he came again into the country to make a longer visit; but at the time he was expected came an account of his death. It seems he waited too long for the return of his friend, Dr. Armstrong, and did not choose to employ any other physician. He had nothing of the gentleman in his person or address; but he made amends for the deficiency by his refined sense, spirited expressions, and a manner of speaking not unlike his friend Quin. He did not talk a great deal, but after a pause of reflection produced something or other that accounted for his delay. *The Seasons* would make a fine poem in Latin. Its turgid phrases would lose their stiffness, and its vulgar idioms acquire a proper majesty; its propriety and description shine the same.

> William Shenstone, c1748, *MS. Note in his Copy of the Seasons*

Placid and good-natured in disposition Thomson undoubtedly always was; sluggish and prone to unconventional habits in later years he must have been, or his friends would not have twitted him so excessively on the matter; but a writer who could put to his credit so much admirable and polished poetical work in a somewhat brief career, could not, on the face of it, have been a trifler once upon a day. The storied peach which he so leisurely plucked from his garden-tree at Richmond has enjoyed a celebrity much exceeding its due; in addition, a man who did his writing chiefly at midnight could not with any sort of fairness be expected to be astir at dawn. Thomson has surely borne undeserved reproach, if not libel, on the score of general inertia. . . . A writer who could put so much bright, wholesome, and spiritual thinking into his poetry has inevitably drawn there for himself a character with dominant traits of the best and finest; and, upon the whole, there is no significant reason to conclude that he was materially untrue to the ideal which he thus upheld. Men like Lyttelton and Rundle, moral purists not only in sentiment but in practice, delighted in him. And if a man's letters to his friends are not cunningly devised pieces of deception, then Thomson must be deemed to have been possessed of uncommon goodness of heart.

William Bayne, 1898, *James Thomson* (*Famous Scots Series*),
pp. 97, 107

The Seasons (1726-30)

Mr. Thomson's poetical diction in *The Seasons* is very peculiar to him: His manner of writing is entirely his own: He has introduced a number of compound words; converted substantives into verbs, and in short has created a kind of new language for himself. His stile has been blamed for its singularity and stiffness; but with submission to superior judges, we cannot but be of opinion, that though this observation is true, yet is it admirably fitted for description. The object he paints stands full before the eye, we admire it in all its lustre, and who would not rather enjoy a perfect inspection into a natural curiosity through a microscope capable of discovering all the minute beauties, though its exterior form should not be comely, than perceive an object but faintly, through a microscope ill adapted for the purpose, however its outside may be decorated. Thomson has a stiffness in his manner, but then his manner is new; and there never yet arose a distinguished genius, who had not an air peculiarly his own. 'Tis true indeed, the tow'ring sublimity of Mr. Thomson's stile is ill adapted for the tender passions, which will appear more fully when we consider him as a dramatic writer, a sphere in which he is not so excellent as in other species of poetry.

Theophilus Cibber, 1753, *Lives of the Poets,* vol. V, p. 202

Of all professed descriptive compositions, the largest and fullest that I am acquainted with, in any language, is Mr. Thomson's *Seasons,* a work which possesses very uncommon merit. The style, in the midst of much splendour and strength, is sometimes harsh, and may be censured as deficient in ease and distinctness. But notwithstanding this defect, Thomson is a strong and a beautiful describer; for he had a feeling heart, and a warm imagination. He had studied and copied nature with care. Enamoured of her beauties, he not only described them properly, but felt their impression with strong sensibility. The impression which he felt, he transmits to his readers; and no person of taste can peruse any one of his *Seasons,* without having the ideas and feelings, which belong to that season, recalled and rendered present to his mind.

Hugh Blair, 1783, *Lectures on Rhetoric and Belles-Lettres,*
ed. Mills, Lecture XL

While virgin Spring, by Eden's flood,
Unfolds her tender mantle green,
Or pranks the sod in frolic mood,
Or tunes the Æolian strains between;
While Summer, with a matron grace,
Retreats to Dryburgh's cooling shade,
Yet, oft delighted, stops to trace
The progress of the spikey blade;
While Autumn, benefactor kind,
By Tweed erects his aged head,
And sees, with self-approving mind,
Each creature on her bounty fed;
While maniac Winter rages o'er
The hills whence classic Yarrow flows,
Rousing the turbid torrent's roar,
Or sweeping, wild! a waste of snows;
So long, sweet Poet of the year!
Shall bloom that wreath thou well hast won,
While Scotia, with exulting tear,
Proclaims that Thomson was her son.

Robert Burns, 1791, *Address to the Shade of Thomson*

In the whole range of British poetry, Thomson's *Seasons* are, perhaps, the earliest read, and most generally admired. He was the Poet of Nature, and, studying her deeply, his mind acquired that placidity of thought and feeling which an abstraction from public life is sure to produce. . . . His pictures of scenery and of rural life are the productions of a master, and render him the Claude of Poets. *The Seasons* are the first book from which we are taught to worship the goddess to whose service the bard of Ednam devoted himself; and who is there that has reflected on the magnificence of an external landscape, viewed the sun as he emerges from the horizon, or witnessed the setting of that glorious orb when he leaves the world to reflection and repose, and does not feel his descriptions rush upon the mind, and heighten the enjoyment?

Sir Nicholas Harris Nicolas, 1831-47, ed.,
Poetical Works of James Thomson

In choosing his subject, therefore, and in the minute loving way in which he dwells upon it, Thomson would seem to have been working in the spirit of his country. But there the Scottish element in him begins and ends. Neither in the kind of landscape he pictures, in the rural customs he selects, nor in the language or versification of his poem, is there much savor of Scottish habits or scenery. His blank verse cannot be said to be a garment that fits well to its subject. It is heavy, cumbrous, oratorical, overloaded with epithets, full of artificial invocations, "personified abstractions," and insipid classicalities. It is a composite style of language formed from the recollection partly of Milton, partly of Virgil's Georgics. Yet in spite of all these obstructions which repel pure taste and natural feeling, no one can read the four books of *The Seasons* through, without seeing that Thomson, for all his false style, wrote with his eye upon Nature, and laid his finger on many a fact and image never before touched in poetry.

John Campbell Shairp, 1877, *On Poetic Interpretation of Nature,*
p. 197

Thomson's descriptions are not always due to the colors thrown upon them by his own hopes and fears for himself; it is only passages here and there that have a direct biographical interest. The gloomy notes of the opening of his poem on Winter are only significant of the mood in which he began the poem; once fairly absorbed in his subject, he seems, as it were, to have been carried on the wings of imagination far above and away from the anxieties of his own life, up into sublime contemplation of the great forces of Nature, and into warm sympathy with the human hardships and enjoyments, horrors and amusements, peculiar to the season.

William Minto, 1894, *The Literature of the Georgian Era,*
ed. Knight, p. 61

The Seasons shows that as far as intrinsic worth is concerned the poems are marked with a strange mingling of merits and defects, but that, considered in their historical place in the development of the poetry of nature, their importance and striking originality can hardly be overstated. Though Thomson talked the language of his day, his thought was a new one. He taught clearly, though without emphasis, the power of nature to quiet the passions and elevate the mind of man, and he intimated a deeper thought of divine immanence in the phenomena of nature. But his great service to the men of his day was that he shut up their books, led them out of their parks, and taught them to look on nature with enthusiasm.

Myra Reynolds, 1896, *The Treatment of Nature in
English Poetry,* p. 89

Between the ages of Pope and Scott, Thomson continued the most popular poet in the English language, and it would be difficult to set a limit to the extent of his influence. His plays, cold and undramatic, were of no great moment; and his political pieces, dreary diatribes and citations, might have remained unwritten. Even his *Castle of Indolence,* with it rich archaic setting and its sensuous and languid splendour, must have exercised a charm always only upon the inner few. But his *Seasons* were a new voice on the earth; their imagery, fresh and exuberant, carried men back to the natural wells of delight—the simple enjoyments of sense, the glory of valley and woodland, and the magic and the majesty of the sea. The verse, moreover, in which they were written was the first blank verse of the modern kind.

> George Eyre-Todd, 1896, *Scottish Poetry of the Eighteenth Century*, vol. I, p. 100

We have grown so accustomed to a more intimate treatment and a more spiritual interpretation of nature, that we are perhaps too apt to undervalue Thomson's simple descriptive or pictorial method. Compared with Wordsworth's mysticism, with Shelley's passionate pantheism, with Byron's romantic gloom in presence of the mountains and the sea, with Keats' joyous re-creation of mythology, with Thoreau's Indian-like approach to the innermost arcana—with a dozen other moods familiar to the modern mind— it seems to us unimaginative. Thomson has been likened, as a colorist, to Rubens; and possibly the glow, the breadth, and the vital energy of his best passages, as of Rubens' great canvases, leave our finer perceptions untouched, and we ask for something more esoteric, more intense. Still there are permanent and solid qualities in Thomson's landscape art, which can give delight even now to an unspoiled taste. To a reader of his own generation, *The Seasons* must have come as the revelation of a fresh world of beauty. Such passages as those which describe the first spring showers, the thunderstorm in summer, the trout-fishing, the sheep-washing, and the terrors of the winter night, were not only strange to the public of that day, but were new in English poetry.

> Henry A. Beers, 1898, *A History of English Romanticism in the Eighteenth Century*, p. 107

MS. Corrections of *The Seasons*

It has long been accepted as a fact among scholars that Pope assisted Thomson in the composition of the *Seasons*. Our original authority for the statement is, I suppose, Joseph Warton. Johnson who had heard, through Savage, a great deal about Thomson, does not mention *this*. . . . But if the best authorities at the Museum many years ago were positive that this handwriting is Pope's, their successors at the present time are equally positive that it is not. On this point the opinion of Mr. Warner, whom Mr. W. Y. Fletcher kindly consulted for me, is very decided. Nor does Mr. Courthope, to whom I have shown the volume, recognize the hand as bearing much resemblance to Pope's. Without pretending to an idependent judgment upon such matters, I must say that it has all along been perplexing to me how the opinion that this was Pope's handwriting could ever have been confidently entertained. . . . At present I am inclined to believe these notes to be the work of a very intimate and even devoted friend. If space permitted, I think I could show that they were written by a man of finer taste—perhaps of greater poetic gift— than Thomson himself.

D. C. Tovey, 1894, "An Interleaved Copy of Thomson's *Seasons*," *The Athenæum*, vol. 2, pp. 131, 132

"Through the black night that sits immense around." Indeed, throughout *The Seasons* Thomson's indebtedness to his corrector is incalculable; many of the most felicitous touches are due to him. Now, who was his corrector? . . . What has long therefore been represented and circulated as an undisputed fact—namely, that Pope assisted Thomson in the revision of *The Seasons*—rests not, as all Thomson's modern editors, have supposed, on the traditions of the eighteenth century, and on the testimony of authenticated handwriting, but on a mere assumption of Mitford. That the volume in question really belonged to Thomson, and that the corrections are originals, hardly admits of doubt, though Mitford gives neither the pedigree nor the history of this most interesting literary relic. It is of course possible that the corrections are Thomson's own, and that the differences in the handwriting are attributable to the fact that in some cases he was his own scribe, in others he employed an amanuensis; but the intrinsic unlikeness of the corrections made in the strange hand to his characteristic style renders this improbable. In any case there is nothing to warrant the assumption that the corrector was Pope.

John Churton Collins, 1897, "A Literary Mare's-Nest," *The Saturday Review*, vol. 84, p. 118

(1) There is no one to whom Thomson would have, between 1738 and 1744, so likely applied for criticism and suggestions as his friend and neighhour, the great Mr. Pope. (2) There is no one but Pope who could, at that time, have written verse equal or nearly equal to that of Thomson. (3) If the writing be certainly not that of Pope, as it is not either that of any other known writer who could be supposed to have been the author of such emendations and additions, there remains only to conclude that the real author used an amanuensis. But instead of Mr. Churton Collins's suggestion (which he himself declares to be improbable, and which seems to me utterly untenable) that the notes are Thomson's while employing an amanuesis, I hold by the notion that, whoever the amanuensis, the notes were dictated by Pope.

Léon Morel, 1898, "Thomson and Pope," *The Saturday Review*, vol. 86. p. 208

The Castle of Indolence (1748)

I conclude you will read Mr. Thomson's *Castle of Indolence*: it is after the
manner of Spenser; but I think he does not always keep so close to his style
as the author of the *School-Mistress,* whose name I never knew until you
were so good as to inform me of it,—I believe the *Castle of Indolence* will
afford you much entertainment; there are many pretty paintings in it; but I
think the wizard' song deserves a preference:

"He needs no muse who dictates from the heart."

Countess Hertford, 1748, *Letter to Lady Luxborough,* May 15

To *The Castle of Indolence* he brought not only the full nature, but the perfect art, of a poet. The materials of that exquisite poem are derived originally from Tasso; but he was more immediately indebted for them to *The
Fairy Queen*: and in meeting with the paternal spirit of Spenser he seems as
if he were admitted more intimately to the home of inspiration.

Thomas Campbell, 1819, *Specimens of the British Poets*

The Castle of Indolence, more thoroughly complete, more delicately finished,
and aspiring to a certain plot and story, displays more of the artist, with
very little less of the poet, than *The Seasons*. It is, certainly, the sweetest
piece of poetic seduction in the world. No hymn to Sleep ever was so soft—
no "dream within a dream," of rest beyond the dreaming land, was so subtle.

George Gilfillan, 1853, ed. *Thomson's Poetical Works,* p. xvii

No work of poetry between the time of Spenser and Thomson is so marked
by this absolutely delicate idealising tendency; nothing like it appears again
till the time of Keats. We do not hear much about the significance of Thomson's part in setting forth anew the "sweet-slipping movement" and charm
of the Spenserian manner as a model for the poets of the nineteenth century
literary renaissance; but there can be no doubt about the validity of his right
in this matter. In the romantic method, so excellently represented by Thomson, Keats may be taken as the most direct successor who understood the
extraordinary richness of the note that was struck in *The Castle of Indolence;* for though there is its mystic glamour in the poetry of Coleridge,
Keats, in his work, combines in a more general way, the main aims in the
literary design of Thomson.

William Bayne, 1898, *James Thomson (Famous Scots Series),*
p. 131

DRAMAS

The town flocks to a new play of Thomson's, called *Tancred and Sigis-munda*: it is very dull; I have read it. I cannot bear modern poetry; these refiners of the purity of the stage and of the incorrectness of English verse are most wofully insipid. I had rather have written the most absurd lines in Lee, than *Leonidas* or *The Seasons;* as I had rather be put into the round-house for a wrong-headed quarrel than sup quietly at eight o'clock with my grandmother.

> Horace Walpole, 1745, *Letter to Sir Horace Mann,* March 29;
> *Letters,* ed. Cunningham, vol. I, p. 347

Mr. Thomson's tragedies seem to me wisely intricated and elegantly writ; they want perhaps some fire, and it may be that his heroes are neither mov-ing nor busy enough, but taking him all in all, methinks he has the highest claim to the greatest esteem.

> François Marie Arouet Voltaire, 1790, *Letter to Lord Lyttelton,*
> May 17

Though *Agamemnon* is not a capital play on the whole, and abounds in languid and long declamatory speeches, yet parts of it are striking, partic-ularly Melisander's account of the desert island to which he was banished, copied from the *Philoctetes* of Sophocles; and the prophetic speeches of Cassandra during the moment of Agamemnon's being murdered, well calc-ulated to fill the audience with alarm, astonishment, and suspense at an awful event, obscurely hinted at in very strong imagery. These speeches are closely copied from the *Agamemnon* of Eschylus, as is a striking scene in his *Eleonora* from the *Alcestis* of Euripides. Thomson was well acquainted with the Greek tragedies, on which I heard him talk learnedly when I was once introduced to him by my friend Mr. W. Collins.

> Joseph Warton, 1797, ed. *Pope's Works,* vol. VII, p. 10

The beautiful fancy, the gorgeous diction, and generous affections of Thom-son, were chilled and withered as soon as he touched the verge of the Drama; where his name is associated with a mass of verbose puerility, which it is difficult to conceive could ever have proceeded from the author of *The Seasons* and *The Castle of Indolence.*

> Francis, Lord Jeffrey, 1822-44, *Contributions to the*
> *Edinburgh Review,* vol. 2, p. 334

It [*Sophonisba*] was a poor imitation of Otway, and there was little oppor-tunity in it for the display of the poet's characteristic excellencies; it was nevertheless sold to Millar for 130 guineas, and went through four editions during the year (several translations appeared, a Russian one in 1786). One line of *Sophonisba* at least has defied oblivion. Nat Lee had written "O Sophonisba, Oh!" Thomson expanded the sentiment in the verse

Oh! Sophonisba, Sophonisba, Oh!

the inanity of which was pointed out, not at the theatre, as has generally been assured, but in an envious little squib, called *A Criticism of the New Sophonisba* (1730). The quick eye of Fielding soon detected the absurdity, which was paraded in his *Tom Thumb the Great,* the line "Oh! Huncamunca, Huncamunca, Oh!" appearing as a kind of refrain. It is noticeable that the line "O Sophonisba, I am wholly thine," was not substituted by Thomson until after 1738.

Thomas Seccombe, 1898, Dictionary of National Biography,
vol. LVI, p. 248

GENERAL

Thomson was blessed with a strong and copious fancy; he has enriched poetry with a variety of new and original images, which he painted from nature itself, and from his own actual observations; his descriptions have, therefore, a distinctness and truth which are utterly wanting to those of poets who have only copied from each other, and have never looked abroad on the subjects themselves. Thomson was accustomed to wander away into the country for days and for weeks, attentive to each rural sight, each rural sound; while many a poet who has dwelt for years in the Strand has attempted to describe fields and rivers, and has generally succeeded accordinly.

Joseph Warton, 1756, Essay on the Genius and Writings of Pope

Just at present Thomson's reputation is a pious tradition rather than a visibly potential reality. It seems strange that this should be so, in an age which gives unmistakable and increasing welcome to the apostles of the new naturalism; for it is no exaggeration to say that the discoveries of Jefferies and of Burroughs were well know to Thomson, and that Thomson presented his transcripts of nature with perfect truth, freedom, and beauty, and subimity of effect. One of the secrets of Thomson's power our new naturalists possess, namely, fulness of knowledge, acquired by careful sympathetic study; but for the felicity of his expression of the phenomena of nature he stands to this day unmatched. His pages are broadcast with these felicities of phrase. Such are his castled clouds, for ever flushing round a flushing sky; the sleepy horror of his waving pines; the still song of his harvests, breathed into the reaper's heart; his sturdy boy grasping the indignant ram by the twisted horns; his lively-shining leopard, the beauty of the waste; his ruddy maid, full as the summer rose blown by prevailing suns; the slender feet of his red-breast, attracted by the table crumbs; his lightfooted dews; his isles amid the melancholy main. One does not need to pick and choose; they start from the opened leaves.

Hugh Haliburton, 1893, "James Thomson," *Good Words*,
vol. 34, p. 467

THE LATER
EIGHTEENTH CENTURY

HENRY FIELDING
1707-1754

Born, at Sharphan Park, Somersetshire, 22 April 1707. Family moved to
East Stour, Dorsetshire, 1710. Educated at Eton (1719?-1725?). At
Leyden, studying Law (1725-27?). Returned to London. First play, *Love
in several Masques,* produced at Drury Lane, Feb. 1728. Probably returned to Leyden for a short time in 1728. Prolific writer of plays, 1727-37.
Married Charlotte Craddock, 1735 (?). Manager of Haymarket Theatre,
1736-37. Entered Middle Temple, 1 Nov. 1737; called to Bar, 20 June
1740. Edited *The Champion,* with J. Ralph; contrib. articles, 27 Nov.
1739 to 12 June 1740. Revised his play, *The Wedding Day,* for Garrick;
produced 17 Feb. 1743. Wife died, 1743 (?). Ed. *The True Patriot,*
5 Nov. 1745 to 10 June 1746. Edited *The Jacobite's Journal,* Dec. 1747 to
Nov. 1748. Married Mary Daniel, 27 Nov. 1747. Lived at Twickenham.
Moved to house in Bow Street, when appointed J. P. for Westminster, Dec.
1748. Chairman of Quarter Sessions, Hick's Hall, May 1749. Ed. *Covent
Garden Journal,* Jan. to Nov. 1752. Severe illness, winter of 1749, and
spring of 1754. Moved to Ealing, May 1754. To Lisbon for health, July
1754. Died there, 8 Oct. 1754; buried in English cemetery there. WORKS:
Love in several Masques, 1728; *Rape upon Rape* (anon.), 1730 (another
edition called: *The Coffee-house Politicians,* 1730); *The Temple Beau,*
1730; *The Author's Farce* (under pseud. "H. Scriblerus Secundus"), 1730;
Tom Thumb (by "Scriblerus Secundus"), 1730 (with additional act,
1731); *The Welsh Opera* (by "Scriblerus Secundus"), 1731 (2nd edn.
same year, called: *The Grub Street Opera*); *The Letter-Writers* (by "H.
Scriblerus Secundus"), 1731; *The Lottery* (anon.), 1732; *The Modern
Husband,* 1732; *The Covent Garden Tragedy* (anon.), 1732; *The Debauchees* (or *The Old Debauchees,* anon.), 1732; *The Mock Doctor*
(anon.; from Molière), 1732; *The Miser,* 1733; *The Intriguing Chambermaid,* 1734 (from Regnard); *Don Quixote in England,* 1734; *An Old
Man taught Wisdom,* 1735; *The Universal Gallant,* 1735; *Pasquin,* 1736;
The Historical Register for the Year 1736 (anon.), 1737; *Eurydice,* 1737;
Tumble-down Dick, 1737; *The Vernon-aid* (anon.), 1741; *The Crisis*
(anon.), 1741; *Miss Lucy in Town* (anon.), 1742; *Letter to a Noble
Lord* (respecting preceding; anon.), 1742; *The History of the Adventures
of Joseph Andrews* (2 vols.; anon.), 1742 (2nd edn. same year); *A Full
Vindication of the Duchess Dowager of Marlborough* (anon.), 1742;
Plutus (from Aristophanes, with W. Young), 1742; *The Wedding Day,*
1743; *Miscellanies* (including *Jonathan Wild* (3 vols.), 1743 (2nd edn.
same year); *Proper Answer to a Scurrilous Libel,* 1747; *The History of
Tom Jones* (6 vols.), 1749; *A Charge delivered to the Grand Jury,* 1749;
A True State of the Case of Bosavern Penlez, 1749; *An Enquiry into the
Causes of the late Increase of Robbers, etc.,* 1751; *Amelia,* 1751; *Examples*

*of the Interposition of Providence, 1752; Proposals for making an effec-
tual Provision for the Poor, 1753; A clear State of the Case of Elizabeth
Canning, 1753.* POSTHUMOUS: *Journal of a Voyage to Lisbon, 1755; The
Fathers, 1778.* He *translated:* Ovid's *Art of Love,* under title *The Lover's
Assistant, 1759;* and *edited:* the 2nd edn. of Sarah Fielding's *Adventures
of David Simple, 1744,* and *Familiar Letters, 1747.* COLLECTED WORKS:
ed. by Murphy, in 4 vols., 1762; ed. by Chalmers, in 10 vols., 1806; ed. by
Roscoe, 1840; ed. by Herbert, 1872; ed. by Leslie Stephen, 10 vols. 1882;
ed. by G. Saintsbury, 12 vols. 1893. *Life:* by F. Lawrence, 1855; by
Austin Dobson, 1883.

R. Farquharson Sharp, 1897, *A Dictionary of English Authors,* p. 99

SEE: *Complete Works,* ed. W. E. Henley and others, 1903, 16 v. (incomplete); *The True Patriot,* ed. Miriam A. Locke, 1965; *An Apology for the
Life of Mrs. Shamela Andrews (1741), with an Introduction* by Ian Watt,
1956; Wilbur L. Cross, *The History of Henry Fielding,* 1918, 3 v.;
F. Homes Dudden, *Henry Fielding: His Life, Work, and Times,* 1952,
2 v.; Frederick T. Blanchard, *Fielding, The Novelist,* 1926; Martin C.
Battestin, *The Moral Basis of Fielding's Art: A Study of 'Joseph Andrews',*
1959; Maurice Johnson, *Fielding's Art of Fiction: Eleven Essays . . . ,*
1961; Henry Knight Miller, *Essays on Fielding's 'Miscellanies': A Commentary on Volume One,* 1961.

PERSONAL

These so tolerated companies gave encouragement to *a broken wit* to collect
a fourth company, who for some time acted plays in the Haymarket. . . .
This enterprising person, I say (whom I do not choose to name, unless it
could be to his advantage, or that it were of importance), had sense enough
to know that the best plays with bad actors would turn but to a very poor
account, and therefore found it necessary to give the public some pieces of
an extraordinary kind, the poetry of which he conceived ought to be so strong
that the greatest dunce of an actor could not spoil it: he knew, too, that
as he was in haste to get money, it would take up less time to be intrepidly
abusive than decently entertaining; that to draw the mob after him he must
rake the channel and pelt their superiors. . . . Such then was the mettlesome
modesty he set out with; upon this principle he produced several frank and
free farces, that seemed to knock all distinctions of mankind on the head—
religion, laws, government, priests, judges, and ministers, were all laid flat,
at the feet of this *Herculean* satirist! this Drawcansir in wit, who spared
neither friend nor foe! who, to make his poetical fame immortal, like another Erostratus, set fire to his stage by writing up to an act of parliament
to demolish it. I shall not give the particular strokes of his ingenuity a chance
to be remembered by reciting them; it may be enough to say, in general
terms, they were so openly flagrant that the wisdom of the legislature thought
it high time to take a proper notice of them.

Colley Cibber, 1740, *Apology*

I wish you had been with me last week when I spent two evenings with Fielding and his sister, who wrote *David Simple*: and you may guess I was very well entertained. The lady, indeed, retired pretty soon, but Russel and I sat up with the poet till one or two in the morning, and were inexpressibly diverted. I find he values, as he justly may, his *Joseph Andrews* above all his writings. He was extremely civil to me, I fancy on my father's account.

Joseph Warton, 1746, Letter to Thomas Warton, Oct.

I am sorry for H. Fielding's death, and not only as I shall read no more of his writings, but I believe he lost more than others, as no man enjoyed life more than he did, though few had less reason to do so, the highest of his preferment being raking in the lowest sinks of vice and misery. I should think it a nobler and less nauseous employment to be one of the staff-officers that conduct the nocturnal weddings. His happy constitution (even when he had, with great pains, half demolished it) made him forget everything when he was before a venison pasty, or over a flask of champaigne; and I am persuaded he has known more happy moments than any prince upon earth. His natural spirits gave him rapture with his cook-maid, and cheerfulness when he was starving in a garret. There was a great similitude between his character and that of Sir Richard Steele. He had the advantage both in learning and, in my opinion, genius: they both agreed in wanting money in spite of all their friends, and would have wanted it, if their hereditary lands had been as extensive as their imagination; yet each of them so formed for happiness, it is pity he was not immortal.

Lady Mary Wortley Montagu, 1755, Letter to the Countess
of Bute, Sept. 22

Mr. Fielding had not been long a writer for the stage, when he married Miss Craddock, a beauty from Salisbury. About that time, his mother dying, a moderate estate, at Stower, in Dorsetshire, devolved to him. To that place he retired with his wife, on whom he doated, with a resolution to bid adieu to all the follies and intemperances to which he had addicted himself in the career of a town-life. But unfortunately a kind of family-pride here gained an ascendant over him; and he began immediately to vie in splendour with the neighbouring country 'squires. With an estate not much above two hundred pounds a-year, and his wife's fortune, which did not exceed fifteen hundred pounds, he encumbered himself with a large retinue of servants, all clad in costly yellow liveries. For their master's honour, these people could not descend so low as to be careful in their apparel, but, in a month or two, were unfit to be seen; the 'squire's dignity required that they should be new-equipped; and his chief pleasure consisting in society and convivial mirth, hospitality threw open its doors, and in less than three years, entertainments, hounds, and horses, entirely devoured a little patrimony, which, had it been managed with economy, might have secured to him a state of independence for the rest of his life. . . . . His passions, as the poet expresses it, were trembling alive all o'er; whatever he desired, he desired ardently; he was alike impatient of disappointment, or illusage, and the same quickness of sensibility rendered him elate in prosperity, and overflowing with gratitude at every instance of friendship or generosity: steady in his private attachments, his affection was warm, sincere, and vehement; in his resentments, he was manly, but temperate, seldom breaking out in his writings into gratifications of ill humour, or personal satire. It is to the honour of those whom he loved, that he had too much penetration to be deceived in their characters; and it is to the advantage of his enemies, that he was above passionate attacks upon them. Open, unbounded, and social in his temper, he knew no love of money; but, inclining to excess even in his very virtues, he pushed his contempt of avarice into the opposite extreme of imprudence and prodigality. When young in life he had a moderate estate, he soon suffered hospitality to devour it; and when in the latter end of his days he had an income of four or five hundred a-year, he knew no use of money, but to keep his table open to those who had been his friends when young, and had impaired their own fortunes. Though disposed to gallantry by his strong animal spirits, and the vivacity of his passions, he was remarkable for tenderness and constancy to his wife, and the strongest affection for his children.

Arthur Murphy, 1762, *An Essay on the Life and Genius of Henry Fielding, Esq., Works,* ed. Chalmers, vol. I, pp. 44, 82

Nor was she (Lady Mary Wortley Montagu) a stranger to that beloved first wife, whose picture he drew in his *Amelia,* where, as she said, even the glowing language he knew how to employ did not do more than justice to the amiable qualities of the original, or to her beauty, although this had suffered a little from the accident related in the novel—a frightful overturn, which destroyed the gristle of her nose. He loved her passionately, and she returned his affection. . . . . His biographers seem to have been shy of disclosing that after the death of this charming woman, he married her maid. And yet the act was not so discreditable to his character as it may sound. The maid had few personal charms, but was an excellent creature, devotedly attached to her mistress, and almost broken-hearted for her loss. In the first agonies of his own grief, which approached to frenzy, he found no relief but from weeping along with her; nor solace when a degree calmer, but in talking to her of the angel they mutually regretted. This made her his habitual confidential associate, and in process of time he began to think he could not give his children a tenderer mother, or secure for himself a more faithful housekeeper and nurse. At least, this was what he told his friends; and it is certain that her conduct as his wife confirmed it, and fully justified his good opinion.

Lady Louisa Stuart, 1837, *Letters and Works of Lady Mary Wortley Montagu,* ed. Wharncliffe, Introductory Anecdotes

I cannot offer or hope to make a hero of Harry Fielding. Why hide his faults? Why conceal his weaknesses in a cloud of periphrasis? Why not show him, like him as he is, not robed in a marble toga, and draped and polished in a heroic attitude, but with inked ruffles, and claret stains on his tarnished lace coat, and on his manly face the marks of good fellowship, of illness, of kindness, of care, and wine. Stained as you see him, and worn by care and dissipation, that man retains some of the most precious and splendid human qualities and endowments. He has an admirable natural love of truth, the keenest instinctive antipathy to hypocrisy, the happiest satirical gift of laughing it to scorn. His wit is wonderfully wise and detective; it flashes upon a rogue and lightens up a rascal like a policeman's lantern. He is one of the manliest and kindliest of human beings: in the midst of all his imperfections, he respects female innocence and infantine tenderness, as you would suppose such a great-hearted, courageous soul would respect and care for them. He could not be so brave, generous, truth-telling as he is, were he not infinitely merciful, pitiful, and tender. He will give any man his purse—he cannot help kindness and profusion. He may have low tastes, but not a mean mind; he admires with all his heart good and virtuous men, stoops to no flattery, bears no rancour, disdains all disloyal arts, does his public duty uprightly, is fondly loved by his family, and dies at his work.

William Makepeace Thackeray, 1853, *The English Humourists of the Eighteenth Century*

The day of reckoning came. In a very short time Fielding found that all was spent and gone—all swallowed up in the abyss of ruin! It seemed like a dream, a wild, incoherent vision. The roar of mirth, the deafening cheer, the splendid liveries, prancing horses, staring rustics, fullmouthed dogs, faded before him like some "insubstantial pageant." He had been generous, hospitable, profuse; and what was his reward? Those who had sat at meat with him now ridiculed his extravagance. Even the gaping boors of the neighbourhood cracked their heavy jokes at his expense. The prudent gentlemen and ladies who had not scrupled to sit at his jovial board, and partake of his cheer, now shook their heads, and gravely condemned his prodigality. Those of his more ambitious neighbours whom he had recently outshone in splendour, rejoiced in his downfall, without attempting to conceal their satisfaction. In the midst of all these untoward circumstances, he had to escape from his creditors as best he might, and to seek for happiness and a livelihood in some other sphere. How bitterly Fielding cursed his folly, and how penitently he bewailed his imprudence, can be well imagined. His sorrow—now, alas; unavailing—was not unmixed with feelings of resentment. The jealousy with which he had been regarded in the height of his ostentatious career, and the treatment he experienced in his reverses, long rankled in his breast. He could not easily forget the sneers and slights of those whom in his heart he so much despised; and from this time forth, therefore, the Squirearchy of England had to expect little mercy at his hands.

Frederick Lawrence, 1855, The Life of Henry Fielding, p. 75

Force, activity, invention, tenderness, all overflowed in him. He had a mother's fondness for his children, adored his wife, became almost mad when he lost her, found no other consolation than to weep with his maid-servant, and ended by marrying that good and honest girl, that he might give a mother to his children; the last trait in the portrait of his valiant plebeian heart, quick in telling all, possessing no dislikes, but all the best parts of man, except delicacy. We read his books as we drink a pure, whole-some, and rough wine, which cheers and fortifies us, and which wants nothing but bouquet.

H. A. Taine, 1871, History of English Literature,
tr. Van Laun, vol. II, bk. iii, ch. vi, p. 170

And what was his reward, after wasting disappointments? The then not very reputable post of Middlesex magistrate at Bow Street. But, to his credit be it told, the corrupt practices which disgraced that important though subordinate seat of criminal justice were swept away by his judicious and indefatigable management, and from being a nest rather for the nursing care of some delinquents than for their utter extermination, it became in his hands the dread of incorrigible evil doers; while the weary and heavy-laden met with compassionate consideration. Of these facts there is no one but must feel assured who has read what may be called his dying words, which are so impressively told in his *Voyage to Lisbon*—his last resting place.

James P. Browne, 1872, ed., Miscellanies and Poems by
Henry Fielding, Preface, p. xviii

DRAMAS

Though it must be acknowledged, that in the whole collection there are few plays likely to make any considerable figure on the stage hereafter, yet they are worthy of being preserved, being the works of a genius, who, in his wildest and most inaccurate productions, yet occasionally displays the talent of a master. Though in the plan of his pieces he is not always regular, yet is he often happy in his diction and style; and, in every groupe that he has exhibited, there are to be seen particular delineations that will amply recompense the attention bestowed upon them.

Arthur Murphy, 1762, *An Essay on the Life and Genius of Henry Fielding, Esq., Works,* ed. Chalmers, vol. I, p. 14

Can any reason be assigned, why the inimitable Fielding, who was so perfect in Epic fable, should have succeeded so indifferently in Dramatic? Was is owing to the peculiarity of his genius, or of his circumstances? to any thing in the nature of Dramatic writing in general, or of that particular taste in Dramatic Comedy which Congreve and Vanburgh had introduced, and which he was obliged to comply with?

William Beattie, 1776-79, *Essays on Poetry and Music,* p. 102, note

None of Fielding's plays, with the exception, perhaps, of his adaptation of *The Miser,* can be said to have "kept the stage;" few even of the students of literature have read them, and those who have read them have dismissed them too hastily. The closest students these plays have ever had were the dramatists of the following generation, whose works, notably those of Sheridan, contain many traces of their assiduity. The tradition about his writing scenes after his return from tavern carousals on the papers in which his tobacco had been wrapt, and his cool reception of Garrick's desire that he should alter some passage in *The Wedding-Day,* have helped the impression that they were loose, ill-considered, ill-constructed productions, scribbled off hastily to meet passing demands. There is only a fraction of truth in this notion. That the plays are not the work of a dull plodder or a mechanician of elaborate ingenuity goes without saying; but, though perhaps rapidly considered and rapidly constructed, they are neither ill-considered nor ill-constructed, and bear testimony to the large and keen intelligence, as well as the overflowing humor and fertile wit of their author.

William Minto, 1879, *Fielding, Encyclopædia Britannica,* vol. IX

As a dramatist he has no eminence; and though his plays do not deserve the sweeping condemnation with which Macaulay once spoke of them in the House of Commons, they are not likely to attract any critics but those for whom the inferior efforts of a great genius possess a morbid fascination. Some of them serve, in a measure, to illustrate his career; others contain hints and situations which he afterwards worked into his novels; but the only ones that possess real stage qualities are those which he borrowed from Regnard and Molière. *Don Quixote in England, Pasquin,* the *Historical Register,* can claim no present consideration commensurate with that which

they received as contemporary satires, and their interest is mainly antiquarian; while *Tom Thumb* and the *Covent-Garden Tragedy,* the former of
which would make the reputation of a smaller man, can scarcely hope to be
remembered beside *Amelia* or *Jonathan Wild.*

Austin Dobson, 1883, Fielding (English Men of Letters), p. 176

Joseph Andrews (1742)

I have myself, upon your recommendation, been reading *Joseph Andrews.*
The incidents are ill laid and without invention; but the characters have a
great deal of nature, which always pleases even in her lowest shapes. Parson
Adams is perfectly well; so is Mrs. Slipslop, and the story of Wilson; and
throughout he shows himself well read in Stage-Coaches, Country Squires,
Inns, and Inns of Court. His reflections upon high people and low people,
and misses and masters, are very good.

Thomas Gray, 1742, Letter to Richard West

The worthy parson's learning, his simplicity, his evangelical purity of heart
and benevolence of disposition, are so admirably mingled with pedantry,
absence of mind, and with the habit of athletic and gymnastic exercise, then
acquired at the universities by students of all descriptions, that he may be
safely termed one of the richest productions of the Muse of Fiction.

Sir Walter Scott, 1820, Henry Fielding

While, however, it is highly probable that he had Cervantes in his eye, it
is certain that the satiric and burlesque portion of *Joseph Andrews* was
suggested to him by the perusal of Richardson's *Pamela,* on the overwrought
refinement and strained sentiment of which it affords a humorous commentary in the adventures of her professed brother, the hero. Besides its intrinsic
wit and excellence, it has thus a twofold attraction in the comic and burlesque spirit it maintains throughout, in the same way as the adventures of
the Spanish knight and his squire, however ludicrous in themselves, are relished with a double zest for the contrast they offer to the dignified bearing
and marvellous deeds of the old Paladins. How exquisitely Fielding has
caught the humour, assumed gravity, and delicate satire of his prototype,
they who have compared the two master-pieces will readily admit; and that
he loses nothing in point of originality.

Thomas Roscoe, 1840, Life and Works of Henry Fielding

Resemblances have been found, and may be admitted to exist, between the
Rev. Charles Primrose and the Rev. Abraham Adams. They were from
kindred genius; and from the manly habit which Fielding and Goldsmith

shared of discerning what was good and beautiful in the homeliest aspects of humanity. In the parson's saddle-bag of sermons would hardly have been found this prison-sermon of the vicar; and there was in Mr. Adams not only a capacity for beef and pudding, but for beating and being beaten, which would ill have consisted with the simple dignity of Doctor Primrose. But unquestionable learning, unsuspecting simplicity, amusing traits of credulity and pedantry, and a most Christian purity and benevolence of heart, are common to both these masterpieces of English fiction; and are in each with such exquisite touch discriminated, as to leave no possible doubt of the originality of either.

John Forster, 1848-54, *The Life and Times of Oliver Goldsmith,*
vol. I, ch. xiii

It is a piece of admirable art, but composed of the basest materials, like a palace built of dung. *Amelia* is not so corrupt, but it is often coarse, and, as a whole, very poor and tedious. *Joseph Andrews* is by far the most delightful of his writings. With less art than *Tom Jones,* it has much more genius. Parson Adams is confessedly one of the most original and pleasing characters in fiction. Goldsmith's *Vicar of Wakefield,* Joseph Cargill in *St. Ronan's Well,* are both copied from him, but have not a tithe of his deep simplicity and delicious *bonhommie.* We predict that, in a century hence, *Joseph Andrews* will alone survive to preserve Fielding's name.

George Gilfillan, 1855, *A Third Gallery of Portraits,* p. 231

What is London in the mouths of Hume, and Richardson, and Boswell? A place of elegant manners, refined ideas, general enlightenment, knowledge, enterprise, wealth, liberality. What are London and England in the pictures of Hogarth and the pages of Fielding? "No better than they should be," certainly: full of poverty, low vice, coarse indulgence, and sheer brutality, relieved now and then by exhibitions of good sense, courage, and love of learning. Parson Adams, the simple-minded clergyman in *Joseph Andrews,* who goes up to London to sell his sermons to some publisher, and meets on the way to and from the country with as many adventures as Don Quixote himself, is a literary creation of unsurpassed merit; nor are the personages that surround him, though less interesting, drawn with less ability.

Thomas Arnold, 1868-75, *Chaucer to Wordsworth,* p. 372

Jonathan Wild (1743)

Jonathan Wild is assuredly the best of all the fictions in which a villain is throughout the prominent character. But how impossible it is by any force of genius to create a sustained attractive interest for such a groundwork,

and how the mind wearies of, and shrinks from, the more than painful interest, the μισητὸν, of utter depravity,—Fielding himself felt and endeavoured to mitigate and remedy by the (on all other principles) far too
large a proportion, and too quick recurrence, of the interposed chapters of
moral reflection, like the chorus in the Greek tragedy,—admirable specimens as these chapters are of profound irony and philosophic satire.

Samuel Taylor Coleridge, 1832, *Notes on Books and Authors;*
Miscellanies, Æsthetic and Literary, ed. Ashe, p. 339

This has never been a favourite among Fielding's readers, because of its
caustic cynicism and the unbroken gloom of its tone, but it is equal to the
best he has left us in force and originality. It is the history of an unmitigated
ruffian, from his baptism by Titus Oates to his death at Newgate on "the
Tree of Glory." The story is intended to mock those relations in which
biographers lose themselves in pompus eulogies of their subjects, for their
"greatness," without consideration of any "goodness," by showing that it
is possible to write the history of a gallows-bird in exactly the same style of
inflated gusto. The inexorable irony which is sustained all through, even
when the most detestable acts of the hero are described, forms rather a
strain at last upon the reader's nerves, and no one would turn to *Jonathan
Wild* for mere amusement. But it shows a marvellous knowledge of the
seamy side of life, the author proving himself in it to be as familiar with
thieves and their prisons as in *Joseph Andrews* he had been with stage-
coaches and wayside taverns; while nothing could be more picturesque
than some of the scenes with Blueskin and his gang, or than the Petronian
passages on board ship.

Edmund Gosse, 1888, *A History of Eighteenth Century
Literature,* p. 253

In *Jonathan Wild* above all Fielding indulges to the full his taste for clearness and unity of intellectual structure. . . . Fielding conducts his narrative
under the dominant influence of one prevailing purpose, in the service of
which he employs all his irony, never suffering the reader for one moment
to forget the main thesis, which is stated at the beginning of the story, re-
stated at the close and illustrated with matchless skill throughout. This thesis
is in effect that the elements of "greatness," in the common acceptation of
the term, when divorced from that plain goodness of heart which is little
likely to foster ambition, are the same in the thief and in men eminent in
more reputable professions, as those can testify "who have lived long in
cities, courts, gaols, or such places." In sketching the history of Wild, and
showing how his career of selfish villainy might have been marred at innumerable points by the slightest liability to humane feeling, Fielding's
polished irony achieves a triumph, and presents a picture of almost "perfect

diabolism." The humour of the author is at its grimmest in this work, not so much in depicting Wild, the horror of whose character is almost forgotten in its artistic unity, as in sundry subordinate details.

Walter Raleigh, 1894, *The English Novel*, pp. 167, 168

Tom Jones (1749)

I have been very well entertained lately with the two first volumes of *The Foundling*, written by Mr. Fielding, but not to be published till January (1749). If the same spirit runs through the whole work, I think it will be much preferable to *Joseph Andrews*.

Lady Hertford (Dutchess of Somerset), 1748,
Letter to Lady Luxborough

Meanwhile, it is an honest pleasure, which we take in adding, that (exclusive of one wild, detach'd, and independent Story of a *Man of the Hill*, that neither brings on Anything, nor rose from Anything that went before it). All the changeful windings of the Author's Fancy carry on a course of regular Design; and end in an extremely moving Close, where Lives that seem'd to wander and run different ways, meet, All, in an instructive Center. The whole Piece consists of an inventive Race of Disappointments and Recoveries. It excites Curiosity, and holds it watchful. It has just and pointed Satire; but it is a partial Satire, and confin'd, too narrowly: It sacrifices to Authority and Interest. Its *Events* reward Sincerity, and punish and expose Hypocrisy; shew Pity and Benevolence in amiable Lights, and Avarice and Brutality in very despicable ones. In every Part It has Humanity for its Intention: In too many, it *seems* wantoner than It was meant to be: It has bold shocking Pictures; and (I fear) not unresembling ones, in high Life, and in low. And (to conclude this too adventurous Guess-work, from a Pair of forward Baggages) woud, every where (we think), *deserve to* please,—if stript of what the Author thought himself most sure to *please by*. And thus, Sir, we have told you our sincere opinion of *Tom Jones*. . . . Your most profest Admirers and most humble servants.

Astræa and Minerva Hill, 1749, *Letter to Samuel Richardson*,
July 27

I must confess, that I have been prejudiced by the Opinion of Several judicious Friends against the truly coarse-titled *Tom Jones*; and so have been discouraged from reading it.—I was told, that it was a rambling Collection of Waking Dreams, in which Probability was not observed: And that it had a very bad Tendency. And I had Reason to think that the Author intended for his Second View (His *first*, to fill his Pocket, by accommodating it to the reigning Taste) in writing it, to whiten a vicious Character, and to make Morality bend to his Practices. What Reason had he to make his Tom illegitimate, in an Age where Keeping is become a Fashion? Why did he make him a common—What shall I call it? And a Kept Fellow, the Lowest of all Fellows, yet in Love with a Young Creature who was traping [trapesing?] after him, a Fugitive from her Father's House?—Why did he draw his Heroine so fond, so foolish, and so insipid?—Indeed he has one excuse—He knows not how to draw a delicate Woman—He has not been accustomed to such Company,—And is too prescribing, too impetuous, too immoral, I will venture to say, to take any other Byass that a perverse and crooked Nature has given him; or Evil Habits, at least, have confirm'd in him. Do Men expect Grapes of Thorns, or Figs of Thistles? But, perhaps, I think the worse of the Piece because I know the Writer, and dislike his Principles both Public and Private, tho' I wish well to the *Man,* and Love Four worthy Sisters of his, with whom I am well acquainted. And indeed should admire him, did he make the Use of his Talents which I wish him to make. For the Vein of Humour, and Ridicule, which he is Master of, might, if properly turned, do great Service to ye Cause of Virtue. But no more of this Gentleman's Work, after I have said, That the favourable Things, you say of the Piece, will tempt me, if I can find Leisure, to give it a Perusal.

Samuel Richardson, 1749, *Letter to Astræa and Minerva Hill,*
Aug. 4

There is lately sprung up amongst us a species of narrative poem, representing likewise the characters of common life. It has the same relation to comedy that the epic has to tragedy, and differs from the epic in the same respect that comedy differs from tragedy; that is, in the actions and characters, both which are much nobler in the epic than in it. It is therefore, I think, a legitimate kind of poem; and, accordingly, we are told, Homer wrote one of that kind, called "Margites," of which some lines are preserved. The reason why I mention it is, that we have, in English, a *poem* of that kind (for so I will call it), which has more of character in it than any work, antient or modern, that I know. The work I mean is, *The History of Tom Jones,* by Henry Fielding, which, as it has more personages brought into the story than any thing of the poetic kind I have ever seen; so all those personages have characters peculiar to them, insomuch, that there is not even an host or an hostess upon the road, hardly a servant, who is not distinguished in that way; in short I never saw any thing that was so much animated, and, as I may say, *all alive* with characters and manners, as *The History of Tom Jones.*

Lord Monboddo (James Burnet), 1779-99, *Of the Origin and
Progress of Language,* vol. III, p. 134

I never saw Johnson really angry with me but once. I alluded to some witty passages in *Tom Jones,* he replied, "I am shocked to hear you quote from so vicious a book. I am sorry to hear you have read it: a confession which no modest lady should ever make. I scarcely know a more corrupt work!" He went so far as to refuse to Fielding the great talents which are ascribed to him, and broke out into a noble panegyric on his competitor, Richardson; who, he said, was as superior to him in talents as in virtue; and whom he pronounced to be the greatest genius that had shed its lustre on this path of literature.

Hannah More, 1780, Memoirs, vol. I, p. 168

A book seemingly intended to sap the foundation of that morality which it is the duty of parents and all public instructors to inculcate in the minds of young people, by teaching that virtue upon principle is imposture, that generous qualities alone constitute true worth, and that a young man may love and be loved, and at the same time associate with the loosest women. His morality, in respect that it resolves virtue into good affections, in contradiction to moral obligation and a sense of duty, is that of lord Shaftesbury vulgarised, and is a system of excellent use in palliating the vices most injurious to society. He was the inventor of that cant-phrase, goodness of heart, which is every day used as a substitute for probity, and means little more than the virtue of a horse or a dog; in short, he has done more towards corrupting the rising generation than any writer we know of.

Sir John Hawkins, 1787, Life of Samuel Johnson, p. 214

I have already given my opinion of Fielding; but I cannot refrain from repeating here my wonder at Johnson's excessive and unaccountable depreciation of one of the best writers that England has produced. *Tom Jones* has stood the test of publick opinion with such success, as to have established its great merit, both for the story, the sentiments, and the manners, and also the varieties of diction, so as to leave no doubt of its having an animated truth of execution throughout.

James Boswell, 1791, Life of Johnson, ed. Hill, vol. II, p. 201

Tom Jones cannot be considered simply a novel: the abundance of philosophical ideas, the hypocrisy of society, and the contrast of natural qualities, are brought into action with an infinity of art; and love, as I have observed before, is only a vehicle to introduce all these.

Madame de Staël, 1800, The Influence of Literature
upon Society, ch. xv

Fielding had all the ease which Richardson wanted, a genuine flow of humour, and a rich variety of comic character; nor was he wanting in strokes of an amiable sensibility, but he could not describe a consistently virtuous character, and in deep pathos he was far excelled by his rival. When we see Fielding parodying *Pamela,* and Richardson asserting, as he does in his letters, that the run of *Tom Jones* is over, and that it would soon be completely forgotten: we cannot but smile on seeing the two authors placed on the same shelf, and going quietly down to posterity together.

Anna Lætitia Barbauld, 1804, ed., *The Correspondence of Samuel Richardson,* vol. I, p. lxxix

As a story, *Tom Jones* seems to have only one defect, which might have been so easily remedied, that it is to be regretted that it should have been neglected by the author. Jones, after all, proves illegitimate, when there would have been no difficulty for the author to have supposed that his mother had been privately married to the young clergyman. This would not only have removed the stain from the birth of the hero, but, in the idea of the reader, would have given him better security for the property of his uncle Allworthy. In fact, in a miserable continuation which has been written of the history of Tom Jones, the wrong headed author (of whom Blifil was the favourite), has made his hero bring an action against Tom after the death of Mr. Allworthy, and oust him from his uncle's property.

John Dunlop, 1814-42, *The History of Fiction,* vol. II, p. 407

In point of general excellence *Amelia* has commonly been considered, no less by critics, perhaps, than by the public, as decidedly inferior to *Tom Jones.* In variety and invention it assuredly is so. Its chief merit depends less on its artful and elaborate construction than on the interesting series it presents of domestic paintings, drawn, as we have remarked, from his own family history. It has more pathos, more moral lessons, with far less vigour and humour, than either of its predecessors. But we agree with Chalmers, that those who have seen much of the errors and distresses of domestic life will probably feel that the author's colouring in this work is more just, as well as more chaste, than in any of his other novels. The appeals to the heart are far more forcible.

Thomas Roscoe, 1840, *Life and Works of Henry Fielding*

The book breathes health. The convention of the time did not forbid a direct picturing of its evil; but the coarse scenes in Fielding's novels are given always for what they are, with no false gloss upon them. Whenever Tom

Jones sins against the purity of his love for Sophia his wrong doing is made in some part to part him from her, and when he pleads toward the close of the story, the difference between men and women, and the different codes of morality by which they are judged in society, Fielding makes Sophia answer, "I will never marry a man who is not as incapable as I am myself of making such a distinction." The charm of genius enters into the whole texture of thought in Fielding's novels. A page of his is to a page of Richardson's as silk to sackcloth.

Henry Morley, 1881, Of English Literature in the Reign of
Victoria, with a Glance at the Past, p. 88

Like *Don Quixote, Tom Jones* is the precursor of a new order of things— the earliest and freshest expression of a new departure in art. But while *Tom Jones* is, to the full, as amusing as *Don Quixote,* it has the advantage of a greatly superior plan, and an interest more skilfully sustained. The incidents which, in Cervantes, simply succeed each other like the scenes in a panorama, are, in *Tom Jones,* but parts of an organised and carefully-arranged progression towards a foreseen conclusion. As the hero and heroine cross and recross each other's track, there is scarcely an episode which does not aid in the moving forward of the story. Little details rise lightly and naturally to the surface of the narrative, not more noticeable at first than the most everyday occurrences, and a few pages farther on become of the greatest importance.

Austin Dobson, 1883, Fielding, p. 118

The scenes are still constructed as in comedy. As we read on, it is as if we were assisting at the representation of a score of comedies, parallel and successive; some pathetic, some burlesque, others possessing the gay wit of Vanbrugh and Congreve—all of which, after a skilfully manipulated revolution of circumstances, are united in a brilliant conclusion. Instead of being burdened, as were the earlier epic romancers, with a number of narratives to be gathered up in the last chapters, Fielding in the main becomes his own story-teller throughout. Character is unfolded, and a momentum is given to his plot by direct, not reported, conversations. All devices to account for his subject-matter, such as bundles of letters, fragmentary or rat-eaten manuscripts, found by chance, or given to the writer in keeping, are brushed aside as cheap and silly. Fielding throws off the mask of anonymity, steps out boldly, and asks us to accept his omniscience and omnipresence.

Wilbur L. Cross, 1899, The Development of the English
Novel, p. 45

Amelia (1751)

You guess that I have not read *Amelia*. Indeed I have read but the first volume. I had intended to go through with it; but I found the characters and situations so wretchedly low and dirty, that I imagined I could not be interested for any one of them; and to read and not care what became of the hero and heroine, is a task I thought I would leave to those who had more leisure than I am blessed with. . . . Booth, in his last piece, again himself; Amelia, even to her noselessness, is again his first wife. His brawls, his jarrs, his gaols, his spunging-houses, are all drawn from what he has seen and known. As I said (witness also his hamper plot) he has little or no invention: and admirably do you observe, that by several strokes in his *Amelia* he designed to be good, but knew not how, and lost his genius, low humour, in the attempt.

> Samuel Richardson, 1752, *Letter to Mrs. Donnellan,*
> *Correspondence*, ed. Barbauld, vol. IV, p. 60

Amelia, which succeeded *Tom Jones* in about *four* years, has indeed the marks of genius, but of a genius beginning to fall into its decay. The author's invention in this performance does not appear to have lost its fertility; his judgment, too, seems as strong as ever; but the warmth of imagination is abated; and, in his landscapes, or his scenes of life, Mr. Fielding is no longer the colourist he was before. . . . And yet *Amelia* holds the same proportion to *Tom Jones* that *The Odyssey* of Homer bears, in the estimation of Longinus, to the *Iliad*. A fine vein of morality runs through the whole; many of the situations are affecting and tender; the sentiments are delicate; and, upon the whole, it is *The Odyssey,* the moral and pathetic work, of Henry Fielding.

> Arthur Murphy, 1762, *An Essay on the Life and Genius*
> *of Henry Fielding, Esq.*

Amelia, whose portrait Fielding drew from that of his second wife, has, indeed, been always a favourite character with readers; but the same cannot be said about her husband, Booth, who, we may suppose, was intended to represent Fielding himself. If so, the likeness which he drew is certainly not a flattering one. Thackeray preferred Captain Booth to Tom Jones, because he thought much more humbly of himself than Jones did, and went down on his knees and owned his weaknesses; but most will be inclined to agree with Scott, who declares that we have not the same sympathy for the ungrateful and dissolute conduct of Booth which we yield to the youthful follies of Jones. However, after all necessary deductions have been made, *Amelia* must be pronounced a wonderful work, full of that rich flow of humour and deep knowledge of human nature which charm us in *Tom Jones* and *Joseph Andrews*.

Henry J. Nicoll, 1882, *Landmarks of English Literature,* p. 219

In *Amelia,* things get better; all things get better; it is one of the curiosities of literature that Fielding, who wrote one book that was engaging, truthful, kind, and clean, and another book that was dirty, dull, and false, should be spoken of, the world over, as the author of the second and not the first, as the author of *Tom Jones,* not of *Amelia.*

Robert Louis Stevenson, 1888, "Some Gentlemen in Fiction,"
Scribner's Magazine, vol. 3, p. 766

GENERAL

It always appeared to me that he estimated the compositions of Richardson too highly, and that he had an unreasonable prejudice against Fielding. In comparing those two writers, he used this expression: "that there was as great a difference between them as between a man who knew how a watch was made, and a man who could tell the hour by looking on the dial-plate." This was a short and figurative state of his distinction between drawing characters of nature and characters only of manners. But I cannot help being of opinion, that the neat watches of Fielding are as well constructed as the large clocks of Richardson, and that his dial-plates are brighter. Fielding characters, though they do not expand themselves so widely in dissertation, are as just pictures of human nature, and I will venture to say, have more striking features, and nicer touches of the pencil; and though Johnson used to quote with approbation a saying of Richardson's, "that the virtues of Fielding's heroes were the vices of a truly good man," I will venture to add, that the moral tendency of Fielding's writings, though it does not encourage a strained and rarely possible virtue, is ever favourable to honour and honesty, and cherishes the benevolent and generous affections. He who is as good as Fielding would make him, is an amiable member of society, and may be led on by more regulated instructors, to a higher state of ethical perfection.

James Boswell, 1791-93, *Life of Johnson,* ed. Hill, vol. II, p. 55

Fielding's novels are, in general, thoroughly his own; and they are thoroughly English. What they are most remarkable for, is neither sentiment, nor imagination, nor wit, nor even humour, though there is an immense deal of this last quality; but profound knowledge of human nature, at least of English nature, and masterly pictures of the characters of men as he saw them existing. This quality distinguishes all his works, and is shown almost equally in all of them. As a painter of real life, he was equal to Hogarth; as a mere observer of human nature, he was little inferior to Shakspeare, though without any of the genius and poetical qualities of his mind. His humour is less rich and laughable than Smollett's; his wit as often misses as hits; he has none of the fine pathos of Richardson or Sterne; but he has brought together a greater variety of characters in common life, marked with more distinct peculiarities, and without an atom of caricature, than any other novel writer whatever.

> William Hazlitt, 1818, *On the English Novelists, Lectures on the English Comic Writers,* Lecture VI

There is not in Fielding much of that which can properly be called ideal—if we except the character of Parson Adams; but his works represent life as more delightful than it seems to common experience, by disclosing those of its dear immunities, which we little think of, even when we enjoy them. How delicious are all his refreshments at all his inns! How vivid are the transient joys of his heroes, in their chequered course—how full and overflowing are their final raptures.

> Thomas Noon Talfourd, 1842, "On British Novels and Romances," *Critical and Miscellaneous Writings,* p. 13

With all his faults, Fielding was one of the greatest novelists that England ever produced. If he were often licentious in sentiment and coarse in expression, these were in no small degree the faults of his times and the true reflex of the society which he portrayed; but his merits were all his own. He painted with the heart of a genius and the hand of an artist. Every character is conceived with truth and delineated with vigour. From the lady of fashion to the chambermaid; from the dissipated man of the town to the humble parson—all are portraits; and though some of them are likenesses of a class that has passed away or been greatly changed, others present to us features that will be fresh in every age, and last for all time.

> John Francis Waller, 1870, *Pictures from English Literature,* p. 47

Fielding, in his public capacity of magistrate, as well as in the public career he pursued, had an infinite variety of characters come under his notice; and his order of mind and natural tendency being that of studying the evolutions of human action, the whole animus of his genius was directed to that order of delineation. Hence is to be noticed in his novels how very meagre are his descriptions of scenery, particularly of rural scenery. Compare them with Walter Scott's, whose order of mind was absolutely panoramic. Scott was a true poet. Fielding had very little *external* imagination, and even less fancy; he never went out of the scenes in which he had been accustomed to move. He busied himself solely with human nature; and rarely has any one turned his studies to more ample account than he. Its principles, and general, intimate, and remote feelings, acting under particular circumstances and impressions, move him to an intense degree. They were ever present with him.

Charles Cowden Clarke, 1872, "On the Comic Writers of England,"
The Gentleman's Magazine, n. s., vol. 8, p. 558

Although Fielding was dramatic, in so far as conversation and incident led the story on from point to point with a certain degree of system, combined with spontaneity, he did not carry the dramatic movement far enough. When all was over, his tale would remain but a rambling, aimless concatenation, terminating in nothing but an end of the adventures. His great powers lay in the observation of manners and natures; but he was content to offer the results of this observation in a crude, digressive form, somewhat lacking—if it may be said—in principle. He was fond of whipping in and out among his characters, in person, and did so with a sufficiently cheery and pleasant defiance of all criticism; but the practice injured his art, nevertheless. In a word, he seems to have written as much for his own amusement as for that of his reader; and although he sedulously endeavoured to identify these two interests, he did not hesitate, when he felt like discharging a little dissertation of love, or classical learning, or what not, to do this at any cost, either of artistic propriety or the reader's patience. And, worst of all, he frequently dissected his *dramatis personæ* in full view of the audience, giving an epitome of their characters off-hand, or chattering garrulously about them, when the mood took him. These short-comings withheld from him the possibility of grouping his keen observations firmly about some centre of steady and assimilative thought. With Fielding, nothing crystallized, but all was put together in a somewhat hastily gathered bundle; and the parts have a semi-detached relation.

George Parsons Lathrop, 1874, "Growth of the Novel,"
The Atlantic Monthly, vol. 33, p. 686

JONATHAN EDWARDS
1703-1758

Edwards was born October 5th, 1703, in East Windsor, Connecticut. He was the son of Rev. Timothy and Esther Stoddard Edwards; was graduated at Yale College in 1720; studied theology at New Haven; from August 1722 to March 1723 preached in New York; from 1724 to 1726 was a tutor at Yale; on the 15th of February, 1727, was ordained at Northampton, Massachusetts; in 1750 was dismissed from the church there, and in 1751 removed to Stockbridge, Massachusetts. He was called to Princeton in 1757, and died there March 22d, 1758.

> Egbert C. Smyth, 1897, *Jonathan Edwards, Library of the World's Best Literature*, ed. Warner, vol. IX, p. 5178

Sermon on Man's Dependence, 1731; Sermon on Spiritual Light, 1734; first Revival at Northampton, 1735; *Narrative of Surprising Conversions*, 1736; publishes sermons on Justification, etc., 1738; The Great Awakening, 1740; Sermon at Enfield, 1741; publishes *Distinguishing Marks*, etc., 1741; *Thoughts on the Revival*, 1742; *Religious Affections*, 1746; troubles at Northampton, 1749; publication of *Qualifications for Full Communion*, 1749; *Reply to Williams*, 1752; *The Freedom of the Will*, 1754; treatises written on *Virtue and End of Creation*, 1755; publication of treatise on *Original Sin*, 1758.

> Charles Wells Moulton, 1901

SEE: *Representative Selections*, ed. C. H. Faust and T. H. Johnson, 1935; Perry Miller, *Jonathan Edwards*, 1949.

PERSONAL

On the Sabbath felt wonderful satisfaction in being at the house of Mr. Edwards. He is a son himself and hath also a daughter of Abraham for his wife. A sweeter couple I have not seen. Their children were dressed, not in silks and satins, but plain, as becomes the children of those who in all things ought to be examples of Christian simplicity. She is a woman adorned with a meek and quiet spirit, and talked so feelingly and so solidly of the things of God, and seemed to be such an helpmeet to her husband, that she caused me to renew those prayers which for some months I have put up to God, that He would send me a daughter of Abraham to be my wife. I find upon many accounts it is my duty to marry. Lord, I desire to have no choice of my own. Thou knowest my circumstances.

> George Whitefield, 1740, *Diary, The Great Awakening*

I have a constitution in many respects peculiarly unhappy, attended with flaccid solids, vapid, sizy, and scarce fluids, and a low tide of spirits; often occasioning a kind of childish weakness and contemptibleness of speech, presence, and demeanor, with a disagreeable dulness and stiffness, much unfitting me for conversation, but more especially for the government of a college. This makes me shrink at the thoughts of taking upon me, in the decline of life, such a new and great business, attended with such a multiplicity of cares, and requiring such a degree of activity, alertness, and spirit of government; especially as succeeding one so remarkably well qualified in these respects, giving occasion to every one to remark the wide difference. I am also deficient in some parts of learning, particularly in algebra, and the higher parts of mathematics, and in the Greek classics; my Greek learning have been chiefly in the New Testament. . . . My method of study, from my first beginning the work of the ministry, has been very much by writing; applying myself, in this way, to improve every important hint; pursuing the clue to my utmost, when any thing in reading, meditation, or conversation, has been suggested to my mind, that seemed to promise light in any weighty point; thus penning what appeared to me my best thoughts, on innumerable subjects, for my own benefit. The longer I prosecuted my studies in this method, the more habitual it became, and the more pleasant and profitable I found it. The farther I travelled in this way, the more and wider the field opened, which has occasioned my laying out many things in my mind, to do in this manner, if God should spare my life, which my heart hath been much upon; particularly many things against most of the prevailing errors of the present day, which I cannot with any patience see maintained (to the utter subverting of the Gospel of Christ) with so high a hand, and so long continued a triumph, with so little control, when it appears so evident to me that there is truly no foundation for any of this glorying and insult.

> Jonathan Edwards, 1757, *Letter to the Trustees of the College of New Jersey,* Oct. 19

He studied the Bible more than all other books, and more than most other divines do. He took his religious principles from the Bible, and not from any human system of body or of divinity. Though his principles were Calvinistic, yet he called no man father. He thought and judged for himself, and was truly very much of an original.

> Samuel Hopkins, 1759, *Life of Edwards,* p. 47

The person of Mr. Edwards, . . . was tall and slender. He was a little more than six feet in stature. His countenance was strongly marked with intelligence and benignity; and his manners were peculiarly expressive of modesty, gentleness, and Christian dignity. His voice, in public speaking, was rather feeble, and he had little or no gesture. Yet such were the gravity of his manner, the weight and solemnity of his thoughts, and the evident earnestness of his delivery, that few preachers were listened to with more fixed attention, or left a more deep and permanent impression. Mr. Edwards was the father of *eleven* children; *three sons* and *eight daughters.* One of these, his second daughter, died eleven years before him, in the 17th year of her age. All the rest survived him, and some of them a number of years. One only of his sons became a minister of the Gospel. This was his *second son, Jonathan,* who greatly resembled his venerable father in metaphysical acuteness, in ardent piety, and in the purest exemplariness of Christian deportment.

> Samuel Miller, 1837, *Life of Jonathan Edwards, Sparks's Library of American Biography,* vol. VIII, p. 168

Edwards was pre-eminently a student. Tall in person, and having even a womanly look, he was of delicate constitution. He was, however, so temperate and methodical in his living that he was usually in good health, and able to give more time to study than most men. Twelve or thirteen hours of every day were commonly allotted to this. So devoted was he to his work as a student that he was most unwilling to allow anything to disturb it. Though he was careful to eat regularly and at certain fixed hours, yet he would postpone his meals for a time if he was so engaged in study that the interruption of eating would interfere with the success of his thinking. He was so miserly also in his craving for time that he would leave the table before the rest of the family and retire to his room, they waiting for him to return again when they had finished their meal, and dismiss them from the table with the customary grace.

> N. H. Eggleston, 1874, "A New England Village,"
> *Harper's Magazine,* vol. 43, p. 823

While Edwards' official connection with Princeton was short and came to an almost tragic close, it is yet true that in an important sense Princeton became the residuary legatee of his name and fame. His spirit has continued to be one of the moulding forces of the college's life. The things in which he believed have been, in the main, the things in which Princeton has believed, and the type of religious life and experience which he prized most highly is the type that has always dominated the religious life and history of Princeton. The library of Edwards graces the University's shelves; his portrait and statue dignify and beautify her walls, and among the presidents of the past he holds a place as one of the trinity of greatest names, Edwards, Witherspoon, McCosh.

> Alexander T. Ormond, 1901, *Jonathan Edwards, A Retrospect,*
> ed. Gardiner, p. 81

GENERAL

There are some things in your New England doctrine and worship, which I do not agree with; but I do not therefore condemn them, or desire to shake your belief or practice of them. We may dislike things that are nevertheless right in themselves. I would only have you make me the same allowance, and have a better opinion both of morality and your brother. Read the pages of Mr. Edwards's late book, entitled *Some Thoughts concerning the present Revival of Religion in New England,* from 367 to 375, and when you judge of others, if you can perceive the fruit to be good, don't terrify yourself that the tree may be evil; but be assured it is not so, for you know who has said, "Men do not gather grapes of thorns and figs of thistles." I have no time to add, but that I shall always be your affectionate brother.

Benjamin Franklin, 1743, *Letter to His Sister*, July 28;
Writings, ed. Sparks, vol. VII, p. 8

Seeds from Edwards have taken root in strange fields. A single stalk from his philosophy has shed beauty and perfume over wastes of modern speculation. Many, of whose opinions all is dross that is not borrowed from him, have exhibited the poverty of their natural powers in assaults upon his system; and others, incapable of penetrating beyond the shell of his logic, and understanding the beauty of his life and doctrine, have done him much greater injury by professing to be of his school.

Rufus Wilmot Griswold, 1845, *The Prose Writers of America*

Edwards's writings, as a whole, display an exceedingly strong and comprehensive memory, great force and perspicuity of thought, and powers of ratiocination equalled by few of that or any other age. These powers, which he possessed in so eminent a degree, were still further strengthened by the most unceasing exertion. His intellectual labors knew no relaxation, and so fixedly that his mind becomes associated with one branch of enquiry, that his whole existence may be said to have been absorbed in it. His mind, shut out as it were by his processes of abstraction from the contemplation of the external world, seemed to concentrate its whole energies in the analysis of those materials which lie deep buried within. The subjection of his being to one particular train of thought, placed his passions and feelings so perfectly under control as to give him the appearance of an individual without those ordinary emotions which characterize the human family; hence we find him under the most exciting circumstances as calm and collected as if he were perfectly indifferent as to the result of his investigations.

James Wynne, 1850, *Lives of Eminent Literary and Scientific Men of America*, p. 167

I may have the usual bias of a discoverer and editor. But I shall be surprised if this treatise [*Treatise on Grace,*] do not at once take rank with its kindred one, on *The Religious Affections*. There is in it, I think, the massive argumentation of his great work on *The Will*; but there is, in addition, a fineness of spiritual insight, a holy fervour not untinged with the pathetic "frenzy" of the English Mystics, as of Peter Sterry and Archbishop Leighton, and—especially towards the close—a rapturous exultation in the "excellency and loveliness" of God, a *glow* in iteration of the wonder and beauty and blessedness of Divine Love, and a splendor of assertion of the CLAIMS, so to speak, of God the Holy Spirit, which it would be difficult to over-estimate.

> Alexander B. Grosart, 1865, *Selections from the Unpublished Writings of Jonathan Edwards of America,* Introduction

As a theologian, as a metaphysician, as the author of *The Inquiry into the Freedom of the Will,* as the mighty defender of Calvinism, as the inspirer and the logical drill-master of innumerable minds in his own country, and in Great Britain, he, of course, fills a large place in ecclesiastical and philosophical history. But even from the literary point of view, and in spite of his own low estimate of his literary merits, he deserves high rank. He had the fundamental virtues of a writer—abundant thought, and the utmost precision, clearness, and simplicity in the utterance of it; his pages, likewise, hold many examples of bold, original, and poetic imagery; and though the nature of his subjects, and the temper of his sect, repressed the exercise of wit, he was possessed of wit in an extraordinary degree, and of the keenest edge. In early life, he was sadly afflicted by the burden of checking the movements of this terrible faculty; but later, it often served him in controversy, not as a substitute for argument, but as its servant; enabling him, especially in the climaxes of a discussion, to make palpable the absurdity of propositions that he had already shown to be untenable.

> Moses Coit Tyler, 1878, *A History of American Literature,* 1676-1765, vol. II, p. 191

Puritanism to such men was a girdle, not a fetter; it held them together and made them march forward in line, instead of straggling along without aim or purpose. But in time the girdle became a chain; the people began to fret under it and threw it off; and this was the very period at which Edwards and Franklin appeared. The one contended stoutly for the old faith, in all its strictness and with all its alarming penalties for sin; the other, with genial and prudent good nature, sought to introduce a milder sway, more friendly to the general development of mankind. Both were powerful forces, and had other forces more powerful behind them; but the time had come for puritanism to withdraw from the scene, and the controversial writings of Edwards furnished the salvo of theological artillery under cover of which the army of the Puritans fell back in good order, leaving the field to Democracy and the philanthropists.

> F. B. Sanborn, 1883, "The Puritanic Philosophy and Jonathan Edwards," *The Journal of Speculative Philosophy,* vol. 17, p. 421

WILLIAM COLLINS
1721-1759

Born, at Chichester, 25 Dec. 1721. Probably educated first at Chichester. Scholar of Winchester College, 19 Jan. 1733. Contributed verses to *Gentleman's Magazine,* (Jan. and Oct. 1739), while still at school. Matriculated at Queen's College, Oxford, 22 March 1740; Demyship at Magdalen College, 29 July 1741; B. A., 18 Nov. 1743. Visit to uncle in Flanders. Thought of entertaining Army or Church, but eventually devoted himself to literature in London. Failing health; visit to France, lived with sister at Chichester on his return. For a time in a madhouse at Chelsea. Visit to Oxford, 1754. Died at Chichester, 12 June 1759. Buried, at St. Andrew's Church, Chichester. WORKS: *Persian Eclogues* (anon.), 1742 (another edn., anon., entitled *Oriental Eclogues,* 1757); *Odes,* 1747 [1746]; *Verses humbly addressed to Sir Thomas Hammer* (anon.), 1743. POSTHUMOUS: *An Ode on the Popular Superstitions of the Highlands,* 1788. COLLECTED WORKS: ed. by Langhorne, with *Life,* 1765, etc.; ed. by Mrs. Barbauld, 1797; cd. by A. Dyce, 1827; ed. by Moy Thomas, with *Life,* 1858.

R. Farquharson Sharp, 1897, *A Dictionary of English Authors,* p. 62

SEE: *Poems,* ed. Edmund Blunden, 1929; *Drafts and Fragments of Verse, edited from the Manuscripts* by J. S. Cunningham, 1956; H. W. Garrod, *Collins,* 1928.

PERSONAL

How little can we venture to exult in any intellectual powers or literary attainments, when we consider the condition of poor Collins. I knew him a few years ago, full of hopes and full of projects, versed in many languages, high in fancy, and strong in retention. This busy and forcible mind is now under the government of those who lately would not have been able to comprehend the least and most narrow of its designs. What do you hear of him? are there hopes of his recovery? or is he to pass the remainder of his life in misery and degradation? perhaps with complete consciousness of his calamity.

Samuel Johnson, 1754, *Letter to Joseph Warton,* March 8

The neglected author of the Persian eclogues, which, however inaccurate, excel any in our language, is still alive. Happy, if *insensible* of our neglect, not *raging* at our ingratitude.

Oliver Goldsmith, 1759, *An Enquiry into the Present State of Polite Learning*

William Collins, the poet, I was intimately acquainted with, from the time he came to reside at Oxford. . . . As he brought with him, for so the whole turn of his conversation discovered, too high an opinion of his school acquisitions, and a sovereign contempt for all academic studies and discipline, he never looked with any complacency on his situation in the university, but was always complaining of the dulness of a college life. . . . When poverty overtook him, poor man, he had too much sensibility of temper to bear with his misfortunes, so fell into a most deplorable state of mind. How he got down to Oxford, I do not know; but I myself saw him under Merton wall, in a very affected situation, struggling, and conveyed by force, in the arms of two or three men, towards the parish of St. Clement, in which was a house that took in such unhappy objects; and I always understood that, not long after, he died in confinement; but when, or where, or where he was buried, I never knew. Thus was lost to the world this unfortunate person, in the prime of life, without availing himself of fine abilities, which, properly improved, must have raised him to the top of any profession, and have rendered him a blessing to his friends, and an ornament to his country. Without books, or steadiness or resolution to consult them if he had been possessed of any, he was always planning schemes for elaborate publications, which were carried no farther than the drawing up of proposals for subscriptions, some of which were published; and in particular, as far as I remember, one for a "History of the Darker Ages." He was passionately fond of music; good natured and affable; warm in his friendships, and visionary in his pursuits; and, as long as I knew him, very temperate in his eating and drinking. He was of moderate stature, of a light and clear complexion, with grey eyes, so very weak at times as hardly to bear a candle in the room; and often raising within him apprehensions of blindness.

Gilbert White, 1781, Gentleman's Magazine

I have lately finished eight volumes of Johnson's *Prefaces, or Lives of the Poets.* In all the number I observe but one man—(a poet of no great fame, —of whom I did not know that he existed till I found him there), whose mind seems to have had the slightest tincture of religion; and he was hardly in his senses. His name was Collins. He sunk into a state of melancholy, and died young. Not long before his death, he was found at his lodgings in Islington by his biographer, with the New Testament in his hand. He said to Johnson, "I have but one book; but it is the best." Of him, therefore, there are some hopes.

William Cowper, 1784, Letter to Mr. Newton, March 19

Much speculation has taken place as to the causes of Collins's irresolution; but human motives are not easily determined. The evidences are too many to doubt, that he was at this time indolent and undecided; but fond of pleasure and eager for excitement. His truest friend has spoken of habits of dissipation and long association with "fortuitous companions." But his studies were extensive, and his scholarship commanded the respect of learned men. As with his friends the Wartons, his taste led him to the study of the older English writers. He was acquainted with the riches of the Elizabethan poets at a time when few English students strayed beyond Cowley; and he read in the Italian, French, and Spanish languages those poems and romances which, to the more sober taste of Johnson, "passed the bounds of nature." At this time he composed his Odes, upon which his fame rests.

W. Moy Thomas, 1858-92, ed., *The Poetical Works of William Collins*, p. xix

The Passions

The Ode to the Passions is, by universal consent, the noblest of Collins's productions, because it exhibits a much more extended invention, not of one passion only, but of all the passions combined, acting, according to the powers of each, to one end. The execution, also, is the happiest, each particular passion is drawn with inimitable force and compression. Let us take on Fear and Despair, each dashed out in four lines, of which every word is like inspiration. Beautiful as Spenser is, and sometimes sublime, yet he redoubles his touch too much, and often introduces some coarse feature or expression, which destroys the spell. Spenser, indeed, has other merits of splendid and inexhaustible invention, which render it impossible to put Collins on a par with him: but we must not estimate merit by mere quantity: if a poet produces but one short piece, which is perfect, he must be placed according to its quality. And surely there is not a single figure in Collins's *Ode to the Passions* which is not perfect, both in conception and language. He has had many imitators, but no one has ever approached him in his own department.

Sir Samuel Egerton Brydges, 1830, *An Essay on the Genius and Poems of Collins*

All that Collins has written is full of imagination, pathos, and melody. The defect of his poetry in general is that there is too little of earth in it: in the purity and depth of its beauty it resembles the bright blue sky. Yet Collins had genius enough for anything; and in his ode entitled *The Passions*, he has shown with how strong a voice and pulse of humanity he could, when he chose, animate his verse, and what extensive and enduring popularity he could command.

George L. Craik, 1861, *A Compendious History of English Literature and of the English Language*, vol. II, p. 284

GENERAL

In simplicity of description and expression, in delicacy and softness of numbers, and in natural and unaffected tenderness, they are not to be equalled by anything of the pastoral kind in the English language.

William Langhorne, 1765-81, *The Poetical Works of William Collins*, Memoir

His diction was often harsh, unskilfully laboured, and injudiciously selected. He affected the obsolete, when it was not worthy of revival; and he puts his words out of the common order, seeming to think, with some later candidates for fame, that not to write prose is certainly to write poetry. His lines commonly are of slow motion, clogged and impeded with clusters of consonants. As men are often esteemed who cannot be loved, so the poetry of Collins may sometimes extort praise when it gives little pleasure.

Samuel Johnson, 1779-81, *Collins, Lives of the English Poets*

He had that true *vivida vis,* that genuine inspiration, which alone can give birth to the highest efforts of poetry. He leaves stings in the minds of his readers, certain traces of thought and feeling, which never wear out, because nature had left them in his own mind. He is the only one of the minor poets of whom, if he had lived, it cannot be said that he might not have done the greatest things. The germ is there. He is sometimes affected, unmeaning and obscure; but he also catches rare glimpses of the bowers of Paradise, and has lofty aspirations after the highest seats of the Muses. With a great deal of tinsel and splendid patchwork, he has not been able to hide the solid sterling ore of genius. In his best works there is an attic simplicity, a pathos, and fervour of imagination, which make us the more lament that the efforts of his mind were at first depressed by neglect and pecuniary embarrassment, and at length buried in the gloom of an unconquerable and fatal malady. . . . I should conceive that Collins had a much greater poetical genius than Gray: he had more of that fine madness which is inseparable from it, of its turbid effervescence, of all that pushes it to the verge of agony or rapture.

William Hazlitt, 1818, *Lectures on the English Poets,* Lecture VI

It is not, however, inconsistent with a high respect for Collins, to ascribe every possible praise to that unrivaled production, the *Ode to the Passions,* to feel deeply the beauty, the pathos, and the sublime conceptions of the Odes to Evening, to Pity, to Simplicity, and a few others, and yet to be sensible of the occasional obscurity and imperfections of his imagery in other pieces, to find it difficult to discover the meaning of some passages, to think the opening of four of his odes which commence with the common-place invocation of "O thou," and the alliteration by which so many lines are disfigured, blemishes too serious to be forgotten, unless the judgment be drowned in the full tide of generous and enthusiastic admiration of the great and extraordinary beauties by which these faults are more than redeemed. That these defects are to be ascribed to haste it would be uncandid to deny; but haste is no apology for such faults in productions which fill a hundred pages, and which their author had ample opportunities to remove.

Sir Harris Nicholas Nicolas, 1831, ed. Collins' Poetical Works,
Memoir

Living both in the age and after an age of critical poetry, Collins, always alien alike from the better and from the worse influences of his day, has shown at least as plentiful a lack of any slightest critical instinct or training as ever did any poet on record, in his epistle to Hanmer on that worthy knight's "inqualifiable" edition of Shakespeare. But his couplets, though incomparably inferior to Gray's, are generally spirited and competent as well as fluent and smooth. The direct sincerity and purity of their positive and straightforward inspiration will always keep his poems fresh and sweet to the senses of all men. He was a solitary song-bird among many more or less excellent pipers and pianists. He could put more spirit of colour into a single stroke, more breath of music into a single note, than could all the rest of his generation into all the labours of their lives. And the sweet name and the lucid memory of his genius could only pass away with all relics and all records of lyric poetry in England.

Algernon Charles Swinburne, 1880, The English Poets,
ed. Ward, vol. III, p. 282

SAMUEL RICHARDSON
1689-1761

Samuel Richardson, 1689-1761. Born, in Derbyshire, 1689. Apprenticed to a stationer, 1706. Afterwards employed as compositor at a printing works. Set up as a printer on his own account, 1719. Married (i.) Martha Wilde. She died, 25 Jan. 1731. Married (ii.) Elizabeth Leake. Began novel writing, 1739. Master of Stationers' Company, 1754. Died, in London, 4 July 1761. Buried in St. Bride's Church. WORKS: *Pamela* (anon.), 1741-42; *Clarissa* (anon.), 1748; *The History of Sir Charles Grandison* (anon.), 1754 (2nd edn. same year). POSTHUMOUS: *Correspondence*, ed. by A. L. Barbauld (6 vols.), 1804. He *edited*: *A Tour thro'* . . . *at Great*

Britain, 1742; Sir T. Roe's *Negotiations in his Embassy to the Ottoman Porte,* 1746; *The Life . . . of Balbe Berton* [1760?]. COLLECTED WORKS: ed. by E. Mangin (19 vols.), 1811; ed. by Leslie Stephen (12 vols.), 1883.

R. Farquharson Sharp, 1897, *A Dictionary of English Authors,* p. 239

SEE: *Novels,* 1929-31, 18 v.; William M. Sale, *Samuel Richardson: Master Printer,* 1950; Morris Golden, *Richardson's Characters,* 1964.

PERSONAL

Short; rather plump than emaciated, notwithstanding his complaints; about five foot five inches; fair wig; lightish cloth coat, all black besides; one hand generally in his bosom, the other a cane in it, which he leans upon under the skirts of his coat usually, that it may imperceptibly serve his as a support, when attacked by sudden tremors or startings, and dizziness, which too frequently attack him, but, thank God, not so often as formerly; looking directly foreright, as passers-by would imagine, but observing all that stirs on either hand of him without moving his short neck; hardly ever turning back; of a light-brown complexion; teeth not yet failing him; smoothish faced, and ruddy-cheeked; . . . a grey eye, too often overclouded by mistinesses from the head; by chance lively; very lively it will be, if he have hope of seeing a lady whom he loves and honours; his eye always on the ladies.

Samuel Richardson, 1749, *Letter to Mrs. Belfour*

Poor Mr. Richardson was seized on Sunday evening with a severe paralytic stroke. How many good hearts will be afflicted by this in many more countries than England! To how many will he be an inexpressible loss! But to consider him at present as lost to himself and perhaps with some sense of that loss is most grievous. It sits pleasantly upon my mind that the last morning we spent together was particularly friendly and quiet and comforting. It was the twenty-eighth of May—he looked then so well! One has long apprehended some stroke of this kind; the disease made its gradual approaches by the heaviness which clouded the cheerfulness of his conversation, that used to be so lively and so instructive; by the increased tremblings which unfitted that hand so peculiarly formed to guide the pen; and by perhaps the querulousness of temper most certainly not natural to so sweet and so enlarged a mind, which you and I have lately lamented as making his family at times not so comfortable as his principles, his study and his delight to diffuse happiness wherever he could, would otherwise have done. Well, his noble spirit will soon now I suppose be freed from its corporeal encumbrance; it were a sin to wish against it, and yet how few such will be left behind.

Miss Talbot, 1761, Letter to Mrs. Carter, Correspondence of
Samuel Richardson, ed. Anna L. Barbauld, 1804, vol. II, p. 209

A literary lady has favoured me with a characteristick anecdote of Richardson. One day at his country-house at Northend, where a large company was assembled at dinner, a gentleman who was just returned from Paris, willing to please Mr. Richardson, mentioned to him a very flattering circumstance,—that he had seen his *Clarissa* lying on the King's brother's table. Richardson observing that part of the company were engaged in talking to each other, affected then not to attend to it. But by and by, when there was a general silence, and he thought that the flattery might be fully heard, he addressed himself to the gentleman, "I think, Sir, you were saying something about,—" pausing in a high flutter of expectation. The gentleman provoked at his inordinate vanity, resolved not to indulge it, and with an exquisite sly air of indifference answered, "A mere trifle, Sir, not worth repeating!" The mortification of Richardson was visible, and he did not speak ten words more the whole day.

James Boswell, 1780, Life of Samuel Johnson,
ed. Hill, vol. IV, p. 34, note

Richardson's conversation was of the preceptive kind, but it wanted the diversity of Johnson's, and had no intermixture of wit or humour. Richardson could never relate a pleasant story, and hardly relish one told by another: he was ever thinking of his own writings, and listening to the praises which, with an emulous profusion, his friends were incessantly bestowing on them, he would scarce enter into free conversation with any one that he thought had not read *Clarissa,* or *Sir Charles Grandison,* and at best, he could not be said to be a companionable man. Those who were unacquainted with Richardson, and had red his books, were led to believe, that they exhibited a picture of his own mind, and that his temper and domestic behaviour could not but correspond with that refined morality which they inculcate, but in this they were deceived. He was austere in the government of his family, and issued his orders to some of his servants in writing only. His nearest female relations, in the presence of strangers, were mutes, and seemed to me, in a visit I once made him, to have been disciplined in the school of Ben Jonson's Morose, whose injunction to his servant was, "Answer me not but with your leg." In short, they appeared to have been taught to converse with him by signs; and it was too plain to me, that on his part,

the most frequent of them were frowns and gesticulations, importing that
they should leave his presence. I have heard it said, that he was what is
called a nervous man; and how far nervosity, with so good an understanding as he is allowed to have possessed, will excuse a conduct so opposite to
that philanthrophy which he laboured to inculcate, I cannot say: his benevolence might have taken another direction, and in other instances be very
strong; for I was once a witness to his putting into the hand of Mr. Whiston
the bookseller, ten guineas for the relief of one whom a sudden accident
had made a widow.

> Sir John Hawkins, 1787, *Life of Samuel Johnson,* p. 384

Richardson, the author of *Clarissa,* had been a common printer, and possessed no literature whatever. He was very silent in company, and so vain
that he never enjoyed any subject but that of himself or his works. He once
asked Douglas, Hishop of Salisbury, how he liked *Clarissa*. The bishop said
he could never get beyond the Bailiff scene. The author, thinking this a condemnation of his book, looked grave; but all was right when the hishop
added, it affected him so much that he was drowned in tears, and could not
trust himself with the book any longer. Richardson had a kind of club of
women about him—Mrs. Carter, Mrs. Talbot, &c.—who looked up to him
as to a superior being; to whom he dictated and gave laws; and with whom
he lived almost entirely. To acquire a facility of epistolary writing he would
on every trivial occasion write notes to his daughters even when they were
in the same house with him.

> Edmond Malone, 1792, *Maloniana,* ed. Prior, p. 439

His moral character was in the highest degree exemplary and amiable. He
was temperate, industrious, and upright; punctual and honourable in all
his dealings; and with a kindness of heart, and a liberality and generosity
of disposition, that must have made him a very general favourite, even if
he had never acquired any literary distinction.—He had a considerable
share of vanity, and was observed to talk more willingly on the subject of
his own works than on any other. The lowness of his original situation, and
the lateness of his introduction into polite society, had given to his manners
a great shyness and reserve; and a consciousness of his awkwardness and
his merit together, rendered him somewhat jealous in his intercourse with
persons in more conspicuous situations, and made him require more court-
ing and attention than every one was disposed to pay. He had high notions
of parental authority, and does not seem always quite satisfied with the
share of veneration which his wife could be prevailed on to shew for him.

He was particularly partial to the society of females; and lived, indeed, as Mrs. Barbauld has expressed it, in a flower-garden of ladies.

> Francis, Lord Jeffrey, 1804, "Richardson," *Edinburgh Review,*
> vol. 5, p. 31

The predominant failing of Richardson seems certainly to have been vanity; vanity naturally excited by his great and unparalleled popularity at home and abroad, and by the continual and concentred admiration of the circle in which he lived. Such a weakness finds root in the mind of every one who has obtained general applause, but Richardson, the gentleness of whose mind was almost feminine, was peculiarly susceptible of this feminine weakness, and he fostered and indulged its growth, which a man of firmer character would have crushed and restrained.

> Sir Walter Scott, 1821, *Samuel Richardson*

Pamela (1740)

What though thy fluttering sex might learn from thee,
That merit forms a rank above degree?
That pride, too conscious, falls from every claim,
While humble sweetness climbs beyond its aim.

> Aaron Hill, 1740 ? *To the Unknown Author of the*
> *Beautiful New Piece, called "Pamela"*

Two booksellers, my particular friends [Mr. Rivington and Mr. Osborne] entreated me to write for them a little volume of Letters in a common style, on such subjects as might be of use to those country readers who were unable to indite for themselves. "Will it be any harm," said I, "in a piece you want to be written so low, if we should instruct them how they should think and act in common cases as well as indite?" They were the more urgent for me to begin the little volume for this hint. I set about it; and, in the progress of it, writing two or three letters to instruct handsome girls who were obliged to go out to service, as we phrase it, how to avoid the snares that might be laid against their virtue, the above story recurred to my thought; and hence sprung *Pamela*.

> Samuel Richardson, c1760, *Correspondence*, ed. Anna L. Barbauld,
> 1804, vol. I, Introduction, p. liii

A work, usually found in the servant's drawer, but which, when so found, has not unfrequently detained the eye of the mistress, wondering all the while by what secret charm she was induced to turn over a book, apparently too low for her perusal, and that charm was—Richardson.

> Anna Lætitia Barbauld, 1804, *Life of Samuel Richardson*

Taking the general idea of the character of a modest and beautiful country girl, and of the ordinary situation in which she is placed, he makes out all the rest, even to the smallest circumstance, by the mere force of a reasoning imagination. It would seem as if a step lost would be as fatal here as in a mathematical demonstration. The development of the character is the most simple, and comes the nearest to nature that it can do, without being the same thing. The interest of the story increases with the dawn of understanding and reflection in the heroine; her sentiments gradually expand themselves, like opening flowers.

William Hazlitt, 1818, "On the English Novelists," *Lectures on the English Comic Writers,* Lecture VI

Thought what fame was on reading in a case of murder that "Mr. Wych, grocer at Tunbbridge, sold some bacon, flour, cheese, and, it is believed some plums, to some gipsy woman accused. He had on his counter (I quote faithfully) a book, the 'Life of Pamela,' which he was tearing for wastepaper, &c. In the cheese was found, &c., and a leaf of *Pamela* wrapt around the bacon!" What would Richardson, the vainest and luckiest of *living* authors (*i. e.,* while alive)—he who, with Aaron Hill, used to prophesy and chuckle over the presumed fall of Fielding (the prose Homer of human nature), and of Pope (the most beautiful of poets)—what would he have said, could he have traced his pages from their place on the French prince's toilets (see Boswell's *Johnson*) to the grocer's counter and the gipsy murderess's bacon!!!

Lord Byron, 1821, *A Journal in Italy,* Jan. 4

This first novel is a flower—one of those flowers which only bloom in a virgin imagination, at the dawn of original invention, whose charm and freshness surpass all that the maturity of art and genius can afterwards cultivate or arrange.

H. A. Taine, 1871, *History of English Literature,* tr. Van Laun, vol. II, bk. iii, ch. vi, p. 160

Few writers—it is a truism to say so—have excelled him in minute analysis of motive, and knowledge of the human heart. About the final morality of his heroine's long-drawn defence of her chastity it may, however, be permitted to doubt; and, in contrasting the book with Fielding's work, it should not be forgotten that, irreproachable though it seemed to the author's admirers, good Dr. Watts complained (and with reason) of the indelicacy of some of the scenes.

Austin Dobson, 1883, *Fielding (English Men of Letters),* p. 71

While the story of *Pamela* suffers as a story from the slowness of movement which, in a less degree (though the slowness is even greater), injures that of Clarissa, the former heroine, unlike the latter, is herself as severe a sufferer *as* a heroine from the delay. Her figure, to begin with, is one which will not stand much de-romanticizing. Mrs. Pamela's virtue, though no doubt quite sincere and genuine, is (as of course it should be) of a very soubrettish type, exceedingly, not to say pharisaically, self-conscious, not refined or elevated by the slightest admixture of delicacy, and obviously associated with a very shrewd eye to the main chance. All this, of course, is true enough to Nature; but truth to Nature becomes useless unless it falls into the impartial hands of Art.

Henry Duff Traill, 1883-97, "Samuel Richardson,"
The New Fiction, p. 116

His "Pamela" survives, not as the virtuous serving-maid he tried to portray, but as a perfectly true picture of an atrocious prude, who well knew how to play her cards to advantage.

Walter Lewin, 1889, "The Abuse of Fiction, *The Forum*,
vol. 7, p. 668

A book the defects of which can hardly be over-stated; whose warped morality, glaring want of taste, and improbability of incident, would seem sufficient to obscure all the merit that cannot be denied to it. It is only when we remember that both plan and subject matter were entirely original, and that the sentiments and treatment correspond to the ordinary tone of lower middle-class feeling at the time, that we can comprehend or sympathise with the immense enthusiasm it excited. It inaugurated a new school of fiction, and if its permanent popularity in England was somewhat impaired by the speedy publication of Fielding's parody, its effect on the literary development of France and Germany, where many imitations were produced, was of the greatest importance.

Clara Linklater Thomson, 1900, *Samuel Richardson,*
A Biographical and Critical Study, p. 170

Clarissa Harlowe (1748)

When I tell you I have lately received this Pleasure (*i. e.,* of reading a new master-piece), you will not want me to inform you that I owe it to the author of *Clarissa*. Such Simplicity, such Manners, such deep Penetration into Nature; such Power to raise and alarm the Passions, few Writers, either ancient or modern, have been possessed of. My Affections are so strongly engaged, and my Fears are so raised, by what I have already read, that I cannot express my Eagerness to see the rest. Sure this Mr. *Richardson* is Master of all that Art which *Horace* compares to Witchcraft

                —Pectus inaniter angit,

Irritat, mulcet, falsis terroribus implet

Ut Magus.——

                    Henry Fielding, 1748, *Jacobite's Journal,* No. 5

I begin by a confession which ought to do some credit to my honesty because it might do little honour to my discernment. Of all the imaginative works I have read, and my self-conceit does not lead me to except my own, none have given me greater pleasure than the one now submitted to the public.

                    Abbé Prévost, 1751, ed. *Clarissa Harlowe,* Preface

I was such an old fool as to weep over *Clarissa Harlowe,* like any milkmaid of sixteen over the ballad of the "Lady's Fall." To say truth, the first volume softened me by a near resemblance of my maiden days; but on the whole 'tis most miserable stuff. Miss How, who is called a young lady of sense and honour, is not only extremely silly, but a more vicious character than Sally Martin, whose crimes are owing at first to seduction, and afterwards to necessity; while this virtuous damsel, without any reason, insults her mother at home and ridicules her abroad; abuses the man she marries; and is impertinent and impudent with great applause. Even the model of affection, Clarissa, is so faulty in her behaviour as to deserve little compassion. Any girl that runs away with a young fellow, without intending to marry him, should be carried to Bridewell or to Bedlam the next day. Yet the circumstances are so laid, as to inspire tenderness, notwithstanding the low style and absurd incidents; and I look upon this and *Pamela* to be two books that will do more general mischief than the works of Lord Rochester.

                    Lady Mary Wortley Montagu, 1752, *Letter to the*
                    Countess of Bute, March 1

The character of Lothario seems to have been expanded by Richardson into that of Lovelace; but he has excelled his original in the moral effect of the fiction. Lothario, with gaiety which cannot be hated, and bravery which cannot be despised, retains too much of the spectator's kindness. It was in the power of Richardson alone, to teach us at once esteem and detestation; to make virtuous resentment overpower all the benevolence which wit, and elegance, and courage, naturally excite; and to lose at last the hero in the villain.

                    Samuel Johnson, 1779-81, *Rowe, Lives of the English Poets*

Except by *Clarissa Harlowe,* I was never so moved by a work of genius as by *Othello.* I read seventeen hours a day at *Clarissa,* and held the book so long up, leaning on my elbows in an armchair, that I stopped the circulation and could not move. When Lovelace writes, "Dear Belton, it is all over, and Clarissa lives," I got up in a fury and wept like an infant, and cursed and d——d Lovelace till exhausted. This is the triumph of genius over the imagination and heart of its readers.

> Benjamin Robert Haydon, 1813, *Autobiography,* March 3

I spoke to him [Lord Macaulay] once about *Clarissa.* "Not read *Clarissa!*" he cried out. "If you have once thoroughly entered on *Clarissa,* and are infected by it, you can't leave it. When I was in India, I passed one hot season at the hills, and there were the governor-general, and the secretary of government, and the commander-in-chief, and their wives. I had *Clarissa* with me; and, as soon as they began to read, the whole station was in a passion of excitement about Miss Harlowe and her misfortunes and her scoundrelly Lovelace! The governor's wife seized the book, and the secretary waited for it, and the chief justice could not read it for tears!" He acted the whole scene: he paced up and down the Athenæum library: I daresay he could have spoken pages of the book,—of that book, and of what countless piles of others!

> William Makepeace Thackeray, 1860, *"Nil Nisi Bonum,"*
> *Cornhill Magazine,* Vol. 1, p. 133

It is like a deluge of very weak and lukewarm green tea, breakfast cup after breakfast cup. After the first of the four volumes, into which the Tauchnitz edition is divided, we gave way. I was much interested with Richardson's method, and admired the particularity with which he puts his characters upon the canvas, and makes them live more in the smallest circumstances of daily life. By force of accumulated details they acquire fulness and reality. But when they come to act, when all the minutiæ of their internal hesitations and emotions are insisted on with wearisome prolixity, one begins to feel that what one wants in Art is something other than the infinite particulars of life. Then Richardson, to my mind, is essentially a bourgeois, his imagination mediocre, his sentiment mawkish.

> John Addington Symonds, 1868, quoted in Horatio F. Brown,
> *John Addington Symonds,* 1903, vol. II, p. 19

Here is an old stationer, fat, well to do, loving money and good living, vain as a peacock, worried to death by small critics who continually gave him dyspepsia and agonies of indigestion, and only soothed by the highly spiced flattery and the spiteful reprisals on his enemies of a circle of foolish female friends; here is, to all appearance, one of the most unfit men in the world, who after making money till he is fifty, is led by the paltry ambition of making more, to write a work which turns out to be utterly different from his first intention, and to prove the author a great moralist, who has the most intimate acquaintance with the human heart, its passions, foibles, strength, and virtues; who can describe almost as minutely as Defoe; who can teach while he amuses, and instruct the heart in virtue while he drives away the admiration for vice; who is powerful, tragic, pathetic, and eminently original; and whose art is so great that his readers follow their enchanter through eight long volumes, heaving a sigh of regret when they lay them down; while the student of morality pronounces them to have been a benefit to the human race.

James Hain Friswell, 1869, *Essays on English Writers*, p. 271

You cannot read through twenty pages of *Clarissa* without feeling that you are mainly in the company, not of the preacher Richardson, but of real live men and women, whose movements, and sentiments, and motives are of importance to watch, and one of whom, the heroine, is a creature to inspire that deep interest always felt in any creature perfectly beautiful: her we can follow into the profoundest misfortunes, and still "in the mid-most heart of grief" can "clasp a secret joy." To show, too, that Richardson felt what other artists feel, that a work of art must be mainly beautiful, the figure of Clarissa is made to occupy a place in his picture far more prominent than any one else; and a vast deal of the material which goes to make up the minor figures grouped about this central perfection, and distributed over the distance and middle distance, a great proportion of the narrative upon which our ideas of the rest are formed, comes to us polarised through the medium of Clarissa's noble and lucid mind; so that, while we are frequently disgusted with the matter, we never lose sight of the perfection of Clarissa, whether as actor or narrator.

Harry Buxton Forman, 1869, "Samuel Richardson as Artist and Moralist," *Fortnightly Review*, vol. 12, p. 434

It has been truly said that *Clarissa Harlowe* is to *La Nouvelle Héloise* what Rousseau's novel is to *Werther;* the three works are inseparably connected, because the bond between them is one of heredity. But while *Werther* and *Héloise* are still read *Clarissa* is scarcely read at all, and this, beyond doubt, is the reason that, while no one thinks of disputing Goethe's indebtedness to Rousseau, it is to-day less easy to perceive the extent to which Rousseau is indebted to Richardson.

Joseph Texte, 1895-99, *Jean-Jacques Rousseau and the Cosmopolitan Spirit in Literature,* tr. Matthews, p. 208

Sir Charles Grandison (1754)

Will you permit me to take this opportunity, in sending a letter to Dr. Young, to address myself to you? It is very long ago that I wished to do it. Having finished your *Clarissa* (oh, the heavenly book!) I could have prayed you to write the history of a manly Clarissa, but I had not courage enough at that time. I should have it no more to-day, as this is only my first English letter—but I have it! It may be because I am now Klopstock's wife (I believe you know my husband by Mr. Honorst,) and then I was only the single young girl. You have since written the manly Clarissa without my prayer. Oh, you have done it to the great joy and thanks of all your happy readers! Now you can write no more, you must write the history of an angel.

> Madame Friedrich Gottlieb Klopstock, 1757,
> *Letter to Richardson*, Nov. 29

Richardson has sent me his *History of Sir Charles Grandison,* in four volumes octavo, which amuses me. It is too long, and there is too much mere talk in it. Whenever he goes *ultra crepidam,* into high life, he grossly mistakes the modes; but, to do him justice, he never mistakes nature, and he has surely great knowledge and skill both in painting and in interesting the heart.

> Philip Dormer Stanhope Lord Chesterfield, 1753,
> *Letter to David Mallet*, Nov. 5

I have now read over Richardson—he sinks horribly in his third volume (he does so in his story of Clarissa). When he talks of Italy, it is plain he is no better acquainted with it than he is with the kingdom of Mancomugi. He might have made his Sir Charles' amour with Clementina begin in a convent, where the pensioners sometimes take great liberties; but that such familiarity should be permitted in her father's house, is as repugnant to custom, as it would be in London for a young lady of quality to dance on the ropes at Bartholomew fair: Neither does his hero behave to her in a manner suitable to his nice notions. It was impossible a discerning man should not see her passion early enough to check it, if he had really designed it. His conduct puts me in mind of some ladies I have known, who could never find out a man to be in love with them, let him do or say what he would, till he made a direct attempt, and then they were so surprised, I warrant you!

> Lady Mary Wortley Montagu, 1755, *Letter to the Countess
> of Bute,* Oct. 20

You admire Richardson, monsieur le marquis; how much greater would be your admiration, if, like me, you were in a position to compare the pictures of this great artist with nature; to see how natural his situations are, however seemingly romantic, and how true his portraits, for all their apparent exaggeration!

Jean-Jacques Rousseau, 1767, Letter to Marquis de Mirabeau

I don't like those long and intolerable novels *Pamela* and *Clarissa*. They have been successful because they excite the reader's curiosity even amidst a medley of trifles; but if the author had been imprudent enough to inform us at the very beginning that Clarissa and Pamela were in love with their persecutors, everything would have been spoiled, and the reader would have thrown the book aside.

Francois Marie Arouet Voltaire, 1767, Letter, May 16

Who will not one of them submit
To be Sir Charles' devoted slave;
And, blindlings still, will not admit
All the Dictator's teachings brave.
But sneer and jeer, and run away,
And hear no more he has to say.

Johann Wolfgang Goethe, 1768, Epistle to Frederika Oeser;
Grimm's Life of Goethe, tr. Adams, p. 152

Throughout the entire composition, the author exhibits great powers of mind; but especially in describing the agitations caused by the passion of love in the bosom of the amiable and enthusiastic Clementina; whose madness is so finely drawn, that Doctor Warton thought it superior to that of Orestes in Euripides; and heightened by more exquisite touches of nature even than that of Shakspeare's Lear. Amongst other beauties in this work may be counted, the truth and delicacy with which the author has sketched the numberless portraits it contains, the innocent love of Emily Jervois, the imposing effect with which Sir Charles is introduced, and the great art shewn in keeping him constantly in view.

Edward Mangin, 1810, ed., The Works of Samuel Richardson,
Sketch, vol. I, p. xxii

But as my friend, Sir Charles Grandison, has no other sin to answer for than that of being very long, very tedious, very oldfashioned, and a prig, I cannot help confessing that, in spite of these faults, and perhaps because of them, I think there are worse books printed, now-a-days and hailed with delight among critics feminine, than the seven volumes that gave such in-finite delight to the beauties of the court of George the Second.

> Mary Russell Mitford, 1851, *Recollections of a Literary Life,*
> p. 412

It would be allowing too much, however, to the third of Richardson's ro-mances, *Sir Charles Grandison,* to say that it reaches the same level of ideal portraiture as *Clarissa Harlowe.* In delineating, at the request of his friends, as he tells us, "the man of true honour," in the person of this irreproachable baronet, Richardson had no such dramatic contrast to inspire him as in his second and greatest romance. Sir Hargrave Pollexfen is but a commonplace and vulgar foil to the virtues of the hero, and there is no thread of pathos or of tragedy running through the story, or indeed appearing in it, except episodically, to give play to the author's strongest powers. Sir Charles Grandison shows himself a man of true honours, in eight volumes; and that is about all that can be said of the romance. Unlike, *Clarissa,* its narrative can not be said to hang fire through the diffuseness of the narrator's method; for in strictness of language it contains no narrative at all.

> Henry Duff Traill, 1883-97, "Samuel Richardson,"
> *The New Fiction,* p. 134

In *Sir Charles Grandison* the story is arrested while the characters are dis-played, contrasting their thoughts, plans, and sentiments. And there is an incessant doubling back on what has gone before; first a letter is written describing what "Has passed," this letter is communicated by its recipient to a third character, who comments on it, while the story waits. This con-stant repercussion of a theme or event between one or more pairs of cor-respondents produces a structure of story very like "The House that Jack Built." Each writer is narrating not events alone, but his or her reflections on previous narrations of the same events. And so, on the next-to-nothing that happened there is superimposed the young lady that wrote to her friend describing it, the friend that approved her for the decorum of the manner in which she described it, the admirable baronet that chanced to find the letter approving the decorum of the young lady, the punctilio of honour that pre-vented the admirable baronet from reading the letter he found, and so on. It is very lifelike, but life can become at times a slow affair, and one of the privileges of the novel-writer is to quicken it. This privilege Richardson foregoes.

> Walter Raleigh, 1894, *The English Novel,* p. 151

GENERAL

This author never deluges the pavement with blood; he does not transport you into distant lands; he does not expose you to the cannibalism of savages; he never loses himself in magic realms. The world where we live is the scene of his action; the basis of his drama is reality; his persons possess all possible actuality; his characters are taken from the midst of society; his incidents from the manners of all polite nations; the passions that he paints are such as I have myself felt; the same objects inspire them, and they have the energy which I know them to possess. The misfortunes and afflictions of his heroes are of the same kind as continually threaten me; he illustrates the ordinary progress of things around me. Without this art my mind, yielding with difficulty to imaginary descriptions, the illusion would be but momentary, and the impression weak and transitory. . . . I still remember the first time that I chanced upon the works of Richardson. I was in the country. How deliciously did their perusal affect me. With every passing minute I saw my happiness diminish by a page. Very soon I experienced the same sensation as men feel who have lived together in intimate friendship and are on the point of separation. At the end I felt as if I were left all alone. . . . He bequeathed to me a lasting and pleasing melancholy; sometimes my friends perceive it and ask me, What is the matter with you? You are not the same as usual; what has happened to you? They question me about my health, my fortune, my relations, my friends. O my friends, *Pamela, Clarissa,* and *Grandison,* are three great dramas! Torn from reading them by important business, I felt an overwhelming distate for it; I neglected my work and returned to Richardson. Beware of opening these enchanting books when you have any important duties to perform. . . . O Richardson, Richardson, first of men in my eyes, you shall be my reading at all times! Pursued by pressing need; if my friend should fall into poverty; if the limitations of my fortunes should prevent me from giving fit attention to the education of my children, I will sell my books; but you shall remain on the same shelf as Moses, Euripides and Sophocles, and I will read you by turns.

Denis Diderot, 1761, *Eloge de Richardson; Works,*
vol. V, pp. 212, 227

Those deplorably tedious lamentations, *Clarissa* and *Sir Charles Grandison,* which are pictures of high life as conceived by a bookseller, and romances as they would be spiritualized by a Methodist teacher. . . . Many English books, I conclude, are to be bought at Paris. I am sure Richardson's Works are, for they have stupified the whole French nation: I will not answer for our best authors.

Horace Walpole, 1764-65, *Letters,* ed. Cunningham,
vol. IV, pp. 305, 396

Erskine. "Surely, Sir, Richardson is very tedious." *Johnson.* "Why, Sir, if you were to read Richardson for the story, your impatience would be so much fretted that you would hang yourself. But you must read him for the sentiment, and consider the story as only giving occasion to the sentiment."

Samuel Johnson, 1772, Life by Boswell, April 6,
ed. Hill, vol. II, p. 200

Voltaire, Rousseau, and Diderot made a frequent and arbitrary use of romance, as being a form eminently adapted to the conveyance of certain peculiar ideas of their own. But if this form be regarded as a distinct poetic species, as regular narrative in prose, sketching the transient features of society, it will be found that, in this respect, too, French writers have frequently copied from English models, but have seldom, if ever, equalled them. In point of originality and power of representation Richardson perhaps occupies the highest place in this peculiar style of composition. If he, likewise, has become antiquated, if his striving after the ideal was not attended with special success owing to exactness of details occasionally tedious, we have a proof of the incompatibility of direct poetic connexion with the hard realities of life, though disguised in prosaic garb. If his genius availed not to solve the problem, it was because its solution was little short of impracticable.

Frederick Schlegel, 1815-59, Lectures on the History
of Literature, p. 311

Richardson has a certain standard, the standard of the respectability of the day, and he tries to raise his readers to it both by showing them what a fine thing his ideal looks when it is endowed with life, and by pointing out that the path of virtue is the path of safety, which cannot be forsaken without peril of imminent disaster. Unfortunately Richardson spoils by his eagerness the moral as well as the artistic effect of his books. He is so bent on showing us that virtue is intrinsically admirable and a good investment into the bargain that he becomes absolutely incredible, and we laugh instead of being convinced. His most morally impressive book is that which is also artistically the greatest—the book which telling of the heroic virtue of Clarissa shows us how it found its reward not in the cheap splendours amidst which we bid farewell to his earliest heroine, but in the solemn quiet of the grave, where the wicked Lovelace can no more trouble her, and she, the weary one, may lie at rest.

James Ashcroft Noble, 1886, Morality in English Fiction, p. 16

Richardson's great forte consists in the art of making his characters *live;* in this particular he has rarely been rivalled, never, I think, excelled, by other authors. He employs not the mental dissecting-knife of modern writers. He affects not to analyze with a pretence of profoundity the implexicable workings of the mind. His method, on the contrary, is that of nature herself. The characters of his creations are revealed to us, like those of our friends, in what they say and do; and with so much of nature, so much of consistency, in the representation, that they grow into our intimacy as our friends themselves; they excite our love, our esteem, our compassion, or it may be our scorn, our detestation, as if they were veritably sentient and sensible beings. In a word, the persons of Richardson's novels are no mere problems in psychology, but, relatively to the reader's affections, real creatures of flesh and blood, a consummation far more difficult of attainment.

William C. Ward, 1890, "Samuel Richardson,"
Gentleman's Magazine, N. S., vol. 44, p. 78

We are not likely to overestimate the historical position of Richardson; we are more likely to underestimate it. Morover, in the logical sequence of minor incident, *Clarissa Harlowe* has been excelled only by the maturest work of George Eliot. And yet the weaknesses and shortcomings of Richardson are apparent, and were apparent in his own time. His ethical system was based upon no wide observation or sound philosophy; it was the code of a Protestant casuist. He was a sentimentalist, creating pathetic scenes for their own sake and degrading tears and hysterics into a manner. His language was not free from the affectations of the romancers; even his friends dared tell him with caution and circumlocution that he was fond of the nursery phrase. He was unacquainted, as he said himself, with the high life he pretended to describe.

Wilbur L. Cross, 1899, *The Development of the English Novel*,
p. 42

LADY MARY WORTLEY MONTAGU
1689-1762

Montagu (*Lady* Mary Wortley), 1689-1762. Born [Mary Pierrepont; Lady Mary in 1690, when her father became Earl of Kingston], in London, 1689; baptized, 26 May. Early taste for literature. Married to Edward Wortley Montagu, 12 Aug. 1712. In favour at Court. Friendship with Pope begun. In Vienna with her husband (appointed Ambassador to the Porte), Sept. 1716 to Jan. 1717; in Constantinople, May 1717 to June 1718. Returned to England, Oct. 1718. Estrangement from Pope, 1722. Lived abroad, apart from husband, July 1739-1762. Died, in England, 21 Aug. 1762. WORKS: *Court Poems* (anon.; surreptitiously published), 1716 (misdated 1706 on title-page); authorised edn., as *Six Town Eclogues* (under initials: Rt. Hon. L. M. W. M), 1747. POSTHUMOUS: *Letters of Lady M——y W——y M——e* (3 vols.), 1763; *Poetical Works of the Right Hon. Lady M——y W——y M——e*, 1781.

> R. Farquharson Sharp, 1897, *A Dictionary of*
> *English Authors*, p. 201

SEE: *Complete Letters*, ed. Robert Halsband, 1966, 3 v.; Robert Halsband, *Life*, 1956.

PERSONAL

Her dress, her avarice, and her impudence must amaze any one that never heard her name. She wears a foul mob that does not cover her greasy black locks, that hang loose, never combed or curled, an old mazarine blue wrapper, that gapes open and discovers a canvas petticoat. Her face swelled violently on one side with the remains of a——, partly covered with a plaister, and partly with white paint, which for cheapness she has bought so coarse.

> Horace Walpole, 1740, *Letter to Conway*, Sept. 25;
> *Letters*, ed. Cunningham, vol. I, p. 57

There is more fire and wit in all the writings of that author than one meets with in almost any other; and whether she is in the humour of an infidel or a devotee, she expresses herself with so much strength that one can hardly persuade oneself she is not in earnest on either side of the question. Nothing can be more natural than her complaint of the loss of her beauty [*vide* the "Saturday" in her *Town Eclogues*]; but as that was only one of her various powers to charm, I should have imagined she would only have felt a very small part of the regret that many other people have suffered on a like misfortune; who have nothing but the loveliness of their persons to claim admiration; and consequently, by the loss of that, have found all their hopes of distinction vanish much earlier in life than Lady Mary's;—for if I do not mistake, she was near thirty before she had to deplore the loss of beauty greater than I ever saw in any face beside her own.

> Lady Hertford (Duchess of Somerset), 1741, *Letters:*
> *Little Memoirs of the Eighteenth Century*, by Paston, p. 33

To Congreve she was all brightness, life and spirit; her silvery laugh sounded like divinest melody; but when I stood before her, scarcely daring to look into those eyes for that sacred love after which I pined, she was cold, severe, and silent. When Pope was near, when Wharton was by her side, gazing at her with his large and earnest eyes, how beautiful she appeared; all her genius shone out of her spirit face; her features glowed with animation; her tongue spake in softest accents, and she seemed a something more than earthly. But when the visitor departed, a magic change came over her —she froze, as it were, into marble; she grew cold, still, selfish, unfeeling, capricious and exacting. One reads in old romances of a beautiful damsel discovered in a forest by some brave, errant knight; she weeps, she prays, she smiles, she fascinates. The gallant adventurer vows to devote his life to her service; she leads him to her bower, or to some faërie castle. Something in her appearance suddenly awakens suspicion, and the noble knight clutches his good sword Excalibar within his mailed hand, and mayhap as an additional precaution lifts up a prayer to God and the Virgin. Scarcely has he done it, when a transformation is seen—a mighty transformation indeed; and the virgin disappears, and he sees only a venomous serpent looking at him with deadly eyes, as Lucifer looked on Eve, and hissing forth cold poison. Such was the difference between my mother before her visitors, and my mother with her son.

> Edward Wortley Montagu, 1776? *An Autobiography*, vol. I, p. 97*

Whatever esteem we may feel for the talents and merits, whatever toleration we may be inclined to extend over the eccentricities and audacities, of such women as Lady Mary Wortley Montague, it is the rankest and most nauseous cant of hypocritical chivalry to pretend that they have a right to expect the same tender and reverent forbearance which all but the vilest of men and subscribers feel for "any woman, womanly."

> Algernon Charles Swinburne, 1886, *Miscellanies*, p. 42

The fact seems to have been that Lady Mary, like many of the men of the eighteenth century, had developed the intellectual and practical side of her nature at the expense of the emotions. There is no proof that she was ever in love with anyone but her husband; and her affection for him began in intellectual companionship, and consisted to a considerable extent in respect, with a touch of fear. Her love-letters are full of business details, plain speaking, and close reasoning. Her lover gives her up rather than violate his principles as to marriage settlements, and she heartily approves him. All this is very sensible, but it is hardly the note of passion, even allowing for the undemonstrative character of the age. Family affection was not strongly developed in Lady Mary: her father's death leaves little impression on her. He had neglected her; why should she mourn him? Her religion, again, was Whig Christianity of the day, the moderately rationalistic, tolerant half-deism of the Georgian Bishops; she never speaks but with contempt of past mystics or present Methodists. Patriotism had little hold on her—she was

---

* A fictitious autobiography, written by Y., who was E. V. H. Kenealy, and published in 1869.

cosmopolitan; and though English defeats galled her a little, English victories left her cold. All her failings—coarseness of phrase, coldness of feeling, want of consideration in the use of her wit, even the slovenliness of dress into which she fell—are the faults of a nature too merely intellectual. One may say that she was all her days a traveller, regarding the world of life as she did the lands through which she journeyed. The joys of existence were but the chance of a fine day, or a good inn on the road; its griefs but the breaking of a wheel, the discomfort of a hovel—all alike to be borne with quietly, because they would be gone and almost forgotten to-morrow. Friends, relations even, were but travelling-companions—here to-day, gone to-morrow.

> Arthur R. Ropes, 1892, ed., *Lady Mary Wortley Montagu,*
> *Select Passages from Her Letters,* Introduction, p. 30

POEMS

The letter of Gold, and the curious illumining of the Sonnets, were not a greater token of respect than what I have paid to *your Eclogues;* they lie inclosed in a monument of red Turkey, written in my fairest hand; the gilded leaves are opened with no less veneration than the pages of the Sibyls; like them, locked up and concealed from all profane eyes, *none but my own* have beheld these sacred remains of yourself; and I should think it as great a wickedness to divulge them, as to scatter abroad the ashes of my ancestors.

> Alexander Pope, 1717, *Letter to Lady Mary Wortley Montagu*

Of her poetical talents it may be observed, that they were usually commanded by particular occasions, and that when she had composed stanzas, as any incident suggested them, little care was taken afterwards; and she disdained the scrupulous labour, by which Pope acquired a great degree of his peculiar praise. But it should be remembered, that the ore is equally sterling, although it may not receive the highest degree of polish of which it is capable. She attempted no poem of much regularity or extent. In the "Town Eclogues," which is the longest, a few illegitimate rhymes and feeble expletives will not escape the keen eye of a critic. The epistle of Arthur Gray has true Ovidian tenderness, the ballads are elegant, and the satires abound in poignant sarcasms, and just reflections on the folly and vices of those whom she sought to stigmatize. There is little doubt, but that if Lady Mary had applied herself wholly to poetry, a near approximation to the rank of her contemporary bards would have been adjudged to her, by impartial posterity.

> J. Dallaway, 1803, ed., *The Works of Lady Mary Wortley*
> *Montagu,* Memoirs, vol. I, p. 97

How coarsely, and even lewdly, she herself could write is proved in the *Epistle from Arthur Grey, the Footman;* a composition which a penny street ballad-monger would now blush to own; and added to its offences against decency is the cruelty of holding up the poor lady, whose notoriety was already sufficiently dreadful, to further ribaldry. Nor does this poem stand alone; the "Town Eclogues" and others of her fugitive pieces are almost equally gross.

> H. Barton Baker, 1877, "A Representative Lady of the
> Last Century," *The Gentleman's Magazine,* vol. 241, p. 86

LETTERS

The publication of these letters will be an immortal monument to the memory of Lady Mary Wortley Montagu, and will shew, as long as the English language endures, the sprightliness of her wit, the solidity of her judgment, the elegance of her taste, and the excellence of her real character. These letters are so bewitchingly entertaining that we defy the most phlegmatic man on earth to read one without going through with them, or, after finishing the third volume, not to wish there was twenty more of them.

> Tobias George Smollett, 1763, *Critical Review*

The letters of Lady Mary Wortley Montague are not unworthy of being named after those of Madame de Sevigné. They have much of the French ease and vivacity; and retain more the character of agreeable epistolary style, than perhaps any letters which have appeared in the English language.

> Hugh Blair, 1783, *Lectures on Rhetoric and Belles-Lettres,*
> ed. Mills, Lecture XXXVII

Lady Mary Wortley Montague is a remarkable instance of an author nearly lost to the nation: she is only known to posterity by a chance publication; for such were her famous Turkish letters, the manuscript of which her family once purchased with an intention to suppress, but they were frustrated by a transcript. The more recent letters were reluctantly extracted out of the family trunks, and surrendered in exchange for certain family documents, which had fallen into the hands of a bookseller. Had it depended on her relatives, the name of Lady Mary had only reached us in the satires of Pope. The greater part of her epistolary correspondence was destroyed by her mother (?); and what that good and Gothic lady spared, was suppressed by the hereditary austerity of rank, of which her family was too susceptible. The entire correspondence of this admirable writer and studious woman (for once, in perusing some unpublished letters of Lady Mary's, I discovered that "she had been in the habit of reading seven hours a day for many years") would undoubtedly have exhibited a fine statue, instead of the torso we now possess; and we might have lived with her ladyship, as we do with Madame de Sévigné.

> Isaac Disraeli, 1791-1824, "Of Suppressors and Dilapidators of Manuscripts," *Curiosities of Literature*

The great charm of her letters is certainly the extreme ease and facility with which every thing is expressed, the brevity and rapidity of her representations, and the elegant simplicity of her diction. While they unite almost all the qualities of a good style, there is nothing of the professed author in them: nothing that seems to have been composed, or to have engaged the admiration of the writer. She appears to be quite unconscious either of merit or of exertion in what she is doing; and never stops to bring out a thought, or to turn an expression, with the cunning of a practised rhetorician.

> Francis, Lord Jeffrey, 1803-1844, "Lady Mary Wortley Montagu," *Contributions to the Edinburgh Review*, vol. IV, p. 427

WILLIAM SHENSTONE
1714-1763

William Shenstone (1714-63), born at the Leasowes, Hales Owen, Worcestershire, studied at Pembroke College, Oxford, in 1737 published anonymously *Poems upon various Occasions*, in 1741 *The Judgment of Hercules*, and next year *The Schoolmistress*. In 1745 he succeeded his father in the Leasowes. His success in beautifying his little domain attracted visitors from all quarters, and brought him more fame than his poetry, but involved him in pecuniary embarrassments. *The Schoolmistress* has secured for him a permanent if humble place among English poets. His other works are mostly insignificant; but his *Pastoral Ballad* has touches of exquisite tenderness. See Life by Dr. Johnson prefixed to Shenstone's *Essays on Men and Manners* (new ed. 1868), and that by G. Gilfillan to an edition of his *Poems* (1854).

> Patrick and Groome, eds., 1897, *Chamber's Biographical Dictionary*, p. 851

SEE: *Poetical Works*, ed. C. C. Clarke, 1880; *Shenstone's Miscellany, 1759-1763*, ed. Ian A. Gordon, 1952; *Letters*, ed. Duncan Mallam, 1939; *Letters*, ed. Marjorie Williams, 1939; Marjorie Williams, *William Shenstone*, 1935.

PERSONAL

His appearance surprised me, for he was a large, heavy, fat man, dressed in white clothes and silver lace, with his gray hairs tied behind and much powdered, which, added to his shyness and reserve, was not at first prepossessing. His reserve and melancholy (for I could not call it pride) abated as we rode along, and by the time we left him at the Admiral's, he became good company,—Garbett, who knew him well, having whispered him, that though we had no great name, he would find us not common men.

Alexander Carlyle, 1758, *Autobiography*, ch. ix

He was no economist; the generosity of his temper prevented him from paying a proper regard to the use of money: he exceeded, therefore, the bounds of his paternal fortune, which, before he died, was considerably encumbered. But when one recollects the perfect paradise he had raised around him, the hospitality with which he lived, his great indulgence to his servants, his charities to the indigent, and all done with an estate not more than three hundred pounds a year, one should rather be led to wonder that he left anything behind him than to blame his want of economy. He left, however, more than sufficient to pay his debts; and by his will appropriated his whole estate for that purpose.

Richard Dodsley, 1764-69, ed. *Shenstone's Works*, Preface

I have read an octave volume of Shenstone's *Letters*; poor man! He was always wishing for money, for fame, and other distinctions; and his whole philosophy consisted in living against his will in retirement, and in a place which his taste had adorned, but which he only enjoyed when people of note came to see and commend it. His correspondence is about nothing else but this place and his own writings, with two or three neighbouring clergymen, who wrote verses too.

Thomas Gray, 1769, *Letter to Mr. Nicholls*, June 24

The pleasure of Shenstone was all in his eye; he valued what he valued merely for its looks; nothing raised his indignation more than to ask if there were any fishes in his water. . . . He is represented by his friend Dodsley as a man of great tenderness and generosity, kind to all who were within his influence, but if once offended not easily appeased; inattentive to economy, and careless of his expenses: in his person he was larger than the middle size, with something clumsy in his form; very negligent of his clothes, and remarkable for wearing his grey hair in a particular manner; for he held that the fashion was no rule of dress, and that every man was to suit his appearance to his natural form. His mind was not very comprehensive, nor his curiosity active; he had no value for those parts of knowledge which he had not himself cultivated.

Samuel Johnson, 1779-81, Shenstone, Lives of the English Poets

Dr. Warton, in his <i>Essay on Pope,</i> has mentioned that three of our celebrated poets died singular deaths. He might have added Shenstone to the number. He had a housekeeper who lived with him in the double capacity of maid and mistress; and being offended with her on some occasion, he went out of the house and set all night in his post-chaise in much agitation, in consequence of which he caught a cold that eventually caused his death.

Edmond Malone, 1783, Maloniana, ed. Prior, p. 340

Mr. Shenstone was too much respected in the neighbourhood to be treated with rudeness: and though his works (frugally as they were managed), added to his manners of living, must necessarily have made him exceed his income, and, of course, he might sometimes be distressed for money, yet he had too much spirit to expose himself to insults from trifling sums, and guarded against any great distress by anticipating a few hundreds; which his estate could very well bear, as appeared by what remained to his executors after the payment of his debts and his legacies to his friends, and annuities of thirty pounds a year to one servant, and six pounds to another: for his will was dictated with equal justice and generosity.

Richard Graves, 1788, Recollections of Some Particulars
of the Life of William Shenstone

He was not formed to captivate; his person was clumsy, his manners disagreeable, and his temper feeble and vacillating. The Delia who is introduced into his elegies, and the Phillis of his pastoral ballad, was Charlotte Graves, sister to the Graves who wrote the <i>Spiritual Quixotte.</i> There was nothing warm or earnest in his admiration, and all his gallantry is as vapid as his character. He never gave the lady who was supposed, and supposed herself, to be the object of his serious pursuit, an opportunity of accepting or rejecting him; and his conduct has been blamed as ambiguous and unmanly. His querulous declamations against women in general, had neither cause nor excuse; and his complaints of infidelity and coldness are equally without foundation. He died unmarried.

Anna Brownell Jameson, 1829, The Loves of the Poets,
vol. II, p. 311

GENERAL

Why have the "Elegies" of Shenstone, which forty years ago formed for many of us the favourite poems of our youth, ceased to delight us in mature life? It is perhaps that these Elegies, planned with peculiar felicity, have little in their execution. They form a series of poetical truths, devoid of poetical expression; truths,—for notwithstanding the pastoral romance in which the poet has enveloped himself, the subjects are real, and the feelings could not, therefore, be fictitious. . . . These Elegies, with some other poems, may be read with a new interest, when we discover them to form the true Memoirs of Shenstone. Records of querulous but delightful feelings! whose subjects spontaneously offered themselves from passing incidents; they still perpetuate emotions, which will interest the young poet, and the young lover of taste.

Isaac Disraeli, 1791-1824, "Shenstone Vindicated,"
Curiosities of Literature

His genius is not forcible, but it settles in mediocrity without meanness. His pieces of levity correspond not disagreeably with their title. His "Ode to Memory" is worthy of protection from the power which it invokes. Some of the stanzas of his "Ode to Rural Elegance" seem to recall to us the country-loving spirit of Cowley, subdued in wit, but harmonized in expression. From the commencement of the stanza in that ode, "O sweet disposer of the rural hour," he sustains an agreeable and peculiarly refined strain of poetical feeling. The ballad of "Jemmy Dawson," and the elegy on "Jessy," are written with genuine feeling. With all the beauties of the Leasowes in our minds, it may be still regretted, that instead of devoting his whole soul to clumping beeches, and projecting mottoes for summerhouses, he had not gone more into living nature for subjects, and described her interesting realities with the same fond and *naïve* touches which give so much delightfulness to his portrait of the "School-mistress."

Thomas Campbell, 1819, Specimens of the British Poets

Shenstone was deficient in animal spirits, and condescended to be vexed when people did not come to see his retirement; but few men had an acuter discernment of the weak points of others and the general mistakes of mankind, as anybody may see by his *Essays*; and yet in those *Essays* he tells us, that he never passed a town or village, without regretting that he could not make the acquaintance of some of the good people that lived there.

Leigh Hunt, 1848, A Jar of Honey from Mount Hybla, p. 173

Most of his verse is artificial and unreal, and has rightly been forgotten, but what remains is of permanent interest. He is best known by the *School-*

mistress, a burlesque imitation of Spenser, which was highly praised by Johnson and by Goldsmith; but many will value equally, in its way, the neatly turned *Pastoral Ballad, in four parts,* written in 1743, which is supposed to refer to the author's disappointment in love, or the gently satirical "Progress of Taste," showing "how great a misfortune it is for a man of small estate to have much taste." Burns warmly eulogised Shenstone's elegies, which are also to some extent autobiographical, though it is difficult to say how far they are sincere.

George A. Aitken, 1897, *Dictionary of National Biography,*
vol. LII, p. 50

CHARLES CHURCHILL
1731-1764

Charles Churchill, 1731-1764. Born, in Westminster, Feb. 1731. Educated at Westminster School, 1739-49(?). Made a "Fleet marriage" with Miss Scot, 1748. Entered at Trinity College, Cambridge, 1749, but did not take up residence. Ordained Curate to South Cadbury, Somersetshire, 1753. Ordained Priest, 1756; took curacy under his father at Rainham. Succeeded father at his death to curacy and lectureship of St. John's Westminster. Added to small income by tuition. Separation from his wife, Feb. 1761. Contrib. to *The Library,* 1761. Resigned lectureship in consequence of protests of parishioners, Jan. 1763. Assisted Wilkes in editing *The North Briton,* 1762-63. Copious publication of satires and poems. At Oxford during Commemoration, 1763. Died, at Boulogne, 4 Nov. 1764. Buried in St. Martin's Churchyard, Dover. WORKS: *The Rosciad* (anon.), 1761; *The Apology, addressed to the Critical Reviewers,* 1761; *Night* (anon.), 1761; *The Ghost,* bks. i., ii. (anon.), 1762; bk. iii., 1762; bk. iv., 1763; *The Prophecy of Famine,* 1763; *The Conference,* 1763; *An Epistle to W. Hogarth,* 1763; *The Author,* 1763; *Poems,* 1763; *Gotham,* 1764; *The Duellist,* 1764 (2nd edn. same year); *The Candidate,* 1764; *The Times* (anon.), 1764; *Independence* (anon.), 1764; *The Farewell* (anon.), 1764. POSTHUMOUS: *Sermons* (possibly by his father), 1765. COLLECTED WORKS: in 4 vols., 1765; in 4 vols., 1774; in 2 vols., with *life,* 1804.

R. Farquharson Sharp, 1897, *A Dictionary of
English Authors,* p. 54

SEE: *Poetical Works,* ed. James Laver, 1933, 2v.; *Poetical Works,* ed. Douglas Grant, 1953; Wallace C. Brown, *Charles Churchill: Poet, Rake and Rebel,* 1953.

PERSONAL

Whenever I am happy in the acquaintance of a man of genius and letters, I never let any mean ill-grounded suspicions creep into my mind to disturb that happiness: whatever he says, I am inclined and bound to believe, and, therefore, I must desire you not to vex yourself with unnecessary delicacy upon my account. I see and read so much of Mr. Churchill's spirit, without having the pleasure of his acquaintance, that I am persuaded that his genius disdains any direction, and that resolutions once taken by him will withstand the warmest importunities of his friends. At the first reading of his *Apology,* I was so charmed and raised with the power of his writing, that I really forgot that I was delighted when I ought to have been alarmed; this puts me in mind of the Highland officer, who was so warmed and elevated by the heat of the battle that he had forgot, till he was reminded by the smarting, that he had received no less than eleven wounds in different parts of his body.

David Garrick, 1761, *Letter to Robert Lloyd*

Possessed of powers and natural endowments which might have made him, under favourable circumstances, a poet, a hero, a man, and a saint, he became, partly through his own fault, and partly through the force of destiny, a satirist, an unfortunate politician, a profligate, died early; and we must approach his corpse, as men do those of Burns and Byron, with sorrow, wonder, admiration, and blame, blended into one strange, complex, and yet not unnatural emotion. Like them, his life was short and unhappy—his career triumphant, yet checquered—his powers uncultivated—his passions unchecked—his poetry only a partial discovery of his genius—his end sudden and melancholy—and his reputation, and future place in the history of letters, hitherto somewhat uncertain. And yet, like them, his very faults and errors, both as a man and a poet, have acted, with many, as nails, fastening to a "sure place" his reputation and the effect of his genius. . . . For the errors of Churchill, as a man, there does not seem to exist any plea of palliation, except what may be found in the poverty of his early circumstances, and in the strength of his later passions. The worst is, that he never seems to have been seduced into sin through the bewildering and bewitching mist of imagination. It was naked sensuality that he appeared to worship, and he always sinned with his eyes open. Yet his moral sense, though blunted, was never obliterated; and many traits of generosity and good feeling mingled with his excesses.

George Gilfillan, 1855, ed., *The Poetical Works of Charles Churchill*, pp. iii, xv

GENERAL

I have read him twice, and some of his pieces three times over, and the last time with more pleasure than the first. . . . He is indeed a careless writer for the most part; but where shall we find in any of those authors who finish their works with the exactness of a Flemish pencil, those bold and daring strokes of fancy, those numbers so hazardously ventured upon and so happily finished, the matter so compressed and yet so clear, and the colouring so sparingly laid on, and yet with such a beautiful effect? In short, it is not his least praise, that he is never guilty of those faults as a writer which he lays to the charge of others. A proof that he did not judge by a borrowed standard, or from rules laid down by critics, but that he was qualified to do it by his own native powers, and his great superiority of genius. For he that wrote so much, and so fast would, through inadvertence hurry unavoidably, have departed from rules which he might have founded in books, but his own truly poetical talent was a guide which could not suffer him to err.

William Cowper, 1786, Letter to Mr. Unwin

A certain simplicity of style—and easy unaffected English—which disclaims the correction of minute blemishes, immingles much of the idiomatic dialect of conversation—which avoids the set of phrases and dancing master steps of practised versifiers—these constitute Churchill's highest merit, and confer on his writings the atticism which preserves them.

William Taylor, 1804, Critical Review, May

His best thoughts are all essentially commonplace; but, in uttering them, there is almost always a determined plainness of words, a free step in verse, a certain boldness and skill in evading the trammel of the rhyme, deserving high praise; while often, as if spurning the style which yet does not desert him, he wears it clinging about him with a sort of disregarded grace.

John Wilson, 1845, "Supplement to Mac-Flecnoe and The Dunciad,"
Blackwood's Magazine, vol. 58, p. 373

Churchill is a Juvenalian; a suckling of the Roman wolf; fierce but jolly; savage yet not unkindly. Of course, too, he has points in common with all the great satirists, for they have the distant likenesses of a clan as well as the nearer likenesses of a family. He has the Aristophanic heartiness, though not the Aristophanic poetry; the good-fellowship of Horace, with far less subtlety and familiar grace; a good deal of Dryden's vigour and eye for the points of a satirical portrait, but inferior penetration of glance, and far less comprehensive sweep, whether of reasoning power, poetic humour, or fancy.

James Hannay, 1866, ed., The Poetical Works of
Charles Churchill, Memoir, p. xxx

The celebrity of the smart verse making of Churchill marks a low point in English taste. It nearly secured him a poet's monument in Westminster Abbey; and it actually secured a poet's rank for a petulant rhymer without a spark of the poet's imagination, of cold heart, natural bad taste, and very little knowledge of that narrow world which he so impudently lampooned. Nothing in Churchill reveals a gleam of genial feeling, or justifies the suspicion that he could take pleasure in what refines or elevates. If we may believes his own account of himself, nature had given him little enough, beyond an ugly face, a sour temperament and a bitter tongue. Yet he was not dissatisfied. He was very willing to be taken for what he was: and if he could not win liking and respect, he was content to be feared. In all this there must have been something of affectation. Yet it is only too clear that the coarse texture of his mind was impermeable to the kindlier and worthier influences of his time. . . . Cowper, we know, had a real admiration for him. His earliest work, *The Rosciad,* is his best, because in it he most adhered to good models. His later works will serve the student as a rich mine of all sorts of errors in taste and judgment. In proportion as he abandoned himself to his own guidance, his work degenerated, and the poverty of his thought appeared; and in three years he had literally written himself out. But in all that he wrote there is a certain fierce manliness which wins attention, and even sympathy for his untutored brain and unsoftened heart, and this effect is heightened by the story of his life and death.

E. J. Payne, 1880, The English Poets, ed. Ward,
vol. III, pp. 389, 391

EDWARD YOUNG
1683-1765

Born at Upham, Hants, June 1683. At Winchester School, 1694-99. Matric. New Coll., Oxford, 3 Oct. 1702. Soon afterwards removed to Corpus Christi Coll. Law Fellowship, All Soul's Coll., 1706; B. C. L., 23 April, 1714; D. C. L., 10 June 1719. Tutor to Lord Burleigh, for a short time before 1719. Play *Busiris* produced at Drury Lane, March 1719; *The Brothers,* Drury Lane, 1753. Ordained, 1727; Chaplain to George II., April 1728; Rector to Welwyn, Herts, 1730-65. Married Lady Elizabeth Leigh, 27 May 1731. Clerk of Closet to Princess Dowager, 1751. Died, at Welwyn, 5 April 1765. Buried there. WORKS: *Epistle to . . . Lord Lansdown,* 1713; *A Poem on the Lord's Day,* 1713 (2nd edn. same year); *The Force of Religion,* 1714; *On the Late Queen's Death,* 1714; *Oratio habita in Coll. Omnium Animarum,* 1716; *Paraphrase on part of the Book of Job,* 1719; *Busiris,* 1719; *Letter to Mr. Tickell,* 1719; *The Revenge,* 1721; *The Universal Passion* (6 pts.; anon.), 1725-28; *The Instalement,* 1726; *Cynthio* (anon.), 1727; *Ocean* 1728; *A Vindication of Providence,* 1728

(2nd edn. same year); *An Apoloyy for Princes*, 1729; *Imperium Pelagi* (anon.), 1730; *Two Epistles to Mr. Pope* (anon.), 1730; *The Sea-Piece*, 1730; *The Foreign Address*, 1734; *Poetical Works* (2 vols.), 1741; *The Complaint; or, Night Thoughts on Life, Death, and Immortality* (anon.; 9 pts.), 1742-46; *The Consolation* (anon.), 1745; *Reflections on the Public Situation of the Kingdom*, 1745; *The Brothers* (anon.), 1753; *The Centaur not Fabulous* (anon.), 1755; *An Argument drawn from the circumstance of Christ's Death*, 1758; *Conjectures on Original Composition* (anon.), 1759 (2nd edn. same year); *Resignation* (anon.), 1762; *Works* (4 vols.), 1764. POSTHUMOUS: *The Merchant*, 1771. COLLECTED WORKS: *Complete Works*, ed. by Dr. Doran (2 vols.), 1854.

R. Farquharson Sharp, 1897, A Dictionary of
English Authors, p. 307

SEE: Henry C. Shelley, *The Life and Letters of Edward Young*, 1914; C. V. Wicker, *Edward Young and The Fear of Death*, 1952.

PERSONAL

When he had determined to go into orders he addressed himself, like an honest man, for the best directions in the study of theology. But to whom did he apply? It may, perhaps, be thought, to Sherlock or Atterbury; to Burnet or Hare. No! to Mr. Pope; who, in a youthful frolic, recommended Thomas Aquinas to him. With this treasure he retired, in order to be free from interruption, to an obscure place in the suburbs. His director hearing no more of him in six months, and apprehending he might have carried the jest too far, sought after him, and found him out just in time to prevent an irretrievable derangement.

Owen Ruffhead, 1769, Life of Pope, p. 291, note

There are who relate, that, when first Young found himself independent, and his own master at All Souls, he was not the ornament to religion and morality which he afterwards became. . . . They who think ill of Young's morality, in the early part of his life, may perhaps be wrong; but Tindal could not err in his opinion of Young's warmth and ability in the cause of religion. Tindal used to spend much of his time at All Souls. "The other boys," said the atheist, "I can always answer, because I always know whence they have their arguments, which I have read a hundred times; but that fellow Young is continually pestering me with something of his own." After all, Tindal and the censurers of Young may be reconcilable. Young might, for two or three years, have tried that kind of life in which his natural principles would not suffer him to wallow long. If this were so, he has left behind him not only his evidence in favour of virtue, but the potent testimony of experience against vice.

Herbert Croft, Jr., 1780, Young, Lives of the English Poets
by Samuel Johnson

Young, whose satires give the very anatomy of human foibles, was wholly governed by his housekeeper. She thought and acted for him, which probably greatly assisted the *Night Thoughts,* but his curate exposed the domestic economy of a man of genius by a satirical novel. If I am truly informed, in that gallery of satirical poets in his "Love of Fame," Young has omitted one of the most striking—his own! While the poet's eye was glancing from "earth to heaven," he totally overlooked the lady whom he married, and who soon became the object of his contempt; and not only his wife, but his only son, who when he returned home for the vacation from Winchester school, was only admitted into the presence of his poetical father on the first and the last day; and whose unhappy life is attributed to this unnatural neglect:—a lamentable domestic catastrophe, which, I fear, has too frequently occurred amidst the ardour and occupations of literary glory.

> Isaac Disraeli, 1796-1818, "Domestic Life," *The Literary Character*

The outline of Young's character is too distinctly traceable in the well-attested facts of his life, and yet more in the self-betrayal that runs through all his works, for us to fear that our general estimate of him may be false. For, while no poet seems less easy and spontaneous than Young, no poet discloses himself more completely. Men's minds have no hiding-place out of themselves—their affections do but betray another phase of their nature. And if, in the present view of Young, we seem to be more intent on laying bare unfavourable facts than on shrouding them in "charitable speeches," it is not because we may have any irreverential pleasure in turning men's characters the seamy side without, but because we see no great advantage in considering a man as he was *not.* Young's biographers and critics have usually set out from the position that he was a great religious teacher, and that his poetry is morally sublime; and they have toned down his failings into harmony with their conception of the divine and the poet. For our own part, we set out from precisely the opposite conviction—namely, that the religious and moral spirit of Young's poetry is low and false; and we think it of some importance to show that the *Night Thoughts* are the reflex of a mind in which the higher human sympathies were inactive. This judgment is entirely opposed to our youthful predilections and enthusiasm. The sweet garden-breath of early enjoyment lingers about many a page of the *Night Thoughts,* and even of the "Last Day," giving an extrinsic charm to passages of stilted rhetoric and false sentiment, but the sober and repeated reading of maturer years has convinced us that it would hardly be possible to find a more typical instance than Young's poetry, of the mistake which substitutes interested obedience for sympathetic emotion, and baptizes egoism as religion.

> George Eliot, 1857, *Worldliness and Other-Worldliness*:
> *The Poet Young; Essays*

One of the greatest sycophants of a very adulatory age; a self-seeking, greedy, worldly man.

> Henry J. Nicoll, 1882, *Landmarks of English Literature,* p. 196

He closed his long career, rich indeed through his marriage with the Earl of Lichfield's daughter, Lady Elizabeth Lee, but petulant, proud, and solitary. The insatiable ambition of Young has been the theme of many moralists, and the tendency of his personal character was indubitably parasitic; but it would be easy to show, on the other hand, that he really was, to an eminent degree, what Hobbes calls an "episcopable" person, and that his talents, his address, his loyalty, and his moral force were qualities which not only might, but for the honour of the English Church should, have been publicly acknowledged by preferment.

> Edmund Gosse, 1888, *A History of Eighteenth Century Literature,* p. 210

Night Thoughts (1742-46)

The title of my poem (*Night Thoughts*) not affected; for I never compose but at night, except sometimes when I am on horseback.

> Edward Young, 1758, *Spence's Anecdotes,* ed. Singer, p. 288

I will venture to say that in point of depth this poet is what Homer and Pindar are in point of grandeur. I should find it difficult to explain the effect produced upon me by my first perusal of this work. I might experience much the same impression in the heart of the desert on a dark and stormy night, when the surrounding blackness is pierced at intervals by flashes of lightning.

> Comte de Bissy, 1762, *Journal étranger,* Feb.

It is all too full of tolling bells, tombs, mournful chants and cries, and phantoms; the simple and artless expression of true sorrow would be a hundred times more effective.

> Frederick Melchior Grimm, 1770, *Correspondance littéraire,*
> May

Looked into Young's *Night Thoughts:* debased throughout with many poor and puerile conceits; such as making "the night weep dew over extinct nature;" the revolving spheres, "a horologe machinery divine;" "each circumstance armed with an aspic, and all a hydra woe;" "each tear mourn its own distinct distress, and each distress heightened by the whole." Frigidity and tumour, obscurity and glare, are the two apparently opposite but striking faults of this popular and imposing poem: yet parts are in good taste: he glows with a natural and genial warmth in describing the charms of social intercourse and the blessings of friendship, towards the close of the 2d Night; and the passage in the 4th, beginning, "O my coævals, remanants of yourselves," is animated and sublime. Johnson perhaps caught his "panting Time toiled after him in vain," from Young's "and leave Praise panting in the distant vale."

Thomas Green, 1779-1810, *Diary of a Lover of Literature,* p. 67

No writer, ancient or modern, had a stronger imagination than Dr. Young, or one more fertile in figures of every kind. His metaphors are often new, and often natural and beautiful. But his imagination was strong and rich, rather than delicate and correct. Hence, in his *Night Thoughts,* there prevails an obscurity, and a hardness in his style. The metaphors are frequently too bold, and frequently too far pursued; the reader is dazzled, rather than enlightened; and kept constantly on the stretch to keep pace with the author.

Hugh Blair, 1783, *Lectures on Rhetoric and Belles-Lettres,*
ed. Mills, Lecture XV

Young's great poem is a notable instance of the want of reserve and poetical economy. In the poetry of Cowper, Burns, Crabbe, we have abundance of sadness, and it is all the more truly and deeply sad, because it seems to come unsought, nay, rather shunned. The poet's soul appears to crave the sunshine: he "does not love the shower nor seek the cold," but only yields to mournful reflections because they force themselves upon him in a world of woe. But when Young so resolutely makes love to Gloom and sets his cap at Melancholy, we suspect that both are in masquerade, and that blooming forms are beneath the sable stole; when he surrounds his head with cypress, we image a snug velvet cap under the dusky wreath; when he "sits by a lamp at mid-day, and has skulls, bones, and instruments of death for the ornaments of his study," we feel disposed to think that he makes sin, death, and sorrow a poetical amusement, and takes up these topics because they offer facilities for impressive writing more than to relieve their pressure on a burdened heart.

Sara Coleridge, 1847, ed. *Coleridge's Biographia Literaria,*
ch. xxiii, note

Although some have called its sublimity "fustian," and its melancholy artificial, its combinations grotesque, its phraseology involved, and its reasoning sometimes confused, it stands, on the whole, as a monument of the inexhaustible wit (in the proper sense of the word) and genius of the author. Its moral is expressly directed against that of Pope in his *Essay on*

Man, wherein the world was taught to be content with the present, without troubling itself about the hereafter. A great portion of Pope's poem consists merely of a versified translation of Pascal's *Thoughts and Maxims;* but the sentiments of Young are, with one or two exceptions, entirely original.

John Doran, 1854, ed., The Complete Works of
Rev. Edward Young, Life

It is difficult to give even a guess whether this remarkable poem will ever recover much or anything of the great reputation which it long held, and which, for two generations at least, it has almost entirely lost. It has against it, the application of phrase and even of thought, merely of an age, to the greatest and most lasting subjects, and a tone only to be described as the theatrical-religious. Its almost unbroken gloom frets or tires according to the mood and temperament of the reader. On the other hand, the want of sincerity is always more apparent than real, and the moral strength and knowledge of human nature, which were the great merits of the eighteenth century, appear most unmistakably. Above all, the poem deserves the praise due to very fine and, in part at least, very original versification. If Young here deserts the couplet, it is, as we have seen, by no means because he cannot manage it; it is because he is at least partly dissatisfied with it, and sees that it will not serve his turn. And his blank verse is a fine and an individual kind. Its fault, due, no doubt, to his practice in drama, is that it is a little too declamatory, a little too suggestive of soliloquies in an inky cloak with footlights in front. But this of itself distinguishes it from the blank verse of Thomson, which came somewhat earlier. It is not a direct imitation either of Milton or of Shakespeare, and deserves to be ranked by itself.

George Saintsbury, 1898, A Short History of English Literature,
p. 561

SATIRES

Young's Satires were in higher reputation when published than they stand in at present. He seems fonder of dazzling than pleasing; of raising our admiration for his wit, than our dislike of the follies he ridicules.

Oliver Goldsmith, 1776, Works, ed. Cunningham, vol. III, p. 439

The chief fault in the satires of Young appear to have arisen from a too great partiality to antithesis and epigrammatic point: occasionally used, they give weight and terseness to sentiment; but, when profusely lavished, offend both the judgment and the ear. The poet likewise, instead of faithfully copying from human life, has too often had recourse to the sources of a fertile imagination; hence his pictures, though vividly and richly coloured, are defective in that truth of representation which can alone impart to them a due degree of moral influence.

Nathan Drake, 1804, Essays Illustrative of the Tatler,
Spectator and Guardian, vol. III, p. 252

DRAMAS

Dr. Young's *Revenge,* is a play which discovers genius and fire; but wants tenderness, and turns too much upon the shocking and direful passions.

Hugh Blair, 1783, Lectures on Rhetoric and Belles-Lettres,
ed. Mills, Lecture XLVI

Young, Thomson, and others who followed the same wordy and declamatory system of composition, contributed rather to sink than exalt the character of the stage. The two first were both men of excellent genius, as their other writings have sufficiently testified; but, as dramatists they wrought upon a false model, and their productions are of little value.

Sir Walter Scott, 1814-23, Essay on The Drama

Young's Tragedies of the *Revenge, Busiris,* and *The Brothers,* are evidently the productions of no ordinary mind. For high and eloquent declamation, they are equal to any thing which the French School has produced, either in its native soil, or in our imitative Country. Though the first is the only one of these three Tragedies which keeps possession of the Stage, yet *Busiris* appears to me to possess the most merit. The principal character is drawn with as much force and decision as *Zanga,* but has more of real human nature in its composition. *Zanga* is a fine Poetical study; the grandeur of the conception, and the power of the execution, are equal; but it has not much of truth or Nature in its composition. Compare it with the Iago of Shakspeare, of which it is evidently a copy, and it is like comparing a lay figure with a Statue. One is a fitting vehicle to convey to us the drapery of the Poet's fancy, and the folds and forms in which he chooses to array it; but the other has the truth and power of Nature stamped upon every limb.

Henry Neele, 1827-29, Lectures on English Poetry, p. 144

The literary genius of E. Young (1681-1765), on the other hand, possessed vigour and variety enough to distinguish his tragedies from the ordinary level of Augustan plays; in one of them he seems to challenge comparison in the treatment of his theme with a very different rival; but by his main characteristics as a dramatist he belongs to the school of his contemporaries.

Adolphus William Ward, 1878, Drama,
Encyclopædia Britannica, vol. VII

GENERAL

Though incapable either of tenderness or passion, he had a richness and activity of fancy that belonged rather to the days of James and Elizabeth, than to those of George and Anne:—But then, instead of indulging it, as the older writers would have done, in easy and playful inventions, in splendid descriptions, or glowing illustrations, he was led, by the restraints and established taste of his age, to work it up into strained and fantastical epigrams, or into cold and revolting hyperboles. Instead of letting it flow gracefully on, in an easy and sparkling current, he perpetually forces it out in jets, or makes it stagnate in formal canals;—and thinking it necessary to write like Pope, when the bent of his genius led him rather to copy what was best in Cowley and most fantastic in Shakespeare, he has produced something which excites wonder instead of admiration, and is felt by every one to be at once ingenious, incongruous, and unnatural.

> Francis, Lord Jeffrey, 1811-44, "Ford's Dramatic Works,"
> *Contributions to the Edinburgh Review*, vol. II, p. 293

He had nothing of Donne's subtle fancy, and as little of the gayety and playfulness that occasionally break out among the quibbles and contortions of Cowley. On the other hand, he has much more passion and pathos than Cowley, and, with less elegance, perhaps makes a nearer approach in some of his greatest passages to the true sublime. But his style is radically an affected and false one; and of what force it seems to possess, the greater part is the result not of any real principle of life within it, but of mere strutting and straining.

> George L. Craik, 1861, *A Compendious History of English
> Literature and of the English Language*, vol. II, p. 285

His influence was not so pure as that of Thomson. The author of *Night Thoughts* was an artist of a force approaching that of genius, but his error was to build that upon rhetoric which he should have based on imagination. The history of Young is one of the most curious in the chronicles of literature. Born far back in the seventeenth century, before Pope or Gay, he wrote in the manner of the Anne wits, without special distinction, through all the years of his youth and middle life. At the age of sixty he collected his poetical works, and appeared to be a finished mediocrity. It was not until then, and after that time, that, taking advantage of a strange wind of funereal enthusiasm that swept over him, he composed the masterpiece by which the next generation knew him, his amazingly popular and often highly successful *Night Thoughts*.

> Edmund Gosse, 1897, *Short History of Modern
> English Literature*, p. 237

LAURENCE STERNE
1713-1768

Born, at Clonmel, 24 Nov. 1713. At school at Halifax, 1723-31. Matriculated Jesus College, Cambridge, 1732; Sizarship, July 1733; Scholar, July 1734; B. A., Jan. 1736; M. A., 1740. Ordained Deacon, March 1736; Priest, Aug. 1738. Vicar of Sutton-on-the-Forest, Yorks., 1738. Prebendary of York Cathedral, Jan. 1741. Married Elizabeth Lumley, 30 March 1741. Vicar of Stillington, 1741. Curate of Coxwold, Yorks., 1760. Lived mainly in France, 1762-67. Died, in London, 18 March 1768. Buried in Burial Ground of St. George's, Hanover Square. WORKS: *The Case of Elijah and the Widow of Zarephath considered*, 1747; *The Abuses of Conscience*, 1750; *The Life and Opinions of Tristram Shandy* (9 vols.), 1759-67; *The Sermons of Mr. Yorick* (7 vols.), 1760-69; *A Sentimental Journey through France and Italy, by Mr. Yorick* (2 vols.), 1768. POSTHUMOUS: *The History of a Good Warm Watch-coat*, 1769; *Letters . . . to his Most Intimate Friends*, ed. by his daughter (3 vols.), 1775; *Letters from Yorick to Eliza*, 1775; *Letters to his Friends on various occasions*, 1775; *Original Letters, never before published*, 1788; *Seven Letters written by Sterne and his Friends, hitherto unpublished* (priv. ptd.), 1844. COLLECTED WORKS: ed. by G. Saintsbury (6 vols.), 1894. *Life*: by P. H. Fitzgerald, 1864.

R. Farquharson Sharp, 1897, *A Dictionary of English Authors*, p. 269

SEE: *Works*, ed. Wilbur L. Cross, 1904, 12 v.; *Sterne. Selected Works*, ed. Douglas Grant, 1950; *Tristram Shandy*, ed. Wilbur L. Cross, 1925; Wilbur L. Cross, *Life and Times of Sterne*, 1929, Second Edition with additions, 1925, rev. 1929; John Traugott, *Tristam Shandy's World: Sterne's Philosophical Rhetoric*, 1954; Margaret R. B. Shaw, *Laurence Sterne: The Making of a Humorist, 1713-1762*, 1957; Alan B. Howes, *Yorick and The Critics: Sterne's Reputation in England 1760-1868*, 1958.

PERSONAL

Tristram Shandy is still a greater object of admiration, the man as well as the book. One is invited to dinner, where he dines, a fortnight beforehand. His portrait is done by Reynolds, and now engraving. *Tristram Shandy*, Dodsley gives £700 for a second edition, and two new volumes not yet written; and tomorrow will come out two volumes of *Sermons* by him. Your friend, Mr. Hall has printed two Lyric Epistles, one to my Cousin Shandy on his coming to town, the other to the grown gentlewomen, the Misses of York: they seem to me to be absolute madness.

Thomas Gray, 1760; *Letter to Thomas Warton*, April 22; *Works*, ed. Gosse, vol. III, p. 36

Shall pride a heap of sculptured marble raise,
Some worthless, unmourned, titled fool to praise,
And shall we not by one poor gravestone learn
Where genius, wit, and humor sleep with Sterne?

David Garrick, 1779 ? *Epitaph on Laurence Sterne*

The celebrated writer Sterne, after being long the idol of this town, died in a mean lodging without a single friend who felt interest in his fate except Becket, his bookseller, who was the only person that attended his interment. He was buried in a graveyard near Tyburn, belonging to the parish of Marylebone, and the corpse being marked by some of the *resurrection men* (as they are called), was taken up soon afterwards and carried to an anatomy professor of Cambridge. A gentleman who was present at the dissection told me, he recognized Sterne's face the moment he saw the body.

Edmond Malone, 1783, *Maloniana*, ed. Prior, p. 373

In the month of January, 1768, we set off for London. We stopped for some time at Almack's house, in Pall-mall. My master afterwards took Sir James Gray's house in Clifford-street, who was going ambassador to Spain. He now began housekeeping, hired a French cook, house-maid, kitchen-maid, and kept a great deal of the best company. About this time, Mr. Sterne, the celebrated author, was taken ill at the silk-bag shop in Old Bond-street. He was sometimes called Tristram Shandy, and sometimes Yorick, a very great favourite of the gentleman's. One day my master had company to dinner, who were speaking about him: the Duke of Roxburgh, the Earl of March, the Earl of Ossory, the Duke of Grafton, Mr. Garrick, Mr. Hume, and Mr. James. "John," said my master, "go and inquire how Mr. Sterne is to-day." I went, returned, and said, "I went to Mr. Sterne's lodging—the mistress opened the door—I enquired how he did. She told me to go up to the nurse; I went into the room, and he was just a-dying. I waited ten minutes; but in five, he said, "Now it is come!" He put up his hand, as if to stop a blow, and died in a minute. The gentlemen were all very sorry, and lamented him very much.

James Macdonald, 1790, *The Life of a Footman*

We are well acquainted with Sterne's features and personal appearance, to which he himself frequently alludes. He was tall and thin, with a hectic and consumptive appearance. His features, though capable of expressing with peculiar effect the sentimental emotions by which he was often affected, had also a shrewd, humorous, and sarcastic character, proper to the wit

and the satirist, and not unlike that which predominates in the portraits of
Voltaire. His conversation was animated, and witty; but Johnson complained that it was marked by licence, better suiting the company of the
Lord of Crazy Castle, than of the great moralist. It has been said, and
probably with truth, that his temper was variable and unequal, the natural
consequence of an irritable bodily frame, and continued bad health. But
we will not readily believe that the parent of Uncle Toby could be a harsh,
or habitually bad-humoured man. Sterne's letters to his friends, and especially to his daughter, breathe all the fondness of affection; and his resources, such as they were, seem to have been always at the command of
those whom he loved.

Sir Walter Scott, 1821, *Laurence Sterne*

So infamous was his private character, that when he entered the pulpit to
preach in York Minister, of which he was a prebend, many of the congre-
gation rose from their seats and left the cathedral. His conduct and temper
so much provoked his wife, a loving and patient woman, that she was compelled to live away from him. With health so broken that his continued
existence appeared almost miraculous, he entered into an intrigue with
a married woman, and, at the age of 54, openly speculating on the prospect
of marrying her, when his own wife as well as the lady's husband should
die! The only redeeming feeling in his life, was his devoted love for his
daughter, for whom, however, he made not the slightest provision. He died,
in lodgings in London, and his attendants robbed him of his gold shirt-
buttons as he lay helpless in bed. His letters, which fully expressed his
profligacy, were published, seven years after his death, by his daughter—
so reduced to poverty by his extravagance that she was compelled to barter
his reputation for bread. It is almost inexplicable how such a man as Sterne
could have lived so loosely and produced such a pure-minded original as
My Uncle Toby, and such a faithful serving man as Corporal Trim, mater-
nal grandfather to Sam Weller, in all probability.

R. Shelton Mackenzie, 1854, ed., *Noctes Ambrosianæ,*
vol. IV, p. 214, note

His patient courtship shows that he was truly in love with his wife. Their
marriage, in the face of inauspicious circumstances, proves that they were
both in earnest; and his frank acknowledgment, a year after, that he was
tired of his conjugal partner, argues no uncommon experience, but a rare
and unjustifiable candor.

Henry T. Tuckerman, 1857, *Essays, Biographical and Critical,*
p. 318

As to the nature of Sterne's love-affairs I have come, though not without hesitation, to the conclusion that they were most, if not all of them, what is called, somewhat absurdly, Platonic. In saying this, however, I am by no means prepared to assert that they would all of them have passed muster before a prosaic and unsentimental British jury as mere indiscretions, and nothing worse. . . . But, as I am not of those who hold that the conventionally "innocent" is the equivalent of the morally harmless in this matter, I cannot regard the question as worth any very minute investigation. I am not sure that the habitual male flirt, who neglects his wife to sit continually languishing at the feet of some other woman, gives much less pain and scandal to others, or does much less mischief to himself and the objects of his adoration, than the thorough-going profligate; and I even feel tempted to risk the apparent paradox that, from the artistic point of view, Sterne lost rather than gained by the generally Platonic character of his amours. For, as it was, the restraint of one instinct of his nature implied the over-indulgence of another which stood in at least as much need of chastenment. If his love-affairs stopped short of the gratification of the senses, they involved a perpetual fondling and caressing of those effeminate sensibilities of his into that condition of hyper-æsthesia which, though Sterne regarded it as the strength, was in reality the weakness, of his art.

H. D. Traill, *Sterne (English Men of Letters)*, pp. 28, 29

Sterne's reasoning faculty was incapable of controlling his constitutional sensitiveness to pain and pleasure. His deficiency in self-control induced a condition of moral apathy, and was the cause alike of the indecency and of the sentimentality which abounded in *Tristram Shandy* and *Sentimental Journey*. Both the indecency and the sentimentality, faithfully and without artifice reflected Sterne's emotional nature. The indelicate innuendoes which he foists on sedate words and situations, and the tears that he represented himself as shedding over dead asses and caged starlings, had an equally spontaneous origin in what was in him the normal state of his nerves. In itself—with the slightest possible reference to the exciting object —his sensibility evoked a pleasurable nervous excitement, and the fulness of the gratification that it generated in his own being discouraged him from seeking to translate its suggestions into act. The divorce of sensibility from practical benevolence will always justify charges of insincerity. All that can be pleaded in extenuation in Sterne's case is that he made no secret that his conduct was the sport of his emotional impulses, and, obeying no other promptings, was guided by no active moral sentiment. Gravity, he warned his readers, was foreign to his nature. Morality, which ordinarily checks the free play of feeling and passion by the exercise of virtuous reason, lay, he admitted, outside his sphere. Such infirmities signally unfitted him for the vocation of a teacher of religion, but his confessions remove hypocrisy from the list of his offences. His declared temperament renders it matter for surprise not that he so often disfigured his career as a husband and author by a wanton defiance of the accepted moral canons, but that he achieved so indisputable a nobility of sentiment as in his creation of Uncle Toby, and so unselfish a devotion as in his relations with his daughter. He was no "scamp" in any accepted use of the term, as Thackeray designates him. He was a volatile, self-centered, morally apathetic man of genius, who was not destitute of generous instincts.

Sidney Lee, 1898, *Dictionary of National Biography*, vol. LIV, p. 216

Tristram Shandy (1759-67)

At present nothing is talked of, nothing admired, but what I cannot help calling a very insipid and tedious performance: it is a kind of novel, called *The Life and Opinions of Tristram Shandy;* the great humour of which consists in the whole narration always going backward. . . . It makes one smile two or three times at the beginning, but in recompense makes one yawn for two hours. The characters are tolerably kept up, but the humour is for ever attempted and missed.

Horace Walpole, 1760, *To Sir David Dalrymple*, April 4; *Letters,* ed. Cunningham, vol. III, p. 298

There are several very dull fellows, who, by a few mechanical helps, sometimes learn to become extremely brilliant and pleasing; with a little dexterity in the management of the eyebrows, fingers, and nose. By imitating a cat, a sow and pigs; by a loud laugh, and a slap on the shoulder, the most ignorant are furnished out for conversation. But the writer finds it impossible to throw his winks, his shrugs, or his attitudes, upon paper; he may borrow some assistance, indeed, by printing his face at the title page; but without wit to pass for a man of ingenuity, no other mechanical help but downright obscenity will suffice. By speaking to some peculiar sensations, we are always sure of exciting laughter, for the jest does not lie in the writer, but in the subject.

Oliver Goldsmith, 1762, *A Citizen of the World*

Nothing odd will do long. *Tristram Shandy* did not last.

Samuel Johnson, 1776, in *Life* by Boswell, ed. Hill, vol. II, p. 521

Voltaire has compared the merits of Rabelais and Sterne as satirists of the abuse of learning, and I think has done neither of them justice. This great distinction is obvious: that Rabelais derided absurdities then existing in full force, and intermingled much sterling sense with the grossest parts of his book; Sterne, on the contrary, laughs at many exploded opinions and forsaken fooleries, and contrives to degrade some of his most solemn passages by a vicious levity. Rabelais flew a higher pitch, too, than Sterne. Great part of the voyage to the Pays de Lanternois, which so severely stigmatizes the vices of the Romish clergy of that age, was performed in more hazard of fire than water.

John Ferriar, 1798-1812, *Illustrations of Sterne, with other Essays*

If we consider Sterne's reputation as chiefly founded on *Tristram Shandy,* he must be regarded as liable to two severe charges:—those, namely, of indecency, and of affectation. Upon the first accusation Sterne was himself peculiarly sore, and used to justify the licentiousness of his humour by representing it as a mere breach of decorum, which had no perilous consequence to morals. The following anecdote we have from a sure source:— Soon after Tristram had appeared, Sterne asked a Yorkshire lady of fortune and condition whether she had read his book. "I have not, Mr. Sterne," was the answer; "and, to be plain with you, I am informed it is not proper for female perusal."—"My dear good lady," replied the author, "do not be gulled by such stories; the book is like your young heir there (pointing to a child of three years old, who was rolling on the carpet in his white tunics), he shows at times a good deal that is usually concealed, but it is all in perfect innocence!" This witty excuse may be so far admitted; for it cannot be said that the licentious humour of *Tristram Shandy* is of the kind which applies itself to the passions, or is calculated to corrupt society. But it is a sin against taste, if allowed to be harmless as to morals. A handful of mud is neither a firebrand nor a stone; but to fling it about in sport, argues coarseness of mind, and want of common manners.

Sir Walter Scott, 1821, *Laurence Sterne*

Even Jean Paul, the greatest of German humorous authors, and never surpassed in comic conception or in the pathetic quality of humor, is not to be named with his master, Sterne, as a creative humorist. What are Siebenkäs, Fixlein, Schmelzle, and Fibel, (a single lay-figure to be draped at will with whimsical sentiment and reflection, and put in various attitudes), compared with the living reality of Walter Shandy and his brother Toby, characters which we do not see merely as puppets in the author's mind, but poetically projected from it in an independent being of their own?

James Russell Lowell, 1866-90, *Lessing;*
Prose Works, Riverside ed., vol. II, p. 170

Figure to yourself a man who goes on a journey, wearing on his eyes a pair of marvellously magnifying spectacles. A hair on his hand, a speck on a tablecloth, a fold of a moving garment, will interest him: at this rate he will not go very far; he will go six steps in a day, and will not quit his room. So Sterne writes four volumes to record the birth of his hero. He perceives the infinitely little, and describes the imperceptible. A man parts his hair on one side: this, according to Sterne, depends on his whole character, which is a piece with that of his father, his mother, his uncle, and his whole ancestry; it depends on the structure of his brain, which depends on the circumstance of his conception and his birth, and these on the fancies of his parents, the humour of the moment, the talk of the preceding hour, the contrarieties of the last curate, a cut thumb, twenty knots made on a bag; I know not how many things besides. . . . His book is like a great store-house of articles of *virtu,* where the curiosities of all ages, kinds and coun-tries lie jumbled in a heap; texts of excommunication, medical consultations, passages of unknown or imaginary authors, scraps of scholastic erudition, strings of absurd histories, dissertations, addresses to the reader. His pen leads him; he has neither sequence nor plan; nay, when he lights upon any-thing orderly, he purposely contorts it; with a kick he sends the pile of folios next to him over the history he has commenced, and dances on the top of them.

H. A. Taine, 1871, History of English Literature, tr. Van Laun,
vol. II, bk. iii, ch. vi, pp. 179, 180

As to its morality, I know good people who love the book; but to me, when you sum it all up, its teaching is that a man may spend his life in low, brutish, inane pursuits and may have a good many little private sins on his conscience,—but will nevertheless be perfectly sure of heaven if he can have retained the ability to weep a maudlin tear over a tale of distress; or, in short, that a somewhat irritable state of the lachrymal glands will be cheerfully accepted by the Deity as a substitute for saving grace or a life of self-sacrifice.

Sidney Lanier, 1881, The English Novel, p. 187

I should have said, with hesitation, that it was one of the most popular books in the language. Go where you will amongst men—old and young, undergraduates at the Universities, readers in our great cities, old fellows in the country, judges, doctors, barristers—if they have any tincture of literature about them, they all know their "Shandy" at least as well as their "Pickwick." What more can be expected? "True Shandeism," its author declares, "think what you will against it, opens the heart and lungs." I will be bound to say Sterne made more people laugh in 1891 than in any previous year; and, what is more, he will go on doing it—" 'that is, if it please God,' said my Uncle Toby."

Augustine Birrell, 1894, Essays about Men, Women and Books,
p. 38

Tristram Shandy, like Charles the Second, has been an unconscionably long time in dying. It would be an exaggeration to say that Mr. Disraeli was the last man who read *Rasselas,* or that no man living has read *Irene.* But references to these classical compositions would in the best educated company fall exceedingly flat, whereas Uncle Toby's sayings are as well known as Falstaff's, and the "sub-acid humour" of Mr. Shandy plays, like the wit of Horace, round the cockles of the heart. It is now a pure curiosity of literature that men have lived who imputed dulness to *Tristram Shandy.*

Herbert Paul, 1896, "Sterne," The Nineteenth Century,
vol. 40, p. 995

It is indeed a strange book, certainly not everybody's book. To start with, it is often tedious, sometimes silly, not seldom downright nasty. It does not begin at the end, because it has no end to begin at; but it does begin very nearly as far on as it ever gets, and goes back great distances in between. If anything at all happens—and it is possible to disentangle two or three events—it happens quite out of its right order; if the vehicle moves at all, it is with the cart before the horse; it is purposely so mixed up that a page of uninterrupted narrative is hardly to be found in it. It is a mass of tricks and affectations, some amusing, and some very wearisome. To say that it has no plot is nothing; it takes the utmost pains to persuade you that it has not a plan. It is sometimes obviously and laboriously imitative. Its pathos, sometimes superb, is sometimes horribly maudlin. We must not ask for good taste, and can by no means rely on decency; there is even a preserve spirit of impropriety which seizes occasions and topics apparently quite innocent. This is not a complete catalogue of its sins; these are only a few points which occur to an old friend, a few characteristics which it is well to mention, lest those who do not know the book should suffer too severe a shock on making its acquaintance. For the difficulty with it is in the beginning; to read it the first time is almost hard; every reading after that goes more easily. Nevertheless, although there are, I believe, fanatic admirers who read all of it every time, I am not of those. I think I have earned the right to skip, and I exercise it freely, without qualms of conscience. What's the use of being on intimate terms with a book if you cannot have that liberty?

Anthony Hope Hawkins, 1897, "My Favorite Novelist
and His Best Book," Munsey's Magazine, vol. 18, p. 352

The Sermons of Mr. Yorick (1760-69)

Have you read his sermons (with his own comic figure at the head of them)? they are in the style, I think, most proper for the pulpit, and shew a very strong imagination and a sensible heart, but you see him often tottering on the verge of laughter, and ready to throw his periwig in the face of his audience.

Thomas Gray, 1760, *Letter to Thomas Warton,* July;
Works, ed. Gosse, vol. III, p. 53

With many serious blemishes, and leavened with much affectation, they are still earnest, dramatic, practical, and simple sermons, with prodigious life and dramatic power and which, when set off by voice and manner, must have been entertaining and instructive. Besides them, the tame conventionalities of Blair read feebly indeed. And there is in them a triumphant answer to those charges of plagiarism which have been so often swung from hoarse and jangling critical bells.

Percy Fitzgerald, 1864, *The Life of Laurence Sterne,*
vol. I, p. 210

Sterne was a pagan. He went into the Church; but Mr. Thackeray—no bad judge—said most justly that his sermons "have not a single Christian sentiment." They are well expressed, vigorous moral essays; but they are no more. . . . There is not much of heaven and hell in Sterne's sermons; and what there is, seems a rhetorical emphasis which is not essential to the argument, and which might perhaps as well be left out.

Walter Bagehot, 1864, "Sterne and Thackeray," *Works,*
ed. Morgan, vol. II, p. 159

The critics who find wit, eccentricity, flashes of Shandyism, and what not else of the same sort in these discourses, must be able—or so it seems to me—to discover these phenomena anywhere. To the best of my own judgment the Sermons are—with but few and partial exceptions—of the most commonplace character; platitudinous with the platitudes of a thousand pulpits, and insipid with the *crambe repetita* of a hundred thousand homilies.

H. D. Traill, 1882, *Sterne (English Men of Letters),* p. 55

A Sentimental Journey (1768)

Sterne has published two little volumes, called *Sentimental Travels.* They are very pleasing, though too much dilated, and infinitely preferable to his tiresome *Tristram Shandy,* of which I never could get through three volumes. In these there is great good-nature and strokes of delicacy.

Horace Walpole, 1768, *To George Montagu,* March 12;
Letters, ed. Cunningham, vol. V, p. 91

I am now going to *charm* myself for the third time with poor Sterne's *Sentimental Journey.*

Frances Burney, 1769, *Early Diary,* ed. Ellis, vol. I, p. 45

And with this pretty dance and chorus, the volume artfully concludes. Even here one cannot give the whole description. There is not a page in Sterne's writing but has something that were better away, a latent corruption—a hint, as of an impure presence. Some of that dreary *double entendre* may be attributed to freer times and manners than ours, but not all. The foul Satyr's eyes leer out of the leaves constantly: the last words the famous author wrote were bad and wicked—the last lines the poor stricken wretch penned were for pity and pardon.

William Makepeace Thackeray, 1853, *The English Humourists
of the Eighteenth Century,* Lecture VI

He loves to suck melancholy out of any passing event "as a weasel sucks eggs;" but he also delights to thrust constantly before our eyes the cap and bells; not that he intends the smile to compete with the tear, but that he prides himself on his personal freedom from the torturing sensibilities over which he claims to have absolute command. Immediately after one of his famous sentimental outbursts, he tells us how good the inn is at Moulines. This is an outrage of a kind he delighted to perpetrate. It seems to say: "Behold! what a master I am! How I can harrow up your feelings! and now I'm off to eat a mutton-chop." It is the grimace of a bad actor before the tragic business is over, before he quits the stage, and while his face is still turned towards his audience.

Hall Caine, 1882, "Sterne," *The Academy,* vol. 22, p. 322

Frenchmen, who are either less awed than we by lecturers in white waistcoats, or understand the methods of criticism somewhat better, cherish the *Sentimental Journey* (in spite of its indifferent French) and believe in the genius that created it. But the Briton reads it with shyness, and the British critic speaks of Sterne with bated breath, since Thackeray told it in Gath that Sterne was a bad man, and the daughters of Philistia triumphed.

A. T. Quiller-Couch, 1891, *Adventures in Criticism,* p. 98

GENERAL

Of Sterne and Rousseau it is difficult to speak without being misunderstood; yet it is impossible to deny the praise of wit and originality to Yorick, or of captivating eloquence to the philosopher of vanity. Their imitators are below notice.

Thomas James Mathias, 1798, *The Pursuits of Literature,*
Eighth ed., p. 59

I have very few heresies in English literature. I do not remember any serious ones, but my moderate opinion of Sterne.

Sir James Macintosh, 1811, *Journal,* May 31,
Life by Macintosh, vol. II, p. 102

His style is . . . at times the most rapid, the most happy, the most idiomatic, of any that is to be found. It is the pure essence of English conversational style. His works consist only of *morceaux,*—of brilliant passages. I wonder that Goldsmith, who ought to have known better, should call him "a dull fellow." His wit is poignant, though artificial; and his characters (though the groundwork of some of them had been laid before) have yet invaluable original differences; and the spirit of the execution, the masterstrokes constantly thrown into them, are not to be surpassed. It is sufficient to name them:—Yorick, Dr. Slop, Mr. Shandy, My Uncle Toby, Trim, Susanna, and the Widow Wadman. In these he has contrived to oppose, with equal felicity and originality, two characters, one of pure intellect and the other of pure good nature, in My Father and My Uncle Toby. There appears to have been in Sterne a vein of dry, sarcastic humour, and of extreme tenderness of feeling; the latter sometimes carried to affectation, as in the tale of Maria, and the apostrophe to the recording angel, but at other times pure and without blemish. The story of Le Fevre is perhaps the finest in the English language. My Father's restlessness, both of body and mind, is inimitable. It is the model from which all those despicable performances against modern philosophy ought to have been copied, if their authors had known anything of the subject they were writing about. My Uncle Toby is one of the finest compliments ever paid to human nature. He is the most unoffending of God's creatures; or, as the French express it, *un tel petit bon homme!* Of his bowling green, his sieges, and his amours, who would say or think any thing amiss!

William Hazlitt, 1818, *Lectures on the English Comic Writers,*
Lecture VI

I think highly of Sterne—that is, of the first part of *Tristram Shandy:* for as to the latter part about the widow Wadman, it is stupid and disgusting;

and the *Sentimental Journey* is poor, sickly stuff. There is a great deal of affectation in Sterne, to be sure; but still the characters of Trim and the two Shandies are most individual and delightful. Sterne's morals are bad, but I don't think they can do much harm to any one whom they would not find bad enough before. Besides, the oddity and erudite grimaces under which much of his dirt is hidden take away the effect for the most part; although, to be sure, the book is scarcely readable by women.

> Samuel Taylor Coleridge, 1833, *Table Talk*,
> ed. Ashe, Aug. 18, p. 251

He terribly failed in the discharge of his duties, still, we must admire in him that sportive kind of geniality and affection, still a son of our common mother, not cased up in buckram formulas as the other writers were, clinging to forms, and not touching realities. And, much as has been said against him, we cannot help feeling his immense love for things around him; so that we may say of him, as of Magdalen, "much is forgiven him, because he loved much." A good simple being after all.

> Thomas Carlyle, 1838, *Lectures on the History of Literature*,
> ed. Greene, p. 179

We think that, on the whole, Mackenzie is the first master of this delicious style. Sterne, doubtless, has deeper touches of humanity in some of his works. But there is no sustained feeling,—no continuity of emotion,—no extended range of thought, over which the mind can brood, in his ingenious and fantastical writings. His spirit is far too mercurial and airy to suffer him tenderly to linger over those images of sweet humanity which he discloses. His cleverness breaks the charm which his feeling spreads, as by magic, around us. His exquisite sensibility is ever counteracted by his perception of the ludicrous and his ambition after the strange. No harmonious feeling breathes from any of his pieces. He sweeps "that curious instrument, the human heart," with hurried fingers, calling forth in rapid succession its deepest and its liveliest tones, and making only marvellous discord. His pathos is, indeed, most genuine while it lasts; but the soul is not suffered to cherish the feeling which it awakens.

> Thomas Noon Talfourd, 1842, *Critical and
> Miscellaneous Writings*

The humour of Sterne is not only very different from that of Fielding and Smollett, but is something unique in our literature. He also was a professed admirer of Cervantes; to as large an extent as Swift he adopted the whimsical and perpetually digressive manner of Rabelais; and there is proof that he was well acquainted with the works of preceding humorists less familiarly known in England. But he was himself a humorist by nature—a British or Irish Yorick, with differences from any of those who might have borne that name before him after their imaginary Danish prototype; and, perpetually as he reminds us of Rabelais, his Shandean vein of wit and fancy is not for a moment to be regarded as a mere variety of Pantagruelism. There is scarcely anything more intellectually exquisite than the humour of Sterne. To very fastidious readers much of the humour of Fielding or of Smollett might come at last to seem but buffoonery; but Shakespeare himself, as one fancies, would have read Sterne with admiration and pleasure.

David Masson, 1859, *British Novelists and Their Styles*, p. 145

There is a singular blend of two qualities in Sterne's writing, as in his character. Humour and pathos are never in their nature far apart; in Sterne they are almost inextricably combined. His laughter and his tears are both so facile, and their springs lie so near together, that the one almost infallibly provokes the other; he will laugh at sorrow and find matter of sentiment in a comical mishap. It is his keenest pleasure to juggle with these effects; a solemn occasion is to him an irresistible provocative to burlesque, and his pathetic sensibility responds to a touch so light that to a less highly strung nature his tears will seem affected. Yet herein lies the delicacy of his writing, and of those exquisite effects, the despair of many a more robust artist, which are as hard to describe as an odour is to remember. His reader must be incessantly on the alert for surprises; it is only prudent, at a funeral where Parson Sterne officiates, for the guest to attend with a harlequin's suit beneath his decent garb of black, prepared for either event.

Walter Raleigh, 1894, *The English Novel*, p. 195

Sterne's reputation increased when it crossed the water. The Germans hailed him as a philosopher. Lessing was taken with him, and when Sterne died, wrote to Nicolai that he would gladly have sacrificed several years of his own life if by so doing he could have prolonged the existence of the sentimental traveller. Goethe writes: "Whoever reads him, immediately feels that there is something free and beautiful in his own soul." The philosophy of Sterne is the most brilliant invention of eighteenth century anglomania.

Joseph Texte, 1895-99, *Jean-Jacques Rousseau and the Cosmopolitan Spirit in Literature*, tr. Matthews, pp. 281, 282

He was a Cambridge man and well taught;—of abundant reading, which he made to serve his turn in various ways, and conspicuously by his stealings; he stole from Rabelais; he stole from Shakespeare; he stole from

Fuller; he stole from Burton's *Anatomy of Melancholy;* not a stealing of ideas only, but of words and sentences and half-pages together, without a sign of obligation; and yet he did so wrap about these thefts with the strings and lappets of his own abounding humour and drollery, as to give to the whole—thieving and Shandyism combined—a stamp of individuality. Ten to one that these old authors who had suffered the pilfering, would have lost cognizance of their expressions, in the new surroundings of the Yorkshire parson; and joined in the common grin of applause with which the world welcomed and forgave them.

> Donald G. Mitchell, 1895, *English Lands Letters and Kings,*
> *Queen Anne and the Georges,* p. 216

Chaotic as it is in the syntactical sense, it is a perfectly clear vehicle for the conveyance of thought. We are rarely at a loss for the meaning of one of Sterne's sentences, as we are, for very different reasons, for the meaning of one of Macaulay's. And his language is so full of life and colour, his tone so animated and vivacious, that we forget we are reading and not listening, and we are as well disposed to be exacting in respect to form as though we were listeners in actual fact. Sterne's manner, in short, may be that of a bad and careless writer, but it is the manner of a first-rate talker; and this of course enhances rather than detracts from the unwearying charm of his wit and humour.

> H. D. Traill, 1895, *English Prose,* ed. Craik, vol. IV, pp. 207, 208

Many critics and writers of eminence—Mr. Carlyle, M. Taine, Mr. Elwin, Mr. Traill—have tried to analyse Sterne's style and methods, contrasting him with Rabelais, Cervantes, Fielding and Dickens. The truth is, our author was so capricious and even fragmentary and disorderly in his system that comparison is impossible. The writers just named were really "monumental" in their handling of their characters, and completed their labour before issuing it to the world. Sterne sent forth his work in fragments, and often wrote what was sheer nonsense to fill his volumes. He allowed his pen to lead him, instead of he himself directing his pen. The whole is so incomplete and disjointed that cosmopolitan readers have not the time or patience to piece the various scraps together. . . . He has given to the world a group of living *characters,* which have become known and familiar even to those who have not read a line of *Tristram.* These are My Uncle Toby, Mr. and Mrs. Shandy, Yorick—his own portrait—and Dr. Slop. There are choice passages, too, grotesque situations and expressions which have become part of the language. Mr. Shandy, I venture to think, is the best of these creations, more piquant and attractive even than My Uncle Toby, because more original and more difficult to touch. It is in this way that Sterne has made his mark, and may be said to be better known than read. A great deal has been written on the false and overstrained sentiment of his pathetic passages such as in the "Story of Le Fever," "Maria of Moulines," "The Dead Ass," and other incidents. No doubt these were somewhat artificially wrought, but it must be remembered they followed the tone of the time. His exquisite humour is beyond dispute, the Shandean sayings, allusions, topics, etc., have a permanent hold; and, as they recur to the recollection, produce a complacent smile, even though the subject be what is called "broad."

Percy Fitzgerald, 1896, The Life of Laurence Sterne,
Preface, vol. I, p. xi

It was a sad day for English fiction when a writer of genius came to look upon the novel as the repository for the crotchets of a lifetime. This is the more to be lamented when we reflect that Sterne, unlike Smollett, could tell a story in a straightforward manner when he chose to do so. Had the time he wasted in dazzling his friends with literary fireworks been devoted to a logical presentation of the wealth of his experiences, fancies, and feelings, he might have written one of the most perfect pieces of composition in the English language. As it is, the novel in his hands, considered from the standpoint of structure, reverted to what it was when left by the wits of the Renaissance.

Wilbur L. Cross, 1899, The Development of the English Novel,
p. 71

THOMAS CHATTERTON
1752-1770

Born, at Bristol, 20 Nov. 1752. Educated at Colston's Hospital, Bristol, Aug. 1760 to July 1767. First poems printed in *Farley's Bristol Journal* 1763 and 1764. Apprenticed to a Bristol attorney, July 1767. First of "Rowley" poems written, 1768. Success with pseudo-antique poems. Apprentice indentures cancelled, April 1770. Left Bristol for London, 24 April 1770. Contributed to various periodicals, but resources gradually failed. Only one poem separately printed in lifetime. Committed suicide, 25 Aug. 1770. Buried in Shoe Lane Workhouse Churchyard. Afterwards transferred to graveyard in Gary's Inn Road. WORKS: *An Elegy on the much lamented death of William Beckford, Esq.* (anon.), 1770. POSTHUMOUS: *The Execution of Sir Charles Baldwin* (ed. by T. Eagles), 1772; *Poems supposed to have been written at Bristol, by Thomas Rowley and others* (ed. by T. Tyrwhitt), 1777 (2nd edn., same year); *Miscellanies in Prose and verse* (ed. by J. Broughton), 1778; *Rowley* poems, ed. by Dean Milles, 1782; Supplement to *Miscellanies*, 1784; *Rowley* poems, ed. by L. Sharpe, 1794; *The Revenge*, 1795. POETICAL WORKS: in 1 vol., 1795; in 3 vols., 1803; in 2 vols., 1875; in 1 vol., 1885. *Life:* by Gregory, 1789;

by Davis (with letters) 1806; by Dix, 1837; by Wilson, 1869, and memoirs in edns. of works.

R. Farquharson Sharp, 1897, *A Dictionary of English Authors*, p. 53

SEE: *Poetical Works*, ed. W. W. Skeat, 1871, 2 v.; *Complete Poetical Works*, with *Life*, ed. H. D. Roberts, 1906, 2 v.; *The Rowley Poems*, ed. M. E. Hare, 1911; Daniel Wilson, *Chatterton: A Biographical Study*, 1869; E. H. W. Meyerstein, *A Life of Thomas Chatterton*, 1930; J. C. Nevill, *Thomas Chatterton*, 1948.

PERSONAL

Sir,—Upon recollection I don't know how Mr. Clayfield could come by his letter; as I intended to have given him a letter, but did not. In regard to my motives for the supposed rashness, I shall observe that I keep no worse company than myself. I never drink to excess; and have, without vanity, too much sense to be attracted to the mercenary retailers of iniquity. No! it is my pride, my damn'd native, unconquerable pride, that plunges me into distraction. You must know that 19-20ths of my composition is pride. I must either live a slave, a servant; have no will of my own, no sentiments of my own which I may freely declare as such; or die!—perplexing alternative. But it distracts me to think of it. I will endeavour to learn humility, but it cannot be here. What it will cost me on the trial Heaven knows! I am your much obliged, unhappy, humble Servant, T. C.

Thomas Chatterton, 1770, *Letter to Mr. Barrett*

EDWIN CROSS, APOTHECARY, BROOK STREET, HOLBORN. Knew the deceased well, from the time he came to live with Mrs. Angell in the same street. Deceased used generally to call on him every time he went by his door, which was usually two or three times in a day: Deceased used to talk a great deal about physic, and was very inquisitive about the natures of different poisons. I often asked him to take a meal with us, but he was so proud that I could never but once prevail on him, though I knew he was half-starving. One evening he did stay, when I unusually pressed him. He talked a great deal, but all at once became silent, and looked quite vacant. He used to go very often to Falcon Court, Fleet Street, to a Mr. Hamilton, who printed a magazine; but who, he said, was using him very badly. I once recommended him to return to Bristol, but he only heaved a deep sigh; and begged me, with tears in his eyes, never to mention the hated name again. He called on me on the 24th August about half-past eleven in the morning, and bought some arsenic, which he said was for an experiment. About the same time next day, Mrs. Wolfe ran in for me, saying deceased had killed himself. I went to his room, and found him quite dead. On his window was a bottle containing arsenic and water; some of the little bits of arsenic were between his teeth. I believe if he had not killed himself, he would soon have died of starvation; for he was too proud to ask of anyone. Witness always considered deceased as an astonishing genius.

Edwin Cross?, 1770, *Testimony at Inquest,* Aug. 27

I am always intending to draw up an account of my intercourse with Chatterton, which I take very kindly you remind me of, but some avocation or other has prevented it. My perfect innocence on having indirectly been an ingredient in his dismal fate, which happened two years after our correspondence, and after he had exhausted both his resources and his constitution, have made it more easy to prove that I never saw him, knew nothing of his ever being in London, and was the first person, instead of the last, on whom he had practiced his impositions, and founded his chimeric hopes of promotion. My very first, or at least second letter, undeceived him in those views, and our correspondence was broken off before he quitted his master's business at Bristol; so that his disappointment with me was but his first ill success; and he resented my incredulity so much, that he never condescended to let me see him. Indeed, what I have said now to you, and which cannot be controverted by a shadow of a doubt, would be sufficient vindication. I could only add to the proofs, a vain regret of never having known his distresses, which his amazing genius would have tempted me to relieve, though I fear he had no other claim to compassion.

Horace Walpole, 1778, *Letter to Rev. William Cole,* May 21;
Letters, ed. Cunningham, vol. VII, p. 70

The activity of his mind is indeed almost unparalleled. But our surprise must decrease, when we consider that he slept but little; and that his whole attention was directed to literary pursuits; for he declares himself so ignorant of his profession, that he was unable to draw out a clearance from his apprenticeship, which Mr. Lambert demanded. He was also unfettered by the study of the dead languages, which usually absorb much of the time and attention of young persons; and though they may be useful to the attainment of correctness, perhaps they do not much contribute to fluency in writing. Mr. Catcott declared, that when he first knew Chatterton, he was ignorant even of Grammar. . . . The person of Chatterton, like his genius, was premature; he had a manliness and dignity beyond his years, and there was a something about him uncommonly prepossessing. His most remarkbale feature was his eyes, which though grey, were uncommonly piercing; when he was warmed in argument, or otherwise, they sparkled with fire, and one eye, it is said, was still more remarkable than the other.

George Gregory, 1779-1803, *Life of Thomas Chatterton,*
ed. Southey, vol. I, pp. lv, lxxi

I thought of Chatterton, the marvellous Boy,
The sleepless Soul that perish'd in his pride.

> William Wordsworth, 1802, *Resolution and Independence*

Thou didst die
A half-blown flow'ret which cold blasts amate.
But this is past: thou art among the stars
Of highest Heaven: to the rolling spheres
Thou sweetly singest: nought thy hymning mars,
Above the ingrate world and human fears.
On earth the good man base detraction bars
From thy fair name, and waters it with tears.

> *John Keats,* 1814, *Sonnet to Chatterton*

A native aptitude to self-sufficiency, pertinacity, and scorn of interference or censure, gave a ready admission into the formation of his character of the unmitigated effect of every thing that, in the circumstances of his situation, tended to create a predominance of the qualities we are describing. Growing up separate and alien, in a great degree, from the social interests and sentiments which bind men together, he was habitually ready and watchful for occasions to practise on their weakness and folly, and to indulge a propensity to annoyance by satire. He would play off the witty malice, no matter who was the object. He was a very Ishmael with this weapon. It is somewhere his own confession that, when the mood was on him, he spared neither foe nor friend. Very greatly amusing as it may well be believed that his company was when he chose to give it, nobody was safe against having his name, with his peculiarities, his hobby, his vanity, hitched into some sarcastic stanza. Men must not be expected to sympathize very kindly with the mortifications of a person, who, whatever be his talents, demands that such temper and habits shall be no obstruction to advancement in society.

> John Foster, 1838-56, *Critical Essays,* ed. Ryland, vol. II, p. 520

Besides being an antiquarian, and a creative genius in the element of the English antique, Chatterton was also, in the year 1769-70, a complete and very characteristic specimen of that long-extinct phenomenon, a thinking young Englishman of the early part of the reign of George III. In other words, reader, besides being, by the special charter of his genius, a poet in the Rowley vein, he was also, by the more general right of his life at that time, very much such a young fellow as your own unmarried great-great-grandfather was.

> David Masson, 1856-74, *Chatterton, A Story of the Year 1770,*
> p. 53

Thomas Chatterton, whose forgery consisted in publishing his own compositions as the poems of Rowley, who lived in the fifteenth century, was an infidel in profession and a libertine in practice; and as he was the most precocious in genius, so was he the most circumstantial in falsehood, of the literary forgers of the age. That his suicide was premeditated is undoubted. . . . He chose to leave Bristol, where he had many friends, to seek his fortune in London, where he had none; and, when he failed, was too proud to return to his native city. To complain of the "cold neglect" of the world with regard to a boy of eighteen, however great his genius, is quite preposterous. But it was the fashion to consider he was neglected and starved, and epigrams, such as the following, were written on him (*Asylum for Fugitive Pieces,* 1785, 118):

> All think, now Chatterton is dead,
>   His works are worth preserving!
> Yet no one, when he was alive,
>   Would keep the bard from starving!

Johnson, Goldsmith, and a hundred others, who were nearly starved at eighteen, persevered and won their way to fame, as Chatterton might have done, had his character been of a higher stamp.

Henry Philip Dodd, 1870, *The Epigrammatists,* pp. 424, 425

Perhaps it may be more than an idle fancy to attribute to heredity the bent which Chatterton's genuis took spontaneously and almost from infancy; to guess that some mysterious antenatal influence—"striking the electric chain wherewith we are darkly bound"—may have set vibrating links of unconscious association running back through the centuries. Be this as it may, Chatterton was the child of Redcliffe Church. St. Mary stood by his cradle and rocked it; and if he did not inherit with his blood, or draw in with his mother's milk a veneration for her ancient pile, at least the waters of her baptismal font seemed to have signed him with the token of her service. Just as truly as *The Castle of Otranto* was sprung from Strawberry Hill, the Rowley poems were born of St. Mary's Church.

Henry A. Beers, 1898, *A History of English Romanticism in the Eighteenth Century,* p. 339

GENERAL

Chatterton's conduct and opinions were early tinctured with irreligion. How must his mind have laboured under the burden of describing pathetically the pleasures of virtue and the rewards of religion; which are so frequently mentioned in these poems, though they had not made their proper impression on his heart!

Jeremiah Milles, 1782, Preliminary Dissertation to
Rowley's Poems

The greatest genius England has produced since the days of Shakespear.

Edmond Malone, 1782, Cursory Observations on the
Poems Attributed to Rowley, p. 41

I cannot find in Chatterton's works anything so extraordinary as the age at which they were written. They have a facility, vigour, and knowledge, which were prodigious in a boy of sixteen, but which would not have been so in a man of twenty. He did not shew extraordinary powers of genius, but extraordinary precocity. Nor do I believe he would have written better had he lived. He knew this himself, or he would have lived. Great geniuses, like great kings, have too much to think of to kill themselves; for their mind to them also "a kingdon is." With an unaccountable power coming over him at an unusual age, and with the youthful confidence it inspired, he performed wonders, and was willing to sct a seal on his reputation by a tragic catastrophe. He had done his best; and, like another Empedocles, threw himself in Ætna, to ensure immortality.

William Hazlitt, 1818, Lectures on the English Poets,
Lecture VI

Curious is it to note that in the long controversy, which followed on the publication by Chatterton of the poems which he ascribcd to a monk Rowlie, living in the fifteenth century, no one appealed at the time to such lines as the following,

"Life, and all its goods I scorn,'

as at once decisive of the fact that the poems were not of the age which they pretended. Warton who rejected, although with a certain amount of hesitation, the poems, and gives reasons, and many of them good ones, for this rejection, yet takes no notice of this little word, which betrays the forgery at once; although there needed nothing more than to point to it, for the disposing of the whole question.

Richard Chenevix Trench, 1855, English Past and Present, p. 101

Perhaps the clearest evidence of his high poetic gifts is to be found in the comparisons instituted between him and other poets. By reason of his very excellence he has been tried by the highest standards, without thought of his immaturity. Grave critics are found testing the Rowley Poems by Chaucer, or matching them with Cowley and Prior; and even finding in the acknowledged satires of a boy of sixteen "more of the luxuriance, fluency, and negligence of Dryden, than of the terseness and refinement of Pope." One of the strongest evidences of his self-originating power is, in reality, to be found in the contrast which his verse presents to that of his own day. In an age when the seductive charm of Pope's polished numbers captivated public taste, Chatterton struck a new chord and evolved principles of harmony which suggest comparison with Elizabethan poets, rather than with those of Anne's Augustan era. But he was no imitator. Amid all the assumption of antique thought, the reader perceives everywhere that he had looked on Nature for himself; and could discern in her, alike in her calm beauty, and in her stormiest moods, secrets hidden from the common eye. He had, moreover, patriotic sympathies as intense as Burns himself. His Goddwyn, Harold, Ælla, and Rycharde, his Hastings, Bristowe, or Ruddeborne, are all lit up with the same passionate fire, to which some of his finest outbursts of feeling were due; and which was still more replete with promise for the future.

Daniel Wilson, 1869, Chatterton: A Biographical Study, p. 316

If he had really taken pains to *read* and *study* Chaucer or Lydgate or any old author earlier than the age of Spenser, the Rowley poems would have been very different. They would then have borne some resemblance to the language of the fifteenh century, whereas they are rather less like the language of that period than of any other. The spelling of the words is frequently too late, or too bizarre, whilst many of the words themselves are too archaic or too uncommon.

Walter W. Skeat, 1871, ed. Chatterton's Poetical Works,
Essay on the Rowley Poems, vol. II, p. xxvii

To try and ascertain the character of Chatterton from his works were as vain as to study Shakespeare with a like object. We cannot trace his personality: in vain do we rub the ring; the genius stubbornly refuses to appear. He belongs to the objective order of poets; his mind is creative rather than reflective. This power of concealing, or effacing, his own identity, while still preserving a thorough sympathy with the character he is delineating, is especially surprising in one so young.

John Richmond, 1888, ed., The Poetical Works of Thomas Chatterton
(Canterbury Poets), Prefatory Notice, p. 25

THOMAS GRAY
1716-1771

Born, in London, 26 Dec. 1716. Early education at Burnham. To Eton, 1727 [?]. To Pembroke Hall, Camb., as Pensioner, summer of 1734; transferred to Peterhouse, 9 Oct. 1734. Took no degree; left University, Sept. 1738. Travelled abroad with Horace Walpole, March 1739 to Sept. 1740. Returned to Peterhouse, Camb., as Fellow-Commoner, Oct. 1742; LL. B., 1743. Lived chiefly at Cambridge for remainder of life. Removed to Pembroke Coll., 6 March 1756. In London, Jan. 1759 to June 1761. Prof. of History and Mod. Languages, Cambridge, 28 July 1768. Increasing ill-health. Died, at Cambridge, 30 July 1771. Buried at Stoke Pogis. WORKS: *Ode on a distant prospect of Eton College* (anon.), 1747; *An Elegy wrote in a Country Churchyard* (anon.), 1751 (2nd-4th edns., same year); *Six Poems*, 1753; *The Progress of Poesy; and, The Bard*, 1758; *Poems* (collected; two independent edns.), 1768; *Ode, performed . . . at the installation of . . . A. H. Fitzroy, Duke of Grafton* (anon.), 1769. POSTHUMOUS: *A Catalogue of the Antiquities . . . in England and Wales* (anon.; priv. ptd.), [1773]; *Life and Letters*, ed. by W. Mason, 1774; *The Bard*, ed. by J. Martin, 1837; *Correspondence with W. Mason*, ed. by J. Mitford, 1853. COLLECTED WORKS: *Poems*, ed. by W. Mason, 1775; *Poems and Letters* (priv. ptd.), 1879; *Works*, ed. by E. Gosse (4 vols.), 1884. LIFE: by E. Gosse, 1882.

R. Farquharson Sharp, 1897, *A Dictionary of English Authors*, p. 118

SEE: *Works*, ed. Edmund Gosse, rev. ed. 1902-6, 4 v.; *Elegy*, ed. F. G. Stokes, 1929; *Correspondence*, ed. Paget Toynbee and Leonard Whibley, 1935, 3 v.; *Selected Letters*, ed. Joseph Wood Krutch, 1952; R. W. Ketton-Cremer, *Thomas Gray: A Biography*, 1955; David Cecil, *The Poetry of Thomas Gray*, 1945 (Warton Lecture).

PERSONAL

He is the worst company in the world. From a melancholy turn, from living reclusely, and from a little too much dignity, he never converses easily; all his words are measured and chosen, and formed into sentences; his writings are admirable; he himself is not agreeable.

Horace Walpole, 1748, *To George Montague*, Sept. 3; *Letters*, ed. Cunningham, vol. II, p. 128

Mr. Gray, our elegant poet, and delicate Fellow-Commoner of Peter House, has just removed to Pembroke Hall, in resentment of some usage he met with at the former place. The case is much talked of, and is this:—He is much afraid of fire, and was a great sufferer in Cornhill; he has ever since kept a ladder of ropes by him, soft as the silky cords by which Romeo ascended to his Juliet, and has had an iron machine fixed to his bedroom window. The other morning Lord Percival and some Petreuchians, going a hunting, were determined to have a little sport before they set out, and thought it would be no bad diversion to make Gray bolt, as they called it, so ordered their man, Joe Draper, to roar out "fire." A delicate white night-cap is said to have appeared at the window; but finding the mistake, retired again to the couch. The young fellows, had he descended, were determined, they said, to have whipped the Butterfly up again.

Rev. John Sharp, 1756, Letter, March 12, Nichols' Illustrations
of Literature of the Eighteenth Century, vol. VI, p. 805

I am sorry you did not see Mr. Gray on his return; you would have been much pleased with him. Setting aside his merit as a poet which, however, is greater in my opinion than any of his contemporaries can boast, in this or any other nation, I found him possessed of the most exact taste, the soundest judgment, and the most extensive learning. He is happy in a singular facility of expression. His composition abounds with original observations, delivered in no appearance of sententious formality, and seeming to arise spontaneously without study or premeditation. I passed two days with him at Glammis, and found him as easy in his manners, and as communicative and frank as I could have wished.

James Beattie, 1765, Letter to Sir William Forbes

I regret that poor Mr. Gray is now no more than Pindar. One fatal moment sets two or three thousand years aside, and brings the account equal. I really believe our British Pindar not unequal in merit to the bard of Thebes. I hope Mr. Gray has left some works yet unpublished.

Elizabeth Montagu, 1772, Letter, Aug. 15; A Lady of the
Last Century, ed. Doran, p. 177

Perhaps he was the most learned man in Europe. He was equally acquainted with the elegant and profound parts of science, and that not superficially, but thoroughly. He knew every branch of history, both natural and civil; had read all the original histories of England, France, and Italy; and was a great antiquarian. Criticism, metaphysics, morals, politics, made a principal part of his study; voyages and travels of all sorts were his favourite amusements; and he had a fine taste in paintings, prints, architecture, and gardening. With such a fund of knowledge, his conversation must have been equally instructing and entertaining; but he was also a good man, a man of virtue and humanity. There is no character without some speck, some imperfection; and I think the greatest defect in his was an affectation in delicacy, or rather effeminacy, and a visible fastidiousness, or contempt and disdain of his inferiors in science.

William Temple, 1772, *Letter to James Boswell,*
London Magazine, March

As the life of Gray advanced, it was still marked by the same studious and secluded habits; but he appears gradually to have left his classical studies for a more extended circle of reading, including history, antiquities, voyages, and travels; and in many of the books in his library, as Fabian's Chronicles, Clarendon, and others, the extreme attention with which he read is seen by his various and careful annotations, and by the margins being filled with illustrations and corrections drawn from State Papers, and other original documents. The latest period of his life seems to have been very much occupied in attention to natural history in all its varied branches, both in the study of books, and in the diligent observation of nature.

John Mitford, 1814-43-53, *Life of Gray*

His contemptuous hatred of theology and of creeds is marked; he had no patience with them; of worship he knew nothing. It has been said that he would have found a medicine for his unhappiness in wedded love; he would have found more than a medicine in religion. The stately pathos of such a life is indisputable. The pale little poet, with greatness written so largely on all his works, with keen, deep eyes, the long aquiline nose, the heavy chin, the thin compressed lips, the halting affected gait, is a figure to be contemplated with serious and loving interest, spoiled for life, as he said, by retirement.

Arthur Christopher Benson, 1888, "Gray,"
Macmillan's Magazine, vol. 59, p. 30

An Elegy in a Country Churchyard (1751)

As you have brought me into a little sort of distress, you must assist me, I believe, to get out of it as well as I can. Yesterday I had the misfortune of receiving a letter from certain gentlemen (as their bookseller expresses it), who have taken the Magazine of Magazines into their hands. They tell me that an *ingenious* Poem, called reflections in a Country Church-Yard, has been communicated to them, which they are printing forth-with; that they are informed that the *excellent* author of it is I by name, and that they beg not only his *indulgence,* but the *honour* of his correspondence, etc. As I am not at all disposed to be either so indulgent, or so correspondent, as they desire, I have but one bad way left to escape the honour they would inflict upon me; and therefore am obliged to desire you would make Dodsley print it immediately (which may be done in less than a week's time) from your copy, but without my name, in what form is most convenient for him, but on his best paper and character; he must correct the press himself, and print it without any interval between the stanzas, because the sense is in some places continued beyond them; and the title must be,—Elegy, written in a Country Church-yard. If he would add a line or two to say it came into his hands by accident, I should like it better. If you behold the Magazine of Magazines in the light I do, you will not refuse to give yourself this trouble on my account, which you have taken of your own accord before now. If Dodsley do not do this immediately, he may as well let it alone.

> Thomas Gray, 1751, *Letter to Horace Walpole*, Feb. 11;
> *Works,* ed. Gosse, vol. II, p. 210

The following Poem came into my hands by accident, if the general approbation with which this little Piece has been spread, may be called by so slight a term as accident. It is this approbation which makes it unnecessary for me to make an Apology but to the Author: as he cannot but feel some Satisfaction in having pleas'd so many Readers already, I flatter myself he will forgive my communicating that Pleasure to many more.

> Robert Dodsley, 1751, *Elegy Written in a Country Church-yard,*
> Advertizement

This is a very fine poem, but overloaded with epithet. The heroic measure, with alternate rhyme, is very properly adapted to the solemnity of the subject, as it is the slowest movement that our language admits of. The latter part of the poem is pathetic and interesting.

> Oliver Goldsmith, 1767, *The Beauties of English Poetry*

The *Church-yard* abounds with images which find a mirror in every mind, and with sentiments to which every bosom returns an echo. The four stanzas, beginning "Yet even these bones" are to me original: I have never seen the notions in any other place; yet he that reads them here persuades himself that he has always felt them. Had Gray written often thus, it had been vain to blame, and useless to praise him.

> Samuel Johnson, 1779-81, *Gray, Lives of the English Poets*

Of smaller poems, the *Elegy* of Gray may be considered as the most exquisite and finished example in the world, of the effect resulting from the intermixture of evening scenery and pathetic reflection.

> Nathan Drake, 1798-1820, *Literary Hours,* No. XXIV,
> vol. II, p. 17

Gray's *Pindaric Odes* are, I believe, generally given up at present: they are stately and pendantic, a kind of methodical borrowed phrensy. But I cannot so easily give up, nor will the world be in any haste to part with, his *Elegy in a Country Churchyard*; it is one of the most classical productions that ever was penned by a refined and thoughtful mind, moralizing on human life. Mr. Coleridge (in his *Literary Life*) says that his friend Mr. Wordsworth had undertaken to show that the language of the *Elegy* is unintelligible: it has, however, been understood.

William Hazlitt, 1818, *Lectures on the English Poets,*
Lecture VI

Had Gray written nothing but his *Elegy,* high as he stands, I am not sure that he would not stand higher; it is the cornerstone of his glory; without it, his odes would be insufficient for his fame.

Lord Byron, 1821, *On Bowles's Strictures on Pope*

I know not what there is of spell in the following simple line:
    "The rude forefathers of the hamlet sleep;"
but no frequency of repetition can exhaust its touching charm. This fine poem overcame even the spiteful enmity of Johnson, and forced him to acknowledge its excellence.

Sir Samuel Egerton Brydges, 1834, *Imaginary Biography*

There is a charm in metre, as there is in music; it is of the same kind, though the relation may be remote; and it differs less in degree, perhaps, than one who has not an ear for poetry can believe. . . . Gray's *Elegy* owes much of its popularity to its strain of verse; the strain of thought alone, natural and touching as it is, would never have impressed it upon the hearts of thousands and tens of thousands, unless the diction and meter in which it was embodied had been perfectly in unison with it. Beattie ascribed its general reception to both causes. . . . Neither cause would have sufficed for producing so general, and extensive, and permanent an effect, unless the poem had been, in the full import of the word, harmonious.

Robert Southey, 1835, *Life of Cowper,* ch. xii

For wealth of condensed thought and imagery, fused into one equable stream of golden song by intense fire of genius, the Editor knows no poem superior to this *Elegy,*—none quite equal. Nor has the difficulty of speaking well on common topics, without exaggeration yet with unfailing freshness and originality, been ever met with greater success. Line after line has the perfection of a flawless jewel: it is hard to find a word that could have been spared, or changed for the better. This condensation, however, has injured the clearness of the poem: the specific gravity of the gem, if we may pursue the image, has diminished its translucent qualities. Many notes have hence been added;—the useful but prosaic task of paraphrase is best left to the reader, who may make one for his benefit, and then burn if for his pleasure.

> Francis Turner Palgrave, 1875, ed., *The Children's Treasury*
> *of English Song,* Notes, p. 292

A popularity due in great measure to the subject,—created for Gray a reputation to which he has really no right. He himself was not deceived by the favour shown to the *Elegy.* "Gray told me with a good deal of acrimony," writes Dr. Gregory, "that the *Elegy* owed its popularity entirely to the subject, and that the public would have received it as well if it had been written in prose." This is too much to say; the *Elegy* is a beautiful poem, and in admiring it the public showed a true feeling for poetry. But it is true that the *Elegy* owed much of its success to its subject, and that it has received a too unmeasured and unbounded praise. Gray himself, however, maintained that the *Elegy* was not his best work in poetry, and he was right. High as is the praise due to the *Elegy,* it is yet true that in other productions of Gray he exhibits poetical qualities even higher than those exhibited in the *Elegy.* He deserves, therefore, his extremely high reputation as a poet, although his critics and the public may not always have praised him with perfect judgment. We are brought back, then, to the question: How, in a poet so really considerable, are we to explain his scantiness of production?

> Matthew Arnold, 1880, *The English Poets,* ed. Ward,
> vol. III, p. 305

It was whilst Gray was quietly vegetating in Bloomsbury that an event occurred of which he was quite unconscious, which yet has singularly endeared him to the memory of Englishmen. On the evening of the 12th of September, 1759—whilst Gray, sauntering back from the British Museum to his lodgings, noted that the weather was cloudy, with a south-south-west wind—on the other side of the Atlantic the English forces lay along the river Montmorency, and looked anxiously across at Quebec and at the fateful heights of Abraham. When night-fall came, and before the gallant four thousand obeyed the word of command to steal across the river, General Wolfe, the young officer of thirty-three, who was next day to win death and immortality in victory, crept along in a boat from post to post to see that all was ready for the expedition. It was a fine, silent evening, and as they pulled along with muffled oars, the General recited to one of his officers who sat with him in the stern of the boat nearly the whole of Gray's *Elegy in a Country Churchyard,* adding as he concluded, "I would prefer being the author of that poem to the glory of beating the French tomorrow." Perhaps no finer compliment was ever paid by the man of action to the man of imagination, and, sanctified, as it were, by the dying lips of the great English hero, the poem seems to be raised far above its intrinsic rank in literature, and to demand our respect as one of the acknowledged glories of our race and language.

Edmund Gosse, 1882, Gray (English Men of Letters), p. 143

ODES

Even my friends tell me they [the Odes] do not succeed, and write me moving topics of consolation on that head; in short, I have heard of nobody but a player [Garrick] and a doctor of divinity [Warburton] that profess their esteem for them.

Thomas Gray, 1757, Letter to Dr. Hurd, Aug. 25;
Works, ed. Gosse, vol. II, p. 325

Talking of Gray's *Odes,* he said, "They are forced plants raised in a hotbed; and they are poor plants; they are but cucumbers after all." A gentleman present, who had been running down Ode-writing in general, as a bad species of poetry, unluckily said, "Had they been literally cucumbers, they had been better things than Odes."—"Yes, Sir (said Johnson), for a *hog.*"

Samuel Johnson, 1780, Life by Boswell, ed. Hill, vol. IV, p. 15

I yet reflect with pain upon the cool reception which those noble odes, *The Progress of Poetry* and *The Bard,* met with at their first publication; it appeared that there were not twenty people in England who liked them.

Thomas Warton, 1781, Letter to Mason, May 29

Gray (to whom nothing is wanting to render him, perhaps, the finest poet in the English language but to have written a little more) is said to have been so much hurt by a foolish and impertinent parody of two of his finest odes, that he never afterwards attempted any considerable work.

Adam Smith, 1801, Theory of Moral Sentiments, vol. I, p. 255

. . . I have this evening been reading a few passages in Gray's Odes. I am very much pleased with them. The *Progress of Poesy* and the *Ode on Eton College* are admirable. And many passages of *The Bard,* though, I confess, quite obscure to me, seem to partake in a great degree of the sublime. *Obscurity* is the great objection which many urge against Gray. They do not consider that it contributes in the highest degree to sublimity;

and he certainly aimed at sublimity in these Odes. Every one admires his Elegy, and if they do not his Odes, they must attribute it to their own want of taste.

Henry Wadsworth Longfellow, 1823, *Letter to His Mother; Life,*
ed. Longfellow, vol. I, p. 29

Compared, not with the work of the great masters of the golden ages of poetry, but with the poetry of his own contemporaries in general, Gray's may be said to have reached, in his style, the excellence at which he aimed; while the evolution, also, of such a piece as his *Progress of Poesy,* must be accounted not less noble and sound than its style.

Matthew Arnold, 1880, *The English Poets,* ed. Ward,
vol. III, p. 316

LETTERS

I find more people like the grave letters than those of humour, and some think the latter a little affected, which is as wrong a judgment as they could make; for Gray never wrote anything easily but things of humour. Humour was his natural and original turn—and though, from his chilhood, he was grave and reserved his genius led him to see things ludicrously and satirically; and though his health and dissatisfaction gave him low spirits, his melancholy turn was much more affected than his pleasantry in writing. You knew him enough to know I am in the right.

Horace Walpole, 1775, *To Rev. William Cole, Letters;*
ed. Cunningham, vol. VI, p. 206

Gray appears to us to be the best letter-writer in the language. Others equal him in particular qualities, and surpass him in amount of entertainment; but none are so nearly faultless. Chesterfield wants heart, and even his boasted "delicacy;" Bolingbroke and Pope want simplicity; Cowper is more lively than strong; Shenstone reminds you of too many rainy days, Swift of too many things he affected to despise, Gibbon too much of the formalist and the *littérateur.* The most amusing of all our letter-writers are Walpole and Lady Mary Wortley Montagu; but though they have abundance of wit, sense, and animal spirits, you are not always sure of their veracity. Now, "the first quality in a companion," as Sir William Temple observes, "is truth;" and Gray's truth is as manifest as his other good qualities. He has sincerity, modesty, manliness (in spite of a somewhat effeminate body), learning, good-nature, playfulness, a perfect style; and if an air of pensiveness breathes all over, it is only of that resigned and contemplative sort which completes our sympathy with the writer. . . . Gray is the "melancholy Jaques" of English literature, without the sullenness or causticity.

Leigh Hunt, 1849, *A Book for a Corner,* Second Series

Everyone knows the letters of Gray, and remembers the lucid simplicity and directness, mingled with the fastidious sentiment of a scholar, of his description of such scenes as the Chartreuse. That is a well-known description, but those in his journal of a "Tour in the North" have been neglected, and they are especially interesting since they go over much of the country in which Wordsworth dwelt, and of which he wrote. They are also the first conscious effort—and in this he is a worthy forerunner of Wordsworth—to describe natural scenery with the writer's eye upon the scene described, and to describe it in simple and direct phrase, in distinction to the fine writing that was then practised. And Gray did this intentionally in the light prose journal he kept, and threw by for a time the refined carefulness and the insistance on human emotion which he thought necessary in poetic description of Nature. In his prose then, though not in his poetry, we have Nature loved for her own sake.

Stopford A. Brooke, 1874, *Theology in the English Poets,* p. 36

GENERAL

I have been reading Gray's Works, and think him the only poet since Shakspeare entitled to the character of sublime. Perhaps you will remember that I once had a different opinion of him. I was prejudiced. He did not belong to our Thursday society, and was an Eton man, which lowered him prodigiously in our esteem. I once thought Swift's letters the best that could be written; but I like Gray's better. His humour, or his wit, or whatever it is to be called, is never ill-natured or offensive, and yet, I think equally poignant with the Dean's.

William Cowper, 1777, *Letter to Joseph Hill,* April 20; *Works,* ed. Southey, vol. II, p. 223

He was indeed the inventor, it may be strictly said so, of a new lyrical metre in his own tongue. The peculiar formation of *his* strophe, antistrophe, and epode, was unknown before him; and it could only have been planned and perfected by a master genius, who was equally skilled by long and repeated study, and by transfusion into his own mind of the lyric composition of ancient Greek and of the higher *"canzoni"* of the Tuscan poets, *"di maggior carme e suono,"* as it is termed in the commanding energy of their language. Antecedent to "The Progress of Poetry," and to "The Bard," no such lyrics had appeared. There is not an ode in the English language which is constructed like these two compositions; with such power, such majesty, and such sweetness, with such proportioned pauses and just cadences, with such regulated measures of the verse, with such master principles of lyric art displayed and exemplified, and, at the same time, with such a concealment of the difficulty, which is lost in the softness and uninterrupted flowing of the lines of each stanza, with such a musical magic, that every verse in it in succession dwells on the ear and harmonizes with that which is gone before.

Thomas James Mathias, 1814, ed., Works of Thomas Gray

Gray failed as a poet not because he took too much pains and so extinguished his animation, but because he had very little of that fiery quality to begin with, and his pains were of the wrong sort. He wrote English verses as his brother Eton school boys wrote Latin, filching a phrase now from one author and now from another. I do not profess to be a person of very various reading; nevertheless, if I were to pluck out of Gray's tail all of the feathers which I know belong to other birds, he would be left very bare indeed. Do not let anybody persuade you that any quantity of good verses can be produced by mere felicity; or that an immortal style can be the growth of mere genius. *"Multa tulit fecit que"* must be the motto of all those who are to last.

William Wordsworth, 1816, Letter to Gillies

Gray and Collins, distinct enough in character to the careful critical inspector, have to the outward eye a curious similarity. They were contemporaries; they wrote very little, and that mostly in the form of odes; they both affected personation and allegorical address to a very unusual extent; both studied effects which were Greek in their precision and delicacy; both were learned and exact students of periods of literature now reinstated in critical authority, but in their day neglected. Yet, while Gray was the greater intellectual figure of the two, the more significant as a man and a writer, Collins possessed something more thrilling, more spontaneous, as a purely lyrical poet. When they are closely examined, their supposed similarity fades away; and, without depreciating either, we discover that each was typical of a class—that Collins was the type of the poet who sings, as the birds do, because he must; and Gray of the artist in verse, who has learned everything which the most consummate attention to workmanship can teach him, when added to the native faculty of a singularly delicate ear. . . . The most important poetical figure in our literature between Pope and Wordsworth.

Edmund Gosse, 1888, A History of Eighteenth Century
Literature, pp. 235, 236

Although Gray's biographers and critics have very seldom spoken of it, the most interesting thing in a study of his poetry—and the thing, of course, that exclusively concerns us here—is the steady progress in the direction of Romanticism. Beginning as a classicist and disciple of Dryden, he ended in thoroughgoing Romanticism. His early poems contain nothing Romantic; his *Elegy* has something of the Romantic mood, but shows many conventional touches; in the Pindaric Odes the Romantic feeling asserts itself boldly; and he ends in enthusiastic study of Norse and Celtic poetry and mythology. Such a steady growth in the mind of the greatest poet of the time shows not only what he learned from the age, but what he taught it. Gray is a much more important factor in the Romantic movement than seems to be commonly supposed. This will appear from a brief examination of his poetry.

William Lyon Phelps, 1893, *The Beginnings of the English Romantic Movement*, p. 157

TOBIAS GEORGE SMOLLETT
1721-1771

Born, in the "Lennox," Dumbartonshire, 1721; baptized, 19 March 1721. Early education at school at Dumbarton. Apprenticed to a doctor. To London, 1739. Entered Navy as Surgeon's Mate, Oct. 1740. After Carthagena expedition, retired from Navy; settled in Jamaica. Married there Anne Lascelles, 1744 [?]. Returned to London, 1744; devoted himself to literature. Visit to Paris. 1749 [?]. M. D., Marischall Coll., Aberdeen, 1750. Edited *Critical Review*, 1756-60. Imprisoned three months for libel, 1759. Edited *British Mag.*, 1760-67; *The Briton*, May 1762 to Feb. 1763. Travelled abroad, June 1763 to spring 1765. To Italy, 1768; settled at Monte Nuovo, near Leghorn. Died there, Sept. 1771. Buried at Leghorn. WORKS: *Advice* (anon.), 1746; *Reproof* (anon.), 1747; *Adventures of Roderick Random* (anon.), 1748; *The Regicide* (anon.), 1749; *The History and Adventures of an Atom* (anon.), 1749; *Adventures of Peregrine Pickle* (anon.), 1751; *Essay on the External Use of Water*, 1752; *Adventures of Ferdinand, Count Fathom* (anon.), 1753; *The Reprisal* (anon.), 1757; *Compleat History of England . . . to the Treaty of Aix-la-Chapelle* (4 vols.), 1757-58; *Continuation* of preceding (5 vols.), 1763-65; *Adventures of Sir Launcelot Greaves* (anon.), 1762; *Travels Through France and Italy* (2 vols.), 1766; *The Present State of All Nations* (8 vols.), 1768-69; *The Expedition of Humphrey Clinker* (anon.), 1771 (misprinted 1671 on title-page of 1st edn.). POSTHUMOUS: *Ode to Independence*, 1773. He *translated*: *Gil Blas* (anon.), 1749; *Don Quixote*, 1755; *Voltaire's Works* (with others), 1761-74; *The Adventures of Telemachus*, 1776; and *edited*: *A Compendium of Authentic and Entertaining Voyages*, 1756. COLLECTED WORKS: in 6 vols., 1790. LIFE: by R. Anderson, 1796.

R. Farquharson Sharp, 1897, *A Dictionary of English Authors*, p. 263

SEE: *Works*, ed. W. E. Henley and Thomas Seccombe, 1899-1901, 12 v.; *Works*, ed. George Saintsbury, 1925, 12 v.; *Letters*, ed. Edward S. Noyes,

1926; Louis L. Martz, *The Later Career of Smollett*, 1942; Lewis Mansfield Knapp, *Tobias Smollett: Doctor of Men and Manners*, 1949; Donald Bruce, *Radical Dr. Smollett*, 1965.

PERSONAL

Smollett was a man of very agreeable conversation and of much genuine humor; and, though not a professional scholar, possessed a philosophical mind, and was capable of making the soundest observations on human life, and of discerning the excellence or seeing the ridicule of every character he met with. Fielding only excelled him in giving a dramatic story to his novels, but, in my opinion, was inferior to him in the true comic vein. He was one of the many very pleasant men with whom it was my good fortune to be intimately acquainted.

Alexander Carlyle, 1753-56-1860, *Autobiography*, p. 216

A most worthless and dangerous fellow, and capable of any mischief.

Horace Walpole, 1770, *To Sir Horace Mann*, March 16;
Letters, ed. Cunningham, vol. V, p. 231

In the practice of physic, Smollett, though possessed of superior endowments, and eminent scientific qualifications, had the mortification, from whatever cause, to be unsuccessful, at a moment when perhaps the neglect he experienced was aggravated by the unaccountable success of many a superficial unqualified contemporary, reaping the harvest of wealth and reputation. It has been supposed, that this want of success in a profession where merit cannot always ensure fame and affluence, was owing to his failing to render himself agreeable to the fair sex, whose favour is certainly of great consequence to all candidates for eminence, whether in physic or divinity. But his figure and address, which were uncommonly elegant and prepossessing, and his unsullied manners, renders this supposition highly improbable. It is more likely that his irritable temper, increased by the teazing and uncomfortable circumstances of the profession, and his contempt for the low arts of servility, suppleness, and cunning, were the real causes of his failure. It may be supposed also, that his publications, as a general satrist and censor of manners, were far more calculated to retard his progress as a physician, than to augment his practice.

Robert Anderson, 1794-1803, *The Life of Tobias Smollett, M.D.*,
p. 47

His learning, diligence, and natural acuteness, would have rendered him eminent in the science of medicine, had he persevered in that profession;

other parts of his character were ill suited for augmenting his practice. He could neither stoop to impose on credulity nor humour caprice.

John Moore, 1797, ed., Works of Smollett, Memoir

We have before us, and painted by his own hand, Tobias Smollett, the manly, kindly, honest and irascible; worn and battered, but still brave and full of heart, after a long struggle against a hard fortune. His brain had been busied with a hundred different schemes; he had been reviewer and historian, critic, medical writer, poet, pamphleteer. He had fought endless literary battles; and braved and wielded for years the cudgels of controversy. It was a hard and savage fight in those days, and a niggard pay. He was oppressed by illness, age, narrow fortune; but his spirit was still resolute, and his courage steady; the battle over, he could do justice to the enemy with whom he had been so fiercely engaged, and give a not unfriendly grasp to the hand that had mauled him. He is like one of those Scotch cadets, of whom history gives us so many examples, and whom, with a national fidelity, the great Scotch novelist has painted so charmingly. Of gentle birth and narrow means, going out from his northern home to win his fortune in the world, and to fight his way, armed with courage, hunger, and keen wits. His crest is a shattered oak tree, with green leaves yet springing from it. On his ancient coat-of-arms there is a lion and a horn; this shield of his was battered and dinted in a hundred fights and brawls, through which the stout Scotchman bore it courageously. You see somehow that he is a gentleman, through all his battling and struggling, and his defeats.

William Makepeace Thackeray, 1853, The English Humourists
of the Eighteenth Century

He was by no means the idle half-reprobate he represents in his Roderick Random. He was often wrong and always irascible, continually fancying himself aggrieved, and always with a quarrel on his hands; but he was as proud, warmhearted, and mettlesome a Scot as had then crossed the Tweed —of a spirit so independent, we are told, that he never asked a favour for himself from any great man in his life; paying his way honestly, and helping liberally those about him who were in distress; and altogether, so far from being a mere pleasure-seeker, that there was probably no man then in or near London, who stayed more at home, or worked more incessantly and laboriously to prevent the world from being a shilling the worse for him. He ruined his health by over-work.

David Masson, 1859, British Novelists and Their Styles, p. 133

In the following year, Smollett died, leaving to his widow little beyond the empty consolations of his great fame. From her very narrow purse she sup-

plied the means of erecting the stone that marks the spot where he lies; and
the pen of his companion . . . [Dr. John Armstrong], furnished an appropriate inscription. The niggardly hands of government remained as firmly
closed against the relief of Mrs. Smollett as they had been in answer to her
husband's own application for himself; an application which must have cost
a severe struggle to his proud spirit, and of which his most intimate literary
friends were probably never aware. He sought favors for others, says Dr.
Moore; but "for himself he never made an application to any great man in
his life!" He was not intemperate, nor yet was he extravagant, but by nature
hospitable and of a cheerful temperament; his house-keeping was never
niggardly, so long as he could employ his pen. Thus his genius was too often
degraded to the hackney-tasks of booksellers; while a small portion of those
pensions which were so lavishly bestowed upon ministerial dependants and
placemen would have enabled him to turn his mind to its congenial pursuits,
and probably to still further elevate the literary civilization of his country.

> W. Sargent, 1859, "Some Unedited Memorials of Smollett,"
> *Atlantic Monthly*, vol. 3, p. 702

His grave is in the old English cemetery in the Via degli Elisi at Leghorn
(the only town in north Italy where protestants at that time had rights of
burial), and the sea lies to the west of him, as of Fielding at Oporto. A
Latin inscription (inaccurate as to dates) was written for his tombstone by
Armstrong, and has recently been recut. Three years later a monument was
erected by the novelist's cousin, Commissary James Smollett, on the banks
of the Leven—a tall Tuscan column, which still attracts the eye of tourists
on their way between the Clyde and Loch Lomond. The inscription was
revised and in part written by Dr. Johnson, who visited Bonhill with Boswell in 1774.

> Thomas Seccombe, 1898, *Dictionary of National Biography*,
> vol. LIII, p. 180

Roderick Random (1748)

I guessed *R. Random* to be his, [Fielding's] though without his name. I
cannot think *Ferdinand Fathom* wrote by the same hand, it is every way
so much below it.

> Lady Mary Wortley Montagu, 1754, *Letter to the*
> *Countess of Bute*, June 23

In none of his succeeding volumes has he equalled the liveliness, force, and
nature of this his first essay. So just a picture of a seafaring life especially
had never before met the public eye. Many of our naval heroes may prob-

ably trace the preference which has decided them in their choice of a profession to an early acquaintance with the pages of *Roderick Random*. He has not, indeed, decorated his scenes with any seductive colours; yet such is the charm of a highly wrought description, that it often induces us to overlook what is disgusting in the objects themselves, and transfer the pleasure arising from the mere imitation to the reality.

Henry Francis Cary, 1821-24-45, *Lives of English Poets,*
ed. Cary, p. 123

In spite of its indecency, the world at once acknowledged it to be a work of genius: the verisimilitude was perfect; every one recognized in the hero the type of many a young North countryman going out to seek his fortune. The variety is great, the scenes are more varied and real than those in Richardson and Fielding, the characters are numerous and vividly painted, and the keen sense of ridicule pervading the book makes it a broad jest from geginning to end. Historically, his delineations are valuable; for he describes a period in the annals of the British marine which has happily passed away, —a hard life in little stifling holds or forecastles, with hard fare,—a base life, for the sailor, oppressed on shipboard, was the prey of vile women and land-sharks when on shore. What pictures of prostitution and indencency! what obscenity of language! what drunken infernal orgies! We may shun the book as we would shun the company, and yet the one is the exact portraiture of the other.

Henry Coppée, 1872, *English Literature*, p. 293

Roderick Random is intentionally modelled on the plan of Lesage, and here, as elsewhere, Smollett shows himself less original than cither Richardson or Fielding. He can hardly be said to invent or to construct; he simply reports. He does this with infinite spirit and variety. Comedy and tragedy, piety and farce, follow one another in bewildering alternation. But although he dazzles and entertains us, he does not charm. The book is ferocious to a strange degree, and so foul as to be fit only for a very well-seasoned reader. The hero, in whom Smollett complacently could see nothing but a picture of "modest merit struggling with every difficulty," is a selfish bully, whose faults it is exasperating to find condoned. The book of course, is full of good things. The hero is three separate times hurried off to sea, and the scenes of rough sailor-life, though often disgusting, are wonderfully graphic. Tom Bowling, Jack Rattlin, and the proud Mr. Morgan are not merely immortal among salt-sea worthies, but practically the first of a long line of sailors of fiction.

Edmund Gosse, 1888, *A History of Eighteenth Century
Literature*, p. 259

Peregrine Pickle (1751)

At candlelight D. D., and I read by turns, and what do *you think* has been part of our study?—why truly *Peregrine Pickle!* We never undertook it before, but *it is wretched stuff;* only Lady V's. history is a curiosity.

> Mrs. Delany (Mary Granville), 1752, *Letter to Mrs. Dewes,*
> *Correspondence,* ed. Llanover, vol. III, p. 162

It has been said, that Smollett was not successful in drawing female characters; yet the principal female in his romances is always of the strictest purity of mind and manners. The character of "Emilia" in *Peregrine Pickle,* the gayest perhaps of them all, is at the same time watchful and spirited. She does not indeed lecture on virtue like a professor of moral philisophy, nor is she decked in all the flowery ornaments with which the heroines of romance are sometimes adorned. She always appears in the simple dress, so becoming, and so peculiarly natural to young English ladies of virtue and good sense.

> John Moore, 1797, ed., *Works of Smollet,* Memoir

It was received with such extraordinary avidity that a large impression was quickly sold in England, another was bought up in Ireland, a translation was executed into the French language, and it soon made its appearance in a second edition with an apologetic "Advertisement" and "Two Letters" relating to the "Memoirs of a Lady of Quality," sent to the editor by "a Person of Honour." This first edition is in our day scarce enough, and sufficiently coarse to fetch an enhanced price.

> David Herbert, 1870, ed., *Works of Smollett,* Life

Peregrine Pickle attacks by a most brutal and cowardly plot the honour of a young girl, whom he wants to marry, and who is the sister of his best friend. We got to hate his rancorous, concentrated, obstinate character, which is at once that of an absolute king accustomed to please himself at the expense of others' happiness, and that of a boor with only the varnish of education. We should be uneasy at living near him; he is good for nothing but to shock or tyrannise over others. We avoid him as we would a dangerous beast; the sudden rush of animal passion and the force of his firm will are so overpowering in him, that when he fails he becomes outrageous. He draws his sword against an inkeeper; he must bleed him, grows mad. Everything, even to his generosities, is spoiled by pride; all, even to his gaieties, is clouded by harshness. Peregrine's amusements are barbarous, and those of Smollett are after the same style.

> H. A. Taine, 1871, *History of English Literature,* tr. Van Laun,
> vol. II, bk. iii, ch. vi, p. 178

Its brightness, and the hearty fun of many of its chapters, like that (ch. xliv.) which describes an entertainment in the manner of the ancients, made the book widely popular and Smollett famous. The pompous gentleman caricatured by Smollett, as the giver of this banquet, was Mark Akenside.

Henry Morley, 1873, A First Sketch of English Literature, p. 836

He keeps the reader's attention even when he offends his taste. He impaired the literary merit of *Peregrine Pickle,* but at the same time added to its dissolute character and its immediate popularity by the forced insertion of the licentious "Memoirs of a Lady of Quality." Now a serious blemish, these memoirs formed at the time an added attraction to the book. They were eagerly read as the authentic account of Lady Vane, a notorious woman of rank, and were furnished to Smollett by herself, in the hope, fully gratified, that her infamous career might be known to future generations.

Bayard Tuckerman, 1882, A History of English Prose Fiction,
p. 214

Ferdinand Count Fathom (1753)

Smollett, nothwithstanding his peculiar propensity for burlesque and broad humour, has, in his *Ferdinand Count Fathom,* painted a scene of natural terror with astonishing effect; with such vigour of imagination indeed, and minuteness of detail, that the blood runs cold, and the hair stands erect from the impression. The whole turns upon the Count, who is admitted, during a tremendous storm, into a solitary cottage in a forest, discovering a body just murdered in the room where he is going to sleep, and the door of which, on endeavouring to escape, he finds fastened upon him.

Nathan Drake, 1798-1820, Literary Hours, vol. I, No. xvii, p. 274

His *Adventures of Count Fathom* is a description of the career of a hideous and perhaps an anomalous scoundrel. The same tendency to exaggerate both incident and character pervades all Smollett's novels. He seems to write under the stimulus of brandy. It is the nature and fancy of madness. The atmosphere of atrocity that surrounds the principal character and his associates in the *Count Fathom* is so black and stifling, and their features are so horrible, that one's imagination takes refuge almost in contempt in order to relieve itself of the disgust they have excited. At the same time it must be owned that there are points in the work which answer to the stimulated energies of an undoubtedly powerful mind by nature. . . . No one of Smollett's works, or indeed of any other writer of fiction that I am acquainted with, contains stronger specimens of real power in invention and language, than this exhibits.

Charles Cowden Clarke, 1872, "On the Comic Writers of England,"
The Gentleman's Magazine, n. s., vol. 8, pp. 572, 573

The Count is a scoundrel, or, at least, tries to be one; but he is so weak, so easily baffled, so utterly unable to succeed except where he is helped by the incredible folly of the virtuous characters; so much more in fact of a dupe than a villain, that whatever feeling he does arouse is one of a rather mild contempt. We hear much of his cleverness, but never see it. Smollett's literary fault in connection with him was not that he drew a greater sinner than any man should put into a book, but that, having introduced his hero as a villain of extraordinary ability, he entirely fails to convince the reader that Count Fathom was other than a very poor rogue indeed. The scene in the Robbers' Hut in the forest is sometimes spoken of as being original, and the model of many others of the same kind, but the praise can hardly have been given with the due recollection of much that is to be found in the "Spanish and French Authors" whom Smollett took as his masters.

David Hannay, 1887, *Life of Tobias George Smollett*, p. 91

Don Quixote (1755)

Smollett inherited from nature a strong sense of ridicule, a great fund of original humour, and a happy versatility of talent, by which he could accommodate his style to almost every species of writing. He could adopt, alternately, the solemn, the lively, the sarcastic, the burlesque, and the vulgar. To these qualifications, he joined an inventive genius, and a vigorous imagination.

Alexander Fraser Tytler (Lord Woodhouselee), 1791, *Essay on the Principles of Translation*

It wants that picturesque and romantic tone which is so great a charm in the original—that tenderness of feeling in the midst of, and modifying, the wildest extravagance of gaiety, which forms as it were the atmosphere of the southern humour, and distinguishes alike the frantic with of the old comedy of Greece, the broad burlesque of the primitive Italian stage, and glows with such a steady and yet subdued radiance through the pages of the gentle Cervantes. Smollett's *Don Quixote* wants *sun*—the sun of La Mancha.

Thomas B. Shaw, 1847, *Outlines of English Literature*, p. 268

A Complete History of England (1757-65)

Smollett had unquestionably talents, but his genius was entirely turned to the low and the ludicrous; of the dignity and beauty of historic composition, he had no conception, much less could he boast of possessing any portion of its all-pervading and philosophical spirit. His work is a dull and often malignant compilation, equally destitute of instruction and amusement.

> William Belsham, 1793, *Memoirs of the Kings of Great Britain of the House of Brunswick; Memoirs of the Reign of George I.*, Preface

Respect for the great name of Smollett will not suffer me to pass over in silence his *History of England,* the most important of his compilations. It is not to the purpose of the present enquiry to observe that the general concoction of the work reminds us rather of the promptings of the bookseller, than of the talents of its author. It is not however to be wondered at, that the style of a work, thus crudely composed, should not be such as to put contemporary authors to the blush.

> William Godwin, 1797, "Of English Style," *The Enquirer,* p. 470

In the beginning of the year 1758, Smollett published his *Complete History of England, deduced from the Descent of Julius Cæsar to the Treaty of Aix-la-Chapelle, in 1748;* in four volumes quarto. It is said that this voluminous work, containing the history of thirteen centuries, and written with uncommon spirit and correctness of language was composed and finished for the press within fourteen months, one of the greatest exertions of facility of composition which was ever recorded in the history of literature. . . . It cannot be denied that, as a clear and distinct narrative of facts, strongly and vigorously told with a laudable regard to truth and impartiality, the Continuation may vie with our best historical works. The author was incapable of being swayed by fear or favour; and where his judgment is influenced, we can see that he was only misled by an honest belief in the truth of his own arguments.

> Sir Walter Scott, 1821, *Tobias Smollett*

But such a work written in fourteen months could hardly compete in manner, and still less in matter, with the eight years' careful labour of Hume. The style is fluent and loose, possessing a careless vigour where the subject is naturally exciting, but composed too hastily to rise above dulness in the record of dry transactions. As regards matter, the historian can make no pretension to original research. He executed the book as a piece of hack-work for a London bookseller, availing himself freely of previous publications, and taking no pains to bring new facts to light.

> William Minto, 1872-80, *Manual of English Prose Literature,* p. 432

Sir Launcelot Greaves (1762)

It is only in externals that this work bears any resemblance to *Don Quixote*. The author seems to have hesitated between making Sir Lancelot a mere madman and making him a pattern of perfectly sane generosity. The fun and the seriousness do not harmonize. The young knight's craze for riding about the country to redress wrongs armed *cap-a-pie* is too harshly out of tune with the rightness of his sympathies and the grave character of the real abuses against which his indignation is directed. In execution the work is very unequal and irregular, but the opening chapters are very powerful, and have been imitated by hundreds of novelists since Smollett's time.

> William Minto, 1887, *Encyclopædia Britannica*,
> Ninth Edition, vol. XXII

Of *Sir Launcelot Greaves,* originally contributed as a serial to *The British Review,* the scheme, as one of the characters remarks, "is somewhat too stale and extravagant." The plot is the merest excuse for variety of scene, and the characters do not live. What he borrowed from Cervantes is as little put to its proper use by Smollett as what he borrowed from Fielding. His work loses its chief merit when he attempts to exchange his own method of reminiscence for a wider imaginative scheme.

> Walter Raleigh, 1894, *The English Novel*, p. 188

Travels Through France and Italy (1766)

I was best pleased with my old and excellent friend Smollett, testy and discontented as he is, he writes with perspicuity; his observations are generally sensible, and even his oddities are entertaining.

> Francis Garden (Lord Gardenstone), 1792-95,
> *Travelling Memoranda*, vol. I

That Smollett, in recording the incidents of such a journey, should have put a good deal of gall into his ink, is not a matter of surprise; but it is rather remarkable that his journal should be so devoid of literary merit. The author of *Humphrey Clinker* seems to have packed his genius away at the bottom of his trunk, and not taken it out during his whole tour. His spirit is all put forth in vituperation; but otherwise he is tame and commonplace.

> George Stillman Hillard, 1853, *Six Months in Italy*, p. 512

Wherever I have been able to test Smollett's accuracy, I have found him so invariably exact and truthful, that I should be inclined to take a good deal for granted on his mere assertion. It is beside my purpose—which is simply that of recalling attention to a book that has been extravagantly abused by some, and unreasonably neglected or forgotten by others—to follow the author through all his various wanderings by sea and land.

W. J. Prowse, 1870, "Smollett at Nice," *Macmillan's Magazine,*
vol. 21, p. 533

Concerning Smollett's *Letters from Abroad* much need not be said. They are far from being without glimpses of the man in his best style, and they light up objects and places to the untravelled man with many vivid touches and references; but they occupy small ground towards forming an estimate of the value of the novelist's intellectual labours.

George Barnett Smith, 1875, "Tobias Smollett,"
Gentleman's Magazine, n. s., vol. 14, p. 735

Humphrey Clinker (1771)

A party novel written by that profligate hireling Smollett to vindicate the Scots and cry down juries.

Horace Walpole, 1797-1845, *Memoirs of the
Reign of King George the Third*

In this novel the author most successively executes, what had scarcely ever been before attempted—a representation of the different effects which the same scenes, and persons, and transactions, have on different dispositions and tempers. He exhibits through the whole work a most lively and humorous delineation, confirming strongly the great moral truth, that happiness and all our feelings are the result, less of external circumstances, than the constitution of the mind.

John Dunlop, 1814-15, *The History of Fiction,* p. 413

The very ingenious scheme of describing the various effects produced upon different members of the same family by the same objects, was not original, though it has been supposed to be so. Anstey, the facetious author of the *New Bath Guide,* had employed it six or seven years before *Humphrey Clinker* appeared. But Anstey's diverting satire was but a light sketch compared to the finished and elaborate manner in which Smollett has, in the first place, identified his characters, and then fitted them with language, sentiments, and powers of observation, in exact correspondence with their talents, temper, condition, and disposition.

Sir Walter Scott, 1821, *Tobias Smollett*

The novel of *Humphrey Clinker* is, I do think, the most laughable story that has ever been written since the goodly art of novel-writing began. Winifred Jenkins and Tabitha Bramble must keep Englishmen on the grin for ages yet to come; and in their letters and the story of their loves there is a perpetual fount of sparkling laughter, as inexhaustible as Bladud's well.

William Makepeace Thackeray, 1853, *The English Humourists of the Eighteenth Century*

The poor peevish author was hastening to his end; but before he sank beneath this life's horizon, his genius shot forth its brightest beam. Disappointed in his last earthly hope—that of obtaining a consulship on some shore of the Mediterranean, where his last hours might be prolonged in a milder air—he travelled to the neighbourhood of Leghorn, and, settling in a cottage there, finished *Humphrey Clinker,* which is undoubtedly his finest work. Lismahago is the best character in this picture of English life; Bath is the principal scene, upon which the actors play their various parts. Scarcely was this brilliant work completed, when Smollett died, an invalided exile, worn out long before the allotted seventy years. His pictures of the navy-men who trod English decks a century ago, are unsurpassed and imperishable. Trunnion, the one-eyed commodore; Hatchway and Bowling, the lieutenants; Ap-Morgan, the kind but fiery Welsh surgeon; Tom Pipes, the silent boatswain, remain as types of a race of men long extinct, who manned our ships when they were, in literal earnest, wooden walls, and when the language and the discipline, to which officers of the royal navy were accustomed, were somewhat of the roughest and the hardest.

William Francis Collier, 1861, *A History of English Literature,* p. 319

It is worth while noticing that in *Humphrey Clinker* the veritable British poorly-educated and poor-spelling woman begins to express herself in the actual dialect of the species, and in the letters of Mrs. Winifred Jenkins to her fellow maid-servant Mrs. Mary Jones at Brambleton Hall, during a journey made by the family to the North, we have some very worthy and strongly-marked originals not only of Mrs. Malaprop and Mrs. Partington, but of the immortal Sairey Gamp and of scores of other descendants in Thackeray and Dickens, here and there.

Sidney Lanier, 1881, *The English Novel,* p. 185

Matthew Bramble and Obadiah Lismahago, the 'squire's sister and her Methodist maid, have passed permanently into literature, and their places are as secure as those of Partridge and Parson Adams, of Corporal Trim and "my Uncle Toby." Not even the Malapropism of Sheridan or Dickens is quite as riotously diverting, as rich in its unexpected turns, as that of Tabitha Bramble and Winifred Jenkins, especially Winifred, who remains delightful even when deduction is made of the poor and very mechanical fun extracted from the parody of her pietistic phraseology. That it could ever have been considered witty to spell "grace" "grease," and "Bible" "byebill," can only be explained by the indiscriminate hostility of the earlier assailants of Enthusiasm. Upon this, as well as upon a particularly evil-smelling taint of coarseness which, to the honour of the author's contemporaries was fully recognized in his own day as offensive, it is needless now to dwell.

Austin Dobson, 1894, Eighteenth Century Vignettes,
Second Series, p. 140

POETRY AND DRAMAS

This ode [*Tears of Scotland*] by Dr. Smollett does rather more honour to the author's feelings than his taste. The mechanical part, with regard to numbers and language, is not so perfect as so short a work as this requires; but the pathetic it contains, particularly in the last stanza but one, is exquisitely fine.

Oliver Goldsmith, 1767, The Beauties of English Poetry

The few poems which he has left have a portion of delicacy which is not to be found in his novels: but they have not, like those prose fictions, the strength of a master's hand. Were he to live over again, we might wish him to write more poetry, in the belief that his poetical talent would improve by exercise; but we should be glad to have more of his novels just as they are.

Thomas Campbell, 1819, Specimens of the British Poets

Of Smollett's poems much does not remain to be said. *The Regicide* is such a tragedy as might be expected from a clever youth of eighteen. The language is declamatory, the thoughts inflated, and the limits of nature and verisimilitude transgressed in describing the characters and passions. Yet there are passages not wanting in poetical vigour. His two satires have so much of the rough flavour of Juvenal, as to retain some relish, now that the occasion which produced them has passed away. The *Ode to Independence,* which was not published till after his decease, amid much of commonplace, has some very nervous lines. The personification itself is but an awkward one. The term is scarcely abstract and general enough to be invested with the attributes of an ideal being. In the *Tears of Scotland,* patriotism has made him eloquent and pathetic; and the *Ode to Leven Water* is sweet and natural. None of the other pieces except the *Ode to*

Mirth, which has some sprightliness of fancy, deserves to be particularly noticed.

Henry Francis Cary, 1821-24-45, *Lives of English Poets,*
ed. Cary, p. 145

The Reprisal, which appeared in 1757, stands alone in two respects in Smollett's life. It was his only successful attempt to reach the stage, and it led to the soldering up of an old quarrel. The plot of this two-act comedy may have given Marryat the first idea of *The Three Cutters,* and is worked up with no small liveliness. Its characters have a distinct comic *vis* of a rather broad kind. The sailors Lyon, Haulyard, and Block, are good as Smollett's sailors always were; Oclabber and Maclaymore, the exiled Jacobites in the French service, are first drafts of the immortal Lismahago. Like most of Smollett's work in those years, this comedy has its touch of journalism.

David Hannay, 1887, *Life of Tobias George Smollett,* p. 144

GENERAL

You ask me what degrees there are between Scott's novels and those of Smollett. They appear to me to be quite distinct in every particular, more especially in their aims. Scott endeavours to throw so interesting and romantic a colouring into common and low characters as to give them a touch of the sublime. Smollett on the contrary pulls down and levels what with other men would continue romance. The grand parts of Scott are within the reach of more minds than the finest humours in Humphrey Clinker. I forget whether that fine thing of the Serjeant is Fielding or Smollett but it gives me more pleasure than the whole novel of the Antiquary. You must remember what I mean. Some one says to the Serjeant: "That's a non-sequitur!"—"If you come to that," replies the Serjeant, "you're another!"

John Keats, 1818, *To George and Thomas Keats,* Jan. 5;
Letters, ed. Colvin, p. 51

Smollett's humour often arises from the situation of the persons, or the peculiarity of their external appearance; as, from Roderick Random's carroty locks, which hung down over his shoulders like a pound of candles, or Strap's ignorance of London, and the blunders that follow from it. There is a tone of vulgarity about all his productions. The incidents frequently resemble detached anecdotes taken from a newspaper or magazine; and, like those in *Gil Blas,* might happen to a hundred other characters. He exhibits the ridiculous accidents and reverses to which human life is liable, not "the stuff" of which it is composed. He seldom probes to the quick, or penetrates beyond the surface; and, therefore, he leaves no stings in the minds of his readers, and in this respect is far less interesting than Fielding. His novels always enliven, and never tire us; we take them up with pleasure, and lay them down without any strong feeling of regret.

William Hazlitt, 1818, *Lectures on the English Comic Writers,*
Lecture VI

So long as his odes to "Leven Water" and to "Independence" exist, Smollett can never fail to be admired as a poet, nor can a feeling of regret be avoided that he did not devote more of his genius to poetic compositions. We cannot take leave of this distinguished Scotchman—distinguished as a historian, as a novelist, and as the author of lines which possess the masculine strength of Dryden—without alluding to a passage in his novel of *Peregrine Pickle,* that passage so inexpressibly touching where the Jacobite exiles stand every morning on the coast of France to contemplate the blue hills of their native land, to which they are never to return!

James Grant Wilson, 1876, *The Poets and Poetry of Scotland,*
vol. I, p. 203

Smollett was placed in a very high rank by his contemporaries. Lady Wortley-Montagu praised her "dear Smollett" to all her friends (including Mrs. Delany and other pious people), Johnson commended his ability, Burke delighted in *Roderick Random,* and Lydia Languish seems to have had an impartial affection for all his novels. Of later generations, Scott readily grants to him an equality with his great rival Fielding. Elia makes his imaginary aunt refer with a sigh of regret to the days when she thought it proper to read *Peregrine Pickle*. Oblivious of Dickens, Leigh Hunt called Smollett the finest of all caricaturists. Talfourd puts his Strap far above Fielding's Patridge, and Thackeray gives to *Clinker* the palm among laughable stories since the art of novel-writing was invented. More critical is the estimate of Hazlitt. Smollett, he says, portrays the eccentricities rather than the characters of human life, but no one has praised so well the charm of *Humphrey Clinker* or the "force and mastery" of many episodes in *Court Fathom*. Taine would appear to sympathise with Mr. Leslie Stephens in a much lower estimate of Smollett as the interpreter of the extravagant humours of "ponderous well-fed masses of animated beefsteak." Of the five great eighteenth century novelists, Defoe, Richardson, Fielding, Smollett, and Sterne, Smollett is now valued the least; yet in the influence he has exercised upon successors he is approached by Sterne alone of his contemporaries.

Thomas Seccombe, 1898, *Dictionary of National Biography,*
vol. LIII, p. 181

CHRISTOPHER SMART
1722-1771

Born, at Shipbourne, Kent, 11 April 1722. Early education at Maidstone and at Durham, 1733-39. Matric. Pembroke Coll., Camb., 30 Oct. 1739; B. A., 1743; Fellow, 1745-53; M. A., 1747. Edited *The Student*, 1750-51. Married Anna Maria Carnan, 1753. Contrib. to *The Universal Visitor, The Midwife, The Old Woman's Mag.*, etc. Confined in a lunatic asylum for two years. Died in King's Bench Prison, 18 May 1770. WORKS: *On the Eternity of the Supreme Being*, 1750; *A Solemn Dirge, sacred to the Memory of . . . Frederic, Prince of Wales*, 1751; *An Occasional Prologue and Epilogue to Othello* [1751]; *On the Immensity of the Supreme Being*, 1751; *On the Omniscience of the Supreme Being*, 1752; *Poems on Several Occasions*, 1752; second series [1763]; *The Hilliad*, 1753; *On the Power of the Supreme Being*, 1754; *Hymn to the Supreme Being*, 1756; *On the Goodness of the Supreme Being*, 1756; *A Song to David*, 1763; *Poems* (priv. ptd.) [1763?]; *Hannah* (oratorio libretto) [1764?]; *Ode to . . . the Earl of Northumberland*, 1764; *Abimelech* (oratorio libretto), [1768?]. He *Translated*: *Carmen Alexandri Pope in S. Cæciliam latine redditum*, 1743; *Horaces' Works* (2 vols.), 1756; *The Poems of Phædrus*, 1765; *The Psalms of David*, 1765; *The Parables of our Lord*, 1768. COLLECTED POEMS: in 2 vols., with memoir, 1791.

R. Farquharson Sharp, 1897, A Dictionary of
English Authors, p. 259

SEE: *Collected Poems*, ed. Normal Callan, 1949, 2 v.; *Poems*, ed. Robert Brittain, 1950; G. G. Ainsworth and Claude E. Jones, *Smart: A Biographical and Critical Study*, 1943; Christopher Devlin, *Poor Kit Smart*, 1961.

PERSONAL

Madness frequently discovers itself merely by unnecessary deviation from the usual modes of the world. My poor friend Smart shewed the disturbance of his mind, by falling upon his knees, and saying his prayers in the street, or in any other unusual place. Now although, rationally speaking, it is greater madness not to pray at all, than to pray as Smart did, I am afraid there are so many who do not pray, that their understanding is not called in question.

Samuel Johnson, 1763, Life by Boswell, ed. Hill, vol. I, p. 459

The author of the *Old Woman's Magazine* and of several poetical productions; some of which are sweetly elegant and pretty—for example: "Harriet's Birthday," "Care and Generosity,"—and many more. This ingenious writer is one of the most unfortunate of men—he has been twice confined in a mad-house—and but last year sent a most affecting epistle to papa, to entreat him to lend him half-a-guinea!—How great a pity so clever, so ingenious a man should be reduced to such shocking circumstances. He is extremely grave, and has still great wildness in his manner, looks, and voice; but 'tis impossible to *see* him and to *think* of his works, without feeling the utmost pity and concern for him.

> Frances Burney, 1768, *Early Diary,* ed. Ellis, Sept. 12,
> vol. I, p. 24

In manner Smart seems to have been abnormally nervous and retiring, but when this shyness was overcome, he was particularly amiable, and had a frank and engaging air which, with children especially, often overflowed with drollery and high spirits. Latterly, however, owing to bad habits, penurious living, and his constitutional melancholia, he became a mere wreck of his earlier self.

> Thomas Seccombe, 1897, *Dictionary of National Biography,*
> vol. LII, p. 388

GENERAL

As a poet his genius has never been questioned by those who censure his carelessness, and commiserated an unhappy vacillation of his mind. He is sometimes not only greatly irregular, but irregularly great. His errors are those of a bold and daring spirit, which bravely hazards what a vulgar mind could never suggest. Shakspeare and Milton are sometimes wild and irregular; but it seems as if originality alone could try experiments. Accuracy is timid and seeks for authority. Fowls of feeble wing seldom quit the ground, though at full liberty, while the eagle unrestrained soars into unknown regions.

> Robert Anderson, 1799, ed., *The British Poets*

No one can afford to be entirely indifferent to the author of verses which one of the greatest of modern writers has declared to be unequalled of their kind between Milton and Keats. . . . Save for one single lyric, that glows with all the flush and bloom of Eden, Smart would take but a poor place on the English Parnassus. His odes and ballads, his psalms and satires, his masques and his georgics, are not bad, but they are mediocre.

> Edmund Gosse, 1891, *Gossip in a Library,* pp. 185, 195

Johnson defended him half-jocularly, but the piece of Smart's work which was least likely to appeal to Johnson is that which has secured him his vogue of late years. This is the now famous *Song to David,* to which the praise given to it in Mr. Ward's *Poets,* and Mr. Browning's allotment to the author of a place in the "Parleying with Certain People of Importance," have given a notoriety certainly not attained by the rest of Smart's work, familiar as, for a century or so, it ought to have been by its inclusion in Chalmers, where the *Song* is not. Smart, as there presented, is very much like other people of his time, giving some decent hackwork, a good deal of intentionally serious matter of no value, and a few light pieces of distinct merit.

> George Saintsbury, 1898, *A Short History of English Literature*, p. 582

PHILIP DORMER STANHOPE
EARL OF CHESTERFIELD
1694-1773

1694, Philip Dormer Stanhope, fourth earl of Chesterfield, born 22nd September, 1712, Chesterfield entered Trinity Hall, Cambridge (as Stanhope). 1715, Appointed Gentleman of the Bed-chamber to the Prince of Wales. 1715, Entered the House of Commons as M. P. for St. Germains. 1723, Appointed Captain of the Guard. 1726, Succeeds to the Earldom, on the death of his father. 1727, Chesterfield appointed Ambassador at the Hague. 1730, Appointed Lord Steward and invested with the Garter. 1732, His son, Philip Stanhope, born. 1733, Dismissed from office by the King, in consequence of his opposition to Walpole's Excise Bill. 1733, Married Melosina de Schoulenberg, Countess of Walsingham (daughter, as supposed, of George I.) She died without issue in 1778. 1737, Speech against Bill for Licensing Theatres. 1739, Commencement of his *Letters to his Son;* continued to the death of the latter in 1768. 1744, Appointed Envoy to the Hague. 1745 and 1746, Lord Lieutenant of Ireland, from May, 1745, to Nov. 18, 1746—residing the last six months in England. 1746, Secretary of State, Offered a Dukedom. 1748, Resigns 6th February, owing to his opposition to the War. 1751, Proposed and carried the Reformation of the Calendar. 1752, His deafness commences. 1755, His Godson and successor, Philip Stanhope, son of Arthur Charles Stanhope, born 28th November. 1761, Commencement of his "Letters to his Godson." 1768, Death of his Son. 1773, Died 24th March.

> Charles Wells Moulton, 1902

SEE: *Letters,* ed. Bonamy Dobrée, 1932, 6v.; Samuel Shellabarger, *Lord Chesterfield and His World,* 1951.

PERSONAL

Lord Chesterfield was allowed by everybody to have more conversable entertaining table-wit than any man of his time; his propensity to ridicule, in which he indulged himself with infinite humour and no distinction, and with inexhaustible spirits and no discretion, made him sought and feared, liked and not loved, by most of his acquaintance; no sex, no relation, no rank, no power, no profession, no friendship, no obligation, was a shield from those pointed, glittering weapons, that seemed to shine only to a stander-by, but cut deep in those they touched. . . . With a person as disagreeable as it was possible for a human figure to be without being deformed, he affected following many women of the first beauty and most in fashion; and, if you would have taken his word for it, not without success; whilst in fact and in truth, he never gained any one above the venal rank of those whom an Adonis or a Vulcan might be equally well with, for an equal sum of money. He was very short, disproportioned, thick and clumsily made; had a broad, rough-featured, ugly face, with black teeth, and a head big enough for a Polyphemus. One Ben Ashurst, . . . told Lord Chesterfield once that he was like a stunted giant which was a humorous idea and really apposite.

John Lord Hervey, 1727-43? *Memoirs of the Reign of
King George the Second,* ed. Croker, ch. iv

Chesterfield is a little, tea-table scoundrel, that tells little womanish lies to make quarrels in families; and tries to make women lose their reputations, and make their husbands beat them, without any object but to give himself airs; as if anybody could believe a woman could like a dwarf baboon.

George II., 1743? *To Lord Hervey*

When, upon some slight encouragement, I first visited your Lordship, I was overpowered, like the rest of mankind, by the enchantment of your address; and could not forbear to wish that I might boast myself *Le vainqueuer du vainqueur de la terre;*—that I might obtain that regard for which I saw the world contending; but I found my attendance so little encouraged, that neither pride nor modesty would suffer me to continue it. When I had once addressed your Lordship in publick, I had exhausted all the art of pleasing which a retired and uncourtly scholar can possess. I had done all that I could; and no man is well pleased to have his all neglected, be it ever so little. Seven years, my Lord, have now past, since I waited in your outward rooms, or was repulsed from your door; during which time I have been pushing on my work through difficulties, of which it is useless to complain, and have brought it, at last, to the verge of publication, without one act of assistance, one word of encouragement, or one smile of favour. Such treatment I did not expect, for I never had a Patron before. The shepherd in Virgil grew at last acquainted with Love, and found him a native of the rocks. Is not a Patron, my Lord, one who looks with unconcern on a man struggling for life in the water, and, when he has reached ground, encumbers him with help? The notice which you have been pleased to take of my labours, had it been early, had been kind; but it has been delayed till

I am indifferent, and cannot enjoy it; till I am solitary, and cannot impart it; till I am known, and do not want it. I hope it is no very cynical asperity not to confess obligations where no benefit has been received, or to be unwilling that the publick should consider me as owing that to a Patron, which Providence has enabled me to do for myself. Having carried on my work thus far with so little obligation to any favourer of learning, I shall not be disappointed though I should conclude it, if less be possible, with less; for I have been long wakened from that dream of hope, in which I once boasted myself with so much exultation.

My Lord,
Your Lordship's most humble,
Most obedient servant.

Samuel Johnson, 1755, *Letter to the Right Honourable*
the Earl of Chesterfield, Feb. 7

Lord Chesterfield however by his perpetual attention to propriety, decorum, *bienséance,* &c., had so *veneered* his manners, that though he lived on good terms with all the world he had not a single *friend.* The fact was I believe that he had no warm affections. His excessive and unreasonable attention to decorum and studied manner attended him almost to his last hour.

Edmond Malone, 1783, *Maloniana,* ed. Prior, p. 357

That Lord Chesterfield must have been mortified by the lofty contempt, and polite, yet keen satire with which Johnson exhibited him to himself in this letter, it is impossible to doubt. He, however, with that glossy duplicity which was his constant study, affected to be quite unconcerned. Dr. Adams mentioned to Mr. Robert Dodsley that he was sorry Johnson had written his letter to Lord Chesterfield. Dodsley, with the true feelings of trade, said "he was very sorry too; for that he had a property in the 'Dictionary,' to which his Lordship's patronage might have been of consequence." . . . Johnson having now explicitly avowed his opinion of Lord Chesterfield, did not refrain from expressing himself concerning that nobleman with pointed freedom: "This man (said he) I thought had been a Lord among wits; but, I find, he is only a wit among Lords!" And when his "Letters" to his natural son were published, he observed, that "they teach the morals of a whore, and the manners of a dancing master."

James Boswell, 1791-93, *Life of Johnson,*
ed. Hill, vol. I, pp. 307, 308

Although one of the genuine aristocracy, owing his title to no modern creation, he made himself a reputation which few of his countrymen equalled in his own day; and, which is perhaps more remarkable, he left his mark upon the mind and manners of the English race so deep, that it will be long before it is entirely effaced. No man ever put into more attractive shape the maxims of a worldly Epicurean philosophy. No man ever furnished, in his own person, a more dazzling specimen of the theory which he recommended. If Cicero came more nearly than any person ever did to the image of the perfect orator which he described, Chesterfield is universally considered as having equally sustained his own idea of the perfect gentleman.

Charles Francis Adams, 1846, "The Earl of Chesterfield,"
North American Review, vol. 63, p. 166

Lord Chesterfield was a man of extraordinary talents, for his own day the veritable king among men of the world, of whom life is built up with an infinity of care and skill upon well-organized, though worldly, self-love and consummate enjoyment of the world; with no negation of religion, but with no interest in it; with a toleration of it, conditional upon its abiding peaceably in its own place, as a hat abides in the hall until it is wanted for going out of doors.

William Ewart Gladstone, 1896, Studies Subsidiary to the
Works of Bishop Butler,</i> p. 134</div>

Chesterfield incurred the dislike of three of the most influential writers of his day—Dr. Johnson, Horace Walpole, and Lord Hervey (Queen Caroline's friend). Their hostile estimates have injured his posthumous reputation, and inspired Dickens's ruthless caricature of him as Sir John Chester in <i>Barnaby Rudge</i>. Chesterfield's achievements betray a brilliance of intellectual gifts and graces which discourages in the critic any desire to exaggerate his deficiency in moral principle. In matter and manner—in delicate raillery and in refinement of gesture—his speeches in parliament were admitted to be admirable by his foes. . . . Chesterfield's wordliness was in point of fact tempered by native common-sense, by genuine parental affections, and by keen appreciation of, and capacity for, literature. Even in his unedifying treatment of the relations of the sexes his solemn warnings against acts which forfeit self-respect or provoke scandal destroyed most of the deleterious effect of the cynical principles on which he took his stand. Nowhere did Chesterfield inculcate an inconsiderate gratification of selfish desires. Very sternly did he rebuke pride of birth or insolence in the treatment of servants and dependents. His habitual text was the necessity from prudential motives of self-control and of respect for the feelings of others. As a writer he reached the highest levels of grace and perspicuity, and as a connoisseur of literature he was nearly always admirable. His critical taste was seen to best advantage in his notices of classical writers.

Sidney Lee, 1898, Dictionary of National Biography,
vol. LIV, p. 34

Letters to his Son (1774)

I have declined the publication of Lord C's letters. The public will see them, and upon the whole, I think with pleasure; but the whole family were strongly bent against it; and especially on d'Eyverdun's account, I deemed it more prudent to avoid making them my personal enemies.

Edward Gibbon, 1773, *Private Letters*, vol. I, p. 195

No modern work, has perhaps been received with such avidity by the public as *Lord Chesterfield's Letters*. The subject, the education of a man of the world, and the author, the most accomplished gentleman of his time, naturally engaged the public attention; and the elegance of composition has, we may say, justified the great expectations that were raised. We have not here simply the speculative opinions of a theorist in his closet, but the conduct and practice of a greater master carrying his work into execution.

Edmund Burke? 1774, *Annual Register*

I have been reading for the first time Lord Chesterfield's *Letters,* with more disgust than pleasure, and more pity than disgust. Such letters must have defeated their own main purpose, and made the poor youth awkward, by impressing him with a continual dread of appearing so. But it is painful to see what the father himself was—not, as it appears, from any want of good qualities, but because there was one *grace* a thought of which never entered his mind.

Robert Southey, 1831, *Correspondence with Caroline Bowles,*
March 8, p. 219

When I said that Chesterfield had lost by the publication of his letters, I of course considered that he had much to lose; that he has left an immense reputation, founded on the testimony of all his contemporaries of all parties, for wit, taste, and eloquence; that what remains of his Parliamentary oratory is superior to anything of that time that has come down to us, except a little of Pitt's. The utmost that can be said of the letters is that they are the letters of a cleverish man; and there are not many which are entitled even to that praise. I think he would have stood higher if we had been left to judge of his powers—as we judge of those of Chatham, Mansfield, Charles Townshend, and many others—only by tradition and by fragments of speeches preserved in Parliamentary reports.

Thomas Babington Macaulay, 1833, *Selection from the
Correspondence of the Late Macvey Napier,* Letter, Oct. 14

These letters were addressed to a natural son—and that circumstance should be constantly kept in mind; it is needful to explain many things that are said, and the only apology for many omissions; but at the same time we must say that if any circumstance could aggravate the culpability of a father's calmly and strenuously inculcating on his son the duties of seduction and intrigue, it is the fact of that son's unfortunate position in the world being the result of that father's own transgression. And when one reflects on the mature age and latterly enfeebled health of the careful unwearied preacher of such a code, the effect is truly most disgusting.

Henry Lord Brougham, 1845, "Collective Edition of
Lord Chesterfield's Letters," Quarterly Review, vol. 76, p. 482

Though as a letter-writer he never equals Johnson at his best, yet in his general level he surpasses him. There is, indeed, more variety in Johnson's letters from the great variety of subjects on which he writes. Nevertheless, in the very uniformity of Chesterfield's there is a certain counter-balancing advantage. Not only are our attention and interest never distracted by sudden transitions, but, moreover, there is a real pleasure in seeing the wonderful dexterity with which, though playing on so few strings, he so rarely repeats the same tune.

George Birkbeck Hill, 1898, Eighteenth Century Letters,
Introduction, p. xxix

GENERAL

The Chesterfield whom we chiefly love to study is therefore a man of wit and of experience, who had devoted himself to business and essayed all the parts of political life only in order to learn their smallest details, and to tell us the result; it is he who, from his youth, was the friend of Pope and of Bolingbroke, the introducer of Montesquieu and of Voltaire into England, the correspondent of Fontenelle and of Madam de Tencin; he whom the Academy of Inscriptions admitted among its members, who combined the spirit of the two nations, and who, in more than one sparkling Essay, but especially in the Letters to his son, exhibits himself to us as a moralist alike amiable and consummate, and one of the masters of life. It is the Rochefoucauld of England whom we are studying.

C. A. Sainte-Beuve, 1850, English Portraits

With the exception of Machiavelli, we know of no other writer whose opinions and precepts have been so ridiculously misrepresented, and that, unfortunately for Chesterfield's fame, not merely by the multitude, but by men who are among the classics of our literature. . . . In times like the present we shall do well to turn occasionally to the writings of Chesterfield, and for other purposes than the acquisition of style. In an age distinguished beyond all precedent by recklessness, charlatanry, and vulgarity, nothing can be more salutary than communion with a mind and genius of the temper of his. We need the corrective—the educational corrective—of his refined good sense, his measure, his sobriety, his sincerity, his truthfulness, his instinctive application of aristocratic standards in attainment, of aristocratic touchstones in criticism. We need more, and he has more to teach us. We need reminding that life is success or failure, not in proportion to the extent of what it achieves in part, and in accidents, but in proportion to what it becomes in essence, and in proportion to its symmetry.

J. C. Collins, 1895, *Essays and Studies*, pp. 196, 262

As a letter-writer, in his few excursions into the essay, and in such other literary amusements as he permitted himself, he stands very high, and the somewhat artificial character of his etiquette, the wholly artificial character of his standards of literary, æsthetic, and other judgment, ought not to obscure his excellence. Devoted as he was to French, speaking and writing it as easily as he did English, he never Gallicised his style as Horace Walpole did, nor fell into incorrectnesses as did sometimes Lady Mary. The singular ease with which, not in the least ostentatiously condescending to them, he adjusts his writing to his boy correspondents is only one function of his literary adaptability. Nor is it by any means to be forgotten that Chesterfield's subjects are extremely various, and are handled with equal information and mother wit. He was not exactly a scholar, but he was a man widely and well read, and the shrewdness of his judgment on men and things was only conditioned by that obstinate refusal even to entertain any enthusiasm, anything high-strung in ethics, æsthetics, religion, and other things, which was characteristic of his age.

George Saintsbury, 1898, *A Short History of
English Literature*, p. 644

OLIVER GOLDSMITH
1730?-1774

Born, at Pallas, Co. Longford, 10 Nov. 1730? Family removed to Lissoy, 1730. At village school, 1734-35; at school at Elphin, 1736-39; at Athlone, 1739-41; at Edgeworthstown, 1741-44. To Trin. Coll., Dublin, as Sizar, 11 June 1744; Symth Exhibition, 1747; B. A., 27 Feb. 1749. With his mother at Ballymahon, 1749-51. Rejected as a clergyman, 1751. Private tutorship, 1751-52. To Edinburgh to study medicine, autumn of 1752. To Leyden, 1754. Travelled on the Continent, 1755-56. Possibly took M. B. degree at Louvain or Padua. Returned to London, Feb. 1756. Set up in practice as physician. Master at school at Peckham, winter of 1756 to 1757. Contrib. to *Monthly Review,* April to Sept., 1757, Dec. 1758; to *Literary Mag.,* Jan. 1757, Jan. to May, 1758; to *Critical Review,* Nov. 1757, Jan. to Aug., 1759, March 1760; to *The Busybody,* Oct. 1759. Ed. *Lady's Mag.,* 1759-60. Friendship with Johnson begun, 1761. Contrib. to *The Public Ledger,* Jan. to Feb. 1760; to *The British Mag.,* Feb. 1760 to Jan. 1763. Visit to Bath for health, 1762. Removed to Islington, winter of 1762. Tried again to set up as physician, 1765. Settled in Temple, 1767; lived there till death. *The Good-natured Man* produced at Covent Garden, 29 Jan. 1768; *She Stoops to Conquer,* Covent Garden, 15 March 1773; *The Grumbler* (adapted from Sedley), Covent Garden, 8 May 1773. Contrib. to *Westminster Mag.,* Jan. to Feb. 1773; to *Universal Mag.,* April 1774. Died, in London, 4 Apr. 1774. Buried in the Temple. WORKS: *Memoirs of a Protestant* (anon.), 1758; *Enquiry into the Present State of Polite Learning* (anon.), 1759; *The Bee* (anon.; 8 nos.), 1759; *A History of the Seven Years' War,* 1761; *A Poetical Dictionary* (anon.), 1761; *History of Mecklenburgh,* 1762; *The Mystery Revealed,* 1742 (1762); *A Citizen of the World* (anon.), 1762; *Life of Richard Nash* (anon.), 1762; *The Art of Poetry on a new Plan* (anon.; attrib. to Goldsmith), 1762; *The Martial Review* (anon.), 1763; *An History of England* (anon.), 1764; *The Traveller,* 1765; *Essays,* 1765; *The Vicar of Wakefield* (2 vols.), 1766; *History of Little Goody Two-Shoes* (anon. attrib. to Goldsmith), 1766; *The Good-natured Man,* 1768; *The Roman History* (2 vols.), 1769 (abridged by Goldsmith, 1772); *The Deserted Village,* 1770; *The Life of Thomas Parnell,* 1770; *Life of . . . Viscount Bolingbroke* (anon.), 1770; *The History of England* (4 vols.) 1771 (abridged, 1774); "Threnodia Augustalis," 1772; *She Stoops to Conquer,* 1773; *Retaliation,* 1774 (2nd to 5th edns. same year); *The Grecian History* (2 vols.), 1774; *A History of the Earth* (8 vols.), 1774. POSTHUMOUS: *Miscellaneous Works,* 1775; *The Haunch of Venison,* 1776; *A Survey of Experimental Philosophy* (2 vols.), 1776; *Poems and Plays,* 1777; *Poetical and Dramatic Works,* 1780; *The Captivity,* 1836; *Asem, the Man-Hater,* 1877. He *translated*: (under pseud. of "James Willington") Bergeracs' *Memoirs of a Protestant,* 1758; Plutarch's *Lives* (with J. Collyer), 1762; Formey's *Concise History of Philosophy,* 1766; Scarron's *Comic Romance,* 1776; and *edited*: Newbery's *Art of Poetry,* 1762; *Poems for Young Ladies* (anon.), 1767; *Beauties of English Poesy,* 1767; *T. Parnell's Poems,* 1770.

R. Farquharson Sharp, 1897, *A Dictionary of English Authors,* p. 114

SEE: *Collected Works,* ed. Arthur Friedman, 1965, 5 v.; *Selected Works,* ed. Richard Garnett, 1950; *New Essays,* ed. R. S. Crane, 1927; *Collected Letters,* ed. K. C. Balderston, 1928; Austin Dobson, *Life of Goldsmith,* 1888, rev. 1899; Ralph M. Wardle, *Oliver Goldsmith,* 1957.

PERSONAL

Of all solemn coxcombs Goldsmith is the first; yet sensible—but affects to use Johnson's hard words in conversation.

Thomas Warton, 1766, *Letter to Joseph Warton,* Jan. 22

He was such a compound of absurdity, envy, and malice, contrasted with
the opposite virtues of kindness, generosity, and benevolence, that he might
be said to consist of two distinct souls, and influenced by the agency of
a good and bad spirit.

Thomas Davies, 1780, *Life of Garrick,* vol. II, p. 147

It has been generally circulated and believed that he was a mere fool in
conversation; but, in truth, this has been greatly exaggerated. He had, no
doubt, a more than common share of that hurry of ideas which we often
find in his countrymen, and which sometimes produces a laughable confusion in expressing them. He was very much what the French call *un
étourdi,* and from vanity and an eager desire of being conspicuous wherever
he was, he frequently talked carelessly without knowledge of the subject,
or even without thought. His person was short, his countenance coarse and
vulgar, his deportment that of a scholar aukwardly affecting the easy gentleman. Those who were in any way distinguished, excited envy in him to so
ridiculous an excess, that the instances of it are hardly credible. When
accompanying two beautiful young ladies with their mother on a tour in
France, he was seriously angry that more attention was paid to them than
to him; and once at the exhibition of the "Fantoccini" in London, when
those who sat next to him observed with what dexterity a puppet was made
to toss a pike, he could not bear that it should have such praise, and exclaimed, "Pshaw! I can do it better myself." He, I am afraid, had no
settled system of any sort, so that his conduct must not be strictly scru-
tinised; but his affections were social and generous, and when he had money
he gave it away very liberally. His desire of imaginary consequence predominated over his attention to truth.

James Boswell, 1791-93, *Life of Johnson,* ed. Hill, vol. I, p. 477

A friend of his paying him a visit at the beginning of March 1759, found
him in lodgings there so poor and uncomfortable that he should not think
it proper to mention the circumstance, if he did not consider it as the
highest proof of the splendour of Doctor Goldsmith's genius and talents,
that by the bare exertion of their powers, under every disadvantage of
person and fortune, he could gradually emerge from such obscurity to the
enjoyment of all the comforts and even luxuries of life, and admission into
the best societies of London. The Doctor was writing his *Enquiry* &c., in
a wretched dirty room in which there was but one chair, and when he,
from civility, offered it to his visitant, himself was obliged to sit in the
window. While they were conversing, some one gently rapped at the door
and being desired to come in, a poor ragged little girl of very decent be-

haviour entered, who, dropping a curtsy, said "My mamma sends her compliments, and begs the favour of you to lend her a chamber-pot full of coals."

Thomas Percy, 1801-7? Memoir of Oliver Goldsmith, p. 60

His death, it has been thought, was hastened by "mental inquietude." If this supposition be true, never did the turmoils of life subdue a mind more warm with sympathy for the misfortunes of our fellow-creatures. But his character is familiar to every one who reads: in all the numerous accounts of his virtues and his foibles, his genius and absurdities, his knowledge of nature and his ignorance of the world, his "compassion for another's woe" was always predominant; and my trivial story of his humouring a froward child weighs but as a feather in the recorded scale of his benevolence.

George Colman, 1830, Random Records

"An inspired-idiot," Goldsmith, hangs strangely about him; though, as Hawkins says, "he loved not Johnson, but rather envied him for his parts; and once entreated a friend to desist from praising him, 'for in doing so,' said he, 'you harrow-up my very soul!' " Yet, on the whole, there is no evil in the "gooseberry-fool;" but rather much good; of a finer, if of a weaker, sort than Johnson's; and all the more genuine that he himself could never become *conscious* of it,—though unhappily never cease *attempting* to become so; the Author of the genuine *Vicar of Wakefield,* nill he, will he, must needs fly towards such a mass of genuine Manhood; and Dr. Minor keep gyrating round Dr. Major, alternately attracted and repelled.

Thomas Carlyle, 1832-69, "Boswell's Life of Johnson,"
Miscellanies, vol. IV, p. 86

Oliver Goldsmith, whose life and adventures should be known to all who know his writings, must be held to have succeeded in nothing that his friends would have had him succeed in. He was intended for a clergyman, and was rejected when he applied for orders; he practised as a physician, and never made what would have paid for a degree. What he was not asked or expected to do, was to write: but he wrote, and paid the penalty. His existence was a continued privation. The days were few, in which he had resources for the night, or dared to look forward to the morrow. There was not any miserable want, in the long and sordid catalogue, which in its turn and in all its bitterness he did not feel. He had shared the experience of those to whom he makes affecting reference in his *Animated Nature,* "people who die really of hunger, in common language of a broken heart;" and when he succeeded at the last, success was but a feeble sunshine on a rapidly approaching decay, which was to lead him, by its flickering light, to an early grave.

> John Forster, 1848-71, *The Life and Times of Oliver Goldsmith,*
> vol. I, p. 1

My trust is that Goldsmith lived upon the whole a life which, though troubled, was one of average enjoyment. Unquestionably, when reading at midnight, in the middle watch of a century which *he* never reached by one whole generation, this record of one so guileless, so upright, or seeming to be otherwise only in the eyes of those who did not know his difficulties, nor could have understood them,—when recurring also to his admirable genius, to the sweet natural gaiety of his oftentimes pathetic humour, and to the varied accomplishments, from talent or erudition, by which he gave effect to endowments so fascinating,—one cannot but sorrow over the strife which he sustained, and over the wrong by which he suffered. A few natural tears fall from every eye at the rehearsal of so much contumely from fools, which he faced unresistingly as one bareheaded under a hailstorm; and worse to bear than the scorn of fools was the imperfect sympathy and jealous self-distrusting esteem which he received to the last from friends. Doubtless he suffered much wrong; but so, in one way or other, do most men: he suffered also this special wrong, that in his lifetime he never was fully appreciated by any one friend: something of a counter movement ever mingled with praise for *him;* he never saw himself enthroned in the heart of any young and fervent admirer; and he was always overshadowed by men less deeply genial, though more showy than himself: but these things happen, and will happen forever, to myriads amongst the benefactors of earth. Their names ascend in songs of thankful commemoration, yet seldom until the ears are deaf that would have thrilled to the music. And these were the heaviest of Goldsmith's afflictions: what are likely to be thought such—viz. the battles which he fought for his daily bread—I do not number amongst them.

> Thomas De Quincey, 1848-57, *Oliver Goldsmith, Works,*
> ed. Masson, vol. IV, p. 289

His name has been used to glorify a sham Bohemianism—a Bohemianism that finds it easy to live in taverns, but does not find it easy, so far as one sees, to write poems like *The Deserted Village*. His experiences as an author have been brought forward to swell the cry about neglected genius— that is, by writers who assume their genius in order to prove the neglect. The misery that occasionally befell him during his wayward career has been made the basis of an accusation against society, the English constitution, Christianity—Heaven knows what. It is time to have done with all this

nonsense. Goldsmith resorted to the hack-work of literature when everything else had failed him; and he was fairly paid for it. When he did better
work, when he "struck for honest fame," the nation gave him all the honor
that he could have desired. With an assured reputation, and with ample
means of subsistence, he obtained entrance into the most distinguished
society then in England—he was made the friend of England's greatest in
the arts and literature—and could have confined himself to that society
exclusively if he had chosen. His temperament, no doubt, exposed him to
suffering; and the exquisite sensitiveness of a man of genius may demand
our sympathy; but in far greater measure is our sympathy demanded for
the thousands upon thousands of people who, from illness or nervous ex-
citability, suffer from quite as keen a sensitiveness without the consolation
of the fame that genius brings.

William Black, 1879, *Goldsmith* (*English Men of Letters*), p. 150

The Citizen of the World (1762)

Goldsmith's *Citizen of the World,* like all his works, bears the stamp of the
author's mind. It does not "go about to cozen reputation without the stamp
of merit." He is more observing, more original, more natural and picturesque than Johnson. His work is written on the model of the "Persian
Letters," and contrives to give an abstracted and somewhat perplexing view
of things, by proposing foreign prepossessions to our own, and thus strip-
ping objects of their customary disguises. Whether truth is elicited in his
collision of contrary absurdities, I do not know; but I confess the process
is too ambiguous and full of intricacy to be very amusing to my plain understanding. For light summer reading it is like walking through a garden full
of traps and pitfalls. . . . Beau Tibbs, a prominent character in this little
work, is the best comic sketch since the time of Addison; unrivalled in his
finery, his vanity, and his poverty.

William Hazlitt, 1818, *Lectures on the English Comic Writers,*
Lecture V

If in any of his writings Goldsmith could be truly said to have echoed the
measured tone of Johnson, it was probably in his most varied and agreeable
Citizen of the World, a work written at a period when his genius was
scarcely yet independent enough to allow of abjuring allegiance to the
reigning powers in literature. Yet even here an imitation is but sometimes
perceptible, and whenever it occurred was, perhaps, only the involuntary
work of the ear taking up the rich and elaborate harmony which it was
most accustomed to hear, and which, in those days, was seldom heard un-
accompanied by unqualified manifestations of almost rapturous approval.

. . . Of that gay and sparkling facetiousness which he himself was wont to admire so highly in other writers, the instances in this collection are innumerable.

Prof. Butler, 1836, "Gallery of Illustrious Irishmen,"
Dublin University Magazine, vol. 7, pp. 44, 45

The Traveller (1765)

Neither the ideas nor the imagery are very new or striking, but it is exquisitely versified (in the rhymed couplet); and its ease, elegance, and tenderness have made many passages pass into the memory and language of society. It is peculiarly admirable for the natural succession and connection of the thoughts and images, one seeming to rise unforcedly, and to be evolved, from the other. It is also coloured with a tender haze, so to say, of soft sentiment and pathos, as grateful to the mind as is to the eye the blue dimness that softens the tints of a distant mountain-range. It is a relief to the reader after Pope, in whom the objects stand out with too much sharpness, and in whom we see too much intense activity of the mere intellect at work. Pope is daylight; Goldsmith is moonlight.

Thomas B. Shaw, 1847, Outlines of English Literature, p. 275

To point out the beauties of this poem, would be to comment upon every passage; and, indeed, it may be safely left to the admiration of its myriad readers. Though praised by Johnson and successful at the start, passing in a few months through four editions, it grew, by degrees, like all works of genius, in popular estimation. The best test of its merit is that now, after the extraordinary production of a new race of poets of the highest powers in the nineteenth century, it is as secure of admiration as ever.

Evert A. Duyckinck, 1873, Portrait Gallery of
Eminent Men and Women,</i> vol. I, p. 39</div>

The Vicar of Wakefield (1766)

I received one morning a message from poor Goldsmith that he was in great distress, and as it was not in his power to come to me, begging that I would come to him as soon as possible. I sent him a guinea, and promised to come to him directly. I accordingly went as soon as I was drest, and found that his landlady had arrested him for his rent, at which he was in a violent passion. I perceived that he had already changed my guinea, and had got a bottle of Madeira and a glass before him. I put the cork into the bottle, desired he would be calm, and began to talk to him of the means by which he might be extricated. He then told me that he had a novel ready for the press, which he produced to me. I looked into it, and saw its merit;

told the landlady I should soon return, and having gone to a bookseller, sold it for sixty pounds. I brought Goldsmith the money, and he discharged his rent, not without rating his landlady in a high tone for having used him so ill.

Samuel Johnson, 1763, Life by Boswell, ed. Hill, vol. I, p. 481

There are a hundred faults in this thing, and a hundred things might be said to prove them beauties. But it is needless. A book may be amusing with numerous errors, or it may be dull without a single absurdity. The hero of this piece unites in himself the three greatest characters upon earth: he is a priest, a husbandman, and the father of a family. He is drawn as ready to teach, and ready to obey; as simple in affluence, and majestic in adversity. In this age of opulence and refinement, whom can such a character please? Such as are fond of high life, will turn with disdain from the simplicity of his country fireside. Such as mistake ribaldry for humor, will find no wit in his harmless conversation; and such as have been taught to deride religion, will laugh at one whose chief stores of comfort are drawn from futurity.

Oliver Goldsmith, 1766, The Vicar of Wakefield, Advertisement

I have this very moment finish'd reading a novel call'd the *Vicar of Wakefield*. It was wrote by Dr. Goldsmith. His style is rational and sensible, and I knew it again immediately. This book is of a very singular kind—I own I began it with distaste and disrelish, having just read the elegant Letters of Henry,—the beginning of it, even disgusted me,—he mentions his wife with such indifference—such contempt—the contrast of Henry's treatment of Frances struck me—the more so, as it is real—while this tale is fictitious —and then the style of the latter is so elegantly natural, so tenderly manly, so unassumingly rational,—I own I was tempted to thro' the book aside— but there was something in the situation of his family, which if it did not interest me, at least drew me on—and as I proceeded, I was better pleased. —The description of his rural felicity, his simple, unaffected contentment— and family domestic happiness, gave me much pleasure—but still, I was not satisfied, a *something* was wanted to make the book satisfy me—to make me *feel* for the Vicar in ever line he writes, nevertheless, before I was half thro' the first volume, I was, as I may truly express myself, *surprised into tears,* and in the second volume I really sobb'd. It appears to me, to be impossible any person could read this book thro' with a dry eye, at the same time the best part of it is that which turns one's griefs out of doors, to open them to laughter.

Frances Burney, 1768, Early Diary, ed. Ellis, vol. I, p. 12

We had lately a poet of the same name with the person just mentioned, perhaps of the same family, but by no means of the same character. His writings, in general, are much esteemed; but his poetry is greatly admired. Few tragedies have been read with stronger emotions of pity than the distressful scenes in the *Vicar of Wakefield;* yet we cannot but regret that the author of the *Traveller* should have undervalued his genius so far as to write a romance.

James Granger, 1769-1824, *Biographical History of England,*
vol. IV, p. 40, note

Now Herder came [in 1770?] and together with his great knowledge brought many other aids, and the later publications besides. Among these he announced to us the *Vicar of Wakefield* as an excellent work, with the German translation of which he would make us acquainted by reading it aloud to us himself. . . . The delineation of this character [that of the "excellent Wakefield"] on his course of life through joys and sorrows, the ever-increasing interest of the story, by the combination of the entirely natural with the strange and the singular, make this novel one of the best which has ever been written. . . . I may suppose that my readers know this work, and have it in memory; whoever hears it named for the first time here, as well as he who is induced to read it again, will thank me.

Johann Wolfgang von Goethe, 1811-31, *From My Own Life,*
tr. Oxenford, vol. I, bk. x, pp. 368, 369

How contradictory it seems that this, one of the most delightful pictures of home and homefelt happiness should be drawn by a homeless man; that the most amiable picture of domestic virtue and all the endearments of the married state should be drawn by a bachelor, who had been severed from domestic life almost from boyhood; that one of the most tender, touching, and affecting appeals on behalf of female loveliness should have been made by a man whose deficiency in all the graces of person and manner seemed to mark him out for a cynical disparager of the sex.

Washington Irving, 1849, *Oliver Goldsmith,* p. 191

Dr. Primrose and his wife, Olivia and Sophia, Moses with his white stockings and black ribbon, Mr. Burchell and his immortal "Fudge," My Lady Blarney and Miss Carolina Wilhelmina Amelia Skeggs—have all become household words. The family picture that could not be got into the house when it was painted; the colt that was sold for a gross of green spectacles; the patter about Sanchoniathon, Manetho, Berosus, and Ocellus Lucanus, with the other humours of Mr. Ephraim Jenkinson—these are part of our stock speech and current illustration. Whether the book is still much read it would be hard to say, for when a work has, so to speak, entered into the blood of a literature, it is often more recollected and transmitted by oral tradition than actually studied. But in spite of the inconsistencies of the plot, and the incoherencies of the story, it remains, and will continue to be, one of the first of our English classics. Its sweet humanity, its simplicity, its wisdom and its common-sense, its happy mingling of character and Christianity, will keep it sweet long after more ambitious, and in many respects abler, works have found their level with the great democracy of the forgotten.

Austin Dobson, 1888, *Life of Oliver Goldsmith,* p. 118

It made its way, not because Goldsmith had written it, but by reason of its domesticity and the simple idyllic charm which attracts in any age. The story of good prevailing over evil as he told it was new-old, and the tale of sure reward for patient submission in adversity is as ancient as the Book of Job. Its motive is to enforce the truth that heroism of soul may rise triumphant over the vanities and trials of daily life.

James Gilbert Riggs, 1896, ed., *The Vicar of Wakefield,*
Introduction, p. 19

As a humorist, Goldsmith set himself squarely against his contemporaries, and, with what little gall there was in him, expressly against Sterne. He never twitches at our nerves with the sentimental scene, but relieves his deepest pathos with a kindly irony. To him there is no humor in the dash, the asterisk, the wink, and the riddle; his sentences always have their logic and their rhythm. He despises ribaldry, and implies, with a grain of truth, that Sterne is only a second Tom D'Urfey, one of the most profane of Restoration wits.

Wilbur L. Cross, 1899, *The Development of the
English Novel,* p. 80

The Deserted Village (1770)

What true and pretty pastoral images has Goldsmith in his *Deserted Village*! They beat all: Pope, and Phillips, and Spenser too, in my opinion;— That is, in the pastoral, for I go no farther.

Edmund Burke, 1780, *Letter to Shackleton,* May 6;
Correspondence, vol. II, p. 347

The Deserted Village is a poem far inferior to *The Traveller,* though it contains many beautiful passages. I do not enter into its pretensions to skill in poetical economy, though, in that respect, it contains a strange mixture of important truths. My business is with the poetry. Its inferiority to its predecessor [*The Traveller*] arises from its comparative want of compression, as well as of force and novelty of imagery. Its tone of melancholy is more sickly, and some of the descriptions which have been most praised are marked by all the poverty and flatness, and indeed are peopled with the sort of comic and grotesque figures, of a Flemish landscape.

Sir Samuel Egerton Brydges, 1808, Life of Goldsmith,
Censura Literaria

A little poem, which we passionately received into our circle, allowed us from henceforward to think of nothing else. Goldsmith's "Deserted Village" necessarily delighted every one at that grade of cultivation, in that sphere of thought. Not as living and active, but as a departed, vanished existence was described, all that one so readily looked upon, that one loved, prized, sought passionately in the present, to take part in it with the cheerfulness of youth. Highdays and holidays in the country, church consecrations and fairs, the solemn assemblage of the elders under the village linden-tree, supplanted in its turn by the lively delight of youth in dancing, while the more educated classes show their sympathy. How seemly did these pleasures appear, moderated as they were by an excellent country pastor, who understood how to smooth down and remove all that went too far,—that gave occasion to quarrel and dispute. Here again we found an honest Wakefield, in his well-known circle, yet no longer in his living bodily form, but as a shadow recalled by the soft mournful tones of the elegiac poet. The very thought of this picture is one of the happiest possible, when once the design is formed to evoke once more an innocent past with a graceful melancholy. And in this kindly endeavour, how well has the Englishman succeeded in every sense of the word! I shared the enthusiasm for this charming poem with Gotter, who was more felicitous than myself with the translation undertaken by us both; for I had too painfully tried to imitate in our language the delicate significance of the original, and thus had well agreed with single passages, but not with the whole.

Johann Wolfgang von Goethe, 1811-31, From My Own Life,
tr. Oxenford, bk. xii, vol. I, p. 474

The Deserted Village is, of all Goldsmith's productions, unquestionably the favorite. It carries back the mind to the early seasons of life, and reasserts the power of unsophisticated tastes. Hence, while other poems grow stale, this preserves its charm. . . . So thoroughly did the author revise *The Deserted Village,* that not a single original line remained. The clearness and warmth of his style is, to my mind, as indicative of Goldsmith's truth, as the candor of his character or the sincerity of his sentiments. It has been said of Pitt's elocution, that it had the effect of impressing one with the idea that the man was greater than the orator. A similar influence it seems to me is produced by the harmonious versification and elegant diction of Goldsmith.

Henry Theodore Tuckerman, 1846-51, *Thoughts on the Poets,*
pp. xxii, xxiii

It is in *The Deserted Village,* his best known poem, that he has most fully shown the grace and truthfulness with which he could touch natural scenes. Lissoy, an Irish village where the poet's brother had a living, is said to have been the original from which he drew. In the poem, the church which crowns the neighboring hill, the mill, the brook, the hawthorn-tree, are all taken straight from the outer world. The features of Nature and the works of man, the parsonage, the school-house, the ale-house, all harmonize in one picture, and though the feeling of desolation must needs be a melancholy one, yet it is wonderfully varied and relieved by the uncolored faithfulness of the pictures from Nature and the kindly humor of those of man. It is needless to quote from a poem which every one knows so well. The verse of Pope is not the best vehicle for rural description, but it never was employed with greater grace and transparency than in *The Deserted Village.* In that poem there is fine feeling for Nature, in her homely forms, and truthful descriptions of these, but beyond this Goldsmith does not venture. The pathos of the outward world in its connection with man is there, but no reference to the meaning of Nature in itself, much less any question of its relation to the Divine Being and a supersensible world.

John Campbell Shairp, 1877, *On Poetic Interpretation
of Nature,* p. 212

The matter is of more importance to him than the manner; and at the same time his ear for music, and familiar acquaintance with good models have enabled him to go on without jarring the reader's ear with crude or false lines. Figures of speech are introduced in sufficient variety, but always from well-understood sources, and never expressed in such a way as to cause any effort in following them or their application. We are not challenged to stop and admire new and glittering constructions, nor ingeniously improvised words. Common speech affords the most of his material; and thus his lines pass again into common speech, and enrich the thought of thousands who are unaffected by the more ambitious masters of verse. He is strikingly free from foreign airs, uses no metrical variations caught from the Continent, and yet, by skilfully varying his pauses, avoids monotony throughout. He has a poet's mastery of epithet. . . . *The Deserted Village* deserves our careful attention from the deep feeling in its thought, the music in its lines, and its entire freedom from affectation. It stands for itself, a graceful example of true English literature.

> Warren Fenno Gregory, 1894, ed. *Oliver Goldsmith's Traveller and Deserted Village*, pp. 43-44

The History of England (1771)

I have published, or Davies has published for me, an *Abridgement of the History of England,* for which I have been a good deal abused in the newspapers, for betraying the liberties of the people. God knows I had no thought for or against liberty in my head; my whole aim being to make up a book of a decent size, that, as Squire Richard says, *would do no harm to nobody.* However, they set me down as an arrant Tory, and consequently an honest man. When you come to look at any part of it, you'll say that I am a sore Whig.

> Oliver Goldsmith, 1772, *Letter to Bennet Langton,* Sept. 7

The History on the whole, however, was well received; some of the critics declared that English history had never before been so usefully, so elegantly, and agreeably epitomized; "and, like his other historical writings, it has kept its ground" in English literature.

> Washington Irving, 1849, *Oliver Goldsmith,* p. 301

As a historian, Goldsmith accomplishes all at which he aims. He does not promise much, but he does more than he promises. He takes, it is true, facts which had been already collected, but he shapes them with an art that is all his own.

> Henry Giles, 1850, *Lectures and Essays,* vol. I, p. 235

COMEDIES

Goldsmith in vain tried to stem the torrent by opposing a barrier of low humour, and dulness and absurdity, more dull and absurd than English sentimental Comedy itself.

> John Pinkerton (Robert Heron), 1785, *Letters of Literature,*
> p. 47

Goldsmith was, perhaps, in relation to Sheridan, what Vanburgh was to Congreve. His comedies turn on an extravagance of intrigue and disguise, and so far belong to the Spanish school. But the ease of his humorous dialogue, and the droll, yet true conception of the characters, made sufficient amends for an occasional stretch in point of probability. If all who draw on the spectators for indulgence, were equally prepared to compensate by a corresponding degree of pleasure, they would have little occasion to complain.

Sir Walter Scott, 1814-23, *The Drama*

His two admirable Comedies of *The Good Natured Man,* and *She Stoops to Conquer,* are the greenest spots in the Dramatic waste of the period of which we are speaking. They are worthy of the Author of *The Vicar of Wakefield;* and to praise them more highly is impossible. Wit without licentiousness; Humour without extravagance; brilliant and elegant dialogue; and forcible but natural delineation of character, are the excellencies with which his pages are prodigally strewn.

Henry Neele, 1827, *Lectures on English Poetry,* p. 152

Goldsmith's immediate predecessors were the playwrights of the sentimental school. His literary taste and keen sense of humour revolted against their general badness and their bathos, and he went back for models to the dramatists of the Restoration,—a term, be it observed, which has much more than a chronological significance,—and both Goldsmith and Sheridan may in a sense be taken to be the last representatives of the great Restoration School of Comedy.

Oswald Crawfurd, 1883, ed., *English Comic Dramatists,* p. 214

She Stoops to Conquer (1773)

Dr. Goldsmith has written a Comedy—no, it is the lowest of all farces. It is not the subject I condemn, though very vulgar, but the execution. The drift tends to no moral, no edification of any kind. The situations, however, are well imagined, and make one laugh, in spite of the grossness of the dialogue, the forced witticisms, and total improbability of the whole plan and conduct. But what disgusts me most is, that though the characters are very low, and aim at a lower humour, not one of them says a sentence that is natural or marks any character at all. It is set up in opposition to sentimental comedy, and is as bad as the worst of them.

Horace Walpole, 1773, *To Rev. William Mason,* May 27;
Letters, ed. Cunningham, vol. V, p. 467

The whole company pledged themselves to the support of the ingenious poet, and faithfully kept their promise to him. In fact he needed all that could be done for him, as Mr. Colman, then manager of Covent Garden theatre, protested against the comedy, when as yet he had not struck upon a name for it. Johnson at length stood forth in all his terrors as champion for the piece, and backed by us his clients and retainers demanded a fair trial. Colman again protested, but, with that salve for his own reputation, liberally lent his stage to one of the most eccentric productions that ever found its way to it, and *She Stoops to Conquer* was put into rehearsal. We were not over-sanguine of success, but perfectly determined to struggle hard for our author: we accordingly assembled our strength at the Shakespear Tavern in a considerable body for an early dinner, where Samuel Johnson took the chair at the head of a long table, and was the life and soul of the corps: the poet took post silently by his side with the Burkes, Sir Joshua Reynolds, Fitzherbert, Caleb Whitefoord and a phalanx of North-British pre-determined applauders, under the banner of Major Mills, all good men and true. Our illustrious president was in inimitable glee, and poor Goldsmith that day took all his raillery as patiently and complacently as my friend Boswell would have done any day, or every day of his life. In the meantime we did not forget our duty, and though we had a better comedy going, in which Johnson was chief actor, we betook ourselves in good time to our separate and allotted posts, and waited the awful drawing up of the curtain. As our stations were pre-concerted, so were our signals for plaudits arranged and determined upon in a manner, that gave every one his cue where to look for them, and how to follow them up. . . . All eyes were upon Johnson, who sate in a front row of a side box, and when he laughed everybody thought themselves warranted to roar. . . . We carried our play through, and triumphed not only over Colman's judgment, but our own.

Richard Cumberland, 1806, Memoirs, vol. I, pp. 366, 368, 369

That delightful comedy, *She Stoops to Conquer,* would indeed deserve a volume, and is the best specimen of what an English comedy should be. It illustrates excellently what has been said as to the necessity of the plot depending on the characters, rather than the characters depending on the plot, as the fashion is at present. . . . What a play! We never tire of it. How rich in situations, each the substance of a whole play! At the very first sentence the stream of humour begins to flow.

Percy Fitzgerald, 1870, Principles of Comedy and
Dramatic Effect, pp. 91, 98

He at least lived long enough to witness the brilliant beginning of a dramatic triumph which has lasted till our day, and which only one other comedy written since, *The School for Scandal,* can be said to have rivaled. Macaulay calls it "an incomparable farce in five acts;" its rollicking drollery and sparkling wit are fitting to amuse all generations, and its dramatic skill is a victory of true inventive genius.

George M. Towle, 1874, "Oliver Goldsmith," *Appleton's Journal,*
vol. 11, p. 461

GENERAL

We do not mean to insinuate that his lucubrations [*The Bee*] are so void of merit as not to deserve the public attention. On the contrary, we much confess ourselves to have found no inconsiderable entertainment in their perusal. His stile is not the worst, and his manner is agreeable enough, in our opinion, however it may have failed of exciting universal admiration. The truth is, most of his subjects are already sufficiently worn out.

William Kenrick, 1760, *Monthly Review,* vol. 22, p. 39

It is in the narrowness of his range, and in the close identity of his characters with his own heart and experience, that we are to find the main cause of Goldsmith's universal and unfading popularity. He had in himself an original to draw from, with precisely those qualities which win general affection. Lovable himself, in spite of all his grave faults, he makes lovable the various copies that he takes from the master portrait. His secret is this—the emotions he commands are pleasurable. He is precisely what Johnson calls him, *"affectuum lenis dominator"—potens* because *lenis.* He is never above the height of the humblest understanding; and, by touching the human heart, he raises himself to a level with the loftiest. He has to perfection what the Germans call *Anmuth.* His muse wears the zone of the Graces. . . . Whether you read *The Deserted Village, The Vicar of Wakefield. The Goodnatured Man,* or *The Citizen of the World,* you find at the close that much the same emotions have been awakened—the heart has been touched much in the same place. But with what pliant aptitude the form and mode are changed and disguised! Poem, novel, essay, drama, how exquisite of its kind! The humour that draws tears, and the pathos that provokes smiles, will be popular to the end of the world.

Edward Bulwer-Lytton, Lord Lytton, 1848-68, *Goldsmith,*
Miscellaneous Prose Works, vol. I, pp. 69, 70

DAVID HUME
1711-1776

Born, in Edinburgh, 26 April 1711. Probably educated at Edinburgh University. Lived in France, 1734-37. Settled at home, at Ninewells, Berwickshire, 1737. Tutor in household of Marquis of Annandale, April 1745 to April 1746. Sec. to Gen. St. Clair in expedition against Canada, 1746-47. With Gen. St. Clair on embassy to Austria and Italy, 1748. Returned to Ninewells, 1749. Removed with his sister to Edinburgh, 1751. Keeper of Advocates' Library, 28 Jan. 1752 to 1757. Prosecuted historical studies. To Paris, as Sec. to Ambassador, Earl of Hartford, Oct. 1763. Pension of £400, 1765. To England, bringing Rousseau with him, Jan. 1766. Returned to Edinburgh, same year. In London, as Under Secretary of State, 1767-68. Settled in Edinburgh, 1769. Died there, 25 Aug. 1776. Buried in Calton Hill Cemetery. WORKS: *A Treatise of Human Nature* (anon.), vols. i, ii, 1739; vol. iii, 1740; *Essays, moral and political* (2 vols., anon.), 1741-42; *Philosophical Essays concerning Human Understanding* (anon.), 1748; *A True Account of the behaviour . . . of Archibald Stewart* (anon.), 1748; *An Enquiry concerning the Principles of Morals*, 1751; *Political Discourses* 1752 (2nd edn. same year); *Essays and Treatises on Several Subjects* (4 vols.), 1753-54; *The History of England* [under the House of Stuart] (2 vols.), 1754-57; *Four Dissertations*, 1757; *The History of England under the House of Tudor* (2 vols.), 1759; *The History of England from the Invasion of Julius Caesar to the accession of Henry VII.* (2 vols.), 1762; *A Concise Account of the dispute between Mr. Hume and Mr. Rousseau* (anon.), 1766; *Scotticisms* (anon.), 1770. POSTHUMOUS: *Autobiography*, 1777; *Two Essays*, 1777; *Dialogues concerning Natural Religion*, 1779.

R. Farquharson Sharp, 1897, *A Dictionary of
English Authors*, p. 141

SEE: *Letters,* ed. J. Y. T. Greig, 1932, 2 v.; *New Letters,* ed. Raymond Klibansky and Ernest C. Mossner, 1954; Ernest C. Mossner, *Life of Hume,* 1954.

PERSONAL

Nature, I believe, never formed any man more unlike his real character than David Hume. The powers of physiognomy were baffled by his countenance; neither could the most skilful in that science pretend to discern the smallest trace of the faculties of his mind in the unmeaning features of his visage. His face was broad and flat, his mouth wide, and without any other expression than that of imbecility; his eyes vacant and spiritless; and the corpulence of his whole person was far better fitted to convey the idea of a turtle-eating alderman than that of a refined philosopher. His speech in English was rendered ridiculous by the broadest Scotch accent, and his French was, if possible, still more laughable; so that wisdom most certainly never disguised herself before in so uncouth a garb.

James Caulfeild, Earl of Charlemont, 1748, *Memoirs of
Political and Private Life by Hardy*, p. 8

At this time David Hume was living in Edinburgh and composing his *History of Great Britain*. He was a man of great knowledge, and of a social and benevolent temper, and truly the best-natured man in the world. He was branded with the title of Atheist, on account of many attacks on revealed religion that are to be found in his philosophical works, and in many places of his History,—the last of which are still more objectionable than the first, which a friendly critic might call only sceptical. Apropos of this, when Mr. Robert Adam, the celebrated architect, and his brother, lived in Edinburgh with their mother, an aunt of Dr. Robertson's, and a very respectable woman, she said to her son, "I shall be glad to see any of your companions to dinner, but I hope you will never bring the Atheist here to disturb my peace." But Robert soon fell on a method to reconcile her to him, for he introduced him under another name, or concealed it carefully from her. When the company parted she said to her son, "I must confess that you bring very agreeable companions about you, but the large jolly man who sat next me is the most agreeable of them all." "This was the very Atheist," said he, "mother, that you was so much afraid of." "Well," says she, "you may bring him here as much as you please, for he's the most innocent, agreeable, facetious man I ever met with." This was truly the case with him; for though he had much learning and a fine taste, and was professed a sceptic, though by no means an atheist, he had the greatest simplicity of mind and manners with the utmost facility and benevolence of temper of any man I ever knew. His conversation was truly irresistible, for while it was enlightened, it was naïve almost to puerility.

Alexander Carlyle, 1753, Autobiography, p. 221

The extreme gentleness of his nature never weakened either the firmness of his mind, or the steadiness of his resolutions. His constant pleasantry was the genuine effusion of good-nature and good-humour, tempered with delicacy and modesty, and without even the slightest tincture of malignity, so frequently the disagreeable source of what is called wit in other men. It never was the meaning of his raillery to mortify; and therefore, far from offending, it seldom failed to please and delight, even those who were the object of it. To his friends, who were frequently the objects of it, there was not perhaps any one of all his great and amiable qualities, which contribute more to endear his conversation. And the gaiety of temper, so agreeable in society, but which is so often accompanied with frivolous and superficial qualities, was in him certainly attended with the most severe application, the most extensive learning, the greatest depth of thought, and a capacity in every respect the most comprehensive. Upon the whole, I have always considered him, both in his lifetime and since his death, as approaching as nearly to the idea of a perfectly wise and virtuous man, as perhaps the nature of human frailty will permit.

Adam Smith, 1776, Letter to William Strahan, Nov. 9

Through the whole of the memorials of Hume's early feelings we find the traces of a bold and far-stretching literary ambition . . . "I was seized very early," he tells us in his *Own Life,* "with a passion for literature, which has been the ruling passion of my life, and a great source of my enjoyments." Joined to this impulse, we find a practical philosophy, partaking far more of the stoical than of that sceptical school with which his metaphysical writings have identified him; a morality of self-sacrifice and endurance for the accomplishment of great ends. . . . He was an economist of all his talents from early youth. No memoir of a literary man presents a more cautious and vigilant husbandry of the mental powers and acquirements. There is no instance of a man of genius who has wasted less in idleness or in unavailing pursuits. Money was not his object, nor was temporary fame; . . . but his ruling object of ambition, pursued in poverty and riches, in health and sickness, in laborious obscurity and amid the blaze of fame, was to establish a permanent name, resting on the foundation of literary achievements, likely to live as long as human thought endured, and mental philosophy was studied.

John Hill Burton, 1846, *Life and Correspondence of David Hume,* vol. I, pp. 17, 18

In a sense, he is inconsistently a thinker who scorns the ordinary levels of thought; a humorist who revels in the pleasures of the passing hour as if life were a play. These apparently contradictory features are as prominent as they have ever appeared in any human life—together they constitute the actual David Hume—philosopher and man of the world.

Henry Calderwood, 1898, *David Hume (Famous Scots Series),* p. 18

GENERAL

If we may judge of him by his writings, will scarcely be charged with the fault of having carried humility to an excess. A pity it is that he hath not made a better use of his abilities and talents, which might have laid a just foundation for acquiring the praise he seems so fond of, as well as rendered him really useful to the world, if he had been so industrious as to employ them in serving and promoting the excellent cause of religion, as he hath unhappily been in endeavouring to weaken and expose it.

John Leland, 1754-56, *A View of the Principal Deistical Writers,* p. 239

"Why, Sir, his style is not English; the structure of his sentences is French. Now the French structure and the English structure may, in the nature of things, be equally good. But if you allow that the English language is established, he is wrong. My name might originally have been Nicholson, as well as Johnson; but were you to call me Nicholson now, you would call me very absurdly."

Samuel Johnson, 1763, Life by Boswell, ed. Hill, vol. I, p. 508

Next comes the Scotch Goliath, David Hume; but where is the accomplished stripling who can cut off his most metaphysical head? Who is he that can stand up before him, and prove the existence of the universe and its Founder? He hath an adroiter wit than all his forefathers in philosophy if he will confound this uncircumcised. The long and dull procession of reasoners that have followed since have challenged the awful shade to duel, and struck the air with their puissant arguments. But as each new comer blazons "Mr. Hume's objections" on his pages, it is plain they are not satisfied the victory is gained. Now, though every one is daily referred to his own feelings as a triumphant confutation of the glozed lies of this deceiver, yet it would assuredly make us feel safer to have our victorious answer set down in impregnable propositions.

Ralph Waldo Emerson, 1823, Letters, ed. Cabot, vol. I, p. 104

Hume is always idiomatic, but his idioms are constantly wrong; many of his best passages are, on that account, curiously grating and puzzling: you feel that they are very like what an Englishman would say, but yet that after all, somehow or other, they are what he never would say,—there is a minute seasoning of imperceptible difference, which distracts your attention and which you are forever stopping to analyze.

Walter Bagehot, 1876, "Adam Smith as a Person," Works,
ed. Morgan, vol. III, p. 296

Hume's place in literature is not, at the present moment, adequate to what we know of his powers of intellect or to his originality as a thinker. He is ackowledged to be a great man, but he is very little read. His History, in fragments, and his Essay on Miracles, which still enjoys a kind of success of scandal, are all that the general reader knows of Hume. If we deplore this fact, it must be admitted that his cool and unimpassioned criticism of belief, his perpetual return to the destructive standpoint, yet without vivacity, as one who undermines rather than attacks an opposing body, his colourless grace, the monotony of his balanced and faultless sentences, offer to us qualities which demand respect but scarcely awaken zeal, and, in short, that Hume although a real is a somewhat uninspiring classic. His great merit as a writer is his lucidity, his perfectly straightforward and competent expression of the particular thing he has it on his mind to say.

Edmund Gosse, 1888, A History of Eighteenth Century
Literature, p. 299

A studied and artful—sometimes a strained—simplicity is the chief characteristic of his style. He never attempts the majestic periods of Johnson or Gibbon; while a certain air of stiffness and precision effectually prevents his being spirited on the one hand, or colloquial on the other. His prose flows on with a steady and even motion, which no obstacle ever retards, nor any passion ever agitates. In the whole of his writings there is scarce one of those outbursts of emotion which at times animate the pages even of the coolest metaphysicians. Scorn there is in abundance; but it is the amused and pitying contempt of a superior being who watches from afar the frailties and vices from which himself is consciously exempt. Enthusiasm, or righteous indignation, was a total stranger to Hume's cast of mind. But his sneer and his sarcasm, though by far less elaborate and less diligently sustained, are hardly less effective and pointed than Gibbon's. . . . Hume's vocabulary is copious and well chosen, but never picturesque. . . . Many men have written English prose with greater ease, fluency, and freedom, and many with greater dignity and effect; but few with more accuracy, and elegance of diction than David Hume.

J. H. Millar, 1895, *English Prose,* ed. Craik, vol. IV, pp. 187, 188

Hume is impeccable in paragraph unity from the point of view of subject analysis. His unity depends on the philosophic scheme, the previsedly careful articulation of framework. It is not the picturesque unity of Macaulay. In spite of occasional extreme sententiousness, and his very sparing use of sentence-connectives, Hume's coherence is always good. The sententiousness is never left unexplained. If the reader is ever delayed it is by the balance of the sentence, but he is never seriously checked by this. In Hume the formal balance breaks in upon the sequence as waves pass beneath a boat and lap it sharply, but only to drive it onward. Hume's favorite order is loose, with a tendency to eschew initiatory sentences. The topic sentence is likely to be somewhat indefinite, becoming clear with the first amplifying sentences. To sum up: Hume represents the long paragraph adapting itself to the Johnsonian balanced sentence. His integers of style are larger than Johnson's, but less unwieldy than Gibbon's. He is retrogressive in percentage of very short sentences.

Edwin Herbert Lewis, 1894, *The History of the English Paragraph,* p. 118

SAMUEL FOOTE

1720-1777

Born, in Truro, Jan. 1720 [?]; baptized 27 Jan. 1720. At school at Worcester. Matric, at Worcester Coll., Oxford, 1 July 1737; took no degree. Became an actor; first appeared at Haymarket Theatre, 6 Feb. 1744. Acted in Dublin same year. Acted in London, 1745-49. Lived in Paris, 1750-52. Acted in London, 1753-57; in Dublin, winter of 1757-58; in Edinburgh, spring of 1759; in Dublin, winter of 1759-60. Manager of Haymarket, 1760; of Drury Lane, 1761. Acted till 1766; in that year lost leg through accident. Granted patent to build a theatre. Opened new theatre in Haymarket, May 1767. Visited Dublin, 1768. Manager of Edinburgh theatre, 1770. Sold patent of London theatre, 16 Jan. 1777. Died, at Dover, 21 Oct. 1777. Buried in West Cloister of Westminster Abbey. WORKS: *The Genuine Memoirs . . . of Sir J. D. Goodere* [1741?]; *A Treatise on the Passions* [1747;] *The Roman and English Comedy Consider'd*, 1747; *Taste*, 1752; *The Englishman in Paris*, 1753; *The Knights*, 1754; *The Englishman Returned from Paris*, 1756; *The Author*, 1757; *The Minor*, 1760; *A Letter . . . to the Reverend Author of the "Remarks . . . on the Minor,"* 1760; *The Orators*, 1762; *The Comic Theatre; being a free Translation of all the best French Comedies, by S. Foote and others* (5 vols.), 1762; *The Lyar* (adapted from Corneille), 1764; *The Mayor of Garratt*, 1764; *The Patron*, 1764; *The Commissary*, 1765; *The Lame Lover*, 1770; *Apology for "The Minor,"* 1771; *A trip to Calais* (under pseud.: *Timothy Timbertoe*), 1775; *The Bankrupt*, 1776. POSTHUMOUS: *The Maid of Bath* (anon.), 1778; *The Devil upon Two Sticks*, 1778; *The Nabob*, 1778; *The Cozeners* (anon.), 1778; *The Capuchin*, 1778. COLLECTED WORKS: in 4 vols., 1763-78; in 3 vols., 1830. LIFE: *Memoirs* (anon.), (1778); by W. Cooke, 1805; by J. Bee, in 1830 edn. of *Works*.

> R. Farquharson Sharp, 1897, *A Dictionary of*
> *English Authors*, p. 101

SEE: Grzegory Sinko, *Samuel Foote: The Satirist of Rising Capitalism*, 1951.

PERSONAL

He was, perhaps, the only man among the set, totally independent of Johnson's monarchy; he had an intrepid wit and pleasantry of his own, and was fearless of any colloquial antagonist.

> George Colman, 1830, *Random Records*

Foote's clothes were, then, tawdily splashed with gold lace; which, with his linen, were generally bedawbed with snuff; he was a Beau Nasty. They tell of him that, in his young days, and in the fluctuation of his finances, he walked about in boots, to conceal his want of stockings, and that, on receiving a supply of money, he expended it all upon a diamond ring, instead of purchasing the necessary articles of hosiery.

> Richard Brinsley Peake, 1841, *Memoirs of the Colman Family*,
> vol. I, p. 395, note

The strength and predominance of Foote's humour lay in its readiness. Whatever the call that might be made upon it, there it was. Other men were humorous as the occasion arose to them, but to him the occasion was never wanting. Others might be foiled or disabled by the lucky stroke of an adversary, but he took only the quicker rebound from what would have laid them prostrate. To put him out was not possible.

John Forster, 1854, "Samuel Foote," *Quarterly Review,*
vol. 95, p. 487

And wittiest among them all, creating roars of laughter by his sallies, or his mimicry of some well-known actor or politician, was a young gentleman of family and fortune, at this time a student of the Inner Temple. Dressed in a frock-suit of green, and silver lace, bag wig, sword, bouquet, and point ruffles, he frequented the place daily, until the carriage of some woman of quality would drive to the door, and Mr. Samuel Foote being inquired for, he would hasten out, hat in hand, and ride away with his lady fair.

J. Fitzgerald Molloy, 1884, *The Life and Adventures of
Peg Woffington,* vol. I, p. 28

GENERAL

BOSWELL. "Foote has a great deal of humour?" JOHNSON, "Yes, Sir." BOSWELL. "He has a singular talent of exhibiting character" JOHNSON. "Sir, it is not a talent; it is a vice; it is what others abstain from. It is not comedy, which exhibits the character of a species, as that of a miser gathered from many misers: it is farce, which exhibits individuals."

Samuel Johnson, 1769, *Life* by Boswell, ed. Hill, vol. II, p. 109

Foote was certainly a great and fertile genius, superior to that of any writer of the age; his dramatic pieces were most of them, it is true, unfinished, and several of them little more than sketches; but they are the sketches of a master, of one who, if he had labored more assiduously, he could have brought them nearer to perfection. Foote saw the follies and vices of mankind with a quick and discerning eye; his discrimination of character was quick and exact; his humour pleasant, his ridicule keen, his satire pungent, and his wit brilliant and exuberant. He described with fidelity the changeable follies and fashions of the times; and his pieces, like those of Ben Jonson, were calculated to please the audience of the day; and for this reason posterity will scarcely know anything of them.

Thomas Davies, 1780, *Life of David Garrick,* vol. II

The plays of Foote, the modern Aristophanes, who ventured, by his powers of mimicking the mind as well as the external habits, to bring living persons on the stage, belong to this period, and make a remarkable part of its dramatic history. But we need not dwell upon it. Foote was an unprincipled satirist; and while he affected to be the terror of vice and folly, was only anxious to extort forbearance-money from the timid, or to fill his theatre at the indiscriminate expense of friends and enemies, virtuous or vicious, who presented foibles capable of being turned into ridicule. It is just punishment of this course of writing, that Foote's plays, though abounding in comic humorous dialogue, have died with the parties whom he ridiculed. When they lost the zest of personality, their popularity, in spite of much intrinsic merit, fell into utter decay.

Sir Walter Scott, 1814-23, *The Drama*

If *The Liar* be his cleverest, *The Mayor of Garratt* retained the largest and the longest popularity: but, alas! it is now consigned to the tomb of the ungenteels. It has not been revived for many years; and when that admirable actor, Dowton, last appeared in Major Sturgeon (and in which performance I can believe that he never was surpassed in richness of humour—even by the author himself), and when Russell played Jerry Sneak (who avowedly exceeded all his predecessors in the part), the piece was pronounced "low," and even hissed. Our "bear-leaders" in society "hates everything as is low; their bears shall dance only to the genteelest of tunes—'Water parted from the sea,' and 'The minute in *Harihadne*' "—and so they turned up their exclusive noses at the major's history of his campaign, and the death of Major Molasses.

Charles Cowden Clarke, 1872, "On the Comic Writers of England,"
Gentleman's Magazine, N. S., vol. 8, p. 315

Foote's prose tracts, like his letters, are forcibly, wittily, and logically written. It is, however, as a dramatist, a wit, and an actor that he has to be judged; in all these qualities he is noteworthy. No complete collection of his plays has been made, more than one of his pieces, chiefly his early entertainments, having never been printed. . . . As a rule the plays are invertebrate, and the manners they sketch are not to be recognized in the present day. Foote had, however, a keen eye to character, and on the strength of the brilliant sketches of contemporary manners which he afforded, and of the wit of the dialogue, they may be read with pleasure to this day. Foote's satire is direct and scathing. Much of it is directed against individuals, not seldom with no conceivable vindication, since Foote singled out those, such as Garrick, to whom he was under deepest obligations. During his lifetime and for some years subsequently Foote was known as the English Aristophanes. Without being deserved, the phrase is less of a misnomer than such terms ordinarily are. As an actor Foote seems to have attracted attention only in his own pieces. Tom Davies, who speaks with something not far from contempt of his general performances, praises his Bayes in *The Rehearsal*. In this, however, Foote, like Garrick, used to introduce allusions to contemporary events.

Joseph Knight, 1889, *Dictionary of National Biography,*
vol. XIX, p. 374

DAVID GARRICK
1717-1779

Born, in Hereford, 19 Feb. 1717. Educated at Lichfield Grammar School, 1727. At Lisbon for a short time to learn wine trade, 1727. Pupil of Samuel Johnson, at Edial, 1736. To London with Johnson, March 1737. Entered at Lincoln's Inn, 9 March 1737. Set up wine business with his brother, 1738. Play *Lethe* produced at Drury Lane, April 1740. Became an actor, 1741. Wrote plays, 1741-75. Played at Goodman's Fields Theatre, 1741-42; in Dublin, 1742; at Drury Lane, 1742-45; in Dublin in 1745 and 1746; at Covent Garden, 1745-47. Joint manager of Drury Lane with Lacy, 1747. Played at Drury Lane, 1747-63, 1765-76. Married Eva Marie Violetti, 22 June 1749. Visited Paris, 1752. Tour in France and Italy, 1763-65. Retired from stage, 1776. Buried in Westminster Abbey. WORKS: *The Lying Valet,* 1741; *Lethe,* 1741; *Lilliput* (anon.), 1747; *Miss in her Teens* (anon.), 1747; *To Mr. Gray on his Odes* (anon.), [1757?]; *The Guardian* (anon.), 1759; *The Enchanter* (anon.), 1760; *The Fribbleraid* (anon.), 1761; *The Farmer's Return from London* (anon.), 1762; *The Sick Monkey* (anon.), 1765; *The Clandestine Marriage* (with G. Colman), 1766; *Neck or Nothing* (anon.), 1766; *Cymon* (anon.), 1767; *A Peep behind the Curtain* (anon.), 1767; *Ode upon dedicating a Building . . . to Shakespeare* (anon.), 1769; *The Theatres* (anon.), 1772; *Love in the Suds* (anon.), 1772; *The Irish Widow* (anon.), 1772; *Albumazar* (anon.), 1773; *A Christmas Tale* (anon.), 1774; *The Theatrical Candidates* (anon.), 1775; *May Day* (anon.), 1775; *Bon Ton* (anon.), 1775; *The Fairies,* 1775. He *adapted* plays by Shakespeare, Beaumont and Fletcher, Wycherley, Jonson, Fagan, Southern, etc. COLLECTED WORKS: *Poetical Works* (2 vols.), 1785; *Dramatic Works* (3 vols.), 1798; *Private Correspondence* (2 vols.), 1831-32. LIFE: by T. Davies, 1780; by Murphy, 1801; by P. Fitzgerald, 1868, rev. 1899 (2 vols.); by Jos. Knight, 1894.

R. Farquharson Sharp, 1897, *A Dictionary of English Authors,* p. 108

SEE: *Letters of David Garrick and Georgiana, Countess Spencer, 1759, 1779,* ed. Earl Spencer and Christopher Dobson, 1961; Carola Oman, *David Garrick,* 1958; Kalman A. Burnim, *David Garrick, Director,* 1961.

PERSONAL

There is a little simple farce at Drury Lane, called *Miss Lucy in Town* in which Mrs. Clive mimics the Muscovita admirably, and Beard Amorevoli tolerably. but all the run is now after Garrick, a wine-merchant, who is turned player at Goodman's-Fields. He plays all parts, and is a very good mimic. His acting I have seen, and may say to you, who will not tell it again here, I see nothing wonderful in it—but it is heresy to say so; the Duke of Argyll says he is superior to Betterton.

Horace Walpole, 1742, Letter to Sir Horace Mann, May 26;
Letters, ed. Cunningham, vol. I, p. 168

I have known one little man support the theatrical world like a David Atlas upon his shoulders, but Préville can't do half as much here, though Mad. Clairon stands by him and sets her back to his. . . . You are much talked of here, and much expected, as soon as the peace will let you. These two last days you have happened to engross the whole conversation at the great houses where I was at dinner. 'Tis the greatest problem in nature in this meridian that one and the same man should possess such tragic and comic powers, and in such an equilibrio as to divide the world from which of the two Nature intended him.

Laurence Sterne, 1762, Letter to David Garrick from Paris

Garrick's appearance forms an epoch in the history of the English theatre, as he chiefly dedicated his talents to the great characters of Shakspeare, and built his own fame on the growing admiration of the poet. Before his time, Shakspeare had only been brought on the stage in mutilated and disfigured alterations. Garrick returned on the whole to the true originals, though he still allowed himself to make some very unfortunate changes. It appears to me that the only excusable alteration of Shakspeare is, to leave out a few things not in conformity to the taste of the time. Garrick was undoubtedly a great actor. Whether he always conceived the parts of Shakspeare in the sense of the poet, I from the very circumstances stated in the eulogies on his acting should be inclined to doubt. He excited, however, a noble emulation to represent worthily the great national poet; this has ever since been the highest aim of actors, and even at present the stage can boast of men whose histrionic talents are deservedly famous.

Augustus William Schlegel, 1809, Dramatic Art and Literature,
ch. xiii

He had no enduring hostility, however, his temper generally being devoid of gall. He carried caution to an excess. Davies says that he acquired through this a hesitation in speech which did not originally characterise him. As a rule he was fairly accessible to authors, and if he produced few masterpieces, the fault was in the writers. In dramatists generally he displayed genuine interest, and after his retirement he took great pains to advance the fortunes of Hannah More. In his disputes the impression conveyed is generally that he was in the right. He generally treated the ebullitions of mortified vanity on the part of authors with tenderness. He kept the masculine portion of his company in fair order, though the feminine portion was generally mutinous. He made many important reforms, some of them learned during his journeys abroad, in discipline, in stage arrangement, and in matters of costume, in which he effected some improvement, pleading as a not very convincing reason for going no further that the public would not stand it. In many cases of difficulty he showed magnanimity, which his enemies sought vainly to stamp as prudence. Fortune fluctuated during his managerial career, but the result was that the property he conducted increased steadily in value during his management, that he retired with a larger fortune than any English actor except Alleyn had made in a similar enterprise, and with the respect and friendship of all the best men of his epoch.

Joseph Knight, 1890, *Dictionary of National Biography,*
vol. XXI, p. 25

GENERAL

Garrick's portentous *Ode,* as you truly call it, has but one line of truth in it, which is where he calls Shakespeare the God *of our Idolatry;* for *sense* I will not allow it; for that which is so highly satirical, he makes the topic of his hero's encomium. The *Ode* itself is below any of Cibber's. Cibber's nonsense was something like sense; but this man's sense, whenever he deviates into it, is much more like nonsense.

William Warburton, 1769, *Letter to Hurd,* Sept. 23

As a writer, we can hardly tell what to say of his powers: we do not know, touching either character, thought, or expression, how much was really in *his* the plays of others. The two-act comedy, at least, was his own. Prologue was his chief province, and his fertility in such compositions, was inexhaustible. *Epigram* he made vigorous court to; and *epitaph,* in some instances, owned no superior. In the light measures of Prior he frolics like that poet himself, or Voltaire, or Gresset in the enchanting *Ver-Vert..*

James Boaden, 1831, *Private Correspondence of David Garrick,*
Memoir, p. lxiv

It is as an actor that Garrick appeals to us, and not as a dramatist. A list of the plays, which were assigned him, or the authorship of which he claimed, may be seen in the *Biographia Dramatica* of Baker, Reed and Jones, to which list of 39 pieces must be added an alteration of *Mahomet* and some similar experiments. A few of Garrick's plays have, as has been said, ingenuity of construction and vivacity. On the whole, like that of Christian in the *Pilgrim's Progress,* his march towards immortality will be the speedier and the more comfortable when the burden of his general dramas falls from him. His occasional verses are sometimes happy. What Johnson said of his talk is almost true of his verses—"Garrick's conversation is gay and grotesque. It is a dish of all sorts, but all good things. There is no solid meat in it: there is a want of sentiment in it." A curiously complex, interesting, and diversified character is that of Garrick. Fully to bring it before the world might have taxed his own powers of exposition.

Joseph Knight, 1894, *David Garrick*, p. 335

SAMUEL JOHNSON
1709-1784

1709, Sep. 18, Johnson born at Lichfield. 1728, goes to Oxford. 1735, translates Lobo's *Abyssinia,* Marries. 1737, goes to London with Garrick. 1738, publishes *London.* 1739, publishes two political pamphlets: *The Complete Vindication* and *Marmor Norfolciense.* 1740-3, writes *Debates in Magna Lilliputia* for *Gentleman's Magazine.* 1744, *Life of Mr. Richard Savage.* 1745, *Miscellaneous Observations on Macbeth.* 1747, *Plan for a Dictionary of the English Language.* 1748, writes *Vanity of Human Wishes.* 1749, *Vanity of Human Wishes* published, *Irene* (written 1736) acted. 1750-2, *The Rambler.* 1752, his wife dies. 1752-3, contributes to Hawkesworth's *Adventurer.* 1755, publishes *The Dictionary.* 1756, issues *Proposals for an Edition of Shakespeare.* 1758-60, writes *The Idler* for the *Universal Chronicle.* 1759, his mother dies; publishes *The Prince of Abyssinia.* 1762, granted a pension. 1763, meets Boswell. 1764, the Literary club is founded; Johnson meets the Thrales. 1765, *Edition of Shakespeare.* 1770, *The False Alarm.* 1771, *Thoughts on the Late Transactions respecting the Falkland Islands.* 1773, tour to Scotland and the Hebrides. 1774 *The Patriot,* tour to North Wales. 1775, *Taxation no Tyranny; Journey to the Western Islands.* 1776, *Political Tracts.* 1777, begins *Lives of Poets.* 1779, publishes four volumes of *Lives;* 1781, last six volumes of *Lives;* Thrale dies. 1784, Mrs. Thrale becomes Mrs. Piozzi; Dec. 13, Johnson dies. 1785, Johnson's *Prayers and Meditations* published; Boswell publishes *Journal of a Tour to the Hebrides;* 1788-9, Johnson's *Sermons.* 1791, *Boswell's Life of Johnson.* 1816, Johnson's *Diary in North Wales.*

Fred N. Scott, 1891, ed. *Rasselas,* p. 25

SEE: *Yale Edition of the Works of Samuel Johnson,* ed. Allen T. Hazen, Walter Jackson Bate, John M. Bullitt, Lawrence F. Powell, and others, 1958-65, 6 v.; *Samuel Johnson. Prose and Poetry,* ed. Mona Wilson, 1950;

The Letters of Samuel Johnson with Mrs. Thrale's Genuine Letters to Him, ed. R. W. Chapman, 1952, 3 v.; James L. Clifford, *Young Sam Johnson,* 1955; *The Life of Samuel Johnson, LL. D., by Sir John Hawkins, Knt.,* ed., abridged by Bertram H. Davis, 1961; William K. Wimsatt, *The Prose Style of Johnson,* 1941; James L. Clifford, *Johnsonian Studies, 1887-1950: a Survey and Bibliography,* 1951; E. L. McAdam, Jr., *Dr. Johnson and the English Law,* 1951; Jean H. Hagstrum, *Samuel Johnson's Literary Criticism,* 1952; Benjamin Beard Hoover, *Samuel Johnson's Parliamentary Reporting: Debates in the Senate of Lilliput,* 1953; Walter Jackson Bate, *The Achievement of Samuel Johnson,* 1955; James H. Sledd and Gwin J. Kolb, *Dr. Johnson's Dictionary: Essays in the Biography of a Book,* 1955; Arthur Sherbo, *Samuel Johnson, Editor of Shakespeare,* 1956; E. A. Bloom, *Samuel Johnson in Grub Street,* 1957; Frederick W. Hilles, ed., *New Light on Dr. Johnson: Essays on the Occasion of His 250th Birthday,* 1959; Donald J. Greene, *The Politics of Samuel Johnson,* 1960.

PERSONAL

He and another neighbour of mine, one Mr. Johnson, set out this morning for London together: Davy Garrick to be with you early the next week; and Mr. Johnson to try his fate with a tragedy, and to see to get himself employed in some translation, either from the Latin or the French. Johnson is a very good scholar and poet, and I have great hopes will turn out a fine tragedy writer.

Gilbert Walmsley, 1736-7, *Letter to Rev. Mr. Colson,* March 2

That great CHAM of literature.

Tobias George Smollett, 1759, *Letter to Wilkes,* March 16

I hope Johnson is a writer of reputation, because, as a writer, he has just got a pension of 300*l.* per annum. I hope, too, that he has become a friend to this constitution and the family on the throne, now he is thus nobly provided for; but I know he has much to *unwrite,* more to *unsay,* before he will be forgiven by the true friends of the present illustrious family for what he has been writing and saying for many years.

John Wilkes, 1762, *The North Briton,* No. 11, Aug. 14

The day after I wrote my last letter to you I was introduced to Mr. Johnson by a friend: we passed through three very dirty rooms to a little one that looked like an old counting-house, where this great man was sat at his breakfast. The furniture of this room was a very large deal writing-desk, an old walnut-tree table, and five ragged chairs of four different sets. I was very much struck with Mr. Johnson's appearance, and could hardly help thinking him a madman for some time, as he sat waving over his breakfast like a lunatic. He is a very large man, and was dressed in a dirty brown coat and waistcoat, with breeches that were brown also (though they had been crimson), and an old black wig: his shirt collar and sleeves were unbuttoned; his stockings were down about his feet, which had on them, by way of slippers, an old pair of shoes. He had not been up long when we called on him, which was near one o'clock: he seldom goes to bed till near two in the morning; and Mr. Reynolds tells me he generally drinks tea about an hour after he has supped. We had been some time with him before he began to talk, but at length he began, and, faith, to some purpose! everything he says is as *correct* as a *second edition:* 'tis almost impossible to argue with him, he is so sententious and so knowing.

Ozias Humphry, 1764, Letter to Rev. William Humphry, Sept. 19

He is, indeed, very ill-favoured; is tall and stout; but stoops terribly; he is almost bent double. His mouth is almost [constantly opening and shutting], as if he was chewing. He has a strange method of frequently twirling his fingers, and twisting his hands. His body is in continual agitation, *sea-sawing* up and down; his feet are never a moment quiet; and, in short, his whole person is in *perpetual motion.* His dress, too, considering the times, and that he had meant to put on his *best becomes,* being engaged to dine in a large company, was as much out of the common road as his figure; he had a large wig, snuff-coloured coat, and gold buttons; but no ruffles to his [shirt] doughty fists, and black worsted stockings. He is shockingly near-sighted, and did not, till she held out her hand to him, even know Mrs. Thrale.

Frances Burney, 1777, Letter to Mr. Crisp, March 28,
Early Diary, ed. Ellis, vol. II, p. 154

Dr. Johnson is as correct and elegant in his common converation as in his writings. He never seems to study either for thoughts or words; and is on all occasions so fluent, so well-informed, so accurate, and even eloquent, that I never left his company without regret. Sir Josh Reynolds told me that from his first outset in life, he had always had this character; and by what means he had attained it. He told him he had early laid it down, as a fixed rule, always to do his best, *on every occasion* and in *every company,* to impart whatever he new in the best language he could put it in; and that by constant practice, and never suffering any careless expression to escape him, or attempting to deliver his thoughts without arranging them in the clearest manner he could, it was now become habitual to him. I have observed, in my various visits to him, that he never relaxes in this respect. When first introduced I was very young; yet he was as accurate in his conversation as if he had been talking with the first scholar in England. I have always found him very communicative; ready to give his opinion on any subject that was mentioned. He seldom however starts a subject himself; but it is very easy to lead him into one.

Edmond Malone, 1783, *Maloniana,* ed. Prior, March, p. 92

His necessary attendance while his play was in rehearsal, and during its performance, brought him acquainted with many of the performers of both sexes, which produced a more favourable opinion of their profession than he had harshly expressed in his *Life of Savage.* With some of them he kept up an acquaintance as long as he and they lived, and was ever ready to show them acts of kindness. He for a considerable time used to frequent the *Green Room,* and seemed to take delight in dissipating his gloom, by mixing in the sprightly chit-chat of the motley circle then to be found there. Mr. David Hume related to me from Mr. Garrick, that Johnson at last denied himself this amusement, from considerations of rigid virtue; saying "I'll come no more behind your scenes, David; for the silk stockings and white bosoms of your actresses excite my amorous propensities."

James Boswell, 1791-93, *Life of Johnson,* ed. Hill, vol. I, p. 233

What Dr. Johnson said a few days before his death of his disposition to insanity was no new discovery to those who were intimate with him. The character of Imlac in *Rasselas,* I always considered as a comment on his own conduct, which he himself practised, and as it now appears very successfully, since we know he continued to possess his understanding in its full vigour to the last. Solitude to him was horror; nor would he ever trust himself alone but when employed in writing or reading. He has often begged me to go home with him to prevent his being alone in the coach. Any company was better than none; by which he connected himself with many mean persons whose presence he could command.

Sir Joshua Reynolds, 1792? *Life and Times of Sir Joshua Reynolds* by Leslie and Taylor, vol. II

Johnson grown old, Johnson in the fulness of his fame and in the enjoyment of a competent fortune, is better known to us than any other man in history. Everything about him, his coat, his wig, his figure, his face, his scrofula, his St. Vitus's dance, his rolling walk, his blinking eye, the outward signs which too clearly marked his approbation of his dinner, his insatiable appetite for fish-sauce and veal pie with plums, his inextinguishable thirst for tea, his trick of touching the posts as he walked, his mysterious practice of treasuring up scraps of orange-peel, his morning slumbers, his midnight disputations, his contortions, his mutterings, his gruntings, his puffings, his vigorous, acute, and ready eloquence, his sarcastic wit, his vehemence, his insolence, his fits of tempestuous rage, his queer inmates, old Mr. Levett and blind Mrs. Williams, the cat Hodge and the negro Frank—all are as familiar to us as the objects by which we have been surrounded from childhood. . . . The club-room is before us, and the table on which stands the omelet for Nugent and the lemons for Johnson. There are assembled those heads which live for ever on the canvas of Reynolds. There are the spectacles of Burke and the tall thin form of Langton; the courtly sneer of Beauclerk and the beaming smile of Garrick; Gibbon tapping his snuff-box, and Sir Joshua with his trumpet in his ear. In the foreground is that strange figure which is as familiar to us as the figures of those among whom we have been brought up—the gigantic body, the huge massy face, seamed with the scars of disease; the brown coat, the black worsted stockings, the gray wig with a scorched foretop; the dirty hands, the nails bitten and paired to the quick. We see the eyes and mouth moving with convulsive twitches; we see the heavy form rolling; we hear it puffing; and then comes the "Why, sir!" and the "What then, sir?" and the "No, sir!" and the "You don't see your way through the question, sir!"

Thomas Babington Macaulay, 1831, "Boswell's *Life of Johnson,*"
Edinburgh Review; Critical and Miscellaneous Essays

Dr. Johnson's fame now rests principally upon Boswell. It is impossible not to be amazed with such a book. But his "bow-wow" manner must have had a good deal to do with the effect produced;— for no one, I suppose, will set Johnson before Burke,—and Burke was a great and universal talker;—yet now we hear nothing of this except by some chance remarks in Boswell. The fact is, that Burke, like all men of genius who love to talk at all, was very discursive and continuous; hence he is not reported; he seldom said the short things that Johnson almost always did, which produce a more decided effect at the moment and which are so much more easy to carry off. Besides, as to Burke's testimony to Johnson's powers, you must remember that Burke was a great courtier; and after all, Burke said and wrote more than once that he thought Johnson greater in talking than writing, and greater in Boswell than in real life.

Samuel Taylor Coleridge, 1833, *Table Talk,* ed. Ashe,
July 4, p. 239

Dr. Johnson was a man of no profound mind,—full of English limitations, English politics, English Church, Oxford philosophy; yet having a large heart, mother-wit, and good sense which impatiently overleaped his customary bounds, his conversation as reported by Boswell has a lasting charm.

Conversation is the vent of character as well as of thought; and Dr. Johnson impresses his company, not only by the point of the remark, but also, when the point fails, because *he* makes it.

Ralph Waldo Emerson, 1880-83, *Clubs; Works,* Riverside ed., vol. VII, p. 223

Given thus, on the one hand, a man of vigorous intellect, strong, though controlled passions, and fascinating conversation, and, on the other, a woman of talent, able and quick to appreciate his merits, and let the two be thrown together intimately for the period of sixteen years, nothing would be more natural than for a feeling to spring up, at least on the part of the man, warmer than mere friendship. Difference of age counts for little in such cases for it is a common saying that the heart never grows old. A man in Johnson's position readily forgets how he actually appears to the woman who flatters and pleases him, and, conscious only of his own youthful feelings, is prone to imagine that he seems to her as young as he does to himself. There is no proof that Mrs. Thrale ever entertained any sentiment for Johnson other than the esteem which in Madame d'Arblay became reverent adoration. Indeed, when spoken to about her supposed passion for him some years afterwards by Sir James Fellows, she ridiculed the idea, saying that she always felt for Johnson the same respect and veneration as for a Pascal. But if the long-continued manifestation of these sentiments, coupled with the most assiduous devotion and tender, wifelike care, had not awakened in him some response beyond mere gratitude, he would have been the most insensible of beings. Love, moreover, is frequently the result of propinquity and habit, and to both these influences Johnson was subjected for more than sixteen years. If he misinterpreted the attentions he received, and was emboldened by them to hope for a return of the passion they aroused, he did only what many a wise man has done under the same circumstances, and will do again.

Thomas Hitchcock, 1891, "Dr. Johnson and Mrs. Thrale," *Unhappy Loves of Men of Genius,* p. 66

POEMS

Dr. Johnson, born no doubt with violent passions, yet with the organs of his senses, thro' which the fancy is stored, if not imperfect, surely far from acute, had from a very early age most cultivated his powers of ratiocination, till by degrees he grew to esteem lightly every other species of excellence: and carrying these ideas into poetry, he was too much inclined to think that to reason in verse, when the harmony of numbers, and especially if something of the ornament of poetical language, was added to the force of truth, was to attain the highest praise of the art.

Sir Samuel Egerton Brydges, 1800, ed. Phillips's Theatrum Poetarum Anglicanorum, Preface, p. xlii

The fame of Dr. Johnson would not have been less widely diffused if the few poetical productions contained in the following pages had never been written; and yet the "Two Satires," and the "Prologue for the Opening of Drury Lane Theatre," are noble productions; and would have been sufficient to throw no mean lustre on the reputation of an ordinary writer. He, like Pope, chose to be the poet of reason; not because he was deficient in imagination, for his Oriental fictions contain much of the elements of the most fanciful poetry, but his mind was so constituted that "he condemned all that had not a direct practical tendency." That he knew how to appreciate the creative faculty of the poet is evident from the character he has drawn of Shakspeare; and he would have done justice to Milton, if his prejudices against the man had not blinded his judgment to the merits of the poet. He had diligently studied the works of Dryden and Pope, and has caught the spirit, vigour and terseness of his great models. . . . Of his lyric effusions much cannot be said: they want the enthusiasm and feeling which is the soul of such compositions. When we recollect the imperfection of two of the senses, sight and hearing, in Johnson, we shall not be surprised that he has not a keen perception of the beauties of nature, or of the powers of harmony; his want of relish for descriptive poetry, and pastoral cannot therefore be wondered at; nor his want of success in his "Odes on the Seasons." He does not paint from nature, but from books.

S. W. Singer, 1822, British Poets, Chiswick, ed.,
vol. 67, pp. 148, 149

That his Tragedy <i>(Irene)</i> was a great failure on the stage has been already related; that it is of extreme dulness, of a monotony altogether insufferable, and therefore tires out the reader's patience quite as much as it did the auditor's, is true; that most of his lesser pieces are only things of easy and of fairly successful execution is likewise certain, with perhaps the exception of his verses on Robert Levett's death, which have a sweetness and tenderness seldom found in any of his compositions. But had he never written anything after the <i>Imitations of Juvenal,</i> his name would have gone down to posterity as a poet of great excellence,—one who only did not reach equal celebrity with Pope, because he came after him, and did not assiduously court the muse. In truth, these two pieces are admirable, both for their matter, their diction, and their versification. . . . Of Johnson's Latin verses it remains to speak, and they assuredly do not rise to the level of his English, nor indeed above mediocrity. The translation of Pope's *Messiah,* however, a work of his boyhood, gave a promise not fulfilled in his riper years.

Henry, Lord Brougham, 1845, Lives of Men of Letters
of the Time of George III

His work in verse is very small, and though all of it is scholarly and some elegant, it is universally composed in obedience to a very narrow and jejune theory of English versification and English poetics generally. Nothing perhaps but the beautiful epitaph on his friend Levett, and the magnificent statement of his religious pessimism in the *Vanity of Human Wishes,* distinctly transcends mediocrity.

George Saintsbury, 1898, A Short History of
English Literature, p. 615

London (1738)

Dr. Johnson's *London, a Satire,* is a noble poem. But his great moral genius was constrained in composition by the perpetual parody on his powerful prototype, Juvenal. To have shown so much genius and so much ingenuity at one and the same time, to have been so original even in imitation, places him in the highest order of minds. But his range was here circumscribed; for he had to move parallel with the Roman,—finding out in every passage corresponding and kindred sins,—and in order to preserve—which he did wondrously—the similitude—

> "To bridle in his struggling muse with pain,
> Which long'd to launch into a nobler strain."

John Wilson, 1828, "The Man of Ton," Blackwood's Magazine,
vol. 23, p. 835

London is marked by genuine public spirit; at the same time we see quite as much of the man as of the moralist in the poet's characteristic allusions to the penalties of poverty, his antipathy to the Whigs, and his dislike of foreigners. The story that "Thales" was meant for Savage, and that the occasion of the poem was the departure of the latter from London after his trial, is confuted by dates, but we may be sure that the poem gives us a real representation of Johnson's feelings as a struggling author and a political partisan.

William John Courthope, 1880, English Poets, ed. Ward,
vol. III, p. 246

Life of Savage (1744)

No finer specimen of literary biography existed in any language, living or dead; and a discerning critic might have confidently predicted that the author was destined to be the founder of a new school of English eloquence.

Thomas Babington Macaulay, 1843, "Samuel Johnson,"
Critical and Historical Essays

In its early days Johnson was the chief contributor to its pages. [*The Gentleman's Magazine*]. He had a room set apart for him at St. John's Gate, where he wrote as fast as he could drive his pen, throwing the sheets off, when completed, to the "copy" boy. The *Life of Savage* was written anonymously, in 1744, and Mr. Harte spoke in high terms of the book, while dining with Cave. The publisher told him afterwards: "Harte, you made a man very happy the other day at my house by your praise of 'Savage's Life.' " "How so? none were present but you and I." Cave replied, "You might observe I sent a plate of victuals behind the screen; there lurked one whose dress was too shabby for him to appear; your praise pleased him much."

Henry Curwen, 1873, A History of Booksellers, p. 59

It is the longest and most elaborate of Johnson's essays in biography, and may still be read with great pleasure, in spite of various patent faults. It recounted, with all detail, a scandal, into the truth of which Johnson had not taken the pains to inquire; it was but careless in the statement of fact which lay easily within the writer's circle of experience; and it treated with extreme indulgence a character which, in a stranger, would have called down the moralist's sternest reproof. The critical passages now escape censure only because so few in the present day read the works examined. But the little book was undeniably lively; it contained several anecdotes admirably narrated, and its graver parts displayed the development of Johnson's studied magnificence of language. Good biography was still rare in England, and *The Account of Savage* attracted a great deal of notice.

Edmund Gosse, 1888, A History of Eighteenth Century
Literature, p. 285

The Vanity of Human Wishes (1749)

The Vanity of Human Wishes is, in the opinion of the best judges, as high an effort of ethick poetry as any language can shew. The instances of variety of disappointment are chosen so judiciously and painted so strongly, that, the moment they are read, they bring conviction to every thinking mind. That of the scholar must have depressed the too sanguine expectations of many an ambitious student. That of the warrior, Charles of Sweden, is, I think, as highly finished a picture as can possibly be conceived.

James Boswell, 1791-93, Life of Samuel Johnson,
ed. Hill, vol. I, p. 225

The Vanity of Human Wishes, the subject of which is in a great degree founded on the Alcibiades of Plato, possesses not the point and fire which animates the *London.* It breathes, however, a strain of calm and dignified philosophy, much more pleasing to the mind, and certainly much more consonant to truth, than the party exaggeration of the prior satire. The poet's choice of modern examples, in place of those brought forward by the ancient bard, is happy and judicious; and he has everywhere availed himself, and in a style the most impressive, of the solemnity, the pathos, and sublime morality of the christian code. In consequence of this substitution of a purer system of ethics, and of a striking selection of characters, among which that of Charles of Sweden is conspicuously eminent, the whole has the air of an original, and, to be understood, requires not to be collated with its prototype.

> Nathan Drake, 1809, *Essays Illustrative of the Rambler,*
> *Adventurer, and Idler,* vol. I, p. 135

Read Johnson's *Vanity of Human Wishes,*—all the examples and mode of giving them sublime, as well as the latter part, with the exception of an occasional couplet. I do not so much admire the opening. I remember an observation of Sharpe's (the *Conversationist,* as he was called in London, and a very clever man), that the first line of his poem was superfluous, and that Pope (the very best of poets, I think), would have begun at once, only changing the punctuation,—

"Survey mankind from China to Peru."

The former line, "Let observation," &c., is certainly heavy and useless. But 'tis a grand poem—and so *true!* true as the tenth of Juvenal himself. The lapse of ages *changes* all things,—time—language—the earth—the bounds of the sea—the stars of the sky, and every thing "about, around, and underneath" man, *except man himself,* who has always been, and always will be, an unlucky rascal. The infinite variety of lives conduct but to death, and the infinity of wishes lead but to disappointment.

> Lord Byron, 1821, *Diary,* Ravenna, Jan. 9

Tennyson admired Samuel Johnson's grave earnestness, and said that certain of his couplets, for these qualities and for their "high moral tone," were not surpassed in English satire. However, he ventured to make merry over:

"Let observation, with extensive view,
Survey mankind, from China to Peru."

"Why did he not say 'Let observation, with extended observation, observe extensively'?"

> Alfred, Lord Tennyson, 1879, *A Memoir by His Son,* vol. II, p. 73

Its strong Stoical morality, its profound and melancholy illustrations of the old and ever new sentiment, *Vanitas Vanitatum,* make it perhaps the most impressive poem of the kind in the language.

Leslie Stephen, 1879, *Samuel Johnson (English Men of Letters),*
p. 35

Irene (1749)

Though uninteresting on the stage, was universally admired in the closet, for the propriety of the sentiments, the richness of the language, and the general harmony of the whole composition.

Arthur Murphy, 1792, *An Essay on the Life and
Genius of Samuel Johnson*

In his tragedy, the dramatis personæ are like so many statues "stept from their pedestal to take the air." They come on the stage only to utter pompous sentiments of morality, turgid declamation, and frigid similes. Yet there is throughout, that strength of language, that heavy mace of words, with which, as with the flail of Talus, Johnson lays everything prostrate before him.

Henry Francis Cary, 1821-24-45, *Lives of English Poets,* p. 90

There are several accounts extant by those who were present on the first night, but that which Dr. Adams gave Boswell is perhaps the most trust-worthy. "Before the curtain drew up there were catcalls whistling which alarmed Johnson's friends. The prologue, which was written by himself in a manly strain, soothed the audience, and the play went off tolerably till it came to the conclusion, when Mrs. Pritchard, the heroine of the piece, was to be strangled on the stage, and was to speak two lines with the bow-string round her neck. The audience cried out 'Murder! Murder!' She several times attempted to speak, but in vain. At last she was obliged to go off the stage alive." The author's annoyance at this interruption must have been a good deal alleviated by the triumph it gave him over Garrick, at whose suggestion the strangling scene had been arranged. Dr. Burney's version is more favourable, but he speaks of a curious story circulated at the time of the author's being "observed at the representation to be dissatisfied with some of the speeches and conduct of the play himself, and, like La Fontaine, expressing his disapprobation aloud." Old Aaron Hill, one of the heroes of *The Dunciad,* who had composed much bad poetry and worse prose, and whose critical judgment may be estimated by his prediction of his own posthumous fame and of Pope's speedy oblivion, wrote to Mallet: "I was at the anomalous Mr. Johnson's benefit, and found the play his proper representative; strong sense, ungraced by sweetness or decorum." Though Irene was not a great success, it escaped positive failure, and Johnson received from copyright and "author's nights," very nearly three hundred pounds.

Frederick Richard Charles Grant, 1887,
Samuel Johnson (*Great Writers*), p. 56

The Rambler (1750-52)

I am inexpressibly pleased with them. . . . I hope the world tastes them; for its own sake I hope the world tastes them. . . . I would not, for any consideration, that they should be laid down through discouragement.

Samuel Richardson, 1750, *Letter to Cave,* Aug. 9

The Rambler, is certainly a strong misnomer: he always plods in the beaten road of his predecessors, following the *Spectator* (with the same pace as a packhorse would do a hunter) in the style that is proper to lengthen a paper. These writers may, perhaps, be of service to the public, which is saying a great deal in their favour. There are numbers of both sexes who never read anything but such productions, and cannot spare time, from doing nothing, to go through a six-penny pamphlet. Such gentle readers may be improved by a moral hint, which, though repeated over and over, from generation to generation, they never heard in their lives. I should be glad to know the name of this laborious author.

Lady Mary Wortley Montagu, 1754, *Letter to the Countess
of Bute,* June 23; *Works,* ed. Dallaway, vol. IV, p. 220

The Rambler may be considered as Johnson's great work. It was the basis of that high reputation which went on increasing to the end of his days. The circulation of those periodical essays was not, at first, equal to their merit. They had not, like the "Spectators," the art of charming by variety; and indeed how could it be expected? The wits of Queen Anne's reign sent their contributions to the *Spectator;* and Johnson stood alone. A stage coach, says Sir Richard Steele, must go forward on stated days, whether there are passengers or not. So it was with the *Rambler,* every Tuesday and Saturday, for two years. In this collection Johnson is the great moral teacher of his countrymen; his essays form a body of ethics; the observations on life and manners are acute and instructive; and the papers, professedly critical, serve to promote the cause of literature. It must, however, be acknowledged, that a settled gloom hangs over the author's mind; and all the essays, except eight or ten, coming from the same fountain-head, no wonder that they have the raciness of the soil from which they spring.

Of this uniformity Johnson was sensible. . . . It is remarkable, that the pomp of diction, which has been objected in to Johnson, was first assumed in *The Rambler.* His *Dictionary* was going on at the same time, and, in the course of that work, as he grew familiar with technical and scholastic words, he thought that the bulk of his readers were equally learned; or at least would admire the splendour and dignity of the style.

> Arthur Murphy, 1792, *An Essay on the Life and*
> *Genius of Samuel Johnson*

The mass of intellectual wealth here heaped together is immense, but it is rather the result of gradual accumulation, the produce of the general intellect, labouring in the mine of knowledge and reflection, than dug out of the quarry, and dragged into the light by the industry and sagacity of a single mind. I am not here saying that Dr. Johnson was a man without originality, compared with the ordinary run of men's minds, but he was not a man of original thought or genius, in the sense in which Montaigne or Lord Bacon was. He opened no new vein of precious ore, nor did he light upon any single pebbles of uncommon size and unrivalled lustre.

> William Hazlitt, 1818, *Lectures on the English Comic Writers,*
> Lecture V

Dr. Johnson seems to have been really more powerful in discoursing *vivâ voce* in conversation than with his pen in hand. It seems as if the excitement of company called something like reality and consecutiveness into his reasonings, which in his writings I cannot see. His antitheses are almost always verbal only; and sentence after sentence in *The Rambler* may be pointed out to which you cannot attach any definite meaning whatever. In his political pamphlets there is more truth of expression than in his other works, for the same reason that his conversation is better than his writings in general. He was more excited and in earnest.

> Samuel Taylor Coleridge, 1833, *Table Talk,* ed. Ashe,
> Nov. 1, p. 266

It would not be easy to name a book more tiresome, indeed, more difficult to read, or one which gives moral lessons, in a more frigid tone, with less that is lively or novel in the matter, in a language more heavy and monotonous. The measured pace, the constant balance of the style, becomes quite intolerable; for there is no interesting truth to be inculcated remote from common observation, nor is there any attack carried on against difficult positions, nor any satirical warfare maintained either with opinions or with persons.

> Henry, Lord Brougham, 1845, *Lives of Men of Letters of*
> *the Time of George III*

The wonder is that Johnson should have managed to continue it for two years, and that with its many obvious defects he should have been able to win for it at last a very substantial popularity. Too much stress is sometimes laid on the pomposity of his diction. For serious topics, which were avowedly his chief aim, his style is well suited, and his use of a balanced, periodic structure, if ludicrous when misapplied, is certainly impressive when it is made the vehicle of his moralizings. . . . Johnson was far from being a pedant, but he wanted the agility to make a graceful descent from the pinnacles of art, and he had not the supreme requisite of being able to conceal the condescensions of learning.

> J. H. Lobban, 1896, *English Essays,* Introduction, pp. xli, xlii

Dictionary (1755)

I think the publick in general, and the republick of letters in particular, are greatly obliged to Mr. Johnson, for having undertaken, and executed, so great and desirable a work. Perfection is not to be expected from man; but if we are to judge by the various works of Johnson already published, we have good reason to believe, that he will bring this as near to perfection as any man could do. The *plan* of it, which he published some years ago, seems to be a proof of it. Nothing can be more rationally imagined, or more accurately and elegantly expressed. I therefore recommend the previous perusal of it to all those who intend to buy the Dictionary, and who, I suppose, are all those who can afford it. . . . It must be owned, that our language is, at present, in a state of anarchy, and hitherto, perhaps, it may not have been the worse for it. During our free and open trade, many words and expressions have been imported, adopted, and naturalized from other languages, which have greatly enriched our own. Let it still preserve what real strength and beauty it may have borrowed from others; but let it not, like the Tarpeian maid, be overwhelmed and crushed by unnecessary ornaments. The time for discrimination seems to be now come. Toleration, adoption, and naturalization have run their lengths. Good order and authority are now necessary. But where shall we find them, and, at the same time, the obedience due to them? We must have recourse to the old Roman expedient in times of confusion, and chuse a dictator. Upon this principle, I give my vote for Mr. Johnson to fill that great and arduous post. And I hereby declare, that I make a total surrender of all my rights and privileges in the English language, as a free-born British subject, to the said Mr. Johnson, during the term of his dictatorship. Nay more, I will not only obey him, like an old Roman, as my dictator, but, like a modern Roman, I will implicitly believe in him as my Pope, and hold him to be infallible while in the chair, but no longer. More than this he cannot well require; for, I presume, that obedience can never be expected, when there is neither terrour to enforce, nor interest to invite it. . . . But a Grammar, a Dictionary, and a History of our Language through its several stages, were still wanting at home, and importunately called for from abroad. Mr. Johnson's labours will now, I dare say, very fully supply that want, and greatly contribute to the farther spreading of our language in other countries. Learners were discouraged, by finding no standard to resort to; and, consequently, thought it incapable of any. They will now be undeceived and encouraged.

Philip Dormer Stanhope, Lord Chesterfield,
The World, 1754, Nov. 28, Dec. 5

Johnson's Dictionary is a most important, and, considered as the work of one man, a most wonderful performance. It does honour to England, and to human genius; and proves, that there is still left among us a force of mind equal to that which formerly distinguished a Stephanus or a Varro. Its influence in diffusing the knowledge of the language, and retarding its decline, is already observable:

Si Pergama dextra
Desendi possent, etiam hac defensa fuissent.

And yet, within the last twenty years, and since this great work was published, a multitude of new words have found their way into the English tongue, and, though both unauthorised and unnecessary, seem likely to remain in it.

James Beattie, 1769, Remarks on the Usefulness of
Classical Learning

The definitions have always appeared to me such astonishing proofs of acuteness of intellect and precision of language, as indicate a genius of the highest rank. This it is which marks the superiour excellence of Johnson's *Dictionary* over others equally or even more voluminous, and must have made it a work of much greater mental labour than mere Lexicons, or *Word-books,* as the Dutch call them. They, who will make the experiment of trying how they can define a few words of whatever nature, will soon be satisfied of the unquestionable justice of this observation, which I can assure my readers is founded upon much study, and upon communication with more minds than my own. A few of his definitions must be admitted to be erroneous. Thus, *Windward* and *Leeward,* though directly of opposite meaning, are defined identically the same way; as to which inconsiderable specks it is enough to observe, that his Preface announces that he was aware there might be many such in so immense a work; nor was he at all disconcerted when an instance was pointed out to him. A lady once asked him how he came to define *Pastern* the *knee* of a horse: instead of making an elaborate defense, as she expected, he at once answered, "Ignorance, Madam, pure ignorance."

James Boswell, 1791-93, *Life of Samuel Johnson*

From a careful examination of this work, and its effect upon the language, I am inclined to believe that Johnson's authority has multiplied instead of reducing the number of corruptions in the English language. . . . I can assure the American public that the errors in Johnson's *Dictionary* are ten times as numerous as they suppose; and that the confidence now reposed in its accuracy is the greatest injury to philology that now exists. I can assure them further that if any man, whatever may be his abilities in other respects, should attempt to compile a new dictionary, or amend Johnson's, without a profound knowledge of etymology, he will unquestionably do as much harm as good.

Noah Webster, 1807, *A letter to Dr. David Ramsay,*
of Charleston, Respecting the Errors in Johnson's Dictionary

Had Johnson left nothing but his *Dictionary,* one might have traced there a great intellect, a genuine man. Looking to its clearness of definition, its general solidity, honesty, insight, and successful method, it may be called the best of all dictionaries. There is in it a kind of architectural nobleness; it stands there like a great solid square-built edifice, finished, symmetrically complete: you judge that a true builder did it.

Thomas Carlyle, 1841, *On Heroes and Hero-Worship*

The public, on this occasion, did Johnson full justice, and something more than justice. The best lexicographer may well be content if his productions are received by the world with cold esteem. But Johnson's Dictionary was hailed with an enthusiasm such as no similar work has ever excited. It was indeed the first dictionary which could be read with pleasure. The definitions show so much acuteness of thought and command of language, and the passages from poets, divines, and philosophers are so skilfully selected, that a leisure hour may always be very agreeably spent in turning over the pages. The faults of the book resolve themselves, for the most part, into one great fault. Johnson was a wretched etymologist. He knew little or nothing of any Teutonic language except English, which indeed, as he wrote it, was scarcely a Teutonic language; and thus he was absolutely at the mercy of Junius and Skinner.

Thomas Babington Macaulay, 1843, "Samuel Johnson,"
Critical and Historical Essays

The publication of Johnson's Dictionary was as the cloud no bigger than a man's hand, heralding the downfall of the patronage system; and the indignant though dignified letter of wounded pride and surly independence which he wrote on February 7, 1755, to the courtly Earl of Chesterfield, who had professed much but had performed little for him at a time when he was friendless and unknown, was as the shrill blast of a trumpeter proclaiming in plain and unmistakable terms that the winter of individual patronage was past and that the summer of public patronage had begun.

William Connor Sidney, 1891, *England and the English in the Eighteenth Century,* vol. II, p. 128

It was a great advance upon its predecessors. The general excellence of its definitions and the judicious selection of illustrative passages make it (as often observed) entertaining as well as useful for reference. Its most obvious defect arises from Johnson's ignorance of the early forms of the language and from the conception then natural of the purpose of a dictionary. Johnson (see his preface) had sensibly abandoned his first impression that he might be able to "fix the language," as he came to see that every living language must grow. He did not aim, however, at tracing the growth historically, but simply at defining the actual senses of words as employed by the "best authors." He held that the language had reached almost its fullest development in the days of Shakespeare, Hooker, Bacon, and Spenser, and thought it needless to go further back than Sidney. He also, as a rule, omitted living authors. The dictionary, therefore, was of no philological value, although it has been the groundwork upon which many later philologists have worked. Taking for granted the contemporary view of the true end of a dictionary, it was a surprising achievement, and made an epoch in the study of the language.

Leslie Stephen, 1892, *Dictionary of National Biography,* vol. XXX, p. 37

Rasselas (1759)

I wish I were not warranted in saying, that this elegant work is rendered, by its most obvious moral, of little benefit to the reader. We would not indeed wish to see the rising generation so unprofitably employed as the Prince of Abyssinia; but it is equally impolitic to repress all hope, and he who should quit his father's house in search of a profession, and return unprovided, because he could not find any man pleased with his own, would need a better justification than that Johnson, after speculatively surveying various modes of life, had judged happiness unattainable, and choice useless.

Sir John Hawkins, 1787, *The Life of Samuel Johnson,* p. 371

To those who look no further than the present life, or who maintain that human nature has not fallen from the state in which it was created, the instruction of this sublime story will be of no avail. But they who think justly, and feel with strong sensibility, will listen with eagerness and admiration to its truth and wisdom. Voltaire's *Candide,* written to refute the system of Optimism, which it has accomplished with brilliant success, is wonderfully similar in its plan and conduct to Johnson's Rasselas; Insomuch, that I have heard Johnson say, that if they had not been published so closely one after another that there was not time for imitation, it would have been in vain to deny that the scheme of that which came latest was taken from the other. Though the proposition illustrated by both these works was the same, namely, that in our present state there is more evil than good, the intention of the writers was very different. Voltaire, I am afraid, meant only by wanton profaneness to obtain a sportive victory over religion, and to discredit the belief of a superintending Providence: Johnson meant, by shewing the unsatisfactory nature of things temporal, to direct the hopes of man to things eternal. *Rasselas,* as was observed to me by a very accomplished lady, may be considered as a more enlarged and more deeply philosophical discourse in prose, upon the interesting truth, which in his *Vanity of Human Wishes* he had so successfully enforced in verse.

James Boswell, 1791-93, *Life of Samuel Johnson,*
ed. Hill, vol. I, p. 396

No prig shall ever persuade me that *Rasselas* is not a noble performance, in design and in execution. Never were the expenses of a mother's funeral more gloriously defrayed by a son than the funeral of Samuel Johnson's mother by the price of *Rasselas,* written for the pious purpose of laying her head decently and honourably in the dust.

John Wilson, 1829, *Noctes Ambrosianæ,* April

The reader who first attempts the "Abyssinian Candide" feels that he has imposed on himself a task rather than found a pleasure, or even a relaxation. The manner is heavy, and little suited to the occasion; the matter is of a very ordinary fabric, if it is safe and wholesome; there is nothing that shines except the author's facility of writing in a very artificial style, as soon as we are informed, by external evidence, of the whole having been written in a few nights. He, perhaps, had some kind of misgiving that it was not a successful effort, for he had never looked at it till two-and-twenty years after it was written, when a friend happening to have it who was travelling with him, Johnson read it with some eagerness.

Henry, Lord Brougham, 1845, *Lives of Men of Letters of
the Time of George III*

Edition of Shakespeare (1765)

The praise is due of having first adopted and carried into execution Dr. Johnson's admirable plan of illustrating Shakspeare by the study of writers of his own time. By following this track, most of the difficulties of the author have been overcome, his meaning (in many instances apparently lost) has been recovered, and much wild unfounded conjecture has been happily got rid of. By perseverance in this plan, he effected more to the elucidation of his author than any if not all his predecessors, and justly entitled himself to the distinction of being confessed the best editor of Shakspeare.

Isaac Reed, 1785-1803, ed. *Shakespeare*, vol. I, p. 3

Johnson compares him who should endeavour to recommend this poet by passages unconnectedly torn from his works, to the pedant in Hierocles who exhibited a brick as a sample of his house. And yet how little, and how very unsatisfactorily, does he himself speak of the pieces considered as a whole! Let any man, for instance, bring together the short characters which he gives at the close of each play, and see if the aggregate will amount to that sum of admiration which he himself, at his outset, has stated as the correct standard for the appreciation of the poet.

Augustus William Schlegel, 1809, *Dramatic Art and Literature,* Lecture XII

Garrick got a better hold of Shakespeare's thought than Dr. Johnson, the John Bull of erudition on whose nose Queen Mab must have skipped about queerly enough, whilst he was writing about the *Midsummer Night's Dream.* He certainly did not know why Shakespeare occasioned him more involuntary irritation and desire to sneeze than any other of the poets he criticised.

Heinrich Heine, 1838-95, *Notes on Shakespeare Heroines,* tr. Benecke, p. 34

When Johnson had issued his proposals twenty years before for an edition of Shakespeare, he pointed to a great novelty for the elucidation of the poet. His intuitive sagacity had discerned that a poet so racy and native required a familiarity both with the idiom and the manners of his age. He was sensible that a complete explanation of an author, not systematic and consequential, but desultory and vagrant, abounding in casual allusions and slight hints, is not to be expected from any single scholiast. He enumerates, however, the desiderata for this purpose; among which we find that of reading the books which Shakespeare read, and to compare his works with those of writers who lived at the same time, or immediately preceded, or immediately followed him. This project, happily conceived, inferred comprehensive knowledge in the proposer; but it was only a reverie,—a dim Pisgah view which the sagacity of the great critic had taken of that future Canaan, which he himself never entered. With this sort of knowledge, and these forgotten writers, which the future commentators of Shakespeare revelled in, Johnson remained wholly unacquainted. But what proved more fatal to the editorial ability of Johnson than this imperfect knowledge of the literature and the manners of the age of Shakespeare, was that the commentator rarely sympathized with the poet; for his hard-witted and unpliant faculties, busied with the more palpable forms of human nature, when thrown amid the supernatural and the ideal, seemed suddenly deserted of their powers: the magic knot was tied which cast our Hercules into helpless impotence; and, in the circle of imaginative creation, we discover the baffled sage resisting the spell by apologizing for Shakespeare's introduction of his mighty preternatural beings!

> Isaac Disraeli, 1841, "Shakespeare," *Amenities of Literature*

He would doubtless have admitted that it would be the height of absurdity, in a man who was not familiar with the works of Æschylus and Euripides to publish an edition of Sophocles. Yet he ventured to publish an edition of Shakspeare, without having ever in his life, as far as can be discovered, read a single scene of Massinger, Ford, Decker, Webster, Marlow, Beaumont, or Fletcher.

> Thomas Babington Macaulay, 1842, "Samuel Johnson,"
> *Critical and Historical Essays*

The larger portion of Johnson's Preface not only to a certain extent represented the tone of opinion in Johnson's age, but was written with so much pomp of diction, with such apparent candour, and with such abundant manifestations of good sense, that, perhaps more than any other production, it has influenced the public opinion of Shakspere up to this day. That the influence has been, for the most part, evil, we have no hesitation in believing.

> Charles Knight, 1849, *Studies of Shakspere*

It is giving the Doctor but little praise to say that he was a better editor than his Reverend predecessor. The majority of his emendations of the text were, nevertheless, singularly unhappy; and his notes, though often learned and sometimes sensible, were generally wanting in just that sort of learning and sense most needful for his task. Strange as it may seem, no one who himself appreciates Shakespeare, can read Johnson's comments and verbal criticisms upon his plays without the conviction that to the "great moralist," the grandest inspirations and most exquisitely wrought fancies of the great dramatist were as a sealed book. Many an humble individual whom the learned bear growled at—we do not hesitate to include even "Bozzy" himself—appreciated Shakespeare better than the literary dictator did.

Richard Grant White, 1854, *Shakespeare's Scholar*, p. 12

Journey to the Western Islands of Scotland (1775)

Dr. Johnson has just published his Journey thro' the western isles; I have read it, and you should read it. It is quite a sentimental Journey, divested of all natural history and antiquities; but full of good sense, and new and peculiar reflections.

Gilbert White, 1775, *Letter to Rev. John White*, Feb. 1;
Life and Letters of Gilbert White, ed. Holt-White, vol. I, p. 277

It is to Johnson that we go to see the life, the houses, the food, the garments —nay, the very speech and manners of the Scotsmen amongst whom he passed, and who were attracted to his personality by the magnetic force of a master-mind. . . . Johnson's Journal has the indescribable but irresistible charm of a monument of literary genius.

Sir Henry Craik, 1901, *A Century of Scottish History*,
vol. II, pp. 40, 41

Lives of the Poets (1779-81)

Johnson, to occasional felicity of diction, great purity of moral, and energy of thought, united a very considerable portion of critical acumen, and his Lives of Dryden and Pope are noble specimens of his powers of discrimination; yet, notwithstanding this rare combination of striking qualities, he was deficient in that sensibility to, and enthusiasm for, the charms of nature, in that relish for the simple and pathetic, so absolutely necessary to just criticism in poetry. To these defalcations were superadded an unreasonable antipathy to blank verse, a constitutional ruggedness of temper, and a bigoted, though well-meant, adhesion to some very extravagant political and religious tenets. His biographical details have suffered much from these peculiarities of temper and of taste; and a Milton, an Akenside, a Collins, a Dyer, and a Gray, might upbraid the Literary Dictator for his bitter and illiberal invective, his churlish and parsimonious praise, his great and various misrepresentations.

Nathan Drake, 1798-1820, *Literary Hours*, vol. I, No. xii, p. 160

There are parts of the *Lives of the Poets* which every lover of literary or moral justice would be glad to see stamped with an indelible brand of reprobation, with a disgrace so signal and conspicuous as to be a perpetual warning against the perversion of criticism and private history by political and religious bigotry and personal spleen.

John Foster, 1808, *Criticism on the English Poets, Essays*

Throughout his *Lives of the Poets,* he constantly betrays a want of relish for the more abstracted graces of the art. When strong sense and reasoning were to be judged of, these he was able to appreciate justly. When the passions or characters were described, he could to certain extent decide whether they were described truly or no. But as far as poetry has relation to the kindred arts of music and painting, to both of which he was confessedly insensible, it could not be expected that he should have much perception of its excellences. . . . When he is most strong, he gives us some good reason for his being so. He is often mistaken, but never trivial and insipid. It is more safe to trust to him when he commends than when he dispraises; when he enlarges the boundaries of criticism which his predecessors had contracted, than when he sets up new fences of his own.

Henry Francis Cary, 1821-24-45, *Lives of English Poets,*
pp. 84, 88

Dr. Johnson's *Lives of the Poets* are necessarily a prominent ornament of every library; as they have been the common theme of admiration of all countries. The style and the reflections are the chief charm of this popular work. Many of the facts must be cautiously admitted. Not that Johnson designedly falsified; but he always wanted time, diligence, and patience, in the collection of his materials; and, he rejoiced to find the fact as he *wished* to find it: without sufficiently weighing it in the balance of impartiality. He *hugged* every thing which he thought might throw a shade on a republican, a whig, or a dissenter; and spared no pains in executing such a picture in his most powerful and overwhelming colours. But toryism and orthodoxy neither require nor recommend such intemperate conduct. Even the very loose reports which had reached him of Dryden's funeral, were inserted without a suspicion of their veracity; and it remained for Mr. Malone (in his admirable edition of Dryden's prose works, to which a biography of the poet is prefixed) to dispel and dissipate this idle story as a barefaced fiction. But Johnson, had he been living, would not have surrendered it without a *growl*. Much that he has inserted in the life of Pope, and more in that of Milton, has been, and will continue to be, corrected and disproved: but who that reads Johnson's criticism on certain portions of the *Paradise Lost,* is not convinced that he is reading one of the most masterly performances of the human intellect? exhibiting an extent of power of conception—a vigour and felicity of diction—such as one knows not where to find equalled in any modern production. His life of Savage, the first in the order of execution, is considered to be the chef-d'œuvre; but this may be because it *was* the first; and because we have long known that Sir Joshua Reynolds read it with such intense interest, as to be unconscious that he was nearly dislocating his arm against a chimney piece, all the time! In consequence, he sought Johnson's acquaintance, and respected and loved the great philologist to his dying day. Still, the lives of Dryden and Pope abound with some of the happiest specimens of Johnson's powers of narrative and criticism. The whole set of Lives is indeed charming: fraught with wisdom and excellent taste.

> Thomas Frognall Dibdin, 1824, *The Library Companion,*
> p. 510, note

The Lives of the Poets has been by far the most popular of his works, and is doubtless the one for which he will be reverenced in future times. It afforded room for the display of every kind of talent; of his critical sagacity, his burning imagination, his learned research, and that memory by which he retained many curious anecdotes and traits of character, which would otherwise have been lost. No doubt a prejudiced air is given to the work by his political prepossessions, and he has done injustice to some distinguished names; but he wrote what he thought, and treated his subjects as he believed they deserved. It is now clear that he was wrong in some respects; but he did not err in malice, and how was it reasonable to expect, that he should follow the prejudices of others in preference to his own.

> W. B. O. Peabody, 1832, "Croker's *Boswell,*"
> *North American Review,* vol. 34, p. 103

The critic was certainly deficient in sensibility to the more delicate, the minor beauties of poetic sentiment. He analyzes verse in the cold-blooded spirit of a chemist, until all the aroma, which constituted its principal charm, escapes in the decomposition. By this kind of process, some of the finest fancies of the Muse, the lofty dithyrambics of Gray, the ethereal effusions of Collins, and of Milton too, are rendered sufficiently vapid. In this sort of criticism, all the effect that relies on *impressions* goes for nothing. Ideas are alone taken into the account, and all is weighed in the same hard, matter-of-fact scales of common sense, like so much solid prose.

> William Hickling Prescott, 1839, *Chateaubriand's Sketches of*
> *English Literature, Biographical and Critical Miscellanies*

Wrote the lives of the poets and left out the poets.

> Elizabeth Barrett Browning, 1842-63, *The Book of the Poets*

The lives of the Poets are, on the whole, the best of Johnson's works. The narratives are as entertaining as any novel. The remarks on life and on human nature are eminently shrewd and profound. The criticisms are often excellent, and, even when grossly and provokingly unjust, well deserve to be studied. For, however erroneous they may be, they are never silly. They are the judgments of a mind trammelled by prejudice and deficient in sensibility, but vigorous and acute. They therefore generally contain a portion of valuable truth which deserves to be separated from the alloy; and, at the very worst, they mean something, a praise to which much of what is called criticism in our time has no pretensions.

Thomas Babington Macaulay, 1843, "Samuel Johnson,"
Critical and Historical Essays

A cry was raised on more grounds than one against his Life of Milton. "I could thrash his old jacket," writes Cowper, "till I made his pension jingle in his pocket." All Cambridge was in arms against what Mackintosh has called "that monstrous example of critical injustice which he entitles the life of Gray." The same feeling was expressed against his criticism on Collins, and only less generally because the reputation of that poet was but then upon the rise. The friends of Lord Lyttelton were annoyed at the contempt, artful and studied as they called it, thrown upon the character of a nobleman who, with all the little foibles he might have, was, in their eyes, one of the most exalted patterns of virtue, liberality, and benevolence. Great displeasure was expressed with equal justice at his account of Thomson, while his censure of Akenside was thought by many what it really is, illiberal, and his criticism on Prior was condemned as "severe and unjust."

Peter Cunningham, 1854, ed. *Johnson's Lives of the Poets,*
vol. I, p. ix

His *Lives of the Poets* do indeed truly stand for what Boswell calls them, "the work which of all Dr. Johnson's writings will perhaps be read most generally and with most pleasure." And in the lives of the six chief personages of the work, the lives of Milton, Dryden, Swift, Addison, Pope, and Gray, we have its very kernel and quintessence; we have the work relieved of whatever is less significant, retaining nothing which is not highly significant, brought within easy and convenient compass, and admirably fitted to serve as a *point de repère,* a fixed and thoroughly known centre of departure and return, to the student of English literature. I know of no such first-rate piece of literature, for supplying in this way the wants of the literary student, existing at all in any other language; or existing in our own language, for any period except the period which Johnson's six lives cover.

A student cannot read them without gaining from them, consciously or unconsciously, an insight into the history of English literature and life.

> Matthew Arnold, 1878, "Johnson's *Lives," Macmillan's Magazine,*
> vol. 38, p. 155

It has generally been acknowledged that Johnson's life of Gray is the worst section in his delightful series. It formed the last chapter but one in the fourth volume of the *Lives of the Poets,* and was written when its author was tired of his task, and longed to be at rest again. It is barren and meagre of fact to the last degree.

> Edmund Gosse, 1882, *Gray (English Men of Letters)*, p. 215

This was a literary task for which he was exactly qualified. Originally he designed to give only a paragraph to minor poets, and four or five pages to the greater; but the flood of anecdote and criticism, as Macaulay happily says, overflowed the narrow channel; and sheets were expanded into volumes. It is instructive to note that, whereas the author's remuneration was three hundred guineas, the publishers reaped nearly six thousand pounds. *Sic vos non vobis!* With this supreme effort of his genius, which continues to be a text-book to literary students to the present day, Johnson's intellectual activity came to an end.

> R. W. Montagu, 1884, ed. *Johnsoniana*

It is no matter that Johnson's standards and view-points are extravagantly and exclusively of his time, so that occasionally—the cases of Milton and Gray are the chief—he falls into critical errors almost incomprehensible except from the historical side. Even these extravagances fix the critical creed of the day for us in an inestimable fashion, while in the great bulk of the Lives this criticism does no harm, being duly adjusted to the subjects. Johnson's estimate of Chaucer doubtless would have been, as his *Rambler* remarks on Spenser actually are, worthless, except as a curiosity. But of Dryden, of Pope, and of the numerous minor poets of their time and his, he could speak with a competently adjusted theory, with admirable literary knowledge and shrewdness, and with a huge store of literary tradition which his long and conversation-loving life had accumulated, and which would have been lost for us had he not written.

> George Saintsbury, 1898, *A Short History of*
> *English Literature*, p. 616

LETTERS

There is little (in *Johnson's Letters*) to gratify curiosity, or to justify impatience. They are such letters as ought to have been *written,* but ought never to have been *printed*. Still they are true letters of friendship, which are meant to show kindness rather than wit. Every place to which he was invited, every dose of physic he took, everybody who sent to ask how he did, is recorded. I can read them with a degree of interest, because I knew and loved the man, and besides was often a party concerned in the dinners he mentions. A few of these letters are very good; sometimes he is moral, and sometimes he is kind—two points of view in which it is always agreeable to consider Johnson. I am often named, never with unkindness, sometimes with favour. The impudence of editors and executors is an additional reason why men of parts should be afraid to die. Burke said to me the other day in allusion to the innumerable lives, anecdotes, remains, etc., which have been published of Johnson—"How many maggots have crawled out of that great body!"

Hannah More, 1788, Letter to Sister

He who found it so easy to talk, rarely took of his own accord to the task of composition. Nor will Johnson, in spite of the plea set up for him by the present editor, be ever known as a great letter-writer, hardly even as a good one. This is not saying that in these two volumes there is not much weighty observation, much acute comment, much that would be found interesting in itself, even did it not have the additional interest of having been written by the most famous literary man that England then possessed. But the indefinable charm of unconscious self-revelation which sets off the hastiest productions of the born letter-writer, is not to be found either among the valuable reflections or the dry details that make up no small share of this correspondence.

Thomas R. Lounsbury, 1892, "Dr. Johnson's Letters,"
The Nation, vol. 54, p. 415

GENERAL

No man had, like him, the faculty of teaching inferior minds the art of thinking. Perhaps other men might have equal knowledge; but few were so communicative.

Sir Joshua Reynolds, 1792? On Johnson's Influence

Johnson's style has pleased many from the very fault of being perpetually translatable; he creates an impression of cleverness by never saying anything in a common way.

Samuel Taylor Coleridge, 1818, "Style," Miscellanies Æsthetic
and Literary, ed. Ashe, p. 182

The structure of his sentences, which was his own invention, and which has been generally imitated since his time, is a species of rhyming in prose, where one clause answers to another in measure and quantity, like the tagging of syllables at the end of a verse; the close of the period follows as mechanically as the oscillation of a pendulum, the sense is balanced with the sound; each sentence, revolving round its centre of gravity, is contained within itself like a couplet, and each paragraph forms itself into a stanza. Dr. Johnson is also a complete balance-master in the topics of morality. He never encourages hope, but he counteracts it by fear; he never elicits a truth, but he suggests some objection in answer to it. He seizes and alternateley quits the clue of reason, lest it should involve him in the labyrinths of endless error: he wants confidence in himself and his fellows. He dares not trust himself with the immediate impressions of things, for fear of compromising his dignity; or follow them into their consequences, for fear of committing his prejudices. His timidity is the result, not of ignorance, but of morbid apprehension.

William Hazlitt, 1818, *Lectures on the English Comic Writers,*
Lecture V

His imagination was not more lively than was necessary to illustrate his maxims; his attainments in science were inconsiderable, and in learning far from the first class; they chiefly consisted in that sort of knowledge which a powerful mind collects from miscellaneous reading, a various intercourse with mankind. From the refinement of abstruse speculation he was withheld, partly, perhaps, by that repugnance to such subtleties which much experience often inspires, and partly also by a secret dread that they might disturb those prejudices in which his mind had found repose from the agitation of doubt. He was a most sagacious and severly pure judge of the actions and motives of men, and he was tempted by frequent detection of imposture to indulge somewhat of that cantemptuous scepticism, respecting the sincerity of delicate and refined sentiments, which affected his whole character as a man and writer.

Sir James Mackintosh, 1835, *Memoirs,* ed. Mackintosh,
vol. II, p. 166

A love of hard and learned words prevailed throughout; and a fondness for balanced periods was its special characteristic. But there was often great felicity in the expression, occasionally a pleasing cadence in the rhythm, generally an epigrammatic turn in the language, as well as in the idea. Even where the workmanship seemed most to surpass the material, and the *word-craft* to be exercised needlessly and the diction to run to waste, there was never any feebleness to complain of, and always something of skill and effect to admire. The charm of nature was ever wanting, but the presence of great art was undeniable. Nothing was seen of the careless aspect which the highest of artists ever give their masterpieces,—the produce of elaborate but concealed pains; yet the strong hand of an able workman was always marked; and it was observed, too, that he disdained to hide from us the far less labour which he had much more easily bestowed. There is no denying that some of Johnson's works, from the meagerness of the material and the regularity of the monotonous style, are exceedingly little adapted to reading. They are flimsy, and they are dull; they are pompous, and, though full of undeniable—indeed, self-evident—truths, they are somewhat empty; they are, moreover, wrapped up in a style so disproportioned in its importance, that the perusal becomes very tiresome, and is soon given up. This character belongs more especially to the *Rambler,* the object of such unmeasured praises among his followers, and from which he derived the title of the Great Moralist.

> Henry, Lord Brougham, 1845, *Lives of Men of Letters*
> *of the Time of George III*

Dr. Johnson's English style demands a few words. So peculiar is it, and such a swarm of imitators grew up during the half century of his greatest fame, that a special name—Johnsonese—has been often used to donate the march of its ponderous classic words. Yet it was not original, and not a many-toned style. There were in our literature, earlier than Dr. Johnson's day, writers who far outdid their Fleet Street disciple in recruiting our native ranks with heavy-armed warriors from the Greek phalanx and the Latin legion. Of these writers Sir Thomas Browne was perhaps the chief. Goldy, as the great Samuel loved to call the author of the *Deserted Village,* got many a sore blow from the Doctor's conversational sledge-hammer; but he certainly contrived to get within the Doctor's guard and hit him home, when he said, *"If you were to write a fable about little fishes, Doctor, you would make the little fishes talk like whales."* Macaulay tells us that when Johnson wrote for publication, he did his sentences out of English into Johnsonese.

> William Francis Collier, 1861, *A History of*
> *English Literature,* p. 349

Johnson first taught literary men the lesson of self-reliance and independence. Of all men of genius he is the only typical Englishman in whose strength, as also in his weakness, we see the national character. He was absolutely free from meanness and jealousy; a mighty soul which disdained tricks and subterfuges. "Like the Monument," in his own language, he stood upright and never stooped; no human power could have torn him from his base. Yet in this strongest of natures there was the gentlest affection, and the deepest reverence and humility. The giant has a heart like a woman or a child.

> Benjamin Jowett, 1871-72, *Life* by Abbott and Campbell,
> vol. II, p. 33

The style of Johnson, deemed so admirable at the time, seems to us now intolerably artificial, pedantic, constrained, and ponderous. His periods are carefully considered and balanced, its proportionate length, emphasis, and weight of heavy words being given to each member: homely and familiar words and phrases, however apposite or expressive, are rejected as undignified; antithesis does duty for brilliancy, and an occasional reversal of the syntax for variety. Each point is handled in the style of a solemn argument: step by step the demonstration proceeds, often leading to a conclusion which would have been admitted upon statement. His utterances are too frequently elaborately dressed-up commonplaces; and a laborious paragraph is employed to evolve a thought which might have been more forcibly expressed in a single terse idiomatic phrase. Thus, his style has no freshness, no individual coloring; we feel that it is the result of a multitude of heterogeneous minds, all ground together in the mill of omnivorous learning. Johnson's criticisms are learned, carefully weighed, but deficient in insight. He had no faculty of entering into other men's natures, and justly appreciating views which he did not himself hold. He was an infatuated, though perfectly honest and disinterested, Tory; and his intense political bias often led him into absurd injustice. In his eyes Voltaire was merely an infidel and cynical buffoon, and Rousseau a miscreant deserving the gallows. Being absolutely destitute of the poetic faculty, he lacked the essential qualification for a critic of poetry; and, while sure to detect a fallacy in reasoning, or a blemish in morals, the finer spirit of poetry he could not appreciate. On the other hand, his writings are everywhere pervaded by a perfect love of truth and justice, and an utter abhorence of falsehood and fraud; by a pure morality, enforced with the strongest emphasis; by a warm admiration for all things good and noble; and by the sincerest spirit of Christian piety; all which qualities he exemplified in his own brave and blameless life. His style, ponderous and constrained as it now appears, was not without many good qualities.

Richard Malcolm Johnston and William Hand Browne, 1872,
English Literature, p. 229

He taught others to look, like himself, through all the fleeting accidents of life to that in which a man can really live, and there were none who came to know him without learning how pure a spring of love and tenderness kept the whole nature fresh within. Firmly attached to the established Church, Johnson was a stout Tory on the religious side of his life and held the First Georges in such contempt as, it may be said, their lives had duly earned for them. But no delusions of party feeling dimmed his sense of human brotherhood, and of the large interests of humanity. Negro slavery was to his mind so gross a wrong that he startled a polite company one day with a a toast "to the next Insurrection of the Blacks." The political corruption of his time caused Johnson in his Dictionary, which appeared

in 1755, to define "Pension" as "a grant made to any one without an equivalent," and 'Pensioner" as "a slave of state, hired by a stipend to obey his
master." . . . Johnson's power had grown with the time, and he so far
shared the reaction against formalism in his style, that the English of his
Lives of the Poets differs distinctly from the English of his *Rambler*.

> Henry Morley, 1881, *Of English Literature in the Reign of*
> *Victoria with a Glance at the Past,* pp. 83, 85

In morals and criticism, it will ever be to his praise that he has assailed all
sentimentalism and licentiousness. His wit, eloquence, and logic were always
enlisted on the side of revealed religion, to deepen and extend, in heart
and practice, the human faith in God. In the fields of Literature, which were
now beginning to be cultivated on all sides, he did more than any of his
contemporaries to create a pure and invigorating atmosphere. His balanced
pomp of antithetic clauses soon had for others, as it had for him, an irresistible charm, and caused a complete revolution, for a time, in English
style. Unhappily, it was too often imitated by inferior writers, who had not
the glow to kindle the massive structure—little fishes talking like whales.
There has been no English prose writer, onward to the present day, whose
style has not been influenced by that of Johnson.

> Alfred H. Welsh, 1883, *Development of English Literature*
> *and Language,* vol. II, p. 178

I hold it more than happy that, during those continental journeys, in which
the vivid excitement of the greater part of the day left me glad to give
spare half-hours to the study of a thoughtful book, Johnson was the one
author accessible to me. No other writer could have secured me, as he did,
against all chance of being misled by my own sanguine and metaphysical
temperament. He taught me carefully to measure life, and distrust fortune;
and he secured me, by his adamantine commonsense, for ever, from being
caught in the cobwebs of German metaphysics, or sloughed in the English
drainage of them.

> John Ruskin, 1885, *Præterita,* vol. I, p. 416

The unfading interest in Dr. Johnson is one of the good signs of English
character. Men do not read his books, but they never cease to care about
him. It shows what hold the best and broadest human qualities always keep
on the heart of man. This man, who had to be coaxed into favor before a
request could be asked, and whose friends and equals were afraid to remonstrate with him except by a round-robin, was yet capable of the truest
delicacy, the purest modesty, the most religious love for all that was greater
and better than himself. But the great value of him was his reality. He was

a perpetual protest against the artificialness and unreality of that strange eighteenth century in which he lived.

Phillips Brooks, 1886-94, "Biography," *Essays and Addresses*, p. 433

Johnson has never been highly estimated as a critic, and on this point he has hardly received fair consideration. His hasty remarks, uttered in the heat of controversy, have been handed down as the result of deliberate judgment, but his literary instincts were more correct than has generally been imagined. Personal feelings undoubtedly often influenced his opinions, and he was unwilling to allow praise to writers of whose principles he disapproved. He could see little merit in the vigorous irony of Swift, and would never acknowledge him to be the author of *The Tale of a Tub!* but there is scarcely any writer from whom Johnson quoted so often in his dictionary. . . . On the other hand, he spoke too favourably of writers whose personal characters he respected. Beattie he loved, and he mentioned his writings in terms which now appear ludicrous. He was under obligations to Richardson, and thought highly of the moral tendency of his works, which in consequence he immensely over-rated, but he admitted that anybody who read Richardson's novels for the sake of the story would be compelled to hang himself, and forgot the fact that it is exactly *for the sake of the story* that novels are generally read, and that, however excellent may be the sentiment, the reader of a work of fiction will soon close the volume if there is no amusement in the plot.

Frederick Richard Charles Grant, 1887, *Life of Samuel Johnson*, pp. 154, 155

When the coffin was lowered into the grave, one able to read the outward signs of coming change might have seen buried with it the whole of the eighteenth century literature, as Johnson understood literature, and not to speak of frivolous productions such as those of Fielding and Smollett, who had also gone before. After Johnson's name in the list of English poets, scholars, and essayists may be drawn a thick black line such as in railway guides they use to indicate that here the train stops. Johnson's train of literature, which started merrily with Pope, Addison, Steele, and a glorious company of wits, had been running slowly of late, and has now come to a final stop. Not only was the old order changing, as happens continually, by the laws of being, but it was completely dead, and its successor as yet was not born. There was to be no more literature of the old school: nothing worth reading on the old lines was to be published; and the world must wait until the new men should begin their work with new thoughts, new ways of looking at things, and new forms of expression.

Sir Walter Besant, 1891, "Over Johnson's Grave," *Harper's Magazine*, vol. 82, p. 927

In style alone, we may justly claim that he is the vertebrate column of our prose. He could not accomplish the impossible. Once more I venture to express the conviction that the highest conceivable perfection of English prose was possible only to the Elizabethans, and that when the task passed unaccomplished from their hands, the hopes of it vanished beyond recall. But what Johnson could do, he did with consummate power. To him it was left to establish a code, to evolve order out of disorderly materials, to found a new ideal of style in absolutely logical precision, adding to that precision dignity and eloquence of force. To ascribe to him a slavish propensity to cumbrous and pendantic sesquipedalianism is to mistake the travesty for the original. His dictatorship in literature, based on native strength, was most unquestioned in the sphere of style; and it is not too much to say that all that is best in English prose since his day is his debtor in respect of not a few of its highest qualities, above all in respect of absolute lucidity, unfailing vigour, and saving common sense.

Henry Craik, 1895, ed., English Prose, Introduction,
vol. IV, p. 10

THOMAS WARTON
The Younger
1728-1790

Born, at Basingstoke, 1728. Matric. Trin. Coll., Oxford, 16 March, 1744; B. A., 1747; M. A., 1750; Fellow, 1751; Professor of Poetry, 1756-66; B. D., 7 Dec., 1767. Rector of Kiddington, 1771. F. S. A., 1771. Camden Prof. of Ancient Hist., Oxford, 1785-90. Poet Laureate, 1785-90. Died, at Oxford, 21 May 1790. Buried in Trin. Coll. Chapel. WORKS: *The Pleasures of Melancholy* (anon.), 1747; *Poems on several Occasions,* 1747; *The Triumph of Isis* (anon.), 1749; *A Description of . . . Winchester* (anon.), 1750; *Newmarket,* 1751; *Ode for Music,* 1751; *Observations on the Faerie Queene,* 1754; *A Companion to the Guide, and a Guide to the Companion* (anon.), 1760; *Life . . . of Ralph Bathurst* (2 vols.), 1761; *Life of Sir Thomas Pope,* 1772; *The History of English Poetry* (4 vols.), 1774-81; *Poems,* 1777; *Enquiry into the authenticity of the poems attributed to Thomas Rowley,* 1782; *Specimen of a History of Oxfordshire* (priv. ptd.), 1782; *Verses on Sir Joshua Reynolds' Painted Window at New College* (anon.), 1782. He *edited: The Union,* 1753; *Inscriptionum Romanorum Metricarum Delectus,* 1758; *The Oxford Sausage,* 1764; C. Cephalas' *Anthologiæ Græcæ,* 1766; *Theocritius' Works,* 1770; Milton's *Poems upon Several Occasions,* 1785. COLLECTED WORKS: *Poetical Works,* ed. by R. Mant, with *memoir* (2 vols.), 1802.

R. Farquharson Sharp, 1897, A Dictionary of
English Authors, p. 294

SEE: *The Three Wartons: A Choice of Their Verse,* ed. Eric Partridge, 1927; *The History of English Poetry: An Unfinished Continuation,* ed.

Rodney M. Baine, 1953; *Correspondence of Thomas Percy and Thomas Warton*, ed. M. G. Robinson and Leah Dennis, 1951; D. Nichol Smith, *Dr. Warton's History of English Poetry*, in *Proceedings of British Academy*, XV (1929).

PERSONAL

The grestest clod I ever saw, and so vulgar a figure with his clunch wig that I took him for a shoemaker at first.

Charlotte Ann Burney, 1783, *Journal*, ed. Ellis, Jan. 14, p. 301

His disposition, with some appearance of indolence, was retired and studious, and he fortunately acquired such preferments as enabled him to pursue his natural bent, and rove unmolested among the treasures of learning which his *alma mater* contains in such profusion. . . . He had less polish in his manner than his brother, Dr. Joseph, but the conversation of the two together was a rich banquet.

Alexander Chalmers, 1808-23, *The British Essayists*,
Preface to the Idler

There are few characters on which I look with so much complacent interest as Warton's. His temper was so sunshiny and benevolent; his manners were so simple; his erudition was so classical and various; his learning was so illuminated by fancy; his love of the country was so unaffected; his images were so picturesque; his knowledge of feudal and chivalrous manners was so minute, curious and lively; his absence of all worldly ambition and show was so attractive; his humour was so good-natured and innocent; his unaffected love of literature was so encouraging and exemplary—that I gaze upon his memory with untired satisfaction. What life can be more innocent, or more full of enjoyment, than a life spent among books, under the control of taste and judgment! I do not think that Warton was of the highest order of genius; he had not enough of warmth and invention; nor dare I say that he was the more happy for this want. But still what pure pleasure must have been continually experienced by him who could write the "Ode on Leaving Wynslade!"

Sir Samuel Egerton Brydges, 1834, *Autobiography*, vol. II, p. 194

History of English Poetry (1774-81)

I am extremely pleased with T. Warton's new edition of his Observations, and have let him know as much by Balguy. I am glad he is in earnest with his project of the History of English Poetry; he will do it well.

William Warburton, 1762, *Letter from a Late Eminent Prelate*,
Nov. 30, p. 338

Well, I have read Mr. Warton's book; and shall I tell you what I think of it? I never saw so many entertaining particulars crowded together with so little entertainment and vivacity. The facts are overwhelmed by one another, as Johnson's sense is by words: they are all equally strong. Mr. Warton has amassed all the parts and learning of four centuries, and all the impression that remains is, that those four ages had no parts or learning at all. There is not a gleam of poetry in their compositions between the Scalds and Chaucer. . . . I have dipped into Mr. Warton's second volume, which seems more unentertaining than the former. . . . I have very near finished Warton, but, antiquary as I am, it was a tough achievement. He has dipped into an incredible ocean of dry and obsolete authors of the dark ages, and has brought up more rubbish than riches; but the latter chapters, especially on the progress and revival of the theatre, are more entertaining; however, it is very fatiguing to wade through the muddy poetry of three or four centuries that had never a poet.

Horace Walpole, 1774-78, *Letter to Rev. W. Cole and Rev. W. Mason; Letters,* ed. Cunningham, vols. VI, p. 72, VII, pp. 50, 54

The late Mr. Warton, with a poetical enthusiasm which converted toil into pleasure, and gilded, to himself and his readers, the dreary subjects of antiquarian lore, and with a capacity of labour apparently inconsistent with his more brilliant powers, has produced a work of great size, and, partially speaking, of great interest, from the perusal of which we rise, our fancy delighted with beautiful imagery, and with the happy analysis of ancient tale and song, but certainly with very vague ideas of the history of English poetry. The error seems to lie in a total neglect of plan and system; for, delighted with every interesting topic which occurred, the historical poet perused it to its utmost verge, without considering that these digressions, however beautiful and interesting in themselves, abstracted alike his own attention, and that of the reader, from the professed purpose of his book. Accordingly, Warton's *History of English Poetry* has remained, and will always remain, an immense commonplace book of *memoirs to serve for such an history.* No antiquary can open it, without drawing information from a mine which, though dark, is inexhaustible in its treasures; nor will he who reads merely for amusement ever shut it for lack of attaining his end; while both may probably regret the desultory excursions of an author, who wanted only system, and a more rigid attention to minute accuracy, to have perfected the great task he has left incomplete.

Sir Walter Scott, 1804, *Critical and Miscellaneous Essays,* vol. I, p. 11

His work, indeed, is one which it will perhaps be always necessary to consult for its facts, its references, and its inferences; and though in many points it needs to be corrected, a long time will certainly elapse before it will be superseded. All this can be said, and be said truly. But while the substantial merits of the chapters on Chaucer need not be denied, they are very far from being perfectly satisfactory. They were marked in particular by the defects which invariably characterize the writings of both the Wartons. In certain ways these two scholars were the most irritating of commentators and literary critics. Their object was never so much to illustrate their author as to illustrate themselves. Instances of this disposition occur constantly in those sections of the *History of English Poetry* which treat of Chaucer. Warton is constantly wandering away from his legitimate subject to furnish information about matters that concerned very remotely, if at all, the business in hand. Much of the material he collected is introduced not to throw light upon the question under consideration, but to parade his knowledge. Still, it is the spirit that pervades the work which is especially objectionable. About it lingered the apologetic air of the eighteenth century, which talked as if it had something of a contempt for itself for taking interest in an age when neither language nor poetry had reached the supreme elegance by which both were then distinguished. Warton's words make upon the mind the impression that he admired Chaucer greatly, and was ashamed of himself for having been caught in the act. Whenever he abandons conventionally accepted ground, we recognize at once the timid utterance of the man who feels called upon to put in a plea in extenuation of the appreciation he has manifested.

> Thomas R. Lounsbury, 1891, *Studies in Chaucer,* vol. III, p. 246

Warton's work may be looked upon as a kind of classic fragment, the incompleteness of which has been emphasized by the glosses and alterations of three generations of commentators. . . . Had Warton chosen to follow the course contemplated by Pope and Gray, few men would have been better qualified to bring the undertaking to a successful issue. His reading was wide, his scholarship sound, his taste fine and discriminating; and though he had no pretensions to be called a great poet, his verse is at least marked by genuine poetic sensibility. Unfortunately he set about his work in the spirit of an antiquary, and in the patience, the industry, and the accuracy, required for this branch of knowledge, he was inferior to men who could not compare with him in capacity as a literary critic.

> W. J. Courthope, 1895, *A History of English Poetry,*
> vol. I, pp. xi, xii

At the outset, Warton's great undertaking was cautiously received. In so massive a collection of facts and dates, errors were inevitable. Warton's arrangement of his material was not flawless. Digressions were very numerous. His translation of old French and English was often faulty. In 1782

Ritson attacked him on the last score with a good deal of bitterness, and Warton, while contemptuously refusing to notice the censures of the "black-letter dog," was conscious that much of the attack was justified. Horace Walpole found the work unentertaining, and Mason echoed that opinion. Subsequently Sir Walter Scott, impressed by its deficiencies of plan, viewed it as "an immense commonplace book of memoirs to serve for" a history; and Hallam deprecated enthusiastic eulogy. On the other hand, Gibbon described it as illustrating "the taste of a poet and the minute diligence of an antiquarian," while Christopher North wrote appreciatively of the volumes as "a mine." But, however critics have differed in the past, the whole work is now seen to be impregnated by an intellectual vigor which reconciles the educated reader to almost all its irregularities and defects. Even the mediæval expert of the present day, who finds that much of Warton's information is superannuated and that many of the generalisations have been disproved by later discoveries, realises that nowhere else has he at his command so well furnished an armoury of facts and dates about obscure writers; while for the student of sixteenth century literature, Warton's results have been at many points developed, but have not as a whole been superseded. His style is unaffected and invariably clear. He never forgot that he was the historian and not the critic of the literature of which he treated. He handled with due precision the bibliographical side of his subject, and extended equal thoroughness of investigation to every variety of literary effort. No literary history discloses more comprehensive learning in classical and foreign literature, as well as in that of Great Britain.

> Sidney Lee, 1899, *Dictionary of National Biography,*
> vol. LIX, p. 434

GENERAL

One of the most beautiful [*Ode on Spring*] and original descriptive poems in our language, and strongly shews the force of poetical imitation in rendering objects that have no beauty in themselves highly beautfiul in description. I suppose there are few scenes less pleasing and picturesque in themselves than the view from Catherine Hill, near Winchester, over the bare adjacent downs, and on the Itchin at its feet, formed into a navigable canal, and creeping through a wide valley of flat water-meadow, intersected often at right angles by straight narrow water-courses. But hear the poet, and observe how the scene appears in the picture he has given of it, without changing the features of the original.

> Henry James Pye, 1788, *Commentary on Aristotle's Poetic*

In one department he is not only unequalled, but original and unprecedented: I mean in applying to modern poetry the embellishment of Gothic manners and Gothic arts; the tournaments and festivals, the poetry, music, painting, and architecture of "elder days." Nor can I here refrain from repeating, that, though engaged in the service, his talents were never prostituted to the undue praise of royalty; nor from adding as a topic of incidental applause, that, though he wanders in the mazes of fancy, he may always be resorted to as supplying at least an harmless amusement; and that with Milton and Gray, whom he resembled in various other points, he shares also this moral commendation, that his laurels, like theirs, are untainted by impurity, and that he has uniformly written (to use the words of another unsullied bard)

Verse that a Virgin without blush may read.

Richard Mant, 1802, *Poetical Works of Thomas Warton, Life,*
vol. I, p. clxi

Thomas Warton is in his poetry chiefly imitative, as was natural in so laborious a student of our early poetical literature. The edition of his poems which was published by his admirer and his brother's devoted pupil, Richard Mant, offers a curious example of a poet "killed with kindness;" for the apparatus of parallel passages from Spenser, Shakespeare, Milton, and others, is enough to ruin any little claim to originality which might have been put forward for him. . . . There are reasons why his genial figure should not be altogether excluded from a representative English anthology. It has often been said that his *History of English Poetry,* with Percy's *Reliques,* turned the course of our letters into a fresh channel; but what is more noticeable here is that his own poetry—or much of it, for he is not always free from the taint of psuedo-classicalism—instinctively deals with materials like those on which the older writers had drawn. In reaction against the didactic and critical temper of the earlier half of his century, he is a student of nature; he is even an "enthusiast," in Whitehead's sense.

Thomas Humphry Ward, 1880, *English Poets,* vol. III, p. 382

BENJAMIN FRANKLIN
1706-1790

Born at Boston, Mass., Jan. 17, 1706; Died at Philadelphia, April 17, 1790. A celebrated American philosopher, statesman, diplomatist, and author. He learned the printer's trade in the office of his elder brother James, and in 1729 established himself at Philadelphia as editor and proprietor of the *Pennsylvania Gazette.* He founded the Philadelphia library in 1731; began the publication of *Poor Richard's Almanac* in 1732; was appointed clerk of the Pennsylvania assembly in 1736; became postmaster of Philadelphia in 1737; founded the American Philosophical Society and the University of Pennsylvania in 1743 and in 1752 demonstrated by experiments made with a kite during a thunderstorm that lightning is a discharge of electricity, a discovery for which he was awarded the Copley medal by the Royal Society in 1753. He was deputy postmaster-general for the British colonies in America 1753-74. In 1754, at a convention of the New England colonies with New York, Pennsylvania, and Maryland, held at Albany, he proposed a plan, known as the "Albany Plan," which contemplated the formation of a self-sustaining government for all the colonies, and which, although adopted by the convention, failed of support in the colonies. He acted as colonial agent for Pennsylvania in England 1757-62 and 1764-75; was elected to the second Continental Congress in 1755; and in 1776 was a member of the committee of five chosen by Congress to draw up a declaration of independence. He arrived at Paris, Dec. 21, 1776, as ambassador to the court of France; and in conjunction with Arthur Lee and Silas Deane concluded a treaty with France, Feb. 6, 1778 by which France recognized the independence of America. In 1782, on the advent of Lord Rockingham's ministry to power, he began a correspondence with Lord Shelburne, secretary of state for home and colonies, which led to negotiations for peace; and in conjunction with Jay and Adams concluded with England the treaty of Paris, Sept. 3, 1783. He returned to America in 1785; was president of Pennsylvania 1785-88; and was a delegate to the constitutional convention in 1787. He left an autobiography, which was edited by John Bigelow in 1868. His works have been edited by Jared Sparks (10 vols., 1836-40) and John Bigelow (10 vols., 1887-1888).

> Benjamin E. Smith, 1894-97, *The Century Cyclopedia*
> *of Names,* p. 408

SEE: *Writings,* ed. A. H. Smyth, 1905-7, 10 v.; *Representative Selections,* ed. F. L. Mott and C. E. Jorgenson, 1936; *Autobiography,* ed. Max Farrand, 1949; Carl Van Doren, *Benjamin Franklin,* 1938.

PERSONAL

As to the charge of subservience to France, . . . two years of my own service with him at Paris, daily visits, and the most friendly and confidential conversations, convinced me it had not a shadow of foundation. He possessed the confidence of that government in the highest degree, insomuch that it may truly be said, that they were more under his influence than he under theirs. The fact is, that his temper was so amiable and conciliatory, his conduct so rational, never urging impossibilities, or even things unreasonably inconvenient to them, in short so moderate and attentive to their difficulties as well as our own, that what his enemies called subserviency I saw was only that reasonable disposition which, sensible that advantages are not all to be on one side, yielding what is just and and liberal, is the more certain of obtaining liberality and justice. Mutual confidence produces of course mutual influence, and this was all which subsisted between Dr. Franklin and the government of France.

> Thomas Jefferson, 1818, *Letter to Robert Walsh,* Dec. 4

Franklin enjoyed, during the greater part of his life, a healthy constitution, and excelled in exercises of strength and activity. In stature he was above the middle size; manly, athletic and well proportioned. His countenance, as it is represented in his portait, is distinguished by an air of serenity and satisfaction, the natural consequence of a vigorous temperament, of strength of mind, and conscious integrity. It is also marked, in visible characters, by deep thought and inflexible resolution. Very rarely shall we see a combination of features, of more agreeable harmony; an aspect in which the human passions are more happily blended or more favourably modified, to command authority, to conciliate esteem, or to excite love and veneration. His colloquial accomplishments are mentioned by those who knew him, in terms of the highest praise.

John Sanderson, 1820-28, *Biography of the Signers to the
Declaration of Independence,* vol. III, p. 132

With placid tranquility, Benjamin Franklin looked quietly and deeply into the secrets of nature. His clear understanding was never perverted by passion, or corrupted by the pride of theory. The son of a rigid Calvinist, the grandson of a tolerant Quaker, he had from boyhood been familiar not only with theological subtilities, but with a catholic respect for freedom of mind. Skeptical of tradition as the basis of faith, he respected reason, rather than authority; and, after a momentary lapse into fatalism, escaping from the mazes of fixed decrees and free will, he gained, with increasing years, an increasing trust in the overruling providence of God. Adhering to none "of all the religions" in the colonies, he yet devoutly, though without form, adhered to religion. But though famous as disputant, and having a natural aptitude for metaphysics, he obeyed the tendency of his age, and sought by observation to win an insight into the mysteries of being. . . . Never professing enthusiasm, never making a parade of sentiment, his practical wisdom was sometimes mistaken for the offspring of selfish prudence; yet his hope was steadfast, like that hope which rests on the Rock of Ages, and his conduct was as unerring as though the light that led him was a light from heaven. He ever anticipated action by theories of self-sacrificing virtue; and yet, in the moments of intense activity, he, from the highest abodes of ideal truth, brought down and applied to the affairs of life the sublimest principles of goodness, as noiselessly and unostentatiously as became the man who, with a kite and hempen string, drew the lightning from the skies.

George Bancroft, 1844, *History of the United States,*
vol. III, p. 378

Humor, indeed, he had so abundantly that it was almost a failing. Like Abraham Lincoln, another typical American, he never shrank from a jest. Like Lincoln, he knew the world well and accepted it for what it was, and made the best of it, expecting no more. But Franklin lacked the spirituality, the faith in the ideal, which was at the core of Lincoln's character. And here was Franklin's limitation: what lay outside of the bounds of common sense he did not see—probably he did not greatly care to see; but common sense he had in a most uncommon degree. One of his chief characteristics was curiosity—in the wholesome meaning of that abused word. He never rested till he knew the why and wherefore of all that aroused his attention.

> Brander Matthews, 1896, *An Introduction to the Study of American Literature*, p. 36

Poor Richard's Almanac (1732-57)

While in this weary state of suspense, a prey to impatience, anxiety, and mortification, Jones happened one day to be looking over an old number of Franklin's Pennsylvania Almanac, when his attention was struck with the saying of Poor Richard: "If you would have your business done, go; if not, send." It immediately occurred to him, that the delay of his own business was in no slight degree owing to his having so long remained at a distance, sending letters to court, instead of going to attend to it in person. He set out forthwith for the capital, and made such good speed in his errand, that, ere many days had elapsed, he received from the reluctant M. de Sartine, the following conclusive letter, dated at Versailles, on the 4th of February, 1779. . . . Feeling that his final success in obtaining a command had been owing to his having adopted the good advice which he had met with in Dr. Franklin's Almanac, and out of compliment to the sage, for whom his veneration was so unbounded, Paul Jones had asked leave, as appears by M. Sartine's letter, to give the ship of which the command was now conferred upon him, the name of the *Bon Homme Richard,* the *Poor Richard;* a name which his heroism was destined to render as enduring as his own.

> Alexander Slidell Mackenzie, 1841, *The Life of Paul Jones,* vol. I, pp. 133, 136

"But, pray, dear father, tell us what made him so famous," said George. "I have seen his portrait a great many times. There is a wooden bust of him in one of our streets; and marble ones, I suppose in some other places. And towns, and ships of war, and steamboats, and banks, and academies, and children, are often named after Franklin. Why should he have grown so very famous?" "Your question is a reasonable one, George," answered his father. 'I doubt whether Franklin's philosophical discoveries, important as they were, or even his vast political services, would have given him all the fame which he acquired. It appears to me that *Poor Richard's Almanac* did more than anything else towards making him familiarly known to the public. As the writer of those proverbs which Poor Richard was supposed to utter, Franklin became the counsellor and household friends of almost every family in America. Thus it was the humblest of all his labors that has done the most for his fame."

Nathaniel Hawthorne, 1842, *Biographical Stories, Works,*
Riverside ed., vol. XII, p. 202

Some of the best fun Franklin ever wrote, occurs in the prefaces to *Poor Richard. . . . Poor Richard,* at this day, would be reckoned an indecent production. All great humorists were more or less indecent before Charles Dickens; *i. e.,* they used certain words which are now never pronounced by polite persons, and are never printed by respectable printers; and they referred freely to certain subjects which are familiar to every living creature, but which, it is now agreed among civilized beings, shall not be topics of conversation. In this respect, *Poor Richard* was no worse, and not much better, than other colonial periodicals, some of which contained things incredibly obscene; as much so as the broadest passages of Sterne, Smollett, Fielding, and Defoe.

James Parton, 1864, *Life and Times of Benjamin Franklin,*
vol. I, pp. 228, 234

The almanac went year after year, for a quarter of a century, into the house of nearly every shopkeeper, planter, and farmer in the American provinces. Its wit and humor, its practical tone, its shrewd maxims, its worldly honesty, its morality of common sense, its useful information, all chimed well with the national character. It formulated in homely phrase and with droll illustration what the colonists more vaguely knew, felt, and believed upon a thousand points of life and conduct. In so doing it greatly trained and invigorated the natural mental traits of the people. *Poor Richard* was the revered and popular schoolmaster of a young nation during its period of tutelage. His teachings are among the powerful forces which have gone to shaping the habits of Americans. His terse and picturesque bits of the wisdom and the virtue of this world are familiar in our mouths today; they moulded our great-grandparents and their children; they have informed our popular traditions; they still influence our actions, guide our ways of thinking, and establish our points of view, with the constant control of acquired habits which we little suspect. If we were accustomed still to read the literature of the almanac, we should be charmed with its humor. The world has not yet grown away from it, nor ever will. Addison and Steele had more polish but vastly less humor than Franklin. *Poor Richard* has found eternal life by passing into the daily speech of the people, while the *Spectator* is fast being crowded out of the hands of all save scholars in literature.

John T. Morse, Jr., 1889, Benjamin Franklin
(American Statesmen), p. 22

Franklin's Almanack, his crowning work in the sphere of journalism, published under the pseudonym of Richard Saunders,—better known since as Poor Richard,—is still one of the marvels of modern literature. Under one or another of many titles the contents of this publication, exclusive of its calenders, have been translated into every tongue having any pretensions to a literature; and have had more readers, probably, than any other publication in the English or indeed in any other language, with the single exception of the Bible. It was the first issue from an American press that found a popular welcome in foreign lands, and it still enjoys the special distinction of being the only almanac ever published that owed its extraordinary popularity entirely to its literary merit. What adds to the surprise with which we contemplate the fame and fortunes of this unpretentious publication, is the fact that its reputation was established by its first number, and when its author was only twenty-six years of age. For a period of twenty-six years, and until Franklin ceased to edit it, this annual was looked forward to by a larger portion of the colonial population and with more impatience than now awaits a President's annual message to Congress.

John Bigelow, 1897, Library of the World's Best Literature,
ed. Warner, vol. X, p. 5926

Autobiography (1782-90)

There is a simplicity in this book which charms us in the same way with the humorous touches of nature in the *Vicar of Wakefield*. Franklin's Boston brother in the printing-office,—irascible, jealous, and mortified on the return of the successful adventurer, who is playing off his prosperity before the workmen, is an artist's picture of life, drawn in a few conclusive touches. So, too, is Keimer as happily hit off as any personage in Gil Blas, particularly in that incident at the break-up of Franklin's system of vegetable diet, which he had adopted; he invites his journeymen and two women friends to dine with him, providing a roast pig for the occasion, which being prematurely served up, is devoured by the enthusiast, before the company arrives; in that effective sketch, in a paragraph of the Philadelphia City Croaker, whose ghost still walks in every city in the world, mocking prosperity of every degree,—"a person of note, an elderly man, with a wise look and a very grave manner of speaking."

Evert A. and George L. Duyckinck, 1855-65-75, Cyclopædia of
American Literature, ed. Simons, vol. I, p. 117

A greater Autobiography than Edward Gibbon's is our own Benjamin Franklin's. Franklin had exactly the genius and temperament of an auto-biographer. He loved and admired himself; but he was so bent upon analysis and measurement that he could not let even himself pass without discrimination. The style is like Defoe. Indeed we are pleased to find that he placed great value both on Defoe and Bunyan, whose stories are told so like his own. He watches his own life as he watched one of his own philosophical experiments. He flies his existence as he flew his kite, and tells the world about it all just as a thoughtful boy might tell his mother what he had been doing—sure of her kindly interest in him. The world is like a mother to Ben Franklin always: so domestic and familiar is his thought of her. He who has read this book has always afterward the boy-man who wrote it clear and distinct among the men he knows.

Phillips Brooks, 1880-94, "Biography," *Essays and Addresses,*
p. 441

The style of this work is inimitable; it is as simple, direct, and idiomatic as Bunyan's; it is a style which no rhetorician can assist us to attain, and which the least touch of the learned critic would spoil.

Francis H. Underwood, 1893, *The Builders of American Literature,* First Series, p. 46

EDWARD GIBBON
1737-1794

Born, at Putney, 27 April, 1737. To school in Putney; afterwards at school at Kingston-on-Thames, Jan. 1746 to 1748 (?). At Westminster School, Jan. 1748 to 1750. To Bath for health 1750. To school at Esher, Jan. 1752. At Magdalen Coll., Oxford, 3 April, 1752 to June 1753. To Lausanne, as pupil of M. Pavillard, June 1753. Returned to England, Aug. 1758. Held commission in Hampshire militia, 12 June 1759 to 1770. In Paris, 28 Jan. to 9 May 1763; at Lausanne, May 1763 to April 1764; in Italy, April, 1764 to May, 1765. Returned to England; lived with father at Buriton. After father's death settled in London, 1772. Prof. of Ancient History at Royal Academy, 1774. M. P. for Liskeard, 11 Oct. 1774 to Sept. 1780. Lord Commissioner of Trade and Plantations, 1779. M. P. for Lymington, June 1781 to March 1784. Settled at Lausanne, Sept. 1783. Visit to England, 1788 to 1793. Died, in London, 16 Jan. 1794. Buried at Fletching, Sussex. WORKS: *Essai sur l'étude de la Littérature* (in French, 1761 Eng. trans., 1764); *Mémoires Littéraires de la Grande-Bretagne* (with Deyverdun), 2 vols., 1767-68; *Critical Observations on the Sixth Book of the Æneid* (anon.), 1770; *History of the Decline and Fall of the Roman Empire* (6 vols.), 1776-88 (2nd and 3rd edns. in same period). POSTHUMOUS: *An Historical View of Christianity* (with Bolingbroke,

Voltaire, and others), 1806; *Antiquities of the House of Brunswick,* ed. by Lord Sheffield, 1814; *Memoirs,* ed. by Lord Sheffield, 1827; *Life* (autobiog.), ed. by H. H. Milman, 1839; *The Autobiographies of Edward Gibbon,* ed. J. Murray, 1896; *Private Letters,* ed. by R. E. Prothero, 1896. COLLECTED WORKS: *Miscellaneous Works,* in 2 vols., 1796; in 5 vols., 1814.

R. Farquharson Sharp, 1897, A Dictionary of
English Authors, p. 111

SEE: *The History of the Decline and Fall of the Roman Empire,* ed. J. B. Bury, 1926-29, 7 v.; *Letters,* ed. J. E. Norton, 1956, 3 v.; G. M. Young, *Gibbon,* 1932; Harold L. Bond, *The Literary Art of Edward Gibbon,* 1960.

PERSONAL

Gibbon is an ugly, affected, disgusting fellow, and poisons our literary club to me.

James Boswell, 1779, Letter to Temple, May 8

Fat and ill-constructed, Mr. Gibbon has cheeks of such prodigious chubbiness, that they envelope his nose so completely, as to render it, in profile, absolutely invisible. His look and manner are placidly mild, but rather effeminate; his voice,—for he was speaking to Sir Joshua at a little distance,—is gentle, but of studied precision of accent. Yet, with these Brobdignatious cheeks, his neat little feet are of a miniature description; and with these, as soon as I turned around, he hastily described a quaint sort of circle, with small quick steps, and a dapper gait, as if to mark the alacrity of his approach, and then, stopping short when full face to me, he made so singularly profound a bow, that—though hardly able to keep my gravity—I felt myself blush deeply at its undue, but palpably intended obsequiousness.

Madame D'Arblay (Fanny Burney), 1782, Letter to
Samuel Crisp, Memoirs of Dr. Burney, p. 170

Mr. Gibbon, the historian, is so exceedingly indolent that he never even pares his nails. His servant, while Gibbon is reading, takes up one of his hands, and when he has performed the operation lays it down and then manages the other—the patient in the meanwhile scarcely knowing what is going on, and quietly pursuing his studies. The picture of him painted by Sir. J. Reynolds, and the prints made from it, are as like the original as it is possible to be. When he was introduced to a blind French lady, the servant happening to stretch out her mistress's hand to lay hold of the historian's cheek, she thought, upon feeling its rounded contour, that some trick was being played upon her with the *sitting* part of a child, and exclaimed, "Fidonc!"

Edmond Malone, 1787, Maloniana, ed. Prior, p. 382

The author of the great and superb *History of the Roman Empire* was scarcely four feet seven to eight inches in height; the huge trunk of his body, with a belly like Silenus, was set upon the kind of slender legs called *drumsticks;* his feet, so much turned in that the point of the right one could often touch the point of the left, were long and broad enough to serve as a pedestal to a statue of five feet six inches. In the middle of his face, not larger than one's fist, the root of his nose receded into the skull more deeply than the nose of a Calmuck, and his very bright but very small eyes were lost in the same depths. His voice, which had only sharp notes, could only reach the heart by splitting the ears. If Jean-Jacques Rousseau had met Gibbon in the Province of Vaud, it is probable that he would have made of him a companion portrait to his funny one of the *Chief Justice.* M. Suard, who cared little to look at, and still less to produce, caricatures, often drew Gibbon, and always as Madam Brown.

M. Garat, 1820, *Dominique Joseph, Memoirs,* vol. II

Thus converted firstly to the Romish communion at Oxford in June, 1753, at the age of sixteen years and two months, he renounced it at Lausanne in December 1754, at the age of seventeen years and eight months. This was precisely, within a few years, what Bayle had done in his youth. In Gibbon's case everything was performed in his head and within the lists of dialectics; one argument had carried it off. He could say, for his own satisfaction, that he owed both the one change and the other to his reading and his solitary meditation alone. Later, when he flattered himself with being wholly impartial and indifferent concerning beliefs, it is allowable to suppose that, even without avowing it, he cherished a secret and cold spite against religious thought, as if it had been an adversary which had one day struck him in the absence of his armour and had wounded him.

C. A. Sainte-Beuve, 1853, *English Portraits,* p. 124

Gibbon's political career is the side of his history from which a friendly biographer would most readily turn away. Not that it was exceptionally ignoble or self-seeking if tried by the standard of the time, but it was altogether commonplace and unworthy of him. The fact that he never even once opened his mouth in the House is not in itself blameworthy, though disappointing in a man of his power. It was indeed laudable enough if he had nothing to say. But why had he nothing to say? His excuse is timidity and want of readiness. We may reasonably assume that the cause lay deeper. With his mental vigour he would soon have overcome such obstacles if he had really wished and tried to overcome them. The fact is that he never tried because he never wished. It is a singular thing to say of such a man, but nevertheless true, that he had no taste or capacity whatever for politics.

James Cotter Morison, 1878, *Gibbon*
(*English Men of Letters*), p. 77

There is usually a tendency to underrate Gibbon's military experiences. . . . He was evidently an officer of more than ordinary intelligence, and possessed some military aptitude. He went beyond the requirements of an infantry captain by closely studying the language and science of tactics; indeed all that pertained to the serious side of soldiering he studied with a perseverance which might have been expected of a man that wrote his memoirs nine times before he was satisfied. While acquiring personal experience he was studying the campaigns of all the great masters of the art of war, in exactly the manner which Napoleon half a century later laid down as the only means of becoming a great captain.

R. Holden, 1895, "Gibbon as a Soldier," *Macmillan's Magazine*,
vol. 71, p. 38

He was a little slow, a little pompous, a little affected and pedantic. In the general type of his mind and character he bore much more resemblance to Hume, Adam Smith, or Reynolds, than to Johnson or Burke. A reserved scholar, who was rather proud of being a man of the world; a confirmed bachelor, much wedded to his comforts though caring nothing for luxury, he was eminently moderate in his ambitions, and there was not a trace of passion or enthusiasm in his nature. Such a man was not likely to inspire any strong devotion. But his temper was most kindly, equable, and contented; he was a steady friend, and he appears to have been always liked and honored in the cultivated and uncontentious society in which he delighted. His life was not a great one, but it was in all essentials blameless and happy. He found the work which was most congenial to him. He pursued it with admirable industry and with brilliant success, and he left behind him a book which is not likely to be forgotten while the English language endures.

William Edward Hartpole Lecky, 1897, *Library of the World's
Best Literature*, ed. Warner, vol. XI, p. 6278

MADEMOISELLE CURCHOD

The cooling-off of Mr. Gibbon has made me think meanly of him. I have been going over his book, and he seems to me to be straining at *esprit*. He is not the man for me; nor can I think that he will be the one for Mademoiselle Curchod. Any one who does not know her value is not worthy of her; but a man who comes to that knowledge and then withdraws himself, is only worthy of contempt. . . . I would sooner a thousand times that he left her poor and free among you than that he brought her rich and miserable away to England.

Jean Jacques Rousseau, 1763, Letter to Moulton

I should be ashamed if the warm season of youth had passed away without any sense of friendship or love; and in the choice of their objects I may applaud the discernment of my head or heart. . . . The beauty of Mademoiselle Curchod, the daughter of a country clergyman, was adorned with science and virtue: she listened to the tenderness which she had inspired; but the romantic hopes of youth and passion were crushed, on my return, by the prejudice or prudence of an English parent. I sighed as a lover, I obeyed as a son; my wound was insensibly healed by time, absence, and the habits of a new life; and my cure was accelerated by a faithful report of the tranquility and cheerfulness of the Lady herself. Her equal behaviour under the tryals of indigence and prosperity has displayed the firmness of her character. A citizen of Geneva, a rich banker of Paris, made himself happy by rewarding her merit; the genius of her husband has raised him to a perilous eminence; and Madame Necker now divides and alleviates the cares of the first minister of the finances of France.

Edward Gibbon, c 1789, Autobiography, Memoir C.,
ed. Murray, p. 238

The letter in which Gibbon communicated to Mademoiselle Curchod the opposition of his father to their marriage still exists in manuscript. The first pages are tender and melancholy, as might be expected from an unhappy lover; the latter becomes by degrees calm and reasonable, and the letter concludes with these words: —<i>C'est pourquoi, Mademoiselle, j'ai l'honneur d'être votre très humble et très obéissant serviteur, Edward Gibbon.</i> He truly loved Mademoiselle Curchod; but every one loves according to his character, and that of Gibbon was incapable of a despairing passion.

M. Suard, 1828, Life

The tone in which Gibbon generally refers to love affairs in his history is not altogether edifying, and hardly implies that his passion had purified or ennobled his mind.

Leslie Stephen, 1898, Studies of a Biographer, vol. I, p. 169

The Decline and Fall of the Roman Empire (1776-88)

As I ran through your volume of History with great avidity and impatience, I cannot forbear discovering somewhat of the same impatience in returning you thanks for your agreeable present, and expressing the satisfaction which the performance has given me. Whether I consider the dignity of your style, the depth of your matter, or the extensiveness of your learning, I must regard the work as equally the object of esteem, and I own that, if I had not previously had the happiness of your personal acquaintance, such a performance from an Englishman in our age would have given me some surprise.

David Hume, 1776, *Letter to Edward Gibbon,* March 18

Gibbon I detect a frequent poacher in the *Philosophical Essays* of *Bolingbroke:* as in his representation of the unsocial character of the Jewish religion; and in his insinuation of the suspicions cast by succeeding miracles, acknowledged to be false, on prior ones contended to be true. Indeed it seems not unlikely that he caught the first hint of his theological chapters from this work.

Thomas Green, 1779-1810, *Diary of a Lover of Literature*

If there be any certain method of discovering a man's real object, yours has been to discredit Christianity in fact, while in words you represent yourself as a friend to it; a conduct which I scruple not to call highly unworthy and mean; an insult to the common sense of the Christian world.

Joseph Priestley, 1782, *A Letter to Edward Gibbon on the Decline and Fall*

I now feel as if a mountain was removed from my breast; as far as I can judge, the public unanimously applauds my compliment to Lord North, and does not appear dissatisfied with the conclusion of my work. I look back with amazement on the road which I have travelled, but which I should never have entered had I been previously apprized of its length.

Edward Gibbon, 1788, *Private Letters,* vol. II, p. 170

I cannot express to you the pleasure it gives me to find, that, by the universal assent of every man of taste and learning whom I either know or correspond with, it sets you at the very head of the whole literary tribe at present existing in Europe.

Adam Smith, 1788, *Letter to Edward Gibbon,* Dec. 10

You desire to know my opinion of Mr. Gibbon. I can say very little about him, for such is the affectation of his style, that I could never get through the half of one of his volumes. If anybody would translate him into good classical English, (such, I mean, as Addison, Swift, Lord Lyttelton, &c.,

wrote), I should read him with eagerness; for I know there must be much curious matter in his work. His cavils against religion, have, I think, been all confuted; he does not seem to understand that part of his subject: indeed I have never yet met with a man, or with an author, who both understood Christianity, and disbelieved it.

James Beattie, 1788, *Letter to Duchess of Gordon*,
November 20th; *Works,* ed. Forbes, vol. III, p. 56

It is a most wonderful mass of information, not only on history, but almost on all the ingredients of history, as war, government, commerce, coin, and what not. If it has a fault, it is in embracing too much, and consequently in not detailing enough, and in striding backwards and forwards from one set of princes to another, and from one subject to another; so that, without much historic knowledge, and without much memory, and much method in one's memory, it is almost impossible not to be sometimes bewildered: nay, his own impatience to tell what he knows, makes the author, though commonly so explicit, not perfectly clear in his expressions. The last chapter of the fourth volume, I own, made me recoil, and I could scarcely push through it. So far from being Catholic or heretic, I wished Mr. Gibbon had never heard of Monophysites, Nestorians, or any such fools! But the sixth volume made ample amends; Mahomet and the Popes were gentlemen and good company. I abominate fractions of theology and reformation.

Horace Walpole, 1788, *To Thomas Barrett,* June 5;
Letters, ed. Cunningham, vol. IX, p. 126

His reflections are often just and profound. He pleads eloquently for the rights of mankind, and the duty of toleration; nor does his humanity ever slumber unless when women are ravished, or the Christians persecuted. . . . He often makes, when he cannot readily find, an occasion to insult our religion, which he hates so cordially that he might seem to revenge some personal insult. Such is his eagerness in the cause, that he stoops to the most despicable pun, or to the most awkward pervsion of language, for the pleasure of turning the Scriptures into ribaldry, or of calling Jesus an impostor.

Richard Porson, 1790, *Letters to Archdeacon Travis,* Preface

I am at a loss how to describe the success of the work without betraying the vanity of the writer. The first impression was exhausted in a few days; a second and third edition were scarcely adequate to the demand; and the bookseller's property was twice invaded by the pyrates of Dublin. My book was on every table, and almost on every toilette; the historian was crowned by the taste or fashion of the day; nor was the general voice disturbed by the barking of any profane critic. . . . It was on the day, or rather, night of the 27th of June, 1787, between the hours of eleven and twelve, that I wrote the last lines of the last page, in a summerhouse in my garden. After laying down my pen, I took several turns in a berceau, or covered walk of acacias, which commands a prospect of the country, the Lake, and the mountains. The air was temperate, the sky was serene, the silver orb of the moon was reflected from the waters, and all nature was silent. I will not dissemble the first emotions of joy on the recovery of my freedom, and perhaps the establishment of my fame. But my pride was soon humbled, and a sober melancholy was spread over my mind, by the idea that I had taken an everlasting leave of an old and agreeable companion, and that, whatsoever might be the future date of my history, the life of the historian must be short and precarious.

Edward Gibbon, 1793, Autobiography, Memoir E.,
ed. Murray, pp. 311, 333

The work of Gibbon excites my utmost admiration; not so much by the immense learning and industry which it displays, as by the commanding intellect, the keen sagacity, apparent in almost every page. The admiration of his ability extends even to his manner of showing his hatred to Christianity, which is exquisitely subtle and acute, and adapted to do very great mischief, even where there is not the smallest avowal of hostility. It is to be deplored that a great part of the early history of the Christian Church was exactly such as a man like him could have wished.

John Foster, 1805, Letters, ed. Ryland, vol. I, p. 262

The author of the *History of the Decline,* &c., appears to have possessed a considerable share of sense, ingenuity, and knowledge of his subject, together with great industry. But these qualities or talents are disgraced, —by *a false taste of composition,* which prompts him continually to employ a verbose, inflated style, in order to obtain the praise of force and energy, —by *a perpetual affectation of wit, irony, and satire,* altogether unsuited to the historic character,—and, what is worse, by *a freethinking, licentious spirit,* which spares neither morals nor religion, and must make every honest man regard him as a bad citizen and pernicious writer. All these miscarriages may be traced up to one common source, an excessive vanity.

Richard Hurd, 1808 ? Commonplace Book, ed. Kilvert, p. 250

A work of immense research and splendid execution. . . . Alternately delighted and offended by the gorgeous colouring with which his fancy invests the rude and scanty materials of his narrative; sometimes fatigued by the learning of his notes, occasionally amused by their liveliness, frequently disgusted by their obscenity, and admiring or deploring the bitterness of his skilful irony—I toiled through his massy tomes with exemplary patience. His style is exuberant, sonorous, and epigrammatic to a degree that is often displeasing. He yields to Hume in elegance and distinctness—to Robertson in talents for general disquisition—but he excels them both in a species of brief and shrewd remark for which he seems to have taken Tacitus as a model, more than any other that I know of.

Thomas Carlyle, 1818, Early Letters, ed. Norton, pp. 68, 69

Gibbon's style is detestable, but his style is not the worst thing about him. His history has proved an effectual bar to all real familiarity with the temper and habits of imperial Rome. Few persons read the original authorities, even those which are classical; and certainly no distinct knowledge of the actual state of the empire can be obtained from Gibbon's rhetorical sketches. He takes notice of nothing but what may produce an effect; he skips on from eminence to eminence, without ever taking you through the valleys between: in fact, his work is little else but a disguised collection of all the splendid anecdotes which he could find in any book concerning any persons or nations from the Antonines to the capture of Constantinople. When I read a chapter in Gibbon I seem to be looking through a luminous haze or fog:—figures come and go, I know not how or why, all larger than life, or distorted or discoloured; nothing is real, vivid, true; all is scenical, and as it were, exhibited by candlelight. And then to call it a History of the Decline and Fall of the Roman Empire! Was there ever a greater misnomer? I protest I do not remember a single philosophical attempt made throughout the work to fathom the ultimate causes of the decline or fall of that empire. How miserably deficient is the narrative of the important reign of Justinian! And that poor scepticism, which Gibbon mistook for Socratic philosophy, has led him to misstate and mistake the character and influence of Christianity in a way which even an avowed infidel or atheist would not and could not have done. Gibbon was a man of immense reading; but he had no philosophy; and he never fully understood the principle upon which the best of the old historians wrote. He attempted to imitate their artificial construction of the whole work—their dramatic ordonnance of the parts—without seeing that their histories were intended more as documents illustrative of the truths of political philosophy than as mere chronicles of events.

Samuel Taylor Coleridge, 1833, Table Talk,
Aug. 15, ed. Ashe, p. 245

Another very celebrated historian, we mean Gibbon—not a man of mere science and analysis, like Hume, but with some (though not the truest or profoundest) artistic feeling of the picturesque, and from whom, therefore, rather more might have been expected—has with much pains succeeded in producing a tolerably graphic picture of here and there a battle, a tumult, or an insurrection; his book is full of movement and costume, and would make a series of very pretty ballets at the Opera house, and the ballets would give us fully as distinct an idea of the Roman empire, and how it declined and fell, as the book does. If we want that, we must look for it anywhere but in Gibbon. One touch of M. Guizot removes a portion of the veil which hid from us the recesses of private life under the Roman empire, lets in a ray of light which penetrates as far even as the domestic hearth of a subject of Rome, and shews us the Government at work making that desolate; but no similar gleam of light from Gibbon's mind ever reaches the subject; *human life,* in the times he wrote about, is not what he concerned himself with.

John Stuart Mill, 1837, "The French Revolution," *Early Essays,*
ed. Gibbs, p. 276

He had three hobbies which he rode to the death (stuffed puppets as they were), and which he kept in condition by the continual sacrifice of all that is valuable in language. These hobbies were *Dignity—Modulation—Laconism.* Dignity is all very well; and history demands it for its general tone; but the being everlastingly on stilts is not only troublesome and awkard, but dangerous. He who falls *en homme ordinaire*—from the mere slipping of his feet—is usually an object of sympathy; but all men tumble now and then, and this tumbling from high sticks is sure to provoke laughter. His modulation, however, is always ridiculous; for it is so uniform, so continuous, and so jauntily kept up, that we almost fancy the writer waltzing to his words. With him, to speak lucidly was a far less merit than to speak smoothly and curtly. There is a way in which, through the nature of language itself, we may often save a few words by talking backwards; and this is, therefore, a favorite practice with Gibbon.

Edgar Allan Poe, 1839-49, *Marginalia, Works,*
ed. Woodberry, vol. VII, p. 338

The great merit of Gibbon is his extraordinary industry, and the general fidelity of his statements, as attested by the constant references which he makes to his numerous and varied authorities—references which enable the "most faithful of historians" to ascertain clearly their accuracy, that is, the truth of his narrative. This is the very first virtue of the historical character; and that merit, therefore, is fully possessed by Gibbon. In it he is the worthy rival of Robertson, and in it he forms a remarkable contrast to Hume. The next great merit of Gibbon is the judgment with which he weighs conflicting authorities and the freedom with which he rejects improbable relations. His sagacity is remarkable; and his attention seems ever awake. . . . The third excellence of his work is its varied learning, distributed in the vast body of notes which accompany the text, and which contain no small portion of a critical abstract, serving for a *catalogue raisonné,* of the works referred to in the page. . . . It must, lastly, be allowed, that the narrative is as lucid as the confused nature of the subject will admit; and that, whatever defects may be ascribed to it, there is nothing tiring or monotonous, nothing to prevent the reader's attention from being kept ever awake. When the nature of the subject is considered, perhaps there may some doubt arise, if the chaster style of Livy, of Robertson, or even of Hume, could have rendered this story as attractive as Gibbon's manner, singularly free from all approach to monotony, though often deviating widely from simplicity and nature.

Henry, Lord Brougham, 1845-6, *Lives of Men of Letters of the Time of George III*

It is acknowledged that Gibbon wrote with a preconceived, speculative object. Cold design overlays every page. His work is rather an elegant oration, pronounced with sustained diction, than a living picture of the past. The order into which he reduced an immense quantity of chaotic material is, perhaps, its most striking charm.

Henry T. Tuckerman, 1849, *Characteristics of Literature,* p. 188

There is no more solid book in the world than Gibbon's history. Only consider the chronology. It begins before the year *one* and goes down to the year 1453, and is a schedule or series of schedules of important events during that time. Scarcely any fact deeply affecting European civilisation is wholly passed over, and the great majority of facts are elaborately recounted. Laws, dynasties, churches, barbarians, appear and disappear. Everything changes; the old world—the classical civilisation of form and definition—passes away, a new world of free spirit and inward growth emerges; between the two lies a mixed weltering interval of trouble and confusion, when everybody hates everybody, and the historical student leads a life of skirmishes, is oppressed with broils and feuds. All through this long period Gibbon's history goes with steady consistent pace; like a Roman legion trough a troubled country— *hæret pede pes;* up hill and down hill, through marsh and thicket, through Goth or Parthian—the firm array passes forward—a type of order, and an emblem of civilisation. Whatever may be the defects of Gibbon's history, none can deny him a proud precision and a style in marching order. . . . . Gibbon's reflections connect the events; they are not sermons between them. But, notwithstanding, the

manner of the *Decline and Fall* is the last which should be recommended
for strict imitation. It is not a style in which you can tell the truth. A monotonous writer is suited only to monotonous matter. Truth is of various kinds
—grave, solemn, dignified, petty. low, ordinary; and an historian who has
to tell the truth must be able to tell what is vulgar as well as what is great,
what is little as well as what is amazing. Gibbon is at fault here.

Walter Bagehot, 1856, "Edward Gibbon," *Literary Studies,*
ed. Hutton, vol. II, pp. 35, 36

If you want to know where the world was, and how it fared with it during
the first ten centuries of our era, read Gibbon. No other writer can do for
you just what he does. No one else has had the courage to attempt his task
over again. The laborious student of history may go to the many and obscure sources from which Gibbon drew the materials for his great work,
and correct or supplement him here and there, as Milman has done; but
the general reader wants the completed structure, and not the mountain
quarries from which the blocks came; and the complete structure you get
in Gibbon. To omit him is to leave a gap in your knowledge of the history
of the world which nothing else can fill. As Carlyle said to Emerson, he "is
the splendid bridge which connects the old world with the new;" very artificial, but very real for all that, and very helpful to any who have business
that way. The case may be even more strongly stated than that. To read
Gibbon is to be present at the creation of the world—the modern world.
. . . Ruskin objects to Gibbon's style as the "worst English ever written by
an educated Englishman." It was the style of his age and country brought
to perfection, the stately curvilinear or orbicular style; every sentence makes
a complete circle; but it is always a real thought, a real distinction that
sweeps through the circle. Modern style is more linear, more direct and
picturesque; and in the case of such a writer as Ruskin, much more loose,
discursive and audacious. The highly artificial buckram style of the age of
Gibbon has doubtless had its day, but it gave us some noble literature, and
is no more to be treated with contempt than the age which produced it is
to be treated with contempt.

John Burroughs, 1886, "Ruskin's Judgment of Gibbon
and Darwin," *The Critic,* May 1

The most important part consists of Memoirs of Mr. Gibbon's life and
writings, a work which he seems to have projected with peculiar solicitude
and attention, and of which he left six different sketches, all in his own
hand-writing. One of these sketches, the most diffuse and circumstantial,
so far as it proceeds, ends at the time when he quitted Oxford. Another at
the year 1764, when he travelled to Italy. A third, at his father's death, in

1770. A fourth, which he continued to a short time after his return to Lausanne in 1788, appears in the form of Annals, much less detailed than the others. The two remaining sketches are still more imperfect. It is difficult to discover the order in which these several pieces were written, but there is reason to believe that the most copious was the last. From all these the following Memoirs have been carefully selected, and put together.

> John Lord Sheffield, 1795, ed., *The Miscellaneous Works of*
> *Edward Gibbon,* Introduction

The private memoirs of Gibbon the historian have just been published. In them we are able to trace with considerable accuracy the progress of his mind. While he was at college, he became reconciled to the Roman Catholic faith. By this circumstance he incurred his father's displeasure, who banished him to an obscure situation in Switzerland, where he was obliged to live upon a scanty provision, and was far removed from all the customary amusements of men of birth and fortune. If this train of circumstances had not taken place, would he ever have been the historian of the *Decline and Fall of the Roman Empire?* Yet how unusual were his attainments in consequence of these events, in learning, in acuteness of research, and intuition of genius.

> William Godwin, 1797, *The Enquirer,* p. 25

Gibbon's miscellaneous work, both in English and French, is not inconsiderable, and it displays his peculiar characteristics; but the only piece of distinct literary importance is his *Autobiography*. This, upon which he seems to have amused himself by spending much pains, was left unsettled for press. Edited with singular judgment and success under the care of his intimate friend and literary executor Lord Sheffield, it has been for three generations one of the favourite things of its kind with all good judges, and is likely to continue so in the *textus receptus,* for which the fussy fidelity of modern literary methods will probably try in vain to substitute a chaos of rough drafts.

> George Saintsbury, 1898, *A Short History of*
> *English Literature,* p. 626

If, as Johnson said, there had been only three books "written by man that were wished longer by their readers," the eighteenth century was not to draw to its close without seeing a fourth added. With *Don Quixote, The Pilgrim's Progress* and *Robinson Crusoe,* the *Autobiography of Edward Gibbon* was henceforth to rank as "a work whose conclusion is perceived with an eye of sorrow, such as the traveller casts upon departing day." It is indeed so short that it can be read by the light of a single pair of candles; it is so interesting in its subject, and so alluring in its turns of thought and its style, that in a second and a third reading it gives scarcely less pleasure than in the first. Among the books in which men have told the story of their own lives it stands in the front rank.

George Birkbeck Hill, 1900, ed., *The Memoirs of the
Life of Edward Gibbon,* Preface, p. v

Letters and Miscellaneous Works (1796-1897)

I shall thus give more satisfaction, by employing the language of Mr. Gibbon, instead of my own; and the public will see him in a new and admirable light, as a writer of letters. By the insertion of a few occasional sentences, I shall obviate the disadvantages that are apt to arise from an interrupted narration. A prejudiced or a fastidious critic may condemn, perhaps, some parts of the letters as trivial; but many readers, I flatter myself, will be gratified by discovering, even in these, my friend's affectionate feelings, and his character in familiar life. His letters in general bear a strong resemblance to the style and turn of his conversation: the characteristics of which were vivacity, elegance, and precision, with knowledge astonishingly extensive and correct. He never ceased to be instructive and entertaining; and in general there was a vein of pleasantry in his conversation which prevented its becoming languid, even during a residence of many months with a family in the country. It has been supposed that he always arranged what he intended to say, before he spoke; his quickness in conversation contradicts this notion: but it is very true, that before he sat down to write a note or letter, he completely arranged in his mind what he meant to express.

John, Lord Sheffield, 1795, *The Autobiography of Edward Gibbon,
Illustrated from his Letters with Occasional Notes and Narratives*

The letters have the ease and freshness of conversations with intimate friends, and, considering the character of the century in which they were written, they present one feature which deserves special notice. Only one short sentence has been omitted as too coarse to be printed. With this solitary exception, the reader knows the worst as well as the best of Gibbon, and there are scarcely a dozen phrases, scattered over 800 pages, which will offend good taste or good feeling.

Rowland E. Prothero, 1896, ed., *Private Letters of
Edward Gibbon,* Preface, vol. I, p. xii

But now that we have the intimate records of his daily life from youth to death in their original form, one wonders anew how so gigantic a work as the *Decline and Fall* was ever completed in about sixteen years amidst all the distractions of country squires, London gaieties, Parliamentary and official duties, interminable worries about his family and property, social scandals and importunate friends. In all these six hundred letters there is not very much about his studies and his writings, but a great deal about politics, society, and pecuniary cares. We are left to imagine for ourselves when the great scholar read, how he wrote, and why he never seemed to exchange a thought with any student of his own calibre of learning. One would think he was a man of fashion, a dilettante man of the world, a wit, a *bon vivant,* and a collector of high-life gossip. All this makes the zest of his *Letters,* which at times seem to recall to us the charm of a Boswell or a Horace Walpole. The world can now have all the fun, as Maria Holroyd said. But it leaves us with the puzzle even darker than before—how did Gibbon, whose whole epoch of really systematic study hardly lasted twenty-five years, acquire so stupendous a body of exact and curious learning?

Frederic Harrison, 1897, "The New Memoirs of Edward Gibbon,"
The Forum, vol. 22, p. 751

GEORGE COLMAN
The Elder
1732-1794

Born, in Florence, March (or April?), 1732. At Westminster School, 1746-51. To Ch. Ch., Oxford, 5 June 1751; B. A., 18 April 1755; M. A., 18 March 1758. Contributed to *The Student,* 1751; to Hawkesworth's *The Adventurer,* Sept. 1753; ed. *The Connoisseur,* with Bonnell Thornton, Jan. 1754 to Sept. 1756. Called to Bar at Lincoln's Inn, 1755. On Oxford Circuit, 1759. Farce, *Polly Honeycombe,* produced at Drury Lane, 5 Dec. 1760; *The Jealous Wife* produced, 12 Feb. 1761. Started *St. James's Chronicle,* with Bonnell Thornton and Garrick, 1761. . . . Purchased Covent Garden Theatre (with Powell, Harris, and Rutherford), and opened it, 14 Sept. 1767. Married Miss Ford, 1767 (?); she died, 29 March 1771. . . . Resigned management, 26 May 1774, and retired to Bath. Contrib. a series of papers called "The Gentleman" to *The London Packet,* July to Dec. 1775. A version of Ben Jonson's *Epicœne* produced at Drury Lane, 13 Jan. 1776; *The Spleen,* 7 March, 1776; *New Brooms,* 21 Sept. 1776. Manager of Haymarket, 1777-85. . . . Pall-bearer at Dr. Johnson's funeral, 20 Dec. 1784. Paralytic stroke, 1785. Mind gradually gave way. Died, in Paddington, 14 Aug. 1794. Buried in vaults of Kensington Church. WORKS: *Polly Honeycombe* (anon.), 1760; *Ode to Obscurity* (anon.), 1760; *The Jealous Wife,* 1761; *Critical Reflections on the Old English Dramatick Writers* (anon.), 1761; *The Clandestine Marriage* (with Garrick), 1761; *The Musical Lady* (anon.), 1762; *The Deuce is in Him* (anon.), 1763; *Terræ Filius* (4 nos., anon.), 1764; *The English Merchant,* 1767; *T. Harris Dissected,* 1768; *True State of the Differences, etc.,* 1768 (2nd edn. same year); *Occasional Prelude,* 1768; *The Portrait,* (anon.; date misprinted MCCCLXX.), 1770; *Man and Wife* (anon.), 1770; *The Oxonian in Town* (anon.), 1769; *The Fairy Prince* (anon.), 1771; *The Man of Business*, 1774; *The Spleen*, 1776; *The Occasional Prelude*, 1776; *New Brooms*, 1776; *Dramatick Works*, 1777; *A Fairy Tale* (adapted, with Garrick, from *A Mid-Summer Night's Dream*), 1777; *The Sheep-shearing* (adapted from *Winter's Tale*), 1777; *The Manager in Distress*, 1780; *Prose on Several Occasions*, 1787; *Tit for Tat* (anon.), 1788; *Ut Pictura Poesis*, 1789. POSTHUMOUS: *Some Particulars of the Life of the late George Colman, written by himself* (ed. by R. Jackson), 1795; *Miscellaneous Works*, 1797. He *translated*: Terence's *Comedies*, 1765; Horace's *Art of Poetry*, 1783; and *edited*: *Poems by Eminent Ladies* (with Bonnell Thornton), 1755; Beaumont and Fletcher's *Philaster*, with alterations, 1763; *Comus*, altered from Milton, 1772; Jonson's *Epicœne*, with alterations, 1776; Beaumont and Fletcher's *Dramatic Works*, 1778; Foote's *Devil Upon Two Sticks*, 1778; Foote's *Maid of Bath*, 1788; Foote's *The Nabob*, 1778; Foote's *A Trip to Calais*, 1778; Lillo's *Fatal Curiosity*, with alterations, 1783. LIFE: In Peake's *Memoirs of the Coleman Family*, 1841.

R. Farquharson Sharp, 1897, A Dictionary of English Authors, p. 63

SEE: E. R. Page, *George Colman the Elder, 1732-1794*, 1935.

PERSONAL

They never admitted Colman as one of the set; Sir Joshua did not invite him to dinner. If he had been in the room Goldsmith would have flown out of it, as if a dragon had been there. I remember Garrick once saying. "D—n his *dishclout* face! His plays would never do, if it were not for my patching them up and acting in them." Another time he took a poem of Colman's and read it backwards to turn it into ridicule. Yet some of his pieces keep possession of the stage, so that there must be something in them.

James Northcote, 1826-27, Conversations, ed. Hazlitt, p. 402

His case was simply this; that he had gout in his habit, which had been indicated so slightly, that he neglected the hints to take care of himself which nature had mildly thrown out. Cold bathing is perhaps one of the most dangerous luxuries in which an elderly man can indulge, when so formidable an enemy is lurking in his constitution. The gout having been repelled by repeated submersion in the sea, not only paralyzed the body, but distempered the brain, and Reason was subverted. But, from the earliest sparks of his disorder at the end of 1785, till it blazed forth unequivocally in June, 1789, an interval of rather more than three years and a half, and again from the last mentioned year to the time of his decease, there was nothing of that "second childishness and mere oblivion," which his biographers have attached to his memory. The assertion that his gradually increasing derangement left him in "a state of idiotism," is directly the reverse of fact. His mind, instead of having grown progressively vacant till it became a blank, was, in the last stages of his malady, filled, like a cabalistic book, with delusions, and crowded with the wildest flights of morbid fancy; it was always active, always on the stretch; and, so far from his exhibiting that moping fatuity which obscured the last sad and silent days of Swift, it might have been said of him, "how pregnant sometimes his replies are! a happiness which reason and sanity would not so prosperously be delivered of."

George Colman (The Younger), 1830, *Random Records*

GENERAL

It is very much to the credit of that excellent writer Mr. Colman, that, while other dramatists were lost in the fashion of sentiment, his comedies always present the happiest medium of nature; without either affectation of sentiment, or affectation of wit. That the able translator of Terence should yet have sufficient force of mind to keep his own pieces clear of the declamatory dullness of that ancient, is certainly a matter deserving of much applause. *The Jealous Wife,* and *The Clandestine Marriage,* with others of his numerous dramas, may be mentioned as the most perfect models of comedy we have: to all the other requisites of fine comic writing they always add just as much sentiment and wit as does them good. This happy medium is the most difficult to hit all composition, and most declares the hand of a master.

John Pinkerton (Robert Heron), 1785, *Letters of Literature,* p. 47

This comedy, by Colman the elder, was written in his youth; and, though he brought upon the stage no less than twenty-five dramas, including those he altered from Shakspeare and other writers, subsequent to this production, yet not one of them was ever so well received by the town, or appears to have deserved so well, as *The Jealous Wife.* To this observation, *The Clandestine Marriage,* may possibly be an exception; but, in that work, Mr. Garrick was declared his joint labourer. It therefore appears, that Mr. Colman's talents for dramatic writing declined, rather than improved, by experience—or, at least, his ardour abated; and all works of imagination require, both in conception and execution, a degree of enthusiasm. . . . Mrs. Oakly is, indeed, so complete a character from life, and so ably adapted to the stage by the genius of the writer, that, performed by an actress possessed of proper abilities for the part, the play might be well supported, were the wit, humor, and repartee, of every other character in the piece annihilated.

Mrs. Elizabeth Inchbald, 1808, "Remarks" on *The Jealous Wife,*
in *The British Theatre,* ed. Elizabeth Inchbald, vol. I

His abilities as a dramatist were not more the subject of praise, than his punctuality as a manager, and his liberal encouragement to other writers for the stage. From the lamentable condition into which he had sunk, both mentally and bodily, his death must have been considered a happy release. A few hours before he expired, he was sized with violent spasms, and these were succeeded by melancholy stupor, in which he drew his last breath. . . . These dramas have considerable merit. In his petite pieces the plots are simple, yet they contain strong character, and aim at ridiculing fashionable and prevailing follies. His comedies have the same merit with the others, as to the preservation of character. The estimation in which the entertainments exhibited under his direction were held by the public, the reputation which the Haymarket Theatre acquired, and the continual concourse of the fashionable world during the height of summer, sufficiently spoke the praises of Mr. Colman's management.

Richard Brinsley Peake, 1841, *Memoirs of the Colman Family,*
vol. II, p. 220

ROBERT BURNS
1759-1796

January 25, 1759, Birth at Ayr, parish of Alloway. 1765, School at Alloway Mill; with Murdoch. 1766-1777, At Mount Oliphant, parish of Ayr (1766). 1768, Early associations on the farm. Taught at home by his father. 1769, Books. Love and song. Jenny Wilson. 1777-84, At Lochlea, parish of Tarbolton. 1778, School at Kirkoswald. 1780, The Bachelor's Club. 1781, Flax-dressing at Irvine. 1782, Finds Fergusson's Poems. 1783, A Freemason. February 1784, His father's death. 1784-1786, At Mossgiel, parish of Mauchline. 1785, Early friends: Gavin Hamilton, Robert Aiken. Struggle with Auld Lichts. Poetic Springtide. Epistles. Satirical Poems. Descriptive Poems. Songs. August, 1786, Kilmarnock (first) edition of poems published. Literary friendships: Dr. Blacklock, Dugald Stewart, Dr. Blair, Rev. Mr. Laurie, Mrs. Dunlop. Visits Katrine, meets Lord Daer and Mrs. Stewart. November 1786, Visits Edinburgh. Among the celebrities. April 1787, Second edition of poems. Travels in Scotland, May, Border Tour. June, Returns to Mossgiel. First Highland Tour. Second Highland Tour. Third Highland Tour. September, Returns to Edinburgh. Johnson's Museum. March 1788, Leaves Edinburgh. 1788-1791, At Ellisland. August 1788, Marries Jean Armour, At Friar's Carse. 1790, Appointed Excise Officer. 1791-1796, at Dumfries. Bank Vennel. Dumfries Volunteers. Thomson's Collection. 1792, Patriotic Songs. 1793, Visits Galloway. 1794, Removes to Mill Hill Brae. Failing Health. July 21, 1796, Death.

Andrew J. George, 1896, ed., *Select Poems
of Robert Burns*, p. 231

SEE: *Complete Writings,* with an Essay by W. E. Henley and Introduction by John Buchan, 1926-27, 10 v.; *Poetry,* ed. W. E. Henley and

Thomas F. Henderson, 1896-97, 4 v., rev. 1897 (one-volume Cambridge ed.); *Poems,* ed. C. S. Dougall, 1927; *Scottish Poems of Robert Burns in His Native Dialect,* ed. Sir James Wilson, 1925; *Burns into English: Renderings of Select Dialect Poems* by William Kean Seymour, 1954; *Letters,* ed. J. DeLancey Ferguson, 1931, 2 v.; *Selected Letters,* ed. J. De Lancey Ferguson, 1954; F. B. Snyder, *The Life of Robert Burns,* 1932; J. De Lancey Ferguson, *Pride and Passion: Robert Burns,* 1939; David Daiches, *Robert Burns,* 1952; Thomas Crawford, *Burns: A Study of the Poems and Songs,* 1960.

PERSONAL

This kind of life—the cheerless gloom of a hermit, with the unceasing moil of a galley-slave, brought me to my sixteenth year; a little before which period I first committed the sin of Rhyme. You know our country custom of coupling a man and woman together as partners in the labours of harvest. In my fifteenth autumn my partner was a bewitching creature, a year younger than myself. My scarcity of English denies me the power of doing her justice in that language; but you know the Scottish idiom—she was a *bonnie sweet, sonie lass.* In short, she altogether, unwittingly to herself, initiated me in that delicious passion, which, in spite of acid disappointment, gin-horse prudence, and book-worm philosophy, I hold to be the first of human joys, our dearest blessing here below! How she caught the contagion, I cannot tell: you medical people talk much of infection from breathing the same air, the touch, &c.; but I never expressly said I loved her, indeed, I did not know myself why I liked so much to loiter behind with her, when returning in the evening from our labours; why the tones of her voice made my heart-strings thrill like an Æolian harp; and particularly my pulse beat such a furious ratan when I looked and fingered over her little hand to pick out the cruel nettlestings and thistles. Among her other love-inspiring qualities, she sung sweetly; and it was her favourite reel to which I attempted giving an embodied vehicle in rhyme. I was not so presumptuous as to imagine that I could make verses like printed ones, composed by men who had Greek and Latin; but my girl sung a song, which was said to be composed by a small country laird's son, on one of his father's maids, with whom he was in love! and I saw no reason why I might not rhyme as well as he; for, excepting that he could smear sheep, and cast peats, his father living in the moor-lands, he had no more scholar-craft than myself.

Robert Burns, 1787, *Letter to Dr. Moore,* Aug. 2;
Burn's Works, ed. Currie

If others have climbed more successfully to the heights of Parnassus, none certainly out-shone Burns in the charms—the sorcery I would almost call it, of fascinating conversation; the spontaneous eloquence of social argument, or the unstudied poignancy of brilliant repartee. His personal endowments were perfectly correspondent with the qualifications of his mind. His form was manly; his action energy itself; devoid, in a great measure, however, of those graces, of that polish, acquired only in the refinement of societies, where in early life he had not the opportunity to mix; but, where, such was the irresistible power of attraction that encircled him, though his appearance and manners were always peculiar, he never failed to delight and to *excel*. His figure certainly bore the authentic impress of his birth and original station in life; it seemed rather moulded by nature for the rough exercises of agriculture, than the gentler cultivation of the *belles lettres*. His features were stamped with the hardy character of independence, and the firmness of conscious, though not arrogant preeminence. I believe no man was ever gifted with a larger portion of the *vivida vis animi:* the animated expressions of his countenance were almost peculiar to himself. The rapid lightenings of his eye were always the harbingers of some flash of genius, whether they darted the fiery glances of insulted and indignant superiority, or beamed with the impassioned sentiment of fervent and impetuous affections. His voice alone could improve upon the magic of his eye; sonorous, replete with the finest modulations, it alternately captivated the ear with the melody of poetic numbers, the perspicuity of nervous reasoning, or the ardent sallies of enthusiastic patriotism.

> Maria Riddell, 1796, *Letter to Dumfries Journal,* Aug. 7,
> *Burn's Works*, ed. Currie

The first time I saw Robert Burns was on the 23d of October, 1786, when he dined at my house at Ayrshire, together with our common friend Mr. John Mackenzie, surgeon, in Mauchline, to whom I am indebted for the pleasure of his acquaintance. . . . His manners were then, as they continued ever afterwards, simple, manly, and independent; strongly expressive of conscious genius and worth; but without any thing that indicated forwardness, arrogance, or vanity. He took his share in conversation, but not more than belonged to him; and listened with apparent attention and deference, on subjects where his want of education deprived him of the means of information. If there had been a little more of gentleness and accommodation in his temper, he would, I think, have been still more interesting; but he had been accustomed to give law in the circle of his ordinary acquaintance; and his dread of any thing approaching to meanness or servility, rendered his manner somewhat decided and hard. Nothing, perhaps, was more remarkable among his various attainments, than the fluency, and precision, and originality of his language, when he spoke in company; more particularly

as he aimed at purity in his turn of expression, and avoided more successfully than most Scotchmen, the peculiarities of Scottish phraseology.

Dugald Stewart, 1800, *Letter to James Currie,*
Currie's *Life of Burns*

Burns died in great povery; but the independence of his spirit, and the exemplary prudence of his wife, had preserved him from debt. He had received from his poems a clear profit of about nine hundred pounds. Of this
sum, the part expended on his library (which was far from extensive) and
in the humble furniture of his house, remained; and obligations were found
for two hundred pounds advanced by him to the assistance of those to whom
he was united by the ties of blood, and still more by those of esteem
and affection. When it is considered, that his expenses in Edinburgh,
and on his various journeys, could not be inconsiderable; that his agricultural undertaking was unsuccessful; that his income, from the Excise
was for some time as low as fifty, and never rose to above seventy
pounds a year; that his family was large and his spirit was liberal—
no one will be surprised that his circumstances were so poor, or that, as
his health decayed, his proud and feeling heart sunk under the secret consciousness of indigence, and the apprehensions of absolute want. Yet poverty never bent the spirit of Burns to any pecuniary meanness. Neither
chicanery nor sordidness ever appeared in his conduct. He carried his dis-
regard of money to blameable excess. Even in the midst of distress he bore
himself loftily to the world, and received with a jealous reluctance every
offer of friendly assistance.

James Currie, 1800, ed., *Works of Robert Burns, Life*

We turned again to Burns's house. Mrs. Burns was gone to spend some time
by the seashore with her children. We spoke to the servant-maid at the door,
who invited us forward, and we sate down in the parlour. The walls were
coloured with a blue wash; on one side of the fire was a mahogany desk,
opposite to the window a clock, and over the desk, a print from "Cotter's
Saturday Night," which Burns mentions in one of his letters having received
as a present. The house was cleanly and neat in the inside, the stairs of stone,
scoured white, the kitchen on the right side of the passage, the parlour on
the left. In the room above the parlour the poet died, and his son after him
in the same room.

Dorothy Wordsworth, Aug. 18, 1803, *Journals*

No person can regret more than I do the tendency of *some* of my Brother's
writings to represent irregularity of conduct as a consequence of genius, and
sobriety the effect of dulness; but surely more has been said on that subject

than the fact warrants: and it ought to be remembered that the greatest part of his writings, having that tendency, *were not published by himself, nor intended for publication.* But it may likewise be observed, and every attentive reader of Burns's Works, must have observed, that he frequently presents a caricature of his feelings, and even of his failings—a kind of mock-heroic account of himself and his opinions, which he never supposed could be taken literally. I dare say it never entered into his head, for instance, that when he was speaking in that manner of Milton's Satan, any one should gravely suppose that was the model on which he wished to form his own character. Yet on such rants, which the author evidently intends should be considered a mere play of imagination, joined to some abstract reasoning of the critic, many of the heavy accusations brought against the Poet for bad taste and worse morals, rest.

> Gilbert Burns, 1814, *Letter to Alexander Peterkin,* Sep. 29;
> *Life and Works of Robert Burns,* ed. Peterkin

The truth is, that the convivial excesses or other errors of Robert Burns, were neither greater nor more numerous than those which we every day see in the conduct of men who stand high in the estimation of society;—of some men, who, like Burns, have, in their peculiar spheres, conferred splendid gifts of genius on their country, and whose names are breathed in every voice, with pride and enthusiasm, as the benefactors of society. Are their errors officiously dragged from the tomb, or emblazoned amidst the trophies of victory without universal reprobation? All we ask is the same measure of justice and mercy for Burns.

> Alexander Peterkin, 1815, ed., *The Life and Works of Robert Burns,* vol. I, p. xlix

One song of Burn's is of more worth to you than all I could think for a whole year in his native country. His misery is a dead weight upon the nimbleness of one's quill; I tried to forget it—to drink toddy without any care—to write a merry sonnet—it won't do—he talked with bitches, he drank with blackguards; he was miserable. We can see horribly clear, in the works of such a man, his whole life, as if we were God's spies.

> John Keats, 1818, *Letters*

Burns was not like Shakspeare in the range of his genius; but there is something of the same magnanimity, directness, and unaffected character about him. He was not a sickly sentimentalist, a namby-pamby poet, a mincing metre ballad-monger, any more than Shakspeare. He would as soon hear "a brazen candlestick tuned, or a dry wheel grate on the axletree." He was as much of a man—not a twentieth as much of a poet—as Shakspeare.

With but little of his imagination or inventive power, he had the same life of mind: within the narrow circle of personal feeing or domestic incidents, the pulse of his poetry flows as healthily and vigorously. He had an eye to see; a heart to feel:—no more.

William Hazlitt, 1818, *Lectures on the English Poets,*
Lecture VII

The multitude who accompanied Burns to the grave went step by step with the chief mourners. They might amount to ten or twelve thousand. Not a word was heard. . . . It was an impressive and mournful sight to see men of all ranks and persuasions and opinions mingling as brothers, and stepping side by side down the streets of Dumfries, with the remains of him who had sung of their loves and joys and domestic endearments, with a truth and a tenderness which none perhaps have since equalled.

Allan Cunningham, 1824, "Robert Burns and Lord Byron,"
London Magazine

I was a lad of fifteen in 1786-7, when he came first to Edinburgh, but had sense and feeling enough to be much interested in his poetry, and would have given the world to know him; but I had very little acquaintance with any literary people, and still less with the gentry of the west country, the two sets that he most frequented. Mr. Thomas Grierson was at that time a clerk of my father's. He knew Burns, and promised to ask him to his lodgings to dinner, but had no opportunity to keep his word, otherwise I might have seen more of this distinguished man. . . . His person was strong and robust: his manners rustic, not clownish; a sort of dignified plainness and simplicity which received part of its effect perhaps from one's knowledge of his extraordinary talents. His features are represented in Mr. Nasmyth's picture, but to me it conveys the idea that they are diminished as if seen in perspective. I think his countenance was more massive than it looks in any of the portraits. I would have taken the poet, had I not known what he was, for a very sagacious country farmer of the old Scotch school—*i. e.* none of your modern agriculturists, who keep labourers for their drudgery, but the *douce gudeman* who held his own plough. There was a strong expression of sense and shrewdness in all his lineaments; the eye alone, I think, indicated the poetical character and temperament. It was large, and of a dark cast, and glowed (I say literally *glowed*) when he spoke with feeling or interest. I never saw such another eye in a human head, though I have seen the most distinguished men in my time. His conversation expressed perfect self-confidence, without the slightest presumption. Among the men who were the most learned of their time and country, he expressed himself with perfect firmness, but without the least intrusive forwardness; and when he differed in opinion, he did not hesitate to express it firmly, yet at the same time with modesty. I do not remember any part of his conversation distinctly enough to be quoted, nor did I ever see him again, except in the street, where he did not recognize me, as I could not expect he should. He was much caressed in Edinburgh, but (considering what literary emoluments have been since his day) the efforts made for his relief were extremely trifling.

Sir Walter Scott, 1827, *Letter to Lockhart, Memoirs* by Lockhart, vol. I, pp. 166, 167

Burns, eager of temper, loud of tone, and with declamation and sarcasm equally at command, was, we may easily believe, the most hated of human beings, because the most dreaded, among the provincial champions of the administration of which he thought fit to disapprove. But that he ever, in his most ardent moods, upheld the principles of those whose applause of the French Revolution was but the mask of revolutionary designs at home, after these principles had been really developed by those that maintained them, and understood by him, it may be safely denied. There is not in all his correspondence, one syllable to give countenance to such a charge. . . . Here, then, as in most other cases of similar controversy, the fair and equitable conclusion would seem to be, "truth lies between." To whatever Burns' excesses amounted, they were, it is obvious, and that frequently, the subject of rebuke and remonstrance even from his own dearest friends— even from men who had no sort of objection to potations deep enough in all conscience. That such reprimands, giving shape and form to the thoughts that tortured his own bosom, should have been received at times with a strange mixture of remorse and indignation, none that have considered the nervous susceptibility and haughtiness of Burns' character, can hear with surprise.

John Gibson Lockhart, 1828, *Life of Robert Burns*, pp. 308, 341

He has a just self-consciousness, which too often degenerates into pride; yet it is a noble pride, for defence, not for offence, no cold, suspicious feeling, but a frank and social one. The peasant poet bears himself, we might say, like a king in exile: he is cast among the low, and feels himself equal to the highest; yet he claims no rank that none may be disputed to him.

Thomas Carlyle, 1828, *Essay on Burns*

In early life he laboured under a disorder of the stomach, accompanied by palpitations of the heart, depression of the spirits, and nervous pains in the head, the nature of which he never appears to have understood, but which evidently arose from dyspepsia. These sufferings, be it remembered, are complained of in his letters years before he had committed any excess; and so far from being the consequence of intemperance, as they are generally considered to have been, the exhaustion they produced was probably the cause which drove him in his moments of hypochondria, to the excitement of the bottle for a temporary palliation of his symptoms.

R. R. Madden, 1833, *Infirmities of Genius,* vol. I, p. 276

Could he have remained always at the plough, and worn always the mantle of inspiration which fell on him there, and enjoyed ever the lawful intoxication of natural scenery and solitary thought, he had been as happy as he was glorious. But night came, and found him weary and jaded in mind and body, thirsting for some new excitement, and eager to pass (O human nature! O hideous anti-climax!) from an Elisha-like plough—to a penny-wedding! There the lower part of his nature found intense gratification and unrestricted play. There the "blood of John Barleycorn" furnished him with a false and hollow semblance of the true inspiration he had met in the solitary field, or on "the side of a plantain, when the wind was howling among the trees, and raving over the plain." And there, through the misty light of the presiding punch-bowl, he saw the most ordinary specimens of female nature transformed into angels; and fancied that, like divinities they should be adored.

George Gilfillan, 1856, ed., *The Poetical Works of Robert Burns,* vol. I, p. xii

Here was a man, a son of toil, looking out on the world from his cottage, on society low and high, and on nature homely or beautiful, with the clearest eye, the most piercing insight, and the warmest heart; touching life at a hundred points, seeing to the core all the sterling worth, nor less the pretence and hollowness of the men he met, the humour, the drollery, the pathos, and the sorrow of human existence; and expressing what he saw, not in the stock phrases of books, but in his own vernacular, the language of his fireside, with a directness, a force, a vitality that tingled to the finger tips, and forced the phrases of his peasant dialect into literature, and made them for ever classical. Large sympathy, generous enthusiasm, reckless abandonment, fierce indignation, melting compassion, rare flashes of moral insight, all are there. Everywhere you see the strong intellect made alive, and driven home to the mark, by the fervid heart behind it. And if the sight of the world's inequalities, and some natural repining at his own obscure lot, mingled from the beginning, as has been said, "some bitterness of earthly spleen and passion with the workings of his inspiration,

and if these in the end ate deep into the great heart they had long tormented," who that has not known his experience may venture too strongly
to condemn him?

John Campbell Shairp, 1879, *Robert Burns*
(*English Men of Letters*), p. 190

Distracted by poetry and poverty and passion, and brought to public shame,
he determined to leave the country, and in 1786, when he was twenty-seven
years old, Burns published his poems by subscription, to get the money to
pay his passage to America. Ah! could that poor, desperate ploughman
of Mossgiel have forseen the day, could he have known that because of
those poems—an abiding part of literature, familiar to every people, sung
and repeated in American homes from sea to sea—his genius would be
honored and his name blessed, and his statue raised with grateful pride to
keep his memory in America green forever, perhaps the amazing vision
might have nerved him to make his life as noble as his genius; perhaps the
full sunshine of assured glory might have wrought upon that great, generous,
wilful soul to

'tak' a thought an' men'."

George William Curtis, 1880, *Robert Burns, an address
Delivered at the Unveiling of the Statue of the Poet, in
Central Park, New York,* October 2; *Orations and
Addresses,* vol. III, p. 310

At least 50,000 people celebrated the centenary of Robert Burns's death,
at Dumfries, on Tuesday. In the morning a long procession, accompanied
by bands, filed through the streets, and hundreds of persons visited the
poet's grave, on which wreaths were laid, many being sent by Scottish
societies in the most distant parts of the world. At two o'clock within the
Drill Hall a conversazione, attended by 4,000 persons was held. . . . Burns
has become the patron saint of Dumfries, and he had borne aloft the
banner of the essential equality of man. At St. Michael's Church-yard,
wreaths presented by 130 Burns and other societies were handed to Lord
Rosebery, who placed them on the poet's tomb. The first wreath laid on
the tomb was that of Lord Rosebery, consisting of arum lilies and eucharis.
The most modest wreath, and yet, probably, the most interesting, was that
from the Glasgow Mauchline Society. It consisted of holly and gowans, the
latter grown on the field at Mossgiel, celebrated by Burns in his poem "To
a Mountain Daisy." The wreath was made up by the granddaughters of
Burns, the daughters of Col. James Glencairn Burns.

Anon, 1896, *Publisher's Circular,* July 25

During his own lifetime Thomson suffered keenly from the charge that he had taken an unfair advantage of Burns, in accepting so much from the poet without making him any substantial pecuniary return. The charge still hangs about Thomson's name in a vague sort of way, for in affairs of this kind the dog who has once acquired a bad repute is likely to retain it. The unfortunate editor, as he puts it himself was assailed, "first anonymously, and afterwards, to my great surprise, by some writers who might have been expected to possess sufficient judgment to see the matter in its true light." He defended himself, in the words of one of his calumniators, "about once every seven years;" but it is not until the appearance of Professor Wilson's onslaught in the *Land of Burns* (1838) that his correspondence begins to show the full extent of his suffering under the lash. . . . The truth is that Burns declined to write deliberately for money. He would—in a patriotic undertaking of this kind at any rate—write for love, or not write at all. If his poems brought him a profit—well, they were not written with that profit directly in view; the pecuniary return was, as it were, but an accident, not affecting in any way the inception of the work. This was practically his view of the matter as expressed to Thomson. It appears that he expressed the same view also to others.

J. Cuthbert Hadden, 1898, George Thomson the
Friend of Burns, pp. 139, 145

While engaged on the farm, which did not pay much, and composing poems, which paid still less, he had time for his favourite wooing, which paid worst of all. His relations with the "sex" were many and migratory. He was no sooner off with the old love than he was on with the new, and even for that he often did not wait. In his tastes he was not fastidious as to the position, quality, or even the looks of his entrancer. "He had always a particular jealousy of people who were richer than himself, or had more consequence," says his brother Gilbert. "His love therefore seldom settled on persons of this description." A buxom barndoor beauty, a servant girl was enough, although she was as devoid of romance as of stockings. He must be the superior. A "fine woman," especially among his humble acquaintance, he could not resist; and seldom could she resist the masterful wooer, with his winning ways, his bewitching talk, his eyes that "glowed like coals of fire."

Henry Grey Graham, 1901, Scottish Men of Letters
in the Eighteenth Century, p. 394

JEAN

Poor ill-advised ungrateful Armour came home on Friday last. You have heard of all the particulars of that affair, and a black affair it is. What she thinks of her conduct now, I don't know; one thing I do know, she has made me completely miserable. Never man loved, or rather adored, a woman, more than I did her; and to confess a truth between you and me, I do still love her to distraction after all, although I won't tell her so if I were to see her, which I don't want to do. My poor, dear, unfortunate Jean, how happy I have been in thy arms! It is not the losing her that made me so unhappy, but for her sake I feel most severely; I forsee she is on the road to—I am afraid—eternal ruin. May Almighty God forgive her ingratitude and perjury to me, as I from my soul forgive her; and may His grace be with her and bless her in all her future life! I can have no nearer idea of the place of eternal punishment than what I have felt in my own heart on her account. I have tried often to forget her. I have run into all kinds of dissipation and riots, mason meetings, drinking matches, and other mischief, to drive her out of my head, but all in vain. And now for a grand cure: the ship is on her way home that is to take me out to Jamaica; then farewell, dear old Scotland; and farewell, dear, ungrateful Jean, for never, never, will I see you more.

Robert Burns, 1786, *Letter to David Brice*

Compared Robert Burns, with Jean Armour, his alleged spouse. They both acknowledged their irregular marriage, and their sorrow for that irregularity, and desiring that the Session will take such steps as may seem to them proper, in order to the solemn confirmation of the said marriage. The Session, taking this affair under their consideration, agree that they both be rebuked for this acknowledged irregularity, and that they be solemnly engaged to adhere faithfully to one another as man and wife all the days of their life. In regard the Session have a title in law to some fine for behoof of the poor, they agree to refer to Mr. Burns his own generosity. The above sentence was accordingly executed, and the Session absolved the said parties from any scandal on this account.

William Auld (Moderator), 1788, *Mauchline Kirk-Session Books,* Aug. 5

Mrs. Burns through the liberality of her children, spent her latter years in comparative affluence, yet "never changed, nor wished to change her place." In March 1843, at the age of sixty-eight, she closed her respectable life in the same room in which her husband had breathed his last thirty-eight years before.

Robert Chambers, 1851-52, *The Life and Works of Robert Burns*

It may be questionable whether any marriage could have tamed Burns; but it is at least certain that there was no hope for him in the marriage he contracted. He did right, but then he had done wrong before; it was, as I said, one of those relations in life which it seems equally wrong to break or to perpetuate. He neither loved nor respected his wife. "God knows," he writes, "my choice was as random as blind man's buff." He consoles himself by the thought that he has acted kindly to her; that she "has the most sacred enthusiasm of attachment to him;" that she has a good figure; that she has a "wood-note wild," "her voice rising with ease to B natural," no less. The effect on the reader is one of unmingled pity for both parties concerned. This was not the wife who (in his own words) could "enter into his favourite studies or relish his favourite authors;" this was not even a wife, after the affair of the marriage lines, in whom a husband could joy to place his trust. Let her manage a farm with sense, let her voice rise to B natural all day long, she would still be a peasant to her lettered lord, and an object of pity rather than of equal affection. She could now be faithful, she could now be forgiving, she could now be generous even to a pathetic and touching degree; but coming from one who was unloved, and who had scarce shown herself worthy of the sentiment, these were all virtues thrown away, which could neither change her husband's heart nor effect the inherent destiny of their relation. From the outset, it was a marriage that had no root in nature; and we find him, ere long, lyrically regretting Highland Mary, renewing correspondence with Clarinda in the warmest language, on doubtful terms with Mrs. Riddel, and on terms unfortunately beyond any question with Anne Park.

Robert Louis Stevenson, 1882, *Familiar Studies of Men and Books*, p. 72

HIGHLAND MARY

He loved Mary Campbell, his "Highland Mary," with as pure a passion as ever possessed a young poet's heart; nor is there so sweet and sad a passage recorded in the life of any other one of all the sons of song. Many such partings there have been between us poor beings—blind at all times, and often blindest in our bliss—but all gone to oblivion. But that hour can never die—that scene will live forever. Immortal the two shadows standing there, holding together the Bible—a little rivulet flowing between—in which, as in consecrated water, they have dipt their hands, water not purer than, at that moment, their united hearts. There are few of his songs more beautiful, and none more impassioned.

John Wilson, 1844, *The Genius and Character of Burns*, p. 15

All the world has heard of Highland Mary—in life a maid-servant in the family of Mr. Hamilton, after death to be remembered with Dante's Beatrice and Petrarch's Laura. How Burns and Mary became acquainted we have little means of knowing—indeed the whole relationship is somewhat obscure—but Burns loved her as he loved no other woman, and her memory is preserved in the finest expression of his love and grief. Strangely enough, it seems to have been in the fierce rupture between himself and Jean that this white flower of love sprang up, sudden in its growth, brief in its passion and beauty. It was arranged that the lovers should become man and wife, and that Mary should return to her friends to prepare for her wedding. Before her departure there was a farewell scene. "On the second Sunday of May," Burns writes to Mr. Thomson, after an historical fashion which has something touching in it, "in a sequestered spot on the banks of the Ayr the interview took place." The lovers met and plighted solemn troth. According to popular statement, they stood on either side of a brook, they dipped their hands in the water, exchanged Bibles—and parted. Mary died at Greenock, and was buried in a dingy church-yard hemmed by narrow streets—beclanged now by innumerable hammers, and within a stone's throw of passing steamers. Information of her death was brought to Burns at Mossgiel; he went to the window to read the letter, and the family noticed that on a sudden his face changed. He went out without speaking; they respected his grief and were silent. On the whole matter Burns remained singularly reticent; but years after, from a sudden geysir of impassioned song, we learn that through all that time she had never been forgotten.

Alexander Smith, 1865, The Poetical Works of Robert Burns,
Life, p. xiii

Little that is positive is known of Mary Campbell except that she once possessed a copy of the Scriptures (now very piously preserved at Ayr), and that she is a subject of a fantasy, in bronze, at Dunoon.

William Ernest Henley, 1897, Life, Genius, Achievement,
The Poetry of Robert Burns, vol. IV, p. 285

By all means let us reject the Mary Campbell tradition, immolate the Bible at Ayr, melt down the "fantasy in bronze" at Dunoon, make building material of the monument at Greenock, reduce all get-at-able Highland Mary literature to pulp, and *for ever more let the story stand as Burns left it.*

Robert M. Lockhart, 1898, "Mr. Henley and Highland Mary,"
The Westminster Review, vol. 149, p. 336

CLARINDA

She called herself "high-spirited," which meant "unyielding;" she mingled romance and strong Calvinistic principles, an almost incompatible mixture;

she was light, vain; a "foolish woman," listening to the rhapsodies of the Ayrshire ploughman when she ought to have been thinking of her children; and her quiet discussion of certain matters relating to her admirer shows her to have been eminently coarse. She also, as one of her family says, "cultivated the Muses." All these elements, combined as it were in one dish, make up a doubtful sort of salad.

Percy Fitzgerald, 1870, "The Loves of Famous Men,"
Belgravia, vol. 12, p. 425

It was at this time Burns met Clarinda once more. She was about to sail for the West Indies, in search of the husband who had forsaken her; the interview was a brief and hurried one, and no account of it remains, except some letters, and a few lyrics which he addressed to her. One of these is distinguished as one of the most impassioned effusions which Burns ever poured forth. It contains that one consummate stanza in which Scott, Byron, and many more, saw concentrated, "the essence of a thousand love-tales."

> Had we never loved so kindly,
> Had we never loved so blindly;
> Never met, or never parted,
> We had ne'er been broken-hearted.

Mrs. Burns is said to have been a marvel of long-suffering and forgiveness, for the way in which she bore the wrongs her husband inflicted upon her by his unfaithfulness. There is no doubt that Burns also tasted self-reproach and

> "Self-contempt, bitterer to drink than blood."

Charlotte A. Price, 1895, "Famous Poets," Belgravia, vol. 87, p. 273

So in the beginning of December he falls in with Mrs. M'Lehose; he instantly proposes to "cultivate her friendship with the enthusiasm of religion;" and the two are languishing in Arcady in the twinkling of a cupid's wing. She was a handsome, womanly creature "of a somewhat voluptuous style of beauty:" a style the Bard appreciated—lively but devout, extremely sentimental yet inexorably dutiful: a grass widow with children—nine times in ten a lasting safeguard—and the strictest notions of propriety—a good enough defense for a time; but young (she was the Bard's own age), clever, "of a poetical fabric of mind," and all the rest. . . . In the prime of life, deserted, sentimental, a tangle of simple instincts and as simple pieties, she had the natural woman's desire for a lover and the religious woman's resolve to keep that lover's passion within bounds. . . . She was plainly an excellent creature, bent on keeping herself honest and her lover straight; and it is impossible to read her letters to Sylvander without a respect, a certain admiration even, which have never been awakened yet by the study of Sylvander's letters to her. From Sylvander's point of view, as M'Lehose was still alive, and an open intrigue with a married woman would have been ruin, only one inference is possible: that he longed for the shepherd's hour to strike for the chimes' sake only; so that, when he thought of his future, as he must have done anxiously and often, he cannot ever have thought of it as Clarinda's, even though in a moment of peculiar exaltation he swore to keep single till that wretch, the wicked husband died.

> William Ernest Henley, 1897, *Life, Genius, Achievement,*
> *The Poetry of Robert Burns,* vol. IV, pp. 304, 305, 306

MRS. DUNLOP

MADAM—I have written you so often without recg. any answer, that I would not trouble you again but for the circumstances in which I am. An illness which has long hung about me in all probability will speedily send me beyond that bourne whence no traveller returns. Your friendship with which for so many years you honored me was a friendship dearest to my soul. Your conversation and especially your correspondence were at once highly entertaining and instructive. With what pleasure did I use to break up the seal! The remembrance yet adds one pulse more to my poor palpitating heart—Farewell!!!

> Robert Burns, 1796, *Last Letter to Mrs. Dunlop*

The friendship of Mrs. Dunlop was of particular value to Burns. This lady, daughter and sole heiress to Sir Thomas Wallace of Craige, and lineal descendant of the illustrious Wallace, the first of Scottish warriors, possesses the qualities of mind suited to her high lineage. Preserving, in the decline of life, the generous affections of youth; her admiration of the poet was soon accompanied by a sincere friendship for the man; which pursued him in after life through good and evil report; in poverty, in sickness, and in sorrow; and which is continued to his infant family, now deprived of their parent.

> James Currie, 1800, ed., *Works of Robert Burns, Life*

The real basis of the friendship was their common warmth and generosity of soul. Mrs. Dunlop's interest in the poet was not purely, or even primarily, intellectual. She was not what would be called a literary lady. She was by no means a pedant. She was simply a woman of good birth and good breeding; old enough and wise enough to have drawn profit from the experiences of life; fond of books and sincerely religious; endowed with good judgment and good sense, with quick womanly sympathy and inextinguishable youthfulness of heart. Being what she was, she won the poet's confidence and sincere affection, and drew out all his finer feelings. His letters to her are not indeed free from that artificiality which characterised the epistolary

style of his day, and marred all his correspondence; but they are less disfigured by it than those addressed to some of his patrons, or to his unknown
literary correspondents—to say nothing of the effusions to "Clarinda."

L. M. Roberts, 1895, "The Burns and Dunlop Correspondence,"
Fortnightly Review, vol. 64, p. 663

The Lochryan MSS., now published for the first time, were in all probability
never seen by Currie. Manifestly none of them has even been handled by
either editor or printer. They are all in a state of beautiful preservation, and
include at least as fine specimens of the poet's handwriting as any that have
seen the light in the original or reproduction. . . . Mrs. Dunlop kept the
Lochryan MSS. at Dunlop till her death, when she left the estate of Lochryan and the MSS. to her grandson, General Sir John Wallace, from whom
the documents descended to his son and heir, the next possessor of Lochryan, who left them by will to his youngest brother the present Colonel
F. J. Wallace, from whom they were recently acquired by Mr. Adam. They
have thus been continuously in the hands of the Dunlop-Wallace family
during the past century. Colonel Wallace states to the best of his knowledge
that they have been kept in a box in the saferoom at Lochryan for the last
fifty years. The interweaving of this new material with the old makes the
Correspondence of Burns and Mrs. Dunlop almost unique in its complete-
ness. A careful search after possible *lacunae* has discovered no more than
four place where it can be definitely stated that the letter of Burns is missing, and of the gross sum of Mrs. Dunlop's it appears that Burns had lost
or destroyed only nine—a circumstance which must have wiped out the
memory of the many proofs the lady had received that he did not always
read her communications with the most respectful care, and at the same
time must have deepened the remorse she felt for her neglect of the poet
during the last eighteen months of his life.

William Wallace, 1898, *Robert Burns and Mrs. Dunlop,*
Preface, vol. I, pp. vi, vii

A curious figure, this Mrs. Dunlop, of Dunlop, and most out of line with
one's notion of a Scotch gentlewoman! To be a lady of sensibility was her
ideal. To go to posterity as the social and, forsooth, the literary mentor of
her gifted neighbor was her ambition. Her religion was of the Genevan type
—not Jean Calvin's, but Jean Jacques Rousseau's. The religion of the heart,
she called it, and had she not been a Sexagenarian and forever occupied
with the births of grandchildren, there is no telling where it would have
landed her. In comparison with her solicitude for Burns, the cares of a
patriarchal household sat light upon her, and with pen in hand she could
say, "as to forming schemes, it is a kind of castle-building that I cannot

resign, as it pleases myself and does little harm to anything else." Scolding, questioning, teasing, advising, and spoiling Burns like a grandmother, she is yet irrepressibly youthful. With all her intellectual fire, and with all her provincial awkwardness, it is impossible not to admire her buoyancy, freshness, and hero-worship. She comes near possessing charm, and is almost a romantic figure.

George McLean Harper, 1898, "Burns in his Correspondence,"
The Book Buyer, vol. 17, p. 20

The Holy Fair (1785)

In Burns's time this poem was much relished by the moderate clergy, and Dr. Blair condescended to suggest the change of a word in order to render its satire more pointed. In these days of better taste, a regret will be generally felt that Burns should have been tempted or provoked into such subjects. This is, however, a general belief in Ayrshire that the "Holy Fair" was attended with a good effect, for since its appearance, the custom of resorting to the "occasion" in neighboring parishes for the sake of holiday making has been much abated, and a great increase of decorous observance has taken place.

Robert Chambers, 1851-52, *The Life and Works
of Robert Burns,* vol. I, p. 270

As a matter of fact, in the history of Scottish literature and religion, this caricature of the Holiest, as some might be inclined to call it, did no harm, but rather good; for the caricature lay undoubtedly to no small extent in the real facts of the case, not in the mere treatment of the poet. Harm to Burns it certainly did do; for it tended to raise a wall of partition between him and the reverential sentiment of the country, which stands in the way of his acceptance with not a few of the most worthy of his countrymen even at the present hour. Harm to the people it could not do; for so far as it was overcharged, the roots of the popular piety had stuck too deep to be shaken by a rude hand; and so far as it was true, the reproof has been so effective that not a shadow of the abuse remains. Had it not been for the polemical relation in which he found himself to the zealous party in the Church, and for the glaring nature of the abuse of sacred ceremonies that forced itself on his observation, I feel certain that Burns was the last man in the world to have wantonly held so sacred a rite up to public ridicule.

John Stuart Blackie, 1888, *Life of Robert Burns
(Great Writers),* p. 51

Of all the satires, however, *The Holy Fair* is the most remarkable. It is in a sense a summing up of all the others that preceded it. The picture it gives of the mixed and motley multitude fairing in the church-yard at Mauchline, with a relay of ministerial mountebanks catering for their excitement, is true to the life. It is begging the question to deplore that Burns was provoked to such an attack. The scene was provocation sufficient to any right-thinking man who associated the name of religion with all that was good and beautiful and true. Such a state of things demanded reformation. The church-yard—that holy ground on which the church was built and sanctified by the dust of pious and saintly men—cried aloud against the desecration to which it was subjected, and Burns, who alone had the power to purify it from such profanities, would have been untrue to himself and a traitor to the religion of his country had he merely shrugged his shoulders and allowed things to go on as they were going.

> Gabriel Setoun, 1896, *Robert Burns*
> (*Famous Scots Series*), p. 51

The Holy Fair, that "joyful solemnity" in which the scandals attending the open-air communions are painted with vivid power and merciless veracity. In these satires there is not *saeva indignatio* at evils he hated, but wild humour over scandals he laughed at. In them he was merely voicing the feelings of the educated classes, and echoing the teaching of the moderate clergy in two-thirds of the Lowland pulpits of Scotland. To say that Burns, by his drastic lines, broke down the despotism of the Church, overthrew the spirit of Puritanism, and dispelled religious gloom in the country, is to speak in ignorance of the real part he played. That work had been begun effectively by others before him, and was to be carried on by others who never felt his influence.

> Henry Grey Graham, 1901, *Scottish Men of Letters*
> *in the Eighteenth Century*, p. 392

The Cotter's Saturday Night (1785)

The Cotter's Saturday Night is tender and moral, it is solemn and devotional, and rises at length into a strain of grandeur and sublimity, which modern poetry has not surpassed. The noble sentiments of patriotism with which it concludes, correspond with the rest of the poem. In no age or country have the pastoral muses breathed such elevated accents, if the Messiah of Pope be excepted, which is indeed a pastoral in form only.

> James Currie, 1800, ed., *Works of Robert Burns, Life*

The Cottar's Saturday Night is, perhaps, of all Burns's pieces, the one whose exclusion from the collection, were such things possible now-a-days, would be the most injurious, if not to the genius, at least to the character, of the man. In spite of many feeble lines, and some heavy stanzas, it appears to me, that even his genius would suffer more in estimation, by being contemplated in the absence of this poem, than of any other single performance he has left us. Loftier flights he certainly had made, but in these he remained but a short while on the wing, and effort is too often perceptible; here the motion is easy, gentle, placidly undulating. There is more of the conscious security of power, than in any other of his serious pieces of considerable length; the whole has an appearance of coming in a full stream from the fountain of the heart—a stream that soothes the ear, and has no glare on the surface.

John Gibson Lockhart, 1828, *Life of Robert Burns,* p. 97

In *The Cottar's Saturday Night,* the poet has so varied his dialect that there are scarcely two consecutive stanzas written according to the same model. An hour of winter evening music on the Æolian harp, when all the winds are on the wing, would hardly be more wild, and sweet, and stern, and changeable than the series. Some of the strains are as purely English as the author could reach; others so racily Scottish as often to require a glossary; while in a third class the two are so enchantingly combined, that no poetic diction can excel the pathos and sublimity, blended with beauty and homeliness, that equally mark them.

James Montgomery, 1833, *Lectures on General Literature, Poetry, etc.,* p. 135

It is the most artificial and the most imitative of Burns's works. Not only is the influence of Gray's *Elegy* conspicuous, but also there are echoes of Pope, Thomson, Goldsmith, and even Milton; while the stanza, which was taken, not from Spenser, whom Burns had not then read, but from Beattie and Shenstone, is so purely English as to lie outside the range of Burns's experience and accomplishment.

William Ernest Henley and Thomas F. Henderson, 1896, ed., *The Poetry of Robert Burns,* vol. I, p. 362, note

Tam O'Shanter (1790)

It is not so much a poem as a piece of sparkling rhetoric; the heart and body of the story still lies hard and dead. He has not gone back, much less carried us back, into that dark, earnest, wondering age, when the tradition was believed, and when it took its rise; he does not attempt, by any new modelling of his supernatural ware, to strike anew that deep mysterious chord of human nature, which once responded to such things, and which lives in us too, and will forever live, though silent, or vibrating with far other notes, and to far different issues. Our German readers will understand us when we say that he is not the Tieck but the Musäus of this tale. Externally it is all green and living; yet look closer, it is no firm growth, but only ivy on a rock. The piece does not properly cohere; the strange chasm which yawns in our incredulous imagination between the Ayr public-house and gate of Tophet is nowhere bridged over; nay, the idea of such a bridge is laughed at; and thus the tragedy of the adventure becomes a mere drunken phantasmagoria painted on ale-vapors, and the farce alone has any reality. We do not say that Burns should have made much more of this tradition; we rather think that, for strictly poetical purposes, not much *was* to be made of it. Neither are we blind to the deep, varied, genial power displayed in what he has actually accomplished; but we find far more "Shakespearean" qualities, as these of *Tam o' Shanter* have been fondly named, in many of his other pieces; nay, we incline to believe that this latter might have been written, all but quite as well, by a man who, in place of genius, had only possessed talent.

Thomas Carlyle, 1828, Essay on Burns

Tam O' Shanter is not so marvellous a creation as *The Dance of the Sevin Deidly Synnis,* though we may find it easier to appreciate the modern poem, in which the tipsy hilarity of the hero gives a familiar aspect to the deviltry of the witches, and robs it of the weirdness and horror that should mark the spectacle of a supernatural world. Burns's humour plays most freely round the incidents of human life, though none can deny the boldness with which it now and again makes a sweep into the realms of superstition.

John Merry Ross, 1884, Scottish History and Literature,
ed. Brown, p. 214

Scarcely excelled in powers of imagination by Shakespeare himself is Burns's weird description of the orgies of the witches, and the infernal scenery in which they are exhibited. . . . The only fault found in this poem is that at the conclusion it falls off in interest. This is said to be owing to Burns having stuck to the popular tale of this hero; for Tam was not a creation of fancy, but a real person. . . . Burns considered *Tam O'Shanter* his masterpiece, and many critics have regarded it in the same light; yet it does not perhaps embody what is brightest and best in his poetry. His address to a mouse on turning up her nest with a plough in November is richer in true poetic light and color. Its companion is that to a daisy. In these and in *The Cotter's Saturday Night* it has been happily remarked that "the poet is seen in his happiest inspiration, his brightest sunshine, and his tenderest tears."

The latter poem is familiar to all, and in true and touching description is almost unrivalled.

Sarah Warner Brooks, 1890, *English Poetry and Poets,* pp. 289, 290, 291

The Jolly Beggars (1785)

Perhaps we may venture to say that the most strictly poetical of all his "poems" is one which does not appear in Currie's edition, but has been often printed before and since under the humble title of *The Jolly Beggars.* The subject truly is among the lowest in nature; but it only the more shows our poet's gift in raising it into the domain of art. To our minds this piece seems thoroughly compacted; melted together, refined; and poured forth in one flood of true *liquid* harmony. It is light, airy, and soft of movement, yet sharp and precise in its details; every face is a portrait: that *raucle carlin,* that *wee Apollo,* that *Son of Mars* are Scottish, yet ideal; the scene is at once a dream, and the very Rag-castle of "Poosie-Nansie." Further, it seems in a considerable degree complete, a real self-supporting whole, which is the highest merit in a poem.

Thomas Carlyle, 1828, *Essay on Burns*

In the world of *The Jolly Beggars* there is more than hideousness and squalor, there is bestiality; yet the piece is a super poetic success. It has a breadth, truth, and power which make the famous scene in Auerbach's Cellar, of Goethe's *Faust,* seem artificial and tame beside it, and which are only matched by Shakespeare and Aristophanes.

Matthew Arnold, 1880, *English Poets,* ed. Ward, Introduction, vol. I, p. xlv

For riotous luxuriance, *The Jolly Beggars* overtops all that Burns ever wrote. Probably no poem more graphic exists in literature. It describes what the writer had actually seen, and not otherwise would its extreme vividness seem to be attainable.

Hugh Walker, 1893, *Three Centuries of Scottish Literature,* vol. II, p. 162

Holy Willie's Prayer

Holy Willie's Prayer is a satirical crucifixion—slow, lingering inexorable, He hated Hypocrisy, he tore its holy robe, and for the outrage Hypocrisy did not forgive him while he lived, nor has it yet learned to forgive him.

Alexander Smith, 1865, *The Complete Works of Robert Burns, Life,* p. xxxix

The unfortunate man, William Fisher, known as "Holy Willie," both Patrick and his wife were little inclined to speak of. When they did so, it was only as a man "neither very bad nor very guid, to ootward appearance." Mrs. Patrick said he must have drawn attention to himself, in his earlier days, as at least a good professor, "to be made an elder o'." Seeing that I knew that the satires of Burns were only too well founded, for he was subsequently dismissed the eldership and died in a ditch after a debauch, they admitted that "he was blaim'd for takin' the kirk bawbees. When standin' at the plate on Sabbath, fowk said, he would boo doon to pat his boots richt, as it were, and slip in a bawbee or so!" Poor man, his punishment has been greater than Burns, with all his indignation against his character, I am sure, meant it to be; for the poet had little anticipation that his fiery words would reach so far and wide when he wrote them, and be so long remembered against their luckless object. Happily, however, in such world-wide pages, the man himself becomes a myth, a mere ideal representative of certain thoughts and actions, which alone remain as the theme of the poem.

William Jolly, 1881, *Robert Burns at Mossgiel;*
With Reminiscences of the Poet by His Herd-Boy, p. 100

This amazing achievement in satire, this matchless parody of Calvinistic intercession—so nice, so exquisite in detail, so overwhelming in effect.

William Ernest Henley and Thomas F. Henderson, 1896, ed.,
The Poetry of Robert Burns, vol. II, p. 320, note

LETTERS

The prose works of Burns consist almost entirely of his letters. They bear, as well as his poetry, the seal and the impress of his genius; but they contain much more bad taste, and are written with far more apparent labour. His poetry was almost all written primarily from feeling, and only secondarily from ambition. His letters seem to have been nearly all composed as exercises, and for display. There are few of them written with simplicity or plainness; and though natural enough as to the sentiment, they are generally very strained and elaborate in the expression. A very great proportion of them, too, relate neither to facts nor feelings peculiarly connected with the author or his correspondent—but are made up of general declamation, moral reflections, and vague discussions—all evidently composed for the sake of effect, and frequently introduced with long complaints of having nothing to say, and of the necessity and difficulty of letter-writing.

Francis, Lord Jeffrey, 1809-44, *Contributions to the*
Edinburgh Review, vol. II, p. 398

His prose-letters are sometimes tinctured with affectation. They seem written by a man who has been admired for his wit, and is expected on all occasions to shine. Those in which he expresses his ideas of natural beauty in reference to Alison's "Essay on Taste," and advocates the keeping up the remembrances of old customs and seasons, are the most powerfully written.

William Hazlitt, 1818, *Lectures on the English Poets,*
Lecture VII

Lord Byron's correspondence exhibits some of the finest specimens of epistolary composition in the language; but the monotony of selfish complaint without cause, petulant aspersion of his fellow-creatures, inexcusable accumulation of oaths, and occasional use of slang, which disfigures it, are faults that must offend the most partial reader. Page after page of sneering, of wilful swearing, or of petty scandal, with scarcely the relief of a single tear, or the sunshine of a single smile, is overwhelming at once to taste and patience. In variety of topic there is nothing in him at all like Burns, and in appropriate diversity of style—on this, or on that theme, as it occurs—there is but little approach to him. In Burns we have sometimes an oath, and sometimes indecorum; but sympathy and sincerity always, and slang never.

Hately Waddell, 1869, *Critical Edition of the
Life and Works of Burns,* vol. II

GENERAL

Some of the poems you have added in this last edition are very beautiful, particularly the "Winter Night," the "Address to Edinburgh," "Green Grow the Rashes," and the two songs immediately following, the latter of which is exquisite. By the way, I imagine you have a peculiar talent for such compositions, which you ought to indulge. No kind of poetry demands more delicacy or higher polishing. Horace is more admired on account of his Odes than all his other writings. But nothing now added is equal to your *Vision* and *Cotter's Saturday Night.* In these are united fine imagery, natural and pathetic description, with sublimity of language and thought. It is evident that you already possess a great variety of expression and command of the English language; you ought, therefore, to deal more sparingly for the future in the provincial dialect; why should you, by using that, limit the number of your admirers to those who understand the Scottish, when you can extend it to all persons of taste who understand the English language? In my opinion, you should plan some larger work than any you have as yet attempted. I mean, reflect upon some proper subject, and arrange the plan in your mind, without beginning to execute any part

of it till you have studied most of the best English poets, and read a little
more of history.

John Moore, 1787, *Letter to Burns*, May 23

Read Burns's poems, and have read them twice: and though they be written
in a language that is new to me, and many of them on subjects much inferior
to the author's ability, I think them, on the whole, a very extraordinary
production. He is, I believe, the only poet these kingdoms have produced
in the lower rank of life since Shakespeare, I should rather say since Prior,
who need not be indebted for any part of his praise as a charitable consideration of his origin, and the disadvantages under which he has laboured.
It will be pity if he should not hereafter divest himself of barbarism, and
content himself with writing pure English, in which he appears perfectly
qualified to excel. . . . Poor Burns loses much of his deserved praise in
this country, through our ignorance of his language. I despair of meeting
with any Englishman who will take the pains that I have taken to understand him. His candle is bright, but shut up in a dark lantern. I lent him
to a very sensible neighbour of mine, but his uncouth dialect spoiled all,
and before he had half read him through, he was quite *ramfeezled*.

William Cowper, 1787, *Letters to Samuel Rose,* July 24,
and Aug. 27; *Life,* ed. Hayley, vol. I, pp. 138, 139

Robert Burns, a natural poet of the first eminence, does not, perhaps appear
to his usual advantage in song—*non omnia possumus*. The political "fragment," as he calls it, inserted in the second volume of the present collection,
has, however, much merit in some of the satirical stanzas, and could it
have been concluded with the spirit with which it is commenced, would
indisputably have been entitled to great praise; but the character of his
favourite minister seems to have operated like the touch of a torpedo; and
after vainly attempting something like a panegyric, he seems under the
necessity of relinquishing the task. Possibly the bard will one day see
occasion to complete his performance as a uniform satire.

Joseph Ritson, 1794, *Historical Essay on Scottish Songs,* p. 71

It is probable that he would have proved a still greater poet if, by strength
of reason, he could have controlled the propensities which his sensibility
engendered; but he would have been a poet of a different class; and certain
it is, had that desirable restraint been early established, many peculiar
beauties which enrich his verses could never have existed, and many
accessary influences, which contribute greatly to their effect, would have
been wanting.

William Wordsworth, 1816, *A Letter to a Friend of Robert Burns*

The field in which Burns's influence has been, as was to be expected, most important and most widely felt, is in the poems of working men. He first proved that it was possible to become a poet and a cultivated man, without deserting his class, either in station or in sympathies; nay, that the healthiest and noblest elements of a lowly born poet's mind might be, perhaps certainly must be, the very feelings and thoughts which he brought up with him from below, not those which he received from above, in the course of his artificial culture. From the example of Burns, therefore, many a working man who would otherwise have "died and given no sign," has taken courage, and spoken out the thought within him, in verse or prose, not always wisely and well, but in all cases, as it seems to us, in the belief that he had a sort of divine right to speak and be heard, since Burns had broken down the artificial ice-wall of centuries, and asserted, by act as well as song, that "a man's a man for a' that.".

Charles Kingsley, 1848? *Burns and his School*

Not Latimer, not Luther struck more telling blows against false theology than did this brave singer. The Confession of Augsberg, the Declaration of Independence, the French Rights of Man, and the *Marseillaise,* are not more weighty documents in the history of freedom than the songs of Burns. His satire has lost none of its edge. His musical arrows yet sing through the air. He is so substantially a reformer that I find his grand plain sense in close chain with the greatest masters—Rabelais, Shakespeare in comedy, Cervantes, Butler and Burns. . . . Yet how true a poet is he! and the poet, too, of poor men, of gray hodden and the guernsey coat, and the blouse. He has given voice to all the experiences of common life; he has endeared the farm-house and cottage, patches and poverty, beans and barley; ale, the poor man's wine; hardship; the fear of debt; the dear society of weans and wife, of brothers and sisters, proud of each other, knowing so few, and finding amends for want and obscurity in books and thoughts. . . . As he was thus the poet of the poor, anxious, cheerful, working humanity, so had he the language of low life. He grew up in a rural district, speaking a *patois* unintelligible to all but natives, and he has made the Lowland Scotch a Doric dialect of fame. It is the only example in history of a language made classic by the genius of a single man.

Ralph Waldo Emerson, 1859, *Address at the Burns Centenary,*
Boston, Jan. 25

Three things may be noted as to the influence of Burns on men's feeling for Nature. First, he was a more entirely open-air poet than any first-rate singer who had yet lived, and as such he dealt with Nature in a more free, close, intimate way than any English poet since the old ballad-singers. He did more to bring the hearts of men close to the outer world, and the outer world to the heart, than any former poet. His keen eye looked directly, with no intervening medium, on the face alike of Nature and of man, and embraced all creation in one large sympathy. With familiar tenderness he dwelt on the lower creatures, felt for their sufferings, as if they had been his own, and opened men's hearts to feel how much the groans of creation are needlessly increased by the indifference or cruelty of man. In Burns, as in Cowper, and in him perhaps more than in Cowper, there was a large going forth of tenderness to the lower creatures, and in their poetry this first found utterance, and in no poet since their time, so fully as in these two. Secondly, his feeling in Nature's presence was not, as in the English poets of his time, a quiet contemplative pleasure. It was nothing short of rapture. Other more modern poets may have been thrilled with the same delight, he alone of all in last century expressed the thrill. In this, as in other things, he is the truest herald of that strain of rejoicing in Nature, even to ecstasy, which has formed one of the finest tones in the poetry of this century. Thirdly, he does not philosophize on Nature or her relation to man; he feels it, alike in his joyful moods and in his sorrowful. It is to him part of what he calls "the universal plan," but he nowhere reasons about the life of Nature as he often does so trenchantly about that of man.

John Campbell Shairp, 1877, On Poetic Interpretation
of Nature, p. 229

Burns, like Chaucer, comes short of a high seriousness of the great classics, and the virtue of matter and manner which goes with that high seriousness is wanting to his work. . . . We arrive best at the real estimate of Burns, I think, by conceiving his work as having truth of matter and truth of manner, but not the accent or the poetic virtue of the highest masters. . . . The freedom of Chaucer is heightened, in Burns, by a fiery, reckless energy; the benignity of Chaucer deepens, in Burns, into an overwhelming sense of the pathos of things;—of the pathos of human nature, the pathos, also, of non-human nature. Instead of the fluidity of Chaucer's manner, the manner of Burns has spring, bounding swiftness. Burns is by far the greater force, though he has perhaps less charm. The world of Chaucer is fairer, richer, more significant than that of Burns; but when the largeness and freedom of Burns gets full sweep, as in *Tam o' Shanter,* or still more in that puissant and splendid production, *The Jolly Beggars,* his world may be what it will, his poetic genius triumphs over it.

Matthew Arnold, 1880, English Poets, ed. Ward,
Introduction, vol. I, pp. xliv, xlv

There is something about Burns peculiarly acceptable to the concrete, human points of view. He poetizes work-a-day agricultural labor and life (whose spirit and sympathies, as well as practicalities, are much the same everywhere), and treats fresh, often coarse, natural occurrences, loves, persons, not like many new and some old poets in a genteel style of gilt and china, or at second or third removes, but in their own born atmosphere, laughter, sweat, unction. Perhaps no one ever sang "lads and lassies"— that universal race, mainly the same, too, all ages, all lands—down on their own plane, as he has. He exhibits no philosophy worth mentioning; his morality is hardly more than parrot-talk—not bad or deficient, but cheap, shopworn, the platitudes of old aunts and uncles to the youngsters (be good boys and keep your noses clean.) Only when he gets at Poosie Nansie's, celebrating the "barley bree," or among tramps, or democratic bouts and drinking generally,

("Freedom and whiskey gang thegither,")

we have, in his own unmistakable color and warmth, those interiors of rake-helly life and tavern fun—the cantabile of jolly beggars in highest jinks—lights and groupings of rank glee and brawny amorousness, out-vying the best painted pictures of the Dutch school, or any school. . . . Never indeed was there truer utterance in a certain range of idiosyncrasy than by this poet. Hardly a piece of his, large or small, but has "snap" and raciness. . . . Finally, in any summing-up of Burns, though so much is to be said in the way of fault-finding, drawing black marks, and doubtless severe literary criticism—(in the present outpouring I have "kept myself in," rather than allow'd any free flow)—after full retrospect of his work and life, the aforesaid "odd-kind chiel" remains to my heart and brain as almost the tenderest, manliest, and (even if contradictory) dearest flesh-and-blood figure in all the streams and clusters of by-gone poets.

Walt Whitman, 1886-88, "Robert Burns as Poet and Person," *November Boughs,* pp. 59, 60, 63, 64

A man of Burns's temperament, born in the middle of that (the 18th) century, was almost bound to combine rationalism in theology with a genuine religious sentiment. It is unnecessary to search very particularly in his actual theological environment for the origins of his religion. He had the same bias in reasoning—towards materialism, empiricism, "common-sense,"—as most of the leadng intellect of the age. . . . It would be a mis-take to try to trace any very close connection between the thought of Burns, so far it was dogmatic, and the doctrines held by the New Light ministers who took the young farmer by the hand, and eulogised the satires which he wrote for their side. The doctrine spread by Auld, Russell and their kind disgusted him; but his polemic against them was purely negative and destructive. . . . The consciousness of the living presence of God in nature was always stronger in him than any theory of redemption. An intellectual sceptic, he was not really interested in theological dogma, though moral and emotional causes preserved in him certain relics of more or less inter-dependent doctrines.

William Wallace, 1896, rev. *The Life and Works of Robert Burns,* ed. by Robert Chambers

Not only does he take whatever the Vernacular School can give in such matters as tone, sentiment, method, diction phrase; but also, he is content to run in debt to it for suggestions as regards ideas and for models in style. . . . It was fortunate for him and for his book, as it was fortunate for the world at large—as, too, it was afterwards to be fortunate for Scots song—that he was thus imitative in kind and thus traditional in practice. He had the sole ear of the Vernacular Muse; there was not a tool in her budget of which he was not master; and he took his place, the moment he moved for it, not so much, perhaps, by reason of his uncommon capacity as, because he discovered himself to his public in the very terms—of diction form, style, sentiment even—with which that public was familiar from of old, and in which it was waiting and longing to be addressed.

William Ernest Henley, 1897, *Life, Genius, Achievement, The Poetry of Robert Burns,* vol. IV, pp. 270, 272

Burns rides the ways of literature hedged by a numerous and terrible guard of devoted Scots, and if any hat is not doffed as he passes the irreverent offender is a marked man. Who dares lay hands on a poet guarded by a nation? . . . Burns, like Homer, is not merely a poet, but a literature. He has succeeded in fulfilling the old savage ideal—he has eaten up all his predecessors, and become possessed of their united powers. It is useless to haggle over much about what he borrowed: one can only envy the gigantic luck of his chance. Such vamps as the one I have analysed from Mr. Henley's notes can only be credited to him as brilliant luck brilliantly used. But the pieces I enumerated of the third class proved that he could write charming songs without such luck; though I think, on the whole, they prove that he wrote still better when he borrowed. . . . Taking him, borrowings and all, the merit of his songs lies in the partly dramatic kind; they display, vividly and pictorially, the life of a whole peasantry, as it has not been displayed in English literature.

Francis Thompson, 1897, "Mr. Henley's Burns," *The Academy,* vol. 51, pp. 273, 274

A stranger freak of burgess criticism is every-day fare in the odd world peopled by the biographers of Robert Burns. The nature of Burns, one would think, was simplicity itself: it could hardly puzzle a ploughman, and two sailors out of three would call him brother. But he lit up the whole of that nature by his marvellous genius for expression, and grave personages have been occupied ever since in discussing the dualism of his character, and professing to find some dark mystery in the existence of this, that, or the other trait—a love of pleasure, a hatred of shams, a deep sense of religion. It is common human nature, after all, that is the mystery, but they seem never to have met with it, and treat it as if it were the poet's eccentricity. They are all agog to worship him, and when they have made an image of him in their own likeness, and given it a tin-pot head that exactly hits their taste, they break into noisy lamentation over the discovery that the original was human, and had feet of clay. They deem "Mary in Heaven" so admirable that they could find it in their hearts to regret that she was ever on earth.

Walter Raleigh, 1897, Style, p. 76

It is of importance that we recognize the fact that in Burns the two literary estates, English and Scottish, were united. Until his time there was a sharp distinction between Scottish and English literature; but after him the literature of the two countries became one, both in nature and in name. This was but natural, when we consider that something of the original impulse which moved Burns's genius was English. When the riches of this noble Scottish house, and of that sister house of Chaucer, Spenser, Shakespeare, and Milton, awaited union in a royal heir, there came a peasant lad from the "auld clay biggin'" in Ayrshire, who, with the simple and graceful dignity of one of nature's noblemen, claimed his own, and there was added a new hereditary peer to the House of Fame.

Andrew J. George, 1897, Carlyle's Essay on Burns, p. 114

JAMES MACPHERSON
1736-1796

Born, at Kingussie, Invernesshire, 27 Oct. 1736. Early education at parish school. Matric., King's Coll., Aberdeen, Feb. 1753. To Marischal Coll., 1755. Probably studied at Edinburgh Univ., winter of 1755-56. After leaving Edinburgh, was master in school at Ruthven; and afterwards private tutor. Contrib. to "Scots Mag.," 1758. Friendship with Home and Dr. Carlyle, who encouraged him in publication of translations of Gaelic poems. Travelled in Highlands, 1760, collecting material. To London, 1761. Sec. to Governor of Pensacola, West Florida, 1764. Returned to England, 1766. Employed by Government to write on political questions. Agent to Nabob of Arcot, 1780. M. P. for Camelford, 1780-96. Died, at Badenoch, Invernesshire, 17 Feb. 1796. Buried in Westminster Abbey.

WORKS: *The Highlander* (anon.), 1758; *Fragments of Ancient Poetry, collected in the Highlands* (anon.), 1760; Ossian's *Fingal,* translated from the Gaelic, 1762; Ossian's *Temora,* translated, 1763; *Introduction to the History of Great Britain and Ireland,* 1771; translation of Homer's *Iliad,* 1773; *A History of Great Britain, from the Restoration to the Accession of the House of Hanover* (2 vols.), 1775; *Original Papers, containing the Secret History of Great Britain* (2 vols.), 1775; *The Rights of Great Britain asserted against the claims of America* (anon.), 1776; *A Short History of the Opposition during the last Session* (anon.), 1779; *The History and Management of the East Indian Company* (anon.), 1779. He edited: *Letters from Mohammed Ali Chang, Nabob of Arcot, to the Court of Directors,* 1779. COLLECTED WORKS: *Poetical Works,* 1802. LIFE: by T. B. Saunders, 1894.

R. Farquharson Sharp, 1897, A Dictionary of
English Authors, p. 181

SEE: *Poems of Ossian,* ed. William Sharp, 1926; *Ossian,* ed O. L. Jiriczek, 1940, 3 v. (Facsimiles); J. S. Smart, *James Macpherson: An Episode in Literature,* 1905; D. S. Thompson, *The Gaelic Sources of Macpherson's Ossian,* 1952.

PERSONAL

I received your foolish and impudent note. Whatever insult is offered me, I will do my best to repel, and what I cannot do for myself, the law shall do for me. I will not desist from detecting what I think a cheat, from any fear of the menaces of a Ruffian. What would you have me retract? I thought your book an imposture; I think it an imposture still. For this opinion I have given my reasons to the public, which I here dare you to refute. Your rage I defy. Your abilities, since your Homer, are not so formidable; and what I hear of your morals inclines me to pay regard, not to what you shall say, but to what you shall prove. You may print this if you will.*

Samuel Johnson, 1775, Letter to Macpherson, Jan. 20

As an original writer Macpherson became more and more discredited, but as an individual more and more wealthy; and, to prove that no honour lies beyond the grasp of unprincipled mediocrity, he was buried in Poet's Corner.

Edmund Gosse, 1888, A History of Eighteenth Century
Literature, p. 336

---

*The original of this well-known letter was sold by auction in 1875, for £50.—Bailey Saunders, 1894, *The Life and Letters of James Macpherson,* p. 250.

He went up to London—was appointed to go with Governor Johnston to Florida, in America; remained there at Pensacola, a year or more; but quarrelled with his chief (he had rare aptitude for quarrelling) and came back in 1766. Some English historical work followed; but with little success or profit. Yet he was a canny Scotchman, and so laid his plans that he became agent for some rich nabob of India (from these pickings winning a great fortune eventually); entered Parliament in 1780; had a country house at Putney, where he entertained lavishly; and at last built a great show place in the highlands near to his birth-place—which one may see to-day—with an obelisk to his memory, looking down on the valley of the Spey; and not so far away from the old coach-road, that passes through Killiecrankie, from Blair Athol to Inverness, but the coach man can show it—as he did to me—with his whip. . . . Yet if his book of Ossianic poems was ten-fold beter than it is, it would hardly give an enduring, or brilliant gloss to the memory of James Macpherson.

> Donald G. Mitchell, 1895, *English Lands, Letters and Kings,*
> *Queen Anne and the Georges,* pp. 224, 228

If none but the great deserved a biography, this book would not have been written. For Macpherson was in no sense a great man: he was a miscellaneous writer of considerable talent, a busy journalist, a member of Parliament, an agent for an Indian prince, a popular and prosperous citizen; and, beyond the fact that he brought out the Ossianic poems at the age of twenty-five, he did little in the sixty years of his life that would entitle him to permanent remembrance. This work of his youth was, as he declared, translated from Gaelic fragments found in the Scottish Highlands. By its wonderful success, and its no less wonderful influence on literature, both in England and on the Continent, it gave him, in his own day, a world-wide reputation. Literary fashions have suffered many changes in the century that has passed since his death, and Macpherson's reputation no longer exists; but his work retains an historical interest of a curious and unique character.

> Bailey Saunders, 1894, *The Life and Letters of*
> *James Macpherson,* Preface, pp. v, vii

Poems of Ossian (1762-63)

Several gentlemen of the Highlands and Isles, generously gave me all the assistance in their power, and it was by their means I was enabled to complete the Epic Poem. How far it comes up to the rules of the Epopœia is the province of criticism to examine. It is only my business to lay it before the reader as I have found it. . . . A man diffident of his abilities might ascribe his own compositions to a person whose remote antiquity and whose situaiton when alive might well answer for faults which would be inexcusable in a writer of this age. . . . But of this I am pursuaded . . . that some will think, notwithstanding the disadvantages with which the works ascribed to Ossian appear, it would be a very uncommon instance of self-denial in me to disown them, were they really of my composition.

James Macpherson, 1762, *Fingal,* Preface

It is as beautiful as Homer.

Friedrich Melchior Grimm, 1762, *Correspondance*
Littéraire, April

I never was able to discover in his most unguarded moments that he was any other than the collector and translator of the works of Ossian, or assumed any other merit that might be derived from thence. But I have heard him express the greatest contempt and disdain for those who thought him the fabricator of them. If there was any person who asserted that Macpherson had owned it to himself, even that would not shake my faith; for I knew him to be of a temper, when he was teased and fretted, to carry his indignation that far.

Alexander Carlyle, 1769-70, *Report of the*
Highland Society, App. p. 68

Homer has been superseded in my heart by the divine Ossian. Through what a world does this angelic bard carry me! With him I wander over barren wastes and frightful wilds; surrounded by whirlwinds and hurricanes, trace by the feeble light of the moon the shades of our noble ancestors; hear from the mountainous heights, intermingled with the roaring of waves and cataracts, their plaintive tones stealing from cavernous recesses; while the pensive monody of some love-stricken maiden, who heaves her departing sighs over the moss-clad grave of the warrior by whom she was adored, makes up the inarticulate concert. I trace this bard, with his silver locks, as he wanders in the valley and explores the footsteps of his fathers. Alas! no vestige remains but their tombs. His thought then hangs on the silver moon, as her sinking beams play upon the rippling main; and the remembrance of deeds past and gone recurs to the hero's mind—deeds of times when he gloried in the approach of danger, and emulation nerved his whole frame; when the pale orb shone upon his bark, laden with the spoils of his enemy, and illuminated his triumphant return. When I see depicted on his countenance a bosom full of woe; when I behold his heroic greatness sinking into the grave, and he exclaims, as he throws a glance at the cold sod which is to lie upon him: "Hither will the traveler who is sensible of my worth bend his weary steps, and seek the soul-enlivening bard, the illustrious son of Fingal; his foot will tread upon my tomb, but his eyes shall never behold me;" at this time it is, my dear friend, that, like some renowned and chivalrous knight, I could instantly draw my sword; rescue my prince from a long, irksome existence of langour and pain; and then finish by plunging the weapon into my own breast, that I might accompany the demi-god whom my hand had emancipated.

> Johann Wolfgang Goethe, 1774, *Sorrows of Werther*, Letter lxviii

Doctor Johnson having asserted in his late publication that the Translator of Ossian's Poems "never could show the original, nor can it be shown by any other," I hereby declare that the originals of *Fingal* and other poems of Ossian lay in my shop for many months in the year 1762, for the inspection of the curious. The public were not only apprised of their lying there for inspection, but even proposals for publishing the originals of the poems of Ossian were dispersed through the kingdom, and advertised in the newspapers. Upon finding that a number of subscribers sufficient to bear the expenses were not likely to appear, I returned the manuscript to the proprietor, in whose hand they still remain.

> Thomas Beckett, 1775, *To the Public*, Jan. 19

I see you entertain a great doubt with regard to the authenticity of the poems of Ossian. You are certainly right in so doing. It is indeed strange that any men of sense could have imagined it possible, that above twenty thousand verses, along with numberless historical facts, could have been preserved by oral tradition during fifty generations, by the rudest, perhaps, of all the European nations, the most necessitous, the most turbulent, and the most unsettled. Where a supposition is so contrary to common sense, any positive evidence of it ought never to be regarded. Men run with great avidity to give their evidence in favour of what flatters their passions and their natural prejudices. You are therefore over and above indulgent to us in speaking of the matter with hesitation.

> David Hume, 1776, *Letter to Gibbon*, March 18;
> *Gibbon's Memoirs*, ed. Hill, p. 197

Mr. Macpherson is by many supposed to be the sole and original author of the compositions which he has published as translations of the works of Ossian; this charge I am enabled to refute, at least in part, having fortunately met with the originals of some of them. Mr. Macpherson, I acknowledge, has taken very great liberties with them; retrenching, adding, and altering as he judged proper: but we must admit that he has discovered great ingenuity in these variations.

Matthew Young, 1784, *Ancient Gaelic Poems respecting the Race of the Fians: Transactions of the Royal Irish Academy*, vol. I, Autiq. p. 43

I was the first person who brought out to the notice of the world, the poems of Ossian: first, by the *Fragments of Ancient Poetry* which I published, and afterwards, by my setting on foot the undertaking for collecting and publishing the *Works of Ossian;* and I have always considered this as a meritorious action of my life.

Hugh Blair, 1787, *Letter to Robert Burns*, May 4

Having had the good fortune to be born and reared in a mountainous country, from my very childhood I have felt the falsehood that pervades the volumes imposed upon the world under the name of Ossian. From what I saw with my own eyes, I knew that the imagery was spurious. In nature everything is indistinct, yet nothing defined into absolute, independent singleness. In Macpherson's work it is exactly the reverse: everything (that is not stolen) is in this manner defined, insulated, dislocated, deadened, yet nothing distinct. It will always be so when words are substituted for things. To say that the characters never could exist; that the manners are impossible; and that a dream has more substance than the whole state of society, as there depicted, is doing nothing more than pronouncing a censure which Macpherson defied. . . . Yet, much as these pretended treasures of antiquity have been admired, they have been wholly uninfluential upon the literature of the country. No succeeding writer appears to have caught from them a ray of inspiration; no author in the least distingushed has ventured formally to imitate them, except the boy, Chatterton, on their first appearance. . . . This incapability to amalgamate with the literature of the Island is, in my estimation, a decisive proof that the book is essenitally unnatural; nor should I require any other to demonstrate it to be a forgery, audacious as worthless. Contrast, in this respect, the effect of Macpherson's publication with the *Reliques* of Percy, so unassuming, so modest in their pretensions.

William Wordsworth, 1800, *Lyrical Ballads, Second Edition, Essay Supplementary to Preface*

Little as we participate in the unqualified enthusiasm expressed by some admirers of Ossian, still the influence exercised by these poems on the public taste is certainly very remarkable. . . . My observations of these Ossianic poems have been founded on the principle of conceding to them the highest possible antiquity, which is at all consistent with historical truth, and at the same time acquiescing at once in their relative authenticity. Certainly, unless the contrary be proved by extraneous circumstances, no internal evidence militates against the supposition that such a hero-race as that of Fingal existed on the northwest coast of Scotland in the ninth and tenth centuries; that it actually produced an Ossian, who, as bard and hero, celebrated his own exploits and those of his race. If his constant recurrence to the melancholy remembrance of departed ancestors, and the earlier period of their glory, become by frequent repetition monotonous and wearying, still the continual interweaving of the person of the bard into the history narrated, affords a happy poetical and universal point of union, and greatly contributes to enhance that fascinating interest with which the poems have inspired so many readers and hearers. This circumstance is, indeed, so peculiarly propitious, that many succeeding bards have adopted the form once suggested, and written and sung as if in Ossian's person.

Frederick Schlegel, 1812, *On the Poetry of the North,*
Æsthetic and Miscellaneous Works, tr. Millington, pp. 248, 256

You ask me about Ossian—now here is truth—the first book I ever bought in my life was Ossian. . . . It is now in the next room. And years before that, the first *composition* I ever was guilty of was something in *imitation* of Ossian, whom I had not read, but *conceived,* through two or three scraps in other books—I never can recollect *not* writing rhymes . . . but I knew they were nonsense even then; *this,* however, I thought exceedingly well of, and laid up for posterity under the cushion of a great armchair. "And now my soul is satisfied"—so said one man after killing another, the death being suggested, in its height of honour, by stars and stars (* * * *). I could not have been five years old, that's one consolation. Years after, when I bought this book, I found a vile dissertation of Laing . . . all to prove Ossian was not Ossian. . . . I would not read it, but could not help knowing the purpose of it, and the pith of the hatefully—irresistible arguments. The worst came in another shape, though . . . an after-gleaning of real Ossianic poems, by a firm believer whose name I forgot—"if this is the *real*"—I thought! Well, to this day I believe in a nucleus for all that haze, a foundation of truth to Macpherson's fanciful superstructure—and I have been long intending to read once again those Fingals and Malvinas.

Robert Browning, 1846, *To Elizabeth Barrett,* Aug. 25;
The Letters of Robert Browning and Elizabeth Barrett,
vol. II, p. 466

The Celts are the prime authors of this vein of piercing regret and passion, of this Titanism in poetry. A famous book, Macpherson's *Ossian,* carried, in the last century, this vein like a flood of lava through Europe. I am not going to criticise Macpherson's *Ossian* here. Make the part of what is forged, modern, tawdry, spurious in the book as large as you please; strip Scotland, if you like, of every feather of borrowed plumes which, on the strength of Macpherson's *Ossian,* she may have stolen from that *vetus et major Scotia,* the true home of the Ossianic poetry, Ireland; I make no objection. But there will still be left in the book a residue with the very soul of the Celtic genius in it, and which has the proud distinction of having brought this soul of the Celtic genius into contact with the nations of modern Europe, and enriched all our poetry by it. Woody Morven, and echoing Sora, and Selma with its silent halls! We all owe them a debt of gratitude, and when we are unjust enough to forget it, may the Muse forget us! Choose any one of the better passages in Macpherson's *Ossian,* and you can see, even at this time of day, what an apparition of newness and power such a strain must have been to the eighteenth century.

Matthew Arnold, 1867, On the Study of Celtic Literature, p. 152

MacPherson got much from Mss. and much from oral recitation. It is most probable that he has given the minor poems exactly as he found them. He may have made considerable changes in the larger ones in giving them their present form, although I do not believe that he, or any of his assistants, added much, even in the way of connecting-links between the various episodes.

Archibald Clerk, 1870, Poems of Ossian in the Original Gaelic,
with a literal translation into English, vol. I, p. 1

Not into literature only did MacPherson's book pour a new lava-steam, but it initiated, in the domain of Historical Science, the most fruitful new researches. Directly springing from, or indirectly stimulated by, the enthusiasm excited by *Ossian,* researches were instituted into the antiquities of all the three great races of Europe—not of the Kelts only, but of the Teutons, and of the Slavs—and collections were made, or edited, of their ancient poesies. It is unnecessary to recall the dates of the several publications. Only this general fact we need here note, that if, in very various degrees, *propter* Ossian, in every case *post* Ossian, were such works as the Welsh *Myvyrian Archæology* and *Mabinogion,* Müller's *Collection of German Poems from the 12th, 13th and 14th Centuries,* and Grimm's *Teutonic Mythology;* and the numberless Slavonic Folk-lore collections which were the antiquarian bases of the great political fact of Panslavonic aspirations. And considering this, we see that by no means was the scope and bearing of the researches springing from, or stimulated by, MacPherson's *Ossian* confined to the sphere of historical theory, and religious belief. Few things are, in the last hundred years, more remarkable than the direct transforma-

tion of historical theories into political forces. Political aspirations of nation-
alities or races to union or re-union are but the transference into the sphere
of practical endeavour of the theories of antiquaries and historians. Yet no
forces have in Europe, in this century, shown themselves more powerful.
And more particularly events are now indicating, with almost daily increasing clearness, that the Keltic Revival, directly, initiated by MacPherson's
Ossian, will show itself hardly less important as a political force than the
Slavonic Revival, indirectly stimulated by *Ossian.*

> J. S. Stuart-Glennie, 1880, "MacPherson, Burns, and Scott in
> their Relation to the Modern Revolution," *Fraser's Magazine,*
> vol. 101, p. 521

Addison had already directed attention to the English ballad-poetry, and
Klopstock, Gleim and others had profited by his example. Bishop Percy's
collection of English ballads was, therefore, received with general rapture
in German, and the sentimental heroic poetry of Celtic origin, which Macpherson sent forth under the name of Ossian, was greeted with enthusiastic
applause by a race of poets full of sentiment and warlike sympathies.

> Wilhelm Scherer, 1883-86, *A History of German Literature,*
> tr. Conybeare, vol. II, p. 56

Ossian points as directly to Byron as the chivalry and ballad revivals point
to Scott. These indicate the two great streams in the Romantic movement.
In Byron's poetry—sincere or feigned—we see constantly manifest the
Ossian feeling. What Byron himself thought of Ossian I have had a good
opportunity to observe by perusing Byron's own manuscript notes in a copy
of the Ossian poems. The following notes I copied directly from Byron's
handwriting: "The portrait which Ossian has drawn of himself is indeed a
masterpiece. He not only appears in the light of a distinguished warrior—
generous as well as brave—and possessed of exquisite sensibility—but of
an aged venerable bard—subjected to the most melancholy vicissitudes of
fortune—weak and blind—the sole survivor of his family—the last of the
race of Fingal. The character of Fingal—the poet's own father—is a highly
finished one. There is certainly no hero in the Iliad—or the Odyssey—who
is at once so brave and amiable as this renowned king of Morven. It is well
known that Hector—whose character is of all the Homeric heroes the most
complete—greatly sullies the lustre of his glorious actions by the insult over
the fallen Patroclus. On the other hand the conduct of Fingal appears uniformly illustrious and great—without one mean or inhuman action to tarnish
the splendour of his fame—He is equally the object of our admiration
esteem and love." Speaking of Ossian's skill in depicting female characters,
he writes, "How happily, for instance, has he characterized his own mistress—afterwards his wife—by a single epithet expressive of that modesty—

softness—and complacency—which constitute the perfection of feminine excellence—'the mildly blushing Everallin.' . . . I am of opinion that though in sublimity of sentiment—in vivacity and strength of description—Ossian may claim a full equality of merit with Homer himself—yet in the invention both of incidents and character he is greatly inferior to the Grecian bard." These quotations are interesting as showing how seriously Byron took Ossian and how carefully and thoughtfully he read him. The influence of Ossian lasted long after the immediate excitement caused by its novelty and professed antiquity had passed away.

William Lyon Phelps, 1893, The Beginnings of the
English Romantic Movement, p. 153

The grandeur and gloom of the Highland mountains, the spectral mists that sweep round the crags, the roar of the torrents, the gleams of sunlight on moor and lake, the wail of the breeze among the cairns of the dead, the unspeakable sadness that seems to brood over the landscape whether the sky be clear or clouded—these features of west Highland scenery were first revealed by Macpherson to the modern world. This revelation quickened the change of feeling, already begun, in regard to the prevailing horror of mountain-scenery. It brought before men's eyes some of the fascination of the mountain-world, more especially in regard to the atmospheric effects that play so large a part in its landscape. It showed the titanic forces of storm and tempest in full activity. And yet there ran through all the poems a vein of infinite melancholy. The pathos of life manifested itself everywhere, now in the tenderness of unavailing devotion, now in the courage of hopeless despair.

Sir Archibald Geikie, 1898, Types of Scenery and
their Influence on Literature, p. 44

GENERAL

His *History* is pronounced by Fox to be full of "impudent" falsehoods; it has long sunk from public notice, and had no charm either of style or thought to relieve it from neglect. Nor is it possible to believe, that one who wrote so dull a history could have produced so wild and imaginative a poem as that which the world has generally attributed to him.

Eugene Lawrence, 1855, Lives of the British Historians,
vol. II, p. 238

That a writer of the stamp of James Macpherson should have been destined to approach history at all was, I think, a remarkable freak of nature. That it should be reserved, however, for the author of the *Ossian* fraud to discover and give to the world important facts, tearing to shreds the character of one of the greatest men that this country has ever produced, is, I submit, a little too hard for belief by rational beings. Is it reasonable to suppose that *Original Papers* on English history produced by the inventor of the Gaelic "Originals" of the Ossian poems are likely to be genuine? The point is, indeed, virtually settled at the outset by the fact which I have mentioned that the manuscripts in question, imputing such fearful crimes to Marlborouh, Godolphin, and their associated helpers in the work of the Revolution, are *not* original. I must ask my readers to keep this steadily in view; for the whole gist of the position taken up by Dalrymple, Hallam, Macaulay, and all more recent followers of Macpherson lies in the assumption that the Nairne papers in the Bodleian library are original state documents, and therefore not to be gainsaid.

Arthur Parnell, 1897, "Macpherson and the Nairne Papers,"
English Historical Review, vol. 12, p. 274

EDMUND BURKE
1729-1797

Born, in Dublin, 12 Jan. (?) 1729. Educated at a school at Ballitore, 1741-43; at Trinity Coll., Dublin, 1743-48; scholarship, 1746; B. A., 1748. To Middle Temple to study Law, 1750. Never called to Bar; gave up legal studies by 1755. Took to literary work. Married Jane Nugent, 1756 (or 1757?). Edited *Annual Register,* 1759-88. Gradually became known by literary work. Private Sec. to William Gerard Hamilton, 1759-64. To Ireland with Hamilton, 1761. Annual pension of £300, 1763. Threw up pension, April 1764. Private Sec. to Lord Rockingham, July 1765. M. P. for Wendover, Dec. 1765. First speech made, 27 Jan. 1766. To Ireland, summer of 1766; received freedom of city of Galway. Purchased estate near Beaconsfield, 1768. Appointed Agent to the Province of New York, 1771. Visit to Paris, Feb. to March 1773. M. P. for Malton after dissolution of Parliament in Sept. 1774; again after dissolution in Sept. 1780; and again in Nov. 1790. Intimacy with Fox begun. Appointed Paymaster of the Forces, 1782. Lord Rector of Glasgow University, 1784 and 1785. Impeachment of Warren Hastings, 10 May 1787; trial begun, 13 Feb. 1788. Grace for conferring Hon. LL.D. degree passed, Dublin Univ., 11 Dec. 1790. Burke apparently never attended to take the degree. Again elected M. P. for Malton, Nov. 1790. Rupture with Fox, 1791. Retired from Parliament, July 1794. Two pensions of £1,200 and £2,500 granted him, Aug. 1794. Interested in foundation of Maynooth Catholic College, 1795. Established, at Beaconsfield, school for sons of French emigrants, 1796. Died at Beaconsfield, 6 July 1797. Buried in Beaconsfield parish church. WORKS: Burke's chief literary works are: *A Vindication of Natural Society* (anon.), 1756; *A Philosophical Inquiry into the Origin of our Ideas of the Sublime and the Beautiful* (anon.), 1757; *An Account of the European Settlements in America* (anon. probably edited by Burke, and written by himself and his cousin, William Burke), 1757; *A Short Account of a Short Administration* (anon.), 1766; *Observations on a late Publication intituled "The Present State of the Nation"* (anon.), 1769; *Thoughts on the Causes of the Present Discontents* (anon.), 1770; *Political Tracts and Speeches*, 1777; *Reflections on the Revolution in France*, 1790 (2nd edn. same year); *Appeals from the New to the Old Whigs* (anon.), 1791 (2nd edn. same year); *Thoughts on the Prospect of a Regicide Peace* (anon.), 1796 (11th edn. same year). [Burke published a number of his speeches, also of political pamphlets and letters, between 1774 and 1791, and many were published posthumously. A complete collection is the *Works and Correspondence* (8 vols.), London, 1852]. POSTHUMOUS: *Correspondence with Dr. Laurence*, 1827; *Letters, 1744-97* (4 vols.), 1844; *Speeches, with Memoir*, 1854; *Letters, Speeches, and Tracts on Irish Affairs*, 1881. COLLECTED WORKS: in 8 vols., 1792-1827; in 8 vols., 1852. LIFE: by MacCormick, 1798; by Bisset, 1798; by Sir James Prior, 5th edn. 1854; by MacKnight, 1858; by Morley ("English Men of Letters" series), 1879.

R. Farquharson Sharp, 1897, A Dictionary of English Authors, p. 39

SEE *Works*, ed. W. Willis and F. W. Raffety, 1906-7, 6 v.; *Select Works*, ed. E. J. Payne, 1874-78, 3 v.; *The Correspondence*, ed. Thomas W. Copeland, Lucy Sutherland, John A. Woods, and others, 1958-   ; *A Notebook of Edmund Burke*, ed. H. V. F. Somerset, 1957; Philip Magnus, *Burke: A Life*, 1939; Thomas W. Copeland, *Our Eminent Friend Burke: Six Essays*, 1949; Charles Parkin, *The Moral Basis of Burke's Political Thought*, 1956; also see *The Burke Newsletter*, ed. Peter J. Stanlis and C. P. Ives.

PERSONAL

It is time I should say who my friend is. His name is Edmond Burke. As a literary man he may possibly be not quite unknown to you. He is the author of a piece which imposed on the world as Lord Bolingbroke's, called, "The Advantages of Natural Society," and of a very ingenious book published last year, called *A Treatise on the Sublime and Beautiful*. I must farther say of him, that his chief application has been to the knowledge of public business, and our commercial interests; that he seems to have a most extensive knowledge, with extraordinary talents for business, and to want nothing but ground to stand upon to do his country very important services.

W. Markham, 1759, Letter to the Duchess of Queensbury, Sep. 25; Chatham Correspondence, vol. I, p. 432

An Irishman, Mr. Burke, is sprung up, in the House of Commons who has astonished every body with the power of his eloquence, and his comprehensive knowledge in all our exterior and internal politics, and commercial interests. He wants nothing but that sort of dignity annexed to rank and property in England to make him the most considerable man in the Lower House.

Arthur Lee, 1766, To the Prince Royal of Poland, Life, p. 290

Here lies our good Edmund, whose genius was such,
We scarcely can praise it, or blame it too much;
Who, born for the universe, narrow'd his mind,
And to party gave up what was meant for mankind;
Though fraught with all learning, yet straining his throat
To persuade Tommy Townshend to lend him a vote;
Who, too deep for his hearers, still went on refining,
And thought of convincing, while they thought of dining;
Though equal to all things, for all things unfit,
Too nice for a statesman, too proud for a wit;
For a patriot, too cool; for a drudge, disobedient;
And too fond of the *right* to pursue the *expedient*.
In short, 'twas his fate, unemploy'd, or in place, sir,
To eat mutton cold, and cut blocks with a razor.

Oliver Goldsmith, 1774, The Retaliation

He must again repeat that all he ever knew of men, that all he ever read in books, that all his reasoning faculties informed him of, or his fancy suggested to him, did not impart that exalted knowledge, that superior information, which he had acquired from the lessons of his right honourable friend. To him he owed all his fame, if fame he had any. And if he (Mr. Fox) should now, or at any time, prevail over him in discussion, he could acknowledge his gratitude for the capability and pride of the conquest in telling him "Hoc ipsum quod vincit id est tuum."

Charles James Fox, 1791, Speech in the House of Commons
on the occasion of his rupture with Mr. Burke

We trust thy liberal views, thy generous heart;
We think of those who, naked, pale and poor,
Relieved and blessed, have wandered from thy door;
We see thee with unwearied step explore
Each track of bloodshed on the farthest shore
Of injured Asia, and thy swelling breast
Harrowing the oppressor, mourning for the oppressed.

William Lisle Bowles, 1792? The Right Honourable
Edmund Burke

There never was a more beautiful alliance between virtue and talents. All his conceptions were grand, all his sentiments generous. The great leading trait of his character, and that which gave it all its energy and its colour, was that strong hatred of vice which is no other than the passionate love of virtue. It breathes in all his writings; it was the guide of all his actions. But even the force of his eloquence was insufficient to transfuse it into the weaker or perverted minds of his contemporaries. This has caused much of the miseries of Europe; this has rendered of no effect towards her salvation the sublimest talents, the greatest and rarest virtues that the beneficence of Providence ever concentrated in a single character for the benefit of mankind. But Mr. Burke was too superior to the age in which he lived. His prophetic genius only astonished the nation which it ought to have governed.

M. Cazalés, 1797, *On the Death of Edmund Burke*

His countenance in early life possessed considerable sweetness, and by his female friends was esteemed handsome. At a later period, it did not appear to be marked, particularly when in a state of quiescence, by that striking expression which, from the well-known qualities of his mind, many persons expected to see; but the lines of thought were evident, and when excited by discussion, there was an occasional working of the brow, occasioned partly by being nearsighted, which let the attentive observer into the secret of the powerful workings within. From this defective state of vision, he almost constantly, from about the year 1780, wore spectacles. . . . Like Mr. Fox, Mr. Burke was somewhat negligent in common dress, being latterly distinguished by a tight brown coat, which seemed to impede all freedom of motion, and a little bob-wig with curls, which, in addition to his spectacles, made his person be recognized by those who had never previously seen him, the moment he rose to speak in the House of Commons.

Sir James Prior, 1824, *Memoir of the Life and Character of the Right Hon. Edmund Burke,* vol. II, pp. 374, 377

It is strange, considering the eminence of the man, and how early his biographers were in the field, what an impenetrable cloud hangs over the life of Edmund Burke, from the time when he left college to his avowed entrance into a public career. The same observation was made long years since by one who knew him personally and well. "It always appeared to Mr. West (*Life of West*) that there was about Mr. Burke *a degree of mystery connected with his early life* which their long intercourse never tended to explain." This mystery was not only maintained during life, but prepared for after death. There is not in existence, as far as we know or have a right to infer from the silence of the biographers, one single letter, paper, or document of any kind,—except a mysterious fragment of one letter,—relating to the domestic life of the Burke's, until long after Edmund Burke became an illustrious and public man,—from brothers to brother, or brothers to sister. Such letters could not, of course, find a place in the formal "Correspondence of the Right Honourable,"—but they were the best possible material for the biographer—for the *man* Burke must grow in and out of them. These letters and documentary evidence must have been intentionally collected and destroyed; and the probabilities are, that they were destroyed by Edmund himself, for he was the last survivor of the family.

Sir Charles Wentworth Dilke, 1853, "Burke," The Papers of a Critic, vol. II, p. 330

He was well versed in Greek and Latin literature, was familiar with the great masters of his own language, and had read the best models of the French. Ancient and modern history he had deeply studied; he was an admirable connoisseur in art; and he was not unfamiliar with some of the natural sciences. To theology and philosophy he paid considerable attention. His acquaintance with English law astonished professional men themselves, while from the Roman jurisprudence he not unfrequently drew happy illustrations; and, as is said of Shakespeare, he loved to converse with laborers and mechanics about their trades. He was a skilful, practical agriculturist; in matters of commerce and finance he was exceedingly well versed, and in the whole science of economics he was far beyond his age.

J. B. Robertson, 1875, Lectures on the Life of Burke

Edmund Burke gave the most striking proofs of his character and genius in the evil days in which his life ended—not when he was a leader in the Commons, but when he was a stricken old man at Beaconsfield. That Burke was a great statesman, no thinking man could read his pamphlets and speeches can deny; but a man may be a great statesman and yet fall very short of being a great man. Burke makes as deep an impression upon our hearts as upon our minds. We are taken captive, not so much by his reasoning, strongly as that moves to its conquest, as by the generous warmth that steals out of him into our hearts. There is a tonic breath of character and of generous purpose in which he writes—the fine sentiment of a pure man; and we are made aware that he who could write thus was great, not so much by reason of what he said or did, as by reason of what he was. What a man was you may often discover in the records of his days of bitterness and pain better than in what is told of his seasons of cheer and hope; for if the noble qualities triumph then and show themselves still sound and sweet, if his courage sink not, if he show himself still capable of self-forgetfulness, if he still stir with a passion for the service of causes and policies which are beyond himself, his stricken age is even greater than his full-pulse years of manhood. This is the test which Burke endures—the test of fire. It has not often been judged so, I know; but let any man of true insight take that extraordinary Letter to a Noble Lord, which was written in 1796, and which is Burke's apologia pro vita sua, and consider the circumstances under which it was written, its tone, its scope, its truth, its self-revelations, and the manner of man revealed, and say whether this be not the real Burke, undaunted, unstained, unchanged in purpose and in principle.

Woodrow Wilson, 1901, "Edmund Burke and the
French Revolution," *The Century Magazine,* vol. 62, p. 784

GENERAL

The most eloquent and rational madman that I ever knew.

Edward Gibbon, 1791, *To Lord Sheffield,* May 31;
Private Letters, ed. Prothero, vol. II, p. 251

With Mr. Burke's book I do not mean to find fault, but to distinguish between what delights me, and what I only respect. I adore *genius;* to *judgement* I pull off my hat, and make it a formal bow; but as I read only to amuse myself, and not to be informed or convinced, I had rather (for my private pleasure) that in his last pamphlet he had flung the reins on the neck of his boundless imagination, as he did in the first. *Genius* creates enthusiasts or enemies; *judgement* only cold friends; and cold friends will sooner go over to your enemies than to your bigots.

Horace Walpole, 1791, *To the Countess of Ossory,* Aug. 22;
Letters, ed. Cunningham, vol. IX, p. 338

Burke was, indeed, a great man. No one ever read history so philosophically as he seems to have done. Yet, until he could associate his general principles with some sordid interest, panic of property, Jacobinism, &c., he was a mere dinner bell. Hence you find so many half truths in his speeches and writings. Nevertheless, let us heartily acknowledge his transcendent greatness. He would have been more influential if he had less surpassed his contemporaries, as Fox and Pitt, men of much inferior minds in all respects.

Samuel Taylor Coleridge, 1833, *Table Talk,* ed. Ashe,
Apr. 8, p. 207

His mind was the reverse of historical: although he had rather a coarse, incondite temperament, not finely susceptible to the best influences, to the most exquisite beauties of the world in which he lived, he yet lived in that world thoroughly and completely. He did not take an interest, as a poet does, in the sublime because it is sublime, in the beautiful because it is beautiful; but he had the passions of more ordinary men in a degree, and of an intensity, which ordinary men may be most thankful that they have not. In no one has the intense faculty of intellectual hatred—the hatred which the absolute dogmatist has for those in whom he incarnates and personifies the opposing dogma—been fiercer or stronger; in no one has the intense ambition to rule and govern—in scarcely any one has the daily ambition of the daily politician—been fiercer and stronger: he, if any man, cast himself upon his time.

> Walter Bagehot, 1856, "Thomas Babington Macaulay," *Works,*
> ed. Morgan, vol. II, p. 84

Considered simply as a master of English prose, Burke has not, in my judgment, been surpassed in any period of our literature. Critics may point to certain faults of haste; the evolution of his thought is sometimes too slow; his majestic march is trammeled by the sweep of his gorgeous rhetoric; or his imagination takes fire, and he explodes into fierce denunciations which shock the reader when the excitement which prompted them has become unintelligible. But, whatever blemishes may be detected, Burke's magnificent speeches stand absolutely alone in the language. They are, literally speaking, the only English speeches which may still be read with profit when the hearer and the speaker have long been turned to dust. His pamphlets, which are written speeches, are marked by a fervour, a richness, and a flexibility of style which is but a worthy incarnation of the wisdom which they embody. It matters little if we dissent from his appreciations of current events, for it is easy to supply the corrective for ourselves. The charge of over-refinement sometimes brought against him is in great part nothing more than the unconscious testimony of his critics that he could see farther than themselves. To a certain degree it is, perhaps, well founded.

> Leslie Stephen, 1876, *History of English Thought*
> *in the Eighteenth Century,* vol. II, p. 219

The varieties of Burke's literary or rhetorical method are very striking. It is almost incredible that the superb imaginative amplication of the description of Hyder Ali's descent upon the Carnatic should be from the same pen as the grave, simple, unadorned *Address to the King* (1777), where each sentence falls on the ear with the accent of some golden-tongued oracle of the wise gods. His stride is the stride of a giant, from the sentimental beauty of the picture of Marie Antoinette at Versailles, or the red horror of the tale of Debi Sing in Rungpore, to the learning, positiveness, and cool judicial mastery of the *Report on the Lord's Journals* (1794), which Phillip Francis, no mean judge, declared on the whole to be the "most eminent and extraordinary" of all his productions. Even in the coolest and dryest of his pieces there is the mark of greatness, of grasp, of comprehension. In all its varieties Burke's style is noble, earnest, deep-flowing, because his sentiments were lofty and fervid, and went with sincerity and ardent disciplined travail of judgment. . . . Burke will always be read with delight and edification, because in the midst of discussions on the local and the accidental, he scatters apophthegms that take us into the regions of lasting wisdom. In the midst of the torrent of his most strenuous and passionate deliverances, he suddenly rises aloof from his immediate subject, and in all tranquility reminds us of some permanent relation of things, some enduring truth of human life or society. We do not hear the organ tones of Milton, for faith and freedom had other notes in the seventeenth century. There is none of the complacent and wise-browed sagacity of Bacon, for Burke's were days of eager personal strife and party fire and civil division. . . . The only great English writer of that age whom we can name along with Burke in the literature of enduring power, is Wordsworth, that great representative in another and a higher field, and with many rare elements added that were all his own, of those harmonising and conciliatory forces and ideas that make man's destiny easier to him through piety in its oldest and best sense; through reverence for the past, for duty, for institutions.

John Morley, 1879, Burke (English Men
of Letters), pp. 210, 211, 212

In one of his elaborated sentences you will sometimes find words and clauses selected and multiplied and arranged and compacted and qualified and de-fined and repeated, for the very purpose of extending and limiting the truth to its exact and undoubted measure. He obviously labors to say just what he means, no more, no less, or other. Still, on the whole, he fails, because he is so elaborately precise in details. The thought is suffocated by the multi-tude of words employed to give it life. It is buried alive. To change the figure, you can divide and subdivide a field into so many, so small, so regular, and so exact patches, that the chief impression it shall leave on your eye is that of the fences. Similar is the impression of an excessively precise style.

Austin Phelps, 1883, English Style in Public Discourse, p. 91

In a well-known canon of style Burke lays it down that the master sentence of every paragraph should involve, first, a thought, secondly, an image, and thirdly, a sentiment. The rule is certainly not one of universal application; it is one not always followed by Burke himself, but it expresses the character of his mind. A thought, an image, a sentiment, and all bearing upon action, —it gives us an intimation that the writer who set forth such a canon was a complete nature, no fragment of a man, but a full-formed human spirit, and that when he came to write or speak, he put his total manhood into his utter-ance. This is, indeed, Burke's first and highest distinction.

Edward Dowden, 1897, The French Revolution and
English Literature, p. 94

HORACE WALPOLE
Earl of Oxford
1717-1797

Born, in London, 24 Sept. 1717. Educated at Eton, April 1727 to Sept.
1734. Entered at Lincoln's Inn, 27 May 1731. To King's Coll., Camb.,
March 1735. Inspector of Imports and Exports, 1737-38; Usher of the
Exchequer, 1738; Comptroller of the Pipe, 1738; Clerk of the Estreats,
1738. Left Cambridge, March 1739. Travelled on Continent, 1739-41.
M. P. for Callington, 1741-44. Settled at Strawberry Hill, 1747. M. P. for
Castle Rising, 1754-57; for King's Lynn, 1757-68. Succeeded to Earldom
of Orford, Dec. 1791. Unmarried. Died, in London, 2 March 1797. Buried
at Houghton. WORKS: *Lessons for the Day* (anon.), 1742; *Epilogue to
Tamerlane* (1746); *Ædes Walpolianæ*, 1747; *Letter from Xo-Ho*, 1757
(5th edn. same year); *Fugitive Pieces in Verse and Prose*, 1758; *Catalogue
of the Royal and Noble Authors of England* (2 vols.), 1758; *Observations
on the Account given of the Catalogue . . . in . . . the Critical Review*,
1759; *Reflections on the Different Ideas of the French and English in
regard to Cruelty* (anon.), 1759; *A Counter-Address to the Public* (anon.),
1764; *The Castle of Otranto* (anon.), 1765 (2nd edn. same year); *An
Account of the Giants lately discovered*, 1766; *The Mysterious Mother*
(priv. ptd.), 1768; *Historic Doubts of the Life and Reign of King Richard
the Third*, 1768 (2nd edn. same year); *Miscellaneous Antiquities* (anon.),
1772; *Description of the Villa . . . at Strawberry Hill*, 1772; *Letter to the
Editor of the Miscellanies of Thomas Chatterton*, 1779; *To Lady H.
Waldegrave* (anon.), (1779); *Hieroglyphick Tales* (anon.), 1785; *Essay
on Modern Gardening*, 1785; *The Press at Strawberry Hill to . . . the
Duke of Clarence* (anon.), (1790?); *Hasty Productions*, 1791. POSTHU-
MOUS: *Letters to . . . Rev. W. Cole and others*, 1818; *Letters to G.
Montagu*, 1819; *Private Correspondence* (4 vols.), 1820; *Memoirs of the
Last Ten Years of the Reign of King George II.*, ed. by Lord Holland (2
vols.), 1822; *Letters to Sir H. Mann* (7 vols.), 1833-44; *Letters*, ed. by
J. Wright (6 vols.), 1840; *Memoirs of the Reign of King George III.*, ed.
by Sir D.Le Marchant (4 vols.), 1845; *Letters to the Countess of Ossory*
(2 vols.), 1848; *Correspondence with W. Mason*, ed. by J. Mitford (2
vols.), 1851; *Letters*, ed. by P. Cunningham (9 vols.), 1857-58; *Journal
of the Reign of King George the Third . . . being a Supplement to his
Memoirs*, ed. by Dr. Doran (2 vols.), 1859; *Supplement to the Historic
Doubts*, ed. by Dr. Hawtrey (priv. ptd.), 1860-61. He *edited*: P. Hentz-
ner's *A Journey into England*, 1757; G. Vertue's *Anecdotes of Painting
in England*, 1762; and *Catalogue of Engravers*, 1763, Lord Herbert of
Cherbury's *Life*, 1764; Count de Grammont's *Memoires*, 1772. COLLECTED
WORKS: in 9 vols., 1798-1825. LIFE: by Austin Dobson, 1890.

R. Farquharson Sharp, 1897, *A Dictionary of
English Authors*, p. 291

SEE: *Correspondence*, ed. W. S. Lewis and others, 1937- , 50 v.;
(Selected) *Letters*, ed. W. S. Lewis, 1951; Robert W. Ketton-Cremer,
Horace Walpole: a Biography, 1940; W. S. Lewis, *Horace Walpole's
Library*, 1957; W. S. Lewis, *Horace Walpole*, 1961.

PERSONAL

When Mr. Horace Walpole came from abroad about the year 1746, he was much of a *Fribble* in dress and manner. Mr. Colman, at that time a school-boy, had some occasion to pay him a visit. He told me he has a strong recol-lection of the singularity of his manner; and that it was then said that Gar-rick had him in thought when he wrote the part of *Fribble,* in *Miss in her Teens.* But I doubt this much; for there is a character in a play called *Tun-bridge Wells,* in which that of *Fribble* seems to be evidently formed. How-ever, Garrick might have had Mr. Walpole in his thoughts. This gentleman (Mr. Walpole) is still somewhat singular in manner and appearance; but it seems only a singularity arising from a very delicate and weak constitution, and from living quite retired among his books, and much with ladies. He is always lively and ingenious; never very solid or energetic. He appears to be very fond of French manners, authors, &c, &c., and I believe keeps up to this day a correspondence with many of the people of fashion in Paris. His love of French manners, and his reading so much of their language, have I think infected his style a little, which is not always so entirely English as it ought to be. He is, I think, a very humane and amiable man.

Edmond Malone, 1782? Maloniana, ed. Prior, p. 86

The letter you sent me of Horace Walpole's is brilliant, and from its sub-ject, inevitably interesting; but do not expect that I can learn to esteem that fastidious and unfeeling being, to whose insensibility we owe the extinction of the greatest poetic luminary Chatterton, if we may judge from the bright-ness of its dawn, that ever rose in our, or perhaps any other hemisphere. This fine wit of Strawberry Hill, is of that order of mortals who swarm, al-ways swarmed, and always will swarm in refined states; whose eyes of ad-miration are in their backs, and who, consequently, see nothing worthy their attention before, or on either side of them; and who, therefore, weary, sicken, and disgust people whose sensibilities are strong and healthy, by their eternal cant about the great *have beens,* and the little *are's.*

Miss Seward, 1787, Letter to Hardinge, Nov. 21

When viewed from behind, he had somewhat of a boyish appearance, owing to the form of his person, and the simplicity of his dress. . . . His laugh was forced and uncouth, and even his smile not the most pleasing. His walk was enfeebled by the gout; which, if the editor's memory do not deceive, he mentioned that he had been tormented with since the age of twenty-five; adding, at the same time, that it was no hereditary complaint, his father, Sir

Robert Walpole, who always drank ale, never having known that disorder, and far less his other parent. This painful complaint not only affected his feet, but attacked his hands to such a degree that his fingers were always swelled and deformed, and discharged large chalkstones once or twice a year; upon which occasions he would observe, with a smile, that he must set up an inn, for he could chalk up a score with more ease and rapidity than any man in England.

John Pinkerton, 1799, *Walpoliana*

The whole spirit of this man was penury. Enjoying an affluent income he only appeared to patronise the arts which amused his tastes,—employing the meanest artists, at reduced prices, to ornament his own works, an economy which he bitterly reprehends in others who were compelled to practise it. He gratified his avarice at the expense of his vanity; the strongest passion must prevail. It was the simplicity of childhood in Chatterton to imagine Horace Walpole could be a patron—but it is melancholy to record that a slight protection might have saved such a youth. Gray abandoned this man of birth and rank in the midst of their journey through Europe; Mason broke with him; even his humble correspondent Cole, this "friend of forty years," was often sent away in dudgeon; and he quarrelled with all the authors and artists he had ever been acquainted with. The Gothic castle at Strawberry-hill was rarely graced with living genius—there the greatest was Horace Walpole himself.

Isaac Disraeli, 1812-13, "The Pain of Fastidious Egotism,"
Calamities of Authors

That cold and false-hearted Frenchified coxcomb, Horace Walpole.

William Wordsworth, 1833, *Letter, Memoirs* by C. Wordsworth,
ed. Reed, vol. II, p. 277

He was, unless we have formed a very erroneous judgment of his character, the most eccentric, the most artificial, the most fastidious, the most capricious of men. His mind was a bundle of inconsistent whims and affectations. His features were covered by mask within mask. When the outer disguise of obvious affectation was removed, you were still as far as ever from seeing the real man. He played innumerable parts, and overacted them all. When he talked misanthropy, he out-Timoned Timon. When he talked philanthropy, he left Howard at an immeasurable distance. He scoffed at courts, and kept a chronicle of their most trifling scandal; at society, and was blown about by its slightest veerings of opinions; at literary fame, and left fair copies of his private letters, with copious notes, to be published after his decease; at rank, and never for a moment forgot that he was an honourable; at the practice of entail, and tasked the ingenuity of conveyancers to tie up his villa in the strictest settlement. The conformation of his mind was such, that whatever was little, seemed to him great, and whatever was great seemed to him little. Serious business was a trifle to him, and trifles were his serious business. To chat with blue-stockings; to write little copies of complimentary verses on little occasions; to superintend a private press; to preserve from natural decay the perishable topics of Ranelagh and White's; to record divorces and bets, Miss Chudleigh's absurdities and George Selwyn's good sayings; to decorate a grotesque house with piecrust battlements; to procure rare engravings and antique chimney-boards; to match odd gauntlets; to lay out a maze of walks within five acres of ground—these were the grave employments of his long life. From these he turned to politics as to an amusement. After the labours of the print-shop and the auction-room, he unbent his mind in the House of Commons. And, having indulged in the recreation of making laws and voting millions, he returned to more important pursuits—to researches after Queen Mary's comb, Wolsey's red hat, the pipe which Van Tromp smoked during his last sea-fight, and the spur which King William struck into the flank of Sorrel.

> Thomas Babington Macaulay, 1833, "Walpole's Letters to
> Sir Horace Mann," *Edinburgh Review,* vol. 58;
> *Critical and Miscellaneous Essays*

Here, at last, we have the prince of letter-writers drawn for us with a sure and graceful touch. Here is the petted child, who, humored in a foolish whim, was carried privately to court at night, to kiss King George's hand. Here is the clever schoolboy, who preferred reading to fighting; whose friends were lads as precocious as himself, and who, in most unboyish fashion, dubbed his play-fellows Oromasdes and Plato instead of plain Ashton and Gray. Here is the one undergraduate of Cambridge who frankly confesses (for which we love him much) that he never mastered even his multiplication table. Here is the young gentleman of leisure who drew a handsome income from sinecures, and who was of real service to his country by traveling abroad, and writing admirable letters home. Here is the valued friend of so many brilliant and distinguished people, who has left us in his vivacious pages those matchless portraits that time can never fade. Here, in a word, is Horace Walpole, whom some loved and not a few hated, whose critics have dealt him heavy censure and faint praise, and who now, from a snug corner in the Elysian fields, must secretly rejoice at finding himself in hands at once sympathetic, tolerant and impartial.

> Agnes Repplier, 1893, "Horace Walpole, A memoir by
> Austin Dobson," *The Cosmopolitan,* vol. 16, p. 250

He was eleven years younger than the rest of his father's children, a circumstance which, taken in connection with his dissimilarity, both personally and mentally, to the other members of the family, has been held to lend some countenance to the contemporary suggestion, first revived by Lady Louisa Stuart (Introduction to Lord Wharncliffe's edition of the *Works of Lady Mary Wortley Montagu*), that he was the son not of Sir Robert Walpole, but of Carr, lord Hervey, the "Sporus" of Pope. His attachment to his mother and his life-long reverence for Sir Robert Walpole, of whom he was invariably the strenuous defender, added to the fact that there is nowhere the slightest hint in his writing of any suspicion on his own part as to his parentage, must be held to discredit this ancient scandal.

Austin Dobson, 1899, Dictionary of National Biography,
vol. LIX, p. 170

STRAWBERRY HILL

Whether Horace Walpole conferred a benefit upon the public by setting of applying the Gothic style of architecture to domestic purposes, may be doubtful; so greatly has the example he gave been abused in practice since. But, at all events, he thus led the professors of architecture to study with accuracy the principle of the art, which has occasioned the restoration and preservation in such an admirable manner of so many of our finest cathedrals, colleges, and ancient Gothic and conventual buildings. This, it must be at least allowed, was the fortunate result of the *rage* for Gothic, which succeeded the building at Strawberry Hill. For a good many years after that event, every new building was *pinnacled* and *turreted* on all sides, however little its situation, its size, or its uses might seem to fit it for such ornaments. Then, as fashion is never constant for any great length of time, the taste of the public rushed at once upon castles; and loop-holes, and battlements, and heavy arches, and buttresses appeared in every direction. Now the fancy of the time has turned as madly to that bastard kind of architecture, possessing, however, many beauties, which, compounded of the Gothic, Castellated, and Grecian or Roman, is called *the Elizabethan,* or *Old English*. No villa, no country-house, no lodge in the outskirts of London, no box of a retired tradesman, is now built, except in some modification of this style.

Lord Dover, 1833, ed. Walpole's Letters to Sir Horace Mann, Life

The fate of Strawberry was still more lamentable. For four and twenty days the apartments, sacred to the Horatian pleasantries, echoed with the hammer of the auctioneer. Circumstances, that need not be more particularly alluded to, rendered this degradation unavoidable, and it was only with difficulty that the most sacred of the family possessions could be preserved from the relentless ordeal of "a public sale!" The shrine which had been visited with so much interest and veneration, was now overrun by a well dressed mob, who glanced at its treasures, and at the copious catalogue in which they were enumerated, apparently with a like indifference. But at the sale this indifference, whether feigned or real, changed to the most anxious desire to obtain possession of some relic of the man whose name was invested with so many pleasant associations; and the more interesting portion of "the thousand trifles" created a degree of excitement which would almost have reconciled their proprietor to such a distribution.

Eliot Warburton, 1852, ed., Memoirs of Horace Walpole
and His Contemporaries, vol. II, p. 568

The position which he occupies with regard to art resembles in many respects that in which he stands as a man of letters. His labours were not profound in either field. But their result was presented to the public in a form which gained him rapid popularity both as an author and a *dilettante*. As a collector of curiosities he was probably influenced more by a love of old world associations than by any sound appreciation of artistic design.

Charles Lock Eastlake, 1871, History of the Gothic Revival, p. 43

As a virtuoso and amateur, his position is a mixed one. He was certainly widely different from that typical art connoisseur of his day—the butt of Goldsmith and of Reynolds—who travelled the Grand Tour to litter a gallery at home with broken-nosed busts and the rubbish of the Roman picture-factories. As the preface to the *Ædes Walpolianae* showed, he really knew something about painting, in fact was a capable draughtsman himself, and besides, through Mann and others, had enjoyed exceptional opportunities for procuring genuine antiques. But his collection was not so rich in this way as might have been anticipated; and his portraits, his china, and his miniatures were probably his best possessions. For the rest, he was an indiscriminate rather than an eclectic collector; and there was also considerable truth in that strange "attraction from the great to the little, and from the useful to the odd" which Macaulay has noted. Many of the marvels at Strawberry would never have found a place in the treasure-houses—say of Beckford or Samuel Rogers.

Austin Dobson, 1890-93, Horace Walpole, A Memoir, p. 286

Horace Walpole's collections were sold at Strawberry Hill by George Robins in April and May 1842, during twenty-four days. The first six days were devoted to the sale of the library, which consisted of 1555 lots, and realised £3900. It was very badly catalogued, and the books and books of prints, collection of portraits, &c., forming the seventh and eight days' sale, were withdrawn, re-catalogued, and extended to a ten days' sale.

Henry B. Wheatley, 1898, Prices of Books, p. 162

The Castle of Otranto (1765)

Shall I even confess to you, what was the origin of this romance? I waked one morning in the beginning of last June from a dream, of which all I could recover was, that I had thought myself in an ancient castle (a very natural dream for a head filled, like mine, with Gothic story), and that, on the uppermost banister of a great staircase I saw a gigantic hand in armour. In the evening I sat down, and began to write, without knowing in the least what I intended to say or relate. The work grew on my hands. . . . In short, I was so engrossed with my tale, which I completed in less than two months, that one evening I wrote from the time I had drunk my tea, about six o'clock, till half an hour after one in the morning.

Horace Walpole, 1765, To Rev. William Cole, March 9;
Letters, ed. Cunningham, vol. IV, p. 328

A series of supernatural appearances, put together under the most interesting form imaginable. Let one be ever so much of a philosopher, that enormous helmet, that monstrous sword, the portrait which starts from its frame and walks away, the skeleton of the hermit praying in the oratory, the vaults, the subterranean passages, the moonshine—all these things make the hair of the sage stand on end, as much as that of the child and his nurse: so much are the sources of the marvellous the same to all men. It is true that nothing very important results at least from all these wonders; but the aim of the author was to amuse, and he certainly cannot be reproached for having missed his aim.

Friedrich Melchior Baron Grimm, 1767? Historical and
Literary Memoirs and Anecdotes, vol. II, p. 218

The actors in the romance are strikingly drawn, with bold outlines becoming the age and nature of the story. Feudal tyranny was, perhaps, never better exemplified than in the character of Manfred. . . . The applause due to chastity and precision of style,—to a happy combination of supernatural agency with human interest,—to a tone of feudal manners and language sustained by characters strongly drawn and well discriminated,—and to unity of action, producing scenes alternately of interest and of grandeur;— the applause, in fine, which cannot be denied to him who can excite the passions of fear and of pity, must be awarded to the author of The Castle of Otranto.

Sir Walter Scott, 1821, Horace Walpole

By way of experiment, in reviving the more imaginative style of romance, Walpole had bethought himself of a mediæval story of an Italian castle, the human tenants of which should act naturally, but should be surrounded by supernatural circumstances and agencies leading them on to their fate. I confess that on reperusing the story the other day, I did not find my nerves affected as they were when I read it first. The mysterious knockings and voices, the pictures starting from the wainscot, the subterranean vaults, and even the great helmet with the nodding black plumes in the courtyard, had lost their horror; and Walpole seemed to me a very poor master of the Gothic business, or of poetic business of any kind. The attempt, however, is interesting as a hark-back to mediævalism, at a time when mediævalism was but little in fashion. As a virtuoso Walpole had acquired a certain artificial taste for the Gothic; and his "Gothic Story," as he called it, did something to bring to the minds of British readers, on its first publication, the recollection that there had been a time in the world, when men lived in castles, believed in the devil, and did not take snuff, or wear powdered wigs.

David Masson, 1859, *British Novelists and Their Styles,* p. 151

There can, however, be no doubt that this story had a very powerful effect on the writers that followed; nay, that it led, amongst other things, to the study of architecture, mediævalism, the love of the Gothic, the writing of Sir Walter Scott's great romances, and even to the revival of the love of colour, glitter, show, and pictorial decoration observable in the religious services of a large portion of the people of this land.

James Hain Friswell, 1869, *Essays on English Writers,* p. 294

It is impossible at this day to take *The Castle of Otranto* seriously, and hard to explain the respect with which it was once mentioned by writers of authority. . . . Walpole's master-piece can no longer make anyone cry even a little; and instead of keeping us out of bed, it sends us there—or would, if it were a trifle longer. For the only thing that is tolerable about the book is its brevity, and a certain rapidity in the action. . . . The book was not an historical romance, and the manners, sentiments, language, all were modern. Walpole knew little about the Middle Ages and was not in touch with their spirit. At bottom he was a trifler, a fribble; and his incurable superficiality, dilettantism, and want of seriousness, made all his real cleverness of no avail when applied to such a subject as *The Castle of Otranto.*

Henry A. Beers, 1898, *A History of English Romanticism in the Eighteenth Century,* pp. 237, 238, 240

LETTERS

Incomparable letters.

> Lord Byron, 1820, *Marino Faliero,* Preface

Read, if you have not read, all Horace Walpole's letters, wherever you can find them;—the best wit ever published in the shape of letters.

> Sydney Smith, 1820, *Letter to Edw. Davenport,* Nov. 19;
> *Memoir of Rev. Sydney Smith*

The best letter-writer in the English language.

> Sir Walter Scott, 1821, *Horace Walpole*

The *Letters* of Mr. Walpole have already attained the highest rank in that department of English literature, and seem to deserve their popularity, whether they are regarded as objects of mere amusement, or as a collection of anecdotes illustrative of the politics, literature, and manners of an important and interesting period.

> John Wilson Croker, 1825, ed., *Letters from the Hon. Horace Walpole to the Earl of Hertford during his Lordship's Embassy in Paris: to which are added Mr. Walpole's Letters to the Rev. Henry Zouch*

The twenty or thirty volumes of Voltaire's correspondence have already furnished a signal example how much a distinguished man will sometimes repeat himself. Yet, as compared with Walpole, he appears to write rather from impulse than meditation, and with the characteristic vivacity of his country. His repeating seems, therefore, to be natural, and like that of a man in conversation upon the same general topics with the succession of individuals. It is not so with Walpole. His phrases are too nicely picked, his anecdotes too carefully told. When they are read the first time, they earn for him the credit of ready wit. But when seen to be transferred from place to place with no essential change, they smack something too much of study. Neither do we detect this solely in his letters. He often produces in his *Memoirs* the counterpart of what he writes to Lord Hertford, or Mann, or Montague. We find the same stories in even the same words. We must, then, already begin to deny him the greatest merit of epistolary composition, its natural and spontaneous flow. But besides this, the repetition of the same thing, however well told, when it is not connected with important events, soon becomes fatiguing.

> Charles Francis Adams, 1845, "Horace Walpole's Letters and Memoirs," *North American Review,* vol. 61, p. 423

These letters have always ranked high since Byron and Scott said they were classic. They are excellently written, and when the subject is good they are delightful, being vivid, amiable, quick, seasoned with allusion, point, and anecdote. But whether they will keep their rank may be questioned. . . . The defect in these letters, as classical compositions, is their lack of freshness. They are a chronicle of faded things—finery, ambitions, sentiments, gossip, criticisms, beaux, dames, and nephews, all musty, and dry, and rubbishy. They do not reveal a nature like Cowper's, nor treasure up refinement, sense, and scholarly associations like Gray's. Invaluable to the historian, and to lovers of old French memoirs, they are not classic in the sense that Cowper's and Gray's letters are—in the sense of being invaluable to the highly-cultivated man. So far as the society they picture is concerned, the candles were burnt out and the play was done long ago. They are the quintessential spirit of the worldliness—the form and feature of the world of which it was anciently said the fashion of it passeth away. They belong to the antiquary; they no longer touch life.

George E. Woodberry, 1884 "Seeley's Walpole,"
The Nation, vol. 38, p. 261

GENERAL

His taste was highly polished; his vivacity attained to brilliancy; and his picturesque fancy, easily excited, was soon extinguished; his playful wit and keen irony were perpetually exercised in his observations on life, and his memory was stored with the most amusing knowledge, but much too lively to be accurate; for his studies were but his sports. But other qualities of genius must distingush the great author, and even him who would occupy that leading rank in the literary republic our author aspired to fill. He lived too much in that class of society which is little favourable to genius; he exerted neither profound thinking, nor profound feeling; and too volatile to attain to the pathetic, that higher quality of genius, he was so imbued with the petty elegancies of society that every impression of grandeur in the human character was deadened in the breast of the polished cynic. . . . All his literary works, like the ornamented edifice he inhabited, were constructed on the same artificial principle; an old paper lodging-house, converted by the magician of taste into a Gothic castle, full of scenic effects.

Isaac Disraeli, 1812-13, "The Pain of Fastidious Egotism,"
Calamities of Authors

"Unhealthy and disorganised mind," "a bundle of whims and affectations," "mask within mask;" these are the phrases that go to make up the popular estimate of a writer who was distinguished by the sincerity of his taste and judgment, and by the quickness and truth of his response to all impressions. Horace Walpole wrote and thought exactly as he pleased; his letters are the expression, direct and clear, of a mind that could not condescend to dull its reflections by any compromise about the values of things, or any concession to opinion. He never tampered with his instinctive appreciation of anything. Whether his judgments are sound in themselves is a question of small importance in comparison with his virtue of self-respect and self-restraint. It is because he had a mind of his own and would not pretend to like what he could not like, that he has been pointed out by the literary demagogue.

W. P. Ker, 1895, *English Prose,* ed. Craik, vol. IV, p. 233

JAMES BOSWELL
1740-1798

Born, at Auchinleck, 29 Oct. 1740. Educated by private tutor; then at private school in Edinburgh; then at Edinburgh High School and Edinburgh Univ. To Glasgow as Student of Civil Law, 8 Jan., 1759. To London, March 1760. In Edinburgh, April, 1761 to Nov. 1762; then returned to London. Contrib. poems to *Collections of Original Poems by Mr. Blacklock,* 1762. First met Johnson, 16 May 1763. In Berlin, July 1764. To Italy, Dec. 1764. To Utrecht, to study Law, Aug. 1765. Tour in Italy and Corsica. Returned to Scotland, Feb. 1766. Admitted Advocate, 26 July 1766. To London on publication of *Account of Corsica,* May 1768. Married Margaret Montgomerie, 25 Nov. 1769. Contrib. to *London Magazine,* 1769-70, 1777-79. Frequent visits to Johnson, mostly in London, between 1772 and 1784. Elected Member of Literary Club, 30 April 1773. Voyage to Hebrides with Johnson, Aug. to Nov. 1773. Began to keep terms at Inner Temple, 1775. Auchinleck estate entailed on him, 7 Aug. 1776. Father died, 30 Aug. 1782. Called to Bar, 1786. Appointed Recorder of Carlisle, 1788. Took chambers in Temple, 1790. *Life of Johnson* appeared, 16 May 1791. Appointed Secretary of Foreign Correspondence to Royal Academy July, 1791. Died, in London, 19 May 1795. Buried at Auchinleck. WORKS: *Ode to Tragedy* (anon.), 1761; *Elegy upon the Death of an amiable Young Lady* (anon.), 1761; *The Cub at Newmarket* (anon.), 1762; *Correspondence with Hon. A. Erskine,* 1763; *Critical Strictures on Mallet's "Elvira"* (with Erskine and Dempster), 1763; *Speeches, Arguments and Determinations* in the Douglas case (anon.), 1767; *Essence of the Douglas Cause* (anon.), 1767; *Dorando,* 1767; Prologue for the Opening of Edinburgh Theatre, 1767; *An Account of Corsica,* 1768; *British Essays in favour of the Brave Corsicans,* 1769; *Decision in the Cause of Hunter v. Donaldson,* 1774; *A Letter to the People of Scotland on the Present State of the Nation,* 1783; *Ode by Samuel Johnson to Mrs. Thrale* (by Boswell; anon.), 1784; *The Journal of a Tour to the Hebrides,* 1785 (2nd ed. same year); *Letter to the People of Scotland on the alarming Attempt to infringe the Articles of Union,* 1786; *The Celebrated Letter from Samuel Johnson, LL. D., to Phillip Dormer Stanhope, Earl of Chesterfield,* 1790; *Conversation between George III. and Samuel Johnson,* 1790; *No Abolition of Slavery* (probably suppressed), 1791; *Life of Johnson,* 1791; (another edn., pirated, 1792;

2nd authorised edn., 1793); *Principal Corrections and Additions to First Edition*, 1793. POSTHUMOUS: *Letters to Rev. J. W. Temple*, 1857; *Boswelliana: the Common-place Book of J. Boswell*, published by Grampian Club, 1874.

      R. Farquharson Sharp, 1897, *A Dictionary of English Authors*, p. 29

SEE: *Life of Samuel Johnson*, ed. G. Birkbeck Hill, 1887, 1934-50 (revised by L. F. Powell), 6 v.; *Boswell's Journal of a Tour of the Hebrides, with Samuel Johnson, LL.D.*, ed. Frederick A. Pottle and Charles H. Bennett, 1936; *Boswell's Column: being his Seventy Contributions to the London Magazine under Pseudonym The Hypochrondiack from 1777 to 1783*, ed. Margery Bailey, 1951; *Yale Edition of the Private Papers*, general editor Frederick A. Pottle: *Boswell in Holland, 1763-1764*, ed. Frederick A. Pottle, 1952; *Boswell on the Grand Tour: Germany and Switzerland, 1764*, ed. Frederick A. Pottle, 1953; *Boswell on the Grand Tour: Italy, Corsica and France, 1765-1766*, ed. Frank Brady and Frederick A. Pottle, 1955; *Boswell in Search of a Wife, 1766-1769*, ed. Frank Brady and Frederick A. Pottle, 1956; *Boswell for the Defense, 1769-1774*, ed. William K. Wimsatt, Jr. and Frederick A. Pottle, 1959; *Boswell: The Ominous Years, 1774-1776*, ed. Charles Ryskamp and Frederick A. Pottle, 1963; also see *Private Papers of James Boswell from Malahide Castle, in the Collection of Ralph Heyward Isham*, ed. Geoffrey Scott, 1928-34, 18 v., *privately printed* (Vols. 17-18 co-edited with Frederick A. Pottle); Chauncey B. Tinker, *Young Boswell*, 1922; Frederick A. Pottle, *The Literary Career of James Boswell, esq.*, 1928.

PERSONAL

I have just seen a very clever letter to Mrs. Montagu, to disavow a jackanapes who has lately made a noise here, one Boswell, by anecdotes of Dr. Johnson.

Horace Walpole, 1786, *To Sir Horace Mann*, March 16;
Letters, ed. Cunningham, vol. IX, p. 45

I fancy Boswell, from some things I heard of him, and it seems confirmed by various passages in his *Life of Johnson,* has a sort of rage for knowing all sorts of public men, good, bad, and indifferent, all one if a man renders himself known he likes to be acquainted with him.

Arthur Young, 1790, *Autobiography*, Oct. 24,
ed. Betham-Edwards, p. 191

I loved the man; he had great convivial powers and an inexhaustible fund of good humour in society; no body could detail the spirit of a conversation in the true style and character of the parties more happily than my friend James Boswell, especially when his vivacity was excited, and his heart exhilarated by the circulation of the glass, and the grateful odour of a well-broiled lobster.

Richard Cumberland, 1806, *Memoirs Written by Himself*,
vol. II, p. 228

He united lively manners with indefatigable diligence, and the volatile curiosity of a *man about town* with the drudging patience of a *chronicler*. With a very good opinion of himself, he was quick in discerning, and frank in applauding, the excellencies of others. Though proud of his own name and lineage, and ambitious of the countenance of the great, he was yet so cordial an admirer of merit, wherever found, that much public ridicule, and something like contempt, were excited by the modest assurance with which he pressed his acquaintance on all the notorieties of his time, and by the ostentatious (but, in the main, laudable) assiduity with which he attended the exile Paoli and the low-born Johnson! These were amiable, and, for us, fortunate inconsistencies. His contemporaries indeed, not without some colour of reason, occasionally complained of him as vain, inquisitive, troublesome, and giddy; but his vanity was inoffensive—his curiosity was commonly directed towards laudable objects—when he meddled, he did so, generally, from good-natured motives— and his giddiness was only an exuberant gaiety, which never failed in the respect and reverence due to literature, morals, and religion; and posterity gratefully acknowledges the taste, temper, and talents with which he selected, enjoyed, and described that polished and intellectual society which still lives in his work, and without his work had perished.

> John Wilson Croker, 1831, ed. *Boswell's Life of Johnson,* Preface

He was, if we are to give any credit to his own account, or to the united testimony of all who knew him, a man of the meanest and feeblest intellect. Johnson described him as a fellow who had missed his only chance of immortality, by not having been alive when the Dunciad was written. Beauclerk used his name as a proverbial expression for a bore. He was the laughing-stock of the whole of that brilliant society which has owed to him the greater part of its fame. He was always laying himself at the feet of some eminent man, and begging to be spit upon and trampled upon. . . . Servile and impertinent—shallow and pedantic—a bigot and a sot—bloated with family pride, and eternally blustering about the dignity of a born gentleman, yet stooping to be a talebearer, an eavesdropper, a common butt in the taverns of London—so curious to know everybody who was talked about, that, Tory and High Churchman as he was, he manœuvered, we have been told, for an introduction to Tom Paine. . . . All the caprices of his temper, all the illusions of his vanity, all the hypochondriac whimsies, all his castles in the air, he displayed with a cool self-complacency, a perfect unconsciousness that he was making a fool of himself, to which it is impossible to find a parallel in the whole history of mankind. He has used many people ill, but assuredly he has used nobody so ill as himself.

> Thomas Babington Macaulay, 1831, "Boswell's *Life of Johnson,*"
> *Edinburgh Review; Critical and Miscellaneous Essays*

In that cocked nose, cocked partly in triumph over his weaker fellow-creatures, partly to snuff up the smell of coming pleasure, and scent it from
afar; in those bag-cheeks, hanging like half-filled wineskins, still able to
contain more; in that coarsely-protruded shelf-mouth, that fat dewlapped
chin; in all this, who sees not sensuality, pretension, boisterous imbecility
enough; much that could not have been ornamental in the temper of a great
man's overfed great man (what the Scotch name *flunky*), though it had
been more natural there? The under part of Boswell's face is of a low,
almost brutish character.

Thomas Carlyle, 1832, *Boswell's Life of Johnson*

"Who *is* this Scotch cur at Johnson's heels?" asked some one, amazed at
the sudden intimacy. "He is not a cur," answered Goldsmith; "You are
too severe. He is only a bur. Tom Davies flung him at Johnson in sport,
and he has the faculty of sticking."

Sir James Prior, 1836, *The Life of Oliver Goldsmith*

That this garrulous, vain, wine-bibbing tattler should ally himself with the
great moralist, may be explained by his love of notoriety and of notables;
but that the austere, intolerant veteran of letters should like—indeed love
such a companion, is a curious problem. Yet, moralist though he was, he
liked, as he said, to "frisk it" now and then,—he loved the Honourable Tom
Hervey, the rake, and Topham Beauclerc, whose morals were far to seek.
Boswell, though not learned, and needing his mentor's advice to "read more
and drink less," knew something of his letters, knew much of the world, was
clever, entertaining, good-natured, and loyal. . . . Meanwhile his wife, a
woman of sense and some wit, had much to endure—her society neglected
for "good company," where he got tipsy, with the usual sequels of fits of
depression and tearful sentiment. He reminds us of Sir Richard Steele with
his bibulous indulgence, and protestations of affection in notelets to his
much suffering spouse: "I am, dear Prue, a little in drink, but all the time
your faitful husband, Richard Steele." All his characteristics remained unchanged; his alternate hypochondria and joviality; his moods of piety and
his lapses from it; his superstitions; his love of excitement—especially for a
hanging, in which he was as keen a connoisseur as George Selwyn himself.
He was ready to kneel down and join in the chaplain's prayers in the prison
cells with the convict in profoundest devotion, and to see him turned off at
Tyburn with the greatest gusto,—to witness fifteen men hanged at once
filled him with the keenest pleasure and the finest moral reflections. Vain
as poor Goldsmith, whose pride in his plum-coloured coat from Filbey's he
laughed at, he would rush in his Court dress from a levee at St. James's to

dazzle compositors at the printing-offices with his magnificence. Few figures were better known in London artistic and literary society than his—paunchy and puffy, with red face, long, cocked nose, protuberant mouth and chin, with mock solemnity of manner and voice, with slow gait and slovenly dress —the clothes being loose, the wig untidy, the gestures restless so as to resemble his great master, of whom he incessantly spoke, and whose big manner and oddities he mimicked with infinite drollery, making listeners convulse with laughter at the exquisite, but irreverent copy of his "revered friend."

Henry Grey Graham, 1901, Scottish Men of Letters
in the Eighteenth Century, pp. 221, 223

An Account of Corsica (1768)

Jamie had taen a toot on a new horn.

Alexander Boswell, 1768, Father of James Boswell

Mr. Boswell's book I was going to recommend to you, when I received your letter: it has pleased and moved me strangely, all (I mean) that relates to Paoli. He is a man born two thousand years after his time! The pamphlet proves what I have always maintained, that any fool may write a most valuable book by chance, if he will only tell us what he heard and saw with veracity. Of Mr. Boswell's truth I have not the least suspicion, because I am sure he could not invent nothing of this kind. The true title of this part of his work is, a Dialogue between a Green-Goose and a Hero.

Thomas Gray, 1768, Letter to Horace Walpole, Feb. 25;
Works, ed. Gosse, vol. III, p. 310

He came to my country, and he fetched me some letter of recommending him; but I was of the belief he might be an impostor, and I supposed in my minte he was espy; for I look away from him, and in a moment I look to him again, and I behold his tablets. Oh! he was to the work of writing down all I say. Indeed I was angry. But soon I discover he was no impostor and no espy; and I only find I was myself the monster he had come to discern. Oh! he is a very good man; I love him indeed; so cheerful, so gay, so pleasant! but at the first, oh! I was indeed angry.

Pascal Paoli, 1782, To Miss Burney, Diary and Letters,
Oct. 15, vol. II, p. 155

Dr. Hill assures us that by every Corsican of education the name of Boswell is known and honoured. One curious circumstance is given. At Pino, when

Boswell fancying himself "in a publick house" or inn, had called for things, the hostess had said *una cosa dopo un altra, signore,* "one thing after another, sir." This has lingered as a memento of Bozzy in Corsica, and has been found by Dr. Hill to be preserved among the traditions in the Tomasi family. Translations of the book in Italian, Dutch, French, and German, spread abroad the name of the traveller who, if like a prophet without honour in his own country, has not been without it elsewhere.

W. Keith Leask, 1897, James Boswell (Famous Scots), p. 52

Journal of a Tour to the Hebrides (1785)

I return you many thanks for Boswell's Tour. I read it to Mrs. Unwin after supper, and we find it amusing. There is much trash in it, as there must always be in every narrative that relates indiscriminately all that passed. But now and then the Doctor speaks like an oracle, and that makes amends for all. Sir John was a coxcomb, and Boswell is not less a coxcomb, though of another kind.

William Cowper, 1789, Letter to Samuel Rose, June 5;
Life, ed. Hayley, vol. I, p. 188

Never, I think, was so unimportant a journey so known of men. Every smart boy in every American school, knows now what puddings he ate, and about the cudgel that he carried, and the boiled mutton that was set before him. The bare mention of these things brings back a relishy smack of the whole story of the journey. Is it for the literary quality of the book which describes it? Is it for our interest in the great, nettlesome, ponderous traveller; or is it by reason of a sneaking fondness we all have for the perennial stream of Boswell's gossip? I cannot tell, for one: I do not puzzle with the question; but I enjoy.

Donald G. Mitchell, 1895, English Lands, Letters and Kings,
Queen Anne and the Georges, p. 137

No better book of travels in Scotland has ever been written than Boswell's *Journal of a Tour to the Hebrides.* The accuracy of his description, his eye for scenes and dramatic effects, have all been fully borne witness to by those who have followed in their track, and the fact of the book being day by day read by Johnson, during its preparation, gives it an additional value from the perfect veracity of its contents—"as I have resolved that the very journal which Dr. Johnson read shall be presented to the publick, I will not expand the text in any considerable degree."

W. Keith Leask, 1897, James Boswell (Famous Scots), p. 109

Life of Johnson (1791-93)

Boswell tells me he is printing *anecdotes* of Johnson, not his *life,* but, as he has the vanity to call it, his *pyramid.* I besought his tenderness of our virtuous and most revered departed friend, and begged he would mitigate some of his asperities. He said, roughly, "He would not cut off his claws, nor make a tiger a cat, to please anybody." It will, I doubt not, be a very amusing book, but I hope not an indiscreet one; he has great enthusiasm, and some fire.

> Hannah More, 1785, *Letter, Memoirs,* ed. Roberts

The labour and anxious attention with which I have collected and arranged the materials of which these volumes are composed, will hardly be conceived by those who read them with careless felicity. The stretch of mind and prompt assiduity by which so many conversations were preserved, I myself, at some distance of time, contemplate with wonder; and I must be allowed to suggest that the nature of the work in other respects, as it consists of innumerable detached particulars, all which, even the most minute, I have spared no pains to ascertain with a scrupulous authenticity, has occasioned a degree of trouble far beyond that of any other species of composition. Were I to detail the books which I have consulted, and the inquiries which I have found it necessary to make by various channels, I should probably be thought ridiculously ostentatious. Let me only observe, as a specimen of my trouble, that I have sometimes been obliged to run half over London, in order to fix a date correctly; which, when I had accomplished I well knew would obtain me no praise, though a failure would have been to my discredit. And after all, perhaps, hard as it may be, I shall not be surprised if omissions or mistakes be pointed out with invidious severity. I have also been extremely careful as to the exactness of my quotations; holding that there is a respect due to the public, which should oblige every author to attend to this, and never to presume to introduce them with, "I think I have read," or, "If I remember right," when the originals may be examined.

> James Boswell, 1791, *The Life of Samuel Johnson,* Advertisement

Highly as this work is now estimated, it will, I am confident, be still more valued by posterity a century hence, when the excellent and extraordinary man, whose wit and wisdom are here recorded, shall be viewed at a still greater distance; and the instruction and entertainment they afford will at once produce reverential gratitude, admiration, and delight.

> Edmond Malone, 1804, ed. *Boswell's Life of Johnson,* Preface

The circle of Mr. Boswell's acquaintance among the learned, the witty, and indeed among men of all ranks and professions, was extremely extensive, as his talents were considerable, and his convivial powers made his company much in request. His warmth of heart towards his friends, was very great; and I have known few men who possessed a stronger sense of piety, or more fervent devotion (tinctured, no doubt, with some little share of superstition which had, probably in some degree, been fostered by his habits of intimacy with Dr. Johnson), perhaps not always sufficient to regulate his imagination, or direct his conduct, yet still genuine, and founded both in his understanding and his heart. His *Life* of that extraordinary man, with all the faults with which it has been charged, must be allowed to be one of the most characteristic and entertaining biographical works in the English language.

Sir William Forbes, 1806, Account of the Life and Writings
of James Beattie, vol. II, p. 378, note

His *Life of Samuel Johnson* exhibits a striking likeness of a confident, overweening, dictatorial pedant, though of parts and learning; and of a weak, shallow, submissive admirer of such a character, deriving a vanity from that very admiration.

Richard Hurd, 1808 ? Commonplace Book, ed. Kilvert, p. 254

Of above *twenty years,* therefore, that their acquaintance lasted, periods equivalent in the whole to about three-quarters of a year only, fell under the personal notice of Boswell. . . . It appears from the Life, that Mr. Boswell visited England a dozen times during his acquaintance with Dr. Johnson, and that the number of days on which they met were about 180, to which is to be added the time of the *Tour,* during which they met daily from the 18th August, to the 22d November, 1773; in the whole about 276 days. The number of pages in the separate editions of the two works is 2528, of which 1320 are occupied by the history of these 276 days; so that a *little less than an hundredth part* of Dr. Johnson's life occupies *above one-half* of Mr. Boswell's works. Every one must regret that his personal intercourse with his great friend was not more frequent or more continued.

John Wilson Croker, 1831, ed. Boswell's Life of Johnson, Preface

The Life of Johnson is assuredly a great, a very great work. Homer is not more decidedly the first of heroic poets, Shakspeare is not more decidedly the first of dramatists, Demosthenes is not more decidedly the first of orators, than Boswell is the first of biographers. He has no second. He has distanced all his competitors so decidedly, that it is not worth while to place them. Eclipse is first, and the rest nowhere. We are not sure that there is in the whole history of the human intellect so strange a phenomenon as this book. Many of the greatest men that ever lived have written biography. Boswell was one of the smallest men that ever lived; and he has beaten them all.

> Thomas Babington Macaulay, 1831, "Boswell's *Life of Johnson*,"
> *Edinburgh Review; Critical and Miscellaneous Essays*

The greatest work of the class which exists in the world. The *Tour to the Hebrides* had shown what was to be expected from a man who seems to have been better fitted for his vocation than anybody else who ever lived, and whose name has supplied the English language with a new word. Every year increases the popularity of Boswell's marvellous work. The world will some day do more justice to his talents, which those who cannot forgive his Toryism are far too prone to run down; for he possessed great dramatic talent, great feeling for humour, and a very keen perception of all the kinds of colloquial excellence. With these men,—and they are not a few,—nine-tenths of whose affected contempt of him rests on the mean foundation that they dislike the very pardonable pride he took in his ancient birth, who would condescend to reason? But if any unprejudiced person doubts the real talent required for doing what Boswell did, let him make the experiment by attempting to describe somebody's conversation himself. Let him not fancy that he is performing a trivial or undignified task; for which of us, in any station, can hope to render a tithe of the service to the world that was conferred on it by the Laird of Auchinleck?

> James Hannay, 1856-61, *Table-Talk, Essays from the*
> *Quarterly Review*, p. 27

No one has ever reported conversations with a skill comparable to that of Boswell—a skill which appears marvellous when compared with the attempts of others; and although there may have been talkers as good as Johnson, no man's reported talk has the variety and force of his. . . . It is Boswell's eternal merit to have deeply reverenced the man whose littlenesses and asperities he could keenly discern, and has courageously depicted; and his work stands almost alone in Biography because he had this vision and this courage. The image of Johnson is not defaced by these revelations, it only becomes more intelligible in becoming more human.

> George Henry Lewes, 1873, *Life and Conversations of*
> *Dr. Samuel Johnson*, ed. Main, Preface, pp. x, xii

Did he (Macaulay) recognise to the full the fact of Boswell's pre-eminence as an artist? Was he really conscious that the *Life* is an admirable work of art as well as the most readable and companionable of books? As, not content with committing himself thus far, he goes on to prove that Boswell was great because he was little; that he wrote a great book because he was an ass, and that if he had not been an ass his book would probably have been at least a small one, incredulity on these points becomes repectable.

William Ernest Henley, 1890, *Views and Reviews,* p. 197

How much the literary Jupiter owes to his literary satellites, particularly to the first one, it is not easy, at this distance of time, to tell. But who reads his *Journey to the Western Islands of Scotland* in these days? How often is his *Dictionary* consulted? What influence has his *Rambler* upon modern letters? What sweet girl graduate or cultivated Harvard "man" of to-day can quote a line from *The Vanity of Human Wishes,* or knows whether that production is in prose or verse? What would the world have thought of Samuel Johnson at the end of a hundred years if a silly little Scottish laird had not made a hero of him, to be worshipped as no literary man was ever worshipped before or since, and if he had not written a biography of him which is the best in any language, and the model for all others.

Laurence Hutton, 1891, *Literary Landmarks of Edinburgh,* p. 20

Wonderful as it is that a man so compact of folly and vanity, so childish and so weak as Boswell, should have produced a book which has enforced the admiration of the world, yet we need not explain that book as a literary miracle. Its success is achieved by the usual means—insight, sympathy, skill, and perseverance; and its author had served an apprenticeship to his art before he began his greatest work.

Henry Craik, 1895, *English Prose,* vol. IV, p. 479

Boswell's book itself may now, in Parliamentary language, be taken for "read." As Johnson said of Goldsmith's *Traveller,* "its merit is established, and individual praise or censure can neither augment nor diminish it." . . . What is most distinctive in Boswell is Boswell's method and Boswell's manner. . . . This faculty of communicating his impressions accurately to his reader is Boswell's most conspicuous gift. Present in his first book, it was more present in his second, and when he began his great biography it had reached its highest point. So individual is his manner, so unique his method of collecting and arranging his information, that to disturb the native character of his narrative by interpolating foreign material, must of necessity impair its specific character and imperil its personal note.

Austin Dobson, 1898, "Boswell's Predecessors and Editors," *Miscellanies,* pp. 110, 124, 125

GENERAL

With all the praise that is lavished upon his biography, the author himself
is rather an underrated man. It is pretty generally supposed that little intellectual power was required for such a production—that it is merely an affair
of memory and observation. Now such powers of memory and observation
are certainly no common endowment. . . . Macaulay, who dilates upon the
meanness of spirit shown in the drawing out of Johnson's opinions, gives no
credit to the ingenuity. Boswell was undoubtedly a man of much social tact,
possessing great general knowledge of human nature, and a most penetrating insight into the thoughts and intents of his habitual companions.

William Minto, 1872-80, *Manual of English
Prose Literature,* p. 481

James Boswell has been treated with the greatest injustice and ingratitude
by nearly all the literary men who have recorded their opinions concerning
him and his work. Sir Walter Scott alone, with characteristic good sense,
stands aloof from the rest in his respectful treatment of the distinguished
biographer. He does not, indeed, seem to be aware that Boswell requires
defence, or that there is any thing particular in a kindly and respectful de-
meanour towards the author of Johnson's Life. He knows that Boswell, in
spite of his faults, was a high-spirited and honourable gentleman, warm-
hearted, and of a most candid and open nature, a sunny temper, and the
most unusual and genuine literary abilities. Accordingly, when Sir Walter
happens to allude to the Laird of Auchinleck it is always in a friendly and
frequently admiring tone—a tone very different from the brutal vituperation
of Macaulay or the superior compassion and humane condescension of the
great Herr Teufelsdrock. James Boswell did not deserve the hatred of the
one or the pity of the other. In standing contrast with the resolute vituperation of the rhetorician and the determined compassion of the prophet, the
honest student of English literature will be always glad to encounter the
kindly, grateful, and admiring language which flows so gracefully and naturally from the pen of Sir Walter in dealing with the character and the
literary performances of Boswell.

Arthur Clive, 1874, "Boswell and his Enemies,"
Gentleman's Magazine, n. s., vol. 13, p. 68

THE BEGINNINGS
OF ROMANTICISM

WILLIAM COWPER
1731-1800

Born, at Great Berkhamstead Rectory, 15 Nov. 1731. At a school in
Market Street, Herts, 1737-39. Under the care of an oculist, 1739-41. At
Westminster School, 1741-49. Student at Middle Temple, 29 April 1748.
Articled to a solicitor for three years, 1750. Called to Bar, 14 June 1754.
Depression of mind began. Commissioner of Bankrupts, 1759-65. Contrib.
nos. 111, 115, 134, 139 to *The Connoisseur,* 1756; to Duncombe's *Trans-
lations from Horace,* 1756-57; to *The St. James's Chronicle,* 1761. Symp-
toms of insanity began to appear; taken to a private asylum at St. Albans,
Dec. 1763. Left there and settled in Huntingdon, June 1765. Began to
board in house of Mr. and Mrs. Unwin there, Nov. 1765. Removed with
Mrs. Unwin and family to Olney, Bucks, autumn of 1767. Assisted John
Newton, curate of Olney, in parochial duties. Fresh attack of insanity,
1773-74. On recovery, showed more activity in literary work. Friendship
with Lady Austen, 1781-83. Contrib. to *Gentleman's Mag.,* June 1784 and
Aug. 1785. Removed from Olney to Weston, Nov. 1786. Attack of insanity, 1787. Contrib. to *Analytical Review,* Feb. 1789. Crown pension
of £300 a year granted, 1794. Visited various places in Norfolk with
Mrs. Unwin, summer of 1795. Settled in Dereham Lodge, Oct. 1795. Died
there, 25 April 1800. Buried in Dereham Church. WORKS: *Olney Hymns*
(anon., with J. Newton), 1779; *Anti-Thelyphthora* (anon.), 1781; *Poems,*
1782; *John Gilpin* (anon.), 1783; *The Task,* 1785 (the fly-leaf bears the
words: *Poems. . . .* Vol. II); Translation of *Iliad and Odyssey,* 1791;
Poems ("On the receipt of my mother's picture"—"The Dog and the
Water Lily"), 1798. POSTHUMOUS: *Adelphi,* 1802; *Life and Posthumous
Writings,* ed. by Hayley, 1803 (2nd edn., 1804; 3rd. entitled *Life and
Letters,* 1809); *Memoir of the early life of William Cowper* (autobiographical), 1816; *Table Talk,* 1817; *Hymns,* 1822; *Private Correspondence* (2 vols.), 1824; *Poems, the early productions of W. Cowper,* ed.
by J. Croft, 1825; *Minor Poems,* 1825; *The Negro's Complaint,* 1826. He
translated: *Homer,* 1791; *The Power of Grace,* by Van Lier, 1792; *Poems
by Mme. De la Motte Guion* (posth.), 1801; Milton's Latin and Italian
poems (posth.), 1808. COLLECTED WORKS: ed. by Newton (10 vols.),
1817; ed. by Memes (3 vols.), 1834; ed. by Grimshawe (8 vols.), 1835;
ed. by Southey (15 vols.), 1836-37. LIFE: by Hayley, 1803; by Bruce,
in Aldine edn. of Works, 1865; by Benham, in Globe edn. of Works, 1870.

R. Farquharson Sharp, 1897, *A Dictionary of
English Authors,* p. 67

SEE: *Poetical Works,* ed. Humphrey Milford, 1905, rev. 1926, 1934
(OSA); *"Memoir of William Cowper: An Autobiography,"* ed. Maurice
J. Quinlan, in *Proceedings of the American Philosophical Society,* XCVII

(1953); *Correspondence,* ed. Thomas Wright, 1904, 4 v.; *Unpublished and Published Letters,* ed. Thomas Wright, 1925; *Selected Letters,* ed. Mark Van Doren, 1951; Thomas Wright, *Life,* 1892, rev. 1921; David Cecil, *The Stricken Deer,* 1929; Norman Nicholson, *William Cowper,* 1951; Maurice J. Quinlan, *William Cowper: A Critical Life,* 1953; Lodwick C. Hartley, *William Cowper: A List of Critical and Biographical Studies Published from 1895 to 1949,* 1950.

PERSONAL

The morning is my writing time, and in the morning I have no spirits. So much the worse for my correspondents. Sleep, that refreshes my body, seems to cripple me in every other respect. As the evening approaches, I grow more alert, and when I am retiring to bed, am more fit for mental occupation than at any other time. So it fares with us whom they call nervous. By a strange inversion of the animal economy, we are ready to sleep when we have most need to be awake, and go to bed just when we might sit up to some purpose. The watch is irregularly wound up, it goes in the night when it is not wanted, and in the day stands still.

William Cowper, 1784, *Letter to John Newton,* Feb. 10

From his figure, as it first appeared to me, in his sixty-second year, I should imagine that he must have been very comely in his youth; and little had time injured his countenance, since his features expressed, in that period of life, all the powers of his mind, and all the sensibility of his heart. He was of a middle stature, rather strong than delicate in the form of his limbs: the colour of his hair was a light brown, that of his eyes a bluish, and his complexion ruddy. In his dress he was neat, but not finical; in his diet temperate and not dainty. He had an air of pensive reserve in his deportment, and his extreme shyness sometimes produced in his manners an indescribable mixture of aukwardness and dignity; but no being could be more truly graceful when he was in perfect health and perfectly pleased with his society. Towards women, in particular, his behaviour and conversation was delicate and fascinating in the highest degree.

William Hayley, 1803, *Life and Posthumous Writings of William Cowper,* vol. II, p. 124

It appears to the present writer, from a careful perusal of that instructive piece of biography published by Mr. Hayley, that Cowper, from his infancy, had a tendency to errations of the mind; and without admitting this fact in some degree, it must seem extremely improbable that the mere dread of appearing as a reader in the house of lords should have brought on his first settled fit of lunacy. Much, indeed, has been said of his uncommon shyness and diffidence, and more, perhaps, than the history of his early life will justify. Shyness and diffidence are common to all young persons who have not been early introduced into company, and Cowper, who had not, perhaps, that advantage at home, might have continued to be shy when other boys are forward. But had his mind been, even in this early period, in a healthful state, he must have gradually assumed the free manners of an ingenuous youth, conscious of no unusual imperfection that should keep him back. At school, we are told, he was trampled upon by the ruder boys who took advantage of his weakness, yet we find that he mixed in their amusements, which must in some degree have advanced him on a level with them: and what is yet more extraordinary, we find him associating with men of more gaiety than pure morality admits, and sporting with the utmost vivacity and wildness with Thurlow and others, when it was natural to expect that he would have been glad to court solitude for the purposes of study, as well as for the indulgence of his habitual shyness, if, indeed, at this period it was so habitual as we are taught to believe.

Alexander Chalmers, 1814, English Poets, Life of Cowper

His prevailing insanity, so far as it could be called insanity at all, in those long intervals of many years, during which his mind was serene and active, his habit of thought playful, and his affections more and more fervent, was simply the exclusion of a personal religious hope to such a degree as to seem like habitual despair. This despair was his insanity, for it could be only madness that could produce it, after such a revelation of the glory of God in the face of Jesus Christ as he had been permitted in the outset to enjoy. If Paul had gone deranged after being let down from his trance and vision in the third heavens, and the type of his derangement had been the despair of ever again beholding his Saviour's face in glory, and the obstinate belief of being excluded by Divine decree from heaven, though his affections were all the while *in* heaven, even that derangement would have been scarcely more remarkable than Cowper's. In the case of so delicate and profound an organization as his, it is very difficult to trace the effect of any entanglement or disturbance from one side or the other between the nervous and mental sensibilities of his frame. There was a set of Border Ruffians continually threatening his peace, endeavoring to set up slavery instead of freedom, and ever and anon making their incursions, and defacing the title-deeds to his inheritance, which they could not carry away; and Cowper might have assured himself with the consolation that those documents would not be destroyed, being registered in heaven, and God as faithful to them, as if their record in his own heart had been always visible.

George B. Cheever, 1843, Lectures on the Life, Genius and
Insanity of Cowper, Introduction, p. vii

If Cowper's retirement was virtuous, it was so because he was actively employed in the exercise of his highest faculties: had he been a mere idler,
secluded from his kind, his retirement would not have been virtuous at all.
His flight from the world was rendered necessary by his malady, and respectable by his literary work; but it was a flight and not a victory. His
misconception was fostered and partly produced by a religion which was
essentially ascetic, and which, while it gave birth to characters of the highest
and most energetic beneficence, represented salvation too little as the reward of effort, too much as the reward of passive belief and of spiritual
emotion.

Goldwin Smith, 1880, *Cowper* (*English Men of Letters*), p. 52

LADY AUSTEN

He was not a famous poet in those days, but a poor invalid recluse, with a
shadow of madness and misery about him, whose story was inevitably
known to all his neighbours, and about whom there could be no delusion
possible; but though all this is against the theory that a brilliant, lively,
charming, and very likely fanciful woman, such as Lady Austen seems to
have been, meant to marry him, it is quite enough to explain the compassionate interest rapidly ripening into warm friendship which moved her at
first. Men like Cowper are always interesting to women, and there can be
little doubt that, in the dull neighborhood of Olney, such company and
conversation as his would be a godsend to any visitor from livelier scenes.
When the new alliance went so far as to induce her to settle in Olney in
the adjoining house, with the famous door in the wall first made to faciliate
communications between Newton and Cowper, reopened, a stronger motive
is no doubt necessary. But it is a vulgar conclusion that marriage must be
thought of wherever a man and woman are concerned, and it was the age
for romantic friendships. At all events, whatever was the cause, Lady
Austen took up her abode in the deserted vicarage.

Margaret O. W. Oliphant, 1882, *Literary History of England
in the End of the Eighteenth and Beginning of the
Nineteenth Century*, vol. I, p. 55

The fact now began to dawn upon his mind that Lady Austen was in love
with him. The only wonder is that he did not perceive it before. Nobody
can blame her for losing her heart to the poet. She saw only the bright and
cheerful side of his character, and knew little or nothing of the canker of
despair that gnawed continually at his heart. . . . As soon as Cowper discovered in what light Lady Austen regarded him, he perceived that matters
could no longer go on as they were. The thought of love—anything more
than a brotherly and sisterly love—had never entered his mind, for since

his last dreadful derangement at the vicarage he had given up all thoughts of marriage (it should be remembered, too, that he was in his fifty-fourth year), and seeing himself called on to renounce either one lady or the other, he felt it to be his bounden duty to cling to Mrs. Unwin, to whose kindness he had been indebted for so many years. It has been said by some that Mrs. Unwin was jealous of Lady Austen. Very likely she was. When we consider how tenderly and patiently she had watched over Cowper in his dark and dreadful hours, how for so many years she had shared his joys and sorrows, and delighted in his companionship, we need not wonder if some feeling akin to jealousy stirred her when she perceived the danger of her place being taken by one who, though more brilliant, could not possibly love him more. But Mrs. Unwin had no need to fear. Cowper's affections for her, his knowledge of her worth, his gratitude for past services, would not allow him to hesitate. He had hoped that it would be possible to enjoy the friendship of both ladies; but when he discovered that it was necessary to decide between one and the other, he bowed to the painful necessity and wrote Lady Austen "a very tender yet resolute letter, in which he explained and lamented the circumstances that forced him to renounce her society." She in anger burnt the letter, and henceforth there was no more communication between them.

Thomas Wright, 1892, The Life of William Cowper, pp. 347, 348

Olney Hymns (1779)

As a hymn-writer, except for one very remarkable composition, Cowper scarcely ranks as high as the Wesleys. He might haven taken a much higher place than they—a higher place than almost any writer of hymns of his own time or since—if he could have applied his genius to the work. That was certainly not possible to him at the time when the Olney hymns were written, and at the other periods when it might have been possible he was occupied with greater things. The defect of his hymns was their severe doctrinal character. They are statements of religious belief, for the most part narrow and despondent; and only occasionally, when they reflect what may have been a passing mood of cheerfulness, do they express the aspirations or contentments of simple piety.

George Cotterell, 1897, "Cowper's Letters," The Argosy,
vol. 64, p. 152

"God Moves in a Mysterious Way." Cowper's hymn has helped multitudes to bear up under the blows of apparently adverse fortune. Within a year of the writing of this beautiful and touching hymn, Cowper's reason reeled, and he endeavoured to commit suicide by drowning in the Ouse. It is some poor consolation to know that his attempt at suicide was not a suicide of despair, but rather the perversion of the spirit of resignation and joyful submission which finds expression in the hymn. Newton says that Cowper tried to take his life, believing it was a sacrifice which God required at his hands. The accepted legend is that he had proposed to commit suicide at a certain place, but as the driver of the postchaise could not find it, he returned home without putting his purpose into execution, and there composed this hymn.

W. T. Stead, 1897, *Hymns that have Helped,* p. 115

The Task (1785)

The Task, beginning with all the peaceful attractions of sportive gaiety, rises to the most solemn and awful grandeur, to the highest strain of religious solemnity. Its frequent variation of tone is masterly in the greatest degree, and the main spell of that inexhaustible enchantment which hurries the reader through a flowery maze of many thousand verses, without allowing him to feel a moment of languor or fatigue. Perhaps no author, ancient or modern, ever possessed, so completely as Cowper, the nice art of passing, by the most delicate transition, from subjects to subjects that might otherwise seem but little or not at all allied to each other, the rare talent.
"Happily to steer
From grave to gay, from lively to severe."

William Hayley, 1803, *The Life and Posthumous Writings
of William Cowper,* vol. II, p. 142

It seems to have been begun without design like a morning's ramble, and to have been continued and completed without labour. Nevertheless, in this walk how many beautiful and even sublime objects rise upon the view. Cowper appears to bear in his style a very great resemblance to the Roman Ovid. There is in both the same elegance of diction and unstudied easiness of expression. But the Christian poet must be allowed to bear the palm from the Pagan in sentiment if he is equalled by him (which I do not think) in other respects. The pious fervour which goes through the page of Cowper will preserve it from oblivion, while the blasphemous scoffings of a witty infidel, should they pass down to another generation, will be viewed only with mingled indignation and contempt.

Connop Thirlwall, 1810, *To John Candler,* Oct. 24;
Letters, eds. Perowne and Stokes, p. 16

Cowper's first volume, partly from the grave character of the longer pieces and the purposely rugged, rambling, slip-shod versification, was long neglected, till *The Task,* the noblest effort of his muse, composed under the inspiration of cheerfulness, hope, and love, unbosoming the whole soul of his affections, intelligence, and piety,—at once made our countrymen feel that neither the genius of poesy had fled from our isle, nor had the heart for it died in the breast of its inhabitants. *The Task* was the first long poem from the close of Churchill's brilliant but evanescent career, that awoke wonder, sympathy, and delight by its own ineffable excellence among the reading people of England.

> James Montgomery, 1833, *Lectures on General Literature,*
> *Poetry, etc.,* p. 303

Where is the poem that surpasses *The Task* in the genuine love it breathes, at once towards inanimate and animate existence—in truthfulness of perception and sincerity of presentation—in the calm gladness that springs from a delight in objects for their own sake, without self-reference—in divine sympathy with the lowliest pleasures, with the most shortlived capacity for pain? . . . How Cowper's exquisite mind falls with the mild warmth of morning sunlight on the commonest objects, at once disclosing every detail and investing every detail with beauty! No object is too small to prompt his song—not the sooty film on the bars, or the spoutless tea-pot holding the bit of mignonette that serves to chear the dingy town-lodging with a "hint that Nature lives;" and yet his song is never trivial, for he is alive to small objects, not because his mind is narrow, but because his glance is clear and his heart is large.

> George Eliot, 1857, *Worldliness and Other-Worldliness:*
> *The Poet Young; Essays,* pp. 72, 73

The great beauties of *The Task*, and its pure and elevated feeling, can hardly be said to make it a poem of the highest class. The very method of its origin was some bar to success. . . . Towards the end of the First Book he again changes his subject, for the purpose of moralizing. The country and the life therein are contrasted with the town, and this affords the opening for satire, which is just touched in the end of the First Book, but forms the staple for the Second. And splendid satire it is, full of vigour, and energy, and point, sometimes mere good humoured badinage, sometimes full of burning indignation. It is satire of a different kind from that of his former poems; it is less bilious, more free from personality. Yet, Antæus-like, the author loses all his power when he ceases to touch his proper sphere. His faculty of keen observation enables him to lash effectively the false pretentions and follies which he sees. But his reflections upon the world without are of the poorest kind. He foresees the end of the world close at hand. He rails at the natural philosopher who attempts to discover the causes of physical calamities, such

as earthquakes and diseases; at the historian who takes the trouble to investigate the motives of remarkable men; at the geologist and the astron-
omer. For the last especially there is nothing but contempt.

William Benham, 1870, ed., *The Poetical Works*
of William Cowper, Introduction, p. lvii

As *Paradise Lost* is to militant Puritanism, so is *The Task* to the religious
movement of its author's time. To its character as the poem of a sect it no
doubt owed and still owes much of its popularity. Not only did it give
beautiful and effective expression to the sentiments of a large religious party,
but it was about the only poetry that a strict Methodist or Evangelical could
read; while to those whose worship was unritualistic and who were debarred
by their principles from the theatre and the concert, anything in the way of
art that was not illicit must have been eminently welcome.

Goldwin Smith, 1880, *Cowper (English Men of Letters),* p. 62

Save for a few occasional—and not always fortunate—lapses into familiarity, Cowper's manner of dealing with the domestic is still the manner of
the earlier century, still radically opposed to these principles of "natural"
poetic diction, on which Wordsworth was afterwards to insist with so much
more zeal than discretion, and to delay for many years the acceptance of
invaluable truth by exaggerating them in his preaching and rendering them
ridiculous in his practice. Cowper is still far from that frank fraternal recognition of the common objects, ideas, and interests of life which is advocated
in the famous preface to the *Lyrical Ballads.* Poetry in his hands will unbend
to common things, but it is always with a too vigilant dignity: she will take
notice of the tea-urn and the silkreels, and the modest indoor pleasures and
employments of the country house, but it is all done with the conscious condescension of the squire's wife at the village school treat. And Cowper,
moreover, clings still to that leisurely diffuseness of utterance which is so
alien to the spirit of the great poetry, pregnant with thought, and eager to
bring it to the birth. One reads him sometimes divided between delight in
his perfect literary finish and irritation at its prolixity.

Henry Duff Traill, 1896, *Social England,* vol. V, p. 443

On the Receipt of My Mother's Picture (1798)

This is no doubt, as a whole, Cowper's finest poem, at once springing from
the deepest and purest fount of passion, and happy in shaping itself into
richer and sweeter music than he has reached in any other. It shows what
his real originality, and the natural spirit of art that was in him, might have

done under a better training and more favorable circumstances of personal situation, or perhaps in another age.

George L. Craik, 1861, *A Compendious History of English Literature and of the English Language,* vol. II, p. 381

A cousin sent him his mother's portrait. He received it in trepidation, kissed it, hung it where it would be seen last at night, first in the morning, and wrote a poem on it, whose tenderness and pathos, flowing in richer and sweeter music than he had elsewhere reached, are unequalled by anything else he has written, and surpassed by little in the language. Springing from the deepest and purest fount of passion, and shaping itself into mobile and fluent verse, it reveals his true originality, as well as that life-like elegance, that natural spirit of art, wherein consists the great revolution of the modern style.

Alfred H. Welsh, 1883, *Development of English Literature and Language,* vol. II, p. 245

SONNETS

Petrarch's sonnets have a more ethereal grace and a more perfect finish; Shakespeare's more passion; Milton's stand supreme in stateliness, Wordsworth's in depth and delicacy. But Cowper's unites with an exquisiteness in the turn of thought which the ancients would have called Irony, and intensity of pathetic tenderness peculiar to his loving and ingenuous nature. —There is much mannerism, much that is unimportant or of now exhausted interest in his poems: but where he is great, it is with that elementary greatness which rests on the most universal human feelings. Cowper is our highest master in simple pathos.

Francis Turner Palgrave, 1861, *The Golden Treasury,* note

They never rise to the highest excellence, neither do they fall much below the level of his average composition. If they embalm no superb thoughts, of which it can be said, as of Herrick's fly in amber:

> "The urn was little but the room
> More rich than Cleopatra's tomb."

and if none of them have lines which have become current for their intrinsic beauty or wealth of thought, or for a breadth of application which has caused them to echo alone the decades from his day till ours, they still present refined and elevated sentiments, gracefully, naturally, and poetically, and clothe them in pure and nervous English.

Charles D. Deshler, 1879, *Afternoons with the Poets,* p. 176

LETTERS

The letters of Cowper . . . form a perfect contrast to Pope's. In the one, I think I see a mind striving to be great, and affecting to be unaffected; in the other, we contemplate, not the studious loftiness, but the playfulness of a mind naturally lofty, throwing at random a ray of sweetness, cheerfulness, and tenderness upon whatever subject occurs, mixed occasionally with severer touches of wisdom, and a mournful, but seldom angry survey of the follies of mankind. We see the playful humour, mingled with melancholy, and the melancholy, mingled with kindness, social feelings, sincerity and tenderness.

William Lisle Bowles, 1806, ed. *Pope's Works*

There is something in the letters of Cowper inexpressibly delightful. They possess excellencies so opposite—a naïve simplicity, arising from perfect goodness of heart and singleness of purpose, contrasted with a deep acquaintance with the follies and vices of human nature, and a keen sense of humour and ridicule. They unite the playfulness of a child, the affectionateness of a woman, and the strong sense of a man; they give us glimpses of pleasures so innocent and pure as almost to realise the Eden of our great poet, contrasted with horrors so deep, as even to exceed his power of imagery to express.

Reginald Heber, 1823, "Private Correspondence of Cowper," *Quarterly Review*, vol. 30, p. 185

The purest and most perfect specimens of familiar letters in the language. Considering the secluded, uneventful course of Cowper's life, the charm in his letters is wonderful; and is to be explained, I believe, chiefly by the exquisite light of poetic truth which his imagination shed upon daily life, whether his theme was man, himself or a fellow-being, or books, or the mute creation which he loved to handle with such thoughtful tenderness. His seclusion did not separate him from sympathy with the stirring events of his time; and, alike in seasons of sunshine or of gloom, there is in his letters an ever-present beauty of quiet wisdom, and a gentle but fervid spirit.

Henry Reed, 1851-55, *Lectures on English Literature, From Chaucer to Tennyson*, p. 409

The charm of Cowper's Correspondence consists in this succession of images, of thought, and of shades of meaning unfolded with varying vivacity, but in an equable and peaceful course. In his letters we can best apprehend the true sources of his poetry, of the true domestic poetry of private life: bantering not devoid of affection, a familiarity which disdains nothing which is

interesting as being too lowly and too minute, but alongside of them, elevation or rather profundity. Nor let us forget the irony, the malice, a delicate
and easy raillery such as appears in the letters I have quoted.

C. A. Sainte-Beuve, 1854, English Portraits, p. 191

His letters are his principal work in prose, if not the best of all his work.
They differ from most of the prose of the time by the same interval as separates the verse of The Task at its best from the verse of The Botanic
Garden. The phrase of Landor, in the preface to the Hellenics, "not pris-
matic but diaphanous," applies more fitly to the style of Cowper in verse
and prose, especially prose, than to any other writer. It is not that the style
is insipid or tame; it is alive and light; but it escapes notice, like the prose
of Southey, by reason of its perfect accommodation to the matter.

W. P. Ker, 1895, English Prose, ed. Craik, vol. IV, p. 424

GENERAL

I received the letter you did me the honour of writing to me, and am much
obliged by your kind present of a book. The relish for reading of poetry had
long since left me, but there is something so new in the manner, so easy, and
yet so correct in the language, so clear in the expression, yet concise, and
so just in the sentiments, that I have read the whole with great pleasure, and
some of the pieces more than once.

Benjamin Franklin, 1782, Letter to Cowper, May 8

It has been thought that Cowper was the first poet who re-opened the true
way to nature and a natural style; but we hold this to be a mistake, arising
merely from certain negations on the part of that amiable but by no means
powerful writer. Cowper's style is for the most part as inverted and artificial
as that of the others; and we look upon him to have been by nature not so
great a poet as Pope; but Pope, from certain infirmities on his part, was
thrown into the society of the world, and thus had to get what he could out
of an artificial sphere:—Cowper, from other and more distressing infirmities
(which by the way the wretched superstition that undertook to heal, only
burnt in upon him) was confined to a still smaller though more natural
sphere, and in truth did not much with it, though quite as much perhaps as
was to be expected from an organization too sore almost to come in contact
with any thing.

Leigh Hunt, 1817, The Examiner

With all his boasted simplicity and love of the country, he seldom launches
out into general descriptions of nature: he looks at her over his clipped

hedges, and from his well-swept garden-walks; or if he makes a bolder experiment now and then, it is with an air of precaution, as if he were afraid of being caught in a shower of rain, or of not being able, in case of any untoward accident, to make good his retreat home. He shakes hands with nature with a pair of fashionable gloves on, and leads his "Vashti" forth to public view with a look of consciousness and attention to etiquette, as a fine gentleman hands a lady out to dance a minuet. He is delicate to fastidiousness, and glad to get back, after a romantic adventure with crazy Kate, a party of gypsies or a little child on a common, to the drawing-room and the ladies again, to the sofa and the tea-kettle—No, I beg his pardon, not to the singing, well-scoured tea-kettle, but to the polished and loud-hissing urn.

William Hazlitt, 1818, Lectures on the English Poets, Lecture V

Considering the tenor and circumstances of his life, it is not much to be wondered at, that some asperities and peculiarities should have adhered to the strong stem of his genius, like the moss and fungus that cling to some noble oak of the forest, amid the damps of its unsunned retirement. It is more surprising that he preserved, in such seclusion, so much genuine power of comic observation. Though he himself acknowledged having written "many things with bile" in his first volume, yet his satire has many legitimate objects: and it is not abstracted and declamatory satire: but it places human manners before us in the liveliest attitudes and clearest colours. There is much of the full distinctness of Theophrastus, and of the nervous and concise spirit of La Bruyè, in his piece entitled "Conversation," with a cast of humour superadded, which is peculiarly English, and not to be found out of England.

Thomas Campbell, 1819, Specimens of the British Poets

Compare the landscapes of Cowper with those of Burns. There is, if we mistake not, the same sort of difference between them, as in the conversation of two persons on scenery, the one originally an enthusiast in his love of the works of nature, the other driven, by disappointment or weariness, to solace himself with them as he might. It is a contrast which every one must have observed, when such topics come under discussion in society; and those who think it worth while, may find abundant illustration of it in the writings of this unfortunate but illustrious pair. The one all overflowing with the love of nature, and indicating, at every turn, that whatever his lot in life, he could not have been happy without her. The other visibly and wisely soothing himself, but not without effort, by attending to rural objects, in default of some more congenial happiness, of which he had almost come to despair. The latter, in consequence, laboriously sketching every object that came in his way: the other, in one or two rapid lines, which operate, as it were, like a magician's spell, presenting to the fancy just that picture, which was wanted to put the reader's minds in unison with the writer's.

John Keble, 1825, "Sacred Poetry," *Quarterly Review,* vol. 32, p. 217

Cowper has not Thomson's genius, but he has much more taste. His range is neither so wide, nor so lofty, but, as far as it extends. it is peculiarly his own. He cannot paint the Plague at Carthagena, or the Snow-storm, or the Earthquake, as Thomson has done; but place him by the banks of the Ouse, or see him taking his "Winter walk at Noon," or accompany him in his rambles through his Flower garden, and where is the Author who can compare with him for a moment? The pictures of domestic life which he has painted are inimitable. It is hard to say whether his sketches of external nature, or of indoor life, are the best. Cowper does not attempt the same variety of scene as Thomson; but in what he does attempt, he always succeeds.

Henry Neele, 1827-29, *Lectures on English Poetry,* p. 184

As a scold, we think Cowper failed. He had a great idea of the use of railing, and there are many pages of laudable invective against various vices which we feel no call whatever to defend. But a great vituperator had need to be a great hater; and of any real rage, any such gall and bitterness as great and irritable satirists have in other ages let loose upon men,—of any thorough, brooding, burning, abiding detestation,—he was as incapable as a tame hare. His vituperation reads like the mild man's whose wife ate up his dinner: "Really, sir, I feel quite *angry!*" Nor has his language any of the sharp intrusive acumen which divides in sunder both soul and spirit, and makes fierce and unforgetable reviling.

Walter Bagehot, 1855, "William Cowper," *Works,*
ed. Morgan, vol. I, p. 428

Cowper has probably few readers now. One sometimes meets with an elderly lady, brought up in an Evangelical family, who, having been made to learn the *Moral Satires* and *The Task* by heart when a child, still remembers a good deal of them, and cherishes for the poet of Evangelicism the tender affections which gathers in old age round the things which belongs to childhood. But we have most of us ceased to be Evangelical, and most of us who love poetry having come under the spell of Goethe and of the lesser poets of the nineteenth century, find poor Cowper a little cramped, a little narrow, and, to tell the truth, a little dull. Yet there are passages in Cowper's poetry which deserve to live and will live, and which will secure him a place, not indeed among English poets of the first rank, but high among those of the second. The pity is that they run great risk of being buried and lost forever in the wilderness of sermons which fills up such a large part of *The Progress of Error* and *The Task*. It is very hard to write sermons that will live, and, as a writer of sermons, I am afraid Cowper is likely to take his place on the very peaceful and dusty upper shelf in our libraries where the divines of the last century repose. But he deserves a better fate than this, and all lovers of English poetry ought to do what they can to save him from it.

J. C. Bailey, 1889, "William Cowper," *Macmillan's Magazine,* vol. 60, p. 261

JAMES BEATTIE
1735-1803

Born, at Laurencekirk, Kincardine, 25 Oct. 1735. To Marischal Coll., Aberdeen, 1749; M. A., 1753. Schoolmaster and parish clerk at Fordoun, 1753-58. Contrib. to *Scots' Magazine.* Master of Aberdeen Grammar School, 1758-60. Professor of Moral Philosophy and Logic, Marishal Coll., 1760-97. Published first vol. of poems, 1761. First visit to London, 1763. Friendship with Gray begun, 1765. Married Mary Dunn, 28 June 1767. Hon. D. C. L., Oxford, 9 July 1773. Crown pension of £200, Aug. 1773. Refused Professorship of Moral Philosophy at Edinburgh, 1773. Active literary work. Failing health from 1793. Died, 18 Aug. 1803. Buried in St. Nicholas Churchyard, Aberdeen. WORKS: *Original Poems and Translations,* 1760; *Judgment of Paris,* 1765; *Verses on the Death of Churchill,* 1765; *Poems on Several Subjects,* 1766; *Essay on Truth,* 1770; The Minstrel, pt. i. (anon.), 1771; pt. ii., 1774; *Poems on Several Occasions,* 1776; *Essays,* 1776 (2nd edn. same year); *Letter to the Rev. H. Blair . . . on the Improvement of Psalmody, in Scotland* (anon., privately printed), 1778; *List of Two Hundred Scotticisms* (anon.), 1779; *Dissertations, Moral and Critical,* 1783; *Evidences of the Christian Religion,* 1786; *The Theory of Language,* 1788; *Elements of Moral Science,* vol. 1, 1790; vol. 11, 1793; *Notes on Addison* (apparently not published), 1790. COLLECTED POEMS: 1805, 1810, 1822, 1831, etc. He *edited: Essays and Fragments,* by his son, J .H. Beattie (privately printed), 1794. LIFE: by Bower, 1804; by Sir W. Forbes, 1806.

R. Farquharson Sharp, 1897, *A Dictionary of English Authors,* p. 20

SEE: *Poetical Works,* ed. Alexander Dyce, 1894; *London Diary, 1773,* ed, R. S. Walker, 1946; *Day-book, 1773-1789,* ed. R. S. Walker, 1948; M. Forbes, *Beattie and His Friends,* 1904.

PERSONAL

I found him pleasant, unaffected, unassuming, and full of conversable intelligence; with a round, thick, clunch figure, that promised nothing either of his works or his discourse, yet his eye, at intervals, . . . shoots forth a ray of genius that instantly lights up his whole countenance. His voice and his manners are particularly and pleasingly mild, and seem to announce an urbanity of character both inviting and edifying. . . . You would be surprised to find how soon you could forget that he is ugly and clumsy, for there is a sort of perfect good-will in his countenance and his smile, that is quite captivating.

Mme. D'Arblay (Fanny Burney), 1787, Diary, July 13

I am happy to think, that the moral effect of his works is likely to be so powerfully increased by the Memoirs of his exemplary life, which you are preparing for the press, while the respect which the public already entertains for his genius and talents, cannot fail to be blended with other sentiments still more flattering to his memory, when it is known with what fortitude and resignation he submitted to a series of trials, far exceeding those which fall to the common lot of humanity; and that the most vigorous exertions of his mind were made, under the continued pressure of the severest domestic affliction, which a heart like this could be doomed to suffer.

Dugald Stewart, 1806, Letter to Sir William Forbes,
Life of Beattie by Forbes, vol. III, p. 255

Of his conduct towards his unhappy wife, it is impossible to speak in terms of too high commendation. It has already been mentioned, that Mrs. Beattie had the misfortune to inherit from her mother, that most dreadful of all human ills, a distempered imagination, which, in a very few years after their marriage, showed itself in caprices and folly, that embittered every hour of his life, while he strove at first to conceal her disorder from the world, and, if possible, as he has been heard to say, to conceal it even from himself; till at last from whim, and caprice, and melancholy, it broke out into downright insanity, which rendered her seclusion from society absolutely necessary. . . . When I reflect on the many sleepless nights and anxious days, which he experienced from Mrs. Beattie's malady, and think of the unwearied and unremitting attention he paid to her, during so great a number of years, in that sad situation, his character is exalted in my mind to a degree which may be equalled, but I am sure never can be excelled, and makes the fame of the poet and the philosopher fade from my remembrance. . . . In his person, Dr. Beattie was of the middle size, though not elegantly, yet not awkwardly formed, but with something of a slouch in his gait. His eyes were black and piercing, with an expression of sensibility, somewhat bordering on melancholy, except when engaged in cheerful and social intercourse with his friends, when they were exceedingly animated. As he advanced in years, and became incapable of taking his usual degree of exercise, he grew corpulent and unwieldly, till within a few months of his death, when he had greatly decreased in size. When I last saw him, the diminution of his form was but too prophetic of the event that soon followed.

Sir William Forbes, 1806, An Account of the Life and Writings
of James Beattie, vol. III, pp. 176, 177, 187

The Minstrel (1771-74)

The design was to trace the progress of a Poetical Genius, born in a rude age, from the first dawning of fancy and reason, till that period at which he may be supposed capable of appearing in the world as a Minstrel, that is, as an itinerant Poet and Musician;—a character which, according to the notions of our forefathers, was not only respectable, but sacred. I have endeavoured to imitate Spenser in the measure of his verse, and in the harmony, simplicity, and variety of his composition. Antique expressions I have avoided; admitting, however, some old words, where they seemed to suit the subject; but I hope none will be found that are now obsolete, or in any degree not intelligible to a reader of English poetry. To those who may be disposed to ask, what could induce me to write in so difficult a measure, I can only answer that it pleases my ear, and seems, from its Gothic structure and original, to bear some relation to the subject and spirit of the Poem. It admits both simplicity and magnificence of sound and of language beyond any other stanza that I am acquainted with. It allows the sententiousness of the couplet, as well as the more complex modulation of blank verse. What some critics have remarked, of its uniformity growing at last tiresome to the ear, will be found to hold true only when the poetry is faulty in other respects.

James Beattie, 1771, The Minstrel, Preface

I read <i>The Minstrel</i> with as much rapture as poetry, in her noblest, sweetest charms, ever raised in my soul. It seemed to me that my once most-beloved minstrel, Thomson, was come down from heaven, refined by the converse of purer spirits than those he lived with here, to let me hear him sing again the beauties of nature, and the finest feelings of virtue, not with human, but with angelic strains.

Lord Lyttelton, 1771, Letter to Mrs. Montagu, March

His fame now rests upon <i>The Minstrel</i> alone. Since its first publication, many poems of a far loftier and more original character have been produced in England; yet still does it maintain its popularity; and still in Edwin, that happy personification of the poetic temperament, do young and enthusiastic readers delight to recognize a picture of themselves. Though we cannot fail to regret that Beattie should have left it incomplete, yet we do not long for the concluding books from any interest which we take in the story, such as is excited by some other unfinished works of genius, the tale of *Cambuscan,* for instance, or the legend of *Christabel.* In *The Minstrel,* indeed, there is but little invention; it is a poem of sentiment and description, conveying to us lessons of true philosophy in language of surprising beauty, and displaying pictures of nature, in her romantic solitudes, painted by a master's hand.

Alexander Dyce, 1831, Beattie's Poems, Aldine ed., Memoir

No poem has ever given more delight to minds of a certain class, and in a certain stage of their progress . . . that class a high one, and that stage perhaps the most delightful in the course of their pilgrimage. It was to this class that the poet himself belonged; the scenes which he delineated were those in which he had grown up, the feelings and aspirations those of his own boyhood and youth, and the poem derived its peculiar charm from its truth.

Robert Southey, 1835, Life of Cowper, p. 340

GENERAL

Dr. Beattie's style is singularly free and perspicuous, and adapted in the highest degree to the purpose of familiar lecturing to his pupils; but for the author we should deem it something less than elegant, and something less than nervous. In early life he took great pains to imitate Addison, whose style he always recommended and admired. . . . In many parts of the letters, we are constrained to perceive a degree of egotism inconsistent with the dignity of a philosopher or a man. The writer seems unwilling to lose any opportunity of recounting the attentions, the compliments, the testimonies of admiration, which he has received from individuals or the public. The complacency with which he expatiates on himself and his performances, is but imperfectly disguised by the occasional and too frequent professions of holding himself and those performances cheap. This is a very usual but unsuccessful expedient, with those who have reflection enough to be sensible that they have rather too much ostentation, but not resolution enough to restrain themselves from indulging in it.

John Foster, 1807, "On Memoir-Writing," Critical Essays,
ed. Ryland, vol. I, pp. 27, 28

He wrote English better than any other of his countrymen, and had formed his style and manner of composition on our Addison; but what he admired in him was his tuneful prose and elegant expression. He had no notion of that writer's original and inimitable humour.

Richard Hurd, 1808, *Commonplace Book, Memoirs,*
ed. Kilvert, p. 244

On the whole, Beattie may be ranked beside, or near, Campbell, Collins, Gray, and Akenside. Deficient in thought and passion, in creative power, and copious imagination, he is strong in sentiment, in mild tenderness, and in delicate description of nature. Whatever become of his Essay on Truth, or even of his less elaborate and more pleasing Essays on Music, Imagination, and Dreams, the world can never, at any stage of its advancement, forget to read and admire *The Minstrel* and the *Hermit,* or to cherish the memory of their warm-hearted and sorely-tried author.

George Gilfillan, 1854, ed. *The Poetical Works of Beattie,
Blair and Falconer,* p. xxiv

CLARA REEVE
1729-1807

Born at Ipswich, the daughter of the rector of Freston, translated Barclay's *Argenis* (1772), and wrote *The Champion of Virtue, a Gothic Story* (1777), renamed *The Old English Baron,* which was avowed an imitation of Walpole's *Castle of Otranto.* She wrote four other novels and *The Progress of Romance* (1785).

Patrick and Groome, eds., 1897, *Chambers's
Biographical Dictionary,* p. 782

SEE: *The Old English Baron,* ed. Henry Morley, 1888; Robert Donald Spector, ed., *Seven Masterpieces of Gothic Horror,* 1963.

GENERAL

Have you seen *The Old Baron,* a Gothic story, professedly written in imitation of Otranto, but reduced to reason and probability? It is so probable, that any trial for murder at the Old Bailey would make a more interesting story. Mrs. Barbauld's *Fragment* was excellent. This is a *caput mortuum.*

Horace Walpole, 1778, *To Rev. William Mason,* April 8;
Letters, ed. Cunningham, vol. VII, p. 51

The various novels of Clara Reeve are all marked by excellent good sense, pure morality, and a competent command of those qualities which constitute a good romance. They were, generally speaking, favorably received at the time, but none of them took the same strong possession of the public mind as *The Old English Baron,* upon which the fame of the author may be considered as now exclusively rested. . . . In no part of *The Old English Baron,* or of any other of her works, does Miss Reeve show the possession of a rich or powerful imagination. Her dialogue is sensible, easy, and agreeable, but neither marked by high flights of fancy, nor strong bursts of passion. Her apparition is an ordinary fiction, of which popular superstition used to furnish a thousand instances, when nights were long, and a family, assembled around a Christmas log, had little better to do than to listen to such tales. Miss Reeve has been very felicitously cautious in showing us no more of Lord Lovel's ghost than she needs must—he is a silent apparition, palpable to the sight only, and never brought forward into such broad daylight as might have dissolved our reverence. And so far, we repeat, the authoress has used her own power to the utmost advantage, and gained her point by not attempting to step beyond it. But we cannot allow that the rule which, in her own case, has been well and wisely adopted, ought to circumscribe a bolder and a more imaginative writer.

Sir Walter Scott, 1821, *Clara Reeve*

As in Walpole's book [in the *Champion of Virtue*], there are a murder and a usurpation, a rightful heir defrauded of his inheritance and reared as a peasant. There are a haunted chamber, unearthly midnight groans, a ghost in armor, and a secret closet with its skeleton. The tale is infinitely tiresome, and is full of that edifying morality, fine sentiment and stilted dialogue— that "old perfumed, powdered D'Arblay conversation," as Thackeray called it—which abound in *Evelina, Thaddeus of Warsaw,* and almost all the fiction of the last quarter of the last century. Still it was a little unkind in Walpole to pronounce his disciple's performance tedious and insipid, as he did.

Henry A. Beers, 1898, *A History of English Romanticism
in the Eighteenth Century,* p. 243

THOMAS PAINE
1737-1809

Born, at Thetford, Norfolk, 29 Jan. 1737. Educated at Thetford Grammar School. At sea, 1755-56. In London, working as staymaker, 1756-58. Removed to Dover, 1758; to Sandwich, 1759. Married (i.) Mary Lambert, 17 Sept. 1759. She died, at Margate, 1760. Returned to Thetford, as Excise Officer, July 1761; to Grantham, Dec. 1762; to Alford, Aug. 1764. Dismissed from Office, Aug. 1765; restored, Feb. 1768; sent to Lewes; dismissed again, April 1774. Married (ii.) Elizabeth Ollive, 26 March 1771; separated from her, June 1774. To Philadelphia, Nov. 1774, with introduction to Franklin (?). Contrib. to *Pennsylvania Journal,* 1775-76.

Editor of *Pennsylvania Mag.*, Jan. 1775 to Aug. 1776. Took part in American War of Independence. Sec. to Committee of Foreign Affairs, April 1777 to Jan. 1779. Clerk to Pennsylvania Assembly, Nov. 1779 to Dec. 1780. M. A., Pennsylvania Univ., 4 July 1780. Sec. to Col. Laurens on Mission to France, Feb. to Aug., 1781. Presented with estate of New Rochelle, 1784. Visit to England in connection with his invention of an iron bridge, 1787-90. To Paris, 1790. French citizen, Aug. 1793; Mem. of Convention, Sept. 1793. On Committee to form Republican Constitution, Oct. 1793. Imprisoned in Paris, Dec. 1793 to Nov. 1794. Returned to America, Oct. 1802. Contrib. to *The Prospect*, 1804-05. Died, in New York, 8 July, 1809. WORKS: *The Case of the Officers of Excise* (anon.), (1772); *Common Sense* (anon.), 1776; *Large Additions to Common Sense* (anon.), 1776; *Epistle to the People called Quakers*, 1776; *Dialogue between Gen. Montgomery and an American Delegate*, 1776; *The American Crisis* (13 nos.; anon.), 1776-83; *The Public Good*, 1780; *Letter addressed to the Abbé Raynal*, 1782; *Thoughts on the Peace*, 1783; *Letter to the Earl of Shelburne*, 1783; *Dissertation on Government*, 1786; *Prospects on the Rubicon* (anon.), 1787; (another edn., called *Prospects on the War*, 1793); *Letter to Sir G. Staunton*, 1788; *The Rights of Man* (2 pts.), 1791-92; *Address and Declaration of the Friends of Universal Peace and Liberty* (1791); *Letter to the Abbé Sièyes*, 1792; *Four Letters on Government*, 1792; *Address to the Republic of France* (1792); *Letter addressed to the Addressers*, 1792; *Speech in Convention on bringing Louis Capet to trial*, 1792; *Lettre . . . au Peuple françois* (1792); *Opinion . . . concernant le judgment de Louis XVI.*, 1792; *Works*, 1792; *Miscellaneous Articles*, 1792; *Reasons for wishing to preserve the life of Louis Capet* (1793); *Prospects on the War and Paper Currency*, 1793; *Rational and Revealed Religion* (anon.), 1794; *The Age of Reason*, pt. i., 1794; pt. ii., 1795; pt. iii., 1811; *Letter to the French Convention*, 1794; *Dissertations on First Principles of Government*, 1795; *The Decline and Fall of the English System of Finance*, 1796; *Letter to George Washington*, 1796; *Agrarian Justice opposed to Agrarian Law*, 1797; *Lettre . . . sur les Cultes*, 1797; *Letter to the Hon. T. Erskine*, 1797; *Letter to Camille Jourdan*, 1797; *Atheism Refuted*, 1798; *Maritime Compact*, 1801; *Letter to Samuel Adams*, 1802; *Letter to Citizens of the United States*, 1802; *Letter to the People of England*, 1804; *To the French Inhabitants of Louisiana*, 1804; *To the Citizens of Pennsylvania*, 1805; *On the Causes of Yellow Fever*, 1805; *On Constitutions, Governments and Charters*, 1805; *Observations on Gunboats*, 1806; *Letter to A. A. Dean*, 1806; *On the Political and Military Affairs of Europe*, 1806; *To the People of New York*, 1807; *On Governor Lewis's Speech*, 1807; *On Mr. Hale's Resolutions*, 1807; *Three Letters to Morgan Lewis*, 1807; *On the question, Will there be War?* 1807; *Essay on Dreams*, 1807. POSTHUMOUS: *Reply to the Bishop of Llandaff*, 1810; *The Origin of Freemasonry*, 1811; *Miscellaneous Letters and Essays*, 1819; *Miscellaneous Poems*, 1819. COLLECTED WORKS: ed. by M. D. Conway, 1894-96, 4 vols.

R. Farquharson Sharp, 1897, *A Dictionary of English Authors*, p. 219

SEE: *Representative Selections*, ed. H. H. Clark, 1944; Moncure Daniel Conway, *The Life of Thomas Paine*, 1892, 2 v.; F. Gould, *Thomas Paine*,

1925; Ray B. Browne, ed, *The Burke-Paine Controversy: Texts and Criticism,* 1963.

PERSONAL

Dear Son, The bearer, Mr. Thomas Paine, is very well recommended to me, as an ingenious, worthy young man. He goes to Pennsylvania with a view of settling there. I request you to give him your best advice and countenance, as he is quite a stranger there. If you can put him in a way of obtaining employment as a clerk, or assistant tutor in a school, or assistant surveyor, (of all which I think him very capable), so that he may procure a subsistence at least, till he can make acquaintance and obtain a knowledge of the country, you will do well, and much oblige your affectionate father.

> Benjamin Franklin, 1774, *Letter to Richard Bache,* Sept. 30;
> *Works,* ed. Sparks, vol. VIII, p. 137

Philadelphia, Feb. 10, 1782.—The subscribers, taking into consideration the important situation of affairs at the present moment, and the propriety and even necessity of informing the people and rousing them into action; considering also the abilities of Mr. Thomas Paine as a writer, and that he has been of considerable utility to the common cause by several of his publications: They are agreed that it will be much for the interest of the United States that Mr. Paine be engaged in their service for the purpose above mentioned. They are therefore agreed that Mr. Paine be offered a salary of $800 per annum, and that the same be paid him by the Secretary of Foreign Affairs. The salary to commence from this day, and to be paid by the Secretary of Foreign Affairs out of monies to be allowed by the Superintendent of Finance for secret services. The subscribers being of opinion that a salary publicly and avowedly given for the above purpose would injure the effect of Mr. Paine's publications, and subject him to injurious personal reflections.

> Robert Morris, Robert Livingston, George Washington

Dear Sir, I have learned since I have been at this place, that you are at Bordentown. Whether for the sake of retirement or economy, I know not. Be it for either, for both, or whatever it may, if you will come to this place, and partake with me, I shall be exceedingly happy to see you. Your presence may remind Congress of your past services to this country; and if it is in my power to impress them, command my best services with freedom, as they will be rendered cheerfully by one who entertains a lively sense of the importance of your works, and who, with much pleasure, subscribes himself, Your sincere friend.

> George Washington, 1783, *Letter to Paine from Rocky Hill,* Sept. 10

The villain Paine came over to the Crown and Anchor; but, finding that his pamphlet had not set a straw on fire, and that the 14th of July was as little in fashion as the ancient gunpowder-plot, he dined at another tavern with a few quaking conspirators; and probably is returning to Paris, where he is engaged in a controversy with the Abbe Sieyes, about the "plus or minus" of the rebellion.

Horace Walpole, 1791, *To the Miss Berrys*, July 26;
Letters, ed. Cunningham, vol. IX, p. 332

I met this interesting personage at the lodgings of the son of a late patriotic American governour [Trumbull]. . . . He was dressed in a snuff-coloured coat, olive velvet vest, drab breeches, coarse hose. His shoe buckles of the size of a half dollar. A bob tailed wig covered that head which worked such mickle woe to courts and kings. If I should attempt to describe it, it would be in the same stile and principle with which the veteran soldier bepraiseth an old standard: the more tattered, the more glorious. It is probable that this was the same identical wig under the shadow of whose curls he wrote *Common Sense* in America, many years before. He was a spare man, rather under size; subject to the extreme of low, and highly exhilarating spirits; often sat reserved in company; seldom mingled in common chit-chat: But when a man of sense and elocution was present, and the company numerous, he delighted in advancing the most unaccountable, and often the most whimsical paradoxes; which he defended in his own plausible manner. If encouraged by success, or the applause of the company, his countenance was animated with an expression of feature which, on ordinary occasion one would look for in vain, in a man so much celebrated for acuteness of thought; but if interrupted by extraneous observation, by the inattention of his auditory, or in an irritable moment, even by the accidental fall of the poker, he would retire into himself, and no persuasion could induce him to proceed upon the most favourite topic.

Royall Tyler, 1797, *The Algerine Captive*

I have received your letter calling for information relative to the life of Thomas Paine. It appears to me that this is not the moment to publish the life of that man in this country. His own writings are his best life, and these are not read at present. The greater part of readers in the United States will not be persuaded, as long as their present feelings last, to consider him in any other light than as a drunkard and a deist. The writer of his life who should dwell on these topics, to the exclusion of the great and estimable traits of his real character, might indeed please the rabble of the age, who do not know him; the book might sell, but it would only tend to render the truth more obscure for the future biographer than it was before. But if the present writer should give us Thomas Paine *complete* in all his character, as one of the most benevolent and disinterested of mankind, endowed with the clearest perception, an uncommon share of original genius, and the greatest breadth of thought; if this piece of biography should analyze his literary labors and rank him, as he ought to be ranked, among the brightest and most undeviating luminaries of the age in which he has lived, yet with a mind assailable by flattery, and receiving through that weak side a tincture of vanity which he was too proud to conceal; with a mind, though strong enough to bear him up and to rise elastic under the heaviest hand of oppression, yet unable to endure the contempt of his former friends and fellow-laborers, the rulers of the country that had received his first and greatest services; a mind incapable of looking down with serene compassion, as it ought, on the rude scoffs of their imitators, a new generation that knows him not; a mind that shrinks from their society, and unhappily seeks refuge in low company, or looks for consolation in the sordid, solitary bottle, till it sinks at last so far below its native elevation as to lose all respect for itself and to forfeit that of his best friends, disposing these friends almost to join with his enemies, and wish, though from different motives, that he would hasten to hide himself in the grave—if you are disposed and prepared to write his life *thus entire,* to fill up the picture to which these hasty strokes of outline give but a rude sketch with great vacuities, your book may be a useful one for another age, but it will not be relished, nor scarcely tolerated, in this. . . . You ask what company he kept. He always frequented the best, both in England and France, till he became the object of calumny in certain American papers (echoes of the English court papers) for his adherence to what he thought the cause of liberty in France—till he conceived himself neglected and despised by his former friends in the United States. From that moment he gave himself very much to drink, and, consequently, to companions less worthy of his better days. It is said that he was always a peevish ingrate. This is possible. So was Lawrence Sterne, so was Torquato Tasso, so was J. J. Rousseau. But Thomas Paine, as a visiting acquaintance and as a literary friend, the only points of view from which I knew him, was one of the most instructive men I have ever known.

Joel Barlow, 1809, *Letter to James Cheetham,*
Life and Letters, ed. Todd, pp. 236, 238

Paine had no good qualities. Incapable of friendship, he was vain, envious, malignant; in France cowardly, and every where tyrannical. In his private dealings he was unjust, never thinking of paying for what he had contracted, and always cherishing deadly resentments against those who by law compelled him to do justice. To those who had been kind to him he was more than ungrateful, for to ingratitude, as in the case of Mr. Munroe, he added mean and detestable fraud. He was guilty of the worst species of seduction; the alienation of a wife and children from a husband, and a father. Filthy and drunken, he was a compound of all the vices.

James Cheetham, 1809, Life of Thomas Paine, p. 313

Mr. Paine in his person was about five feet ten inches high, and rather athletic; he was broad shouldered, and latterly stooped a little. His eyes, of which the painter could not convey the exquisite meaning, was full, brilliant, and singularly piercing; it had in it the "muse of fire." In his dress and person he was generally very cleanly, and wore his hair cued, with side curls, and powdered, so that he looked altogether like a gentleman of the old French school. His manners were easy and gracious; his knowledge was universal and boundless; in private company and among his friends his conversation had every fascination that anecdote, novelty and truth could give it. In mixt company and among strangers he said little, and was no public speaker.

Thomas C. Rickman, 1819, The Life of Thomas Paine

Paine lies in a little hole under the grass and weeds of an obscure farm in America. There, however, he shall not lie, unnoticed, much longer. He belongs to England. His fame is the property of England; and if no other people will show that they value that fame, the people of England will. Yes, amongst the pleasures that I promise myself, that of seeing the name of Paine honoured in every part of England; where base corruption caused him, while alive, to be burnt in effigy.

William Cobbett, 1819, On the Remains of Thomas Paine

Poverty was his mother—Necessity his master. He had more brains than books; more sense than education; more courage than politeness; more strength than polish. He had no veneration for old mistakes—no admiration for ancient lies. He loved the truth for the truth's sake, and for man's sake. . . . The result of his investigations was given to the world in The Age of Reason. From the moment of its publication he became infamous. He was caluminated beyond measure. To slander him was to secure the thanks of the Church. All his services were instantly forgotten, disparaged or denied. He was shunned as though he had been a pestilence. Most of his old friends forsook him. He was regarded as a moral plague, and at the bare mention of his name the bloody hands of the Church were raised in horror. He was denounced as the most despicable of men. Not content with following him to his grave, they pursued him after death with redoubled fury, and recounted with infinite gusto and satisfaction the supposed horrors of his death-bed; gloried in the fact that he was forlorn and friendless, and gloated like fiends over what they supposed to be the agonizing remorse of his lonely death. It is wonderful that all his services were thus forgotten. It is amazing that one kind word did not fall from some pulpit; that some one did not accord to him, at least—honesty. Strange, that in the general denunciation some one did not remember his labor for liberty, his devotion to principle, his zeal for the rights of his fellow-men. . . . He had made it impossible to write the history of political freedom with his name left out. He was one of the creators of light; one of the heralds of the dawn. He hated tyranny in the name of kings, and in the name of God, with every drop of his noble blood. He believed in liberty and justice, and in the sacred doctrine of human equality. Under these divine banners he fought the battle of his life. In both worlds he offered his blood for the good of man. In the wilderness of America, in the French Assembly, in the sombre cell waiting for death, he was the same unflinching, unwavering friend of his race; the same undaunted champion of universal freedom. And for this he has been hated; for this the Church has violated even his grave.

Robert G. Ingersoll, 1874, *The Gods and Other Lectures*, pp. 122, 135

The bones of Thomas Paine were landed in Liverpool November 21, 1819. The monument contemplated by Cobbett was never raised. There was much parliamentary and municipal excitement. A Bolton town-crier was imprisoned nine weeks for proclaiming the arrival. In 1836 the bones passed with Cobbett's effects into the hands of a Receiver (West). The Lord Chancellor refusing to regard them as an asset, they were kept by an old day-laborer in 1844, when they passed to B. Tilley, 13 Bedford Square, London, a furniture dealer. In 1849 the empty coffin was in possession of J. Chennell Guildford. The silver plate bore the inscription "Thomas Paine, died June 8, 1809, aged 72." In 1854, Rev. R. Ainslie (Unitarian) told E. Truelove that he owned "the skull and the right hand of Thomas Paine," but evaded subsequent inquiries. The removal caused excitement in America. Of Paine's gravestone the last fragment was preserved by his friends of the Bayeaux family, and framed on their wall. In November, 1839, the present marble monument at New Rochelle was erected.

Moncure Daniel Conway, 1892, *The Life of Thomas Paine*, vol. II, p. 427, note

In private life Paine was uncorrupted by the worst vices of his generation. He was never abstemious, and during the Reign of Terror he drank to excess; but, if there be any truth in the accounts of drunkenness of his later years, it lies in the very occasional indulgence at a time when gentlemen slept under the table and awoke still gentlemen. The stories of his filthy habits are slander, though towards the close of his life, he became more careless of his dress, and maybe did not brush his coat after each pinch of snuff. He was always gentle to children and to animals. In manner he was kindly, and in conversation intelligent; but he was intolerant of contradiction, and not disinclined to assume the god in a gathering of friends. Like most vain men, Paine had little pride. His repeated requests for money for his services grate harshly enough, but their origin was not in meanness. . . . His tasks were not all done wisely, but they were done bravely. Too often his light was darkness; but he walked steadfastly in its path, and the goal which he sought was the happiness of his fellow-men.

> Ellery Sedgwick, 1899, *Thomas Paine,* pp. 145, 147

Common Sense (1776)

A few more of such flaming arguments as were exhibited at Falmouth and Norfolk, added to the sound doctrine and unanswerable reasoning contained in the pamphlet *Common Sense,* will not leave numbers at a loss to decide upon the propriety of separation.

> George Washington, 1776, *Letter to Joseph Reed,* Jan. 31;
> *Writings,* ed. Ford, vol. III, p. 396

Had in him the seeds of something like genius. . . . Though Burke moves in an intellectual sphere altogether superior to that in which Paine was able to rise, and though the richness of Burke's speculative power is as superior to Paine's meager philosophy as his style is superior in the amplitude of its rhetoric, it is not to be denied that Paine's plain-speaking is more fitted to reach popular passions, and even that he has certain advantages in point of argument.

> Leslie Stephen, 1876. *History of English Thought
> in the Eighteenth Century,* vol. II, p. 261

Like all his works, this pamphlet was written in clear, racy, vivid English, and with much power of popular reasoning; and, like most of his works, it was shallow, violent, and scurrilous.

> William Edward Hartpole Lecky, 1882, *A History of England
> in the Eighteenth Century,* vol. III, p. 489

No other pamphlet published during the Revolution is comparable with *Common Sense* for interest to the reader of today, or for value as an historical document. Therein as in a mirror is beheld the almost incredible England, against which the colonies contended. And therein is reflected the moral, even religious, enthusiasm which raised the struggle above the paltriness of a rebellion against taxation to a great human movement,—a war for an idea. The art with which every sentence is feathered for its aim is consummate.

Moncure Daniel Conway, 1892, *The Life of Thomas Paine,*
vol. I, p. 66

The Rights of Man (1791-92)

Mr. Paine's answer to Burke will be a refreshing shower to their minds. It would bring England itself to reason and revolution if it was permitted to be read there.

Thomas Jefferson, 1791, *Letter to Benjamin Vaughan,* May 11;
Writings, ed. Ford, vol. V, p. 334

With respect to Paine's book, the first impression was seized by the government, and the circulation of it stopped as much as possible, but still many copies have got abroad, and, as I am just informed, have done much mischief. Your help, therefore, is as much wanted and as strongly called for as ever. I will venture to say, that the eyes of many are fixed on *you* at this important crisis.

Beilby Porteus, 1793, *Letter to Hannah More, Memoirs,*
ed. Roberts, vol. I, p. 424

I have had the ill or good fortune to provoke two great men of this age to the publication of their opinions: I mean Citizen Thomas Paine, and his Grace the *** of *** I am not so great a leveller as to put these two great men on a par, either in the state, or the republic of letters; but "the field of glory is a field for all." It is a large one, indeed; and we all may run, God knows where, in chase of glory, over the boundless expanse of that wild heath whose horizon always flies before us. I assure his Grace, (if he will yet give men leave to call him so), whatever may be said on the authority of the clubs or the bar, that Citizen Paine (who, they will have it, hunts with me in couples, and who only moves as I drag him along) has a sufficient activity in his own native benevolence to dispose and enable him to take the lead for himself. He is ready to blaspheme his God, to insult his king, and to libel the Constitution of his country, without any provocation from me or any encouragement from his Grace.

Edmund Burke, 1795, *A Letter to William Elliot,*
Works, vol. I, p. iii

This work should be read by every man and woman. It is concise, accurate, natural, convincing, and unanswerable. It shows great thought; and intimate knowledge of the various forms of government; deep insight into the very springs of human action, and a courage that compels respect and admiration. The most difficult political problems are solved in a few sentences. The venerable arguments in favor of wrong are refuted with a question—answered with a word. For forcible illustration, apt comparison, accuracy and clearness of statement, and absolute thoroughness, it has never been excelled.

Robert G. Ingersoll, 1874, The Gods and Other Lectures, p. 130

The Age of Reason (1794-95-1811)

How exceedingly superficial and frivolous are the hacknied objections to Christianity, and how entirely they arise from the grossest ignorance of the subject, will appear from my animadversions on Mr. Paine's boasted work. He would have written more to the purpose, if he had been acquainted with the writings of Voltaire, and other better informed unbelievers. But he seems entirely unread on the subject, and thereby to be acquainted with the ground on which either the friends or the enemies of Christianity must stand. Had he been better acquainted with the Scriptures which are a constant subject of his ridicule, he might have made a more plausible attack upon them.

Joseph Priestley, 1794, Letters to a Philosophical Unbeliever
in Answer to Mr. Paine's Age of Reason

This volume, the hornbook of vulgar infidelity, is now before us, and we have doubted how far we ought to refer to it, or what use to make of it. It has passed utterly out of the world's thoughts, and we have a repugnance, not easily to be overcome, in bringing it to light again. Its blasphemies are enough to sicken the heart; but still it may not be useless, in one view, to show the Christian reader to what dregs infidelity, beginning with refinement and high-bred speculation, will at last come.

W. B. Read, 1843, "The Life and Character of Thomas Paine,"
North American Review, vol. 57, p. 49

That hasty pamphlet of his which he named The Age of Reason, written to alleviate the tedium of his Paris prison, differs from other deistical works only in being bolder and honester. It contains not a position which Franklin, John Adams, Jefferson, and Theodore Parker would have dissented from; and, doubtless, he spoke the truth when he declared that his main purpose in writing it was to "inspire mankind with a more exalted idea of the

Supreme Architect of the Universe." I think his judgment must have been impaired before he could have consented to publish so inadequate a performance.

James Parton, 1874, *Life of Thomas Jefferson*, p. 591

The man who was the most influential assailant of the orthodox faith was Thomas Paine. He was the arch infidel, the infidel *par éminence,* whom our early and later theologians have united in holding up as a monster of iniquity and unbelief. The truth is that Paine was a dogmatic, well-meaning iconoclast, who attacked religion without having any religious experience or any imaginative perception of the vital spiritual phenomena on which religious faith is based. Nobody can read his *Age of Reason,* after having had some preparatory knowledge derived from the study of the history of religions, without wondering at its shallowness. Paine is, in a spiritual application of the phrase, color-blind. He does not seem to know what religion is. The reputation he enjoyed was due not more to his masterly command of all the avenues to the average popular mind than to the importance to which he was lifted by his horrified theological adversaries. His merit as a writer against religion consisted in his hard, almost animal, common-sense, to whose tests he subjected the current theological dogmas.

Edwin Percy Whipple, 1886, *American Literature and Other Papers*

As an exponent of religious views, had a position in his day somewhat similar to that of Robert Ingersoll with us. He made a determined and vigorous attack upon a faith of whose true character he was irremediably ignorant. He was devoid of Ingersoll's quick wit and poetic genius; but he had his rough and ready knowledge of human nature, his love of destruction, his hard common sense, his spiritual color-blindness, and, perhaps, more than his earnestness. As in Ingersoll's case, too, the consternation which his attacks upon religion produced among clergymen and church members greatly increased his weight and importance as an "infidel." His *Age of Reason,* is a shallow production, but it had its effect when it was written. Religion, it needs hardly be said, sustained no permanent injury at Paine's hands.

Julian Hawthorne and Leonard Lemmon, 1891, *American Literature*, p. 27

Paine's book is the uprising of the human HEART against the Religion of Inhumanity. . . . But here is one man, a prisoner, preparing for his long silence. He alone can speak for those slain between the throne and the altar. In these outbursts of laughter and tears, these outcries that think not of literary style, these appeals from surrounding chaos to the starry realm of order, from the tribune of vengeance to the sun shining for all, this passionate horror of cruelty in the powerful which will brave a heartless heaven or hell with its immortal indignation,—in all these the unfettered mind may hear the wail of enthralled Europe, sinking back choked with its blood, under the chain it tried to break. So long as a link remains of the same chain, binding reason or heart, Paine's *Age of Reason* will live. It is not a mere book—it is a man's heart.

Moncure Daniel Conway, 1892, The Life of Thomas Paine,
vol. II, pp. 198, 222

The Age of Reason damaged Paine's reputation in America, where the name of "Tom Paine" became a stench in the nostrils of the godly, and a synonym for atheism and blasphemy. His book was denounced from a hundred pulpits, and copies of it were carefully locked away from the sight of "the young," whose religious beliefs it might undermine. It was, in effect, a crude and popular statement of the deistic argument against Christianity. . . . The contest between skepticism and revelation has long since shifted to other grounds. Both the philosophy and the temper of *The Age of Reason* belong to the eighteenth century. But Paine's downright pugnacious method of attack was effective with shrewd, half-educated doubters; and in America well-thumbed copies of his book passed from hand to hand in many a rural tavern or store, where the village atheist wrestled in debate with the deacon or the schoolmaster.

Henry A. Beers, 1895, Initial Studies in American Letters

CHARLES BROCKDEN BROWN
1771-1810

Charles Brockden Brown was born in Philadelphia, Jan. 17, 1771, and died in the same city, of consumption, Feb. 22, 1810. By his own statement, made in a letter just before his death, we learn that he never had more than one continuous half-hour of perfect health. In spite of his short life and his ill-health he accomplished much. At first he studied law, but abandoned it for literature. He was a frequent contributor to the magazines of the time and was himself editor of the *Monthly Magazine and American Review* (1799), and the *Literary Magazine and American Register* (1803-8). His first published work, *The Dialogue of Alcuin* (1797), dealt with questions of marriage and divorce, and he was also the author of several essays on political, historical, and geographical subjects. His novels followed each other with astonishing rapidity: *Sky Walk; or the Man Unknown to Himself* (1798, not published), *Wieland; or the Transformation* (1798), *Ormond; or the Secret Witness* (1799),

Arthur Mervyn; or Memoirs of the year 1793 (1799-1800), *Edgar Huntley; or Memoirs of a Sleep-Walker* (1801), *Jane Talbot* (1801), and *Clara Howard or the Enthusiasm of Love* (1801). They met with an equally astonishing success, and constitute the first important contribution to American fiction.

> George Rice Carpenter, 1898, ed.,
> *American Prose*, p. 84

SEE: *Novels*, 1827, 7 v., 1887, 6 v.; *Ormond*, ed. Ernest Marchand, 1937; Harry R. Warfel, *Charles Brockden Brown: America's Gothic Novelist*, 1949.

PERSONAL

Acted as if he had no use for money. . . . Without system in every thing. . . . Was negligent of personal appearance, even to slovenliness. . . . In mixed company often silent and absent. . . . Fitful and irregular.

> William Dunlap, 1815, *Life of Charles Brockden Brown*,
> vol. I, pp. 56, 57

We believe Brown to have been one of the purest of men. The intellectual so predominated in him, and he seems so to have loathed the sensual, that perhaps he was not aware of the great strength of certain temptations over others.

> Richard Henry Dana, 1827-50, *The Novels of Charles Brockden Brown, Poems and Prose Writings*, vol. II, p. 335

His religious views were unsettled in the early period of his life, but in the preface of his Magazine he emphatically professes his faith in Christianity. His moral character was unexceptionable. He was much beloved by his friends and relatives, and was liberal notwithstanding his poverty, receiving his sisters-in-law, on their father's death, into his own family. In person, Brown was tall and strongly framed, but extremely thin. His complexion was pale and sallow, his hair straight and black. The expression of his face was strongly marked with melancholy. "I saw him," says Sully, the painter "a little before his death. I had never known him—never heard of him—never read any of his works. He was in a deep decline. It was in the month of November—our Indian summer—when the air is full of smoke. Passing a window one day, I was caught by the sight of a man, with a remarkable physiognomy, writing at a table in a dark room. The sun shone directly upon his head. I never shall forget it. The dead leaves were falling then—it was Charles Brockden Brown."

> Evert A. and George L. Duyckinck, 1855-65-75, *Cyclopædia of American Literature*, ed. Simons, vol. I, p. 611

He had little of the spirit of adventure, and on one occasion said he would rather consort with a ploughman or an old market-woman forever, than expose himself to the hundredth part of the perils which beset the heels of a Ledyard or a Park. He was careless of money, and slovenly in dress, but he was habitually careful in his diet. He abstained from spirituous liquors long before temperance societies were established, and he wrote papers in one of his magazines on the deleterious effects of intemperance, and of the use of greasy articles of food.

George Barnett Smith, 1878, "Brockden Brown,"
Fortnightly Review, vol. 30, p. 408

GENERAL

Brown owes his reputation to his novels. He wrote them indeed principally for his amusement, and preferred publishing them when unfinished to labouring upon them after they had lost their interest to himself: they are proofs or signs of power rather than the result of its complete and steady exertion; but they shew the character of his mind and will justify our curiosity to examine it. In attempting this, we do not feel as if we were bringing forward a deserving but neglected author; he has received honourable notice from distinguished men abroad, and his countrymen discerned his merits without waiting till a foreign glory had shone on and revealed them. Still he is very far from being a popular writer. There is no call, as far as we know, for a second edition of any of his works. He is rarely spoken of but by those who have an habitual curiosity about everything literary, and a becoming pride in all good writing which appears amongst ourselves. They have not met with the usual success of leaders, in matters of taste, since, with all their admiration, they have not been able to extend his celebrity much beyond themselves. . . . We should not pronounce Brown a man of genius, nor deny him that distinction, from his style. It might have been acquired by care and study, but it is the result only and never betrays the process.

Gulian Crommelin Verplanck, 1819, "Charles Brockden Brown,"
North American Review, vol. 9, pp. 63, 76

The very want of variety has given such an air of truth to what he is about, showing such an earnest singleness of purpose, that perhaps no writer ever made his readers more completely forget that they were not reading a statement of some serious matter of fact; and so strong is this impression, that we even become half reconciled to improbabilities which so vex us in fiction, though often happening in daily life. This enables us, also, to bear better with his style; for, along with something like a conviction that the man who had vivacity of genius enough for such inventions could never have delivered himself with such dull poverty and pedantry of phrase, we at last are almost driven to the conclusion, that, however extraordinary they may be, they are nevertheless facts; for the man never could have made them, and things must have happened pretty much as he tells us they did.

Richard Henry Dana, 1827-50, *The Novels of Charles Brockden Brown, Poems and Prose Writings,* vol. II, p. 329

He may be rather called a philosophical than a poetical writer; for, though he has that intensity of feeling which constitutes one of the distinguishing attributes of the latter, yet in his most tumultuous bursts of passion we frequently find him pausing to analyze and coolly speculate on the elements which have raised it. This intrusion, indeed, of reason, *la raison froide,* into scenes of the greatest interest and emotion, has sometimes the unhappy effect of chilling them altogether.

William H. Prescott, 1834, "Charles Brockden Brown," *Biographical and Critical Miscellanies,* p. 38

We have long been ashamed that one who ought to be the pride of the country, and who is, in the highest qualities of the mind, so far in advance of our other novelists, should have become almost inaccessible to the public. It has been the custom to liken Brown to Godwin. But there was no imitation, no second-hand in the matter. They were congenial natures, and whichever had come first might have lent an impulse to the other. Either mind might have been conscious of the possession of that peculiar vein of ore without thinking of working it for the mint of the world, till the other, led by accident, or overflow of feeling, showed him how easy it was to put the reveries of his solitary hours into words and upon paper for the benefit of his fellow men. . . . Brown is great as ever human writer was in showing the self-sustaining force of which a lonely mind is capable. He takes one person, makes him brood like the bee, and extract from the common life before him all its sweetness, its bitterness, and its nourishment.

Margaret Fuller Ossoli, 1845-59, *Papers on Literature and Art,* ed. Fuller, pp. 322, 324

He had more genius than talent, and more imagination than fancy. It has been said that he outraged the laws of art by gross improbabilities and inconsistencies, but the most incredible of his incidents had parallels in true history, and the metaphysical unity and consistency of his novels are apparent to all readers familiar with psychological phenomena. His works, generally written with great rapidity, are incomplete, and deficient in method. He disregarded rules, and cared little for criticism. But his style was clear and nervous, with little ornament, free of affectations, and indicated a singular sincerity and depth of feeling.

> Rufus Wilmot Griswold, 1845, ed., "Intellectual History, Condition and Prospects of the Country," *The Prose Writers of America,* p. 29

Judged by the standards set by Poe and Hawthorne, his work is crude and defective in art. The story is at times tediously spun out; character is dissected with disgusting minuteness; the plots are glaringly improbable; the characters either monsters or angels. He is not even a "clumsy Poe," as some have called him, so vastly inferior is his art to his who produced *The Fall of the House of Usher.* Brown's excellences are his graphic portrayals of action and his descriptions of wild nature. He had the art of stimulating expectations;—it is hard to lay down one of his romances unfinished; one reads on and on in a sort of ghastly dream until at length the end of the book completes the hideous nightmare.

> Fred Lewis Pattee, 1896, *A History of American Literature,* p. 104

The first imaginative writer worth mentioning in America. . . . He was also the first to exert a positive influence, across the Atlantic, upon British literature, laying thus early a few modest strands towards an ocean-cable of thought. As a result of this influence concealed doors opened in lonely houses, fatal epidemics laid cities desolate, secret plots were organized, unknown persons from foreign lands died in garrets leaving large sums of money; the honor of innocent women was occasionally endangered, though usually saved in time; people were subject to somnambulism and general frenzy; vast conspiracies were organized with small aims and smaller results. His books, published between 1798 and 1801, made their way across the ocean with a promptness that now seems inexplicable; and Mrs. Shelley in her novel of *The Last Man* founds her description of an epidemic on "the mastery delineations of the author of *Arthur Mervyn.*" Shelley himself recognized his obligations to Brown; and it is to be remembered that Brown himself was evidently familiar with Godwin's philosophical writings, and that he may have drawn from those of Mary Wollstonecraft his advanced views as to the rights and education of women, a subject on which his first book, *Alcuin,* provided the eariest American protest.

> Thomas Wentworth Higginson, 1898, *American Prose,* ed. Carpenter, p. 84

THOMAS PERCY
1729-1811

> Bishop of Dromore, 1729-1811. Born, at Bridgnorth, Shropshire, 13 April 1729. Early education at Bridgnorth Grammar School. Matric., Christ

Church, Oxford, 7 July 1746; B. A., 1750; M. A., 1753. Vicar of Easton-Maudit, Northamptonshire, 1753-82. Rector of Wilby, 1756-82. Married Anne Gutteridge, 1759. Active literary life. Chaplain to George II., 1769. D. D., Camb., 1770. Dean of Carlisle, 1778-82. Bishop of Dromore, 1782. Suffered from blindness in last years of life. Died at Dromore, 30th Sept. 1811. Buried at Dromore Cathedral. WORKS: *Hau Kiou Choaun; or, the Pleasing History* (from the Chinese; 4 vols., anon.), 1761; *Miscellaneous Pieces relating to the Chinese* (2 vols., anon.), 1762; *Five Pieces of Runic Poetry from the Islandic Language* (anon.), 1763; *The Song of Solomon, newly translated"* (anon.), 1764; *Reliques of Ancient English Poetry* (3 vols.), 1765; *A Letter describing the ride to Hulme Abbey from Alnwich* (anon.), (1765); *Four Essays* (anon.), 1767; *A Key to the New Testament,* 1769; *A Sermon* (on John xiii, 35), 1769; *Northern Antiquities* (anon.), 1770; *The Hermit of Warkworth* (anon.), 1771; *The Matrons* (anon.), 1772; *Life of Dr. Oliver Goldsmith* (anon.), 1774; *A Sermon* (on Prov. xxii, 6), 1790; *An Essay on the Origin of the English Stage,* 1793. He *translated*: P. H. Mallet's *Northern Antiquities,* 1770; and *edited*: Surrey's *Poems,* 1763; the *Household Book of the Earl of Northumberland,* 1768.

R. Farquharson Sharp, 1897, *A Dictionary of English Authors*, p. 226

SEE: *Reliques of Ancient English Poetry,* ed. Henry B. Wheatley, 1906, 2 v.; *Letters,* ed. D. Nichol Smith, Cleanth Brooks, and others, 1944-61, 6 v.

PERSONAL

He is a man very willing to learn, and very able to teach; a man out of whose company I never go without having learned something. It is sure that he vexes me sometimes, but I am afraid it is by making me feel my own ignorance. So much extention of mind, and so much minute accuracy of inquiry, if you survey your whole circle of acquaintance, you will find so scarce, if you find it at all, that you will value Percy by comparison. Lord Hailes is somewhat like him; but Lord Hailes does not, perhaps, go beyond him in research; and I do not know that he equals him in elegance. Percy's attention to poetry has given grace and splendour to his studies of antiquity. A mere antiquarian is a rugged being.

Samuel Johnson, 1778, *Letter to Boswell,* April 23; *Boswell's Life of Johnson*

Percy had natually a hot temper, but this cooled down with time, and the trials of his later life were accepted with Christian meekness. One of his relations, who as a boy could just recollect him, told Mr. Pickford "that it was quite a pleasure to see even then his gentleness, amiability, and fondness for children. Every day used to witness his strolling down to a pond in the palace garden, in order to feed his swans, who were accustomed to come at the well-known sound of the old man's voice." He was a pleasing companion and a steady friend. His duties, both in the retired country village and in the more elevated positions of dean and bishop, were all performed with a wisdom and ardour that gained him the confidence of all those with whom he was brought in contact. The praise given to him in the inscription on the tablet to his memory in Dromore Cathedral does not appear to have gone beyond the truth. It is there stated that he resided constantly in his diocese, and discharged "the duties of his sacred office with vigilance and zeal, instructing the ignorant, relieving the necessitous, and comforting the distressed with pastoral affection." He was revered for his piety and learning, and beloved for his universal benevolence, by all ranks and religious denominations.

> Henry B. Wheatley, 1891, ed. *Percy's Reliques of Ancient
> English Poetry,* General Introduction, vol. I, p. lxxix

Reliques of Ancient English Poetry (1765)

You have heard me speak of Mr. Percy. He was in treaty with Mr. James Dodsley for the publication of our best old ballads in three volumes. He has a large folio MS. of ballads which he showed me, and which, with his own natural and acquired talents, would qualify him for the purpose as well as any man in England. I proposed the scheme to him myself, wishing to see an elegant edition and good collection of this kind.

> William Shenstone, 1761, *Letter to Graves,* March 1

The reader is here presented with select remains of our ancient English Bards and Minstrels, an order of men, who were once greatly respected by our ancestors, and contributed to soften the roughness of a martial and unlettered people by their songs and by their music. The greater part of them are extracted from an ancient folio manuscript, in the Editor's possession, which contains near two hundred Poems, Songs, and Metrical Romances. This MS. was written about the middle of the last century; but contains compositions of all times and dates, from the age prior to Chaucer, to the conclusion of the reign of Charles I. This manuscript was shown to several learned and ingenious friends, who thought the contents too curious to be consigned to oblivion, and importuned the possessor to select some of them and give them to the press. As most of them are of great simplicity, and seem to have been merely written for the people, he was long in doubt, whether, in the present state of improved literature, they could be deemed worthy the attention of the public. At length the importunity of his friends prevailed, and he could refuse nothing to such judges as the Author of the Rambler and the late Mr. Shenstone.

> Thomas Percy, 1765, *Reliques of Ancient English Poetry,* Preface

I remember well the spot where I read these volumes for the first time. It was beneath a huge platanus tree, in the ruins of what had been intended for an old-fashioned arbor in the *garden* I have mentioned. The summer-day sped onward so fast, that notwithstanding the sharp appetite of thirteen, I forgot the hour of dinner, was sought for with anxiety, and was still found entranced in my intellectual banquet. To read and to remember was in this instance the same thing, and henceforth I overwhelmed my school-fellows, and all who would hearken to me, with tragical recitations from the ballads of Bishop Percy. The first time, too, I could scrape a few shillings together, which were not common occurrences with me, I bought unto myself a copy of these beloved volumes; nor do I believe I ever read a book half so frequently, or with half the enthusiasm.

Sir Walter Scott, 1808, Autobiography, in Life by Lockhart,
vol. I, ch i

The late Bishop of Dromore, if he merit no other distinction, is entitled to the proud praise of being the Father of Poetical Taste, in that department of literature which he has the exclusive merit of having first brought into public notice. His *Reliques* is a publication that reflects lasting honour upon his name; and it has proved the germ of a rich harvest in the same field of the muses.

Thomas Frognall Dibdin, 1817, The Bibliographical Decameron,
vol. III, p. 339

I never take up these three heavily-bound volumes, the actual last edition, at which Dr. Johnson was wont to scoff, without feeling a pleasure quite apart from that excited by the charming book itself; although to that book, far more than to any modern school of minstrelsy we owe the revival of the taste for romantic and lyrical poetry, which had lain dormant since the days of the Commonwealth. This pleasure springs from a very simple cause. The associations of these ballads with the happiest days of my happy childhood.

Mary Russell Mitford, 1851, Recollections of a Literary Life, p. 1

The publication of the *Reliques,* then, constitutes an epoch in the history of the great revival of taste, in whose blessings we now participate. After 1765, before the end of the century, numerous collections of old ballads, in Scotland and England, by Evans, by Pinkerton, Herd, Ritson, were made. The noble reformation, that received so great an impulse in 1765, advanced thenceforward steadily. The taste that was awakened never slumbered again. The recognition of our old life and poetry that *Reliques* gave, was at last gloriously confirmed and established by Walter Scott.

John W. Hales, 1868, Bishop Percy's Folio Manuscript,
The Revival of Ballad Poetry in the Eighteenth Century,
vol. II, p. xxix

The *Reliques of Ancient English Poetry,* published in 1765 by Bishop Thomas Percy, produced a purer and more lasting effect than Macpherson's "Ossian." They are the fruit of the industry of a loving and careful collector, and proved to every susceptible mind that the essence of poetry is not to be found in formalism, and in sober reflection, but in true and strong feelings. In Percy's *Reliques* we again meet with undisguised nature, with simple feeling, and with energetic action; they are the poetic reflection of an age of national heroes and whose traditions are closely interwoven with English thought and feeling. Hence the powerful and rapid influence these ancient relics of minstrelsy acquired in England and Scotland, an influence which may be traced in the development of English poetry down to our own days.

J. Scherr, 1874, *A History of English Literature,* tr. M. V., p. 167

Percy's *Reliques* is commonly mentioned as the turning-point in the taste of the last century, but it was quite as much the result, as the cause, of the renewed interest in old ballads. Percy did more completely what had been done feebly before. Still, it is well to bear in mind the date of the publication, 1765, as mnemonic point, for this was by far the most important of the collections. A copy of the book fell into the hands of Bürger (1748-94), who translated many of the ballads into German, and was inspired by it to write his own *Lenore.* . . . It would be fair to say that Percy's *Reliques* had more influence in Germany than in England. Bürger and his fellow-poets of the "Hainbund," who were all young men with a confused hatred of tyrants and great affection for the full moon, took to writing more ballads after the old pattern, as illustrated by Percy's *Reliques* and explained by Herder, and soon Herder established the new lines in which German thought was destined to run, substituting the intelligent study of the past for the faithful following of academic rules.

Thomas Sergeant Perry, 1883, *English Literature in the Eighteenth Century,* pp. 422, 423

Percy was a critic of admirable poetical taste and literary skill, but he was not altogether proof against the temptations to which these qualities exposed him. In the collection of ballads which he "edited" from the MS. in his possession, he did not scruple to alter and supplement the original text whenever he thought that by so doing he could improve the general effect. By these practices he roused the wrath of an able and relentless antagonist.

W. J. Courthope, 1895, *A History of English Poetry,* vol. I, p. 428

Percy not only rescued, himself, a number of ballads from forgetfulness; what was equally important, his book prompted others to hunt out and publish similar relics before it was to late. It was the occasion of collections like Herd's (1769), Scott's (1802-03), and Motherwell's (1827), and many more, resting on purer texts and edited on more scrupulous principles than his own. Furthermore, his ballads helped to bring about a reform in literary taste and to inspire men of original genius. Wordsworth, Coleridge, Southey, Scott, all acknowledged the greatest obligations to them. Wordsworth said that English poetry had been "absolutely redeemed" by them. "I do not think there is a writer in verse of the present day who would not be proud to acknowledge his obligations to the *Reliques*. I know that it is so with my friends; and for myself, I am happy in this occasion to make a public avowal of my own." Without the *Reliques, The Ancient Mariner, The Lady of the Lake, La Belle Dame sans Merci, Stratton Water,* and *The Haystuck in the Floods* might never have been. Perhaps even the *Lyrical Ballads* might never have been, or might have been something quite unlike what they are.

Henry A. Beers, 1898, *A History of English Romanticism in the Eighteenth Century*, p. 299

GENERAL

Dr. Percy was so abashed by the ridicule flung upon his labours from the ignorance and insensibility of the persons with whom he lived, that, though while he was writing under a mask he had not wanted resolution to follow his genius into the regions of true simplicity and genuine pathos (as is evinced by the exquisite ballad of "Sir Cauline," and by many other pieces), yet when he appeared in his own person and character as a poetical writer, he adopted, as in the tale of the "Hermit of Warkworth," a diction scarcely in any one of its features distinguishable from the vague, the glossy, and unfeeling language of his day. I mention this remarkable fact with regret, esteeming the genius of Dr. Percy in this kind of writing superior to that of any other man by whom in modern times it has been cultivated.

William Wordsworth, 1815, *Poems, Essay Supplementary to the Preface*

Percy was not, perhaps, a man of much originality of genius, or great strength, or richness of mind. Johnson was probably right when he said, "He runs about with little weight upon his mind." Yet he was unquestionably endowed with certain rare qualities. He had ardent enthusiasm, an enthusiasm which, like that of Scott, was the same in kind, although different in direction, from that of his warlike ancestors; he had a vivid sympathy with the old writers, and could think their thoughts, feel their passions, and talk their language; he had invincible diligence, an enormous memory, and had written some ballads of his own, such as "Sir Cauline," which entitle him to an independent and considerable poetical reputation.

George Gilfillan, 1858, ed. *Reliques of Ancient English Poetry, Life of Thomas Percy,* p. 9

RICHARD BRINSLEY SHERIDAN
1751-1816

Born, in Dublin, 30 Oct. 1751. Parents removed to London, 1758. Educated at Harrow, 1762-68. Parents removed to Bath, 1771. Eloped with Elizabeth Linley, 1772; secretly married to her at Calais. Formally married in London, 13 April 1773. Settled in London, spring of 1774. *The Rivals* produced at Covent Garden, 17 Jan. 1775; *St. Patrick's Day; or, The Scheming Lieutenant,* Covent Garden, May 1775; *The Duenna,* Covent Garden, 21 Nov. 1775. Purchased a share in Drury Lane Theatre, June 1776; Manager, Sept. 1776 to Feb. 1809. *A Trip to Scarborough* (adapted from Vanbrugh's *The Relapse*) produced at Drury Lane, 24 Feb. 1777; *The School for Scandal,* Drury Lane, 8 May 1777; *The Critic,* Drury Lane, 30 Oct. 1779. M. P. for Stafford, 1780. Under Secretary of State, 1782. Concerned in impeachment of Warren Hastings, 1787-88. Intimacy with Prince of Wales begun, 1787. Wife died, 1792. Drury Lane Theatre rebuilt, 1792-94; new house opened, 21 April 1794. Married (ii.) Esther Ogle, 27 April 1795. *Pizarro* (adapted from Kotzebue's *Spaniards in Peru*) produced at Drury Lane, 24 May 1799. Privy Councillor and Treasurer of Navy, 1799. Receiver of Duchy of Cornwall, 1804. Drury Lane Theatre burnt down, 24 Feb. 1809. Died, in London, 7 July 1816. Buried in Westminster Abbey. WORKS: *Clio's Protest* (under pseud.: "Asmodeo") (1771); *The Rivals,* 1775; *St. Patrick's Day; or, The Scheming Lieutenant,* 1775; *The General Fast* (anon.), (1775?); *The Duenna,* 1775; *A Trip to Scarborough,* 1777; *The School for Scandal,* (anon.), 1777; *Verses to the Memory of Garrick,* 1779; *The Critic,* 1781; *The Legislative Independence of Ireland* (a speech), 1785; *Speech . . . against Warren Hastings,* 1788; *A Comparative Statement of the two Bills for the better Government of the British Possessions in India,* 1788; *Dramatic Works* (1795?); *Pizarro,* 1799; *Speech . . . on the Motion to address His Majesty* (1798); *Speech . . . on the Union with Ireland,* 1799; *Speech . . . on the Army Estimates,* 1802. POSTHUMOUS: *Speeches* (5 vols.), 1816; *An Ode to Scandal,* 2nd edn. 1819; *Speeches in the Trial of Warren Hastings,* ed. by E. A. Bond (4 vols.), 1859-61. He *translated: The Love Epistles of Aristænetus* (with N. B. Halhed), 1771. COLLECTED WORKS: ed. by F. Stainforth, 1874. LIFE: by T. Moore, 1825; by Mrs. Oliphant, 1883; by W. F. Rae, 1896.

R. Farquharson Sharp, 1897, *A Dictionary of English Authors,* p. 255

SEE: *Plays and Poems,* ed. R. Crompton Rhodes, 1928, 3 v.; *Dramatic Works,* ed. Joseph Knight, 1924 (OSA); Walter Sichel, *Sheridan, from New and Original Material,* 1909, 2 v.; R. Crompton Rhodes, *Harlequin Sheridan: The Man and the Legends,* 1933.

PERSONAL

Mr. Sheridan has a very fine figure, and a good though I don't think a handsome face. He is tall, and very upright, and his appearance and address are at once manly and fashionable, without the smallest tincture of foppery or modish graces. In short, I like him vastly, and think him every way worthy his beautiful companion. . . . He evidently adores her, and she as evidently idolises him. The world has by no means done him justice.

> Mme. D'Arblay (Fanny Burney), 1779, *Diary and Letters,*
> vol. I, ch. IV

It was some Spirit, SHERIDAN! that breathed
O'er thy young mind such wildly-various power!
My soul hath marked thee in her shaping hour,
Thy temples with Hymettian flow'rets wreathed:
And sweet thy voice, as when o'er Laura's bier
Sad music trembled through Vauclusa's glade;
Sweet, as at dawn the love-lorn serenade
That wafts soft dreams to Slumber's listening ear.
Now patriot Rage and Indignation high
Swell the full tones! And now thy eyebeams dance
Meanings of Scorn and Wit's quaint revelry!

> Samuel Taylor Coleridge, 1795, *To Richard Brinsley Sheridan*

Sheridan is very little consulted at present; and it is said, will not have a seat in the cabinet. This is a distressing necessity. His habits of daily intoxication are probably considered as unfitting him for trust. The little that has been confided to him he has been running about to tell; and since Monday, he has been visiting Sidmouth. At a dinner at Lord Cowper's on Sunday last, where the Prince was, he got drunk as usual, and began to speak slightingly of Fox. From what grudge this behaviour proceeds I have not learned. The whole fact is one to investigate with candour, and with a full remembrance of Sheridan's great services, in the worst times, to the principles of liberty.

> Francis Horner, 1806, *Memoirs and Correspondence,* vol. I, p. 357

I find things settled so that £150 will remove all difficulty. I am absolutely undone and broken-hearted. I shall negotiate for the Plays succesfully in the course of a week, when all shall be returned. I have desired Fairbrother to get back the Guarantee for thirty. They are going to put the carpets out of window, and brake into Mrs. S.'s room and *take me—* for God's sake let me see you.

> Richard Brinsley Sheridan, 1816, *Letter to Samuel Rogers,*
> May 15; *Moore's Memoirs of Sheridan,* vol. II, p. 454

Long shall we seek his likeness—long in vain,
And turn to all of him which may remain,
Sighing that Nature form'd but one such man.
And broke the die—in moulding Sheridan.

Lord Byron, 1816, Monody on the Death of the
Rt. Hon. R. B. Sheridan, Spoken at Drury-Lane Theatre

I must differ from Moore in his view of Sheridan's heart. Notwithstanding his passion for Miss Linley and his grief for his father's death, who used him ill, I question his having a "really good heart." His making love to Pamela, Madame de Genlis's daughter, so soon after his lovely wife's death, and his marriage, in two years, with a young girl as a *compliment* to her remembrance, renders one very suspicious of the real depth of his passion. No man of wit to the full extent of the word can have a good heart, because he has by nature less regard for the feelings of others than for the brilliancy of his own sayings. There must be more mischief than love in hearts of all radiant wits. Moore's life of him wants courage.

Benjamin Robert Haydon, 1825, To Miss Mitford, Dec. 10;
Life, Letters and Table Talk, ed. Stoddard, p. 226

Sheridan was a man of quick but not deep feelings; of sudden but not lasting excitements. He was not one of those who suffer a single passion to influence the whole course of their lives. Even the desire to dazzle by his wit, great as was its power over him, was not always awake, for we are told that he would sometimes remain silent for hours in company, too lazy to invent a smart saying for the occasion, but idly waiting for the opportunity to apply some brilliant witticism already in his memory. . . . His griefs might have been violent, but they were certainly brief, and he quickly forgot them when he came to look again at the sunny side of things. Even his political disappointments do not seem in the least to have soured his temper, or abated his readiness to adopt new hopes and new expedients.

William Cullen Bryant, 1826-84, "The Character of Sheridan,"
Prose Writings, ed. Godwin, vol. II, p. 368

The account of Sheridan's death-bed is as nearly fabulous as any narration can be; but it is the current "copied" account, and passes muster with the rest. And now, we may fairly ask, if such "biographies" be true, how came this man, so abused, so run down, whose faults were so prodigious, whose merits were *nil,* to occupy the position he did when living? . . . How did it happen, then, that a man labouring under such a disadvantage of birth, and also described as a commonplace swindler, drunkard, and driveller, excelled in everything he attempted, and, from the obscure son of the Bath actor and schoolmaster, became minister of state and companion of princes? What dazzled fools does it make all his contemporaries that *they* admitted him unquestioned to a superiority which is now denied to have existed! What an extraordinary anomaly does that famous funeral in Westminster Abbey present, amid a crowd of onlookers so dense that they seemed "like a wall of human faces," if it was merely the carrying of a poor old tipsy gentleman to his grave by a group of foolish lords!

> Hon. Caroline Norton, 1861, "Sheridan and His Biographers,"
> *Macmillan's Magazine,* vol. 3, p. 177

He was the contemporary of Beaumarchais, and resembled him in his talent and in his life. The two epochs, the two schools of drama, the two characters correspond. Like Beaumarchais, he was a lucky adventurer, clever, amiable, and generous, reaching success through scandal, who flashed up and shone in a moment, scaled with a rush the empyrean of politics and literature, settled himself, as it were, among the constellations, and, like a brilliant rocket, presently went out in the darkness. Nothing failed him; he attained all at the first leap, without apparent effort, like a prince who need only show himself to win a place. All the most surpassing happiness, the most brilliant in art, the most exalted in worldly position, he took as his birthright. The poor unknown youth, wretched translator of an unreadable Greek sophist, who at twenty walked about Bath in a red waistcoat and a cocked hat, destitute of hope, and ever conscious of the emptiness of his pockets, had gained the heart of the most admired beauty and musician of her time, and carried her off from ten rich, elegant, titled adorers, had fought with the best-hoaxed of the ten, beaten him, had carried by storm the curiosity and attention of the public. Then, challenging glory and wealth, he placed successively on the stage the most diverse and the most applauded dramas, comedies, farce, opera, serious verse; he bought and worked a large theatre without a farthing, inaugurated a reign of success and pecuniary advantages, and led a life of elegance amid the enjoyments of social and domestic joys, surrounded by universal admiration and wonder. Thence, aspiring yet higher, he conquered power, entered the House of Commons, showed himself a match for the first orators. . . . Whatever the business, whoever the man, he persuaded; none withstood him, every one fell under his charm. What is more difficult than for an ugly man to make a young girl forget his ugliness? There is one thing more difficult, and that is to make a creditor forget you owe him money. There is something more difficult still, and that is, to borrow money of a creditor who has come to demand it. . . . In the morning, creditors and visitors filled the rooms in which he lived; he came in smiling, with an easy manner, with so much loftiness and grace, that the people forgot their wants and their claims, and looked as if they had only come to see him. His animation was irresistible; no one had a more dazzling wit; he had an inexhaustible fund of puns, contrivances, sallies, novel ideas. Lord Byron, who was a good judge, said that he had never heard nor conceived of a more extraordinary conversation. Men spent nights in listening to him.

H. A. Taine, 1871, *History of English Literature*,
tr. Van Laun, vol. I, bk iii, ch. i, pp. 524, 525

Doubtless, in any attempt to judge of Sheridan as he was apart from his works, we must make considerable deductions from the mass of floating anecdotes that have gathered round his name. It was not without reason that his granddaughter Mrs. Norton denounced the unfairness of judging of the real man from unauthenticated stories about his indolent procrastination, his wrecklessness in money matters, his drunken feats and sallies, his wild gambling, his ingenious but discreditable shifts in evading and duping creditors. The real Sheridan was not a pattern of decorous respectability, but we may fairly believe that he was very far from being as disreputable as the Sheridan of vulgar legend. Against the stories about his reckless management of his affairs we must set the broad facts that he had no source of income but Drury Lane theatre, that he bore from it thirty years all the expenses of a fashionable life, and that the theatre was twice burnt to the ground during his proprietorship. Enough was lost in those fires to account ten times over for all his debts. His biographers always speak of his means of living as a mystery. Seeing that he started with borrowed capital, it is possible that the mystery is that he applied much more of his powers to plain matters of business than he affected or got credit for.

William Minto, 1886, *Encyclopædia Britannica*,
Ninth edition, vol. XXI, p. 836

It is impossible to close this rapid and slight sketch without one word at least on Mrs. Sheridan. One of the strong titles of Sheridan to the favour of posterity is to be found in the warm attachment of his family and his descendants to his memory. The strongest of them all lies in the fact that he could attract, and could retain through her too short life, the devoted affections of this admirable woman, whose beauty and accomplishments, remarkable as they were, were the least of her titles to praise. Mrs. Sheridan was certainly not strait-laced: not only did she lose at cards fifteen and twenty-one guineas on two successive nights, but she played cards, after the fashion of her day, on Sunday evenings. I am very far from placing such exploits among her claims on our love. But I frankly own to finding it impossible to read the accounts of her without profoundly coveting, across the gulf of all these years, to have seen and known her. Let her be judged by the incomparable verses (presented to us in these volumes) in which she opened the floodgates of her bleeding heart at a moment when she feared that she had been robbed, for the moment, of Sheridan's affections by the charms of another. Those verses of loving pardon proceed from a soul advanced to some of the highest Gospel attainments. She passed into her rest when still under forty; peacefully absorbed for days before her departure, in the contemplation of the coming world.

> William Ewart Gladstone, 1896, "Sheridan," *The Nineteenth Century,*
> vol. 39, p. 1041

The Rivals (1775)

In such a play as *The Rivals* the reader is kept in a state of continual hilarious delight by a profusion of sallies, rejoinders, blunders, contrasts, which seem to exhaust all the resources of the ludicrous. Mrs. Malaprop's "parts of speech" will raise the laughter of unborn generations, and the choleric generous old father will never find a more perfect representative than Sir Anthony Absolute.

> Thomas Arnold, 1868-75, *Chaucer to Wordsworth,* p. 371

The Rivals from the date of its first night's failure, has neither merited nor enjoyed a like measure of success as, throughout the world, has followed *The School for Scandal;* while I venture to think the incidents of the comedy are too fragile and farcical to bear such elaborate scenic treatment as we endeavoured to depict of last-century life, when Beau Nash reigned in the pumproom at Bath.

> Sir Squire Bancroft, 1896, in *Sheridan,*
> *A Biography* by Rae, vol. II, p. 321

The Rivals is artificial comedy, inclining on one side to farce, and, in the parts of Falkland and Julia, to the sentimental. But it is, on its own rather artificial plan, constructed with remarkable skill and tightness; and the characters of Sir Anthony Absolute, Mrs. Malaprop, Sir Lucius O'Trigger, and Bob Acres, with almost all the rest, combine fun with at least theatrical verisimilitude in a very rare way. Indeed, Sir Anthony and Mrs. Malaprop, though heightened from life, can hardly be said to be false to it, and though in the other pair the license of dramatic exaggeration is pushed to its farthest, it is not exceeded. The effect could not have been produced without the sparkling dialogue, but this alone could not have given it.

> George Saintsbury, 1898, *A Short History of*
> *English Literature,* p. 641

The Duenna (1775)*

This drama has a charm for the public beyond its own intrinsic worth—it was written by Richard Brinsley Sheridan. If that name has no power over the reader's imagination, so as to give to every sentence a degree of interest, let him throw aside the book, and forbear to seek after literary pleasures, for he has not the taste to enjoy them. Although *The Duenna's* highest claim to notice depends, now, upon the reputation of its author, yet the author was first indebted to *The Duenna* for the honour of ranking among poets, and of receiving from the fashionable world all those animating caresses, so dear to a poet's heart. . . . Divested of all adventitious aid, the value of the opera consists in the beautiful poetry of many of the songs; for though it is a production of much ingenuity and skill, it does not give a presage, either in wit or incident, of such a work, from the same hand, as *The School for Scandal*.

> Mrs. Elizabeth Inchbald, 1808, "Remarks" on *The Duenna*, in
> *The British Theatre*, ed. Elizabeth Inchbald, vol. II

The Duenna is partly a *pasticcio*, consisting of original music mingled with popular airs, glees, &c., adapted to new words; and it appears from the above passages in Sheridan's letters, that he himself had a hand in the selection and adaptation of the old music. Several of the original pieces were contributed by Thomas Linley, the composer's eldest son. These were, the overture; the songs, "Could I each fault remember," "Friendship is the bond of reason," and "Sharp is the woe;" the duet, "Turn thee round, I pray thee;" and the trio which concludes the first act. These are all charming things, and do honour to the genius of a young musician, who, but for his untimely fate, would undoubtedly have achieved the highest triumphs in his art.

> George Hogarth, 1838, *Memoirs of the Musical Drama*,
> vol. II, p. 433

With the progress of musical compositions, especially in connexion with the Drama, *The Duenna,* greatly admired as it was on its first production, passed out of fashion; and in spite of the simplicity and the charm of many of the melodies composed for the work by Linley, in spite, above all, of the ingenuity, wit and humour of the piece, it may be doubted whether Sheridan's *Duenna,* will ever be played again in its original form. . . . A justly admired composer of our time, Mr. J. L. Roeckel, has set to music Sheridan's ancient opera-book with such lyrical additions as the taste and fashion of the day

---

*Written in 1775, this play titled *The Governess* was published in a pirated edition in Dublin in 1777 and in London in 1794 under the title, *The Duenna,* by which it is now known.

seemed to render necessary, but with no change whatever in the original dialogue, and *The Duenna* with music by Roeckel will probably supersede *The Duenna* with music by Linley, just as the operatic version of Beaumarchais' *Barber of Seville* with music by Rossini has displaced the older operatic version of the same work with music by Paisiello.

Sutherland Edwards, 1896, in *Sheridan, A Biography*
by Rae, vol. I, p. 305

The School for Scandal (1777)

I have seen Sheridan's new comedy, and liked it much better than any I have seen since *The Provoked Husband*. There is a great deal of wit and good situations; but it is too long, has two or three bad scenes that might easily be omitted, and seemed to me to want nature and truth of character; but I have not read it, and sat too high to hear it well.

Horace Walpole, 1778, *To Rev. Wm. Mason*, May 16;
Letters, ed. Cunningham, vol. VII, p. 67

The School for Scandal is, if not the most original, perhaps the most finished and faultless comedy which we have. When it is acted you hear people all around you exclaiming: "Surely it is impossible for anything to be cleverer." The scene in which Charles sells all the old family pictures but his uncle's, who is the purchaser in disguise, and that of the discovery of Lady Teazle when the screen falls, are mong the happiest and most highly wrought that comedy, in its wide and brilliant range, can boast. Besides the wit and ingenuity of this play, there is a genial spirit of frankness and generosity about it that relieves the heart as well as clears the lungs. It professes a faith in the depravity of human nature. While it strips off the mask of hypocrisy it inspires a confidence between man and man. As often as it is acted it must serve to clear the air of the low creeping pestilent fog of cant and mysticism, which threatens to confound every native impulse, or honest conviction, in the nauseous belief of a perpetual lie, and the laudable profession of systematic hypocrisy.

William Hazlitt, 1818, *Lectures on the English Comic Writers*,
Lecture VIII

Amidst the mortifying circumstances attendant upon growing old, it is something to have seen *The School for Scandal* in its glory. This comedy grew out of Congreve and Wycherley, but gathered some allays of the sentimental comedy which followed theirs. It is impossible that it should be now *acted*, though it continues, at long intervals, to be announced in the bills. Its hero, when Palmer played it at least, was Joseph Surface. When I remember the gay boldness, the graceful solemn plausibility, the measured step, the insinuating voice—to express it in a word—the downright *acted* villainy of the part, so different from the pressure of conscious actual wickedness,—the hypocritical assumption of hypocrisy,—which made Jack so deservedly a favourite in that character, I must needs conclude the present generation of playgoers more virtuous than myself, or more dense. I freely confess that he divided the palm with me with his better brother; that, in fact, I liked him quite as well. . . . You did not believe in Joseph with the same faith with which you believed in Charles. The latter was a pleasant reality, the former a no less pleasant poetical foil to it. The comedy, I have said is incongruous; a mixture of Congreve with sentimental incompatibilities: the gaiety upon the whole is buoyant; but it required the consummate art of Palmer to reconcile the discordant elements.

Charles Lamb, 1824? *On the Artificial Comedy*
of the Last Century

The beauties of this Comedy are so universally known and felt, that criticism may be spared the trouble of dwelling upon them very minutely. With but little interest in the plot, with no very profound or ingenious development of character, and with a group of personages, not one of whom has any legitimate claims upon either our affection or esteem, it yet, by the admirable skill with which its materials are managed,—the happy contrivance of the situations, at once both natural and striking,—the fine feeling of the ridiculous that smiles throughout, and that perpetual play of wit which never tires, but seems, like running water, to be kept fresh by its own flow, —by all this general animation and effect, combined with a finish of the details almost faultless, it unites the suffrages, at once, of the refined and the simple, and is not less successful in ministering to the natural enjoyment of the latter, than is satisfying and delighting the most fastidious tastes among the former.

Thomas Moore, 1825, *Memoirs of the Life of the*
Right Honourable Richard Brinsley Sheridan, vol. I, p. 245

The surpassing merits of *The School for Scandal* become the more brilliant, the more minutely they are scanned, and the more fairly the faults of the play are in juxtaposition with its beauties. Its merits are not so much to be sought in the saliency of any predominating excellence as in the harmonious combination of great varieties of excellence, in a unity of purpose sufficiently philosophical for the intellect of comedy, but not so metaphysical as to mar the airy playfulness of comic mirth. The satire it conveys is directed, not to rare and exceptional oddities in vice or folly, but to attributes of human society which universally furnish the materials and justify the ridicule of satire. It is one of the beauties of this great drama, that its moral purpose is not rigidly narrowed into the mere illustration of a maxim—that the outward plot is indeed carried on by personages who only very indirectly serve to work out the interior moral.

Edward Bulwer-Lytton, 1863-68, *Caxtoniana, Miscellaneous Prose Works,* vol. III, p. 457

Sheridan is not of course to be likened to Molière: the Frenchman had a depth and a power to which the Irishman could not pretend. But a comparison with Beaumarchais is fair enough, and it can be drawn only in favor of Sheridan; for brilliant as *The Marriage of Figaro* is, it lacks the solid structure and the broad outlook of *The School for Scandal.* Both the French wit and the Irish are masters of fence, and the dialogue of these comedies still scintillates as steel crosses steel. Neither of them put much heart into his plays; and perhaps *The School for Scandal* is even more artificial than *The Marriage of Figaro,*—but it is wholly free from the declamatory shrillness which today mars the masterpiece of Beaumarchais.

Brander Matthews, 1897, *Library of the World's Best Literature,* ed. Warner, vol. XXIII, p. 13320

The Critic (1779-81)

Sir Fretful, between his two tormenters, and the cheerful bustle and assured confidence of Mr. Puff, have held their ground when hundreds of sensational dramas have dropped and died. Never was a more wonderful literary feat. The art of puffing has been carried to a perfection unsuspected by Mr. Puff, and not one person in a thousand has the most remote idea who Cumberland was; but *The Critic* is as delightful as ever, and we listen to the gentlemen talking with as much relish as our grandfathers did. Nay, the simplest-minded audience, innocent of literature, and perhaps not very sure what it all means, will still answer to the touch and laugh till they cry over the poor author's wounded vanity and the woes of Tilburina. Shakspeare, it is evident, found the machinery cumbrous, and gave up the idea of making Sly and his mockers watch the progress of *The Taming of the Shrew,* and Beaumont and Fletcher lose our interest altogether in their long-drawn-out by-play, though the first idea of it is comical in the highest degree. Nor could Fielding keep the stage with his oft-repeated efforts, notwithstanding the wit and point of many of his dialogues. But Sheridan at last, after so many attempts, found out the right vein.

Margaret O. W. Oliphant, 1883, *Sheridan (English Men of Letters),* p. 97

The Critic is perhaps the highest proof of Sheridan's skill as a dramatist, for in it he has worked out, with perfect success for all time, a theme which, often as it has been attempted, no other dramatist has ever succeeded in redeeming from tedious circumstantiality and ephemeral personalities. The laughtable infirmities of all classes connected with the stage,—authors, actors, patrons, and audience,—are touched off with the lightest of hands; the fun is directed, not at individuals, but at absurdities that grow out of the circumstances of the stage as naturally and inevitably as weeds in a garden.

William Minto, 1886, *Encyclopædia Britannica,*
Ninth edition, vol. XXI, p. 835

GENERAL

Sheridan's was a brillant, shallow intellect, a shifty, selfish nature; his one great quality, his one great element of success as a dramatist, as an orator and as a man, was mastery of effect. His tact was exquisitely nice and fine. He knew how to say and how to do the right thing, at the right time, in the right way. This was the sum of him; there was no more. Without wisdom, without any real insight into the human heart, without imagination, with a flimsy semblance of fancy, entirely devoid of true poetic feeling, even of the humblest order, incapable of philosophic reflection, never rising morally above the satirizing of the fashionable vices and follies of his day, to him the doors of the great theatre of human life were firmly closed. His mind flitted lightly over the surface of society, now casting a reflection of himself upon it, now making it sparkle and ripple with a touch of his flashing wing. He was a surface man, and the name of the two chief agents in the plot of his principal comedy is so suitable to him as well as to their characters, that the choice of it would seem to have been instinctive and intuitive. He united the qualities of his Charles and Joseph Surface; having the wit, the charming manner, the careless good-nature of the one, with at least a capacity of the selfishness, the duplicity, the crafty design, but without the mischief and the malice, of the other.

Richard Grant White, 1883, ed., *The Dramatic Works of*
Richard Brinsley Sheridan, Introduction

Compared even with Congreve himself, he stands high as a dialoguist, for though his wit is not quite so keen or so nimble, or his style quite so polished, his epigrams and jests seem to grow more naturally and unforcedly out of the circumstances of the play; his geniality, too, is much greater, and is contagious. After a play of Sheridan's we feel on better terms with human nature. His plots are admirable—not solutions of any of the problems of social life as, according to some critics, comedies should be, but easy, pleasant, and fluent, and full, as such ease and pleasantness implies, of much concealed art. The spirit of Sheridan's plays is so thoroughly modern, they are salted with so good and true a wit, have so much of honest stagecraft in them, and are so full of a humour which is wholly that of the present period, that a play of his adequately put upon the stage will hold its own to this day triumphantly against the most successful of modern pieces.

Oswald Crawfurd, 1883, ed., *English Comic Dramatists*, p. 262

The real risk to which *The School for Scandal* is more and more exposed as the years roll by, is lest it may be found trespassing on the borderlands of truth and reality, and evoking genuine feeling; for as soon as it does this, the surroundings must become incongruous and therefore painful. Too long ago, when Miss Ellen Terry used to act Lady Teazle at the Vaudeville with a moving charm still happily hers, I remember hearing behind me a youthful voice full of tears and terror (it was of course when Joseph Surface was making his insidious proposals to Lady Teazle) exclaim, "Oh, mother, I hope she won't yield!" and I then became aware of the proximity of some youthful creature to whom all this comic business (for one knew the screen was soon to fall) was sheer tragedy. It made me a little uncomfortable. To Sheridan, it was all pure comedy. We see this from the boisterous laughter with which Charles Surface greets the *dénouement*. Charles was no doubt a rake, but he was not meant to be a heartless rake after the fashion of the Wildairs of an earlier day. Had he not refused five hundred pounds for a trumpery picture of his uncle, for whose fortune he was waiting? It was all comedy to Sheridan, and if it ever ceases to be all comedy to us, it will be the first blow this triumphant piece has ever received.

Augustine Birrell, 1896, *The School for Scandal and The Rivals,* Introduction

JANE AUSTEN
1775-1817

No other English woman of letters ever lived a life so entirely uneventful. . . . Born on the 16th of December, 1775. In the year 1796 and '97, before she was twenty-three years old, she wrote the novel *Pride and Prejudice,* in 1797 and '98 *Sense and Sensibility,* and *Northanger Abbey.* These works, however, waited fifteen years for a publisher; and Jane, who wrote merely for her own amusement, seems to have possessed her soul in patience. In 1801 the family removed to Bath; in 1805 the Rev. George Austen died, and they again removed to Southampton. In 1809 they settled at Chawton, Hampshire; and in 1811 Jane was at length enabled to publish *Sense and Sensibility.* It was followed in 1813 by

Pride and Prejudice. Mansfield Park appeared in 1814, and *Emma* in 1816. Jane Austen died on the 18th of July, 1817. After her death her early novel *Northanger Abbey,* and *Persuasion,* a mature work which has the same mellower quality as *Emma,* together with a pathos peculiarly its own, were published.

Helen Gray Cone and Jeannette L. Gilder, 1887,
Pen-Portraits of Literary Women, vol. I, p. 195

SEE: *Novels,* ed. R. W. Chapman, 1923-54, 6 v.; *Letters,* ed. R. W. Chapman, 1932, 2 v. (one-vol. edition in 1952); Mary Lascelles, *Jane Austen and Her Art,* 1939, repr. 1963; A Walton Litz, *Jane Austen: A Study of Her Artistic Development,* 1965.

PERSONAL

There were twenty dances, and I danced them all, and without fatigue. I was glad to find myself capable of dancing so much and with so much satisfaction as I did; from my slender enjoyment of the Ashford halls, I had not thought myself equal to it, but in cold weather and with few couples I fancy I could just as well dance for a week together as for half an hour.

Jane Austen, 1799, *To her Sister,* Dec. 24; *Letters,* ed. Brabourne

A friend of mine, who visits her now, says that she has stiffened into the most perpendicular, precise, taciturn piece of "single blessedness" that ever existed, and that, till *Pride and Prejudice* showed what a precious gem was hidden in that unbending case, she was no more regarded in society than a poker or a fire-screen, or any other thin upright piece of wood or iron that fills its corner in peace and quietness. The case is very different now; she is still a poker, but a poker of whom every one is afraid. It must be confessed that this silent observation from such an observer is rather formidable. . . . After all, I do not know that I can quite vouch for this account, though the friend from whom I received it is truth itself; but her family connections must render her disagreeable to Miss Austen, since she is the sister-in-law of a gentleman who is at law with Miss A.'s brother for the greater part of his fortune.

Mary Russell Mitford, 1815, *Letter to Sir Wm. Elford,*
April 3; *Life,* ed. L'Estrange

In person she was very attractive; her figure was rather tall and slender, her step light and firm, and her whole appearance expressive of health and animation. In complexion she was a clear brunette with a rich colour; she had full round cheeks, with mouth and nose small and well formed, bright hazel eyes, and brown hair forming natural curls close round her face. If not so regularly handsome as her sister, yet her countenance had a peculiar charm of its own to the eyes of most beholders. . . . She was well acquainted with the old periodicals from *The Spectator* downwards. Her knowledge of Richardson's works was such as no one is likely again to acquire, now that the multitude and the merits of our light literature have called off the attention of readers from that great master.

J. E. Austen Leigh, 1870, A Memoir of Jane Austen,
by her Nephew, pp. 82, 84

During her whole life she remained to a great extent engrossed by the interest of her family and their limited circle of old and intimate friends. This was as it should be—so far, but there may be too much of a good thing. The tendency of strictly restricted family parties and sets—when their members are above small bickerings and squabblings—when they are really superior people in every sense, is to form "mutual admiration" societies, and neither does this more respectable and amiable weakness act beneficially upon its victims. . . . Fondly loved and remembered as Jane Austen has been, with much reason, among her own people, in their considerable ramifications, I cannot imagine her as greatly liked, or even regarded with anything save some amount of prejudice, out of the immediate circle of her friends, and in general society. . . . What I mean is, that she allowed her interests and sympathies to become narrow, even for her day, and that her tender charity not only began, but ended, in a large measure, at home.

Henrietta Keddie (Sarah Tytler), 1880,
Jane Austen and Her Works, pp. 15, 16

All the time that she was writing her three best novels she had no private study: she wrote in the general sittingroom at her little mahogany desk, and when visitors interrupted, a handkerchief or a newspaper was thrown over the tell-tale MSS. Very often her nephews and nieces rushed in, and she was always ready to break off from her writing to tell them long delightful fairy stories.

Catherine J. Hamilton, 1892, Women Writers,
First Series, p. 203

No book published in Jane Austen's lifetime bore her name on the title-page; she was never lionized by society; she was never two hundred miles from home; she died when forty-two years of age, and it was sixty years before a biography was attempted or asked for. She sleeps in the cathedral at Winchester, and not so very long ago a visitor, on asking the verger to see her grave, was conducted thither, and the verger asked, "Was she anybody in particular? so many folks ask where she's buried, you know!" But this is changed now, for when the verger took me to her grave and we stood by that plain black marble slab, he spoke intelligently of her life and work. And many visitors now go to the cathedral only because it is the resting-place of Jane Austen, who lived a beautiful, helpful life and produced great art, yet knew it not.

Elbert Hubbard, 1897, *Little Journeys to the Homes of Famous Women*, p. 353

Pride and Prejudice (1796-1813)

Read again, and for the third time at least, Miss Austen's very finely written novel of *Pride and Prejudice*. That young lady had a talent for describing the involvements, and feelings, and characters of ordinary life, which is to me the most wonderful I ever met with. The Big Bow-wow strain I can do myslef like any now going; but the exquisite touch, which renders ordinary commonplace things and characters interesting, from the truth of the description and the sentiment, is denied to me. What a pity such a gifted creature died so early.

Sir Walter Scott, 1826, *Diary*, March 14; *Memoirs*, ed. Lockhart, ch. lxviii

Why do you like Miss Austen so very much? I am puzzled on that point. What induced you to say that you would rather have written *Pride and Prejudice,* or *Tom Jones,* than any of the Waverly Novels? I had not seen *Pride and Prejudice* till I read that sentence of yours—then I got the book. And what did I find? An accurate daguerreotyped portrait of a common-place face; a carefully fenced, high-cultivated garden, with neat borders and delicate flowers; but no glance of a bright, vivid physiognomy, no open country, no fresh air, no blue hill, no bonny beck. I should hardly like to live with her ladies and gentlemen, in their elegant but confined houses. . . . She (George Sand) is sagacious and profound—Miss Austen is only shrewd and observant. . . . You say I must familiarize my mind with the fact that "Miss Austen is not a poetess, has no 'Sentiment,' no eloquence, none of the ravishing enthusiasm of poetry."—and then you add, I *must* "learn to acknowledge her as *one of the greatest artists, of the greatest painters of human character,* and one of the writers with the nicest sense of means to an end that ever lived." The last point only will I ever acknowledge. Can there be a great artist without poetry?

Charlotte Brontë, 1848, *Letters to G. H. Lewes, Life of Brontë by Gaskell*, pp. 313, 319

To say nothing of the supreme excellence of the dialogue, there is scarcely a page but has its little gem of exact and polished phrasing; scarcely a chapter which is not adroitly opened or artistically ended; while the whole book abounds in sentences over which the writer, it is plain, must have lingered with patient and loving craftsmanship. . . . Criticism has found little to condemn in the details of this capital novel.

Austin Dobson, 1895, ed., *Pride and Prejudice,* Introduction

Perhaps *Pride and Prejudice* is the only one where the general design can be almost undeservedly praised, but even in this, which is undoubtedly the finest of her novels, there is one serious defect that is absent in none of them, namely, an inadequate sense of dramatic climax. It may be ungenerous to find fault with the author for the perfunctory manner in which she disposes of the minor figures in her story after the main interest has been exhausted. . . . It was entirely inexcusable that she should invariably fail to realise the opportunity of making emotional capital out of the supreme psychological moment of her *dénoûment.*

James Oliphant, 1899, *Victorian Novelists,* pp. 26, 27

One can use the style of Jane Austen as a model for study in the schoolroom. There is repression in every detail; the plot is made simple; the adjective is cut out of the sentences; every detail of finish is subordinated to a requirement of sincerity, to a limited and selected variety. The humor is cultivated, genial; it is the humor of an observer—of a refined, satisfied observer—rather than the humor of a reformer; it is the humor of one who sees the incongruities, but never dreams of questioning the general excellence of the system as a whole. All this is the method of a completed ideal; a method of manifest limits, but within its limits absolutely true. Still further we may claim that this novel is not only an expression of a complete novel form; it is not only an expression of a complete literary method; it is also an embodiment of completed ideals.

Francis Hovey Stoddard, 1900, *The Evolution of
the English Novel,* pp. 53, 55

Sense and Sensibility (1797-1811)

I think the title of the book is misleading to modern ears. Sensibility in Jane Austen's day meant warm, quick feeling, not exaggerated or over keen, as it really does now; and the object of the book, in my belief, is not to contrast the sensibility of Marianne with the sense of Elinor, but to show how with equally warm, tender feelings the one sister could control her sensibility by means of her sense when the other would not attempt it. These qualities come still more prominently forward when Mrs. Dashwood and her daughters have found a home at Barton Cottage. . . . There can be little doubt that in *Sense and Sensibility* we have the first of Jane Austen's revised and finished works, and in several respects it reveals an inexperienced author.

The action is too rapid, and there is a want of dexterity in getting the characters out of their difficulties. Mrs. Jennings is too vulgar, and in her, as in several of the minor characters, we see that Jane Austen had not quite shaken off the turn for caricature, which in early youth she had possessed strongly.

Mrs. Charles Malden, 1889, Jane Austen
(Famous Women), pp. 60, 77

To contend, however, for a moment that the present volume is Miss Austen's greatest, as it was her first published, novel, would be a mere exercise in paradox. There are, who swear by *Persuasion,* there are, who prefer *Emma* and *Mansfield Park;* there is a large contingent for *Pride and Prejudice;* and there is even a section which advocates the pre-eminence of *Northanger Abbey.* But no one, as far as we can remember, has ever put *Sense and Sensibility* first, nor can I believe that its author did so herself. And yet it is she herself who has furnished the standard by which we judge it, and it is by comparison with *Pride and Prejudice,* in which the leading characters are also two sisters, that we assess and depress its merit. The Elinor and Marianne of *Sense and Sensibility* are only inferior when they are contrasted with the Elizabeth and Jane of *Pride and Prejudice,* and even then, it is probably because we personally like the handsome and amiable Jane Bennet rather better than the obsolete survival of the sentimental novel represented by Marianne Dashwood. Darcy and Bingley again are much more "likeable" (to use Lady Queensberry's word) than the colourless Edward Ferrars and the stiff-jointed Colonel Brandon.

Austin Dobson, 1896, Sense and Sensibility, Introduction

Northanger Abbey (1797-1818)

The behaviour of the General in *Northanger Abby,* packing off the young lady without a servant or the common civilities which any bear of a man, not to say gentleman, would have shown, is quite outrageously out of drawing and out of nature.

Maria Edgeworth, 1818, Letters, vol. I, p. 246

I read Dickens' *Hard Times.* One excessively touching, heartbreaking passage and the rest sullen socialism. The evils which he attacks he caricatures grossly, and with little humor. Another book of Pliny's letters. Read *Northanger Abbey,* worth all Dickens and Pliny together. Yet it was the work of a girl. She was certainly not more than twenty-six. Wonderful creature!

Thomas Babington Macaulay, 1854, Journal, Aug. 12;
Life and Letters, ed. Trevelyan

Her style deserves the highest commendation. It has all the form and finish of the eighteenth century, without being in the least degree stilted or unnatural. It has all the tone of good society without being in the least degree insipid. For a specimen of crisp, rich English, combining all the vigour of the masculine with all the delicacy of the feminine style, we suggest the opening chapter of *Northanger Abbey* as a model for any young lady writer of the present age.

T. E. Kebbel, 1870, "Jane Austen," *Fortnightly Review*, vol. 13, p. 193

Mansfield Park (1814)

It is certainly not *incumbent* on you to dedicate your work now in the press to His Royal Highness; but if you wish to do the Regent that honour either now or at any future period I am happy to send you that permission, which need not require any more trouble or solicitation on your part. Your late works, Madam, and in particular *Mansfield Park,* reflect the highest honour on your genius and your principles. In every new work your mind seems to increase its energy and power of discrimination. The Regent has read and admired all your publications.

J. S. Clarke, *Librarian,* 1815; *Letter to Miss Austen,* Nov. 16

How well I recall the greatest literary pleasure of my life, its time and place! A dreary winter's day without, within a generous heat and glow from the flaming grate, and I reclining at my ease on the library lounge, *Mansfield Park* in hand. Then succeed four solid hours of literary bliss, and an absorption so great that when I mechanically close the book at the last page it is only by the severest effort that I come back to the real world of pleasant indoors and bleak outdoors. I was amazed that I, a hardened fiction reader, should be so transported by this gentle tale of Miss Austen's, and yet I enjoyed to the full the after-taste of her perfect realistic art. This first enthusiasm, however, soon abated, and I began to see flaws, to note the prolixity and unevenness of the work, and to feel that it was almost schoolgirlish in tone and sentiment. While the verisimilitude is, indeed, fascinating, the realization is far from profound. And the characters are too one-sided for full human beings—are only puppets, each pulled by a single string. Edmund Bertram is, perhaps, the most woodeny of these marionettes. Lady Bertram, the languid beauty, seems often overdrawn. Mrs. Norris is a perfect busybody, but a pettiness so absolutely consistent at length rouses our suspicions and irritates us. We feel that human nature, outside of the madhouse, does not fulfill the single types so completely. But in Fanny Price we find no flaw or artistic presentment. Here comes before our eyes a real, a free, a complex human being. . . . I am acquainted with no more charming figure in fiction than Fanny; she is so completely, perfectly, deliciously feminine in instinct, feeling, manner and intelligence.

Hiram M. Stanley, 1897, Essays on Literary Art, p. 47

Emma (1816)

We, therefore, bestow no mean compliment upon the author of *Emma* when we say that, keeping close to common incidents, and to such characters as occupy the ordinary walks of life, she has produced sketches of such spirit and originality, that we never miss the excitation which depends upon a narrative of uncommon events, arising from the consideration of minds, manners and sentiments, greatly above our own. In this class she stands almost alone; for the scenes of Miss Edgeworth are laid in higher life, varied by more romantic incident, and by her remarkable power of embodying and illustrating national character. But the author of *Emma* confines herself chiefly to the middling classes of society; her most distinguished characters do not rise greatly above well-bred country gentlemen and ladies; and those which are sketched with most originality and precision, belong to a class rather below that standard.

Sir Walter Scott, 1815, "Emma," Quarterly Review,
vol. 14, p. 193

I have likewise read one of Miss Austen's works—*Emma*—read it with interest and with just the degree of admiration which Miss Austen herself would have thought sensible and suitable. Anything like warmth or enthusiasm—anything energetic, poignant, heart-felt is utterly out of place in commending these works: all such demonstration the authoress would have met with a well-bred sneer, would have calmly scorned as outré and extravagant. She does her business of delineating the surface of the lines of genteel English people curiously well. There is a Chinese fidelity, a miniature delicacy in the painting. She ruffles her reader by nothing vehement, disturbs him by nothing profound. The passions are perfectly unknown to her; she rejects even a speaking acquaintance with that stormy sisterhood. Even to the feelings she vouchsafes no more than an occasional graceful but distant recognition—too frequent converse with them would ruffle the smooth elegance of her progress. Her business is not half so much with the human heart as with the human eyes, mouth, hands, and feet. What sees keenly, speaks aptly, moves flexibly, it suits her to study; but what throbs fast and full, though hidden, what the blood rushed through, what is the unseen seat of life and the sentient target of death—this Miss Austen ignores. She no more, with her mind's eye, beholds the heart of her race than each man, with bodily vision, sees the heart in his heaving breast. Jane Austen was a complete and most sensible lady, but a very incomplete and rather insensible (not senseless) woman. It this is heresy, I cannot help it.

Charlotte Brontë, 1850, Letter to W. S. Williams, April 12;
Charlotte Brontë and her Circle, by Shorter, p. 339

Persuasion (1818)

Persuasion—excepting the tangled, useless histories of the family in the first fifty pages—appears to me, especially in all that relates to poor Anne and her lover, to be exceedingly interesting and natural. The love and the lover admirably well drawn: don't you see Captain Wentworth, or rather don't you in her place feel him taking the boisterous child off her back as she kneels by the sick boy on the sofa? And is not the first meeting after their long separation admirably well done?

Maria Edgeworth, 1818, Letters, vol. I, p. 247

The book shows broader sympathies, deeper observation, and perhaps more perfect symmetry, balance, poise, than the others. The always flexible, unobtrusive style, in which reduction of emphasis is carried sometimes to the verge of equivocation, concealing the author, yet instinct with her presence, in none of her books approximates more nearly to Cardinal Newman's definition—"a thinking out into language." In general, the qualities that appear in the others are in *Persuasion* perhaps more successfully fused than before.

W. B. Shubrick Clymer, 1891, "A Note on Jane Austen,"
Scribner's Magazine, vol. 9, p. 384

Persuasion represents the ripest development of Jane Austen's powers, that latest phase of her thoughts and feelings. It is a novel which, while not wanting in the several excellences of those which preceded it, has a mellower tone and a more finished grace of style than any of the others. It was written at a time when bodily strength had given place to weakness; and although her mind was more active than ever, her physical condition insensibly influenced her thought, giving this latest of her books that deeper note of feeling, that finer touch of sympathy and tenderness, which make *Persuasion* the greatest of all her works.

Oscar Fay Adams, 1891-96, The Story of Jane Austen's Life, p. 254

It was Miss Austen's last story, and has more depth of feeling and pathos than most of hers. . . . The delicate minature painting of the characters in these tales is apt not to be appreciated by the young, and the tone of county society of that day disgusts them; but as they grow older they perceive how much ability and insight is displayed in the work, and esteem the forbearance, sweetness, and self-restraint of such a heroine as Anne.

Charlotte M. Yonge, 1893, "Anne Elliot," *Great Characters of Fiction*, ed. Townsend, pp. 18, 19

GENERAL

Miss Austin's works may be safely recommended, not only as among the most unexceptionable of their class, but as combining, in an eminent degree, instruction with amusement, though without the direct effort at the former, of which we have complained as sometimes defeating its object. For those who cannot or will not *learn* anything from productions of this kind, she has provided entertainment which entitles her to thanks; for mere innocent amusement is in itself a good, when it interferes with no greater; especially as it may occupy the place of some other that may *not* be innocent. The Eastern monarch who proclaimed a reward to him who should deserve a new pleasure, would have deserved well of mankind had he stipulated that it should be blameless. Those, again, who delight in the study of human nature, may improve in the knowledge of it, and in the profitable application of that knowledge by the perusal of such fictions as those before us.

Archbishop Whately, 1821, "*Northanger Abbey* and *Persuasion*," *Quarterly Reiew*, vol. 24, p. 375

The delicate mirth, the gently hinted satire, the feminine, decorous humor of Jane Austen, who, if not the greatest, is surely the most faultless of female novelists. My Uncle Southey and my father had an equally high opinion of her merits, but Mr. Wordsworth used to say that though he admitted that her novels were an admirable copy of life, he could not be interested in productions of that kind; unless the truth of nature were presented to him clarified, as it were, by the pervading light of imagination, it had scarce any attractions in his eyes.

Sara Coleridge, 1834, *Letter to Miss Emily Trevenen,* Aug.; *Memoirs and Letters,* ed. by her Daughter, p. 77

It is the constant manner of Shakspeare to represent the human mind as lying, not under the absolute dominion of one domestic propensity, but under a mixed government, in which a hundred powers balance each other. Admirable as he was in all parts of his art, we most admire him for this, that, while he has left us a greater number of striking portraits than all other dramatists put together, he has scarcely left us a single caricature.

Shakspeare has had neither equal nor second. But among the writers who, in the point which we have noticed, have approached nearest to the manner of the great master, we have no hesitation in placing Jane Austen, a woman of whom England is justly proud. She has given us a multitude of characters, all, in a certain sense, commonplace, all such as we meet every day. Yet they are all as perfectly discriminated from each other as if they were the most eccentric of human beings.

Thomas Babington Macaulay, 1842, "Madame D'Arblay,"
Critical and Miscellaneous Essays

All in all, as far as my information goes, the best judges unanimously prefer Miss Austen to any of her contemporaries of the same order. They reckon her *Sense and Sensibility,* her *Pride and Prejudice,* her *Mansfield Park* and her *Emma* (which novels were published in her lifetime), and also her *Northanger Abbey* and her *Persuasion* (which were published posthumously) as not only better than anything else of the kind written in her day, but also among the most perfect and charming fictions in the language. I have known the most hard-headed men in ecstasies with them; and the only objection I have heard of as brought against them by ladies is, that they reveal too many of their secrets.

David Masson, 1859, *British Novelists and Their Styles,* p. 189

Miss Austen is, of all his successors, the one who most nearly resembles Richardson in the power of impressing reality upon her characters. There is a perfection in the exhibition of Miss Austen's characters which no one else has approached; and truth is never for an instant sacrificed in that delicate atmosphere of satire which pervades her works. . . . She has been accused of writing dull stories about ordinary people. But her supposed ordinary people are really not such very ordinary people. Let any one who is inclined to criticize on this score, endeavour to construct one character from among the ordinary people of his own acquaintance that shall be capable of interesting any reader for ten minutes. It will then be found how great has been the discrimination of Miss Austen in the selection of her characters and how skillful is her treatment in the management of them.

W. F. Pollock, 1860, "British Novelists," *Fraser's Magazine,*
vol. 61, pp. 30, 31

The extraordinary skill which Miss Austen displayed in describing what Scott called "the involvements and feelings and characters of ordinary life," places her as a novelist above her predecessor, Miss Burney. But it is more doubtful whether she is entitled to rank above her contemporary Miss Edgeworth. In Macaulay's opinion Madame de Stael was certainly the first woman of her age; Miss Edgeworth the second; and Miss Austen the third. Yet Miss Austen has one advantage over Miss Edgeworth which is very important. In reading Miss Austen no one ever thinks of the moral of the story, everyone becomes insensibly the better person for perusing it.

Spencer Walpole, 1878, *A History of England from the Conclusion of the Great War in 1815,* vol. 1, p. 378

A distinguished English scholar said to a lecturer who had extolled the tales of Charlotte Brontë, "I am afraid you do not know that Miss Austen is the better novelist." If the scholar had explained doubtless he would have said, in comparing Miss Brontë or George Eliot with Miss Austen,—and the three are the chief of their sex in this form of English literature—that her distinction and superiority lie in her more absolute artistic instinct. She writes wholly as an artist, while George Eliot advocates views, and Miss Brontë's fiery page is often a personal protest. In Miss Austen, on the other hand, there is in kind, but infinitely less in degree, the same clear atmosphere of pure art which we perceive in Shakespeare and Goethe. It is a thread of exceeding fineness with which she draws us, but it is spun of pure gold. There are no great characters, no sweep of passion, no quickening of soul and exaltation of purpose and sympathy, upon her page, but there is the pure pleasure of a Watteau. . . . Miss Austen's art is not less in the choice than in the treatment. She does not, indeed, carve the Moses with Michael Angelo, but she moulds the delicate cup, she cuts the gem.

George William Curtis, 1881, "Editor's Easy Chair," *Harper's Magazine,* vol. 62, p. 309

To-day, more than seventy long years have rolled away since the greater part of them [*Letters*] were written; no one now living can, I think, have any possible just cause of annoyance at their publication, whilst, if I judge rightly, the public never took a deeper or more lively interest in all that concerns Jane Austen than at the present moment. Her works, slow in their progress towards popularity, have achieved it with the greater certainty, and have made an impression the more permanent from its gradual advance. The popularity continues, although the customs and manners which Jane Austen describes have changed and varied so much as to belong in a great measure to another age.

Edward Lord Brabourne, 1884, ed., *Letters of Jane Austen,* Introduction, vol. I, p. xii

It is a curious fact that Paris, to which the works of Jane Austen were lately as unknown as if she were an English painter, has just discovered her existence. Moreover, it has announced that she, and she only, is the founder of that realistic school which is construed to include authors so remote from each other as the French Zola and the American Howells. The most decorous of maiden ladies is thus made to originate the extreme of indecorum; and the good loyal Englishwoman, devoted to Church and King, is made sponsor for the most democratic recognition of persons whom she would have loathed as vulgar. There is something extremely grotesque in the situation; and yet there is much truth in the theory. It certainly looked at one time as if Miss Austen had thoroughly established the claim of her sex to the minute delineation of character and manners, leaving to men the bolder school of narrative romance. . . . But the curious thing is that of the leading novelists in the English tongues to-day it is the men, not the women, who have taken up Miss Austen's work, while the women show more inclination, if not to the "big bow-wow style" of Scott, at least to the novel of plot and narrative. Anthony Trollope among the lately dead, James and Howells among the living, are the lineal successors of Miss Austen. Perhaps it is an old-fashioned taste which leads me to think that neither of these does his work quite so well as she.

Thomas Wentworth Higginson, 1887,
Women and Men, pp. 156, 157

The perfection of Miss Austen's workmanship has been seized upon by unfavourable critics and used as a weapon of offence. She is perfect, they allege, only as some are virtuous, because she has no temptation; she lives in an abject world, dead to poetry, visited by no breath of romance, and is placidly contented with her ant-hill, which she describes with great accuracy and insight. It would be unjust to this type of criticism to interpret it merely as a complaint that one who was of unsurpassed power in comedy and satire did not forego her gifts and take up with romance and tragedy. If it has a meaning worth considering, it means that even the comedy of life has in it shades of pathos and passion to which she is constitutionally blind. And this is to mistake her art. The world of pathos and passion is present in her work by implication; her delicious quiet mirth, so quiet as to be inaudible to gross ears, is stirred by the incongruity between the realities of the world, as she conceives them, and these realities as they are conceived by the puppets. The kingdom of Lilliput has its meaning only when it is seen through the eyes of Gulliver. A rabbit fondling its own harmless face affords no matter of amusement to another rabbit, and Miss Austen has had many readers who have perused her works without a smile. Sympathy with her characters she frequently has, identity never. Not in the high-spirited Elizabeth Bennet, not even in Anne Elliot of *Persuasion,* is the real Jane Austen to be found. She stands forever aloof. Those who wish to enjoy her art must stand aloof too, and must not ask to be hurried through

her novels on a personally conducted tour, with their admirations and dislikes prepared for them.

Walter Raleigh, 1894, The English Novel, p. 263

MATTHEW GREGORY LEWIS
1775-1818

Born, in London, 9 July 1775. At Westminster School, June 1783 to 1790.
Matric., Ch. Ch., Oxford, 27 April 1790; B. A., 1794; M. A., 1797. Visit
to Paris, 1791; to Weimar, autumn 1792-93. Attaché to British Embassy
at the Hague, 1794. M. P., for Hindon, 1796-1802. Play, *The Castle
Spectre,* produced at Drury Lane, 14 Dec. 1797; *The East Indian* (afterwards called; *Rich and Poor*), Drury Lane, 24 April 1799; *Adelmorn,*
Drury Lane, 4 May 1801; *Alphonso,* Covent Garden, 15 Jan. 1802; *The
Captive,* Covent Garden, 1803; *The Harper's Daughter,* Covent Garden,
4 May 1803; *Rugantino,* Covent Garden, 1805; *Adelgitha,* Drury Lane,
1807; *The Wood Demon* (afterwards called *One o'clock*), Covent Garden, 1807; *Venoni,* Drury Lane, 1 Dec. 1808; *Timour the Tartar,* Covent
Garden, 29 April, 1811. In West Indies, Jan. to March 1816. In Italy, May
1816 to Dec. 1817. In West Indies, Feb. to May 1818. Sailed for England,
4 May; died at sea, 14 May 1818. Works: *The Monk,* (anon.), 1796;
Village Virtues (anon.), 1796; *The Castle Spectre,* 1798; *Tales of Terror,*
1799 (?); *The Love of Gain* (from Juvenal), 1799; *The East Indian,* 1799;
Adelmorn, 1801 (2nd edn. same year); *Alfonso, King of Castile,* 1801;
Tales of Wonder (with Scott and Southey), 1801; *Adelgitha,* 1806; *Feudal
Tyrants,* 1806; *Romantic Tales,* 1808; *Venoni,* 1809; *One o'clock,* 1811;
Timour the Tartar, 1812; *Poems,* 1812; *Koenigsmark the Robber* (1815?).
Posthumous: *Raymond and Agnes* (1820?); *The Isle of Devils,* 1827;
Journal of a West Indian Proprietor, 1834; *My Uncle's Garret Window,*
1841. He *translated*: Schiller's *The Minister* (*Kabale and Liebe*), 1798;
Kotzebue's *Rolla,* 1799; Zschokke's *The Bravo of Venice* (Abellino), 1805.
Life: *Life and Correspondence* (2 vols.), 1839.

R. Farquharson Sharp, 1897, A Dictionary of
English Authors, p. 168

See: *The Monk,* ed. Louis F. Peck, 1952; Louis F. Peck, *A Life of
Matthew Lewis,* 1961.

Personal

Talked of poor Monk Lewis: his death was occasioned by taking emetics
for seasickness, in spite of the advice of those about him. He died lying on
the deck. When he was told all hope was over, he sent his man down below
for pen, ink, and paper; asked him to lend him his hat; and upon that, as he
lay, wrote a codicil to his will. Few men, once so talked of, have ever produced so little sensation by their death. He was ruining his Negroes in

Jamaica, they say, by indulgence, for which they suffered severely as soon as his back was turned; but he has enjoined it to his heirs, as one of the conditions of holding his estate, that the Negroes were to have three additional holidays in the year.

Thomas Moore, 1818, *Diary*, Sept. 7; *Memoirs, Journal and Correspondence*, ed. Russell, vol. II, p. 183

Lewis was a good man, a clever man, but a bore. . . . My only revenge or consolation used to be, setting him by the ears with some vivacious person who hated bores, especially, Me de Stael or Hobhouse, for example. But I liked Lewis: he was a jewel of a man had he been better set. I don't mean *personally,* but less *tiresome,* for he was tedious, as well as contradictory to every thing and every body.

Lord Byron, 1821, *Detached Thoughts*

Mat had queerish eyes—they projected like those of some insects, and were flattish on the orbit. His person was extremely small and boyish—he was indeed the least man I ever saw, to be strickly well and neatly made. . . . This boyishness went through life with him. He was a child, and a spoilt child, but a child of high imagination; and so he wasted himself on ghost-stories and German romances. He had the finest ear for rhythm I ever met with—finer than Byron's.

Sir Walter Scott, 1825, *Lockhart's Life of Scott,* ch. ix

When he was still a schoolboy, quarrels arose in his home, which resulted in a separation between his parents, and the pretty, proud, frivolous mother, left her husband's house. Henceforward, the precocious boy became her affectionate friend, protector, and champion, dividing his schoolboy means with her, when her thoughtless expenditure had exhausted her own, writing her long tender letters about all that was going on, sympathising, guiding, deferring to her opinion, confiding all his plans, literary and otherwise, to her. A more touching picture could not be than that of this curious pair, in themselves so imperfect, the faded, extravagant, foolish, but loving mother, and her fat little undergraduate, so sensible, so tender, so constant, so anxious to anticipate all her wants, scarcely betraying the consciousness that these wants are sometimes unreasonable, and while he pours out all his heart to her, still remaining loyally just and faithful to the father, whose liberality he will not hear impugned.

Margaret O. W. Oliphant, 1882, *Literary History of England, XVIII-XIX Century,* vol. III, p. 136

The Monk

There is one publication at the time too peculiar, and too important to be passed over in a general reprehension. There is nothing with which it may be compared. A legislator in our own parliament, a member of the House of Commons of Great Britain, an elected guardian and defender of the laws, the religion, and the good manners of the country, has neither scrupled nor blushed to depict, and to publish to the world, the arts of lewd and systematick seduction, and to thrust upon the nation the most open and unqualified blasphemy against the very code and volume of our religion. And all this, with his name, style, and title, prefixed to the novel or romance called *The Monk*. And one of our publick theatres has allured the publick attention *still more* to this novel, by a scenick representation of an Episode in it.

Thomas James Mathias, 1797, *The Pursuits of Literature,*
Eighth ed., p. 239

Lewis's acquaintance with literature, and especially with the German resuscitations of feudalism, monasticism, ghosts, and hobgoblins, enabled him to fill his museum of atrocities with a large variety of articles of vertu, including the Inquisition, the wandering Jew, and the bleeding nun. But his imagination is gross, boyish, and vulgar, and his horrors rests mainly on a physical basis. He was foolish enough to throw over all the restraints that Mrs. Radcliffe had observed, and to attempt explicit climax.

Walter Raleigh, 1894, *The English Novel,* p. 234

The Monk used, and abused, the now familiar apparatus of Gothic romance. It had Spanish grandees, heroines of dazzling beauty, bravoes and forest banditti, foolish duennas and gabbing domestics, monks, nuns, inquisitors, magic mirrors, enchanted wands, midnight incantations, sorcerers, ghosts, demons; haunted chambers, wainscoted in dark oak; moonlit castles with ruined towers and ivied battlements, whose galleries rang with the shrieks and blasphemies of guilty spirits, and from whose portals issued, when the castle clock tolled one, the spectre of a bleeding nun, with dagger and lamp in hand. There were poisonings, stabbings, and ministrations of sleeping potions; beauties who masqueraded as pages, and pages who masqueraded as wandering harpers; secret springs that gave admittance to winding stairs leading down into the charnel vaults of convents, where erring sisters were immured by cruel prioresses and fed on bread and water among the loathsome relics of the dead. With all this, *The Monk* is a not wholly contemptible work. There is a certain narrative power about it which puts it much above the level of *The Castle of Otranto*. And though it partakes of the stilted dialogue and false conception of character that abound in Mrs. Radcliffe's romances, it has neither the excess of scenery nor of sentiment which distinguishes that very prolix narrator.

Henry A. Beers, 1898, *A History of English Romanticism in the Eighteenth Century,* p. 410

GENERAL

As a man of truly original powers, M. G. Lewis was far behind either Godwin or Coleridge, and stood much on the level of his successor Maturin: but what his imagination lacked in grandeur was made up by energy: he was a high-priest of the intense school. Monstrous and absurd in many things, as were the writings of Lewis, no one could say that they were deficient in interest. Truth and nature, to be sure, he held utterly at arm's-length; but, instead, he had a life-in-death vigour, a spasmodic energy, which answered well for all purposes of astonishment.

D. M. Moir, 1850-51, *Sketches of the Poetical Literature of the Past Half-Century,* p. 18

One of his best novels was *The Bravo of Venice,* published in 1804. . . . He contrives to make this hero respected, even admired to a degree; and artfully employs the poetry and witchery of Venice, that unique city in the world,—half land, half sea,—to give a tinge of appropriateness and even congruity to his wild romance. The *Bravo* is as good a specimen of the improbable and yet conceivable as any work of fiction earlier than Scott.

William Edward Simonds, 1894, *An Introduction to the Study of English Fiction*

Nothing can be worse in kind, and nothing, of its kind, can well be better than *Alonso the Brave.* It was Lewis's *rôle* to fling the orts and refuse of German Romanticism about the soil of England. It was his luck rather than merit to have once or twice thrown them where they nourished good seed, and now and then to have grasped a flower among his handfuls of treasured weeds. His false ballads helped to elicit the true ones of Scott, and the respectable ones of Southey, and he introduced to the author of *Manfred* what he doubtless regarded as that capital "Tale of Wonder," Goethe's *Faust.*

C. H. Herford, 1897, *The Age of Wordsworth,* p. 94

THE NINETEENTH CENTURY:
Romanticism

JOHN KEATS
1795-1821

Born, in London 31 Oct. 1795. At school at Enfield, at irregular periods between 1801 and 1810. His mother removed to Edmonton, 1806. Apprenticed to surgeon at Edmonton, 1810. To London 1814. Studied medicine at St. Thomas's and Guy's Hospitals. Appointed Dresser at Guy's, March 1816. Licentiate of Apothecaries' Hall, 25 July 1816. Contrib. to *The Examiner,* 1816-17. Friendship with Leigh Hunt and Haydon begun about this time. Abandoned medical career, 1817. Visit to Oxford, Sept. to Oct. 1817. Contrib. poems to *The Champion,* 1817; wrote dramatic criticism for it, Dec. 1817 to Jan. 1818. At this period resided mainly with his brothers at Hampstead. Walking tour with Charles Armitage Brown in Northern England and Scotland, June to Aug. 1818. Engaged to Fanny Brawne, Dec. 1818. One brother married and went to America, June 1818; the other died, Dec. 1818. Lived at Shanklin and Winchester successively during early part of 1819; settled in Westminster, Oct. 1819. Contrib. "Ode to a Nightingale" to *Annals of the Fine Arts,* 1819; "La Belle Dame Sans Merci" to *The Indicator,* 1820. Consumption set in, Feb. 1820. Sailed with Joseph Severn to Italy, Sept. 1820; arrived at Naples in Oct.; at Rome in Nov. Died, in Rome, 23 Feb. 1821. Buried in Old Protestant Cemetery there. WORKS: *Poems,* 1817; *Endymion,* 1818; *Lamia; Isabella; the Eve of St. Agnes,* 1820. POSTHUMOUS: *Life, Letters and Literary Remains,* ed. by R. Monckton Milnes, 1848; *Letters to Fanny Brawne,* ed. by H. Buxton Forman, 1878; *Letters,* ed. by H. Buxton Forman, 1895. COLLECTED WORKS: ed. by H. Buxton Forman (4 vols.), 1883. LIFE: by Lord Houghton, revised edn. 1867; by W. M. Rossetti, 1887; by Sidney Colvin, 1887.

R. Farquharson Sharp, 1897, *A Dictionary of English Authors,* p. 154

SEE: *Complete Works,* ed. H. Buxton Forman, 1900-1, 5 v., rev. by M. B. Forman as *Poetical Works and Other Writings,* 1938-39, 8 v.; *Poems,* ed. Ernest de Selincourt, 1905, Fifth Edition 1926; *Poetical Works,* ed. H. W. Garrod, 1939, rev. 1956 (OSA); *Complete Poems and Selected Letters,* ed. C. D. Thorpe, 1935; *Letters,* ed. M. B. Forman, 1930, 1935, 1947; *Letters, 1814-1821,* ed. Hyder E. Rollins, 1958, 2 v.; *The Keats Circle: Letters and Papers, 1816-1878,* ed. Hyder E. Rollins, 1948, 2 v.; Sidney Colvin, *John Keats: His Life and Poetry,* 1917; Amy Lowell, *John Keats,* 1925; Walter Jackson Bate, *John Keats,* 1963; Aileen Ward, *John Keats, The Making of a Poet,* 1963; J. Middleton Murry, *Studies in Keats,* 1939 (rev. 1949 as *The Mystery of Keats*); E. R. Wasserman, *The Finer Tone: Keats' Major Poems,* 1953.

PERSONAL

He is gone. He died with the most perfect ease—he seemed to go to sleep. On the 23rd, about four, the approaches of death came on. "Severn—I— lift me up. I am dying—I shall die easy. Don't be frightened: be firm, and thank God it has come." I lifted him up in my arms. The phlegm seemed boiling in his throat, and increased until eleven, when he gradually sunk into death, so quiet that I still thought he slept. I cannot say more now. I am broken down by four nights' watching, no sleep since, and my poor Keats gone. Three days since the body was opened: the lungs were completely gone. The doctors could not imagine how he had lived these two months. I followed his dear body to the grave on Monday [February 26th], with many English. . . . The letters I placed in the coffin with my own hand.

Joseph Severn, 1821, *Journal,* Feb. 27

The genius of the lamented person to whose memory I have dedicated these unworthy verses was not less delicate and fragile than it was beautiful; and where canker-worms abound, what wonder if its young flower was blighted in the bud? The savage criticism on his *Endymion* which appeared in the *Quarterly Review* produced the most violent effect on his susceptible mind; the agitation thus originated ended in a rupture of a bloodvessel in the lungs; a rapid consumption ensued; and the succeeding acknowledgements from more candid critics of the true greatness of his powers were ineffectual to heal the wound thus wantonly inflicted.

Percy Bysshe Shelley, 1821, *Adonais,* Preface

Keats was a victim to personal abuse and the want of power to bear it. . . . He began life full of hope. . . . He expected the world to bow at once to his talents, as his friends had done. . . . Goaded by ridicule, he distrusted himself and flew to dissipation. For six weeks he was hardly ever sober. . . . He told me that he once covered his tongue and throat, as far as he could reach, with Cayenne pepper, in order to enjoy "the delicious coolness of claret in all its glory." . . . He had great enthusiasm for me, and so had I for him, but he grew angry latterly because I shook my head at his proceedings. I told him, I begged of him to bend his genius to some definite object. I remonstrated on his absurd dissipation, but to no purpose. The last time I saw him was at Hampstead, lying on his back in a white bed, helpless, irritable, and hectic. He had a book, and enraged at his own feebleness, seemed as if he were going out of the world with a contempt for this, and no hopes of a better. He muttered as I stood by him that if he did not recover, he

would "cut his throat." I tried to calm him, but to no purpose. . . . Poor
dear Keats!

Benjamin Robert Haydon, 1821, *Letter to Miss Mitford,*
Apr. 21; *Life, Letters and Table Talk,*
ed. Stoddard, pp. 207, 208, 209

One night at eleven o'clock, he came into the house in a state that looked
like fierce intoxication. Such a state in him, I knew, was impossible; it therefore was the more fearful. I asked hurriedly, "What is the matter? you are
fevered." "Yes, yes," he answered, "I was on the outside of the stage this
bitter day till I was severely chilled—but now I don't feel it. Fevered!—of
course, a little." He mildly and instantly yielded, a property in his nature
towards any friend, to my request that he should go to bed. I followed with
the best immediate remedy in my power. I entered his chamber as he leapt
into bed. On entering the cold sheets, before his head was on the pillow, he
slightly coughed, and I heard him say, "That is blood from my mouth." I
went towards him; he was examining a single drop of blood upon the sheet.
"Bring me the candle, Brown, and let me see this blood." After regarding
it steadfastly, he looked up in my face with a calmness of countenance that
I can never forget, and said, "I know the colour of that blood—it is arterial
blood—I cannot be deceived in that colour—that drop of blood is my death-
warrant—I must die."

Charles Armitage Brown, 1841? *Houghton MSS*

He had a soul of noble integrity, and his common sense was a conspicuous
part of his character. Indeed his character was, in the best sense, manly. . . .
With his friends, a sweeter tempered man I never knew than was John
Keats. Gentleness was indeed his proper characteristic, without one particle
of dullness, or insipidity, or want of spirit. . . . In his letters he talks of
suspecting everybody. It appeared not in his conversation. On the contrary,
he was uniformly the apologist for poor frail human nature, and allowed
for people's faults more than any man I ever knew, and especially for the
faults of his friends. But if any act of wrong or oppression, of fraud or
falsehood, was the topic, he rose into sudden and animated indignation.

Benjamin Bailey, 1848, *Letter to Lord Houghton, Houghton MSS*

Keats, when he died, had just completed his four-and-twentieth year. He
was under the middle height; and his lower limbs were small in comparison
with the upper, but neat and well-turned. His shoulders were very broad for
his size; he had a face in which energy and sensibility were remarkably
mixed up; and eager power, checked and made patient by ill health. Every
feature was at once strongly cut, and delicately alive. If there was any

faulty expression it was in the mouth, which was not without something of a character of pugnacity. The face was rather long than otherwise; the upper lip projected a little over the under; the chin was bold, the cheeks sunken; the eyes mellow and glowing; large, dark, and sensitive. At the recital of a noble action, or a beautiful thought, they would suffuse with tears, and his mouth trembled. In this there was ill health as well as imagination, for he did not like these betrayals of emotion; and he had great personal as well as moral courage. He once chastised a butcher, who had been insolent, by a regular stand-up fight. His hair, of a brown color, was fine, and hung in natural ringlets. The head was a puzzle for the phrenologists, being remarkably small in the skull; a singularity which he had in common with Byron and Shelley, whose hats I could not get on. Keats was sensible of the disproportion above noticed, between his upper and lower extremities; and he would look at his hand, which was faded and swollen in the veins, and say that it was the hand of a man of fifty. He was a seven months' child.

Leigh Hunt, 1850-60, Autobiography, vol. II, ch. xvi

A lady, whose feminine acuteness of perception is only equalled by the vigour of her understanding, thus describes Keats as he appeared about this time (1818) at Hazlitt's lectures:—"His eyes were large and blue, his hair auburn; he wore it divided down the centre, and it fell in rich masses on each side his face; his mouth was full, and less intellectual than his other features. His countenance lives in my mind as one of singular beauty and brightness; it had the expression as if he had been looking on some glorious sight. The shape of his face had not the squareness of a man's, but more like some women's faces I have seen—it was so wide over the forehead and so small at the chin. He seemed in perfect health, and with life offering all things that were precious to him."

Richard Monckton Milnes, 1869, ed., The Poetical Works
of John Keats, Memoir, p. xxvii

In the early part of his school-life John gave no extraordinary indications of intellectual character; but it was remembered of him afterwards, that there was ever present a determined and steady spirit in all his undertakings: I never knew it misdirected in his required pursuit of study. He was a most orderly scholar. . . . Not the less beloved was he for having a highly pugnacious spirit, which, when roused, was one of the most picturesque exhibitions—off the stage—I ever saw. One of the transports of that marvellous actor, Edmund Kean—whom, by the way, he idolized—was its nearest resemblance; and the two were not very dissimilar in face and figure. . . . His passion at times was almost ungovernable; and his brother George, being considerably the taller and stronger, used frequently to hold him down by main force, laughing when John was in one of his moods, and was endeavoring to beat him. It was all, however, a wisp-of-straw conflagration; for he had an intensely tender affection for his brothers, and proved it upon the most trying occasions. He was not merely the "favorite of all," like a pet prizefighter, for his terrier courage; but his high-mindedness, his utter unconsciousness of a mean motive, his placability, his generosity, wrought so general a feeling in his behalf, that I never heard a word of disapproval from any one, superior or equal, who had known him. . . . The character and expression of Keats's features would arrest even the casual passenger in the street. . . . Reader, alter in your copy of the *Life of Keats,* vol. i., page 103, "eyes" *light hazel,* "hair" *lightish brown and wavy.*

Charles Cowden Clarke, 1874-78, "Keats," Recollections of
Writers, pp. 122, 123, 133, 154

I confess there is something in the personality of Keats, some sort of semiphysical aroma wafted from it, which I cannot endure; and I fear these letters will be very redolent of this. What a curious thing is that undefinable flavour of personality—suggestion of physical quality, odour of the man in his unconscious and spontaneous self-determination, which attracts or repels so powerfully, and is the very root of love or dislike.

John Addington Symonds, 1878, Letter to Edmund Gosse,
Feb. 16; quoted in Horatio F. Brown, John Addington Symonds,
1903, vol. II, p. 147

Unluckily Keats died, and his death was absurdly attributed to a pair of reviews which may have irritated him, and which were coarse and cruel even for that period of robust reviewing. But Keats knew very well the value of these critiques, and probably resented them not so much more than a football player resents being "hacked" in the course of the game. He was very willing to see Byron and Wordsworth "trounced," and as ready as Peter Corcoran in his friend's poem to "take punishment" himself. The character of Keats was plucky, and his estimate of his own genius was perfectly sane. He knew that he was in the thick of a literary "scrimmage," and he was not the man to flinch or to repine at the consequences.

Andrew Lang, 1889, Letters on Literature, p. 197

FANNY BRAWNE

Mr. Severn tells me that Mrs. and Miss Brawne felt the keenest regret that they had not followed him and Keats to Rome; and, indeed, I understand that there was some talk of a marriage taking place before the departure.

Even twenty years after Keat's death, when Mr. Severn returned to England, the bereaved lady was unable to receive him on account of the extreme painfulness of the associations connected with him.

> Harry Buxton Forman, 1877, *Letters of John Keats to Fanny Brawne,* Introduction, p. lxii

Her ways and presence at first irritated and after a little while completely fascinated him. From his first sarcastic account of her written to his brother, as well as from Severn's mention of her likeness to the draped figure in Titian's picture of Sacred and Profane Love, and from the full-length silhouette of her that has been preserved, it is not difficult to realize her aspect and presence. A brisk and blooming very young beauty, of the far from uncommon English hawk blonde type, with aquiline nose and retreating forehead, sharp-cut nostril and gray-blue eye, a slight, shapely figure, rather short than tall, a taking smile, and good hair, carriage and complexion— such was Fanny Brawne externally, but of her character we have little means of judging. She was certainly high-spirited, inexperienced, and self-confident; as certainly, though kind and constant to her lover, in spite of prospects that before long grew dark, she did not fully realise what manner of man he was. Both his men and women friends, without thinking unkindly of her, were apparently of one opinion in holding her no mate for him either in heart or mind, and in regarding the attachment as unlucky.

> Sidney Colvin, 1887, *Keats (English Men of Letters),* p. 129

Though she was inexperienced and self-confident, she was constant and kind to her lover in spite of prospects which soon grew very dark. She never, however, fully realized what manner of man he was, though some of the things said by his friends, who did not approve of her or of his frenzy of passion for her, were most unkind and entirely unjustified. As I have been guilty in previous writings of repeating at least one such unkind remark, I most cheerfully acknowledge that better evidence has convinced me that she loved Keats dearly, and when he was dead tenderly cherished his memory.

> John Gilmer Speed,* 1895, "The Real John Keats," *McClure's Magazine,* vol. 5, p. 468

LOVE LETTERS

The thirty-seven letters of Keats to Fanny Brawne I have read with great pain inasmuch as from them I now understand *for the first* time the sufferings and death of the Poet.—He did not confide to me this serious pas-

---

*Grand-nephew of Keats.

sion and it now seems to me *but for this cause he might have lived many years*—I can now understand his want of courage to speak as it was consuming him in body and mind. . . . Perhaps I view the work more painfully as I was not aware of such torment existing in the Poet's mind and as I saw him struck down from health and vigour to sickness and death you will not wonder at my emotion now that I find the fatal cause.

Joseph Severn, 1878, *Letter to Harry Buxton Forman,* Feb. 5;
The Poetical Works and Other Writings of John Keats,
vol. IV, pp. 218, 219

The character of the letters is such as obtains in similar productions, only it is intensified a thousand-fold. I know of nothing comparable with them in English literature—know nothing that is so unselfish, so longing, so adoring —nothing that is so mad, so pitiful, so utterly weak and wretched. John Keats was a great genius, but he had not one particle of common-sense— for himself. Few men of genius ever do have; it is only the Master Shakespeare and the Masters Milton and Wordsworth, who are able to cope with the world. Why, a boy might have told Keats that the way to woo and win a woman was not to bare his heart before her, as he did before Fanny Brawne, and not to let her know, as he did, that he was her captive. If he had had the least glimmer of common-sense, he never would have surrendered at discretion. . . . Miss Fanny Brawne made John Keats ridiculous in the eyes of his friends in his lifetime, and now she (through her representatives) makes him ridiculous in the eyes of the world. She (and they) have had fifty-seven years in which to think about it—she forty-four years as maid and wife; they thirteen years as her children. Why did she keep his letters all those years? What *could* she keep them for but to minister to her vanity, and to remind her that once upon a time a crazy young English poet was desperately in love with her, was her captive and her slave? What else could she keep them for? She revered the memory of Keats, did she? This is how she revered it!

Richard Henry Stoddard, 1878, "John Keats and Fanny Brawne,"
Appleton's Journal, vol. 19, pp. 381, 382

A man who writes love-letters in this strain is probably predestined, one may observe, to misfortune in his love-affairs; but that is nothing. The complete enervation of the writer is the real point for remark. We have the tone, or rather the entire want of tone, the abandonment of all reticence and all dignity, of the merely sensuous man, of the man who "is passion's slave." Nay, we have them in such wise that one is tempted to speak even as *Blackwood* or the *Quarterly* were in the old days wont to speak, one is tempted to say that Keats's love-letter is the lover-letter of a surgeon's apprentice. It has in its relaxed self-abandonment something underbred and ignoble, as of a youth ill brought up, without the training which teaches us that we must put some constraint upon our feelings, and upon the expression of them. It is the sort of love-letter of a surgeon's apprentice which one might hear read out in a breach of promise case, or in the Divorce Court. The sensuous man speaks in it, and the sensuous man of a badly bred and badly trained sort. That many who are themselves, also, badly bred and badly trained should enjoy it, and should even think it a beautiful and characteristic production of him whom they call their "lovely and beloved Keats," does not make it better.

> Matthew Arnold, 1880, *The English Poets,* ed. Ward,
> vol. IV, p. 429

While admitting that neither his love-letters nor the last piteous outcries of his wailing and shrieking agony would ever have been made public by merciful or respectful editors, we must also admit that, if they ought never to have been published, it is no less certain that they ought never to have been written; that a manful kind of man or even a manly sort of boy, in his love-making or in his suffering, will not howl and snivel after such a lamentable fashion.

> Algernon Charles Swinburne, 1882-86, "Keats,"
> *Encyclopædia Britannica; Miscellanies,* p. 212

Keats seems to me, throughout his love-letters, unbalanced, wayward, and profuse; he exhibts great fervour of temperament, and abundant caressingness, without the inner depth of tenderness and regard. He lives in his mistress, for himself. As the letters pass further and further into the harsh black shadows of disease, he abandons all self-restraint, and lashes out right and left; he wills that his friends should have been disloyal to him, as the motive of his being disloyal to them. To make allowance for all this is possible, and even necessary; but to treat it as not needing that any allowance should be made would seem to me futile.

> William Michael Rossetti, 1887, *Life of John Keats*
> (*Great Writers*), p. 45

Endymion (1818)

Knowing within myself the manner in which this Poem has been produced, it is not without a feeling of regret that I make it public. What manner I mean, will be quite clear to the reader, who must soon perceive great inexperience, immaturity, and every error denoting a feverish attempt, rather than a deed accomplished.

> John Keats, 1818, *Endymion,* Preface

Reviewers have been sometimes accused of not reading the works which they affected to criticise. On the present occasion we shall anticipate the author's complaint, and honestly confess that we have not read his work. Not that we have been wanting in our duty—far from it—indeed, we have made efforts almost as superhuman as the story itself appears to be, to get through it; but with the fullest stretch of our perseverance, we are forced to confess that we have not been able to struggle beyond the first of the four books of which this Poetic Romance consists. We should extremely lament this want of energy, or whatever it may be, on our parts, were it not for one consolation—namely, that we are no better acquainted with the meaning of the book through which we have so painfully toiled, than we are with that of the three which we have not looked into. It is not that Mr. Keats (if that be his real name, for we almost doubt that any man in his senses would put his real name to such a rhapsody) it is not, we say, that the author has not powers of language, rays of fancy, and gleams of genius:—he has all these; but he is unhappily a disciple of the new school of what has been somewhere called Cockney poetry; which may be defined to consist of the most incongruous ideas in the most uncouth language. . . . Of the story we have been able to make out but little; it seems to be mythological, and probably relates to the loves of Diana and Endymion; but of this, as the scope of the work has altogether escaped us, we cannot speak with any degree of certainty; and must therefore content ourselves with giving some instances of its diction and versification.

William Gifford, 1818, "Keats's *Endymion*," *Quarterly Review,*
vol. 19, pp. 204, 205

Warmly as I admire the poetry of Keats, I can imagine that an intelligent man might read the *Endymion* with care, yet think that it was not genuine poetry; that it showed a sheer misuse of abundant fancy and rhythmical power. For its range is narrow; like the artificial comedy it has a world of its own, and this world is more harmonious within itself, made up of light rich materials; but it is not deep enough or wide enough to furnish satisfaction for the general heart and mind.

Henry Nelson Coleridge, 1843, ed., *S. T. Coleridge's
Biographia Literaria*, Introduction

As reasonably, and as hopefully in regard to human sympathies, might a man undertake an epic poem upon the loves of two butterflies. The modes of existence in the two parties to the love-fable of the *Endymion,* their relations to each other and to us, their prospects finally, and the obstacles to the *instant* realisation of these prospects,—all these things are more vague and incomprehensible than the reveries of an oyster. Still, the unhappy subject, and its unhappy expansion, must be laid to the account of childish years and childish inexperience.

Thomas De Quincey, 1845-57, "Gilfillan's Literary Portraits,"
Works, ed. Masson, vol. XI, p. 392

Let any man of literary accomplishment, though without the habit of writing poetry, or even much taste for reading it, open *Endymion* at random, (to say nothing of the later and more perfect poems), and examine the characteristics of the page before him, and I shall be surprised if he does not feel that the whole range of literature hardly supplies a parallel phenomenon. As a psychological curiosity, perhaps Chatterton is more wonderful; but in him the immediate ability displayed is rather the full comprehension of and identification with the old model, than the effluence of creative genius. In Keats, on the contrary, the originality in the use of his scanty materials, his expansion of them to the proportions of his own imagination, and above all, his field of diction and expression extending so far beyond his knowledge of literature, is quite inexplicable by any of the ordinary processes of mental education. If his classical learning had been deeper, his seizure of the full spirit of Grecian beauty would have been less surprising; if his English reading had been more extensive, his inexhaustible vocabulary of picturesque and mimetic words could more easily be accounted for; but here is a surgeon's apprentice, with the ordinary culture of the middle classes, rivalling in æsthetic perceptions of antique life and thought the most careful scholars of his time and country, and reproducing these impressions in a phraseology as complete and unconventional as if he had mastered the whole history and the frequent variations of the English tongue, and elaborated a mode of utterance commensurate with his vast ideas.

Richard Monckton Milnes (Lord Houghton), 1848-67,
Life and Letters of John Keats, p. 330

Luscious and luxuriant in intention— for I cannot suppose that Keats aimed at being exalted or ideal—the poem becomes mawkish in result: he said so himself, and we need not hesitate to repeat it. Affectations, conceits, and puerilities, abound, both in thought and in diction: however willing to be pleased, the reader is often disconcerted and provoked. The number of clever things said cleverly, of rich things richly, and of fine things finely, is however abundant and superabundant; and on one who peruses *Endymion* with a true sense for poetic endowment and handling can fail to see that it is peculiarly the work of a poet.

William Michael Rossetti, 1887, *Life of John Keats*
(*Great Writers*), p. 178

Lamia (1820)

Perhaps there is no poet, living or dead, except Shakspeare, who can pretend to anything like the felicity of epithet which characterizes Keats. One word or phrase is the essence of a whole description or sentiment. It is like the dull substance of the earth struck through by electric fires, and converted into veins of gold and diamonds. For a piece of perfect and inventive description, that passage from *Lamia,* where, Lycius gone to bid the guests to his wedding, Lamia, in her uneasy excitement, employs herself and her demon powers in adorning her palace, is unrivaled.

William Howitt, 1846, *Homes and Haunts of the
Most Eminent British Poets,* vol. I, p. 482

No one can deny the truth of Keats's own criticism on *Lamia* when he says, "I am certain there is that sort of fire in it which must take hold of people in some way—give them either pleasant or unpleasant sensation." There is, perhaps, nothing in all his writing so vivid, or that so burns itself in upon the mind, as the picture of the serpent-woman awaiting the touch of Hermes to transform her, followed by the agonized process of the transformation itself. . . . This thrilling vividness of narration in particular points, and the fine melodious vigour of much of the verse, have caused some students to give *Lamia* almost the first, if not the first, place among Keats's narrative poems. But surely for this it is in some parts too feverish and in others too unequal. It contains descriptions not entirely successful, as, for instance, that of the palace reared by Lamia's magic, which will not bear comparison with other and earlier dream-palaces of the poet's building.

Sidney Colvin, 1887, *Keats (English Men of Letters),* p. 166

The Eve of St. Agnes (1820)

To the description before us, it would be a great injury either to add or diminish. It falls at once gorgeously and delicately upon us, like the colours of the painted glass. Nor is Madeline hurt by all her encrusting jewelry and rustling silks. Her gentle, unsophisticated heart is in the midst, and turns them into so many ministrants to her loveliness.

Leigh Hunt, 1820, *The Indicator*

The glory and charm of the poem is in the description of the fair maiden's antique chamber, and of all that passes in that sweet and angel-guarded sanctuary: every part of which is touched with colours at once rich and delicate—and the whole chastened and harmonised, in the midst of its gorgeous distinctness, by a pervading grace and purity, that indicate not less clearly the exaltation than the refinement of the author's fancy.

> Francis, Lord Jeffrey, 1820-44, "Keats's Poems,"
> *Contributions to the Edinburgh Review,* vol. III, p. 116

What a gorgeous gallery of poetic pictures that *Eve of St. Agnes* forms, and yet how slim the tissue that lies below! How thin the canvas on which the whole is painted! For vigorous sense, one deep-thoughted couplet of Dryden would make the whole kick the beam. And yet what can be more exquisite in their way than those pictures of the young poet! Even the old worn out gods of Grecian mythology become life-like when he draws them. They revive in his hands, and become vital once more.

> Hugh Miller, 1856-62, *Essays,* p. 452

The Eve of St. Agnes, aiming at no doubtful success, succeeds in evading all casual difficulty in the line of narrative; with no shadow of pretence to such interest as may be derived from stress of incident or depth of sentiment, it stands out among all other famous poems as a perfect and unsurpassable study in pure color and clear melody—a study in which the figure of Madeline brings back upon the mind's eye, if not as moonlight recalls a sense of sunshine, the nuptial picture of Marlow's Hero, and the sleeping presence of Shakespeare's Imogen. Besides this poem should always be placed the less famous but not less precious *Eve of St. Mark* a fragment unexcelled for the simple perfection of its perfect simplicity, exquisite alike in suggestion and in accomplishment.

> Algernon Charles Swinburne, 1882-86, *Keats,*
> *Encyclopædia Britannica; Miscellanies,* p. 213

The Eve of St. Agnes is *par excellence* the poem of "glamour." It means next to nothing; but means that little so exquisitely, and in so rapt a mood of musing or of trance, that it tells as an intellectual no less than a sensuous restorative. Perhaps no reader has ever risen from "The Eve of St. Agnes" dissatisfied. After a while he can question the grounds of his satisfaction, and may possibly find them wanting; but he has only to peruse the poem again, and the same spell is upon him.

> William Michael Rossetti, 1887, *Life of John Keats*
> (*Great Writers*), p. 183

Pure and passionate, surprising by its fine excess of color and melody, sensuous in every line, yet free from the slightest taint of sensuality, is unforgettable and unsurpassable as the dream of first love.

> Henry Van Dyke, 1895, "The Influence of Keats,"
> *The Century,* vol. 50, p. 912

Hyperion (1820)

His fragment of *Hyperion* seems actually inspired by the Titans, and is as sublime as Æschylus.

> Lord Byron, 1821, *Observations upon an Article in*
> *Blackwood's Magazine*, note

Keat's new volume has arrived to us, and the fragment called *Hyperion* promises for him that he is destined to become one of the first writers of the age.

> Percy Bysshe Shelley, 1820, *Correspondence of*
> *Leigh Hunt*, vol. I, p. 158

Though there are passages of some force and grandeur, it is sufficiently obvious, from the specimen before us, that the subject is too far removed from all the sources of human interest, to be successfully treated by any modern author. Mr. Keats has unquestionably a very beautiful imagination, a perfect car for harmony, and a great familiarity with the finest diction of English poetry; but he must learn not to misuse or misapply these advantages; and neither to waste the good gifts of nature and study on intractable themes, nor to luxuriate too recklessly on such as are more suitable.

> Francis, Lord Jeffrey, 1820-44, "Keats's Poems,"
> *Contributions to the Edinburgh Review*, vol. III, p. 119

The very midsummer madness of affectation, of false vapoury sentiment, and of fantastic effeminacy, seemed to me combined in Keats's *Endymion*, when I first saw it, near the close of 1821. The Italian poet Marino had been reputed the greatest master of gossamery affectation in Europe. But *his* conceits showed the palest of rosy blushes by the side of Keats's bloody crimson. Naturally I was discouraged at the moment from looking further. But about a week later, by pure accident, my eye fell upon his *Hyperion*. The first feeling was that of incredulity that the two poems could, under change of circumstances or lapse of time, have emanated from the same mind. The *Endymion* trespasses so strongly against good sense and just feeling that, in order to secure its pardon, we need the whole weight of the imperishable *Hyperion*, which, as Mr. Gilfillan truly says, "is the greatest of poetical torsos." The first belongs essentially to the vilest collection of waxwork filigree or gilt gingerbread, the other presents the majesty, the austere beauty, and the simplicity of a Grecian temple enriched with Grecian sculpture.

> Thomas De Quincey, 1845-57, *Gilfillan's Literary Portraits*,
> *Works*, ed. Masson, vol. XI, p. 389

As a *story*, *Endymion* deserves all that its worst enemies ever said of it. *Hyperion* shows a remarkable advance, but it is well that Keats left it a fragment, for it is plain that, with his effeminate notion of Apollo, he could never have invented any kind of action which would have interested the reader in learning how the old Titan Sun-God was turned out of his kingdom.

> William John Courthope, 1885, *The Liberal Movement in English Literature,* p. 184

The opening promises well; we are conscious at once of a new musical blank verse, a music both sweet and strong, alive with imagination and tenderness. There and throughout the poem are passages in which Keats, without losing his own individuality, is as good as Milton, where Milton is as good as Virgil; and such passages rank with the best things that Keats ever did; but in other places he seems a little overshadowed by Milton, while definite passages of the *Paradise Lost* are recalled, and in some places the imitation seems frigid.

> Robert Bridges, 1894, *Poems of John Keats,* ed. Drury, Introduction, vol. I, p. xli

Odes (1820)

I have come to that pass of admiration for him now, that I dare not read him, so discontented he makes me with my own work; but others must not leave unread, in considering the influence of trees upon the human soul, that marvellous ode to Psyche.

> John Ruskin, 1860, *Modern Painters,* pt. vi, ch. ix

If one may say a word *obiter,* out of the fulness of one's heart—I am often inclined to think for all-in-all,—that is, for thoughts most mortally compacted, for words which come forth, each trembling and giving off light like a morning-star, and for the pure beauty of the spirit and strength and height of the spirit,—which, I say, for all-in-all, I am often inclined to think [*Ode on Melancholy*], reaches the highest height yet touched in the lyric line.

> Sidney Lanier, 1881, *The English Novel,* p. 95

The *Ode to a Nightingale,* one of the finest masterpieces of human work in all time and for all ages.

> Algernon Charles Swinburne, 1882-86, "Keats," *Encyclopædia Britannica; Miscellanies,* p. 211

I make bold to name one of our shorter English lyrics that still seems to me, as it seemed to me ten years ago, the nearest to perfection, the one I would surrender last of all. What should this be save the *Ode to a Night-*

ingale, so faultless in its varied unity and in the cardinal qualities of language, melody, and tone? A strain that has a dying fall; music wedded to ethereal passion, to the yearning that floods all nature.

Edmund Clarence Stedman, 1884, "Keats,"
The Century, vol. 27, p. 600

The *Ode on a Grecian Urn* wonderfully enshrines the poet's kinship with Greece, and with the spirit of her worship. There is all the Greek measure and moderation about it also; a calm and classic grace, with severe loveliness of outline. In form it is perfect. There is an exquisiteness of expression—not that which is often mistakenly so designated, but a translucence, as of silver air, or limpid water, that both reveals and glorifies all fair plants, or pebbles, or bathing lights.

Roden Noel, 1886, "Keats," *Essays on Poetry and Poets,* p. 169

In the five odes there is naturally some diversity in the degrees of excellence. . . . Considered intellectually, we might form a kind of symphony out of them, and arrange it thus—1, "Grecian Urn;" 2, "Psyche;" 3, "Autumn;" 4, "Melancholy;" 5, "Nightingale;" and, if Keats had left us nothing else, we should have in this symphony an almost complete picture of his poetic mind, only omitting, or representing deficiently, that more instinctive sort of enjoyment which partakes of gaiety. Viewing all these wondrous odes together, the predominant quality which we trace in them is an extreme susceptibility to delight, close-linked with after thought—pleasure with pang—or that poignant sense of ultimates, a sense delicious and harrowing, which clasps the joy in sadness, and feasts upon the very sadness in joy. The emotion throughout is the emotion of beauty. Beauty intensely perceived, intensely loved, questioned of its secret like the sphinx, imperishable and eternal, yet haunted (as it were) by its own ghost, the mortal throes of the human soul. As no poet had more capacity for enjoyment than Keats, so none exceeded him in the luxury of sorrow. Few also exceeded him in the sense of the one moment irretrievable; but this conception in its fulness belongs to the region of morals yet more than of sensation, and the spirit of Keats was almost an alien in the region of morals.

William Michael Rossetti, 1887, *Life of John Keats*
(*Great Writers*), p. 194

SONNETS

"Nature's Eremite:" like a solitary thing in Nature.—This beautiful Sonnet was the last word of a poet deserving the title "marvellous boy" in a much higher sense than Chatterton. If the fulfilment may ever safely be prophesied from the promise, England appears to have lost in Keats one whose gifts in Poetry have rarely been surpassed.

Francis Turner Palgrave, 1861, *The Golden Treasury*

Do you remember that last sonnet? Let us repeat it solemnly, and let the words wander down with the waters of the river to the sea. . . . How the star-sheen on the tremulous tide, and that white death-like "mask," haunt the imagination! Had the poet, who felt the grass grow over him ere he was five-and-twenty, been crowned with a hundred summers, could he have done anything more consummate? I doubt it.

John (Shirley) Skelton, 1862, *Nugæ Criticæ*, p. 236

Though Keats has never been and probably never will be a really popular poet, his influence on other poets and on poetic temperaments generally has been quite incalculable. Some of his sonnets are remarkable for their power and beauty, while others are indifferent and a few are poor. With all his love for the beauty of isolated poetic lines—music condensed into an epigram more concise than the Greeks ever uttered—as, for example, his own splendid verse,
            There is a budding morrow in mid-night—
and with all that sense of verbal melody which he manifested so remarkably in his odes, it is strange that in his sonnets he should so often be at fault in true harmony.

William Sharp, 1886, *Sonnets of this Century*, Introduction, p. lv

GENERAL

Sir,—We regret that your brother ever requested us to publish this book, or that our opinion of its talent should have led us to acquiesce in undertaking it. We are, however, much obliged to you for relieving us from the unpleasant necessity of declining any further connexion with it, which we must have done, as we think the curiosity is satisfied, and the sale has dropped. By far the greater number of persons who have purchased it from us have found fault with it in such plain terms, that we have in many cases offered to take the book back rather than be annoyed with ridicule which has, time after time, been showered upon it. In fact, it was only on Saturday last that we were under the mortification of having our own opinion of its merits flatly contradicted by a gentleman, who told us he considered it "no better than a take in." These are unpleasant imputations for any one in business to labour under, but we should have borne them and concealed their existence from you had not the style of your note shewn us that such delicacy would be quite thrown away. We shall take means without delay for ascertaining the number of copies on hand, and you shall be informed accordingly. Your most, &c.

C. and J. Ollier, 1817, Letter to George Keats, April 29

To witness the disease of any human understanding, however feeble, is distressing; but the spectacle of an able mind reduced to a state of insanity is of course ten times more afflicting. It is with such sorrow as this that we have contemplated the case of Mr. John Keats. This young man appears to have received from nature talents of an excellent, perhaps even of a superior order—talents which, devoted to the purposes of any useful profession, must have rendered him a respectable if not an eminent citizen. His friends, we understand, destined him to the career of medicine, and he was bound apprentice some years ago to a worthy apothecary in town. But all has been undone by a sudden attack of the malady to which we have alluded. . . . We venture to make one small prophecy, that his bookseller will not a second time venture 50*l.* on anything he can write. It is a better and a wiser thing to be a starved apothecary than a starved poet; so back to the shop Mr. John, back to "plasters, pills, and ointment-boxes," &c. But, for Heaven's sake, young Sangrado, be a little more sparing of extenuatives and soporifics in your practice than you have been in your poetry.

John Gibson Lockhart, 1818, "The Cockney School of Poetry,
No. 4," Blackwood's Magazine, vol. 3, pp. 519, 524

Mr. Keats, we understand, is still a very young man; and his whole works, indeed, bear evidence enough of the fact. They are full of extravagance and irregularity, rash attempts at originality, interminable wanderings, and excessive obscurity. They manifestly require, therefore, all the indulgence that can be claimed for a first attempt:—But we think it no less plain that they deserve it: For they are flushed all over with the rich lights of fancy; and so coloured and bestrewn with the flowers of poetry, that even while perplexed and bewildered in their labyrinths, it is impossible to resist the intoxication of their sweetness, or to shut our hearts to the enchantments they so lavishly present.

Francis, Lord Jeffrey, 1820-44, "Keats's Poems,"
Contributions to the Edinburgh Review, vol. III, p. 102

I am inclined to think that Mr. Matthew Arnold, a critic with whose judgments I rarely find myself in dissent, makes a somewhat misleading remark when he insists that Keat's master passion was not the passion of the sensuous or sentimental poet, but was an intellectual or spiritual passion. If the words sensuous and sentimental were intended in an opprobrious sense, the remark might be useful; but if they are used in the literal meaning, and then contrasted with intellectual and spiritual, their tendency is to withdraw the reader of Keats from the main characteristics of his poetry.

William Minto, 1894, *The Literature of the Georgian Era,*
ed. Knight, p. 304

In spite of this earnestness and philosophy, it is certainly true that Keats's mind was of a luxurious habit; and it must have been partly due to this temperament that he showed so little severity towards himself in the castigation of his poems, though that was, as I said before, chiefly caused by the prolific activity of his imagination, which was always providing him with fresh material to work on. In this respect he is above all poets an example of what is meant by inspiration: the mood which all artists require, covet, and find most rare was the common mood with him; and I should say that being amply supplied with this, what as an artist he most lacked was self-restraint and self-castigation,—which was indeed foreign to his luxurious temperament, unselfish and devoted to his art as he was,—the presence of which was most needful to watch, choose, and reject the images which crowded on him as he thought or wrote.

Robert Bridges, 1894, *Poems of John Keats,*
ed. Drury, Introduction, vol. I, p. ci

The perfection of Keats's art, the sureness of success with which he translated into words, feelings that but for him those who underwent them would have abandoned as inexpressible, make rather startling the suggestion that there was anything to which he was inadequate because for it "he was not ripe." Indeed it is the very ripeness of Keats's art at its best that distinguishes it above the work of so many generations of his elders, and makes it so astonishing as the work of a youth, so far is it removed, in its security and ease of mastery, from the struggles for expression of immaturity, from the mere glibness of precocity. It is the sense rather of overripeness than of unripeness that it gives of a sensibility hectic and excessive.

Montgomery Schuyler, 1895, "The Centenary of Keats,"
The Forum, vol. 20, p. 362

The Cap and Bells is a melancholy example of what a great poet can produce who is consumed by a hopeless passion and wasted by disease. . . . In his first sonnet on Fame, Keats, in a saner mood, puts by the temptation which would withdraw him from the high serenity of conscious worth. In the second, wherein he seems almost to be seeing Fanny Brawne, mocking behind the figure of Fame, he shows a more scornful attitude. There is little doubt that notwithstanding his close companionship with poets living and dead Keats never could long escape from the allurements of this "wayward girl," yet it may surely be said that his escape was most complete when he was fulfilling the highest law of his nature and creating those images of beauty which have given him Fame while he sleeps.

Horace E. Scudder, 1899, *The Complete Poetical Works and Letters of John Keats,* Cambridge ed., Biographical Sketch, pp. xxiii, xxiv

PERCY BYSSHE SHELLEY
1792-1822

Born, at Field Place, near Horsham, Sussex, 4 Aug. 1792. Educated privately, 1798-1802; at a school at Brentford, 1802-04; at Eton, July 1804 to 1809. Wrote poetry while at Eton. Matric., University Coll., Oxford, 10 April 1810. Expelled (with Hogg) from Oxford for publication of *The Necessity of Atheism,* 25 March 1811. Married (i.) Harriet Westbrook, 28 Aug. 1811. Lived for a few weeks with Hogg in Edinburgh; then to Keswick, Nov. 1811. Friendship formed there with Southey. Friendship with Godwin begun, Jan. 1812. In Dublin, spring of 1812; at Lynmouth, June to Sept. 1812; in Carnarvonshire, Sept. 1812 to Feb. 1813; in Ireland, Feb. to April 1913; to London, April 1813. Removed to Bracknell, July 1813; in Edinburgh, winter 1813-14; returned to Bracknell, spring of 1814. On account of his having been married in Scotland as a minor, he remarried his wife in London, 24 March 1814. Estrangement from his wife, and meeting with Mary Godwin, 1814. To Continent with Mary Godwin, 28 July 1814; returned with her to England, Sept. 1814. Friendship with Byron begun, 1816. At Geneva with him, summer of 1816. Mrs. Shelley committed suicide, Dec. 1816. He married (ii.) Mary Godwin, 30 Dec. 1816; settled with her at Marlow, spring of 1817. Friendship with Keats begun, 1817. Removed to Italy, March 1818. Drowned, 8 July 1822. His body cremated on the shore near Via Reggio, 16 Aug. 1822. His ashes buried in old Protestant Cemetery, Rome, Dec. 1822. WORKS: *Zastrozzi* (under initials: P. B. S.), 1810; *Original Poetry: by Victor and Cazire* (no copy known (?)), 1810; *Posthumous Fragments of Margaret Nicholson,* 1810 (priv. ptd., ed. by H. B. Forman, 1877); *St. Irvyne* (anon.), 1811; *Poetical Essay on the Existing State of Things,* 1811; *The Necessity of Atheism,* 1811; *An Address to the Irish People,* 1812; *Proposals for an Association,* 1812; *Declaration of Rights,* 1812; *Letters to Lord Ellenborough* (1812); *The Devil's Walk,* 1812; *Queen Mab,* 1813; *A Vindication of Natural Diet* (anon.), 1813; *A Refutation of Deism* (anon.), 1814; *Alastor,* 1816; *Proposal for putting reform to the Vote* (anon.), 1817; *History of a Six Weeks' Tour through a Part of France* (with his wife; anon.), 1817; *Laon and Cythna,* 1818 (1817) (recalled; and reissued as *The Revolt of Islam,* (1817); *Address to the People on the Death of Princess Charlotte* (1818); *Rosalind and Helen,* 1819; *The Cenci,* 1819; *Prometheus Unbound,* 1820; *Œdipus Tyrannus* (anon.), 1820; *Epipsychidion* (anon.), 1821; *Adonais,* 1821; *Hellas,* 1822. POSTHUMOUS: *Posthumous Poems,* ed. by Mrs. Shelley (1824); *The Masque of Anarchy,* ed. by Leigh Hunt, 1832; *The Shelley Papers* (from *Athenæum*)

1833; *Essays, etc.,* by Mrs. Shelley, 1840; *The Dæmon of the World,* ed. by H. B. Forman (priv. ptd.), 1876; *Notes on Sculptures in Rome and Florence* (ed. by H. B. Forman; priv. ptd.), 1879. COLLECTED WORKS: ed. by H. Buxton Forman (8 vols.), 1880 (1876-80). LIFE: by Prof. Dowden, 1886.

R. Farquharson Sharp, 1897, A Dictionary of
English Authors, p. 254

SEE: *Complete Works,* ed. Roger Ingpen and Walter F. Peck, 1927, 10 v.; *Complete Poetical Works,* ed. Thomas Hutchinson, 1905(OSA); *The Early Collected Editions of Shelley's Poems: A Study in the History and Transmission of the Printed Text,* ed. Lawrence John Zillman, 1958; *Shelley's "Prometheus Unbound": A Variorum Edition,* ed. Lawrence John Zillman, 1959; *The Essaile Notebook: A Volume of Early Poems,* ed. Kenneth Neill Cameron, 1964; *Notebooks,* ed. H. Buxton Forman, 1911, 3 v.; *Letters,* ed. Roger Ingpen, 1909, 2 v.; Newman Ivey White, *Shelley,* 1940, 2 v., rev. 1945 as *Portrait of Shelley,* one vol.; Kenneth Neill Cameron, *The Young Shelley: Genesis of a Radical,* 1951; Kenneth Neill Cameron, ed., *Shelley and His Circle, 1773-1822,* Vols. I, II, 1961; M. T. Solve, *Shelley: His Theory of Poetry,* 1927; Carl Henry Grabo, *The Magic Plant,* 1936; Carlos Baker, *Shelley's Major Poetry,* 1948; also see *Letters of Mary Shelley,* ed. F. L. Jones, 1944, 2 v.; *Mary Shelley's Journal,* ed. F. L. Jones, 1947; *New Shelley Letters,* ed. W. S. Scott, 1949.

PERSONAL

I went to Godwin's. Mr. Shelley was there. I had never seen him before. His youth and a resemblance to Southey, particularly in his voice, raised a pleasing impression, which was not altogether destroyed by his conversation, though it is vehement, and arrogant, and intolerant. He was very abusive towards Southey, whom he spoke of as having sold himself to the Court. And this he maintained with the usual party slang. . . . Shelley spoke of Wordsworth with less bitterness, but with an insinuation of his insincerity, etc.

Henry Crabb Robinson, 1817, Diary, Nov. 6

The author of *Prometheus Unbound,* has a fire in his eye, a fever in his blood, a maggot in his brain, a hectic flutter in his speech, which mark out the philosophic fanatic. He is sanguine-complexioned, and shrill-voiced. As is often observable in the case of religious enthusiasts, there is a slenderness of constitutional stamina, which renders the flesh no match for the spirit. His bending, flexible form appears to take no strong hold of things, does not grapple with the world about him, but slides from it like a river,—

> "And in its liquid texture mortal wound
> Receives no more than can the fluid air."

William Hazlett, 1821, "On Paradox and the Commonplace,"
Table-Talk, p. 355

"You should have known Shelley," said Byron, "to feel how much I must regret him. He was the most gentle, most amiable, and *least* worldly-minded person I ever met; full of delicacy, disinterested beyond all other men, and possessing a degree of genius, joined to a simplicity as rare as it is admirable. He had formed to himself a *beau-idéal* of all that is fine, high-minded, and noble, and he acted up to this ideal even to the very letter. He had a most brilliant imagination, but a total want of worldly wisdom. I have seen nothing like him, and never shall again, I am certain. I never can forget the night that his poor wife rushed into my room at Pisa, with a face as pale as marble, and terror impressed on her brow, demanding, with all the tragic impetuosity of grief and alarm, where was her husband? Vain were all our efforts to calm her; a desperate sort of courage seemed to give her energy to confront the horrible truth that awaited her; it was the courage of despair. I have seen nothing in tragedy or on the stage so powerful, or so affecting, as her appearance; and it often presents itself to my memory. I knew nothing then of the catastrophe, but the vividness of her terror communicated itself to me, and I feared the worst,—which fears were, alas! too soon fearfully realized."

> Marguerite Countess Blessington, 1834, *Conversations with*
> *Lord Byron*, ch. iv

The qualities that struck any one newly introduced to Shelley, were,—First, a gentle and cordial goodness that animated his intercourse with warm affection and helpful sympathy. The other, the eagerness and ardour with which he was attached to the cause of human happiness and improvement; and the fervent eloquence with which he discussed subjects. His conversation was marked by its happy abundance, and the beautiful language with which he clothed his poetic ideas and philosophical notions. To defecate life of its misery and its evil was the ruling passion of his soul: he dedicated to it every power of his mind, every pulsation of his heart. He looked on political freedom as the direct agent to affect the happiness of mankind; and thus any new-sprung hope of liberty inspired a joy and an exultation more intense than he could have felt for any personal advantage.

> Mary Godwin Shelley, 1839, *Shelley's Poetical Works,* Preface

Can we imagine the case of an angel touched by lunacy? Have we ever seen the spectacle of a human intellect, exquisite by its functions of creation, yet in one chamber of its shadowy house already ruined before the light of manhood had cleansed its darkness? Such an angel, such a man— if ever such there were—such a lunatic angel, such a ruined man, was Shelley whilst yet standing on the earliest threshold of life. . . . Something of a similar effect arises to myself when reviewing the general abstract of

Shelley's life—so brief, so full of agitation, so full of strife. When one thinks of the early misery which he suffered, and of the insolent infidelity which, being yet so young, he wooed with a lover's passion, then the darkness of midnight begins to form a deep, impenetrable background, upon which the phantasmagoria of all that is to come may arrange itself in troubled phosphoric streams, and in sweeping processions of woe. Yet, again, when one recurs to his gracious nature, his fearlessness, his truth, his purity from all fleshliness of appetite, his freedom from vanity, his diffusive love and tenderness, suddenly out of the darkness reveals itself a morning of May, forests and thickets of roses advance to the foreground, and from the midst of them looks out "the eternal child," cleansed from his sorrow, radiant with joy, having power given him to forget the misery which he suffered, power given him to forget the misery which he caused, and leaning with his heart upon that dove-like faith against which his erring intellect had rebelled.

Thomas De Quincey, 1845-57, *Gilfillan's Literary Portraits,*
Works, ed. Masson, vol. XI, pp. 358, 376

Innocent and careless as a boy, he possessed all the delicate feelings of a gentleman, all the discrimination of a scholar, and united, in just degrees, the ardor of the poet with the patience and forbearance of the philosopher. His generosity and charity went far beyond those of any man (I believe) at present in existence. He was never known to speak evil of any enemy, unless that enemy had done some grievous injustice to another; and he divided his income of only one thousand pounds with the fallen and the afflicted. This is the man against whom such clamors have been raised by the religious and the loyal, and by those who live and lap under their tables.

Walter Savage Landor, 1846, *Imaginary Conversations*

His features were small—the upper part of his face not strictly regular—the eyes unusually prominent, too much so for beauty. His mouth was moulded after the finest modelling of Greek art, and wore an habitual expression of benevolence, and when he smiled, his smile irradiated his whole countenance. His hands were thin, and expressed feeling to the fingers' ends; . . . his hair, profuse, silken, and naturally curling, was at a very early period interspersed with gray. . . . He did not look so tall as he was, being nearly five feet eleven, for his shoulders were a little bent by study. . . . owing to his being near-sighted, and leaning over his books, and which increased the narrowness of his chest.

Thomas Medwin, 1847, *The Life of Percy Bysshe Shelley*

Shelley, when he died, was in his thirtieth year. His figure was tall and slight, and his constitution consumptive. He was subject to violent spasmodic pains, which would sometimes force him to lie on the ground till they were over; but he had always a kind word to give to those about him, when his pangs allowed him to speak. . . . Though well-turned, his shoulders were bent a little, owing to premature thought and trouble. The same causes had touched his hair with gray; and though his habits of temperance and exercise gave him a remarkable degree of strength, it is not supposed that he could have lived many years.

Leigh Hunt, 1850, Autobiography

Brown's four novels, Schiller's *Robbers,* and Goethe's *Faust,* were, of all the works with which he was familiar, those which took the deepest root in his mind, and had the strongest influence in the formation of his character. He was an assiduous student of the great classical poets, and among these his favourite heroines were Nausicaa and Antigone. I do not remember that he greatly admired any of our old English poets, excepting Shakspeare and Milton. He devotedly admired Wordsworth and Coleridge, and in a minor degree Southey: these had great influence on his style, and Coleridge especially on his imagination; but admiration is one thing and assimilation is another; and nothing so blended itself with the structure of his interior mind as the creations of Brown. Nothing stood so clearly before his thoughts as a perfect combination of the purely ideal and possibly real, as Constantia Dudley. . . . He had a prejudice against theatres which I took some pains to overcome. I induced him one evening to accompany me to a representation of *The School for Scandal.* When, after the scenes which exhibited Charles Surface in his jollity, the scene returned, in the fourth act, to Joseph's library, Shelley said to me,—"I see the purpose of this comedy. It is to associate virtue with bottles and glasses, and villainy with books." I had great difficulty to make him stay to the end. He often talked of "the withering and perverting spirit of comedy." I do not think he ever went to another.

Thomas Love Peacock, 1858, "Memoirs of Percy Bysshe Shelley,"
Fraser's Magazine, vol. 57, pp. 657, 658

After the fire was well kindled we repeated the ceremony of the previous day; and more wine was poured over Shelley's dead body than he had consumed during his life. This with the oil and salt made the yellow flames glisten and quiver. The heat from the sun and fire was so intense that the atmosphere was tremulous and wavy. The corpse fell open and the heart was laid bare. The frontal bone of the skull, where it had been struck with the mattock, fell off; and, as the back of the head rested on the redhot bottom bars of the furnace, the brains literally seethed, bubbled, and boiled, as in a cauldron, for a very long time. Byron could not face this scene, he withdrew to the beach and swam off to the *Bolivar*. Leigh Hunt remained in the carriage. The fire was so fierce as to produce a white heat on the iron, and to reduce its contents to grey ashes. The only portions that were not consumed were some fragments of bones, the jaw, and the skull; but what surprised us all was that the heart remained entire. In snatching this relic from the fiery furnace, my hand was severely burnt; and had any one seen me do the act I should have been put into quarantine.

Edward John Trelawny, 1858-78, Records of Shelley,
Byron and the Author, p. 144

At the commencement of Michaelmas term, that is, at the end of October, in the year 1810, I happened one day to sit next to a freshman at dinner; it was his first appearance in hall. His figure was slight, and his aspect remarkably youthful, even at our table, where all were very young. He seemed thoughtful and absent. He ate little, and had no acquaintance with any one. . . . His figure was slight and fragile, and yet his bones and joints were large and strong. He was tall, but he stooped so much, that he seemed of a low stature. His clothes were expensive, and made according to the most approved mode of the day; but they were tumbled, rumpled, unbrushed. His gestures were abrupt, and sometimes violent, occasionally even awkward, yet more frequently gentle and graceful. His complexion was delicate and almost feminine, of the purest red and white; yet he was tanned and freckled by exposure to the sun, having passed the autumn, as he said, in shooting. His features, his whole face, and particularly his head, were, in fact, unusually small; yet the last *appeared* of a remarkable bulk, for his hair was long and bushy, and in fits of absence, and in the agonies (if I may use the word) of anxious thought, he often rubbed it fiercely with his hands, or passed his fingers quickly through his locks unconsciously, so that it was singularly wild and rough. . . . His features were not symmetrical (the mouth, perhaps, excepted), yet was the effect of the whole extremely powerful. They breathed an animation, a fire, an enthusiasm, a vivid and preternatural intelligence, that I never met with in any other countenance. Nor was the moral expression less beautiful than the intellectual; for there was a softness, a delicacy, a gentleness, and especially (though this will surprise many) that air of profound religious veneration, that characterises the best works, and chiefly the frescoes (and into these they infused their whole souls), of the great masters of Florence and of Rome.

Thomas Jefferson Hogg, 1858, The Life of Percy Bysshe Shelley,
vol. I, pp. 51, 54, 55

The ashes of Shelley were deposited in the Protestant burial ground at Rome, by the side of his son William, and of his brother-poet Keats. An inscription in Latin, simply putting forth the facts, was written by Leigh Hunt, and Mr. Trelawny added a few lines from Shakspeare's *Tempest* (one of Shelley's favorite plays):—

> "Nothing of him that doth fade,
> But doth suffer a sea-change
> Into something rich and strange."

The same gentleman also planted eight cypresses round the spot, of which seven were flourishing in 1844, and probably are still. And so the sea and the earth closed over one who was great as a poet, and still greater as a philanthropist; and of whom it may be said, that his wild, spiritual character seems to have fitted him for being thus snatched from life under circumstances of mingled terror and beauty, while his powers were yet in their spring freshness, and age had not come to render the ethereal body decrepit, or to wither the heart which could not be consumed by fire.

Lady Shelley, 1859, ed., *Shelley Memorials from Authentic Sources*, p. 219

The lovers of Shelley as a man and a poet have done what they could to palliate his conduct in this matter. But a question of morals, as between man and society, cannot be reduced to any individual standard, however exalted. Our partiality for the man only heightens our detestation of the error. The greater Shelley's genius, the nobler his character and impulses, so much the more startling is the warning. If we make our own inclinations the measure of what is right, we must be the sterner in curbing them. A woman's heart is too delicate a thing to serve as a fulcrum for the lever with which a man would overturn any system, however conventional. The misery of the elective-affinity scheme is that men are not chemical substances, and that in nine cases in ten the force of the attraction works more constantly and lastingly upon the woman than the man.

Charles Eliot Norton, 1865, *Shelley's Poetical Works,* Memoir

To prove that Shelley as a man was deficient in passion we need mention one incident only in his life. Some time after his separation from Harriet, he proposed that she should return to him and take up a place as a member of his household, not as his wife, but side by side with the friend for whom she had been abandoned, and who still shared his bed. This extraordinary proposal arose out of the most self-oblivious generosity, but what a commentary it affords on Shelley's masculinity!

Hall Caine, 1883, *Cobwebs of Criticism,* p. 229

Mary Shelley returned to England in the autumn of 1823. On February 21, 1851, she died. Shelley's son, Percy Florence, succeeded to the baronetcy on the death of his grandfather in April, 1844. In the monument, by Weekes, which Sir Percy and Lady Shelley have erected in the noble parish church of Christchurch, Hants, the feeling of Mary's heart, confided to the pages of her journal after her husband's death, is translated into monumental marble. In Boscombe Manor, Bournemouth, in an alcove devoted to that purpose, the portraits, of Shelley and Mary, duly ordered by Lady Shelley's hands, are preserved with love and reverence. The murmur of pine woods, and the resonance and silvery flash of the waves of our English sea, are near to solemnize and to gladden the heart.

Edward Dowden, 1886, *Life of Percy Bysshe Shelley,*
vol. II, p. 538

What a set! what a world! is the exclamation that breaks from us as we come to an end of this history of "the occurrences of Shelley's private life." I used the French word *bête* for a letter of Shelley's; for the world in which we find him I can only use another French word, *sale*. Godwin's house of sordid horror, and Godwin preaching and holding the hat, and the green-spectacled Mrs. Godwin, and Hogg the faithful friend, and Hunt the Horace of this precious world, and, to go up higher, Sir Timothy Shelley, a great country gentleman, feeling himself safe while "the exalted mind of the Duke of Norfolk [the drinking Duke] protects me with the world," and Lord Byron with his deep grain of coarseness and commonness, his affection, his brutal selfishness—what a set! . . . Mrs. Shelley, after her marriage and during Shelley's closing years, becomes attractive; up to her marriage her letters and journal do not please. Her ability is manifest, but she is not attractive. In the world discovered to us by Professor Dowden as surrounding Shelley up to 1817, the most pleasing figure is poor Fanny Godwin; after Fanny Godwin, the most pleasing figure is Harriet Shelley herself.

Matthew Arnold, 1888, "Shelley," *The Nineteenth Century,*
vol. 23, p. 34, *Essays in Criticism,* vol. II

Shelley's moral character was really no better than Byron's; but one was a cynic, and the other a sentimentalist who perhaps did not always carry his feelings into action. Without going back to Shelley's former life, it is sufficient to study his relations to Emilia Viviani, to Jane Williams, and, indeed, to all the women whom he met frequently, or to read his poem, *Epipsychidion,* which inculcates the necessity of loving more than one woman in the interest of art and of the higher spiritual culture.

Eugene Schuyler, 1888-1901, *Italian Influences,* p. 143

What Shelley was at first he remained to the last: a beautiful, effeminate, arrogant boy—constitutionally indifferent to money, generous by impulse, self-indulgent by habit, ignorant to the end of all that it most behooves a responsible being to know, and so conceited that his ignorance was incurable; showing at every turn the most infallible sign of a feeble intellect, a belief in human perfectibility; and rushing at once to the conclusion, when he or others met with suffering, that some one, not the sufferer, was doing grievous wrong.

Coventry Patmore, 1889-98, Principle in Art, p. 87

He never could clearly realise the aspect which his relations with Mary bore to the world, who merely saw in him a married man who had deserted his wife and eloped with a girl of sixteen. He thought people should understand all he knew, and credit him with all he did not tell them; that they should sympathise and fraternise with him, and honour Mary the more, not the less, for what she had done and dared. Instead of this, the world accepted his family's estimate of its unfortunate eldest son, and cut him.

Mrs. Julian Marshall, 1889, The Life and Letters of
Mary Wollstonecraft Shelley, vol. I, p. 128

Shelley was nineteen. He was not a youth, but a man. He had never had any youth. He was an erratic and fantastic child during eighteen years, then he stepped into manhood, as one steps over a door-sill. He was curiously mature at nineteen in his ability to do independent thinking on the deep questions of life and to arrive at sharply definite decisions regarding them, and stick to them—stick to them and stand by them at cost of bread, friendships, esteem, respect, and approbation. For the sake of his opinions he was willing to sacrifice all these valuable things, and did sacrifice them; and went on doing it, too, when he could at any moment have made himself rich and supplied himself with friends and esteem by compromising with his father, at the moderate expense of throwing overboard one or two indifferent details of his cargo of principles.

Samuel Langhorne Clemens (Mark Twain), 1897, "In Defence
of Harriet Shelley," How to Tell a Story and Other Essays, p. 24

The Necessity of Atheism (1811)

At a meeting of the Master and Fellows held this day, it was determined that Thomas Jefferson Hogg, and Percy Bysshe Shelley, commoners, be publicly expelled for contumaciously refusing to answer questions proposed to them, and for also repeatedly declining to disavow a publication entitled *The Necessity of Atheism.*

Records, University of Oxford, 1811

The importance of *The Necessity of Atheism* is rather biographical and illustrative than literary. It is true the little tract is put together cleverly, and apparently with perfect good faith; but from a strictly literary stand-point it could not be said that an irreparable loss would be sustained by its destruction. None the less its recovery seems to me a matter for great congratulation. So much hung upon this tract,—Shelley's expulsion and all its momentous issues,—so much has been said and written about it,— that to have it before us exactly as it issued from the Press at Worthing and was offered to the Oxford worthies and undergraduates was highly desirable.

> Harry Buxton Forman, 1880, ed., *The Prose Works of Percy Bysshe Shelley,* vol. I, p. xviii

His "Essay on Christianity" is full of noble views, some of which are held at the present day by some of the most earnest believers. At what time of his life it was written we are not informed; but it seems such as would insure his acceptance with any company of intelligent and devout Unitarians.

> George Macdonald, 1882, *The Imagination and Other Essays,* p. 271, note

Queen Mab (1813)

An extravagant expression of his zeal for the improvement of the world, full of vague fantastic notions, but also, like all his poems, replete with delicate, lofty, and brilliant ideas. The book, published by a treacherous bookseller against the poet's wish, was condemned. Shelley had excited persecution specially by the notes he had added to the text. These notes, which contain an argument against Christianity, revealed great youthful incompetence; he forgot that it would be simple folly to deny the effects of Christianity in the history of the world. . . . It does not belong to a particular class; it is a series of sketches, lyrical, descriptive, polemic, didactic, in changing metres.

> J. Scherr, 1874, *A History of English Literature,* tr. M. V., p. 246

We cannot include *Queen Mab,* in spite of its sonorous rhetoric and fervid declamation, in the canon of his masterpieces. It had a *succès de scandale* on its first appearance, and fatally injured Shelley's reputation. As a work of art it lacks maturity and permanent vitality.

> John Addington Symonds, 1879, *Shelley* (*English Men of Letters*), p. 69

Ridiculed in so far as it was not ignored at the time of its appearance, it has in later times and in some quarters been absurdly overpraised; but, with all its defects and excesses of youth, an impartial criticism can hardly hesitate to pronounce it the most striking and powerful work of imagination, and by far the richest in promise, that has ever sprung from the brain of a poet who had not yet passed his twentieth year.

Henry Duff Traill, 1896, Social England, vol. V, p. 586

The radical character of *Queen Mab,* which was made a part of the evidence against his character, on the occasion of the trial which resulted in his being deprived of the custody of his children by Lord Eldon, was a main element in the contemporary obloquy in which his name was involved in England, though very few persons could ever have read the poem then; but it may be doubted whether in the end it did not help his fame by the fascination it exercises over a certain class of minds in the first stages of social and intellectual revolt or angry unrest so widespread in this century.

George Edward Woodberry, 1901, ed., Complete Poetical
Works of Percy Bysshe Shelley, Cambridge ed., p. 2

Alastor (1815)

In *Alastor* we at last have the genuine, the immortal Shelley. It may indeed be said that the poem, though singularly lovely and full—charged with meaning, has a certain morbid vagueness of tone, a want of firm human body: and this is true enough. Nevertheless, *Alastor* is proportionately worthy of the author of *Prometheus Unbound* and *The Cenci,* the greatest Englishman of his age.

William Michael Rossetti, 1870-78-86,
Memoir of Percy Bysshe Shelley, p. 57

The first of his poems, which really was worthy of his powers—*Alastor*—was written in the first year of this union. It is the first real indication of the new voice which had awakened in English literature. It was like nothing else then existing; nor do we know to what to compare it in the past. Shelley had no story to tell, no character to disclose; his was pure poetry, music such as charmed the ear and filled the mouth with sweetness. Never was poet so eager to teach, or with so many wild assertions to make, or so strong a conviction of the possibility of influencing humanity and changing the world; but the soul of his poetry was the same as that of music, not definite, scarcely articulate, only melodious, ineffably sweet.

Margaret O. W. Oliphant, 1882, Literary History of England,
XVIII-XIX Century, vol. III, p. 46

The Revolt of Islam (1817)

Even in its amended form it probably presents a better key to the poet's wild opinions than any other of his works. It is a protest against the ordinary usages of society, which Shelley calls "custom." Cythna and Laon declare war against this custom. The reader finds some difficulty in following the fertile imagination of the poet through the phases of alternate suffering and victory which the hero and the heroine experience. He fails to comprehend the means which enabled Cythna to enthrone herself as the Goddess of Liberty, or to appreciate the causes which produced the sudden downfall of her authority. Her flight with Laon on the black Tartarian steed is absurdly unnatural; and her subsequent conduct, or the narrative of it, is grossly indecent. Custom, in short, or, to speak more correctly, the custom which had made matrimony a necessity, was the tyranny against which Shelley's eloquence is directed, and the poem is thus fitly dedicated, in some of the most beautiful verses Shelley ever wrote, to the lady who, for his sake, had broken the bands of custom.

> Spencer Walpole, 1878, *A History of England from the Conclusion of the Great War in 1815,* vol. I, p. 366

The storms are even better than the sunsets and dawns. The finest is at the beginning of *The Revolt of Islam*. It might be a description of one of Turner's storm-skies. The long trains of tremulous mist that precede the tempest, the cleft in the storm-clouds, and seen through it, high above, the space of blue sky fretted with fair clouds, the pallid semicircle of the moon with mist on its upper horn, the flying rack of clouds below the serene spot —all are as Turner saw them; but painting cannot give what Shelley gives —the growth and changes of the storm.

> Stopford A. Brooke, 1880, "Some Thoughts on Shelley," *Macmillan's Magazine,* vol. 42, p. 129

Julian and Maddalo (1818)

Is a Conversation or Tale, full of that thoughtful and romantic humanity, but rendered perplexing and unattractive by the veil of shadowy or of glittering obscurity, which distinguished Mr. Shelley's writings. The depth and tenderness of his feelings seem often to have interfered with the expression of them, as the sight becomes blind with tears. A dull, waterish vapour clouds the aspect of his philosophical poetry, like that mysterious gloom which he has himself described as hanging over the Medusa's Head of Leonardo de Vinci.

> William Hazlitt, 1824, "Shelley's Posthumous Poems," *Edinburgh Review,* vol. 40, p. 499

The familiarity of *Julian and Maddalo* is almost as foreign to that of *Beppo* as to that of the *Idiot Boy*. It is high-bred, poetic familiarity, equally remote from the cynicism verging on vulgarity of the one, and from the rusticity verging on ugliness of the other; a manner happily mediating between the abstract intensity of Shelley's ordinary verse and the rich concrete talk of Byron, under the "intoxication" of which it arose.

C. H. Herford, 1897, *The Age of Wordsworth*, p. 245

Prometheus Unbound (1819)

To our apprehensions, Prometheus is little else but absolute raving; and were we not assured to the contrary, we should take it for granted that the author was a lunatic—as his principles are ludicrously wicked, and his poetry a mélange of nonsense, cockneyism, poverty, and pedantry.

Anon, 1820, *Literary Gazette*, Sept. 9

In short, it is quite impossible that there should exist a more pestiferous mixture of blasphemy, sedition, and sensuality, than is visible in the whole structure and strain of this poem—which, nevertheless, and notwithstanding all the detestation its principles excite, must and will be considered by all that read it attentively, as abounding in poetical beauties of the highest order —as presenting many specimens not easily to be surpassed, of the moral sublime of eloquence—as overflowing with pathos, and most magnificent in description. Where can be found a specacle more worthy of sorrow than such a man performing and glorying in the performance of such things?

Anon, 1820,*"Prometheus Unbound," Blackwood's Magazine,*
vol. 7, p. 680

In Mr. Shelley's poetry, all is brilliance, vacuity, and confusion. We are dazzled by the multitude of words which sound as if they denoted something very grand or splendid: fragments of images pass in crowds before us; but when the procession has gone by, and the tumult of it is over, not a trace of it remains upon the memory. The mind, fatigued and perplexed, is mortified by the consciousness that its labour has not been rewarded by the acquisition of a single distinct conception; the ear, too, is dissatisfied; for the rhythm of the verse is often harsh and unmusical; and both the ear and the understanding are disgusted by new and uncouth words, and by the awkward and intricate construction of the sentences. The predominating characteristic of Mr. Shelley's poetry, however, is its frequent and total want of meaning.

Anon, 1821, "Shelley," *Quarterly Review*, vol. 26, p. 169

Prometheus Unbound is the most ambitious of his poems. But it was written too fast. It was written, too, in a state of over-excitement, produced by the intoxication of an Italian spring, operating upon a morbid system, and causing it to flush over with hectic and half-delirious joy. Above all, it was written twenty years too soon, ere his views had consolidated, and ere his thought and language were cast in their final mould. Hence, on the whole, it is a strong and beautiful disease. Its language is loose and luxuriant as a "Moenad's hair"; its imagery is wilder and less felicitous than in some of his other poems. The thought is frequently drowned in a diarrhœa of words; its dialogue is heavy and prolix; and its lyrics have more flow of sound than beauty of image or depth of sentiment;—it is a false gallop rather than a great kindling race. Compared with the *Prometheus* of Æschylus, Shelley's poem is wordy and diffuse; lacks unity and simplicity; above all, lacks whatever human interest is in the Grecian work. Nor has it the massive strength, the piled-up gold and gems, the barbaric but kingly magnificence of Keats' *Hyperion*.

George Gilfillan, 1855, *A Third Gallery of Portraits,* p. 431

The *Prometheus Unbound* gives perhaps the most perfect expression anywhere to be found of the thought and passion of a great period of English poetry. It fully initiates the earnest student into the ideals of the Revolution —those ideals which, in their development, are determining the trend of our modern life. There is no need to speak of the imaginative fervor and pure lyricism of the drama: few English poems can be more effective to quicken and train æsthetic sensitiveness. So far as difficulty is concerned, the student who can understand *The Faery Queen* can understand the *Prometheus Unbound. . . .* The supreme æsthetic glory of the *Prometheus Unbound* is not its nature-descriptions nor its color-treatment, but its music. Never did melody so enfold the spirit of a poet. The form is transparent and supple as clear flame. Blank verse rises into the long, passionate swing of the anapæst, or is broken by the flute-like notes of short trochaic lines, or relieved by the half-lyrical effect of rhymed endings. The verse lends itself with equal beauty to the grandeur of sustained endurance, to the passionate yearning of love, to severe philosophic inquiry, to the ethereal notes of spirit-voices dying on the wind. The variety of metres is marvellous. Thirty-six distinct verse-forms are to be found, besides the blank verse. These forms are usually simple; but at times the versification-scheme is as complex as that of the most elaborate odes of Dryden or Collins. Yet the artificial and labored beauty of the eighteenth century verse is replaced in Shelley by song spontaneous as that of his own skylark. The conventions, the external barriers of poetry, are completely swept away by the new democracy.

Vida D. Scudder, 1892, èd., *Prometheus Unbound,*
Preface and Introduction, pp. iii, 1

The Cenci (1819)

I have read the tragedy of *Cenci,* and am glad to see Shelley at last descending to what really passes among human creatures. The story is certainly an unfortunate one, but the execution gives me a new idea of Shelley's powers. There are passages of great strength, and the character of Beatrice is certainly excellent.

> William Godwin, 1820, *Letter to Mrs. Shelley,* March 30;
> C. K. Paul, *William Godwin,* vol. II, p. 272

This is evidence enough that if Shelley had lived *The Cenci* would not now be the one great play written in the great manner of Shakespeare's men that our literature has seen since the time of these. The proof of power is here as sure and as clear as in Shelley's lyric work; he has shown himself, what the dramatist must needs be, as able to face the light of hell as of heaven, to handle the fires of evil as to brighten the beauties of things. This latter work indeed he preferred, and wrought at it with all the grace and force of thought and word which give to all his lyrics the light of a divine life; but his tragic truth and excellence are as certain and absolute as the sweetness and the glory of his songs. The mark of his hand, the trick of his voice, we can always recognise in their clear character and individual charm; but the range is various from the starry and heavenly heights to the tender and flowering fields of the world wherein he is god and lord: with here such a flower to gather as the spinners' song of Beatrice, and here such a heaven to ascend as the Prologue to Hellas, which the zealous love of Mr. Garnett for Shelley has opened for us to enter and possess for ever; where the pleadings of Christ and Satan alternate as the rising and setting of stars in the abyss of luminous sound and sonorous light.

> Algernon Charles Swinburne, 1869, "Notes on the
> Text of Shelley," *Fortnightly Review,* vol. 11, p. 561

Admiration is often expressed of his dramatic ability, and *The Cenci* has been spoken of as the greatest English tragedy since Shakespeare. In truth there seems to be little that is dramatic in it. It is a nightmare of a drama. We are plunged at once into the deepest gloom, and kept at the highest pitch of excitement all through till the final catastrophe. There is no relief except in the very last half-dozen lines, when we know that the women are to be executed. In rapidity of action *The Cenci* much resembles *Macbeth,* but what a contrast in other respects! Every one must feel the extreme beauty of the scene where Duncan is riding towards the castle and is met by Lady Macbeth, and Banquo tells us of the "temple-haunting martlet," and how it is increased by contrast with the horrors that are so soon to follow. The mutual relations of Beatrice and Count Cenci are wonderfully depicted, and Beatrice's character skilfully developed; but who could suppose that such a perfect monster as Cenci ever existed? His utter shamelessness and selfishness are superhuman. We feel, too, the fatal want of humour, but we are always on the solid ground, the sentiments are obvious enough, and the play had consequently some success, being the only one of Shelley's poems that reached a second edition in his lifetime.

R. C. Seaton, 1881, "Shelley," *The Temple Bar,* vol. 61, p. 234

Adonais (1821)

There is much in *Adonais* which seems now more applicable to Shelley himself, than to the young and gifted poet whom he mourned. The poetic view he takes of death, and the lofty scorn he displays towards his calumniators, are as a prophecy on his own destiny, when received among immortal names, and the poisonous breath of critics has vanished into emptiness before the fame he inherits.

Mary Wollstonecraft Shelley, 1839, ed.
Shelley's Poetical Works, p. 328

An elegy only equalled in our language of *Lycidas,* and in the point of passionate eloquence even superior to Milton's youthful lament for his friend.

John Addington Symonds, 1879, *Shelley*
(*English Men of Letters*), p. 143

As an utterance of abstract pity and indignation, *Adonais* is unsurpassed in literature; with its hurrying train of beautiful spectral images, and the irresistible current and thrilling modulation of its verse, it is perhaps the most perfect and sympathetic effect of Shelley's art; while its strain of transcendental consolation for mortal loss contains the most lucid exposition of his philosophy. But of Keats as he actually lived the elegy presents no feature, while the general impression it conveys of his character and fate is erroneous.

Sidney Colvin, 1887, *Keats (English Men of Letters),* p. 207

GENERAL

There is no *Original Poetry* in this volume: [*Original Poetry by Victor and Cazire*]: there is nothing in it but downright scribble. It is really annoying to see the waste of paper which is made by such persons as the putters-together of these 64 pages. There is, however, one consolation for the critics who are obliged to read all this sort of trash. It is that the crime of publishing is generally followed by condign punishment in the shape of bills from the stationer and printer, and in the chilling tones of the bookseller, when, to the questions of the anxious rhymer how the book sells, he answers that not more than a half-a-dozen copies have been sold.

Anon, 1810-11, *The Poetical Register and*
Repository of Fugitive Poetry

I can no more understand Shelley than you can. His poetry is "thin-sown with profit or delight." . . . For his theories and nostrums, they are oracular enough, but I either comprehend 'em not, or there is "miching malice" and mischief in 'em; but, for the most part, ringing with their own emptiness. Hazlitt said well of 'em, "Many are the wiser or better for reading Shakspeare, but nobody was ever wiser or better for reading Shelley."

Charles Lamb, 1824, *To Bernard Barton*, Aug. 24;
Life and Letters, ed. Talfourd

Mr. Shelley's style is to poetry what astrology is to natural science—a passionate dream, a straining after impossibilities, a record of fond conjectures, a confused embodying of vague abstractions,—a fever of the soul, thirsting and craving after what it cannot have, indulging its love of power and novelty at the expense of truth and nature, associating ideas by contraries, and wasting great powers by their application to unattainable objects.

William Hazlitt, 1824, "Shelley's Posthumous Poems,"
Edinburgh Review, vol. 40, p. 494

Shelley is one of the best *artists* of us all: I mean in workmanship of style.

William Wordsworth, 1827, *Miscellaneous Memoranda;*
in *Memoirs* by Christopher Wordsworth, vol. II, p. 484

The strong imagination of Shelley made him an idolater in his own despite. Out of the most indefinite terms of a hard, cold, dark, metaphysical system, he made a gorgeous Pantheon, full of beautiful, majestic, and life-like forms. He turned atheism itself into a mythology, rich with visions as glorious as the gods that live in the marble of Phidias, or the virgin saints that smile on us from the canvas of Murillo. The Spirit of Beauty, the Principle of Good, the Principle of Evil, when he treated of them, ceased to be abstractions. They took shape and colour. They were no longer mere words, but "intelligible forms"; "fair humanities"; objects of love, of adoration, or of fear. As there can be no stronger sign of a mind destitute of the poetical faculty than that tendency which was so common among the writers of the French school to turn images into abstractions,—Venus, for example, into Love, Minerva into Wisdom, Mars into War, and Bacchus into festivity,—so there can be no stronger sign of a mind truly poetical than a disposition to reverse this abstracting process, and to make individuals out of generalities. Some of the metaphysical and ethical theories of Shelley were certainly most absurd and pernicious. But we doubt whether any modern poet has possessed in an equal degree the highest qualities of the great ancient masters. The words bard and inspiration, which seem so cold and affected when applied to other modern writers, have a perfect propriety when applied to him. He was not an author, but a bard. His poetry seems not to have been an art, but an inspiration. Had he lived to the full age of man, he might not improbably have given to the world some great work of the very highest rank in design and execution.

> Thomas Babington Macaulay, 1831, "Southey's edition of
> *The Pilgrim's Progress,*" *Edinburgh Review,* vol. 54, p. 454

If ever mortal "wreaked his thoughts upon expression," it was Shelley. If ever poet sang (as a bird sings) impulsively, earnestly, with utter abandonment, to himself solely, and for the mere joy of his own song, that poet was the author of *The Sensitive Plant.* Of art—beyond that which is the inalienable instinct of genius—he either had little or disdained all. He really disdained that Rule which is the emanation from Law, because his own soul was law in itself. His rhapsodies are but the rough notes, the stenographic memoranda of poems,—memoranda which, because they were all-sufficient for his own intelligence, he cared not to be at the trouble of transcribing in full for mankind. In his whole life he wrought not thoroughly out a single conception. For this reason it is that he is the most fatiguing of poets. Yet he wearies in having done too little, rather than too much; what seems in him the diffuseness of one idea, is the conglomerate concision of many; and this concision it is which renders him obscure. With such a man, to imitate was out of the question; it would have answered no purpose—for he spoke to his own spirit alone, which would have comprehended no alien tongue;—he was, therefore, profoundly original.

> Edgar Allan Poe, 1845? "Miss Barrett's *A Drama of Exile,*"
> *Works of Poe,* ed. Stedman and Woodberry, vol. VI, p. 317

I would rather consider Shelley's poetry as a sublime fragmentary essay towards a presentment of the correspondency of the universe to Deity, of the natural to the spiritual, and of the actual to the ideal, than I would isolate and separately appraise the worth of many detachable portions which might be acknowledged as utterly perfect in a lower moral of view, under the mere conditions of art.

> Robert Browning, 1851, *Letters of Percy Bysshe Shelley,*
> Introductory Essay

It is impossible to deny that he loved with a great intensity; yet it was with a certain narrowness, and therefore a certain fitfulness. Possibly a somewhat wider nature, taking hold of other characters at more points,—fascinated as intensely but more variously, stirred as deeply but through more complicated emotions,—is requisite for the highest and most lasting feeling; passion, to be enduring, must be many-sided. Eager and narrow emotions urge like the gadfly of the poet, but they pass away; they are single; there is nothing to revive them. Various as human nature must be the passion which absorbs that nature into itself. Shelley's mode of delineating women has a corresponding peculiarity; they are well described, but they are described under only one aspect. Every one of his poems, almost, has a lady whose arms are white, whose mind is sympathizing, and whose soul is beautiful. She has many names,—Cythna, Asia, Emily; but these are only external disguises; she is indubitably the same person, for her character never varies. No character can be simpler; she is described as the ideal object of love in its most simple and elemental form; the pure object of the essential passion. She is a being to be loved in a single moment, with eager eyes and gasping breath; but you feel that in that moment you have seen the whole,—there is nothing to come to afterwards. The fascination is intense, but uniform; there is not the ever-varying grace, the ever-changing charm, that alone can attract for all time the shifting moods of a various and mutable nature.

Walter Bagehot, 1856, "Percy Bysshe Shelley,"
Works, ed. Morgan, vol. I, p. 117

Let it not be supposed that I mean to compare the sickly dreaming of Shelley over clouds and waves with the masculine and magnificent grasp of men and things which we find in Scott.

John Ruskin, 1856, *Modern Painters,* pt. iii, sec. ii, ch. iv, note

Florence to the living Dante was not more cruelly unjust than England to the living Shelley. Only now, nearly forty years after his death, do we begin to discern his true glory. It is well that this glory is such as can afford to wait for recognition; that it is one of the permanent stars of heaven, not a rocket to be ruined by a night of storm and rain. I confess that I have long been filled with astonishment and indignation at the manner in which he is treated by the majority of our best living writers. Emerson is serenely throned above hearing him at all; Carlyle only hears him "shriek hysterically"; Mrs. Browning discovers him "blind with his white ideal"; Messrs. Ruskin and Kingsley treat him much as senior schoolboys treat the youngster who easily "walks over their heads" in class—with reluctant tribute of admiration copiously qualified with sneers, pinches, and kicks. Even Bulwer (who, intellectually worthless as he is, now and then serves well as a straw to show the way the wind blows among the higher and more educated classes), even Bulwer can venture to look down upon him with pity, to pat him patronisingly on the back, to sneer at him—in *Earnest Maltravers* —with a sneer founded upon a maimed quotation. . . . These distinctive marks of the highest poetry I find displayed in the works of Shelley more gloriously than in those of any other poet in our language. As we must study Shakespeare for knowledge of idealised human nature, and Fielding for knowledge of human nature unidealised, and Carlyle's *French Revolution* as the unapproached model of history, and Currer Bell's *Villette* to learn the highest capabilities of the novel, and Ruskin for the true philosophy of art, and Emerson for quintessential philosophy, so must we study, and so will future men more and more study Shelley for quintessential poetry.

James Thomson ("B. V."), 1860-96, *Biographical and Critical Studies,* pp. 270, 280

This uncritical negligence, the want of minute accuracy in the details of his verse, seems to us intimately connected with the whole character of Shelley's mind, and especially with the lyrical sweep and intensity of his poetical genius. He had an intellect of the rarest delicacy and analytical strength, that intuitively perceived the most remote analogies, and discriminated with spontaneous precision the finest shades of sensibility, the subtilest differences of perception and emotion. He possessed a swift soaring and prolific imagination that clothed every thought and feeling with imagery in the moment of its birth, and instinctively read the spiritual meanings of material symbols. His fineness of sense was so exquisite that eye and ear and touch became, as it were, organs and inlets not merely of sensitive apprehension, but of intellectual beauty and ideal truth. Every nerve in his slight but vigorous frame seemed to vibrate in unison with the deeper life of nature in the world around him, and, like the wandering harp, he was swept to music by every breath of material beauty, every gust of poetical emotion. Above all, he had a strength of intellectual passion and a depth of ideal sympathy that in moments of excitement fused all the powers of his mind into a continuous stream of creative energy, and gave the stamp of something like inspiration to all the higher productions of his muse. His very method of composition reflects these characteristics of his mind. He seems to have been urged by a sort of irresistible impulse to write, and displayed a vehement and passionate absorption in the work that recalls the old traditions of poetical frenzy and divine possession.

Thomas S. Baynes, 1871, "Rossetti's Edition of Shelley," *Edinburgh Review,* vol. 133, p. 428

How shall we name the third class of men, who live for the ideal alone, and yet are betrayed into weakness and error, and deeds which demand an atonement of remorse; men who can never quite reconcile the two worlds in which we have our being, the world of material fact and the spiritual world above and beyond it; who give themselves away for love or give themselves away for light yet sometimes mistake bitter for sweet, and darkness for light; children who stumble on the sharp stones and bruise their hands and feet, yet who can wing their way with angelic ease through spaces of the upper air. These are they whom we say the gods love, and who seldom reach the four-score years of Goethe's majestic old age. They are dearer perhaps than any others to the heart of humanity, for they symbolise, in a pathetic way, both its weakness and its strength. We cannot class them with the exact and patient craftsmen; they are ever half defeated and can have no claim to take their seats beside their conquerors. Let us name them lovers; and if at any time they have wandered far astray, let us remember their errors with gentleness, because they have loved much. It is in this third class of those who serve mankind that Shelley has found a place.

> Edward Dowden, 1887, "Last Words on Shelley,"
> *Fortnightly Review,* vol. 48, p. 481

It is his poetry, above everything else, which for many people establishes that he is an angel. Of his poetry I have not space now to speak. But let no one suppose that a want of humour and a self-delusion such as Shelley's have no effect upon a man's poetry. The man Shelley, in very truth, is not entirely sane, and Shelley's poetry is not entirely sane either. The Shelley of actual life is a vision of beauty and radiance, indeed, but availing nothing, effecting nothing. And in poetry, no less than in life, he is "a beautiful *and ineffectual* angel, beating in the void his luminous wings in vain."

> Matthew Arnold, 1888, "Shelley," *The Nineteenth Century,*
> vol. 23, p. 39; *Essays in Criticism,* vol. II

It [*Defence of Poetry*] expresses Shelley's deepest thoughts about poetry, and marks, as clearly as any writing of the last hundred years, the width of the gulf that separates the ideals of recent poetry from those of the century preceding the French Revolution. It may be compared with Sidney's *Apologie* on the one hand, and with Wordsworth's Preface to the *Lyrical Ballads,* or the more abstract parts of Carlyle's critical writings upon the other. The fundamental conceptions of Shelley are the same as those of the Elizabethan critic and of his own great contemporaries. But he differs from Sidney and Wordsworth, and perhaps from Carlyle also, in laying more stress upon the outward form, and particularly the musical element, of poetry; and from Sidney in laying less stress upon its directly moral associations. He thus attains to a wider and truer view of his subject; and, while insisting as strongly as Wordsworth insists upon the kinship between the matter of poetry and that of truth or science, he also recognizes, as Wordsworth commonly did not, that there is a harmony between the imaginative conception of that matter and its outward expression, and that beautiful thought must necessarily clothe itself in beauty of language and of sound. There is not in our literature any clearer presentment of the inseparable connection between the matter and form of poetry, nor of the ideal element which, under different shapes, is the life and soul of both.

C. E. Vaughan, 1896, ed., *English Literary Criticism,* p. 160

Happily, Shelley's treatment of Nature—his landscape would be too limiting a word—in those instances where he has concentrated his mind upon his object, I should myself hold, as in the case of Keats, on the whole, his most precious achievement in poetry. . . . Without adopting M. Arnold's judgment that Shelley's prose will prove his permanent memorial, I must here (with all due respect and apology) make the confession, probably unpopular, reached after long reluctance, that no true poet of any age has left us so gigantic a mass of wasted effort, exuberance so Asiatic, such oceans (to speak out) of fluent, well-intended platitude—such ineffectual beating of his wings in the persistent effort to scale heights of thought beyond the reach of youth;—youth closed so prematurely, so lamentably. Hence the difference between Shelley's best and what is not best is enormous; the sudden transition from mere prose rendered more prosaic by its presentation in verse, to the most ethereal and exquisite poetry, frequent; and hence, also, it is in his shorter and mostly later lyrics that we find Shelley's very finest, uniquest, most magically delightful work. Yet even here at times the matter is attenuated as the film of the soap-bubble, gaining through its very thinness its marvellous iridescent beauty.

Francis Turner Palgrave, 1896, *Landscape in Poetry,* pp. 218, 219

Shelley's love-poems may be very good evidence, but we know well that they are "good for this day and train only." We are able to believe that they spoke the truth for that one day, but we know by experience that they could not be depended on to speak it the next. That very supplication for a rewarming of Harriet's chilled love was followed so suddenly by the poet's plunge into an adoring passion for Mary Godwin that if it had been a check it would have lost its value before a lazy person could have gotten to the bank with it.

Samuel Langhorne Clemens (Mark Twain), 1897, "In Defence of Harriet Shelley," *How to Tell a Story and Other Essays,* p. 81

.ck on 7 Feb. 1823. She was interred at the chapel-of-ease in the Bays-
ater Road (the resting-place of Laurence Sterne and of Paul Sandby)
oelonging to St. George's Hanover Square.

Richard Garnett, 1896, *Dictionary of National
Biography*, vol. XLVII, p. 121

GENERAL

I have read some of the descriptive verbose tales, of which your Ladyship
says I was the patriarch by several mothers. (Miss Reeve and Mrs. Radcliffe?) All I can say for myself is that I do not think my concubines have
produced issue more natural for excluding the aid of anything marvellous.

Horace Walpole, 1794, *To Countess of Ossory*, Sept. 4;
Letters, ed. Cunningham, vol. IX, p. 440

In the productions of Mrs. Radcliffe, the Shakspeare of Romance Writers,
and who to the wild landscape of Salvator Rosa has added the softer graces
of a Claude, may be found many scenes truly terrific in their conception, yet
so softened down, and the mind so much relieved, by the intermixture of
beautiful description, or pathetic incident, that the impression of the whole
never becomes too strong, never degenerates into horror, but pleasurable
emotion is ever the predominating result.

Nathan Drake, 1798-1820, *Literary Hours*,
vol. I, No. xvii, p. 273

In the writings of this author there is a considerable degree of uniformity
and mannerism, which is perhaps the case with all the productions of a
strong and original genius. Her heroines too nearly resemble each other, or
rather they possess hardly any shade of difference. They all have blue eyes
and auburn hair—the form of each of them has "the airy lightness of a
nymph"—they are all fond of watching the setting sun, and catching the
purple tints of evening, and the vivid glow or fading splendour of the western horizon. Unfortunately they are all likewise early risers. I say unfortunately, for in every exigency Mrs. Radcliffe's heroines are provided with
a pencil and paper, and the sun is never allowed to rise or set in peace. Like
Tilburina in the play, they are "inconsolable to the minuet in Ariadne," and
in the most distressing circumstances find time to compose sonnets to sun-
rise, the bat, a sea-nymph, a lily, or a butterfly.

John Dunlop, 1814-42, *The History of Fiction*, vol. II, p. 412

Her descriptions of scenery, indeed, are vague and wordy to the last degree;
they are neither like Salvator nor Claude, nor nature nor art; and she dwells

on the effects of moonlight till we are sometimes weary of them; her characters are insipid,—the shadows of a shade, continued on, under different
names, through all her novels; her story comes to nothing. But in harrowing up the soul with imaginary horrors, and making the flesh creep and the
nerves thrill with fond hopes and fears, she is unrivalled among her fair
countrywomen. Her great power lies in describing the indefinable, and embodying a phantom. She makes her readers twice children. . . . All the
fascination that links the world of passion to the world unknown is hers,
and she plays with it at her pleasure: she has all the poetry of romance, all
that is obscure, visionary, and objectless in the imagination.

> William Hazlitt, 1818, *Lecture on the English Novelists*

Up to the close of *The Italian,* her mind seems gradually to have ascended;
and perhaps she felt as if the next step might be downward. It may be that
she was right. *Gaston de Blondeville*—not given to the world till after her
death, and written scarcely five years after *The Italian,*—though showing a
surprising improvement in style, discovers, at the same time, a subsiding of
those energies by which she had held us with such fearful mastery.

> Richard Henry Dana, 1827-50, "Radcliffe's *Gaston de Blondeville,*"
> *Poems and Prose Writings,* vol. II, p. 317

Her landscapes, even now, though literature has done a great deal since
then in the pictorial art, are full of an elaborate and old-fashioned yet tender beauty. She is not familiar with them, nor playful, but always at the
height of a romantic strain; not graphic, but refined and full of perception.
There are scenes that remind us of the learned Poussin, and some that have
a light in them not unworthy of Claude before he was put down from his
throne by the braggart energy and rivalship of Turner—since when the
modern spectator has scarcely had eyes for those serene horizons and
gleaming moonlight seas. Perhaps of all others Mrs. Radcliffe's art is most
like that of the gentle painter whom people call Italian Wilson. There is a
ruined temple in the distance, a guitar laid against a broken column; but
the lights, how mellow and soft, the skies how full of tempered radiance,
the pastoral valleys unprofaned by ungracious foot—full of the light that
never was on sea or shore!

> Margaret O. W. Oliphant, 1882, *The Literary History of England,*
> *XVIIIth-XIXth Century,* vol. II, pp. 232, 233

There is generally some mystery afloat; when one has been cleared up, we
are not suffered long to breathe freely before we are caught in the toils of
another. Yet all the time only human agents are at work; there is nothing

improbable except the extraordinary combination of circumstances, nothing supernatural except in the superstitious imaginings of the personages of the story. Every thing that seemed as if it must be the work of spirits is carefully and fully explained as the story goes on. Mrs. Radcliffe has been censured for these explanations, as if they were a mistake in point of art, destroying the illusion and making us ashamed of ourselves for having been imposed upon. This censure I can regard only as an affectation, unless when it comes from a convinced believer in ghosts. Such persons might resent the explanation as casting doubts upon their cherished belief. But for other people I can see nothing that could be gained by leaving the mysterious incidents unexplained, except by the authoress, who would undoubtedly have saved herself an immense deal of trouble if she had made free use of ghosts and other supernatural properties, whenever she required them, without taking any pains to explain how the facts occurred. I read the story myself with a double interest; I enjoy the excitement of superstitious wonder and awe while the illusion lasts, and when the mystery is cleared up, and the excitement is gently subsiding, I am in a mood to get additional enjoyment from reflecting on the ingenuity of the complication that gave to the illusion for the moment the force of truth. Yet it was no less a person than Sir Walter Scott that set the fashion of objecting to Mrs. Radcliffe's explanations.

William Minto, 1894, *The Literature of the Georgian Era,*
ed. Knight, p. 126

Mrs. Radcliffe wrote for the story, and not for the characters, which are all types, and soon became conventional. There is always the young lover, a gentleman of high birth, usually in some sort of disguise, who, without seeing the face of the heroine, may fall in love with her "distinguished air of delicacy and grace" or "the sweetness and fine expression of her voice." The only variation in the heroine is that she may be either dark or fair. The beautiful creature is confined in a castle or a convent because she refuses to marry some one whom she hates. She finally has her own way and marries her lover. The tyrant is always the same man under different names; add to him a little softness, and he becomes the Byronic hero.

Wilbur L. Cross, 1899, *The Development of
the English Novel,* p. 106

Does any one now read Mrs. Radcliffe, or am I the only wanderer in her windy corridors, listening timidly to groans and hollow voices, and shielding the flame of a lamp, which, I fear, will presently flicker out, and leave me in the darkness? People know the name *The Mysteries of Udolpho;* they know that boys would say to Thackeray, at school, "Old fellow, draw us Vivaldi in the Inquisition." But have they penetrated into the chill galleries of the Castle of Udolpho? Have they shuddered for Vivaldi in face of the sable-clad and masked Inquisition? Certainly Mrs. Radcliffe, within the memory of man, has been extremely popular. The thick double-columned volume in which I peruse the works of the Enchantress belongs to a public library. It is quite the dirtiest, greasiest, most dog's-eared, and most be-scribbled tome in the collection. Many of the books have remained, during the last hundred years, uncut, even to this day, and I have had to apply the paper knife to many an author, from Alciphron (1790) to Mr. Max Müller, and Dr. Birkbeck Hill's edition of Bozzy's *Life of Dr. Johnson.* But Mrs. Radcliffe has been read diligently, and copiously annotated. . . . Mrs. Radcliffe does not always keep on her highest level, but we must remember that her last romance, *The Italian,* is by far her best. She had been feeling her way to this pitch of excellence, and, when she had attained to it, she published no more. . . . *The Italian* is an excellent novel. The Prelude, "the dark and vaulted gateway," is not unworthy of Hawthorne, who, I suspect, had studied Mrs. Radcliffe.

Andrew Lang, 1900, "Mrs. Radcliffe's Novels,"
Cornhill Magazine, vol. 82, pp. 23, 24, 33

GEORGE NOEL GORDON, LORD BYRON
1788-1824

Born, in London, 22 Jan. 1788. Lame from birth. Early years spent with mother in Aberdeen. Educated at private schools there, and at grammar school, 1794-98. Succeeded to title on death of grand-uncle, May 1798. To Newstead with his mother, autumn of 1799. Made ward in Chancery under guardianship of Lord Carlisle. To school at Nottingham. To London for treatment of lameness, 1799. To Dr. Glennie's school at Dulwich, 1799. At Harrow, summer of 1801 to 1805. To Trinity Coll., Cambridge, Oct. 1805; M. A., 4 July 1808. On leaving Cambridge, settled at New-stead. Took seat in House of Lords, 13 March 1809. Started on "grand tour," 2 July 1809, to Spain, Malta, Turkey, Greece. Returned to England, July 1811. Settled in St. James's Street, London, Oct. 1811. Spoke for first time in House of Lords, 27 Feb. 1812. Married Anne Isabella Mil-banke, 2 Jan. 1815. Settled in Piccadilly Terrace, London, March 1815. Daughter born, 10 Dec. 1815. Separation from wife, Feb. 1816. Left England, 24 April 1816. To Belgium, Germany, Switzerland, Italy. Amour with Miss Clairmont, 1816-17. Daughter born by her, Jan. 1817 (died April 1822). Settled in Venice, 1817. Amour with Countess Guiccioli, April to Oct., 1819. To Ravenna, Christmas 1819. Prolific literary pro-duction. *Marino Faliero* performed at Drury Lane, spring of 1821. To Pisa, Oct. 1821. *The Liberal* published (4 nos. only), with Leigh Hunt and Shelley, 1823. Elected member of Greek Committee in London, 1823. Sailed from Genoa for Greece, 15 July 1823. Raising Suliote troops on behalf of Greeks against Turks at Missolonghi, Dec. 1823. Serious illness, Feb. 1824. Died, 19 April 1824. Buried in England, at Hucknall Torkard. WORKS: *Fugitive Pieces* (privately printed, all destroyed except two copies), 1806 (a facsimile privately printed, 1886); *Poems on Various Occasions* (anon., same as preceding, with omissions), 1807; *Hours of Idleness*, 1807; *English Bards and Scotch Reviewers* (anon.), 1809 (2nd edn. same year); Poems contrib. to J. C. Hobhouse's *Imitations and Translations*, 1809; *Childe Harold*, cantos 1 and 2, 1812 (2nd-5th edns., same year); *The Curse of Minerva* (anon.), 1812; *The Waltz* (under pseud. of "Horace Hornem"), 1813; *The Giaour*, 1813; *The Bride of Abydos*, 1813 (2nd-5th edns., same year); *The Corsair*, 1814; *Ode to Napoleon Buonaparte* (anon.), 1814; *Lara* (anon., with Rogers's *Jacqueline*), 1814; *Hebrew Melodies*, 1815; *Siege of Corinth* (anon.), 1816; *Parisina*, 1816 (second edn., with preceding work, same year); *Poems*, 1816; *Poems on his Domestic Circumstances*, 1816; *The Prisoner of Chillon*, 1816; *Childe Harold*, canto 3, 1816; *Monody on the Death of Sheridan* (anon.), 1816; *Fare Thee Well!* 1816; *Manfred*, 1817 (2nd edn., same year); *The Lament of Tasso*, 1817; *Poems Written by Somebody* (anon.), 1818; *Childe Harold*, canto 4, 1818; *Beppo* (anon.), 1818; *Suppressed Poems*, 1818; *Three Poems not included in the Works of Lord Byron*, 1818; *Don Juan*, cantos 1 and 2 (anon.), 1819; *Mazeppa*, 1819; *Marino Faliero*, 1820; *Don Juan*, cantos 3-5 (anon.), 1821; *The Prophecy of Dante* (with 2nd edn. of *Marino Faliero*), 1821; *Sardanapalus, The Two Foscari*, and *Cain*, 1821; *Letter . . . on the Rev. W. L. Bowles's Strictures on Pope*, 1821; *Werner*, 1822; *Don Juan*, cantos 6-14 (anon.), 1823; *The Liberal*, with Leigh Hunt and Shelley, 4 nos.), 1823; *The Age of Bronze* (anon.), 1823; *The Island*, 1823 (2nd edn., same year); *The Deformed Transformed*, 1823; *Heaven and Earth* (anon.), 1824; *Don Juan*, cantos 15, 16 (anon.), 1824 (canto 17 of *Don Juan*, 1829, and *Twenty Suppressed Stanzas*, 1838, are spurious); *Parliamentary Speeches*, 1824; *The Vision of Judgment* (anon., reprinted from pt. i. of *The Liberal*), 1824. POSTHUMOUS: *Correspondence with a Friend* (3 vols.), 1825; *Letters and Journals*, edited by T. Moore (2 vols.), 1830. COLLECTED WORKS: in 8 vols., 1815-17; in 5 vols., 1817; in 8 vols., 1818-20; in 4 vols., 1828; *Life and Works* (17 vols.), 1832-35, etc. LIFE: *Lord Byron and Some of His Contemporaries*, by Leigh Hunt, 1828; life by Moore, 1830; by Galt, 1830; by Jeaffreson, 1883; by Roden Noel ("Great Writers" series), 1890.

R. Farquharson Sharp, 1897, A Dictionary of English Authors, p. 45

SEE: *Poetical Works*, ed. E. H. Coleridge, 1898-1904, 7 v.; *Poetical Works*, ed. E. H. Coleridge, 1905(OSA); *Poetic and Dramatic Works*, ed. Paul Elmer More, 1905 (Cambridge ed.); *Selections from Poetry, Letters and Journals*, ed. Peter Quennell, 1949; *Correspondence*, ed. John Murray, 1922, 2 v.; *Letters and Journals*, ed. R. E. Prothero, 1898-1904, 6 v.; *Letters and Diaries, 1798 to 1824*, ed. Peter Quennell, 1950, 2 v.; Ethel C. Mayne, *Byron*, 1912, rev. 1924, 2 v.; Leslie A. Marchand, *Byron: A Biography*, 1957, 3 v.; Doris Langley Moore, *The Late Lord Byron*, 1961; Samuel C. Chew, *Byron in England. His Fame and After-fame*, 1924; Elizabeth F. Boyd, *Byron's Don Juan*, 1945; Bonamy Dobrée's *Byron's Dramas*, 1962.

PERSONAL

Of Lord Byron I can tell you only that his appearance is nothing that you would remark.

> Maria Edgeworth, 1813, *Letters,* vol. I, p.206

I called on Lord Byron to-day, with an introduction from Mr. Gifford. Here, again, my anticipations were mistaken. Instead of being deformed, as I had heard, he is remarkably well built, with the exception of his feet. Instead of having a thin and rather sharp and anxious face, as he has in his picture, it is round, open, and smiling; his eyes are light, and not black; his air easy and careless, not forward and striking; and I found his manners affable and gentle, the tones of his voice low and conciliating, his conversation gay, pleasant, and interesting in an uncommon degree.

> George Ticknor, 1815, *Journal,* June 20;
> *Life Letters and Journals,* vol. I, p. 58

A countenance, exquisitely modeled to the expression of feeling and passion, and exhibiting the remarkable contrast of very dark hair and eyebrows, with light and expressive eyes, presented to the physiognomist the most interesting subject for the exercise of his art. The predominating expression was that of deep and habitual thought, which gave way to the most rapid play of features when he engaged in interesting discussion; so that a brother poet compared them to the sculpture of a beautiful alabaster vase, only seen to perfection when lighted up from within. The flashes of mirth, gayety, indignation, or satirical dislike which frequently animated Lord Byron's countenance, might, during an evening's conversation, be mistaken by a stranger, for the habitual expression, so easily and happily was it formed for them all; but those who had an opportunity of studying his features for a length of time, and upon various occasions, both of rest and emotion, will agree with us that their proper language was that of melancholy.

> Sir Walter Scott, 1816, *"Childe Harold,* Canto iii, and
> Other Poems," *Quarterly Review,* vol. 16, p. 176

If you had seen Lord Byron, you could scarcely disbelieve him. So beautiful a countenance I scarcely ever saw—his teeth so many stationary smiles, his eyes the open portals of the sun—things of light and for light—and his forehead so ample, and yet so flexible, passing from marble smoothness into a hundred wreaths and lines and dimples correspondent to the feelings and sentiments he is uttering.

> Samuel Taylor Coleridge, 1816, *Letter,* April 10; *Life* by Gillman

I was introduced, at the theatre, to Lord Byron.—What a grand countenance!—it is impossible to have finer eyes!—the divine man of genius!—He is yet scarcely twenty-eight years of age, and he is the first poet in England, probably in the world; when he is listening to music it is a countenance worthy of the *beau-ideal* of the Greeks. For the rest, let a man be ever so great a poet, let him besides be the head of one of the most ancient families in England, this is too much for our age, and I have learnt with pleasure that *Lord Byron is a wretch*. When he came into the drawing-room of Madame de Staël, at Copet, all the English ladies left it. Our unfortunate man of genius had the imprudence to marry,—his wife is very clever, and has renewed at his expense the old story of "Tom Jones and Blifil." Men of genius are generally mad, or at the least very imprudent! His lordship was so atrocious, as to take an actress into keeping for two months. If he had been a blockhead, nobody would have concerned themselves with his following the example of almost all young men of fashion; but it is well known that Mr. Murray, the bookseller, gives him two guineas a line for all the verses he sends him. He is absolutely the counterpart of M. de Mirabeau; the feudalists, before the Revolution, not knowing how to answer the "Eagle of Marseilles," discovered that he was a monster.

Henri Beyle (Stendhal), 1817,
Rome, Naples and Florence, June 27

I come at once to his lordship's charge against me, blowing away the abuse with which it is frothed, and evaporating a strong acid in which it is suspended. The residuum, then, appears to be, that "Mr. Southey, on his return from Switzerland (in 1817), scattered abroad calumnies, knowing them to be such, against Lord Byron and others." To this I reply with *a direct and positive denial*. If I had been told in that country that Lord Byron had turned Turk, or monk of La Trappe,—that he had furnished a *harem,* or endowed a hospital, I might have thought the report, whichever it had been, possible, and repeated it accordingly, passing it, as it had been taken, in the small change of conversation, for no more than it was worth. In this manner I might have spoken of him as of Baron Gerambe, the Green Man, the Indian Jugglers, or any other *figurante* of the time being. There was no reason for any particular delicacy on my part in speaking of his lordship; and, indeed, I should have thought anything which might be reported of him would have injured his character as little as the story which so greatly annoyed Lord Keeper Guilford—that he had ridden a rhinoceros. He may ride a rhinoceros, and though every one would stare, no one would wonder. But making no inquiry concerning him when I was abroad, because I felt no curiosity, I heard nothing, and had nothing to repeat.

Robert Southey, 1822, *To the Editor of The Courier,* Jan. 5

I was told it all alone in a room full of people. If they had said the sun or the moon was gone out of the heavens, it could not have struck me with the idea of a more awful and dreary blank in the creation than the words, "Bryon is dead."

Jane Welsh, 1824, *Letter to Thomas Carlyle,*
in *Life* by Froude, vol. I, p. 173

Poor Byron! alas, poor Byron! the news of his death came upon my heart like a mass of lead; and yet, the thought of it sends a painful twinge through all my being, as if I had lost a brother. O God! that so many souls of mud and clay should fill up their base existence to its utmost bound; and this the noblest spirit in Europe should sink before half his course was run. Late so full of fire and generous passion and proud purposes; and now for ever dumb and cold. Poor Byron! and but a young man, still struggling amidst the perplexities and sorrows and aberrations of a mind not arrived at maturity, or settled in its proper place in life. Had he been spared to the age of three-score and ten, what might he not have done! what might he not have been! But we shall hear his voice no more. I dreamed of seeing him and knowing him; but the curtain of everlasting night has hid him from our eyes. We shall go to him; he shall not return to us. Adieu. There is a blank in your heart and a blank in mine since this man passed away.

Thomas Carlyle, 1824, *Letter to Jane Welsh,*
in *Life* by Froude, vol. I, p. 173

I never met with any man who shines so much in conversation. He shines the more, perhaps, for not seeking to shine. His ideas flow without effort, without his having occasion to think. As in his letters, he is not nice about expressions or words;—there are no concealments in him no injunctions to secresy. He tells everything that he has thought or done without the least reserve, and as if he wished the whole world to know it; and does not throw the slightest gloss over his errors. . . . He hates argument, and never argues for victory. He gives every one an opportunity of sharing in the conversation, and has the art of turning it to subjects that may bring out the person with whom he converses.

Thomas Medwin, 1824, *Conversations of Lord Byron Noted
During a Residence with his Lordship at Pisa in the Years
1821 and 1822,* p. 334

I have just finished Lord Byron's *Conversations.* . . . Fifty years hence our descendants will see which is remembered best, the author of *The Excursion,* or of *Childe Harold.* But he seems to me to have wanted the power of admiration, the organ of veneration; to have been a cold, sneering, vain, Voltairish person, charitable as far as money went, and liberal so far as it

did not interfere with his aristocratic notions; but very derisive, very un-
English, very scornful. Captain Medwyn speaks of his suppressed laugh.
How unpleasant an idea that gives! The only thing that does him much
credit in the whole book is his hearty admiration of Scott. . . . Well, I think
this book will have one good effect, it will disenchant the whole sex.

Mary Russell Mitford, 1824, Letter to B. R. Haydon, Nov. 2

Of his face the beauty may be pronounced to have been of the highest order,
as combining at once regularity of features with the most varied and interesting expression. The same facility, indeed, of change observable in the
movements of his mind was seen also in the free play of his features, as the
passing thoughts within darkened or shone through them. His eyes, though
of a light grey, were capable of all extremes of expression, from the most
joyous hilarity to the deepest sadness, from the very sunshine of benevolence
to the most concentrated scorn or rage. . . . But it was in the mouth and
chin that the great beauty as well as expression of his fine countenance lay.
. . . His head was remarkably small,—so much so as to be rather out of
proportion with his face. The forehead, though a little too narrow, was
high, and appeared more so from his having his hair (to preserve it, as he
said) shaved over the temples; while the glossy, dark-brown curls, cluster-
ing over his head, gave the finish to its beauty. When to this is added, that
his nose, though handsomely, was rather thickly shaped, that his teeth were
white and regular, and his complexion colourless, as good an idea perhaps
as it is in the power of mere words to convey may be conceived of his features. In height he was, as he himself has informed us, five feet eight inches
and a half, and to the length of his limbs he attributed his being such a good
swimmer. His hands were very white, and—according to his own notion of
the size of hands as indicating birth—aristocratically small. The lameness
of his right foot, though an obstacle to grace, but little impeded the activity
of his movements; and from this circumstance, as well as from the skill with
which the foot was disguised by means of long trowsers, it would be difficult to conceive a defect of this kind less obtruding itself as a deformity;
while the diffidence which a constant consciousness of the infirmity gave
to his first approach and address made, in him, even lameness a source of
interest.

Thomas Moore, 1830-31, Life of Lord Byron, vol. II, pp. 534, 535

The young peer had great intellectual powers; yet there was an unsound
part in his mind. He had naturally a generous and tender heart; but his
temper was wayward and irritable. He had a head which statuaries loved to
copy, and a foot the deformity of which the beggars in the streets mimicked.
Distinguished at once by the strength and by the weakness of his intellect,

affectionate yet perverse, a poor lord and a handsome cripple, he required if ever man required, the firmest and the most judicious training. But, capriciously as nature had dealt with him, the relative to whom the office of forming his character was intrusted was more capricious still. She passed from paroxysms of rage to paroxysms of fondness. At one time she stifled him with her caresses, at another time she insulted his deformity. He came into the world, and the world treated him as his mother treated him— sometimes with kindness, sometimes with severity, never with justice. It indulged him without discrimination, and punished him without discrimination. He was truly a spoiled child; not merely the spoiled child of his parents, but the spoiled child of nature, the spoiled child of fortune, the spoiled child of fame, the spoiled child of society.

> Thomas Babington Macaulay, 1830, "Moore's *Life of Lord Byron*," *Critical and Miscellaneous Essays*

Byron had the strangest and most perverse of all vanities—the desire to surprise the world by showing, that, after all his sublime and spiritual flights, he could, on nearer inspection, be the lowest, the coarsest, the most familiar, and the most sensual of the low: and this, it is said, he exhibited in the MS. autobiography which was burnt. This is a most incomprehensible fact,—even more incomprehensible than some of the mad Confessions of Rousseau. Byron's, perhaps, arose from the vanity of wishing to be considered a man of the world, and a man of fashion—a very mean and contemptible wish. I scorn hypocrisy; but who in a sane mind would blacken his own character with disgraceful vice beyond the truth?

> Sir Samuel Egerton Brydges, 1834, *Autobiography*, vol. II, p. 229

He died among strangers, in a foreign land, without a kindred hand to close his eyes; yet he did not die unwept. With all his faults and errors, and passions and caprices, he had the gift of attaching his humble dependents warmly to him. One of them, a poor Greek, accompanied his remains to England, and followed them to the grave. I am told, that during the ceremony, he stood holding on by a pew in an agony of grief, and when all was over, seemed as if he would have gone down into the tomb with the body of his master.—A nature that could inspire such attachments, must have been generous and beneficent. . . . His love for Miss Chaworth, to use Lord Byron's own expression, was "the romance of the most romantic period of his life," and I think we can trace the effect of it throughout the whole course of his writings, coming up every now and then, like some lurking theme which runs through a complicated piece of music, and links it all in a pervading chain of melody.

> Washington Irving, 1849, "Newstead Abbey," *The Crayon Miscellany*, pp. 296, 316

In external appearance Byron realised that ideal standard with which imag-ination adorns genius. He was in the prime of life, thirty-four; of middle height, five feet eight and a half inches; regular features, without a stain or furrow on his pallid skin, his shoulders broad, chest open, body and limbs finely proportioned. His small highly-finished head and curly hair had an airy and graceful appearance from the massiveness and length of his throat: you saw his genius in his eyes and lips. In short, Nature could do little more than she had done for him, both in outward form and in the inward spirit she had given to animate it. But all these rare gifts to his jaundiced imagin-ation only served to make his one personal defect (lameness) the more ap-parent, as a flaw is magnified in a diamond when polished; and he brooded over that blemish as sensitive minds will brood until they magnify a wart into a wen. His lameness certainly helped to make him sceptical, cynical, and savage. There was no peculiarity in his dress, it was adapted to the climate: a tartan jacket braided—he said it was the Gordon pattern, and that his mother was of that race. A blue velvet cap with a gold band, and very loose nankeen trousers strapped down so as to cover his feet; his throat was not bare, as represented in drawings. . . . He would exist on biscuits and soda-water for days together.

Edward John Trelawny, 1858-78, Records of Shelley,
Byron and the Author, pp. 18, 51

The man in Byron is of nature even less sincere than that of the poet. Under-neath this Beltenebros there is hidden a coxcomb. He posed all through his life. He had every affectation—the writer's, the roué's, the dandy's, the conspirator's. He was constantly writing, and he pretends to despise his writings. To believe himself, he was proud of nothing but his skill in bodily exercises. An Englishman, he affects Bonapartism; a peer of the realm, he speaks of the Universal Republic with the enthusiasm of a schoolboy of fifteen. He plays at misanthropy, at dissillusion: he parades his vices; he even tries to make us believe that he has committed a crime or two. Read his letters—his letters written nominally to friends, but handed about from hand to hand in London. Read his journal—a journal kept ostensibly for himself, but handed over afterwards by him to Moore with authority to publish it. The littleness which these things show is amazing.

Edmond Scherer, 1863-91, in Taine's History of English Literature,
Essays on English Literature, tr. Saintsbury

Byron was always mean. He could pretend affection to Shelley in Italy, while he was secretly joining in the cry against him in England. He betrayed Leigh Hunt; he betrayed every hand that ever touched his. The only good thing that can be said of him is, that he finally came to despise himself; and

he probably entered the Greek struggle, where he fell, from sheer despera-
tion at the glimpse of his own degradation. As for this new revelation by
Mrs. Stowe, I don't see that it should sink Byron another degree in the
opinion of any one were it proved true; it would suggest the plea of diseased
instincts, which is the best that can be offered for his crimes; but his cowardice, his affectation, his deliberate meanness—pah!

M. D. Conway, 1870, "Southcoast Saunterings in England,"
Harper's Magazine, vol. 40, p. 525

Had he survived he might possibly have become, as H. E. W. surmises,
King of Greece, and perhaps not altogether a bad one. How strange a vista
of the possibilities of history is opened by such a suggestion! Against Byron's
vices and miserable affectations, and the false *ring* of his whole character—
which was so ludicrously exemplified by his writing "Fare thee well, and if
for ever" on the back of an unpaid butcher's bill—must always be set the
honour of his self-devotion and heroism in the Greek war. If he was somewhat of a Sardanapalus, it was a Sardanapalus who could fight for a noble
cause not his own. Expressing once to Mazzini my own sense that Byron
could scarcely take rank as a poet, compared to Shelley, the Italian *patriot*
replied: "Ah! but you forget that Shelley was only a poet in words and
feeling; Byron translated his poetry into action, when he went to fight for
Greece."

Frances Power Cobbe, 1882, *Letter to The Temple Bar*,
vol. 64, p. 318

In the domain of the affections he was, from boyhood till his hair whitened,
a man of so acute a sensibility that it may well be termed morbid. To this
excessive sensibility, and the various kinds of emotionality that necessarily
attended it, must be attributed the quickness with which his "passions"
succeeded one another. . . . With women he was what they pleased to make
or take him for. But he was most pleased with them when they treated him
as nearly as possible like "a favorite and sometimes forward sister." The
reader may smile, but must not laugh; it was as "a favorite and sometimes
forward sister" that he was thought of and treated by Hobhouse and other
men. What then more natural for him to like to be thought of and treated
by women in the same way?

John Cordy Jeaffreson, 1883, *The Real Lord Byron*, pp. 65, 172

LADY BYRON

She is a very superior woman, and very little spoiled; which is strange in an
heiress, a girl of twenty, a peeress that is to be in her own right, an only
child, and a savante, who has always had her own way. She is a poetess, a

mathematician, a metaphysician; yet, withal, very kind, generous, and gentle, with very little pretension. Any other head would be turned with half her acquisitions and a tenth of her advantages.

Lord Byron, 1815, Journal

> Fare thee well! and if for ever
>   Still for ever, fare *thee well;*
> Even though unforgiving, never
>   'Gainst thee shall my heart rebel.
>
>   .   .   .   .
>
> Though my many faults defaced me,
>   Could no other arm be found,
> Than the one which once embraced me,
>   To inflict a cureless wound?

Lord Byron, 1816, Fare Thee Well, March 17

Lord and Lady Byron are, you know, separated. He said to Rogers that Lady Byron had parted with him, apparently in good friendship, on a visit to her father, and that he had no idea of their being about to part, when he received her decision to that effect. He stated that his own temper, naturally bad, had been rendered more irritable by the derangement of his fortune, and that Lady Byron was entirely blameless. The truth is, he is a very unprincipled fellow.

Sydney Smith, 1816, To Francis Jeffrey,
A Memoir of Sidney Smith by Lady Holland

Lord Byron's was a marriage of convenience,—certainly at least on his own part. . . . He married for money, but of course he wooed with his genius; and the lady persuaded herself that she liked him, partly because he had a genius, and partly because it is natural to love those who take pains to please us. Furthermore, the poet was piqued to obtain his mistress, because she had a reputation for being delicate in such matters; and the lady was piqued to become his wife, not because she did not know the gentleman previously to marriage, but because she did, and hoped that her love and her sincerity, and her cleverness, would enable her to reform him. The experiment was dangerous, and did not succeed. . . . The "Farewell' that he wrote, and that set so many tender-hearted white handkerchiefs in motion, only resulted from his poetical power of assuming an imaginary position, and taking pity on himself in the shape of another man. He had no love for the object of it, or he would never have written upon her in so different a style afterwards.

Leigh Hunt, 1828, Lord Byron and Some of His
Contemporaries, vol. I, pp. 9, 11

The accounts given me after I left Lord Byron, by the persons in constant intercourse with him, added to those doubts which had before transiently occurred to my mind as to the reality of the alleged disease; and the reports of his medical attendant were far from establishing the existence of anything like lunacy. Under this uncertainty, I deemed it right to communicate to my parents, that, if I were to consider Lord Byron's past conduct as that of a person of sound mind, nothing could induce me to return to him. It therefore appeared expedient, both to them and myself, to consult the ablest advisers. For that object, and also to obtain still further information respecting the appearances which seemed to indicate mental derangement, my mother determined to go to London. She was empowered by me to take legal opinions on a written statement of mine, though I had then reasons for reserving a part of the case from the knowledge even of my father and mother. Being convinced by the result of these inquiries, and by the tenor of Lord Byron's proceedings, that the notion of insanity was an illusion, I no longer hesitated to authorize such measures as were necessary in order to secure me from being ever again placed in his power. Conformably with this resolution, my father wrote to him on the 2d of February to propose an amicable separation. Lord Byron at first rejected this proposal; but when it was distinctly notified to him, that, if he persisted in his refusal, recourse must be had to legal measures, he agreed to sign a deed of separation.

Lady (A. I. Noel) Byron, 1830, Letter to the Public, Feb. 19

Miss Milbanke knew that he was reckoned a rake and a *roué;* and although his genius wiped off, by impassioned eloquence in love-letters that were felt to be irresistible, or hid the worst stain of that reproach, still Miss Milbanke must have believed it a perilous thing to be the wife of Lord Byron. . . . But still, by joining her life to his in marriage, she pledged her troth, and her faith, and her love, under probabilities of severe, disturbing, perhaps fearful trials in the future. . . . But I think Lady Byron ought not to have printed that Narrative. Death abrogates not the rights of a husband to his wife's silence, when speech is fatal . . . to his character as a man. Has she not flung suspicion over his bones interred, that they are the bones of—a monster?

John Wilson (Christopher North), 1830, "Noctes Ambrosianæ,"
Blackwood's Magazine, vol. 27, pp. 823, 824

Many excellent reasons are given for his being a bad husband; the sum of which is, that he was a very bad man. I confess I was rejoiced then, and am rejoiced now, that he was driven out of England by public scorn; because his vices were not in his passions, but in his principles.

Daniel Webster, 1833, Letter to George Ticknor, April 8

I have said enough to show him as he was, a thoroughly spoilt man. Lady Byron was equally spoilt in an opposite direction—self-willed, intolerant, jealous, and vindictive. She was a rigid Puritan: they are a brave and undaunted sect in self-reliance on their superiority over all other people, and fear nothing. Saints armed in righteousness prefer doing battle with great sinners, confident of their cause. Lady Byron, with the pertinacity of a zealot, plied the poet with holy texts from Scripture and moral maxims from pious writers. . . . Any one could live with him excepting an inflexible and dogmatic saint; not that he objected to his wife's piety, for he saw no harm in that, but her inflicting it on him. The lady's theory was opposed to this: her mission was to reform him by her example and teaching. She had a smattering of science, mathematics, and metaphysics—a toy pet from her childhood, idolized by her parents, and considered as a phenomenon by her country neighbours.

> Edward John Trelawny, 1858-78, *Records of Shelley,*
> *Byron and the Author,* pp. 40, 41

Never was a young creature led to the altar more truly as a sacrifice. She was rash, no doubt; but she loved him, and who was not, in the whole business, more rash than she? At the altar she did not know that she was a sacrifice: but before sunset of that winter day she knew it, if a judgment may be formed from her face and attitude of despair when she alighted from the carriage on the afternoon of her marriage-day. It was not the traces of tears which won the sympathy of the old butler who stood at the open door. The bridegroom jumped out of the carriage and walked away. The bride alighted, and came up the steps alone, with a countenance and frame agonized and listless with evident horror and despair. The old servant longed to offer his arm to the young, lonely creature, as an assurance of sympathy and protection. From this shock she certainly rallied, and soon. The pecuniary difficulties of her new home were exactly what a devoted spirit like hers was fitted to encounter. He husband bore testimony, after the catastrophe, that a brighter being, a more sympathizing and agreeable companion, never blessed any man's home. When he afterwards called her cold and mathematical, and over-pious, and so forth, it was when public opinion had gone against him, and when he had discovered that her fidelity and mercy, her silence and magnanimity, might be relied on, so that he was at full liberty to make his part good, as far as she was concerned. . . . She loved him to the last with a love which it was not in his power to destroy. She gloried in his fame; and she would not interfere between him and the public who adored him, any more than she would admit the public to judge between him and her. As we have said, her love endured to the last.

> Harriet Martineau, 1860-69, *Biographical Sketches,* pp. 284, 287

She has been called, after his words, the moral Clytemnestra of her husband. Such a surname is severe: but the repugnance we feel to condemning a woman cannot prevent our listening to the voice of justice, which tells us that the comparison is still in favor of the guilty one of antiquity; for *she* driven to crime by fierce passion overpowering reason, at least only deprived her husband of physical life, and, in committing the deed, exposed herself to all its consequences; while Lady Byron left her husband at the very moment that she saw him struggling amid a thousand shoals in the stormy sea of embarrassments created by his marriage, and precisely when he more than ever required a friendly, tender, and indulgent hand to save him from the tempests of life. Besides, she shut herself up in silence a thousand times more cruel than Clytemnestra's poniard: *that* only killed the body; whereas Lady Byron's silence was destined to kill the soul,—and such a soul!—leaving the door open to calumny, and making it to be supposed that her silence was magnanimity destined to cover over frightful wrongs, perhaps even depravity. In vain did he, feeling his conscience at ease, implore some inquiry and examination. She refused, and the only favor she granted was to send him, one fine day, two persons to see whether he were not mad.

Countess Guiccoli, 1868-69, *My Recollections of Lord Byron,*
tr. Jerningham, p. 540

Supposing Mrs. Stowe's narrative to have been really a "true story," and that we had meant to reveal the whole of our grandmother's history, I do not see what defence that is to Mrs. Stowe against the charge of repeating what was told her in a "private, confidential conversation." But it is not true that Lady Anne Blunt and I ever intended to publish correspondence of the nature mentioned. About three years ago a manuscript in Lady Noel Byron's handwriting was found among her papers, giving an account of some circumstances connected with her marriage, and apparently intended for publication after her death; but as this seemed not quite certain, no decision as to its publication was come to. In the event of a memoir being written, this manuscript might, perhaps, be included, but hitherto it has not been proposed to publish any other matter about her separation. This statement in Lady Byron's own handwriting does not contain any accusation of so grave a nature as that which Mrs. Stowe asserts was told her, and Mrs. Stowe's story of the separation is inconsistent with what I have seen in various letters, &c., of Lady Byron's. . . . I, for one, cannot allow that Mrs. Stowe's statement is substantially correct.

Lord Wentworth, 1869, *Pall Mall Gazette,* Sept. 3

It appears by Dr. Lushington's statements, that, when Lady Byron did
speak, she had a story to tell that powerfully affected both him and Romilly,
—a story supported by evidence on which they were willing to have gone to
public trial. Supposing, now, she had imitated Lord Byron's example, and,
avoiding public trial, had put her story into private circulation; as he sent
Don Juan to fifty confidential friends, suppose she had sent a written
statement of her story to fifty judges as intelligent as the two that had
heard it; or suppose she had confronted his autobiography with her own,—
what would have been the result? The first result would have been Mrs.
Leigh's utter ruin. The world may finally forgive the man of genius anything;
but for a woman there is no mercy and no redemption. This ruin Lady Byron
prevented by her utter silence and great self-command. Mrs. Leigh never
lost position. Lady Byron never so varied in her manner toward her as to
excite the suspicions even of her confidential old servant. To protect Mrs.
Leigh effectually, it must have been necessary to continue to exclude even
her own mother from the secret, as we are assured she did at first; for, had
she told Lady Milbanke, it is not possible that so highspirited a woman
could have restrained herself from such outward expressions as would at
least have awakened suspicion. There was no resource but this absolute
silence.

Harriet Beecher Stowe, 1870, Lady Byron Vindicated, p. 73

If the case is looked at calmly, a simple explanation is not difficult to find.
A woman who could ask such a husband in a voice of provoking sweetness
"when he meant to give up his bad habit of making verses," a woman who
never lost her temper, never gave up her point, and inflicted the most
malignant stabs in the tenderest places with angelic coolness, possessed the
power of goading a sensitive, impetuous man to frenzy. She had a maid, for
example, to whom Byron entertained a violent aversion, because he suspected her of poisoning his wife's mind against him. Lady Byron listened to
all his furious tirades with unruffled meekness, but never consented to send
the woman away. She was quite as jealous of her dignity, quite as resentful
of slights, real or supposed, as himself; and in their differences of opinion
she had the inestimable advantage of a temper perfectly under control, and
a command of all the sweet resignation of a martyr, combined with the most
skilful ingenuity of provoking retort. Byron, with his liability to fits of un-
controllable passion, could never have been an easy man to live with; but if
his wife had been a loving, warm-hearted woman, with the unconscious
tact that such women have, the result would probably have been very different.

William Minto, 1894, The Literature of the Georgian Era,
ed. Knight, p. 272

Hours of Idleness (1807)

The poesy of this young lord belongs to the class which neither gods nor men are said to permit. Indeed, we do not recollect to have seen a quantity of verse with so few deviations in either direction from that exact standard. His effusions are spread over a dead flat, and can no more get above or below the level, than if they were so much stagnant water. As an extenuation of this offence, the noble author is peculiarly forward in pleading minority. We have it in the title-page, and on the very back of the volume; it follows his name like a favourite part of his *style*. Much stress is laid upon it in the preface, and the poems are connected with this general statement of his case, by particular dates, substantiating the age at which each was written. Now, the law upon the point of minority we hold to be perfectly clear. It is a plea available only to the defendant; no plaintiff can offer it as a supplementary ground of action. . . . Whatever judgment may be passed on the poems of this noble minor, it seems we must take them as we find them, and be content; for they are the last we shall ever have from him. . . . What right have we poor devils to be nice? We are well off to have got so much from a man of this Lord's station; who does not live in a garret, but "has the sway" of Newstead Abbey. Again, we say, let us be thankful; and, with honest Sancho, bid God bless the giver, nor look the gift horse in the mouth.

Henry, Lord Brougham, 1808, "Lord Byron's Poems,"
Edinburgh Review, vol. 11, pp. 285, 289

Yet though there were many, and those not the worst judges, who discerned in these juvenile productions, a depth of thought and felicity of expression which promised much at a more mature age, the errors did not escape the critical lash; and certain brethren of ours yielded to the opportunity of pouncing upon a titled author, and to that which most readily besets our fraternity, and to which we dare not pronounce ourselves wholly inaccessible, the temptation, namely, of shewing our own wit, and entertaining our readers with a lively article without much respect to the feelings of the author, or even to the indications of merit which the work may exhibit.

Sir Walter Scott, 1816, *"Childe Harold,* Canto iii, and
Other Poems," *Quarterly Review,* vol. 16, p. 174

Hours of Idleness were poorish and pretentious verses, certainly with less of promise in them than the first productions of most other great poets. Yet they had some, and there was little excuse for the smart but stupid *Edinburgh Review* article upon them. However, this had the good effect of rousing Byron to put forth his power.

Roden Noel, *The Poets and the Poetry of the Century,
Southey to Shelley,* ed. Miles, p. 375

English Bards and Scotch Reviewers (1809)

As to the *Edinburgh Reviewers,* it would indeed require an Hercules to crush the Hydra; but if the author succeeds in merely "bruising one of the heads of the serpent," though his own hand should suffer in the encounter, he will be amply satisfied.

> Lord Byron, 1809, *English Bards and Scotch Reviewers,* Preface

If I could envy any man for successful ill-nature, I should envy Lord Byron for his skill in satirical nomenclature.

> Sydney Smith, 1810, *To Lady Holland,* June;
> *Memoir* by Lady Holland

[It] is the last angry reverberation of the literary satire of Dryden and Pope. It is a kind of inverted *Dunciad;* and novice falls upon the masters of his day, as the Augustan master upon the nonentities of his, and emulates Pope's stiletto with a vigorous bludgeon. Only those who, like Rogers or Campbell, in some sort also maintained the tradition of Pope, came off without a gibe. But the invective, though as a rule puerile as criticism, shows extraordinary powers of malicious statement, and bristles with the kind of epigram which makes satire stick, when it is too wildly aimed to wound.

> C. H. Herford, 1897, *The Age of Wordsworth,* p. 222

Childe Harold (1812-18)

The Third Canto of *Childe Harold* exhibits, in all its strength and in all its peculiarities, the wild, powerful and original vein of poetry which, in the preceding cantos, first fixed the public attention upon the author. If there is any difference, the former seems to us to have been rather more sedulously corrected and revised for the publication, and the present work to have been dashed from the author's pen with less regard to the subordinate points of expression and versification. Yet such is the deep and powerful strain of passion, such the original tone and colouring of description, that the want of polish in some of its minute parts rather adds to than deprives the poem of its energy.

> Sir Walter Scott, 1816, *"Childe Harold,* Canto iii, and
> Other Poems," *Quarterly Review,* vol. 16, p. 189

The effect was, accordingly, electric; his fame had not to wait for any of the ordinary gradations, but seemed to spring up, like the palace of a fairy tale, in a night. As he himself briefly described it in his memoranda, "I awoke one morning and found myself famous."

> Thomas Moore, 1830, *Life of Lord Byron,* vol. I, p. 274

On taking up a fairly good version of *Childe Harold's Pilgrimage* in French or Italian prose, a reader whose eyes and ears are not hopelessly sealed against all distinction of good from bad in rhythm or in style will infallibly be struck by the vast improvement which the text has undergone in the course of translation. The blundering, floundering, lumbering and stumbling stanzas, transmuted into prose and transfigured into grammar, reveal the real and latent force of rhetorical energy that is in them: the gasping, ranting, wheezing, broken-winded verse has been transformed into really effective and fluent oratory. A ranter, of course, it is whose accents we hear in alternate moan and bellow from the trampled platform of theatrical misanthropy: but he rants no longer out of tune: and we are able to discern in the thick and troubled stream of his natural eloquence whatever of real value may be swept along in company with much drifting rubbish. It is impossible to express how much *Childe Harold* gains by being done out of wretchedly bad metre into decently good prose: the New Testament did not gain more by being translated out of canine Greek into divine English.

Algernon Charles Swinburne, 1886, "Wordsworth and Byron," *Miscellanies*, p. 75

But no English poet has used the Spenserian stanza with the grand *vigor* with which Byron has used it in his *Childe Harold*. His impetuous spirit imparts a character to the stanza quite distinct from its peculiar Spenserian character. Even the stanzas in which his gentler and more pensive moods are embodied, bear little or no similarity to the manner of Spenser.

Hiram Corson, 1892, *A Primer of English Verse*, p. 125

The demerits of *Childe Harold* lie on the surface; but it is difficult for the modern reader, familiar with the sight, if not the texture, of "the purple patches," and unattracted, perhaps demagnetized, by a personality once fascinating and always "puissant," to appreciate the actual worth and magnitude of the poem. We are "o'er informed"; and as with Nature, so with Art, the eye must be couched, and the film of association removed, before we can see clearly. But there is one characteristic feature of *Childe Harold* which association and familiarity have been powerless to veil or confuse— originality of design. "By what accident," asks the Quarterly Reviewer (George Agar Ellis), "has it happened that no other English poet before Lord Byron has thought fit to employ his talents on a subject so well suited to their display?" The question can only be answered by the assertion that it was the accident of genius which inspired the poet with a "new song." *Childe Harold's Pilgrimage* had no progenitors, and, with the exception of some feeble and forgotten imitations, it has had no descendants.

Ernest Hartley Coleridge, 1899, ed., *The Works of Lord Byron, Poetry*, vol. II, p. 13

The Giaour (1813)

I suppose you have read Lord Byron's *Giaour*,—and which edition? because there are five, and in every one he adds about fifty lines; so that the different editions have rather the sisterly likeness which Ovid says the Nereids had, than the identity expected by the purchasers of the same work. And pray do you say Lord Byron, or Byron, in defiance of the *y* and our old friend in Sir Charles Grandison? And do you pronounce Giaour hard *g* or soft *g*? And do you understand the poem at first reading?—because Lord Byron and the Edinburgh Reviewers say you are very stupid if you don't; and yet the same Reviewers have thought proper to prefix the story to help your apprehension. All these, unimportant as you may think them, are matters of discussion here.

Anna Lætitia Barbauld, 1813, Works, vol. II, p. 96

The Giaour is, as he truly called it, "a string of passages," not a work moving by a deep internal law of development to a necessary end; and our total impression from it cannot but receive from this, its inherent defect, a certain dimness and indistinctness. But the incidents of the journey and death of Hassan, in that poem, are conceived and presented with a vividness not to be surpassed; and our impression from them is correspondingly clear and powerful.

Matthew Arnold, 1881, The Poetry of Byron, Preface

The Corsair (1814)

To me Byron's *Corsair* appears the best of all his works. Rapidity of execution is no sort of apology for doing a thing ill, but when it is done well, the wonder is so much the greater. I am told he wrote this poem at ten sittings—certainly it did not take him more than three weeks.

Earl of Dudley, 1818, Letters

His Corsair is marred by classic elegancies: the pirates' song at the beginning is no truer than a chorus at the Italian opera; his scamps propound philosophical antitheses as balanced as those of Pope. A hundred times ambition, glory, envy, despair, and the other abstract personages, whose images in the time of the Empire the French used to set upon their drawing-room clocks, break in amidst living passions. The noblest passages are disfigured by pedantic apostrophes, and the pretentious poetic diction sets up its threadbare frippery and conventional ornaments. Far worse, he studies effect and follows the fashion.

H. A. Taine, 1871, History of English Literature,
tr. Van Laun, vol. II, bk. iv, ch. ii, p. 284

The Prisoner of Chillon (1816)

Next day beautiful drive to Vevey, as you know. After visiting Chillon, where Lord Byron's name and *coat of arms* are cut upon Bonnivar's pillar, I read the poem again, and think it most sublime and pathetic. How can that man have perverted so much feeling as was originally given to him!

> Maria Edgeworth, 1820, *Letters,* vol. II, p. 12

No one of Byron's poems is so purely narrative, or has such a unity of lofty and tender interest, uninterrupted by a single distracting image. But this very perfection makes it tame and cold among the heat and animation of the rest: it is the only one in which Byron is left out.

> Margaret O. W. Oliphant, 1882, *Literary History of England, XVIII-XIX Century,* vol. III, p. 56

Detained by bad weather at Ouchy, he wrote in two days *The Prisoner of Chillon.* with its glorious introductory sonnet to Liberty. This tale is a very beautiful composition, having unity, graphic description, tenderness, and pathos.

> Roden Noel, 1890, *Life of Lord Byron* (*Great Writers*), p. 120

Manfred (1817)

There are great faults, it must be admitted, in this poem;—but it is undoubtedly a work of genius and originality. It worst fault, perhaps, is that it fatigues and overawes us by the uniformity of its terror and solemnity. Another is the painful and offensive nature of the circumstance on which its distress is ultimately founded.

> Francis, Lord Jeffrey, 1817-44, *Contributions to the Edinburgh Review,* vol. II, p. 386

His [Goethe's] *Faust* I never read, for I don't know German; but Matthew Monk Lewis, in 1816, at Coligny, translated most of it to me *vivá voce,* and I was naturally much struck with it; but it was the "Staubach" and the "Jungfrau," and something else, much more than Faustus, that made me write *Manfred.*

> Lord Byron, 1820, *Letter to Mr.* [*John*] *Murray,* June 7

Byron's tragedy, *Manfred,* was to me a wonderful phenomenon, and one that closely touched me. This singular intellectual poet has taken my *Faustus* to himself, and extracted from it the strangest nourishment for his hypochondriac humour. He has made use of the impelling principles in his own

way, for his own purposes, so that no one of them remains the same; and it is partcularly on this account that I cannot enough admire his genius. The whole is in this way so completely formed anew that it would be an interesting task for the critic to point out, not only the alterations he has made, but their degree of resemblance with, or dissimilarity to, the original; in the course of which I cannot deny that the gloomy heat of an unbounded and exuberant despair becomes at last oppressive to us. Yet is the dissatisfaction we feel always connected with esteem and admiration. We find thus in this tragedy the quintessence of the most astonishing talent born to be its own tormentor.

> Johann Wolfgang Goethe, 1820, *Review of Manfred,* tr. Hoppner

Lord Byron's *Manfred* is in parts intensely poetical; yet the delicate mind naturally shrinks from the spirit which here and there reveals itself, and the basis on which the drama is built. From a perusal of it we should infer, according to the above theory, that there was right and fine feeling in the poet's mind, but that the central and consistent character was wanting. From the history of his life we know this to be the fact.

> John Henry Newman, 1829-71, *Poetry with Reference to Aristotle's Poetics; Essays Critical and Historical,* vol. I, p. 22

Byron's grandest poem is *Manfred.* Henri Taine compares it with *Faust,* and says that *Manfred* is the poem of individuality, and *Faust* the poem of humanity. I should call *Manfred* the poem of sentiment, and *Faust* the poem of ideas; *Manfred* the poem of nature, and *Faust* the poem of history. Both poems represent the disenchantment which is produced within the limits of human existence. Faust himself is weary after having thought, and Manfred after having lived. The one dies, as becomes a German doctor, after having studied medicine, alchemy, the theological sciences and philosophy, and having found them but ashes. The other expires after having felt, struggled, and loved in vain; after having ascended the gigantic ladder formed by the Alps, without finding anything more than the piercing wind eternally moaning, the white frost falling, the pines amid the snow-flakes, the cold desert of crystal fatal to life, the profound abyss where light is extinguished; beneath, men are like insects; above, the eagles fly in endless circles, breaking the immensity and the silence by their cries of hunger; a spectacle which reminds him of another desolation, the moonlight night in which he trod the ground of the Colosseum, the ruins overgrown with nettles, and heard nothing but owls, whose melancholy cries were an elegy over the ashes of the martyrs and gladiators of the past. . . . Byron *feels* the evil and Goethe *thinks* it.

> Emilio Castelar, 1873-75, *Life of Lord Byron and Other Sketches,* tr. Arnold, pp. 169, 176

He could exhibit only two squeaking and disjointed puppets: there is, as far as I can remember, just one passage in the whole range of his writings which shows any power of painting any phase of any kind of character at all: and this is no doubt a really admirable (if not wholly original) instance of the very broadest comedy—the harangue addressed by Donna Julia to her intruding husband.

Algernon Charles Swinburne, 1886, Wordsworth and Byron,
Miscellanies, p. 85

Some of Byron's most powerful writing is found in <i>Don Juan</i>; some of his tenderest; and the possible flexibility of the English language is often fully realized. But when he wrote this poem, his better nature was more or less eclipsed; but wherever it asserts itself, we feel its presence in the moulding of the verse, as much as we do in the sentiments expressed.

Hiram Corson, 1892, A Primer of English Verse, p. 29

Cain (1821)

Though it abounds in beautiful passages, and shows more *power* perhaps than any of the author's dramatical compositions, we regret very much that it should ever have been published. It will give great scandal and offence to pious persons in general—and may be the means of suggesting the most painful doubts and distressing perplexities, to hundreds of minds that might never otherwise have been exposed to such dangerous disturbance.

Francis, Lord Jeffrey, 1822-44, Contributions to the
Edinburgh Review, vol. II, p. 362

I said that I had lately been reading Byron's *Cain,* and had been particularly struck by the third act, and the manner in which the murder is brought about. "It is, indeed, admirable," said Goethe. "Its beauty is such as we shall not see a second time in the world." *"Cain,"* said I, "was at first prohibited in England; but now everybody reads it, and young English travellers usually carry a complete Byron with them." "It was folly" said Goethe; "for, in fact, there is nothing in the whole of *Cain* which is not taught by the English bishops themselves."

Johann Wolfgang Goethe, Conversations, ed. Eckermann,
vol. I, p. 419

Like a lion impatiently beating against the iron bars of his cage, so Byron precipitates himself in this poem on the mysteries of revealed faith. He never, indeed, succeeds in bursting his cage; rather he remains in a state of indecision, and never comes to a positive conclusion in either direction. To Englishmen this scepticism was, with few exceptions, an insurmountable stone of offence. In England freedom of action is cramped by the want of freedom in thought; the converse is the case with us Germans: freedom of thought is restricted by the want of freedom in action. To us this scepticism presents nothing in the least degree fearful; we, like Faust, are afraid neither of the devil nor of hell.

Karl Elze, 1870-72, *Lord Byron*, p. 415

Cain is the most complete and finished work of the poet, and we cannot contradict Shelley when he calls it the greatest of Byron's poems. Cain is a Titanic *Manfred,* a creation similar to Job and Prometheus. The spirit Æschylus seems to breath in the poem, and with the exception of a few passages in *Paradise Lost* and in *Faust,* modern poetry has produced nothing similar in boldness and in grandeur to Cain's flight with Lucifer through illimitable space, and the conversations of the two in Hades. In England the poem was appreciated by few at first, and Byron called it jestingly "the Waterloo of my [his] popularity." But it is an æsthetic truth that the creation of Satan in *Cain* must be considered as one of the greatest achievements of modern poetry. There are altogether only four poets who have succeeded in portraying Satan: Vandel, Milton, Goethe, and Byron. Vandel's Satan was created fourteen years before that of Milton; it is a powerful conception, and undoubtedly the greatest poetical figure which Holland has produced. Goethe's Mephisto is such a peculiar impersonation of the Satanic idea that he cannot be compared to the others. Byron's Satan ranks next to Milton's. Dante's detailed delineation only produces a somewhat ridiculous monster which leaves us perfectly indifferent, while Milton's and Byron's Satan is a colossal extention of the human form surrounded by a darkness as of thunder-clouds, and exciting our terror as well as a feeling of sympathy.

J. Scherr, 1874, *A History of English Literature,* tr. M. V., p. 236

LETTERS

The Letters, at least those which were sent from Italy, are among the best in our language. They are less affected than those of Pope and Walpole; they have more matter in them than those of Cowper. Knowing that many of them were not written merely for the person to whom they were directed, but were general epistles, meant to be read by a large circle, we expected to find them clever and spirited, but deficient in ease. We looked with vigilance for instances of stiffness in the language, and awkwardness in the transitions. We have been agreeably disappointed; and we must confess, that if the epistolary style of Lord Byron was artificial, it was a rare and admirable instance of that highest art which cannot be distinguished from nature.

Thomas Babington Macaulay, 1830, "Moore's *Life of Lord Byron,*"
Edinburgh Review; Critical and Miscellaneous Essays

GENERAL

His verse, with all its lofty aspirations and endowments, is lost in the mazes of infidelity and despair; groping in a vast crowd of strange unearthly shapes conjured up by midnight fancy, it deifies only a morbid heroism, which it invests with the gloomy spell of varied passion. This atheistic inspiration was not altogether alien to German poetry at an earlier epoch; but a purer sphere was soon attained, the monstrosities of false tragic grandeur being banished to the extreme confines of the drama. In the higher regions of art it was speedily discovered that modern poetry cannot flow in a transparent stream from the turbid eddy of forward passion; but founded on eternal hope, it must become a glorified admixture of Faith and Love, radiant as the rainbow after the storm, or the dawn of morn after the shades of night.

Friedrich Schlegel, 1815-59, *Lectures on the
History of Literature*

What, then, should be said of those for whom the thoughtlessness and inebriety of wanton youth can no longer be pleaded, but who have written in sober manhood, and with deliberate purpose?—men of diseased hearts and depraved imaginations, who, forming a system of opinions to suit their own unhappy course of conduct, have rebelled against the holiest ordinances of human society, and, hating that revealed religion, which, with all their efforts and bravadoes, they are unable entirely to disbelieve, labour to make others as miserable as themselves, by infecting them with a moral virus that eats into the soul! The school which they have set up may properly be called the Satanic School; for, though their productions breathe the spirit of Belial in their lascivious parts, and the spirit of Moloch in those loathsome images of atrocities and horrors which they delight to represent, they are more especially characterized by a satanic pride and audacious impiety, which still betrays the wretched feeling of hopelessness wherewith it is allied.

Robert Southey, 1821, *The Vision of Judgment,* Preface

The Pilgrim of Eternity, whose fame
Over his living head like Heaven is bent,
An early but enduring monument,
Came, veiling all the lightnings of his song
In sorrow.

Percy Bysshe Shelley, 1821, *Adonais,* st. xxx

It seems, to my ear, that there is a sad want of harmony in Lord Byron's verses. Is it not unnatural to be always connecting very great intellectual power with utter depravity? Does such a combination often really exist *in rerum naturâ?*

Samuel Taylor Coleridge, 1822, *Table-Talk,*
ed. Ashe, Dec. 29, p. 16

There are things in Byron's poetry so exquisite, that fifty or five hundred years hence, they will be read, felt, and adored throughout the world. . . . No, no! give me Byron, with all his spite, hatred, depravity, dandyism, vanity, frankness, passion, and idleness, to Wordsworth, with all his heartless communion with woods and grass.

Benjamin Robert Haydon, *Letter to Mary Russell Mitford;*
Life, Letters and Table Talk, ed. Stoddard, pp. 217, 218

Lord Byron is to be regarded as a man, as an Englishman, and as a great talent. His good qualities belong chiefly to the man, his bad to the Englishman and the peer, his talent is incommensurable. . . . He is a great talent, a born talent, and I never saw the true poetical power greater in any man than in him. In the apprehension of external objects, and a clear penetration into past situations, he is quite as great as Shakspeare. But as a pure individuality, Shakspeare is his superior. This was felt by Byron, and on this account, he does not say much of Shakspeare, although he knows whole passages by heart. He would willingly have denied him altogether; for Shakspeare's cheerfulness is in his way, and he feels that he is no match for it. Pope he does not deny, for he had no cause to fear him. On the contrary, he mentions him, and shews him respect when he can, for he knows well enough that Pope is a mere foil to himself.

Johann Wolfgang Goethe, 1825, *Conversations,*
ed. Eckermann, vol. I, p. 209

Byron has been extolled as the sublimest of poets. There are passages in all his poems which I have thought charming, but mixed with so much that was disgusting that I never believed his popularity would be lasting. His versification is so destitute of sustained harmony, many of his thoughts are so strained, his sentiments so unamiable, his misanthropy so gloomy, his images so grossly indelicate, his libertinism so shameless, his merriment such grinning of a ghastly smile, that I have always believed his verses would soon rank with forgotten things. . . . This person has now been seven years dead, and the public interest in him has not abated. He was one of the wonders of his age, and was, like Napoleon Bonaparte, the torso of a Hercules. A "grand homme manqué"—a club-footed Apollo—in mind as in person. There are sublime and beautiful passages of detail in his poetry; and if he had finished his *Don Juan* it would have been a worthy companion to Voltaire's *Pucelle*, in the Temple of Cloacina upon the summit of Parnassus.

John Quincy Adams, 1830, *Memoirs*, vol. VIII, pp. 218, 248

Lord Byron has abundance of wit, and extremely diversified wit, but of a kind that agitates and has a baneful influence. He has read Voltaire, and he frequently imitates him. In following the great English poet step by step, we are forced to acknowledge that he aims at effect, that he rarely loses sight of himself, that he is almost always in attitude; that he looks at himself with complacency; but the affection of eccentricity, singularity, originality, belongs to the English character in general. If, however, Lord Byron has atoned for his genius by certain foibles, futurity will not concern itself about such paltry matters, or rather it will know nothing about them; the poet will hide the man, and will interpose talent between the man and future generations: through this divine veil posterity will discern nothing but the god.

François René, Vicomte de Chateaubriand, 1837,
Sketches of English Literature, vol. II, p. 344

In Byron there is much to admire but nothing to imitate: for energy is beyond the limits of imitation. Byron could not have written better than he did. Altho' he seems negligent in many places, he was very assiduous in correcting his verses. His poetry took the bent of a wayward and perverted mind often weak, but oftener perturbed. Tho' hemp and flax and cotton are the stronger for being twisted, verses and intellects certainly are not. . . . It is unfortunate that Ariosto did not attract him (Byron) first. Byron had not in his nature amenity enough for it, and chose Berni in preference, and fell from Berni to Casti. But his sorching and dewless heat burnt up their flowery meadows.

Walter Savage Landor, 1845, *To Mrs. Paynter*, Aug. 3;
Letters, ed. Wheeler, p. 146

The truth is, that what has put Byron out of favour with the public of late, is not his faults, but his excellencies. His artistic good taste, his classical polish, his sound shrewd sense, his hatred of cant, his insight into humbug, above all, his shallow, pitiable habit of being always intelligible; these are the sins which condemn him in the eyes of a mesmerizing, table-turning, spirit-rapping, Spiritualizing, Romanizing generation, who read Shelley in secret, and delight in his bad taste, mysticism, extravagance, and vague and pompus sentimentalism. The age is an effeminate one; and it can well afford to pardon the lewdness of the gentle and sensitive vegetarian, while it has no mercy for that of the sturdy peer, proud of his bull-neck and his boxing, who keeps bears and bull-dogs, drilled Greek ruffians at Missolonghi, and "had no objection to a pot of beer"; and who might, if he had reformed, have made a gallant English gentleman.

Charles Kingsley, 1853, "Thoughts about Shelley and Byron,"
Fraser's Magazine, vol. 48, p. 571

Dr. Elze ranks the author of *Harold* and *Juan* among the four greatest English poets, and claims for him the intellectual parentage of Lamartine and Musset, in France, of Espronceda, in Spain; of Puschkin, in Russia; with some modifications, of Heine, in Germany, of Berchet and others in Italy. So many voices of so various countries cannot be simply set aside: unless we wrap ourselves in an insolent insularism, we are bound at least to ask what is the meaning of their concurrent testimony. . . . We may learn much from him still, when we have ceased to disparage, as our fathers ceased to idolize, a name in which there is so much warning and so much example.

John Nichol, 1880, *Byron (English Men of
Letters)*, pp. 205, 206, 212

Wordsworth has an insight into permanent sources of joy and consolation for mankind which Byron has not; his poetry gives us more which we may rest upon than Byron's,—more which we can rest upon now, and which men may rest upon always. I place Wordsworth's poetry, therefore, above Byron's, on the whole, although in some points he was greatly Byron's inferior, and although Byron's poetry will always, probably, find more readers than Wordsworth's, and will give pleasure more easily. But these two, Wordsworth and Byron, stand, it seems to me, first and preëminent in actual performance, a glorious pair, among the English poets of this century.

Matthew Arnold, 1881, *The Poetry of Byron*, Preface

It is by the vast strength and volume of his powers, rather than by any one perfect work, that he is to be estimated. He does not seem to have had any delicacy of ear for the refinements of metre, or to have studied the intricacies of it. But, when the impulse came, he poured himself forth with wonderful rapidity, home-thrusting directness, and burning eloquence—eloquence that carries you over much that is faulty in structure, and imperfect, or monotonous in metre. He himself did not stay to consider the way he said things, so intent was he on the things he had to say. Neither any more does the reader. His cadences were few, but they were strong and impressive, and carried with them, for the time, every soul that heard them.

John Campbell Shairp, 1881, "Modern English Poetry,"
Aspects of Poetry, p. 146

It is remarkable that the influence of Byron's poetry has been far greater on the Continent than it has been in England. No English poet, except Shakespeare, has been so much read or so much admired by foreigners. His works, or parts of them, have been translated into many European languages, and numerous foreign writers have been affected by their ideas and style. The estimate that has been formed of them is extraordinarily high. Charles Nodier said: "The appearance of Lord Byron in the field of European literature is one of those events the influence of which is felt by all peoples and through all generations"; and his judgment in this respect by no means stands alone. The chief reason of this, independently of the splendour of his compositions, is to be found in his political opinions. Byron's poetry, like that of most of his English contemporaries— Wordsworth, Coleridge, Southey, and Shelley—was the outcome of the French Revolution; but whereas the three first-named of these poets, disgusted with the excesses of that movement, went over into the opposite camp, and the idealism of Shelley was too far removed from the sphere of practical politics to be a moving force, Byron became, almost unintentionally, the apostle of the principles which it represented. . . . Thus his writings became a political power throughout Europe, and more so on the Continent than in England, in proportion as the loss of liberty was more keenly felt by foreign nations. Wherever aspirations for independence arose, Byron's poems were read and admired.

H. F. Tozer, 1885, ed., Childe Harold's Pilgrimage

Byron wrote as easily as a hawk flies, and as clearly as a lake reflects, the exact truth in the precisely narrowest terms; not only the exact truth, but the most central and useful one. Of course I could no more measure Byron's greater powers at that time than I could Turner's; but I saw that both were right in all things that *I* knew right from wrong in; and that they must henceforth be my masters, each in his own domain.

John Ruskin, 1885, Præterita, vol. I, p. 258

Byron . . . seems to me a poet distinctly of the second class, and not even of the best kind of second, inasmuch as his greatness is chiefly derived from a sort of parody, a sort of imitation, of the qualities of the first. His verse is to the greatest poetry what melodrama is to tragedy, what plaster is to marble, what pinchbeck is to gold. He is not indeed an impostor; for his sense of the beauty of nature and of the unsatisfactoriness of life is real, and his power of conveying this sense to others is real also. He has great, though uncertain, and never very *fine,* command of poetic sound, and a considerable though less command of poetic vision. But in all this there is a singular touch of illusion, of what his contemporaries had learnt from Scott to call gramarye. The often cited parallel of the false and true Florimels in Spenser applies here also. The really great poets do not injure each other in the very least by comparison, different as they are. Milton does not "kill" Wordsworth; Spencer does not injure Shelley; there is no danger in reading Keats immediately after Coleridge. But read Byron in close juxtaposition with any of these, or with not a few others, and the effect, to any good poetic taste, must surely be disastrous; to my own, whether good or bad, it is perfectly fatal. The light is not that which never was on land or sea; it is that which is habitually just in front of the stage: the roses are rouged, the cries of passion even sometimes (not always) ring false. I have read Byron again and again; I have sometimes, by reading Byron only and putting a strong constraint upon myself, got nearly into the mood to enjoy him. But let eye or ear once catch sight or sound of real poetry, and the enchantment vanishes.

George Saintsbury, 1896, A History of
Nineteenth Century Literature, p. 80

To acquire a right feeling for Byron and his poetry is a discipline in equity. It is easy to yield to a sense of his power, to the force and sweep of his genius; it is easy to be repelled by his superficial insincerity, his license, his cynicism, his poverty of thought, his looseness of construction, his carelessness in execution. To know aright the evil and good is difficult. It is difficult to feel justly towards this dethroned idol (presently, perhaps, to be re-enthroned), an idol in whose composition iron and clay are mingled with fine gold. . . . We must take him or leave him as he is,—the immortal spoilt by his age, great and petty, weak and strong, exalted and debased. A glorious wave that curls upon the sea-beach, though it leave sea-wrack and refuse on the sands, is more stimulating, more health-giving, than a pitcher of such salt water in one's dressing-room, even if it be free from every floating weed. . . . He was a democrat among aristocrats and an aristocrat among democrats; a sceptic among believers and a believer among sceptics. And yet his line of advance was not a *via media,* nor was it determined by a spirit of moderation or critical balance.

Edward Dowden, 1897, The French Revolution and
English Literature, pp. 261, 262, 264

On the continent of Europe there can be no Byronic revival, for the reason that there has never been a decline. English critics might do what they would to "bear" the market—our readers will perhaps remember Mr. Saintsbury's exploit in this line—Byron stock has always stood well in the literary and academic bourses of Germany and France. His poetry is very seriously studied at the universities; dissertations on Byron and Shakspere, treatises on "Byron der Uebermensch," and the like, have abounded.

George Lyman Kittredge, 1898, "Two New Editions
of Byron," The Nation, vol. 67, p. 132